Law and Economics

In the 1940s economists re-discovered that their discipline was not only about economic activities in the strictest sense of the word but were also about institutions and, in particular, legal rules. The works and analyses that developed were gathered under the label "law and economics".

This Reader discusses the historical and methodological foundations of "law and economics" and "economic analyses of the law". The first part of the book is based on the claim that "law and economics" can really be understood through an understanding of its basic methodological assumptions; that is, an understanding of why and how economic analyses of legal systems are possible. It focuses on the history and meaning of the labels and demonstrates why and how they were used. The latter part of the book explains the origins and nature of legal rules and the functioning of legal systems as a whole, rather than the economic studies devoted to specific domains of the law. The book contains a selection of important works from key scholars in law and economics, including Ronald Coase, Richard A. Posner, and David Friedman.

Topics covered include:

- Economic analysis of law
- Economics of legal systems, including common, civil and public law
- Judicial decision making
- Efficiency and the common law

This book brings together the most authoritative articles on law and economics, the interaction between the two disciplines, and the use of economic tools to analyze legal problems. Its focus on fundamental issues, as well as a variety of easily accessible material, makes this book an essential resource for students with little prior subject knowledge and provides an exciting introduction to a key economic discipline.

Alain Marciano is Associate Professor at the University of Reims Champagne-Ardenne.

"Law and economics has become a field that all interested in the social sciences – the scientific explanation of social behaviour – must understand. Professor Marciano has compiled and solicited a set of essays excellent both in their introduction to the field and in explaining the insights of law and economics for the understanding of the operation of legal institutions and of social behavior in response to the law. All interested in this field should read this book."

George Priest,
Professor of Law and Economics,
Yale Law School, USA

"What would you expect from hiking on a well recommended route over the premises of Law and Economics? To find variety? Profoundness? Innovation? And, of course, synopsis?

This new reader, edited by the profound *affectionado* Alain Marciano of the University of Reims, comprises all this. However, it is not a book on the state of art in the typical areas of application, such as tort, contract, crime, finance and so on. It is more on principles, the emergence of views and methodology, judicial decisionmaking, the legal system and its efficiency.

The high quality is secured by a careful selection of authors as well as a careful selection of paper topics. Most of the authors are widely renowned scholars and all of them give very obliging proof of their skills. On top of this, one receives guidance through brief though comprehensive introductions to each of the chapters of the book, and recommendations for further reading.

So taking all in all this is a very valuable addition to the existing body of publications in the field of law and economics."

Wolfgang Weigel,
Associate Professor,
Department of Economics,
University of Vienna, Austria

Law and Economics

A reader

Edited by Alain Marciano

Routledge
Taylor & Francis Group

LONDON AND NEW YORK

First published 2009 by Routledge
2 Park Square, Milton Park, Abingdon, Oxon, OX14 4RN

Simultaneously published in the USA and Canada
by Routledge
270 Madison Avenue, New York, NY 10016

Routledge is an imprint of the Taylor & Francis Group, an informa business

Typeset in Perpetua and Bell Gothic by Keyword Group Ltd.
Printed and bound in Great Britain by CPI Antony Rowe Ltd, Chippenham, Wiltshire

British Library Cataloguing in Publication Data
A catalogue record for this book is available from the British Library

Library of Congress Cataloging in Publication Data
A catalog record for this book has been requested

ISBN 13: 978-0-415-44559-7 (hbk)
ISBN 13: 978-0-415-44560-3 (pbk)

ISBN 10: 0-415-44559-0 (hbk)
ISBN 10: 0-415-44560-4 (pbk)

Contents

Foreword

Richard A. Posner

When I began my scholarly career in "law and economics" (that is, economic analysis of law) in the late 1960s, it was a very tiny field. By the mid-1970s it was growing rapidly, and its growth continues to be rapid. The field has also spread geographically. Once almost exclusively American (although one of its major founders, Ronald Coase, is English, he has lived and worked in the United States since the 1950s), the field is now genuinely international.

It is now a large field. And with size come problems. How to introduce young scholars, along with judges and practicing lawyers, to the field? The answers have been various. There are textbooks and treatises, including my textbook-treatise; there are review articles; there are even encyclopedias; there are handbooks; and there are numerous books of readings. It is the latter genre to which Professor Marciano's new reader belongs.

The scholarly literature on law and economics is now so vast that no single book of readings can encompass it. The Edward Elgar publishing company has published a number of books of readings in particular subfields of law and economics, such as the economic analysis of tort law. None of these books attempts to introduce the new scholar, judge, or lawyer to the field as a whole; nor would it be possible to squeeze into one volume or even several volumes a set of readings that would span the entire field.

Professor Marciano, whose goal is to produce a book of readings that would provide a general introduction, as no other book of readings has done, has wisely confined his selections to writings that deal with *fundamental* issues, as distinct from specific doctrines and procedures. The fundamental issues that his book covers are the emergence of the modern field of law and economics (for there were predecessors); the evolution of the modern field; the economic relation between law and the norms and customs that inform law; the economic differences between common law and civil law; the economics of judicial decision making, a topic of central importance because of the role of judges, especially in common law systems, as creators as well as appliers of law; and whether, despite or perhaps because of its decentralized and judge-shaped character, the common law is an efficient method of social and economic regulation – perhaps more efficient than civil law systems, as Max Weber believed.

The readings that Professor Marciano has chosen for each of these areas are extremely apt and will give the readers of the book an excellent sense of the major insights and controversies in each area. But of particular value are his introductions to each section. These are brief and lucid, without any sacrifice of depth or sophistication. They are not only valuable introductions to the readings, but in their own right a superb introduction to law and economics.

This book is a distinguished contribution to law and economics. All those who labor in the field are in Professor Marciano's debt.

Acknowledgements

The publishers would like to thank the following for their permission to reprint their material.

American Economic Association for permission to reprint Posner, Richard A. (1987) "The Law and Economics Movement", *American Economic Review*, 77(2): 1–13; Peyton Young, H. (1996) "The Economics of Conventions", *Journal of Economic Perspectives*, 10(1): 105–122.

Duke University Press for permission to reprint Medema, Steve (1998) "Wandering the Road From Pluralism to Posner: The Transformation of Law and Economics, 1920s–1970s", in *The Transformation of American Economics: From Interwar Pluralism to Postwar Neoclassicism: History of Political Economy*, Annual Supplement 30: 202–224. Copyright 1998 Duke University Press. All rights reserved.

Elsevier for permission to reprint Miceli, Thomas J. and Metçin M. Cosgel (1994) "Reputation and Judicial Decision-making", *Journal of Economic Behavior and Organization*, 23(1): 31–51.

Harvard Society for Law & Public Policy, Inc. for permission to reprint Aranson, Peter A. (1992) "Bruno Leoni in Retrospect", *Harvard Journal of Law and Public Policy*, 11: 661–711.

Northwest University School of Law for permission to reprint Zywicki, Todd J. (2003) "The Rise and Fall of Efficiency in the Common Law: A Supply-Side Analysis", *Northwestern Law Review*, 97(4): 1551–1633, reprinted by special permission of Northwestern University School of Law.

Oxford University Press for permission to reprint Posner, Richard A. (2000) "An Economic Analysis of the Use of Citations in the Law", *American Law and Economic Review*, 2(2): 381–406; Ellickson, Robert C. (2001) "The market for social norms", *American Law and Economics Review*, 3 (1): 1–49.

Princeton University Press for permission to reprint Jolls, Christine (2007) "Behavioral Law and Economics", in Diamond, P. (ed.), *Economic Institutions and Behavioral Economics*, copyright 2007 by Princeton University Press.

Springer for permission to reprint Witt, U. (1989) "The Evolution of Economic Institutions as a Propagation Process", *Public Choice*, 62(2): 155–172; Wagner, Richard E. (1992) "Crafting Social Rules: Common Law vs. Statute Law, Once Again", *Constitutional Political Economy*, 3(3): 381–397; Backhaus, Juergen. (1999) "The German Civil Code of 1896: An Economic Interpretation", *European Journal of Law and Economics*, 7: 5–14; Webster, Thomas J. (2004) "Economic Efficiency and the Common Law", *Atlantic Economic Journal*, 32(1): 39–48.

University of Chicago Press for permission to reprint Coase, Ronald. H. (1978) "Economics and Contigious Discipline", *Journal of Law and Economics*, 3 (2): 201–211; Friedman, David (1979) "Private Creation and Enforcement of Law: A Historical Case", *Journal of Legal Studies*, 8 (2): 399–415; Whitman, Douglas G. (2000) "Evolution of the Common Law and the Emergence of Compromise", *Journal of Legal Studies*, 29(2): 753–781; reprint Rubin, Paul H. (2005) "Micro and Macro Legal Efficiency: Supply and Demand", *Supreme Court Economic Review*, 13: 19–34.

University of Michigan Press for permission to reprint Landes, William M. (1998) "The Art of Law and Economics: An Autobiographical Essay", in Szenberg, M. (ed.), *Passion and Craft, Economists at Work*, Ann Arbor: The University of Michigan Press, copyright 1998 The University of Michigan Press.

The publishers have made every effort to contact authors and copyright holders of works reprinted in this book. This has not been possible in every case however, and we would welcome correspondence from individuals or companies we have been unable to trace.

Introduction

"**L** AW AND ECONOMICS**"** is certainly not a modern invention. On the contrary, as Steve Medema notes, "law and economics is as old as economics itself" (1998). As Medema explains, from the first Greek philosophers to the early American Institutionalists, in passing by, among others, Adam Smith and Jeremy Bentham, Karl Marx and Henry Sidgwick, many were those economists who were convinced that their discipline could be practised only by taking institutions, in general, and legal rules, in particular, into consideration. They were all *political economists*, that is they believed that economic activities are embedded in social and legal structures; and, for some of them, reciprocally, that legal phenomena have economic aspects. As a consequence, any *economic* analyses necessarily have a legal dimension; the economic concepts are defined as legal concepts (for instance, the price of a good or its value are grounded in property rights). Or, legal analyses rest on economic concepts. Therefore, many of the economic contributions developed since the origins of economics can also be viewed as contributions to law and economics. It would therefore be too complicated and too difficult to list all those economic analyses that have a legal flavor.

This reader concerns the analyses that were developed after economists rediscovered the importance of legal rules in the second half of the twentieth century as *old* then *new* "law and economics" and then as "economic analyses of the law". Therefore, it would be impossible to summarize the particularly large number of articles and books that are regularly published in the many journals and collective volumes devoted to this field, but the list of topics and issues that are discussed in these scholarly publications is nonetheless important. Anyone interested in detailed presentations and discussions should refer to the various encyclopedias, companions and textbooks that cover the field and present it in its diversity. From this perspective, the *Encyclopedia of Law and Economics* (edited by Boudewjin Bouckaert and Gerrit de Geest) as well as Jürgen Backhaus's *Elgar Companion to Law and Economics* and Peter Newman's

New Palgrave Dictionary of Economics and the Law are necessary references. They come near to exhaustive coverage of the entire field and provide a complete and up-to-date list of references. In addition, there exist many textbooks that can be used as references; Posner's is one of the most important. Another notable book is the second edition of *Economics and the Law. From Posner to Post-Modernism and Beyond,* by Steve Medema and Nicolas Mercuro, who help put in perspective the different streams of research that have developed in law and economics since the beginning of the twentieth century in very clear fashion.

It would be impossible to be as complete and as exhaustive as these books are. I have thus chosen to restrict my attention to and to concentrate upon two different sets of works. The first two sections of this book present the works that discuss the historical and methodological foundations of (old or new) "law and economics" and of "economic analyses of the law". My purpose is to explain the meaning of these labels and to show why and how they were used. Our claim is that "law and economics" can really be understood through an understanding of its basic methodological assumptions; that is, an understanding of why and how economic analyses of legal systems are possible. This is in effect the second *parti-pris* (parts 3 to 6): to focus on the works that explain the origins and nature of legal rules and the functioning of legal systems, as a whole, or at the macro-level rather than the economic studies devoted to specific domains of the law. Legal rules cover every aspect of the social life of human beings and the economic analyses that have developed are far too many to be summarized in such a volume. Alternatively, the understanding of the origins and functioning of the rules that order societies is a basic and fundamental question. Their importance is reinforced if one adopts a political economy perspective, from which one accepts that economics is about institutions, in general, and the law in particular.

Further reading

Backhaus, Juergen. 2005. *Elgar Companion to Law and Economics,* Aldershot: Edward Elgar.

Bouckaert, Boudewijn and Gerrit De Geest. 2000. *Encyclopedia in Law and Economics,* Aldershot: Edward Elgar (available on-line at: http://encyclo.findlaw.com).

Medema, Steve and Nicolas Mercuro. 2007. *Economics and the Law. From Posner to Post-modernism and Beyond,* Princeton University Press.

Newman, Peter. 1998. *The New Palgrave Dictionary of Economics and the Law,* London: Palgrave-MacMillan.

Posner, Richard. 2007. *Economic Analysis of Law,* 7th edition, Harvard University Press.

PART 1

From old to new law and economics

Old law and economics: before Coase

THE FIRST ATTEMPTS to analyze "law and economics" date back to the establishment of a research program on anti-trust regulation at the University of Chicago just after World War II, when Aaron Director was hired as an economist at the Law School in 1949 (the history of these early days is particularly well documented in van Horn, 2006, and van Horn and Mirowski, 2006). The project, named the "Antitrust Project", was managed by Director and subsidized by funds that did not come from the University but from private, mostly liberal, organizations, among which the Volker Fund was one of the most generous, even agreeing to pay Director's salary for five years. The Volker Fund wanted to finance a project, as its name unambiguously indicates, not only in order to study capitalism and private enterprise but with the purpose of providing a better understanding of the role of anti-trust legislation in the functioning of a capitalist economy. Therefore, once the obvious ideological dimension of the project is put to one side, what remains particularly significant is the theoretical perspective within which the project developed, i.e. the methodological purpose of its participants; from this perspective, they – and Director in particular – were interested in economics, in economic activities and industrial organization. They were not interested in legal issues as such – their purpose was not to explain the law; they were interested in economic questions and the legal rules which influence the economy. This aspect of these early analyses is important to stress and this did not change even after the emergence of Ronald Coase.

New law and economics: what did Coase change?

However, despite the many works carried out under the auspices of this and other projects, "law and economics" remained barely visible, a marginal field of research in economics.

A transformation occurred in 1960 when the *Journal of Law and Economics* published *The Problem of the Social Cost*, an article written by Ronald Coase, then professor of Economics at Chicago and who went on to become the 1991 Nobel laureate in Economics. Coase's article is usually praised for being a turning point in the evolution of the "law and economics" movement. More than that: the change is so dramatic that, as George Stigler puts it, "[i]n the field of law and/or economics, B.C. means Before Coase" (1992, p. 456) and therefore must be distinguished from what happened *After Coase*. Coase and his article mark the entering into a new era; at least, this is how people once saw it.

Many things could be said about this paper; and a lot has already been said (see, in particular, Medema). To grasp its importance, i.e. to understand why it supposedly played such an important role in the evolution of the field, one might say that *The Problem of the Social Cost* became "the most cited article in the literature of the field, perhaps in the entire literature of economics" (Stigler, 1992, p. 456) and, one must add, also among legal scholars. Indeed, economists (respectively legal scholars) first became properly acquainted with law (respectively, economics) and with "law and economics" by reading this simple article. In addition, Coase's article allowed them to become better acquainted with the original "law and economics", as previously practised. "Law and economics", argued Coase, "continued the early Chicago tradition" (Priest, 2006, p. 358) initiated by Director more than ten years before. Therefore, and despite the standard perception of the evolution of the field, "law and economics" does not qualitatively change before and after Coase's article, although this does not mean to suggest that Coase's article is unimportant, only that it does not represent a rupture in the history of "law and economics", as is often portrayed. This explanation is provided by Medema in his 1998 article, in which it is shown that the same kind of works were published in the journals and the same topics were investigated before and after Coase. Coase may well have given birth to a "new" form of law and economics, but his analyses nonetheless belong to "old" law and economics: *The Problem of the Social Cost* is "an unintended result of law and economics of the old variety" (Medema, 1998, p. 213).

The explanation of this continuity is relatively simple. Coase shares with Director the same interest in economics and in economic activities and he became interested in the law, in legal rules only from this perspective, i.e. as "an economist" (see, for instance, Coase in Epstein *et al.*, 1997, p. 1138). This is exactly what Coase says about his work and he insists on when characterizing his approach to "law and economics". He argues: "in *The Problem of Social Cost* I used the concept of transaction costs to demonstrate the way in which the legal system could affect the working of the economic system, and I did not press beyond this" (Coase, 1988, p. 35). He adds: "[f]or me, *The Problem of Social Cost* was an essay in economics. It was aimed at economists. What I wanted to do was to improve our analysis of the working of the economic system" (Coase, 1993, p. 250). Coase finds it necessary to deal with legal rules because they affect the economy as is made clear in the 1960 article (pp. 27–28). For him, this is the only reason why legal decisions must be drawn into the analysis: to evidence the impact of the law on the economy. In law and economics as Coase conceives it, economists "study ... legal cases both to learn about the details of actual business practices (information largely absent in the economics literature), and to appraise the impact on them of the law. I (and no doubt others) have used the legal cases to illustrate the economic problem" (1996, p. 104).

For Coase, to be an economist bears a specific meaning. It relates to the specific definition of the discipline that Coase associates with Alfred Marshall and, perhaps more surprisingly, with George Stigler. In effect, both Marshall and Stigler refer to economics in terms of an object to study and of the activities that form this object and "emphasize that economists study certain kinds of activities" (Coase, 1978, p. 206; emphasis added; on Marshall, see also Coase, 1975). From this perspective, it is not only assumed that there exists a specific area in human activities that is defined by the nature of these activities and that is called "the economy", but also that economists have to restrict their analyses to these activities. In other words, this means that there exists a subject matter or an object of study for economists and that it consists in analyzing economic or market activities. Such is the perspective adopted by Coase, who for instance writes: "I think economists do have a subject matter: the study of the working of the economic system, a system in which we earn and spend our incomes" (Coase, 1998, p. 93). In slightly different terms, he had already written earlier that economists "study the economic system [...] What economists study is the working of the social institutions which bind together the economic system: firms, markets for goods and services, labour markets, capital markets, the banking system, international trade, and so on" (Coase, 1978, pp. 206–207).

References

Summary

To get acquainted with (either old or new) law and economics, that is, to understand the definitions, the boundaries of the field, we recommend familiarization with three types of works. First, there are those that explain the context in which "law and economics" emerged, i.e. the works that explain why and how economists became interested in legal phenomena or in the impact of legal rules on economic phenomena. With regard to the modern period – that is, the second half of the twentieth century – this means going back to events that occurred at and around the Law School of the University of Chicago. From this perspective, one should refer to the fascinating studies carried out by Robert van Horn and Philip Mirowski, who detail the conditions in which economists and legal scholars interact with each other and with the representatives of liberal think-tanks to develop economic analyses of the legal dimensions of economic activities. These analyses can be complemented by a second set of articles: the enlightening personal recollections of certain of the participants in the emergence of the field (Coase, 1993; Epstein, 1997; Kitch, 1983; Priest, 2006; Manne, 2006). These articles serve a twofold purpose: they allow us to understand what "law and economics" is and also the distinction between this and an "economic analysis of the law".

These works are important, but they can only be properly understood in the light of the writings of one of the founder of law and economics, Ronald Coase. His foundational paper is worth reading because of the role it played, but this is obviously not enough. A genuine understanding of Coase's theory requires a detour via the methodological explanations given by Coase himself on economics and law and economics. This is particularly important because it allows us to understand precisely why Coase's contributions can be classified as "old" law and economics and, more importantly, as shown in Medema's historical study, why Coase's analysis is close to the works of the institutionalists (see also Bertrand, 2006; Medema, 1994).

Further reading

Bertrand, Élodie. 2006. "The Coasean analysis of lighthouse financing: myths and realities", *Cambridge Journal of Economics*, 30, pp. 389–402.

Coase, Ronald H. 1960. "The Problem of Social Cost", *Journal of Law and Economics*, 3 (October), pp. 1–44.

Coase, Ronald H. 1975. "Marshall on Method", *Journal of Law and Economics*, 18 (1), pp. 25–31.

Coase, Ronald H. 1978. "Economics and Contiguous Discipline", *Journal of Legal Studies*, 7 (2), June, pp. 201–211.

Coase, Ronald H. 1993. "Law and Economics at Chicago", *Journal of Law and Economics*, 36 (1), Part 2, John M. Olin Centennial Conference in Law and Economics at the University of Chicago (April), pp. 239–254.

Coase, Ronald H. 1996. "Law and Economics and A. W. Brian Simpson", *Journal of Legal Studies*, 25 (1) (January), pp. 103–119.

Coase, Ronald H. 1998. "The New Institutional Economics", *American Economic Review*, 88 (2), May, pp. 72c74.

Epstein, Richard A., Gary S. Becker, Ronald H. Coase, Merton H. Miller and Richard A. Posner. 1997. "The Roundtable Discussion", *University of Chicago Law Review*, 64 (4), pp. 1132–1165.

Kitch, Edmund W. 1983. "The Fire of Truth: A Remembrance of Law and Economics at Chicago, 1932-1970", *Journal of Law and Economics*, 26 (1), pp. 163–234.

Manne, Henry. 2006. "How Law and Economics was Marketed in a Hostile World: A Very Personal History", in *The Origins of Law and Economics: Essays by the Founding Fathers*, edited by Francesco Parisi and Charles K. Rowley, Cheltenham: Edward Elgar, pp. 309–327.

Medema, Steven G. 1994. *Ronald H. Coase*, London: Macmillan.

Medema, Steve. 1998. "Wandering the Road From Pluralism to Posner: The Transformation of Law and Economics, 1920s–1970s", in *The Transformation of American Economics: From Interwar Pluralism to Postwar Neoclassicism, History of Political Economy Annual Supplement*, 30, pp. 202–24.

Priest, George. 2006. "The Rise of Law and Economics: A Memoir of the Early Years", in *The Origins of Law And Economics: Essays By The Founding Fathers*, edited by Francesco Parisi and Charles K. Rowley, Cheltenham: Edward Elgar, Chapter 14, pp. 350–382.

Stigler, George J. 1992. "Law or Economics? Law or Economics?", *Journal of Law and Economics*, 35 (2), pp. 455–468.

Van Horn, Rob. 2008. "Reinventing Monopoly and the Role of Corporations: The Roots of Chicago Law and Economics." In Philip Mirowski and D. Plehwe, eds, *The Making of the Neoliberal Thought Collective*. Cambridge, MA: Harvard University Press.

Van Horn, Rob and Mirowski, Philip. 2008. "The Rise of the Chicago School of Economics and the Birth of Neoliberalism." In Philip Mirowski and D. Plehwe, eds, *The Making of the Neoliberal Thought Collective*. Cambridge, MA: Harvard University Press.

Chapter 1

Ronald H. Coase

ECONOMICS AND CONTIGUOUS DISCIPLINES

I WISH TO START with two general observations. First, what I have to say is largely based on my knowledge of developments within the United States and Britain. But I have sufficient confidence in the international character of science to believe that what can be observed in these countries is paralleled by similar developments elsewhere. My second observation is that a paper which deals with what is happening within a series of disciplines and which ranges so widely within economics itself, must inevitably mean, at any rate in my case, that it deals with many subjects about which the writer's knowledge is extremely vague. What I have to say will often have the character of assertion rather than of a conclusion based on a careful study of the literature in the many fields covered by my subject. I believe that such a careful study would confirm what I assert. But it is equally true that it may refute my views. Papers presented at international conferences are not usually high-risk ventures, but this one is. However, I do not think what is called for at this stage is a paper guarded by qualifications and difficult to attack because it says so little except what is generally accepted.

What is the subject with which I am dealing? What I am concerned with is what determines the boundaries between disciplines, in particular with what determines the boundaries between economics and the other social sciences: sociology, political science, psychology and the like (without excluding the possibility that there may be overlaps). What the boundaries are at any particular time can, of course, be discovered by examining the range of activities engaged in by members of any given professional association, by the subjects treated in the journals devoted to particular disciplines, by the courses given in university departments, by the topics covered in textbooks and by the books collected in libraries concerned with the various areas of knowledge. A forecast of the boundaries of a discipline is, thus, a forecast of what topics will be covered by professional associations, journals, libraries and the like. I have long considered the definition of economics which Boulding attributed to Viner, and has since often been repeated, "Economics is what economists do,"[1] as essentially sound but only if it were accompanied, which it never is, by a description of the activities in which economists actually engage.

If the question is asked, how do these boundaries between disciplines come to be what they are, the broad answer I give is that it is determined by competition. The process is essentially the same as that which determines the activities undertaken by firms or, to take another example, the extent of empires. Gibbon describes how Augustus came to accept the boundaries of the Roman Empire. Gibbon says that it was easy for Augustus to discover that

> Rome, in her present exalted situation, had much less to hope than to fear from the chance of arms; and that, in the prosecution of remote wars, the undertaking became everyday more difficult, the event more doubtful, and the possession more precarious, and less beneficial.[2]

The same kind of calculation ultimately led, and this is Gibbon's grand theme, to an abandonment of much of what had been contained within the Roman Empire and, finally, to its division within quite another set of boundaries. It is much the same with disciplines. The practitioners in a given discipline extend or narrow the range of the questions that they attempt to answer according to whether they find it profitable to do so, and this is determined, in part, by the success or failure of the practitioners in other disciplines in answering the same questions. Since different people are satisfied with different answers, victory is not necessarily clear-cut, and different answers and different ways of tackling the same question may exist side by side, each satisfying its own market. One group of practitioners need not drive another group from the field, but may merely, to use an economist's terminology, increase their market share. Of course, when the number of those who are satisfied with the answers given by any group of practitioners becomes so small and/or the questions for which this is true are few or trivial, the field may be abandoned altogether except by those whose competence is so low elsewhere that they cannot compete in a wider, more active, and more profitable market.

If we look at the work that economists are doing at the present time, there can be little doubt that economics is expanding its boundaries or, at any rate, that economists are moving more and more into other disciplines. They have been conspicuously active in political science, where they have developed an economic theory of politics and have done a great deal of empirical work analysing voting behaviour.[3] Economists have also moved into sociology and we now have an economic theory of marriage.[4] Nor should we be surprised that there is also an economic theory of suicide.[5] Other subjects on which economists have worked are linguistics,[6] education,[7] and national defence.[8] I am sure that it is only my lack of familiarity with what is going on in the other social sciences which restricts my list. One striking example, with which I am familiar, is the use of economics in the study of law.[9] The general movement is clear. Economists are extending the range of their studies to include all of the social sciences, which I take to be what we mean when we speak of economics' contiguous disciplines.

What is the reason why this is happening? One completely satisfying explanation (in more than one sense) would be that economists have by now solved all of the major problems posed by the economic system, and, therefore, rather than become unemployed or be forced to deal with the trivial problems which remain to be solved, have decided to employ their obviously considerable talents in achieving a similar success in the other social sciences. However, it is not possible to examine any area of economics with which I have familiarity without finding major puzzles for which we have no agreed solutions or, indeed, questions to which we have no answers at all. The reason for this movement of economists into neighbouring fields is certainly not that we have solved the problems of the economic system; it would perhaps be more plausible to argue that economists are looking for fields in which they can have some success.

Another explanation for this interest in neighbouring fields might be that modern economists have had a more broadly based education than those who preceded them and that, in consequence, their interests are wider, with the result that they are naturally dissatisfied with being restricted to so narrow a range of problems as that presented by the economic system. Such an explanation seems to me largely without merit. If we think of Adam Smith or John Stuart Mill or Alfred Marshall, the range of questions with which they deal is greater than is commonly found in a modern work on economics. This impression is reinforced if we have regard to the articles which appear in most of the economics journals, which, to an increasingly great extent, tend to deal with highly formal technical questions of economic analysis, usually treated mathematically. The general impression one derives, particularly from the journals, is of a subject narrowing, rather than extending, the range of its interest. This seems inconsistent with the concurrent movement of economists into the other social sciences, but I believe that there is a connection between these two apparently contradictory developments.

If we are to attempt to forecast what the scope of economists' work is likely to be in the future—which is surely what is needed if we are to be helpful to the librarians and others for whose benefit this conference was planned—we have to understand the reason why economists have been moving into the other social sciences and what the situation is likely to be in future. To do this, we have to consider what it is that binds together a group of scholars so that they form a separate profession and enables us to say that someone is an economist, someone else a sociologist, another a political scientist, and so on. It seems to me that what binds such a group together is one or more of the following: common techniques of analysis, a common theory or approach to the subject, or a common subject matter. I need not conceal from you at this stage my belief that in the long run it is the subject matter, the kind of question which the practitioners are trying to answer, which tends to be the dominant factor producing the cohesive force that makes a group of scholars a recognizable profession with its own university departments, journals, and libraries. I say this, in part, because the techniques of analysis and the theory or approach used are themselves, to a considerable extent, determined by what it is that the group of scholars is studying, although scholars in a particular discipline may use different techniques or approaches in answering the same questions. However, in the short run, the ability of a particular group in handling certain techniques of analysis, or an approach, may give them such advantages that they are able to move successfully into another field or even to dominate it. In making these distinctions, I do not wish to deny that techniques, approaches, and subject matter will all exert some influence at any given time. Nor would I argue that it is inevitable that techniques and approach should exert their influence only in the short run. They could be dominant in the long run as well. But I believe that there are reasons for thinking that this will not usually be the case. If my description of the binding forces of a scholarly discipline is correct and if my assessment of their long- and short-run influences is also valid, then we will have to decide whether the current movement by economists into the other social sciences is the triumph of a technique or of an approach, or whether such an extension of their work illuminates, and is interrelated with, the solution of the central questions which economists attempt to answer, that is, is necessitated by the nature of the subject matter which they study. To the extent that this movement is based on technique or approach, we can expect a gradual displacement of economists from their newly-won ground. To the extent that it is necessitated by their subject matter, we may expect the range of studies undertaken by economists to be permanently enlarged.

My first example of a technique, linear programming, is one which I am particularly unqualified to discuss, but, fortunately, extensive discussion is not called for.[10] It is, if I understand correctly, a mathematical method for discovering the proportions in which inputs should be combined in order to achieve a certain result at minimum cost. Such a technique has, potentially, applications in many fields. It is, however, difficult to believe that such a highly mathematical technique could not be as easily acquired or as well handled by suitably endowed scholars in other disciplines. Indeed, some of these might find such a technique easier to acquire or handle than would most economists. To the extent that economists have moved into other fields using linear programming, I would expect the forces of competition to be such that they would be largely displaced, although individual economists might still do useful work using linear programming. In any case, it seems improbable that knowledge of a technique such as linear programming would become such an essential part of any discipline as to outweigh command of the theory or knowledge of the subject matter. One would not expect economists to dominate such fields as nutrition or oil refinery engineering even if (which seems improbable) economists as a class were particularly adept in linear programming.

The employment of quantitative methods, now so commonly part of the equipment of the modern economist, has also enabled a number of economists to move into neighbouring disciplines. To the extent that economists find it easier to acquire these techniques and/or can handle them with greater dexterity than can their colleagues in the other social sciences (in part because they use them so frequently), it is possible that this may offset their unfamiliarity with the subject matter of these other disciplines and the analytical framework within which these other social scientists work. But it seems a rather fragile basis for predicting a long-run movement by economists into the other social sciences.

My next example, cost-benefit analysis, is more difficult to discuss.[11] My guess would be that the great bulk of the incursions made by economists into contiguous and not-so-contiguous disciplines in recent years have been in connection with the undertaking of cost-benefit studies. Cost-benefit analysis seems to me best described as a technique. But since it is essentially applied price theory, having as its aim the giving of a monetary value to what is gained and what is lost by following a particular course of action, it is certainly an activity in which economists have some obvious advantages. However, since these studies are usually carried out with a view to facilitating decision-making, particularly by public bodies, with the problem to be investigated selected by such bodies, rather than with a view to understanding the system of which these public bodies are a part, and since economists working in unfamiliar fields will tend to rely on the work of others for their data, economists engaged in these studies will tend to play a useful but subordinate role, except to the extent that the particular decisions being investigated are closely related to their main concerns.

More important and more persuasive is the view, which I associate with the name of Gary Becker, that economic theory or the economic approach can form the means by which economists can work in, if not take over, the other social sciences.[12] But before examining this point of view, I will consider what I believe to be the normal binding force of a scholarly profession, its subject matter.

What do economists study? What do they do? They study the economic system. Marshall, in the first edition of the *Principles of Economics* defined economics thus: "Political Economy, or Economics, is a study of man's actions in the ordinary business of life; it inquires how he gets his income and how he uses it."[13] A modern economist, Stigler, has phrased it differently: "Economics is the study of the operation of economic organizations, and economic organizations are social (and rarely individual) arrangements to deal with the production and distribution of economic goods and services."[14] Both of these definitions of economics emphasize that economists study certain kinds of activity. And this accords well with the actual topics dealt with in a book on economics. What economists study is the working of the social institutions which bind together the economic system: firms, markets for goods and services, labour markets, capital markets, the banking system, international trade, and so on. It is the common interest in these social institutions which distinguishes the economics profession.

A very different kind of definition is that of Robbins: "Economics is the science which studies human behaviour as a relationship between ends and scarce means which have alternative uses."[15] Such a definition makes economics a study of human choice. It is clearly too wide if regarded as a description of what economists do. Economists do not study all human choices, or, at any rate, they have not done so as yet. However, the view that economics is a study of all human choice, although it does not tell us the nature of the economic theory or approach which is to be employed in all of the social sciences, certainly calls for the development of such a theory.

I said earlier that there are, at present, two tendencies in operation in economics which seem to be inconsistent but which, in fact, are not. The first consists of an enlargement of the scope of economists' interests so far as subject matter is concerned. The second is a narrowing of professional interest to more formal, technical, commonly mathematical, analysis. This more formal analysis tends to have a greater generality. It may say less, or leave much unsaid, about the economic system, but, because of its generality, the analysis becomes applicable to all social systems. It is this generality of their analytical systems which, I believe, has facilitated the movement of economists into the other social sciences, where they will presumably repeat the successes (and the failures) which they have had within economics itself.

The nature of this general approach has been described by Posner in his *Economic Analysis of Law*:

> Economics, the science of human choice in a world in which resources are
> limited in relation to human wants, explores and tests the implications of

the assumption that man is a rational maximizer of his ends in life, his satisfactions—what we shall call his 'self-interest.'[16]

By defining economics as the "science of human choice," economics becomes the study of all purposeful human behaviour and its scope is, therefore, coterminous with all of the social sciences. It is one thing to make such a claim, it is quite another to translate it into reality. At a time when the King of England claimed to be also King of France, he was not always welcome in Paris. The claim that economics is the science of human choice will not be enough to cause sociologists, political scientists, and lawyers to abandon their field or, painfully, to become economists. The dominance of the other social sciences by economists, if it happens, will not come about simply by redefining economics, but because of something which economists possess and which enables them to handle sociological, political, legal, and similar problems better than the practitioners in these other social sciences. I take it to be the view of Becker and Posner that the decisive advantage which economists possess in handling social problems is their theory of, or approach to, human behaviour, the treatment of man as a rational, utility-maximizer.

Since the people who operate in the economic system are the same people who are found in the legal or political system, it is to be expected that their behaviour will be, in a broad sense, similar. But it by no means follows that an approach developed to explain behaviour in the economic system will be equally successful in the other social sciences. In these different fields, the purposes which men seek to achieve will not be the same, the degree of consistency in behaviour need not be the same and, in particular, the institutional framework within which the choices are made are quite different. It seems to me probable that an ability to discern and understand these purposes and the character of the institutional framework (how, for example, the political and legal systems actually operate) will require specialized knowledge not likely to be acquired by those who work in some other discipline. Furthermore, a theory appropriate for the analysis of these other social systems will presumably need to embody features which deal with the important specific interrelationships of that system.

I am strengthened in this view by a consideration of the part played by utility theory in economic analysis. Up to the present it has been largely sterile. To say that people maximize utility tells us nothing about the purposes for which they engage in economic activity and leaves us without any insight into why people do what they do. As Stigler has told us, the chief implication of utility theory is that, "if consumers do not buy less of a commodity when their incomes rise, they will surely buy less when the price of the commodity rises."[17] But that consumers demand more at a lower price is known to everyone, whether an economist or not, who is at all familiar with the operation of a market. Utility theory seems more likely to handicap than to aid economists in their work in contiguous disciplines. Recently, the work of Lancaster on "characteristics analysis"[18] and of Becker on "commodities,"[19] which relate the satisfactions derived from goods and services to certain, specified, more fundamental needs, shows promise of being more fruitful. But it seems improbable that the list of the important "commodities," to use Becker's term, will be the same in the various social sciences or that they will be uncovered, except by specialists in those disciplines.

Economics, it must be admitted, does appear to be more developed than the other social sciences. But the great advantage which economics has possessed is that economists are able to use the "measuring rod of money." This has given a precision to the analysis, and since what is measured by money are important determinants of human behaviour in the economic system, the analysis has considerable explanatory power. Furthermore, the data (on prices and incomes) is generally available, so that hypotheses can be examined and checked. Marshall said that

> the steadiest motive to ordinary business work is the desire for the pay which is the material reward of work. The pay may be on its way to be spent selfishly or unselfishly, for noble or base ends.... But the motive is supplied by a definite amount of money: and it is this definite and exact money measurement of the steadiest motives in business life, which has enabled economics to outrun every other branch of the study of man.[20]

If it is true that the more developed state of economics, as compared to the other social sciences, has been due to the happy chance (for economics) that the important factors determining economic behaviour can be measured in money, it suggests that the problems faced by practitioners in these other fields are not likely to be dissipated simply by an infusion of economists, since in moving into these fields, they will commonly have to leave their strength behind them. The analysis developed in economics is not likely to be successfully applied in other subjects without major modifications.

If I am right about the relative unimportance of technique as a basis for the choice of professional groupings, if subject matter is really the dominant factor, with the theory or approach in large part determined by the subject matter, what is the outlook for the work of economists in the other social sciences? I would not expect them to continue indefinitely their triumphal advance and it may be that they will be forced to withdraw from some of the fields which they are now so busily cultivating. But such a forecast depends on the practitioners in the other disciplines making a competitive response. The success of economists in moving into the other social sciences is a sign that they possess certain advantages in handling the problems of those disciplines. One is, I believe, that they study the economic system as a unified interdependent system and, therefore, are more likely to uncover the basic interrelationships within a social system than is someone less accustomed to looking at the working of a system as a whole. Another is that a study of economics makes it difficult to ignore factors which are clearly important and which play a part in all social systems. Such a factor would be that, to a large extent, people choose their occupations on the basis of money incomes. Another would be that a higher price lowers the demand. Such factors may appear in various guises, but an economist is likely to see through them. Punishment, for example, can be regarded as the price of crime. An economist will not debate whether increased punishment will reduce crime; he will merely try to answer the question, by how much? The economist's analysis may fail to touch some of the problems found in the other social systems, but often the analysis can be brought to bear. And the economist will take full advantage of those opportunities which occur when the "measuring rod of money" can be used.

But if the main advantage which an economist brings to the other social sciences is simply a way of looking at the world, it is hard to believe, once the value of such economic wisdom is recognized, that it will not be acquired by some practitioners in these other fields. This is already happening in law and political science. Once some of these practitioners have acquired the simple, but valuable, truths which economics has to offer, and this is the natural competitive response, economists who try to work in the other social sciences will have lost their main advantage and will face competitors who know more about the subject matter than they do. In such a situation, only the exceptionally endowed economist is likely to be able to make a significant contribution to our knowledge of the other social sciences.

Economists may, however, study other social systems, such as the legal and political ones, not with the aim of contributing to law or political science, but because it is necessary if they are to understand the working of the economic system itself. It has come to be realized by many economists in recent times that parts of these other social systems are so intermeshed with the economic system as to be as much a part of that system as they are of a sociological, political, or legal system. Thus, it is hardly possible to discuss the functioning of a market without considering the nature of the property right system, which determines what can be bought and sold and which, by influencing the cost of carrying out various kinds of market transactions, determines what is, in fact, bought and sold, and by whom.[21] Similarly, the family or household and the educational system are of concern to the sociologist, but their operations affect the supply of labour to different occupations and the patterns of consumption and production and are, therefore, also of concern to the economist. In the same way, the administration of the regulatory agencies and antitrust policy, while part of the legal system and, as such, studied by lawyers, also provides the framework within which firms and individuals decide on their actions in the economic sphere.

The need to take into account the influence of other social systems, above all the legal system, in analysing the working of the economic system, is now widely accepted by economists. It has resulted in numerous studies of the effect of the legal system on the performance of the economic system.[22] Such work, because of its focus on the economic system, is likely, in general, to be best done by economists. Unlike the movement by economists into the other social sciences which has as its aim, the improvement of these other social sciences, a movement which, for reasons I have already given, seems to me likely to be temporary, the study by economists of the effects of the other social systems on the economic system will, I believe, become a permanent part of the work of economists. It cannot be done effectively by social scientists unfamiliar with the economic system. Such work may be carried out in collaboration with other social scientists, but it is unlikely to be well done without economists. For this reason, I think we may expect the scope of economics to be permanently enlarged to include studies in other social sciences. But the purpose will be to enable us to understand better the working of the economic system.

Notes

1   Kenneth E. Boulding, Economic Analysis 3 (3rd ed. 1955).
2   Edward Gibbon, The Decline and Fall of the Roman Empire ch. 1, at 1–2 (Modern Library ed.).
3   Among the works on the economic theory of politics are: Duncan Black, The Theory of Committees and Elections (1958); Anthony Downs, An Economic Theory of Democracy (1957); James Buchanan and Gordon Tullock, The Calculus

of Consent (1962); Mancur Olson, The Logic of Collective Action (1965); William A. Niskanen, Jr., Bureaucracy and Representative Government (1971). For a study of voting behaviour, see George J. Stigler, General Economic Conditions and National Elections, 63 Am. Econ. Rev. 160 (Papers & Proceedings, May1973).

4   Gary S. Becker, A Theory of Marriage: Part 1, 81 J. Pol. Econ. 813 (1973); and *id.,* A theory of Marriage: Part II, 82 J. Pol. Econ. 511 (March/April 1974).

5   Daniel S. Hamermesh and Neal M. Soos, An Economic Theory of Suicide, 82 J. Pol. Econ. 83 (1974).

6   J. Marschak, Economics of Language, 10 Behavioral Sci. 135 (1965).

7   John Vaizey, The Economics of Education (1962); Theodore W. Schultz, The Economic Value of Education (1963); *id.,* Investment in Human Capital (1970).

8   Charles J. Hitch and Roland N. McKean, The Economics of Defense in the Nuclear Age (1960).

9   Richard A. Posner, Economic Analysis of Law (2nd ed. 1977).

10   J. R. Hicks, Linear Theory, 70 Econ. J. 671 (1960).

11   On cost-benefit analysis, see A. R. Priest and R. Turvey, Cost-Benefit Analysis: A Survey, 75 Econ. J. 683 (1965); E. J. Mishan, Cost-Benefit Analysis (1971); G. H. Peters, Cost-Benefit Analysis and Public Expenditures (1966).

12   See Gary S. Becker, The Economic Approach to Human Behavior ch. 1, at 3–14 (1976).

13   Alfred Marshall, Principles of Economics 131 (9th variorum ed. 1961).

14   George J. Stigler, The Theory of Price 1 (1952).

15   L. C. Robbins, An Essay on the Nature and Significance of Economic Science 15 (1932).

16   Richard A. Posner, *supra* note 9, at 3.

17   George J. Stigler, The Development of Utility Theory, in Essays in the History of Economics 155 (1965).

18   Kelvin J. Lancaster, A New Approach to Consumer Theory, 74 J. Pol. Econ. 132 (1966); *id.,* Consumer Demand (1971).

19   Gary S. Becker & Robert T. Michael, On the New Theory of Consumer Behavior, 75 Sw. J. Econ. 378 (1973).

20   Alfred Marshall, *supra* note 13, at 14.

21   On property rights, see Erik Furubotn and Svetozar Pejovich, Property Rights and Economic Theory: A Survey of Recent Literature, 10 J. Econ. Lit. 1137 (1972).

22   It is necessary here only to refer to the kind of articles which appear in the Journal of Law and Economics and the Journal of Legal Studies.

Chapter 2

Steven G. Medema

WANDERING THE ROAD FROM PLURALISM TO POSNER

The transformation of law and economics in the twentieth century

O NE OF THE DEFINING FEATURES of post-World War II economics is the application of neoclassical economic reasoning to areas traditionally considered non economic—political science, sociology, the law, and so on—the most successful of which is arguably the field of law and economics. If one spends much time examining the current literature in the field, including surveys of law and economics and its development, one comes away with the distinct impression that law and economics is a post-1960 phenomenon, dating roughly from the founding of the *Journal of Law and Economics* in the late 1950s and the publication of Ronald H. Coase's "Problem of Social Cost" in 1960.[1] In fact, of course, law and economics, conceived of as the study of the interrelations between legal and economic processes, is as old as economics itself, as evidenced, for example, in the ancient Greek discussions of the regulatory environment in the ideal state and the Scholastic discussions of usury and pricing (undertaken in light of Roman civil law). Moving a bit more in the direction of the present, Adam Smith, Karl Marx, Henry Sidgwick, the German historical school, A. C. Pigou, and, inter alia, the early American institutionalists devoted significant attention to legal-economic relationships. Yet the existence of such work is noted only barely, if at all, in contemporary legal-economic scholarship, and, when noted, it is largely waved aside as something very different from (and irrelevant to) contemporary practice.

This much having been said, it is certainly not the case that law and economics was a prominent topic in legal and economic discourse prior to the twentieth century.[2] However, the first four decades of the twentieth century witnessed a surge of interest in both the legal and the economics communities in law and economics, most of which was of a form very different from contemporary law and economics, not just in the techniques brought to bear but in the general approach to and conception of the subject. Yet this type of analysis—indeed, law and economics generally—all but disappeared after World War II, only to reemerge in a vastly different form in the early 1960s.

Since law and economics is an interdisciplinary subject, one might correctly expect that the underlying reasons for its transformation lie in the respective intellectual environments of economics and law during these periods. Although much has been written about the influence of the legal environment on these developments (e.g., Posner 1987; Duxbury 1995), what has been neglected, by and large, is the economics side of the issue: What forces within the *economics* community drove the transformation of law and economics, as practiced by economists?

This essay will attempt to probe this question, not with the goal of providing a singular, definitive answer but with the more modest goal of suggesting possible reasons for the transformation in the hope of providing a springboard for further work on this topic and perhaps some insights into the larger transformative processes within economics during the period in question. The transformation of law and economics as described herein will turn on the publication of Coase's "Problem of Social Cost" in 1960. While it is hardly novel to trace the rise of modern law and economics to this source, the point to be made here is rather different from the traditional view: "The Problem of Social Cost" is actually an essay written in the "old" law and economics tradition, but the reasons behind its writing and the form in which it was written raised an entirely new set of questions that were very much amenable to examination using modern microtheoretic analysis.

The next two sections briefly lay out the defining features of the "old" and the "new" law and economics.[3] Then the role of "The Problem of Social Cost" within this transformation process is discussed, and the underlying reasons for the decline of the old law and economics and the rise of the new are probed. Finally, some concluding comments are made on the recent developments in law and economics and their implications for the future of the field.

Old law and economics

In 1897, Oliver Wendell Holmes wrote that "for the rational study of law the black-letter man may be the man of the present, but the man of the future is the man of statistics and the master of economics" (469). It was not long before legal scholars attempted to bring this prediction to fruition, at least to some degree. The legal realists, largely forsaking the doctrinaire approach of traditional precedential jurisprudence, argued instead that law was a means to promote chosen ends and that those ends (and the best means of pursuing them) could be revealed by the study of, among other things, the economic impact of legal rules (Duxbury 1995; Mercuro and Medema 1997).

However, the push for greater interaction between law and economics was not confined to the legal community. Economists, sometimes hand in hand with the realists and sometimes apart from them, increasingly recognized the need for integrating legal and economic analysis. Calls for the integration of law and economics and the undertaking of studies toward this end were evidenced in American Economic Association (AEA) presidential addresses, sessions at the annual meetings of the AEA, and numerous books and journal articles (Samuels 1993). Many, but by no means all, of the economists involved in this scholarship were either tightly or loosely allied with institutional economics—Walton Hamilton (1932), Henry Carter Adams ([1887/1897] 1954), Robert Lee Hale (1952), John R. Commons (1924, 1925), and

Gardiner C. Means (Berle and Means 1932), for example. But regardless of school affiliation (and the lines between schools were very blurred during this era), the individuals urging this integration were not fringe players but ranked among the profession's most prominent members.

The defining feature of this analysis (as compared with contemporary law and economics) was that it saw the study of the legal process as an important facet of the study of the economic system. This view reflects the definition of "economics" as the study of the economic system rather than as an approach or a tool kit for the analysis of individual behavior. As such, the basic goal of the analysis was to do either or both of the following:

1. The analysis sought to explore the legal underpinnings of the economic system and how changes in legal rules impact the economic system, in particular, the allocation and distribution of resources and wealth in society. The perceived need for such analysis arose out of the belief that, because of the problem of scarcity, the economic system, including the operation of markets, is governed by the legal system, which, through rights creation, definition, and modification, channels power, opportunity, and so on—and thus allocation and distribution—in particular directions. This was evidenced in legal decisions as to the types of contracts that would be enforced; the valuation of property for pricing purposes (and the regulation thereof); and rules governing combination of firms and workers, hours of work, allowable levels of concentration, and so on.
2. The analysis examined the influence of the economic system on law. The interest in this vein of research was based on the recognition that economic forces are significant factors in the promotion of legal change, which, in turn, affects economic performance. In particular, economic forces exert pressures for and against legal change, both to promote new economic interests and to protect old ones. As such, law is seen as an instrument of control—a means by which certain ends can be achieved—and competing interests bring pressure to bear on government in the attempt to use law to promote their own ends.

These two facets of legal-economic scholarship were evidenced in the work of a variety of scholars writing from very different perspectives and paradigms (as exemplified in Samuels 1993), including individuals as diverse as John Bates Clark, Irving Fisher, Hale, and Commons.

Although Clark's marginal-productivity theory of distribution made him something of an apologist for the status quo (in contrast with, e.g., Adams, Hale, and Commons), he was nonetheless very interested in the relationship between the legal framework and the competitive market system. Clark (1894) believed that natural laws (such as the marginal-productivity theory) govern the competitive market system but that these laws are themselves subject to the influence of man-made law; the operation of natural law is channeled through the malleable legal institutions of society, and these legal institutions can facilitate or inhibit the development of the competitive market process. Although he believed that the outcomes dictated by natural law would ultimately triumph (and thus he believed in the primacy of economy over law), Clark felt that a study of legal-economic relations could reveal the legal measures that should be removed and the legal rules that should be employed to speed up the development of the competitive market system.

Fisher opens *The Nature of Capital and Income* ([1906] 1965) with a discussion of the concept of "wealth," followed by a chapter on the notion of "property." Noting that wealth implies ownership, which in turn involves rights over resources (18), Fisher argues that the study of wealth necessarily "brings economics into contact with the whole subject of legal and custom-sanctioned relations" (20), for "there can be no wealth without property rights applying to it, nor property rights without the wealth to which they apply" (22). As such, the presence or absence and the form (complete or partial) of rights influence wealth, the potential for creating wealth, the distribution of wealth, and the uses of wealth (36–40).

Two prominent figures identified with the study of law and economics during the interwar period were Hale and Commons. Hale's emphasis on the integration of economics and law was reflected both in his teaching—particularly his course Legal Factors in Economic Society—and in his writing, much of which dealt with the regulation of railroads and public utilities, fields in which an understanding of the interface between economics and law has always been fundamental.[4] Hale wrote extensively on the legal and economic theory of rate-base valuation, as well as on the regulation of rate structure and level, and his writings were instrumental in the adoption by the courts of the "prudent investment" doctrine of valuation for public utilities (Dorfman [1959] 1969, 161).

Consistent with the realism of the day, Hale's work was very much a challenge to and a critique of the dominant tradition of laissez-faire capitalism. Hale saw legal and economic processes as inseparable and described the economy as a structure of coercive power arrangements and relationships, which necessitated an understanding of the formation and structure of the underlying distribution of economic power. Moreover, he believed that the courts must undertake an intelligent balancing of the gains and losses resulting from the particular statutes brought before them, a process that required "a realistic understanding of the economic effect of the legislation" (quoted in Dorfman [1959] 1969, 163). Although Hale (1924, 1927) believed that ethical judgments ultimately must be the basis for the court's decisions, he felt that the judicial application of economic principles was necessary to ascertain the economic consequences—allocative and distributive—of the legislation whose constitutionality the court was asked to evaluate.

Commons optimistically believed that the primary economic institutions could be formed and reshaped (as needed) to conform to the social changes inherent in a society, a belief that led him to extensively probe the impact of institutions, such as the law, on economic structure and performance and to become actively involved in various reform activities. Commons ([1896] 1996, 225) believed that "no economic problem is more important than the just estimate of the part played by customary and statutory law in social evolution," and, perhaps not surprisingly, much of Commons's work involved an examination of the legal foundations of the capitalist economic system, particularly in his classic treatise, *Legal Foundations of Capitalism* (1924), which benefited from Commons's close contact with law through his involvement with the courts, government commissions, and the drafting of legislation. The emphasis of the book is on describing the role of law and the courts in determining the elements of an economic system. Commons undertook an analysis of a wide variety of cases, working rules, and statutes to probe their impact on the development of modern capitalism and thereby to illuminate the interrelations between legal and economic processes.

Commons's primary interest was to uncover the values underlying the working rules that govern social-economic relations, and he found them in the courts' use of the term "reasonable value." He discovered that legal history showed certain well-defined tendencies on the part of the courts to eliminate the destructive practices of capitalistic institutions, while at the same time ascertaining the "reasonable" policies that should be followed in a competitive system. Thus, "reasonable values" could be used to ground policies that would bring about compromises in arenas of economic conflict—namely, labor disputes, public utility-rate making, tax policy, pricing, and so forth (Bell 1967, 556–57). As the definition of the types of activities that were considered reasonable evolved over time, so too did the legal rules governing social-economic relations. For example, Commons examined the effects of law on the employment relation within the firm, on the market mechanism, and on the wage bargain, as well as, inter alia, the effects of the transformation of the legal definition of property and its impact on business relationships and practices. Through this analysis, Commons fleshed out the workings of the legal-economic nexus—the reciprocal interdependence of economy and law—and the implications thereof for the capitalist economic system.[5]

Although the realist-institutionalist interaction of the 1920s and 1930s did a great deal to bring law and economics together, a similar interaction, but with a distinctly different flavor, commenced in the 1930s at the University of Chicago. (For a more detailed discussion of the Chicago school during this period, see Ross B. Emmett's essay in this volume.[*]) In 1934, Henry Simons, who had been a student of Frank Knight, published a pamphlet titled *A Positive Program for Laissez Faire*, in which he set down a blueprint for a legal/regulatory regime that would ensure the maintenance of competitive conditions in the face of increasing concentration in corporate America. Simons's proposals range from nationalization to placing legal limits on advertising to redefining the courts' criterion regarding the maximum firm size consistent with competition.

A debate over Simons's reappointment in the Economics Department was resolved by giving him a half-time appointment in the law school, where he taught a course titled Economic Analysis of Public Policy, and his appointment there inaugurated the tradition that an economist would serve on the law school faculty. Although Simons was best known for his work in monetary theory, his price-theoretic perspective had a significant influence on, for example, Aaron Director, Milton Friedman, George Stigler, Gordon Tullock, and Warren Nutter. Moreover, his view that law should be structured so as to preserve competition reflected a perspective that has been one of the cornerstones of Chicago law and economics.

Simons helped ensure the continuity and growth of Chicago law and economics by bringing to the law school the individual most responsible for firmly establishing the Chicago law and economics tradition—Aaron Director. Director was a member of the economics faculty in the early 1930s, and his work had a distinct Chicago price-theoretic flavor. In 1946, he assumed the directorship of a university center affiliated with the law school that was dedicated to undertaking "a study of a suitable legal and institutional framework of an effective competitive system" (Coase 1993, 246), and upon Simons's death, he took over responsibility for teaching the course Economic Analysis of Public Policy.

---

[*] Emmett, Ross B. "Entrenching Disciplinary Competence: The Role of General Education and Graduate Study in Chicago Economics", *History of Political Economy*, 1998, 30(4), pp. 134–150.

Director was subsequently invited by Edward Levi to collaborate in teaching the antitrust course (an area of law particularly open to the influence of economic ideas), and through his teachings, he had a formidable influence on Chicago law students, including several individuals—for example, Robert Bork—who went on to become prominent scholars. Director formally established the nation's first law and economics program, founded the *Journal of Law and Economics*, and continued to trumpet the theme that regulation was the proper function of markets, not government, a message that often resulted in legal reasoning losing out to economic analysis.

The most substantial and enduring impact of early Chicago law and economics unquestionably has been in the field of antitrust law, the goal of which, within the Chicago tradition, is the promotion of efficiency.[6] Reflecting the Chicago emphasis on the efficacy of the competitive system, monopoly was viewed as occasional, unstable, and transitory—a potential outcome of the competitive process, but one that would soon be removed (in effect if not in reality) by competitive pressures. Thus rigorous antitrust enforcement was thought to be unnecessary, and even when monopolies were shown to generate long-term inefficiencies, the governmental cure was often thought to be worse than the disease because of the inefficiencies of government.

Although the events in the law school laid the foundation for the development of law and economics at Chicago, a full understanding of this development necessitates an appreciation of the scholarship generated by the faculty of the Economics Department, both before and after World War II.[7] Of the significant figures associated with the early Chicago school, Knight had the biggest impact on what has come to be known as Chicago law and economics. In simple terms, proponents of the early Chicago approach generally accepted the propositions that had been at the heart of economics since the writing of Adam Smith: In a liberal democracy, the rational pursuit of economic self-interest by economic actors was taken as given, competition was seen as inherent in and intrinsic to economic life, and market-generated outcomes were thought to be superior to those resulting from government interference with the market mechanism. Although during the 1930s these propositions (the latter two in particular) were increasingly called into question within the profession at large, their continuity within the Chicago school set the Chicago perspective apart from much of the rest of the economics profession.

The new generation of Chicago economists undertook to elaborate and extend these insights, demonstrating, in formal terms, the detailed nexus between competitive markets and efficient outcomes. Following the lead of Friedman and Stigler, postwar Chicago economists, buttressed by empirical research, argued for less government intervention, fewer wealth redistribution policies, reliance on voluntary exchange and on the common law for mediating conflicts, and an across-the-board promotion of more private enterprise, which, based on the evidence provided by their empirical research, would facilitate a more efficient allocation of resources.

A further early contribution to Chicago law and economics came through the work of Armen Alchian (1961) and Harold Demsetz (1964, 1967) on the economics of property rights.[8] The property rights approach emerged as some economists began to (re)appreciate that legal-institutional arrangements that constrain the behavior of individuals and firms might have a crucial effect on the allocation of society's scarce resources. The main postulate of the economics of property rights is that the nature and form of property rights have a fundamental effect on the allocation of resources and the distribution of income in the economy, with the resulting implication that the study of alternative property right regimes could uncover insights into the performance of the economy. The argument consisted of two parts, one reflecting the influence of law on economy and the other the influence of economy on law. First, it was argued that the value of resources is tied directly to the bundles of rights associated with the resources; that is, the more complete and definite the specification of property rights (i.e., the less attenuated the rights structure), the more uncertainty is diminished, which, in turn, tends to promote a more efficient allocation of resources. Second, proponents of the property rights approach inquired whether the standard theory of production and exchange was capable of explaining the emergence of the institution of property rights over scarce resources. Their empirical research suggested an affirmative answer to this question: The emergence and development of new property rights can be explained as a consequence of value-seeking behavior brought on by new technologies and market opportunities.

New law and economics

The new law and economics has drawn its inspiration from several sources, most prominently Coase's "Problem of Social Cost" (1960) and Guido Calabresi's "Some Thoughts on Risk Distribution and the Law of Torts" (1961). Although the stimulation of economists' interest in this line of research came primarily from Coase (1960), both these articles showed, really for the first time, the wide applicability of the basic tools of neoclassical microeconomic theory and welfare economics to the evaluation of legal rules and their incentive effects. It was not long before economic analysis was being applied to assess the effects of all manner of legal rules: common-law rules of property, contract, and tort; statutes; criminal law; and constitutional law.

This scholarship represented one of the earliest applications of the tools of economic theory to the analysis of noneconomic phenomena and reflected a larger process in which economic analysis came to be viewed as an approach, method, or tool kit applicable to all areas of life in which choices are made rather than simply as the study of the economic system per se. The goal of this analysis was to elucidate how legal rules affect individual behavior within the legal arena through the adjustment of incentives.

1.   In contrast to the standard legal view of individuals as reasonable agents behaving according to the norms and customs of society as reflected in legal rules, the economic approach posits agents as rational maximizers of their satisfactions.
2.   Legal rules are viewed as prices that are taken as given by individuals and used by them in the process of calculating their utility/profit-maximizing response to these legal rules. Changes in legal rules thus function as changes in the constraints subject to which individuals maximize, with corresponding implications for individual behavior.

One of the implications of these first two points is that, whereas the traditional approach to law considers lawbreaking and lawbreakers unreasonable, the economics approach considers both lawbreakers and non-lawbreakers rational, their behavioral differences accounted for by the different constraints under which they maximize utility.

3.   The assessment of legal rules proceeds on the basis of the efficiency of the out-
     comes generated by these rules, in contrast with the "justice" or "fairness" crite-
     rion underlying traditional legal reasoning (although Posner [1981] has argued
     strongly that efficiency comports with the dictates of justice).

A simple example will illustrate the economic approach at work and its contrast
to the traditional approach to common-law questions. First, consider a factory, in an
isolated location, that dumps chemical waste into a river. Suppose that land down-
stream is subsequently developed by farmers who use the water from the river to
irrigate their crops. Finding that the chemicals in the river cause substantial damage
to their crops ($1 million per year), the farmers file suit, asking that the factory be
forced to compensate them for the crop damage. Under the traditional common-law
rule of "coming to the nuisance," the factory would be allowed to continue its dump-
ing in the river. However, suppose that the factory could install filtering devices that
would eliminate the chemical pollution at a cost of $0.5 million per year. The
economic approach would suggest that the factory should be forced to compensate
the farmers for the damage, in which case the factory would choose to install the
filters, since the cost of doing so would be less than the cost of paying the damages.
In this case, the traditional common-law rule leads to an inefficient outcome, since
it does not generate the least-cost response to the nuisance dispute.

What remains is to shed some light on what triggered the development of
contemporary law and economics and why, along the way, the economic analysis of
law was transformed from the study of broad questions of the relationship between
law and economic activity into an exercise in applying microeconomic theory and
welfare economics to the analysis and evaluation of legal rules.

The transformation of law and economics: Coase as "Accidental Tourist"

Perhaps the greatest irony of the transformation of law and economics is that
the work on which this transformation turns, "The Problem of Social Cost," was an
unintended result of law and economics of the *old* variety, originating in Coase's study
of the broadcasting industry in the United States that was itself a continuation of
his earlier study of the British broadcasting industry.[9]

In "The Federal Communications Commission" (1959), Coase took issue with the
fiat-based mechanism by which broadcasting licenses were issued in the United States,
arguing that since frequencies were scarce and valuable resources, greater attention
should be paid to the efficiency of their allocation toward the end of enhancing the
efficiency of the broadcasting industry. Noting that the market seemingly was never
considered as a mechanism for allocating frequencies, Coase showed that a perfectly
functioning market would cause frequencies to be allocated to those who valued
them most highly and, more generally, that in any situation of well-defined rights and
costless transacting, rights will be allocated efficiently, regardless of who initially
receives them. But recognizing that markets always function at least somewhat imper-
fectly, Coase went on to consider the various impediments to achieving the allocation
implied by a perfectly functioning market, considerations relevant to the issue of how

a market in broadcast frequencies might actually work in practice. The culmination of his discussion was what might best be described as a plea to the policy makers for a comparative institutional analysis that took into consideration both the existence of alternative institutional structures for frequency allocation and the imperfections of each.

When Coase's conclusions regarding the efficacy of markets were challenged by a number of the leading figures of the Chicago school, Coase wrote "The Problem of Social Cost" in an attempt both to more fully develop and to generalize his earlier analysis. To illustrate his point about the efficiency of smoothly functioning markets in resolving disputes over rights, Coase invoked several British common-law cases to show, hypothetically, how rights would be rearranged among agents to end up in their highest-valued use, regardless of the legal rule in force. But recognizing that, in most cases, transaction costs would preclude such efficient voluntary reallocations, Coase went on to argue that the economic interests of society would be best served if externality policy were designed to promote the greatest possible value of output in society, which, given the inefficiencies associated with the operations of government, might involve using markets or Pigovian remedies or simply doing nothing at all about the externality problem. Most important for present purposes, Coase applied this perspective to the courts, arguing that judges should, at a minimum, take allocational considerations into account in making decisions about rights that impact economic performance.

But Coase (1960, 19) then went a step further, arguing that "it is clear from a cursory study [of the case record] that the courts have often recognized the economic implications of their decisions and are aware (as many economists are not) of the reciprocal nature of the [externality] problem." Moreover, he said, while "the courts do not always refer very clearly to the economic problems posed by the cases brought before them ... it seems probable that in the interpretation of words and phrases like 'reasonable' or 'common or ordinary use' there is some recognition, perhaps largely unconscious and certainly not very explicit, of the economic aspects of the questions at issue" (22)—a sentiment also found in Commons 1924. Coase went on to illustrate these points with examples.

Viewed from the perspective of the present, "The Problem of Social Cost" immediately calls to mind contemporary work in law and economics. Yet it was a work in the older mode,[10] aimed not at legal scholars and legal scholarship but rather at economists and the practice of economics. "What I wanted to do," said Coase (1993, 251), "was to improve our analysis of the working of the economic system. Law came into the article because, in a regime of positive transaction costs, the character of law becomes one of the main factors determining the performance of the economy." Coase consciously distanced himself from Posner, whose "main interest is in the legal system" (251), by noting that "I have no interest in lawyers or legal education" (quoted in Kitch 1983, 192) and acknowledging that "in the development of the economic analysis of the law [i.e., the new law and economics], ... Posner has clearly played the major role" (Coase 1993, 251). In fact, Coase's work in the field subsequent to the publication of "The Problem of Social Cost" has consisted largely of further inquiries into the U.S. broadcasting industry and other regulatory institutions in an attempt to come to grips with what he has called "the institutional structure of production." This work is decidedly *not* along the Coase-theorem-related lines implied by what many took to be the message of "The Problem of Social Cost" (Medema 1994). Coase's rejection of the assumption of rational utility-maximizing consumers (see, e.g., Coase 1984) is instructive here, particularly considering subsequent developments in the field of law and economics.

The study of the relationship between law and economy came naturally for Coase, who had taken several courses in law and whose mentor, Arnold Plant (1974), had done pioneering work on the analysis of the economic implications of rules governing patents, copyrights, and intellectual property generally. Coase believed that important lessons could be learned by examining the relationship between law and economy—namely, by "examining cases, examining business practices, and showing that there was some sense to them, but it wasn't the sense that people had given to them before" (quoted in Kitch 1983, 193). This perspective, initially applied at Chicago in the area of antitrust, was expanded to various aspects of law, largely through the influence of Director and Coase as editors of the *Journal of Law and Economics*, "the aim of which," according to Coase (1993, 251), "was said to be the examination, of public policy issues of interest to lawyers and economists."

Of course, Coase could not have anticipated the direction that law and economics would take subsequent to "The Problem of Social Cost." But his analysis (and Calabresi's) raised many issues for both economists and lawyers, including the choice-theoretic nature of the questions of legal analysis and the potential applicability of economic theory to the analysis of legal rules and legal decision making.

Explaining the transformation of law and economics

The basic differences of approach between the old and the new law and economics can be described at two different levels of sophistication. At a basic level, the old law and economics was concerned with analyzing the interaction between the law and the economy (as an important or even necessary component of the economic theorizing process), whereas the new law and economics was concerned with applying economic theory to analyze agent behavior within the legal arena and had little or nothing to do with understanding the legal bases of the economic system. At a more sophisticated level, the old and the new law and economics represent distinctive versions of social theory. The old law and economics reflected a multifaceted, pluralistic (as regards the method of economic theorizing), interdisciplinary approach to the analysis of the institutional structure of society, one in which law and economy are mutually determined and determining. The new law and economics, in contrast, was part of a larger imperialist project within economics that, in effect, presented neoclassical microeconomic theory as social theory. Rational-choice analysis was presented as the key to understanding (and, in the hands of many, normatively prescribing) the behavior of agents in all manner of social contexts. That is, it was an overtly neoclassical enterprise that consciously reached beyond the boundaries of economics into other fields to influence the scholarship in those fields rather than to influence our understanding of the operation of the economic system.

What accounts for the demise of the old law and economics and its replacement by the new? One can see the evolution of law and economics from its "law and the economy" bent to the economic analysis of law in the pages of the *Journal of Law and*

Economics, and by the early 1970s, the economic analysis of law had developed to such a point that Posner (1973) could write a substantial treatise on the subject.

Although the growth of law and economics stirred up much controversy within the legal community (such as academic turf wars, the issue of the applicability of the economic model of human behavior, and the "efficiency as justice" issue), no such qualms were evident within the economics community. Although there was some initial questioning of the appropriate boundaries for applying microtheoretic tools of analysis, many economists saw the application of economic tools to legal theory as a natural extension of the economic paradigm, a precedent for which already existed in public-choice analysis, which was well along the development path by this time.

The transformation of law and economics is in some ways a microcosm of the larger transformation within economics during this time, the major aspects of which I leave to other contributors to this volume. For present purposes, the key feature of these transformative processes was the expansion of the domain of economics but the narrowing of its scope and perspective in the postwar era.

The problem of pinpointing the causes for the decline of the old law and economics is compounded by the facts that the old law and economics was not homogeneous or monolithic and that the demise occurred in stages over time. The branch of law and economics rooted in the institutionalist-realist tradition was all but dead as an influential academic phenomenon by the mid-1950s. (For a discussion of the influence of the Social Gospel movement on the rise and fall of institutionalism and an attempt to assess the reasons for the "reproductive failure" of Wisconsin institutionalism, see Bradley W. Bateman's and Jeff Biddle's essays in this volume, respectively.*) Meanwhile, old-style Chicago law and economics only really came into its own in the late 1950s, as evidenced by the establishment of the *Journal of Law and Economics* in 1958. This brand of law and economics held firm within the Chicago school well into the 1960s, before beginning a decline matched by the ascendance of the new law and economics.

That much having been said, we can trace the decline of the old law and economics to certain larger professional forces. First, the old law and economics, although by no means exclusively the property of the institutionalists, was, part and parcel, concerned with the study of institutions. As economics became increasingly defined around the neoclassical paradigm in the postwar era, however, it became progressively a-institutional. The questions addressed by economists, and thus the scope of economics itself, became increasingly defined by the Samuelsonian and Walrasian tools of analysis, which were singularly ill suited to tackle the analysis of institutions such as the legal-economic nexus.

Moreover, the spirit of complementarity and inclusion that characterized the interwar period diminished radically during the postwar period. The bounds of what passed for theory became increasingly narrowly defined, often, or even usually, being equated with the presence of formal mathematical models. The more intuitive approach characteristic of the old law and economics was no longer considered solid economic theory. This was particularly the case for institutional law and economics, as the institutionalists were increasingly denigrated as atheoretical or antitheoretical fact gatherers.

---

* Bateman, Bradley W. "Cleaning the Ground: The Demise of the Social Gospel Movement and the Rise of Neoclassicism in American Economics", History of Political Economy, 1998, 30(4), pp. 29–52. Biddle, Jeff. "Institutional Economics: A Case of Reproductive Failure?", *History of Political Economy*, 1998, 30(4), pp. 108–133.

This was true not just within the profession at large but also within the law and economics community, as witnessed by Stigler's comment that institutional economics "had nothing in it but a stance of hostility to the standard theoretical tradition. There was no positive agenda of research, there was no set of problems or new methods they wanted to invoke" (quoted in Kitch 1983, 170). Furthermore, lacking the "aesthetic appeal" of post-war theory, with its elegant systems of equations and high-powered empirical techniques, the more intuitive and non quantitative empirical nature of the old law and economics was not nearly as attractive to budding scholars, nor was such research the road to professional rewards. (See Roger E. Backhouse's essay in this volume for evidence regarding the increasingly mathematical and quantitative nature of articles published in leading U.S. economics journals during this period.*)

Another important factor at work was the increasing professional emphasis on the search for determinate, optimal solutions to the questions of economic theory and policy in the postwar era. Although the old law and economics did a great deal to elucidate the relationships between legal and economic processes, what it did not do (with the exception of certain aspects of early Chicago law and economics) or even attempt to do was set forth a framework for determining the optimal legal structure for the economic system. As such, this type of theorizing was bound to be discarded as having little to offer to a profession increasingly preoccupied with the search for such solutions.

While the search for determinate, optimal solutions to questions of economic theory and policy in part accounts for the decline of the old law and economics, it also plays an important role in accounting for the rise of the new approach. Most of the standard problems of public economics were quickly absorbed within this framework, but the Coase theorem and the illustrations Coase drew from the legal cases showed that the analysis of legal rules, too, could be placed squarely within the economist's world of determinate optimal solutions. Coase showed, as a means of setting up his analysis of how legal rules affect market outcomes in the real world of positive transaction costs, that within the standard neoclassical (zero transaction cost) framework the form of legal institutions has no impact on the working of markets. What economists seized on, however, was not Coase's intended message (the need for a change of approach to the questions of economic policy analysis) but rather the notion of modeling contests over rights in a neoclassical price-theoretic framework. Since any given assignment of rights expands the opportunity sets of some agents while restricting those of others, legal decision making could easily be converted into an exercise in optimal allocations, based upon which one could derive, in relatively straightforward fashion, the efficient legal rules to govern human behavior.

Thus, by a curious reconstructive twist, Coase's analysis of how legal institutions influence economic performance was twisted around to provide the supposed basis for the analysis of all manner of legal rules within the maximization-plus-equilibrium framework so much in vogue in postwar economics. And seeing a potentially fruitful extension of the economic paradigm into the legal arena, economists were quick to begin mining the new territory.

Moreover, Coase's suggestions regarding judges' applications of economic logic in their thinking stimulated a number of scholars—Posner in particular—to examine

---

* Backhouse, Roger. "The Transformation of U.S. Economics, 1920–1960, Viewed through a Survey of Journal Articles", *History of Political Economy*, 1988, 30(4), pp. 85–107.

whether an efficiency logic might be underlying the development of legal rules across the common law. Doing so involved the rather straightforward application of individual decision-making calculus to agents faced with constraints imposed by common-law rules and the assessment of the resulting outcomes according to the dictates of Paretian welfare economics. And of course, where extant rules were found to be inefficient, the determination of rules that would induce optimal behavior was a natural extension.

A further reason for the openness among economists to the application of economic theory to legal reasoning (which perhaps led to a more positive reception to law and economics than to, e.g., economic sociology, at least early on) is that many of the legal questions the economists addressed had a substantial identifiable economic (i.e., dollar-valued) component, as illustrated in the previous example. Rights are valuable: Alternative assignments of rights generate alternative patterns and levels of benefits and costs among the affected parties. Moreover, legal rules, when established as precedents, provide incentives that channel individual decisions and actions in particular directions. From these points, it was just a short and natural leap to the conclusion that it is important to assess the degree to which legal rules promote the efficient allocation of resources, just as economists for decades had proposed efficiency-enhancing regulations through the political process. And it was just a further short leap to the analysis of *all* classes of legal rules (including those involving non-dollar-valued claims), given the assumption of a consistency of individual reasoning across the legal spectrum.

Coupled with this was the view (among economists) of economics as the queen of the social sciences, a perception flowing in part from its rigorous, testable theoretical models, which the other social sciences lacked. Although this factor helped fuel the imperialist tendencies of economists, it took on particular import for the success of the law and economics movement because law was at this time engaged in a search for moorings following the decline of legal realism (Posner 1987). The idea of establishing a "scientific" basis for law through the application of economic theory created a degree of receptiveness within the legal community to economists' attempts at void filling that might well not have been present at another time, and economists were happy to attempt to fill this void.

Although the overriding concern of the present discussion is with positive law and economics, I would be remiss if I did not address the normative overtones that, at the very least, fueled the early development of the new law and economics within certain quarters. It goes without saying that the so-called interventionisin of the institutionalists contrasts starkly with the Chicago approach to antitrust and the market-oriented nature of the Chicago approach generally. (For example, the institutionalists were prominently represented within the U.S. economic-planning bureaucracy described in Marcia L. Balisciano's essay in this volume. Anne Mayhew's essay in this book provides some insights into the normative features underlying the institutionalist and Chicago views of antitrust regulation.[*]) But the post-1960 developments in law and economics provided a rather sturdy intellectual foundation for a market-oriented approach to legal decision making. The Coase theorem opened the door to the analysis of rights allocation within a traditional market framework and to the

---

[*] Mayhew, Anne. "How American Economists Came to Love the Sherman Antitrust Act", History of Political Economy, 1998, 30(4), pp. 179–201.

asking of a relatively simple question: If rights over scarce resources are allocated through the market for all manner of goods, why would the same not apply to rights over pollution, the ability to breach contracts, tortious harms, and so on? To a mind-set that finds market allocation most congenial, the Coase theorem opened up a vast new scope for the operation of markets. If market processes are allowed to work, legal outcomes will be exactly those dictated by the laws governing competitive markets. The implications of this insight were straightforward and quickly seized upon: (1) Let the market work in allocating rights; (2) facilitate the working of the market by removing legal impediments to its operation; and (3) when (1) and (2) are not possible, assign rights or design legal rules to mimic the outcome of a competitive market, the outcome that would have obtained in any event had there not been impediments to the market's operation.

This argument is amazingly powerful, since it implies that the law should simply be structured to let people do what they would naturally do if transaction costs did not preclude them from doing so. And in an era in which so-called activist judges were making decisions that often seemed to conflict with the ideology of the market, the implications of the economic analysis of law were welcome ammunition for those who favored the market. Thus it is not surprising that the new law and economics movement was launched from within the Chicago school, even given its important place within law and economics of the old variety. In addition, the willingness of certain conservative organizations to provide financial support for the law and economics movement (such as the John M. Olin Foundation, which provides substantial funding for a number of law and economics programs across the United States) helped facilitate both the program of research and the classroom dissemination of these ideas. (For a more general discussion of the influence of external funding on the direction of economic research over the course of the twentieth century, see Craufurd D. Goodwin's essay in this volume.[*])

It bears emphasizing that none of these normative conclusions is inherent in the examination of legal rules using the tools of neoclassical economic analysis, and it is both incorrect and irresponsible to equate the new law and economics with conservative ideology. Indeed, the scholars working in the field come from a wide variety of perspectives and draw many conclusions at odds with conservative ideology. However, it would be difficult to deny that law and economics has been used to promote certain normative agendas, not unlike, at times, institutionalist-realist law and economics. When combined with the goal of facilitating competitive market outcomes, the Pandora's box opened by "The Problem of Social Cost" gave ample opportunity for individuals so inclined to design legal rules that would comport with the dictates of competitive markets.

Conclusion

This essay has attempted to document, from the perspective of economics, the transformation in law and economics over the course of the twentieth century. Although the growth of the new law and economics was fueled by forces at work in both the

---

[*]   Goodwin, Craufurd D. "The Patrons of Economics in a Time of Transformation," *History of Political Economy*, 1998, 30(4), pp. 53–81.

legal and the economics communities, I have attempted to shed some light on the forces that attracted economists to the economic analysis of law and led them to neglect the issues raised by law and economics of the older variety.

The present essay takes us into the 1970s, when law and economics hit its stride, but much has changed since that time. In particular, the scope of law and economics—particularly in the methods employed and problems examined—has expanded greatly. For example, recent work on the foundations of behavior in the legal arena has challenged certain standard conclusions in the field (Medema 1997). More important for present purposes, there has been a substantial resurgence of interest in law and economics of the older variety, as evidenced in the work of Oliver Williamson, Douglass North, Yoram Barzel, Thráinn Eggertsson, Warren J. Samuels, and A. Allan Schmid, to name just a few.[11] Although certain aspects of this analysis have commonalities with the new law and economics examined above, what is important is that economists have begun to turn back to an examination of the institutional (including legal) underpinnings of the economic system—that is, to the roots of law and economics.

Notes

1   This literature also tends to convey the impression that law and economics is a rather homogeneous neoclassical enterprise, which is also somewhat misleading (Mercuro and Medema 1997).

2   This statement is false if one defines law and economics broadly to include the general interrelationships between government and economy. For present purposes, however, I define law and economics somewhat more narrowly.

3   For expositional convenience, I use the term "old" law and economics to refer to the law and economics associated with the interwar period and with the Chicago school prior to the early 1960s. Certain aspects of my discussion of old law and economics are based on Mercuro and Medema 1997. The "new" law and economics refers to the post-1960 law and economics associated with Posner and others.

4   Extensive discussions of Hale can be found in Samuels 1973; Dorfman [1959] 1969; and Duxbury 1995.

5   Through his work on proportional representation, Commons ([1907] 1974) made an early contribution to the economic analysis of political choices by exploring the manner in which rules influence the determination of whose preferences will count within the political process.

6   A useful overview of antitrust from a Chicago perspective is contained in Posner 1976.

7   See, for example, Reder 1982 and the references cited therein,

8   For a concise overview of the early economics of property rights literature, see Furubotn and Pejovich 1972.

9   To understand the origins of "The Problem of Social Cost" one must examine the greater corpus of Coase's analysis of institutions. See Medema 1994 for discussions of these various works.

10   See Medema 1996 for a discussion of the commonalities between the law and economics of Coase and of the institutionalists.

11   See Eggertsson 1990 and Mercuro and Medema 1997, chaps. 4–5, for surveys of this literature.

References

Adams, Henry C. [1887/1897] 1954. *Relation of the State to Industrial Action and Economics and Jurisprudence*. Edited by Joseph Dorfman. New York: Viking.

Alchian, Armen, A. 1961. *Some Economics of Property*. Santa Monica, Calif.: RAND Corporation.

Bell, John F. 1967. *A History of Economic Thought*. New York: Ronald Press.

Berle, Adolf A., and Gardiner C. Means. 1932. *The Modern Corporation and Private Property*. New York: Macmillan.

Calabresi, Guido. 1961. Some Thoughts on Risk Distribution and the Law of Torts. *Yale Law Journal* 70 (March): 499–553.

Clark, John Bates. 1894. The Modern Appeal to Legal Forces in Economic Life. *American Economic Association Publications* 9.

Coase, Ronald H. 1959. The Federal Communications Commission. *Journal of Law and Economics* 2 (October): 1–40.

———. 1960. The Problem of Social Cost. *Journal of Law and Economics* 3 (October): 1–44.

———. 1984. The New Institutional Economics. *Journal of Institutional and Theoretical Economics* 140 (March): 229–31.

———. 1993. Law and Economics at Chicago. *Journal of Law and Economics* 36 (April, part 2): 239–54.

Commons, John R. [1896] 1996. Political Economy and Law. *The Kingdom* 24 January. Reprinted in *John R. Commons: Selected Essays*. Edited by Malcolm Rutherford and Warren J. Samuels. London: Routledge.

———. [1907] 1974. *Proportional Representation*. 2d ed. Reprint, New York: Augustus M. Kelley.

———. 1924. *Legal Foundations of Capitalism*. New York: Macmillan.

———. 1925. Law and Economics. *Yale Law Journal* 34 (February): 371–82.

Demsetz, Harold. 1964. The Exchange and Enforcement of Property Rights. *Journal of Law and Economics* 7 (October): 11–26.

———. 1967. Toward a Theory of Property Rights. *American Economic Review* 57 (May): 347–59.

Dorfman, Joseph. [1959] 1969. *The Economic Mind in American Civilization*. Vols. 4 and 5, 1918–1933. Reprint, New York: Augustus M. Kelley.

Duxbury, Neil. 1995. *Patterns of American Jurisprudence*. Oxford: Oxford University Press.

Eggertsson, Thráinn. 1990. *Economic Behavior and Institutions*. Cambridge: Cambridge University Press.

Fisher, Irving. [1906] 1965. *The Nature of Capital and income*. Reprint, New York: Augustus M. Kelley.

Furubotn, Eirik G., and Svetozar Pejovich. 1972. Property Rights and Economic Theory: A Survey of the Literature. *Journal of Economic Literature* 10 (December): 1137–62.

Hale, Robert Lee. 1924. Economic Theory and the Statesman. In *The Trend of Economics*. Edited by Rexford G. Tugwell. New York: Knopf.

———. 1927. Economics and the Law. In *The Social Sciences and Their Interrelations*. Edited by William F. Ogbum and Alexander A. Goldenweiser. Boston: Houghton Mifflin.

———. 1952. *Freedom through Law*. New York: Columbia University Press.

Hamilton, Walton H. 1932. Property according to Locke. *Yale Law Journal* 41 (April): 864–80.

Holmes, Oliver Wendell. 1897. The Path of Law. *Harvard Law Review* 10 (March): 457–78.

Kitch, Edmund W., ed. 1983. The Fire of Truth: A Remembrance of Law and Economics at Chicago, 1932–1970. *Journal of Law and Economics* 26 (April): 163–234.

Medema, Steven G. 1994. *Ronald H. Coase*. New York: St. Martin's.

——. 1996. Ronald Coase and American Instifutionalism. *Research in the History of Economic Thought and Methodology* 14:51–92.

——. 1997. On the Trial of *Homo Economicus:* What Law and Economics Tells Us about the Development of Economic Imperialism. In *New Economics and Its Writing. HOPE* 27 supplement. Edited by John B. Davis. Durham, N.C.: Duke University Press.

Mercuro, Nicholas, and Steven G. Medema. 1997. *Economics and the Law: From Posner to Post Modernism*. Princeton, N.J.: Princeton University Press.

Plant, Sir Arnold. 1974. *Selected Economic Essays and Addresses*. London: Routledge and Kegan Paul.

Posner, Richard A. 1973. *Economic Analysis of Law*. 1st ed. Boston: Little, Brown.

——. 1976. *Antitrust Law: An Economic Perspective*. Chicago: University of Chicago Press.

——. 1981. *The Economics of Justice*. Cambridge, Mass.: Harvard University Press.

——. 1987. The Decline of Law as an Autonomous Discipline, 1962–1987. *Harvard Law Review* 100 (February): 761–80.

Reder, Melvin W. 1982. Chicago Economics: Permanence and Change. *Journal of Economic Literature* 20 (March): 1–38.

Samuels, Warren J. 1973. The Economy as a System of Power and Its Legal Bases: The Legal Economics of Robert Lee Hale. *University of Miami Law Review* 27 (spring/summer): 261–371.

——. 1993. Law and Economics: Some Early Journal Contributions. In *Economic Thought and Discourse in the Twentieth Century*. Edited by Warren J. Samuels, Jeff Biddle, and Thomas W. Patchak-Schuster. Aldershot, England: Edward Elgar.

PART 2

Towards an economic analysis of law

THAT RONALD COASE and his *Problem of Social Cost* has played a role of the utmost importance in the evolution of "law and economics", there is no doubt. It certainly transformed the field, as well as making it more visible among economists, lawyers and legal scholars in academia. However, this was not sufficient in itself. Firstly, one should not neglect the fact that the field's visibility has also been assured by the action of very influential conservative think-tanks. Secondly, the expansion and growth of the "law and economics" movement also depended on its success outside universities and law schools. It was very important not only to convince economics and law professors, but lawyers and judges as well. In this respect, Henry Manne played a particularly important role as an "intellectual entrepreneur". He contributed like no other to establish "law and economics" in and outside academia through the creation of various centers of research in law and economics and the organization of seminars in which judges and advocates would participate (see the autobiographical recollection Manne gives of his role, 2006; and Teles, 2008, pp. 90–134). After a decade of scientific and institutional activities, at the turn of the 70s, "law and economics" was thus established and accepted as an important area of research. It was then that another dramatic change occured, with the birth of an "economic analysis of law".

It can be argued that Guido Calabresi, law professor at Yale Law School, had already developed economic analyses of legal problems ten years before William Landes, Isaac Ehrlich and Richard Posner. Calabresi dealt with problems raised in tort law and accident law and focused on the costs of accidents and the assignment of liability (see for instance, 1961, 1965, 1970, and Calabresi and Melamed, 1972, among other important writings). Calabresi (in fact, anticipated and) extended Coase's analysis and developed a theory that defended a strict liability rule as a means to internalize the costs of accidents. In other words, Calabresi dealt at the same time with a legal problem – the choice of a liability rule – using economic tools, as well as an economic problem, namely to reduce the costs of accidents. These analyses were and remain particularly rich and important and it would be wrong to say that they were ignored. However, they were published at a time when "law and economics" was not yet fully accepted. It probably explains why Calabresi's economic analysis of law did not gain the recognition Posner's work was to enjoy. In fact, Calabresi's works gained indirect recognition in the late 60s and direct recognition in the early 70s, when "law and economics" was being transformed into an "economic analysis of law", under the influence of William Landes, Isaac Ehrlich (two economists) and Richard A. Posner (a lawyer).

The transformation of "law and economics" into an "economic analysis of law" assumed a quantitative and qualitative form that can be explained by the fact that – in contrast to other contributors to "law and economics", including Calabresi – Posner, Landes and Ehrlich did not employ the same definition of economics and did not use the same economic analysis.

A quantitative change

The use of a new label – which corresponds to the title of a textbook written by Posner (1973) – clearly indicates the change of perspective and accordingly emphasizes the differences between the new approach and the older one: in contrast to "law and economics", Posner's "economic analysis of law" no longer set out to understand the functioning of the economy but rather aimed to analyze the working of the legal system. Thus, as Posner writes in his 1975 article: "[t]he hallmark of the 'new' law and economics is the application of the theories and empirical methods of economics to the *central institutions of the legal system*" (p. 39; emphasis added). One finds confirmation that Posner intended adopting a new perspective in the titles of the articles and books that he wrote at that time. Among the books, one may quote an *Economic Analysis of Law* (1973a, 2007 for the 7th edition), *Antitrust Law: An Economic Perspective* (1976, 2001); and among the articles, there are "An Economic Approach to Legal Procedure and Judicial Administration" (1973b), "An Economic Analysis of Legal Rulemaking" (co-authored with Isaac Ehrlich in 1974), "The Economic Approach to Law" (1975) and "The Rule of Reason and the Economic Approach: Reflections on the Sylvania Decision" (1977). Posner therefore clearly puts forward that for an "economic analysis of the law", by contrast with the "law and economics" perspective, those problems analyzed are on the legal and no longer on the economic, side; economics being then viewed as "an especially apt" (1971c, p. 202) or "powerful" (1973a, [1986], p. 3; 1973b, p. 399) "tool".

This is significant as a change and even reversal of the perspective adopted by Coase. In effect, Posner does not assume that there exists a subset of the activities of human beings that are specifically of economic nature and that can be analyzed by economists. In more specific words, Posner adopts a perspective in which economics is no longer defined by its subject matter or in reference to a specific object of study. On the contrary, according to Posner, there is no such thing as a subject matter specific to economics and to which economists should restrict their attention. To him, economic analysis is based on certain concepts not focused on certain topics: "when used in sufficient density these concepts make a work of scholarship 'economic' *regardless of its subject matter or its author's degree*" (1987, p. 2, emphasis added). In other words, it is not the nature of the problem analyzed that does or does not trigger the use of economic tools: on the contrary, an economic problem is what can be analyzed with economic tools. By arguing that economics is just such a set of tools, Posner suggests that no restriction can be imposed on the use of these tools. Any kind of problem or phenomenon – including noneconomic and in particular legal ones – can be analyzed with economic tools.

This change of methodological perspective on the nature of economics implied a quantitative transformation of "law and economics": in other words, an "economic analysis of law" that is not as limited as "law and economics". The result is an increase in the quantity of topics that can be analyzed by economists or lawyer-economists. Thus, Henry Manne suggests that Posner's Economic Analysis of the Law was "revolutionary" because it "demonstrate[s] the universal applicability of economic analysis to every area of law" – in which "universal" bears a quantitative meaning. After Posner, "[n]ever again would Law and Economics be thought of as exclusively the domain of antitrust and corporate law. Now its domain was the very heart of the legal system, torts, property, contracts, domestic relations, procedure, even constitutional law".

And indeed, that which is labelled "law and economics" but should be labelled "economic analysis of law" is concerned with all the dimensions of the law and legal system; it would be too long and, above all, too fastidious a task to list these topics.

A qualitative extension of "law and economics"

In the process of transformation of "law and economics" into an "economic analysis of law", one should not forget the role and influence of 1992 Nobel Prize winner Gary Becker (acknowledged and emphasized by Posner; see, in particular, 1993). In effect, Posner and Landes and Ehrlich used the methodological perspective – economics as a set of tools, without a precise subject matter – that Becker adopted in the late 1960s and which he explained in his writings in the early 1970s. This is no surprise. Posner made his acquaintance in 1970 when he became involved, along with William Landes and Isaac Ehrlich, two former Ph.D. students of Becker, in a research program sponsored by the National Bureau of Economic Research in law and economics (for details see Posner, 1993; Landes, 1998).

Now, at that time, Becker has already claimed that economics should not be restricted to the analysis of a priori defined economic activities. On the contrary, he argued, economics can be used to understand how human beings behave in any aspects of their life. For Becker, there is no reason to limit the domain of application of economics because there is no reason to make a difference between behaviors that can be analyzed by economic science and others that should not; there is no reason to assume a discontinuity in the attitude of individuals on markets and their attitude towards rules because no discontinuity exists: "human behavior is not compartmentalized, sometimes based on maximizing, sometimes not, sometimes motivated by stable preferences, sometimes by volatile ones, sometimes resulting in an optimal accumulation of information, sometimes not" (Becker, 1976, p. 14).

Therefore, there is no legitimacy in assuming that individuals are rational in certain circumstances and irrational in others. To adopt an economic *approach* means assuming that human beings are consistently rational because economics is a science that analyzes *rational* choice under the constraint of scarcity rather than a science that analyzes certain activities.

Posner agrees with this perspective on economics and bases his *Economic Analysis of Law* on Becker's definition: "[a]s conceived in this book, economics is the science of rational choice in a world – our world – in which resources are limited in relation to human wants" (1973, p. 3) and "[the] domain of economics is broader than [. . .] the study of inflation, unemployment, business cycles and other mysterious macroeconomic phenomena remote from the day-to-day concern of the legal system" (ibid.).

An economic analysis of law therefore assumes that the individuals who participate in the functioning of the legal system behave as economists assume they do: they are, or behave as if they were, rational utility maximizers. Let us note that this does not necessarily mean that individuals actually are rational utility maximizers, or that only economic explanations, based on this assumption, are possible and acceptable. There are alternative ways of approaching legal phenomena but for those who use neo-classical economics, as Becker, Landes and Posner do, modeling the functioning of the legal system with economic tools necessarily implies that one has to adopt the assumptions on which these models rest and, in particular, those which concern individual behaviors.

Becker initiated the movement with his analysis of behaviors on the demand side of the legal market, with his famous article entitled *Crime and Punishment: An Economic Approach* (1968), and Ehrlich pushed it further. On their side, Landes, and above all Posner, were the first to use economics to model the supply side of the legal market: courts' behavior and legal decision making. In an afterword to the *Journal of Legal Studies* he launched in 1972, Posner even presented the development of a scientific theory of legal decision-making as one of the major goals of the newly founded *Journal*. To some extent, one may argue that this is what made an "economic analysis of law" so specific. In effect, before Posner, the behavior of courts and judicial decision-making was either ignored or viewed from a law and economics angle. Nothing is said about the process that leads to the decision, the origins of legal rules or the way judges make their decisions. In other words, the behavior of judges remains outside of the scope of the analysis. All this changed with Posner, who can therefore be viewed as a genuine innovator: legal rules are no longer given but become an object of analysis for economics; and judges become rational individuals who produce these goods (we will go into more detail about this in subsequent sections).

Beyond an "economic analysis of law"

The use of economics – defined as a science of rational choice – to analyze any kind of legal phenomenon that Posner put forward was indeed a new area of research in the 70s. Posner's personality and the novelty of his "economic analysis of law" attracted a lot of scholars. Young scholars, in particular, were much taken with the analysis and, as Michael Graetz recalls, "thought that it was something that [they] had to read and understand" (quoted in Teles, 2008, p. 99). But visibility has drawbacks. The field very rapidly attracted the attention of opponents and rivals, from the left but also from the right, economists as well as legal scholars. This gave birth to a lot of criticisms, on the grounds that the economic analyses of the law were (complementarily or alternatively) ideologically or politically biased and methodologically flawed.

Among them, let us mention the criticisms of James Buchanan (1974) and Ronald Coase himself (1978, 1993). This is particularly interesting because Buchanan is one of the founders of *public choice* theory and *constitutional political economy* and Coase, as discussed earlier, practically launched "law and economics". They nonetheless opposed the use of economics – as a science of rational choice – to analyze legal phenomena more or less for the same reason: they did not retain the same definition of economics as Posner and failed to share Posner's confidence in individual rationality as utility maximization. To Coase and to Buchanan, legal rules should not be analyzed by economists. The former took them as given and this leads us back to "law and economics"; the latter assumes that they emerge from the interactions between individuals and therefore cannot be analyzed by economists.

A criticism of the same kind can be found in the work of F. A. Hayek. The criticism remains implicit – Hayek never explicitly criticized "law and economics" and "economic analyses of the law" – but his contributions to "law and economics" are based on the assumption that human beings have limited cognitive capacities and therefore should not be modeled as rational utility maximizers; put differently, Hayek disagrees with the traditional behavioral assumptions of economic analysis, and this perspective has important and multiple consequences in terms of "law and economics". There exists an "austrian law and economics" which mainly rests on the assumption that legal rules must not be viewed from the top – as objects produced by judges, as in standard "economic analyses of law" – but must be viewed from the bottom: legal rules emerge from the interactions that take place among individuals.

Interestingly, Hayek's writings on the limited capacity of human cognition parallels what economists and psychologists have put forward on human psychology. Like the former, the latter have evidenced – essentially through experiments – that the standard behavioral assumption used in economics is unrealistic. Human beings do not actually behave as economists assume they do. Their rationality is limited and they may err in their judgement; their decisions rest on the way they perceive their environment and those perceptions are constrained or biased by, among other factors, the context in which their actions take place or the conditions they are faced with; also, individuals are not as self-interested as economics usually assumes. Those findings on human psychology and human behavior have led some economists to question the standard economic models — arguing that their predictions should be erroneous because they were based on an unrealistic image of human beings — and to build new models and develop new analyses more sophisticated than the standard economic models. Those economists develop a new area of research, namely "behavioral economics". In "law and economics", this area of research is known as "behavioral law and economics". "Behavioral law and economics" thus consists of the analysis of legal phenomena that takes into account those behavioral imperfections and biases, as well as the limitations that obviously characterize human beings. In other words, while "economic analyses of the law" are based on the assumptions that individuals react rationally to incentives and that legal rules are themselves incentives, "behavioral law and economics" argues that individuals do not react to incentives – at least in the way economic models predict they should do.

References

Summary

The key developments described above can be found in the vast array of works of the scholars involved in the emergence of an "economic analysis of law", leading to the extension and transformation of "law and economics". It would be too lengthy a task to mention all those who participated in the process and the references listed in section 3.4.3 below are useful to understand the evolution from "law and economics" to an "economic analysis of law". However, if one were to restrict one's attention to the major contribution to an "economic analysis of law", Posner's works are of the utmost importance, not only because he was at the center of the evolution of the field but also because of the simplicity with which he explains particularly complex ideas. In particular, the introductory section of his *Economic Analysis of Law* is of great interest because of his methodological statements. Similarly, an article published in the *Texas Law Review* is worth reading because it was written for an audience of jurists and legal scholars; one can find enlightening details about how to define economics and law and economics or economic analysis of law. The economic equivalent of this paper – which we have included in this volume – was published in the *American Economic Review* a few years later; his interest lies in the fact that Posner explains to economists the very nature of what being an economist means.

As explained in our introduction, Posner is not the only contributor to the emergence of law and economics. William Landes and Isaac Ehrlich have also played an important role in the emergence of an economic analysis of law. Landes has given a clear and detailed presentation of how things happened in the early 1970s between him, Ehrlich, Posner and Becker. The latter, in particular, has played an important role in the evolution of "law and economics" and its transformation into an economic analysis of law, not because of his relatively scarce contributions to the field but because of his methodological influence. This is explained by Posner in an article published in 1993. One of the best summaries of Becker's methodological claims can be found in his Nobel lecture published in the *Journal of Political Economy*, also in 1993.

The limits, drawbacks and flaws have been discussed in a large number of articles that remain important to take into account because they help to understand the reception of the "economic analysis of law" in the 1970s (Baker, 1975; Cranston, 1977; Horwitz, 1981; Kennedy, 1981; Veljanovski, 1980). Then, to understand the likely future of an "economic analysis of law", it is important to read articles dealing with "behavioral law and economics". From this perspective, a lot of contributions have been made looking at the different possible applications of a behavioral law and economics framework but general articles are less frequent. Among them (Korobkin and Ulen, 2000; Sunstein, 1997 a, b, 2001; Sunstein, Jolls, Thaler, 1998), a recent up-date can be found in a 2007 book chapter written by Christine Jolls.

Further reading

Baker, Edwin C. 1975. "The Ideology of the Economic Analysis of Law", *Philosophy and Public Affairs*, 5 (1), pp. 3–48.

Becker, Gary S. 1976. *The Economic Approach to Human Behavior*, Chicago: University of Chicago Press.

Becker, Gary S. 1993. "Nobel Lecture: The Economic Way of Looking at Behavior", *Journal of Political Economy*, 101 (3), pp. 385–409.

Buchanan, James M. 1974. "Good Economics – Bad Law", *Virginia Law Review*, 60 (3), pp. 483–492.

Calabresi, Guido. 1961. "Some Thoughts on Risk Distribution and the Law of Torts", *Yale Law Journal*, 70 (4), pp. 499–553.

Calabresi, Guido. 1965. "The Decision for Accidents: An Approach to Nonfault Allocation of Costs", *Harvard Law Review*, 78 (4), pp. 713–745.

Calabresi, Guido. 1970. *The Costs of Accidents: A Legal and Economic Analysis*, New Haven: Yale University Press.

Calabresi, Guido and Douglas A. Melamed. 1972. "Property Rules, Liability Rules, and Inalienability: One View of the Cathedral", *Harvard Law Review*, 85 (6), pp. 1089–1128.

Coase, Ronald H. 1978. "Economics and Contiguous Disciplines", *Journal of Legal Studies*, 7 (2), 201–211.

Coase, Ronald H. 1993. "Law and Economics at Chicago", *Journal of Law and Economics*, 36 (1), Part 2, John M. Olin Centennial Conference in Law and Economics at the University of Chicago (April), pp. 239–254.

Cranston, Ross. 1977. "Creeping Economism: Some Thoughts on Law and Economics", *British Journal of Law and Society*, 4 (1), pp. 103–115.

Garoupa, Nuno. 2003. "Behavioral Economic Analysis of Crime: A Critical Review", *European Journal of Law and Economics*, 15 (1), pp. 5–15.

Horwitz, Morton. 1980. "Law and economics: science or politics? ", *Hofstra. Law Review*, 8: 903–912.

Jolls Christine. 2007. "Behavioral Law and Economics", in *Economic Institutions and Behavioral Economics*, edited by Peter Diamond, Princeton University Press, p. 46.

Jolls Christine, Cass R. Sunstein and Richard Thaler. 1998. "A Behavioral Approach to Law and Economics", *Stanford Law Review*, 50 (5), pp. 1471–1550.

Kennedy, Duncan. 1981. "Cost-Benefit Analysis of Entitlement Problems: A Critique", *Stanford Law Review*, 33 (3), pp. 387–445.

Korobkin Russell B. and Thomas S. Ulen. 2000. "Law and Behavioral Science: Removing the Rationality Assumption from Law and Economics", *California Law Review*, 88 (4), pp. 1051–1144.

Landes, William. 1998. "The Art of Law and Economics: An Autobiographical Essay", *The American Economist*, 1 (Spring 1997), reprinted in *Passion and Craft, Economists at Work*, reprinted in this volume.

Manne, Henry. 2006. "How law and economics was marketed in a hostile world: a very personal history", in *The Origins of Law and Economics: Essays by the Founding Fathers*, edited by Francesco Parisi and Charles K. Rowley, Cheltenham, Edward Elgar, Chapter 12, pp. 309–327.

Medema, Steve. 2006. From "Law and Economics" to an "Economic Analysis of Law", mimeo.

Posner, Richard A. 1975. "The Economic Approach to Law", *Texas Law Review*, 53, pp. 757–782.

Posner, Richard A. 1993. "Gary Becker's Contribution to Law and Economics", *Journal of Legal Studies*, 22 (2), pp. 211–215.

Posner, Richard A. 2007 [1973]. *Economic Analysis of Law*, Aspen's Publishers.

Sunstein, Cass R. 1997a. "Behavioral Analysis of Law", *University of Chicago Law Review*, 64 (4), pp. 1175–1195.

Sunstein, Cass. 1997b. "behavioral Law and Economics: A Progress Report", *American Law and Economics Review*, 1 (1), pp. 115–157.

Sunstein, Cass R. 2001. *Behavioral Law and Economics*, Cambridge: Cambridge University Press.

Teles, Steven M. 2008. *The Rise of the Conservative Legal Movement*, Princeton: Princeton University Press.

Veljanovski, Cento G. 1980. "The Economic Approach to Law: A Critical Introduction", *British Journal of Law and Society*, 7 (2), pp. 158–193.

Chapter 3

Richard A. Posner

THE LAW AND ECONOMICS MOVEMENT

I N THE LAST THIRTY YEARS, the scope of economics has expanded dramatically beyond its traditional domain of explicit market transactions.[1] Today there is an economic theory of property rights, of corporate and other organizations, of government and politics, of education, of the family, of crime and punishment, of anthropology, of history, of information, of racial and sexual discrimination, of privacy, even of the behavior of animals—and, overlapping all these but the last, of law.[2]

Some economists oppose this expansion, in whole or (more commonly) in part.[3] There are a number of bad reasons, all I think closely related, for such opposition, and one slightly better one.

1) One bad reason is the idea that economics *means* the study of markets, so that nonmarket behavior is simply outside its scope. This type of argument owes nothing really to economics, but instead reflects a common misconception about language—more specifically a failure to distinguish among three different types of word or concept. The first type, illustrated by the term "marginal cost," is purely conceptual. The term is rigorously and unambiguously defined by reference to other concepts, just as numbers are; but (again like numbers) there is no observable object in the real world that it names. (Try finding a firm's marginal costs on its books of account!) The second type of word, illustrated by "rabbit," refers to a set of real-world objects. Few such words are purely referential; one can speak of a pink rabbit or a rabbit the size of a man without misusing the word, even though one is no longer using it to describe anything that exists. Nevertheless, the referential function dominates. Finally, there are words like "law," "religion," "literature" —and "economics" —which are neither conceptual nor referential. Such words resist all efforts at definition. They have, in fact, no fixed meaning, and their dictionary definitions are circular. They can be used but not defined.[4]

One cannot say that economics is what economists do, because many noneconomists do economics. One cannot call economics the science of rational choice, either. The word "rational" lacks a clear definition; and, passing that difficulty, there can be noneconomic theories of rational choice, in which few predictions of ordinary economics may hold; for example, because the theory assumes that people's preferences are unstable.

There can also be nonrational economic theories; an example is the type of survival theory in industrial organization in which firms that randomly hit on methods of lowering their costs expand vis-à-vis their rivals; another example is Marxism. One cannot call economics the study of markets either, not only because that characterization resolves the question of the domain of economics by an arbitrary definitional stop but also because other disciplines, notably sociology, anthropology, and psychology, also study markets. About the best one can say is that there is an open-ended set of concepts (such concepts as perfect competition, utility maximization, equilibrium, marginal cost, consumers' surplus, elasticity of demand, and opportunity cost), most of which are derived from a common set of assumptions about individual behavior and can be used to make predictions about social behavior; and that when used in sufficient density these concepts make a work of scholarship "economic" regardless of its subject matter or its author's degree. When economics is "defined" in this way, there is nothing that makes the study of marriage and divorce less suitable a priori for economics than the study of the automobile industry or the inflation rate.

2) The "extension" of economics from market to nonmarket behavior is sometimes thought to be premature until the main problems in the study of explicit markets have been solved. How can economists hope to explain the divorce rate when they can't explain behavior under oligopoly? But this rhetorical question is just a variation on the first point, that economics has a fixed subject matter, a predefined domain. The tools of economics may be no good for solving a number of important problems in understanding explicit markets; that is no reason to keep hitting one's head against the wall. Economics does not have a predestined mission to dispel all the mysteries of the market. Maybe it will do better with some types of nonmarket behavior than with some types of market behavior.

3) Next is the idea that to do economics in fields that have their own scholarly traditions, such as history or law, an economist must master so much noneconomic learning that his total educational investment will be disproportionate to the likely fruits of "interdisciplinary" research; hence economists should steer clear of these fields. Besides disregarding the possibility of collaboration between economists and practitioners of other disciplines, this argument assumes that economics means something done by people with a Ph.D. in economics. It may be easier for an anthropologist to learn economics than for an economist to learn anthropology. Maybe the fraction of one's training in economics that is irrelevant to the economic analysis of anthropological phenomena is larger than the fraction of anthropological training that is irrelevant; or maybe economic theory is more compact than the body of knowledge we call anthropology. (It probably is easier to learn economics well than to learn Chinese well.) Or it might simply be (this has happened in law and economics) that a given anthropologist had more of a knack for economics than a given economist had a knack for anthropology. It is only by defining economics, in rather a medieval way, as the work done by members of a particular guild (the guild of economics Ph.D.s) that one will be led to conclude that if the economics of law is done by lawyers, or the economics of history by historians, it cannot be "real" economics. The emergence of nonmarket economics may have resulted in a vast but unrecognized increase in the number of economists!

The idea that nonmarket economics is somehow peripheral to economics is connected with the fact that there has been little fruitful analysis of explicit markets besides economics, though admirers of Max Weber's analysis of the role of Protestantism in the rise of capitalism may want to challenge this assertion. Almost by default, explicit markets became thought of as the natural subject matter of economics. But the fact that other areas of social behavior, such as law, have been extensively studied from other angles than the economic is no reason for concluding that these areas cannot be studied profitably with the tools of modern economic theory.

4) Still another bad reason for hostility to nonmarket economics is fear that it will bring economics into disrepute by associating the economist with politically and morally distasteful, bizarre, or controversial practices (such as capital punishment, polygamy, or slavery before the Civil War) and proposals—whether specific policy proposals such as education vouchers, or the idea, which is basic to nonmarket economics, that human beings are rational maximizers throughout the whole, or at least a very broad, range of their social interactions. If economics becomes associated with highly sensitive topics, it may lose some of the appearance of scientific objectivity that economists have worked so hard to cultivate in the face of obvious difficulties including the fact that much of traditional microeconomics and macroeconomics is already politically and ethically controversial, as is evident from current debates over free trade, deregulation, and deficit spending. But this complaint, too, is part of the fallacious idea that there is a fixed domain for economics. If there were, it would be natural to recoil from economic ventures at once peripheral and controversial. But if I am right that there is no fixed, preordained, or natural domain for economics—that politics, punishment, and exploitation are, at least a priori, as appropriate subjects for economics as the operation of the wheat market—then it is pusillanimous to counsel avoidance of particular topics because they happen to be politically or ethically (are these different?) controversial at the present time.

5) A slightly better reason for questioning the expansion of economics beyond its traditional boundaries is skepticism that economic tools will work well in the new fields or that adequate data will be available in them to test economic hypotheses. Maybe these are domains where emotion dominates reason, and maybe economists can't say much about emotion. And explicit markets generate substantial quantitative data (prices, costs, output, employment, etc.), which greatly facilitate empirical research—though only a small fraction of economists actually do empirical research. These points suggest a functional as distinct from a definitional answer to the question of the appropriate bounds of economics: economics is the set of fruitful applications of economic theory. But a detailed survey of nonmarket economics is not necessary in order to make the point that the economic approach has been shown to be fruitful in dealing with such diverse non-market subjects as education, economic history, the causes of regulatory legislation, the behavior of nonprofit institutions, divorce, racial and sexual wage differentials, the incidence and control of crime, and (I shall argue) the common law rules governing property, torts, and contracts[5] —successful enough at any rate to establish nonmarket economics as a legitimate branch of economics and to counsel at least a temporary suspension of disbelief by the skeptics and doubters. Indeed, so familiar have some of these areas of nonmarket economics become in recent years (for example, education viewed through the lens of human capital theory) that many young economists no longer think of them as being outside the traditional

boundaries of economics. The distinction between "market" and "non-market" economics is fraying.

I

A

The particular area of nonmarket economics that I want to focus on is the economics of law, or "law and economics" as it is often called. Because of the enormous range of behavior regulated by the legal system, law and economics could be defined so broadly as to be virtually coextensive with economics. This would not be a useful definition. Yet to exclude bodies of law that regulate explicit markets—such as contract and property law, labor, antitrust and corporate law, public utility and common carrier regulation, and taxation—would be cripplingly narrow. But if these bodies *are* included, in what sense is law and economics a branch of *non* market economics? (I do not suggest that this is an important question; it may, indeed, be an argument for discarding an increasingly uninteresting distinction.)

As with any nonreferential, nonconceptual term, the only possible criterion for a definition of law and economics is utility—not accuracy. The purpose of carving out a separate field and calling it law and economics (or better, because clearer, "economics of law") is to identify the area of economic inquiry to which a substantial knowledge of law in both its doctrinal and institutional aspects is relevant. Many economic problems in such areas of law as taxation and labor do not require much legal knowledge to solve. Although taxes can be imposed only by laws, often the details of the tax law either are not relevant to the analyst, as where he is asking what the effect on charitable giving of reducing the marginal income tax rate is likely to be, or are transparent and unproblematic.

Similarly, in the field of labor, you can study the effects of unemployment insurance on unemployment without knowing a great deal about the state and federal laws governing unemployment insurance, though you must know something. But suppose you wanted to study the consequences of allowing the defendant in an employment discrimination case to deduct from the lost wages awarded the plaintiff (if the plaintiff succeeds in proving that he was fired because of race or sex or some other forbidden criterion), any unemployment benefits that the plaintiff might have received after being fired. You could not get far in such a study without knowing a fair amount of nonobvious employment discrimination law: Is there a uniform judicial rule on deduction or non-deduction of such benefits? Could the benefits be deducted but then be ordered paid to the state or the federal government rather than kept by the employer? Does the law insist that the employee who wants damages for employment discrimination search for work? How are those damages computed? The economics of law is the set of economic studies that build on a detailed knowledge of some area of law; whether the study is done by a "lawyer," an "economist," someone with both degrees, or a lawyer-economist team has little significance.

The law and economics movement has made progress in a number of areas of legal regulation of explicit markets. These include antitrust law, and the regulation of public utilities and common carriers; fraud and unfair competition; corporate bankruptcy, secured transactions, and other areas of commercial law; corporate law and securities regulation; and taxation, including state taxation of interstate commerce, an area that the courts regulate under the commerce clause of the Constitution.[6] In none of these areas is participation by economists, or (if we insist on guild distinctions) by economics-minded lawyers, particularly controversial any more, though some die-hard lawyers continue to resist the encroachments of economics and of course there is disagreement among economists over many particular issues; this is notable in antitrust. An area of legal regulation of explicit markets that is just beginning to ripen for economics is intellectual property, with special reference to copyrights and trademarks. Patents have long been an object of economic study.

The areas of law and economics about which economists and lawyers display considerable unease are the (sometimes arbitrarily classified as) nonmarket areas— crime, torts, and contracts; the environment; the family; the legislative and administrative processes; constitutional law; jurisprudence and legal process; legal history; primitive law; and so on. All the reasons that I gave at the outset for why some economists resist the extension of economics beyond its traditional domain of explicit market behavior coalesce in regard to these areas. And because they are also close to the heart of what lawyers think distinctive about law—of what they think makes it something more than a method of economic regulation—this branch of economic analysis of law dismays many lawyers. Furthermore, lawyers tend to have more rigid, stereotyped ideas of the boundaries of economics than economists do, in part because most lawyers are not aware of the extension (which is recent, though its roots go back to Adam Smith and Jeremy Bentham) of economics to non-market behavior. Indeed, a demarcation which places secured financing on one side of the divide and contract law on the other seems entirely artificial. The distinction between market and non-market economics may be as arbitrary as it is uninteresting.

B

I want to try to convey some sense of the economic analysis of "nonmarket" law. Its basic premises are two:

1) People act as rational maximizers of their satisfactions in making such nonmarket decisions as whether to marry or divorce, commit or refrain from committing crimes, make an arrest, litigate or settle a lawsuit, drive a car carefully or carelessly, pollute (a nonmarket activity because pollution is not traded in the market), refuse to associate with people of a different race, fix a mandatory retirement age for employees.

2) Rules of law operate to impose prices on (sometimes subsidize) these nonmarket activities, thereby altering the amount or character of the activity.

   A third premise, discussed at greater length later, guides some research in the economics of nonmarket law:

3) Common law (i.e., judge-made) rules are often best explained as efforts, whether or not conscious, to bring about either Pareto or Kaldor-Hicks efficient outcomes.

The first two premises lead to such predictions as that an increase in a court's trial queue will lead to a reduction (other things being equal—a qualification applicable to all my examples) in the number of cases tried, that awarding prejudgment interest to a prevailing plaintiff will reduce settlement rates, that "no-fault" divorce will redistribute wealth from women to men, that no-fault automobile accident compensation laws will increase the number of fatal accidents even if the laws are not applicable to such accidents, that substituting comparative for contributory negligence will raise liability and accident insurance premium rates but will not change the accident rate (except insofar as the increase in the price of liability insurance results in fewer drivers or less driving), that increasing the severity as well as certainty of criminal punishment will reduce the crime rate, that making the losing party in a lawsuit pay the winner's attorney's fees will *not* reduce the amount of litigation, that abolition of the reserve clause in baseball did not affect the mobility of baseball players (the Coase theorem, restated as a hypothesis), that the 1978 revision of the bankruptcy laws led to more personal-bankruptcy filings and higher interest rates, and that abolishing the laws that forbid the sale of babies for adoption would reduce rather than increase the full price of babies.

I have given a mixture of obvious and nonobvious hypotheses derived from my basic premises. Notice that I do not say intuitive and counterintuitive hypotheses, because all are counterintuitive to people who believe, as many economists and most lawyers do, that people are not rational maximizers except when transacting in explicit markets, or that legal rules do not have substantial incentive effects, perhaps because the rules are poorly communicated or the sanctions for violating them are infrequently or irregularly imposed.

C

Thus far in my discussion of the economic analysis of legal regulation of nonmarket behavior I have focused on the effects of legal change on behavior. One can reverse the sequence and ask how changes in behavior affect law. To make this reversal, though, one needs a theory of law, parallel to the rational-maximization theory of behavior. The economic theory of the common law, defined broadly as law made by judges rather than by legislatures or constitutional conventions or other nonjudicial bodies, is that the common law is best understood not merely as a pricing mechanism but as a pricing mechanism designed to bring about an efficient allocation of resources, in the Kaldor-Hicks sense of efficiency.[7] This theory implies that when behavior changes, law will change. Suppose that at first people live in very close proximity to each other. Natural light will be a scarce commodity in these circumstances, so its value in exchange may well exceed the cost of enforcing a property right in it. Later, people spread out, so that the value of natural light (in the economic sense of value—exchange value rather than use value) falls; then the net social value of the property right (i.e., the value of the right minus the cost of enforcing it) may be negative. These two states of the world correspond roughly to the situations in England and America in the eighteenth century. The English recognized a limited right to natural light; they called this right "ancient lights." When American courts after independence decided which parts of the English common law to adopt, they rejected the doctrine of ancient lights—as the economic theory of the common law predicts they would.

Another example is the adoption of the appropriation system of water rights in the arid American West. In wet England and the wet eastern United States, the riparian system prevailed. This was a system of communal rights, which is a kind of halfway house between individual rights and no rights, and is inefficient for scarce goods.

The appropriation system is one of individual rights, and was and is more efficient for areas that are dry (i.e., where water is scarce rather than plentiful)—which is where we find the appropriation system, as the economic theory of common law predicts. Or consider the different responses of the eastern and the western states to the problem of fencing out vs. fencing in. Fencing out refers to a property rights system in which damage caused by straying cattle is actionable at law only if the owner of the crops or other goods damaged by the cattle has made reasonable efforts to fence. Fencing in refers to a system where this duty is not imposed, so that the owner of the cattle must fence them in if he wants to avoid liability. The former system is more efficient if the ratio of crops to cattle is low, for then it is cheaper for the farmer than the rancher to fence. If the ratio is reversed, fencing in is a more efficient system. In fact, the cattle states tended to adopt fencing out, and England and the eastern states fencing in. Many similar examples could be given.[8]

Two objections to this branch of economic analysis of law must be considered:

1)   One is that a theory of law is not testable, because when one is examining the effects of behavior on law rather than of law on behavior, the dependent variable tends not to be quantitative: it is not a price or output figure but a pattern of rules. However, the scientific study of social rules is not impossible; what else is linguistics? Fencing in vs. fencing out (or ancient lights vs. no ancient lights, or riparian vs. appropriative water rights) is a dichotomous dependent variable, which modern methods of statistical analysis can handle. And if a continuous variable is desired, it can be created by using the year in which the particular law was adopted (earlier adoption implying a more strongly supported law), the severity of the sanctions, or the expenditures on enforcement, to distribute states or nations along a continuum.

2)   James Buchanan (1974), along with a number of neo-Austrian economists, holds that law should not be an instrumental variable designed to maximize wealth. Judges should not be entrusted with economic decisions—they lack the training and information to make them wisely. They should use custom and precedent to construct a stable but distinctly background framework for market and nonmarket behavior. But this is an objection to normative economic analysis of law—to urging, for example, that the common law (and perhaps other law) be changed to make it approximate the economic model of efficient law better—and the more interesting and promising aspect of economic analysis of law is the positive. I say this not because of a general preference for positive to normative inquiry, but because so little of a systematic nature is known about law. Law is not so well understood that one can hold a confident opinion about whether the right way to improve it is to make the judges more sophisticated economically or more obedient to precedent and tradition.

II

Much of what I have said so far is old hat, at least to those familiar with the law and economics movement, so let me turn to some novel applications of economic analysis to law: applications to free speech and religious freedom, respectively.

A

It has long been recognized that the process by which truth emerges from a welter of competing ideas resembles competition in a market for ordinary goods and services: hence the influential metaphor of the "marketplace of ideas." It is also well known that because of the incompleteness of patent and copyright law as a system of property rights in ideas, the production of ideas frequently generates external benefits. Aaron Director (1964) and Ronald Coase (1974) have emphasized the peculiarity of the modern "liberal" preference for freedom in the market for ideas to freedom in markets for ordinary goods and services (both freedoms having been part of the nineteenth-century concept of liberty), and have attributed this preference to the self-interest of intellectuals.

Economists have paid scant attention, however, to the details of legal regulation in this area. Over the past seventy years or so, the courts have developed an elaborate body of doctrine through interpretation of the First Amendment's guarantee of free speech. Both the effects of this body of doctrine on the marketplace of ideas and the economic logic (if any) of the doctrines present interesting issues for economic analysis.

So far as effects are concerned, I suspect they have been few. Despite the highflown rhetoric in which our courts discuss the right of free speech, they have countenanced a large number of restrictions—on picketing, on obscenity, on employer speech in collective bargaining representation elections, on commercial advertising, on threats, on defamatory matter, and on materials broadcast on radio and television. Although Americans appear to enjoy greater freedom of speech than citizens of the Western European nations, Japan, and other democratic nations at an equivalent level of development to the United States, the gap appears to have narrowed, not broadened, since the Supreme Court began to take an aggressive stance toward protection of free speech in the 1940's. It may be that as nations become wealthier and their people better educated and more leisured, the gains from restricting free speech—gains that have to do mainly with preserving social and political stability—decline relative to the costs in hampering further progress and in reducing the welfare of producers and consumers of ideas. These trends, I conjecture, are sufficiently pronounced to bring about (save possibly in totalitarian counties) dramatic increases in free speech regardless of the specifics of free-speech law.

The American law[9] has several interesting economic characteristics.

1) In the evolution of free-speech law, the first mode of regulation to go is censorship of books and other reading matter; the law's greater antagonism to censorship than to criminal punishment or other *ex post* regulation (for example, suits for defamation) being expressed in the rule that "prior restraints" on speech are specially disfavored. Censorship is a form of *ex ante* regulation, like a speed limit. The less common the substantive evil (the costs resulting from an accident due to carelessness, in the case of the speed limit, or the costs resulting from a treasonable or defamatory newspaper article, in the case of censorship), and also the more solvent the potential injurer,[10] the weaker the case for *ex ante* regulation is. With the growth of education and political stability, the social dangers of free speech have declined; and suppose the fraction of books and magazine articles that contain seriously harmful matter is today very small. Then the costs of a scheme in which a publisher must obtain a license from the public censor to publish each book are likely to swamp the benefits in weeding out

the occasional prohibitable idea, especially since publishers have sufficient resources to pay fines or damage judgments for any injuries they inflict. It makes more economic sense in these circumstances to rely on *ex post* regulation (through criminal punishment or tort suits) of those ideas that turn out to be punishable. Censorship is retained, however, in areas, such as that of classified government documents, where the probability of harm is high and where in addition the magnitude of the harm if it occurs may be so great (for example, from disclosing sensitive military secrets) that the threat of punishment will not deter adequately because the wrongdoer will lack sufficient resources.

Many of these arguments could of course be made against *ex ante* regulation of safety, as by the Food and Drug Administration and OSHA. One difference is that while the First Amendment forbids overregulating the marketplace of ideas (and also, as we are about to see, the religious marketplace), no constitutional provision seems directed at forbidding overregulation of markets in conventional goods and services.

2) Consider now the onerous limitations that the Supreme Court has placed on efforts to sue the media for defamation. If we assume that news confers external benefits, then, since a newspaper or television station cannot obtain a significant property right in news, there is an argument for subsidizing the production of news. A direct subsidy, however, would involve political risks—though we have run them occasionally, as in the establishment of the Corporation for Public Broadcasting. A form of indirect subsidy is to make the victims of defamation bear some of the costs of defamation that the tort system would otherwise shift to the defamer. Notice, however, the curious effect of this method of subsidization, which may make it on balance inefficient. Because it is impossible to insure one's reputation, the victims of defamation cannot spread the costs of being defamed to other members of the community. The costs are concentrated on a narrow group, resulting in a deadweight loss if risk aversion is assumed. Moreover, public service is made less desirable, resulting in a decline in the quality of government. It would be difficult to prevent the decline by raising government salaries. The salary increase would have to be large enough to cover not only the expected cost of uncompensated defamation, but also the risk premium that risk-averse people would demand because they cannot buy insurance. Even if salaries are raised, the composition of public service will shift in favor of risk preferrers and people with little reputation capital. Finally, the difficulty of monitoring government outputs leads to heavy emphasis on economizing on visible inputs, for example by paying low salaries to government officials; and the problem of false economies is aggravated if the costs of government service are raised by curtailing the right of government officials to protect their reputations through suits for defamation.

3) The Supreme Court has distinguished between public and private figures, giving private figures a broader right to sue for defamation than public ones. This distinction may make economic sense. The external benefits of information about public figures are greater than those of information about private figures, and therefore the argument for allowing some of the costs to be externalized is stronger. Moreover, a public figure, being by definition newsworthy, has some substitute for legal action: he can tell his side of the story, which the news media will pick up.

4) A related point is that if the main reason for limiting efforts by government to regulate the marketplace of ideas is to foster the provision of external benefits, we would expect, and to a certain extent find, that the limitations on regulation are more severe the greater the likelihood of such benefits. Consider: Maximum protection for freedom of speech is provided to scientific and political thought, in which property rights cannot be obtained. Slightly less protection is given art, which enjoys a limited property right under the copyright laws.[11] Even less constitutional protection is given to pornography and commercial advertising. And none is given to threats and other utterances that manifestly create net external costs.

Pornography appears to create no external benefits (no one but the viewer or reader himself benefits—and he pays), and may create external costs. Commercial advertising, a particularly interesting case, also creates few external benefits—since most such advertising is brand-specific and its benefits are captured in higher sales of the advertised brand—and it creates some external costs: competitor A's advertising may go largely to offset B's, and vice versa. This analysis implies that if the logic of free-speech law is basically an economic logic, commercial advertising that is not brand-specific, such as advertising extolling the value of prunes as a laxative, would receive greater legal protection than brand-specific advertising.

B

The First Amendment also forbids the government to make any law (1) respecting an establishment of religion or (2) prohibiting the free exercise of religion. The Supreme Court has enforced both clauses aggressively in recent years.[12] The economic effects of the Court's doctrines as well as their possible economic logic are interesting topics that economists (with the partial exception of Adam Smith) have not addressed.

There is, it is true, a nascent economic analysis of religion. Corry Azzi and Ronald Ehrenberg (1975) have formulated a simple (maybe too simple, given the variety of religious beliefs) economic model of religion, which assumes that people want to increase their expected utility from a happy afterlife.[13] The model leads to such predictions as that women will spend more time in church than men because the cost to women in foregone earnings is less, and that men will spend more time in church as they get older because as they approach the end of their working life it is optimal for them to switch from investing further in their earning capacity to investing in the production of afterlife utility. The authors find support in the data for their predictions.[14] My focus is different. I ask, what have been the effects on religious belief and observance of the Supreme Court's enforcement of the First Amendment? To avoid potential misunderstanding, I emphasize that I am offering no opinion on either the validity of any religious belief or the legal soundness of any of the Court's decisions.

Three major strands in the Court's modern decisions should be distinguished:

1) In its school-prayer decisions, and other decisions under the establishment clause, the Court has interpreted the concept of an "establishment" of religion very broadly, in effect forbidding the states and the federal government to provide direct support, financial or even symbolic, for religion. These decisions make a kind of economic

sense, though perhaps only superficially. Public education (the principal arena of modern disputes over establishment of religion) involves the subsidizing of schoolchildren and their parents. Parents willing to pay the full costs of their children's education can and often do send their children to private schools. If they choose a public school instead, this may be because some of the costs will be paid by others, including persons who do not have school-age children as well as taxpayers in other parts of the state or nation. The principal economic argument for externalizing some of the costs of education is that education (with possible exceptions, as for vocational education and "phys. ed.") confers external benefits; that we all (or most of us, anyway) benefit from living in a nation whose population is educated. Therefore, to justify on economic grounds a public school's spending money on prayer and other religious activities, either these activities would have to be shown to produce positive externalities also (as by making schoolchildren more moral, or at least better behaved in school), or there would have to be economies from combining secular and religious instruction in the same facility, or private persons would have to volunteer to pay the incremental cost of the public school's religious activities, so that there would not be a subsidy.

If the Supreme Court were willing to accept any of these justifications—provided, of course, that they were adequately supported by evidence—then one might conclude that the Court was taking an economic approach to the issue in religion in the public schools. But, in fact, the modern Court forbids virtually every public school religious activity, whether or not any of these justifications is present. If none is present, it can indeed be argued that religious persons would be enjoying a public subsidy of religion if the activity were permitted. Parents willing to pay the full costs of education in a school that conducts prayer or engages in other religious activities can always send their children to a private school that offers such activities, thereby bearing the full cost of those activities rather than shifting a part of it to others in the community. Concern with public subsidies of religion may explain the Court's insistence that Christmas nativity scenes supported by public funds have a secular purpose, that is, confer benefits on nonreligious as well as religious persons. But the Court has not worried about the fact that the benefits may be greater for the latter persons, so that an element of subsidy remains. Nor has it explained its unwillingness to search for similar secular justifications for public school religious activity—such justifications as reducing the rowdiness of schoolchildren.

Further complicating the picture, the Supreme Court has declined to hold that the exemption of church property from state and local taxes is an unconstitutional establishment of religion. However, the consequence of the exemption is that the churches receive public services for which they do not pay. This is fine if they generate benefits for which they cannot charge, but the Court has not required that they show that. So here may be a large judicially sanctioned public subsidy of religion.

2) In its "free exercise" decisions, the Court has sometimes required public bodies to make costly accommodations to religious observance. An example is forbidding the denial of unemployment benefits to a person whose religion forbids him to accept a job offer that would require working on Saturdays. So the Court with one hand (establishment clause cases) forbids the subsidizing of religion and with the other (free-exercise cases) requires such subsidies.

3) In cases involving contraception, abortion, illegitimacy, obscenity, and other moral questions about which religious people tend to hold strong views, the Court in recent years has almost always sided with the secular against the religious point of view.

The decisions in both groups 1 and 2 favor religious rivalry or diversity (not competition in the economic sense: as we shall see in a moment, to subsidize rivalry as in 2 retards rather than promotes competition in the economic sense). Any public establishment of religion will tend to favor major religious groups over minor ones and can thus be compared to government's placing its thumb on the scales in a conventional marketplace, by granting subsidies or other benefits to politically influential firms. Refusing to accommodate fringe religious groups will have effects similar to those of establishing a religion because employment policies, and other public policies and customs, are chosen to minimize conflict with the dominant religious groupings.[15] It is no accident that the official day of rest in this country is the sabbath recognized by the mainline Christian groups. Fringe groups will therefore benefit from a rule requiring accommodation of their needs.

But since the costs of accommodation are borne by employers, consumers, taxpayers, other employees, etc., the group 2 cases actually subsidize fringe religious groups. And since it is no more efficient for government to subsidize weak competitors than strong ones, it may not be possible to defend the accommodation cases by reference to notions of efficiency. In addition, the group 1 cases may go further than necessary to prevent public subsidies of established religious groups, by neglecting the various justifications that might be offered for public support of religion—although allowing the property-tax exemption may correct (or for that matter, overcorrect) that tendency. The most important point to note, however, is that the Supreme Court has required government to subsidize fringe religious groups both directly and by discouraging religious establishments that inevitably would favor the beliefs and practices of the dominant sects in the community. By doing these things, the Court probably has increased religious diversity and may therefore have promoted religion, on balance, notwithstanding the "antireligion" flavor of some of its establishment cases.

The group 3 decisions favor religion, too—more precisely, private religious organizations—but in a subtler sense, which may be entirely unintended, even unrecognized, by the courts. By marking a powerful agency of government (the federal judiciary) as secularist, and, more important, by undermining traditional values through invalidation of regulations that express or enforce those values, these decisions increase the demand for organized religion, viewed as a preserver of traditional values. If the government enforced the value system of Christianity, as it used to do, people would have less to gain from being Christian. The group 1 cases have a similar effect. By forbidding teachers paid by the state to inculcate religious values, the courts have increased the demand for the services provided by religious organizations. And allowing the property-tax exemption lowers the costs of these organizations.

Of course, there may be no net increase in the provision of religious services if a public school in which teachers lead prayers or read to students from the Bible is treated as a religious organization, but my concern is with the effect on private organizations. Similarly, a government that rigorously repressed abortion might be thought of as the enforcement arm of the Christian sects that regard abortion as immoral; but by thereby assuming one of the functions of private religious organizations, it would be competing with those organizations and thus reducing the demand for the services provided by them.

There is a further point. As Adam Smith pointed out (1937, pp. 740–50), the effectiveness of a private group's monitoring and regulating the behavior of its members is apt to be greater, the smaller the group (this is the essence of cartel theory), from which Smith inferred that the more religious sects there were, and hence the smaller each one was on average, the more effective would religion be in regulating behavior. This implies that legal regulations which have the effect of atomizing rather than concentrating religious organization may improve the society's moral tone even if they diminish the role of government in inculcating moral values directly.

It may be hard to believe that the moral tone of our society has actually improved since the Supreme Court adopted its aggressively secularist stance, but economic analysis suggests that the situation might be worse rather than better if the Court had weakened private religious organizations by allowing government to compete more effectively with them in inculcating or requiring moral behavior. Since government and organized religion are substitutes in promoting moral behavior, an expansion in the government's role as moral teacher might reduce the demand for the services of organized religion. I say "might" rather than "would" because, to the extent that the government's role as moral teacher is taken seriously, a government that seeks to promote religiously based moral values may help "sell" religious values, and the organizations that promote them, over their secular substitutes. But this assumes what history suggests is unlikely: that the government will find a way of supporting religion on a genuinely nonsectarian basis rather than establishing a particular sect and thereby weakening competing sects and maybe religion as a whole.

To prove, in the face of the conventional wisdom to the contrary, that the Supreme Court's apparently antireligious decisions have promoted religion would be a formidable undertaking, and here I offer only two fragments of evidence. The first is the rapid growth in recent years of evangelical Christianity, formerly a fringe religious grouping and one marked by emphatic adherence to traditional values.[16] The second is the startling difference in religiosity between the United States and Western Europe. Not only does a far higher percentage of Americans believe in an afterlife than the population of any western European country other than Ireland,[17] but this percentage has been relatively constant in the United States since the 1930's, while it has declined substantially in Europe over the same interval.[18] Almost all Western European nations have an established (i.e., a taxpayer-supported and legally privileged) church (or churches, as with the state churches of Germany), and some require prayer in public schools.[19] To the extent that establishment discourages the rise of rival sects, it reduces the religious "product variety" offered to the population, and I would expect the demand for religion to be less. The American system fosters a wide variety of religious sects. Almost every person can find a package of beliefs and observances that fits his economic and psychological circumstances. And by preventing the government from playing a shaping role in the moral sphere the Supreme Court in recent years has, I have conjectured, increased the demand for religion as a substitute institution for the regulation of morals.

No doubt the Supreme Court's causal role in all this is smaller than I have suggested. The tradition of religious diversity in the United States is very old, and the Court's contribution to maintaining it may be slight. Nevertheless, economic analysis suggests that the religious leaders who denounce the course of the Court's decisions and the secular leaders who defend it may be arguing contrary to their institutional self-interest.

C

My discussions of free speech and religion can be connected as follows. One possible reading of the First Amendment (I do not suggest the only, or a complete one) is that it forbids government to interfere with the free market in two particular "goods"— ideas, and religion. Government may not regulate these markets beyond what is necessary to correct externalities and other impediments to the efficient allocation of resources. This seems an appropriate description of how modern courts interpret the amendment; the principal though not only exceptions are the cases that forbid what might be called "efficient" establishments (establishments that do not involve a subsidy to religious persons beyond what can be justified on secular grounds) and the cases requiring accommodation of religion in the sense of subsidizing fringe religious groups. There is no compelling economic argument for such a subsidy unless something can be made of Adam Smith's point that the more separate religious sects there are, the more effective religion is in bringing about moral behaviour—and morals supplement law in correcting negative externalities such as crime and fostering positive ones such as charity.

But a lecture is not the place to prove a new economic theory. All that is feasible is to suggest that a particular theory holds promise and is thus worth pursuing. I hope I have persuaded you that what may loosely be called the economic theory of law has a significant potential to alter received notions, generate testable hypotheses about a variety of important social phenomena, and in short enlarge our knowledge of the world.

Notes

1   See, for example, Gary Becker (1976); Jack Hirshleifer (1985, p. 53); George Stigler (1984); Gerard Radnitzky and Peter Bernholz (1986).
2   For a recent conspectus of economic analysis of law, see my book (1986).
3   See, for example, Ronald Coase (1978). Coase is of course a leading figure in the economics of property rights, so his opposition is far from total.
4   For an excellent discussion, see John Ellis (1974, ch. 2).
5   For a few examples see Becker (1981; 1975); Orley Ashenfelter and Albert Rees (1973); Robert Fogel and Stanley Engerman (1971); Isaac Ehrlich (1974); David Pyle (1983); Stigler (1971).
6   The work in these areas is summarized in my book (pts. 3–5 and ch. 26). It is of some interest to note that the economic analysis of secured financing is now dominated by economically inclined lawyers. See Robert Scott (1986) and references cited there.
7   See my book (pt. 2); and William Landes and myself (1987).
8   See sources cited in fn. 7, from which the above examples are taken.
9   Well summarized, and in a form accessible to nonlawyers, in Geoffrey Stone et al. (1986, pt. 7).

10   If the probability of apprehension and punishment is substantially less than one, the expected punishment may not deter wrongdoing even if the punishment, when imposed, takes away the offender's entire wealth and utility.

11   Only the specific work of art is protected; an artistic innovation (perspective, chiaroscuro, the sonnet, blank verse, etc.) is not.

12   See Stone et al. (pt. 8).

13   See also Ehrenberg (1977); Paul Pautler (1977); Barbara Redman (1980).

14   For criticism of some of their results, see Holley Ulbrich and Myles Wallace (1984).

15   As stressed in Michael McConnell (1985).

16   See *The Gallup Report* (1985, pp. 3, 11).

17   See *The Gallup Report*, p. 53.

18   See *The Gallup Report*, pp. 9–10, 40, 42, 53.

19   On the religious establishments of Western Europe, see, for example, E. Jürgen Moltman (1986); E. Garth Moore (1967); Franklin Scott (1977, pp. 571–75); Frederic Spotts (1973).

References

Ashenfelter, Orley and Rees, Albert, *Discrimination in Labor Markets*, Princeton: Princeton University Press, 1973.

Azzi, Corry and Ehrenberg, Ronald, "Household Allocation of Time and Church Attendance," *Journal of Political Economy*, February 1975, *83*, 27–56.

Becker, Gary S., *The Economic Approach to Human Behavior*, Chicago: University of Chicago Press, 1976.

———, *Human Capital: A Theoretical and Empirical Analysis, With Specific Reference to Education*, NBER, New York: Columbia University Press, 2d ed., 1975.

———, *A Treatise on the Family*, Cambridge: Harvard University Press, 1981.

Buchanan, James M., "Good Economics—Bad Law," *Virginia Law Review*, March 1974, *60*, 483–92.

Coase, Ronald H., "Economics and Contiguous Disciplines," *Journal of Legal Studies*, June 1978, 7, 201–11.

———, "The Market for Goods and the Market for Ideas," *American Economic Review Proceedings*, May 1974, *64*, 384–91.

Director, Aaron, "The Parity of the Economic Market Place," *Journal of Law and Economics*, October 1964, 7, 1–10.

Ehrenberg, Ronald G., "Household Allocation of Time and Religiosity: Replication and Extension," *Journal of Political Economy*, April 1977, *85*, 415–23.

Ehrlich, Isaac, "Participation in Illegitimate Activities: An Economic Analysis," in Gary S. Becker and William M. Landes, eds., *Essays in the Economics of Crime and Punishment*, NBER, New York: Columbia University Press, 1974, 68–134.

Ellis, John M., *The Theory of Literary Criticism: A Logical Analysis*, Berkeley: University of California Press, 1974.

Fogel, Robert W. and Engerman, Stanley L., *The Reinterpretation of American History*, New York: Harper & Row, 1971.

Gallup Report, Report No. 236, Princeton: The Gallup Poll, May 1985.

Hirshleifer, Jack, "The Expanding Domain of Economics," *American Economic Review*, December 1985, Suppl., *75*, 53–68.

Landes, William M. and Posner, Richard A., *The Economic Structure of Tort Law*, Cambridge: Harvard University Press, forthcoming 1987.

McConnell, Michael, "Accommodation of Religion," *Supreme Court Review*, Chicago: University of Chicago Press, 1985, 1–59.

Moltmann, E. Jürgen, "Religion and State in Germany; West and East," *Annals of the American Academy of Political and Social Science*, January 1986, *483*, 110–17.

Moore, E. Garth, *An Introduction to English Canon Law*, Oxford: Clarendon Press, 1967.

Pautler, Paul A., "Religion and Relative Prices," *Atlantic Economic Journal*, March 1977, *5*, 69–73.

Posner, Richard A., *Economic Analysis of Law*, Boston: Little, Brown, 3d ed., 1986.

Pyle, David J., *The Economics of Crime and Law Enforcement*, New York: St. Martin's Press, 1983.

Radnitzky, Gerard and Bernholz, Peter, *Economic Imperialism: The Economic Approach Applied Outside the Field of Economics*, New York: Paragon House, 1986.

Redman, Barbara J., "An Economic Analysis of Religious Choice," *Review of Religious Research*, Summer 1980, *21*, 330–42.

Scott, Franklin D., *Sweden: The Nation's History*, Minneapolis: University of Minnesota Press, 1977.

Scott, Robert E., "A Relational Theory of Secured Financing," *Columbia Law Review*, June 1986, *86*, 901–77.

Smith, Adam, in Edwin Cannan, ed., *The Wealth of Nations*, London: Methuen, 1937.

Spotts, Frederic, *The Churches and Politics in Germany*, Middletown: Wesleyan University Press, 1973.

Stigler, George J., "Economics—The Imperial Science?," *Scandinavian Journal of Economics*, No. 3, 1984, *86*, 301–13.

——, "The Theory of Economic Regulation," *Bell Journal of Economics*, Spring 1971, *2*, 3–21.

Stone, Geoffrey R. et al., *Constitutional Law*, Boston: Little, Brown, 1986, pts. 7 and 8.

Ulbrich, Holley and Wallace, Myles, "Women's Work Force Status and Church Attendance," *Journal for the Scientific Study of Religion*, December 1984, *23*, 341–50.

Chapter 4

William M. Landes

THE ART OF LAW AND ECONOMICS
An autobiographical essay[1]

Introduction

IN HIS ESSAY "How I Work," Paul Krugman points out that the increasing formalism of modern economics leads most graduate students in economics today to acquire the necessary mathematical skills before they enter graduate school.[2] I strongly suspect the converse holds as well: the student who lacks a technical background will be deterred from choosing a career in economics. This was not always the case. Like Krugman, I came to economics from a liberal arts background, picking up technical skills as needed both during and after graduate school. My journey, however, was more circuitous and unplanned than Krugman's. That I ended up a professor of economics and law is the outcome of an unlikely chain of events.

I started out as an art major at the High School of Music & Art in New York City. Although art majors also were required to take the standard fare of academic courses, it was not a strenuous academic program, and it was possible to do reasonably well without much effort. The emphasis was clearly on the arts, and many graduates went on to specialized art and music colleges in the New York area. I ruled that out since I was only an average art student. I also experimented with architecture in high school. But here I fared no better and decided not to pursue it further, in part, because my closest friend had far more talent than I.[3]

When I entered Columbia College at seventeen I was not well prepared for its demanding academic program (which remains largely intact to this day). I had a good background in the arts but undeveloped study habits. Playing tennis and piano, frequenting jazz clubs and just hanging around Greenwich Village with my high school friends held my interest more than studying western civilization and humanities. But in one respect Music and Art taught me a valuable lesson. It impressed upon me the importance of being creative and imaginative in one's work. I have carried that lesson with me throughout my academic career. I strive to be imaginative both in my choice of topics and my approach to them. Rarely have I come up with a topic by sifting through the economics literature or scouring footnotes hoping to find loose ends to tidy up. I have often stumbled upon a good topic while preparing my classes, participating in seminars and workshops, auditing law school classes, talking to colleagues or just reading the newspaper. The trick is to recognize what one has stumbled upon, or as Robertson Davies writes in his latest novel: "to see what is right in front of one's nose; that is the task . . ."[4]

Early training as an economist

I took my first economics course in my junior year at college. Two things still stand out in my mind about that course. One was that little effort was made to show that microeconomics could illuminate real world problems. I and my classmates came away from the course believing that the assumptions of microeconomics were so unrealistic that economics couldn't have any bearing on real world problems. The other was the professor's condemnation of advertising as a monstrous social waste, a view shared by most of the economics profession at that time. By default, I became an economics major in my senior year at Columbia and took courses in public finance and money and banking, and a seminar for economics majors. After graduation I went to work on Wall Street at a brokerage firm producing colorful charts (my art background helped) tracking the movements in earnings per share, net working capital, etc. of different companies in the hope that I or one of the senior members of the research department could detect likely trends in stock prices. I soon realized that school was more fun and challenging than work, so after four months on Wall Street I returned to Columbia on a part-time basis. My intention was to get a master's degree in economics and ultimately work for some government agency. Becoming an economics professor or even getting a Ph.D. was not on my radar screen.

Unlike more selective graduate schools, Columbia had pretty much an open door policy, admitting large numbers of students and letting Darwinian survival principles operate. There were always a few exceptional students at Columbia who went on to get their doctorates in four or five years but most didn't survive. They either got a master's degree or lost interest after a year or two and dropped out. (At the other extreme, Columbia was also home to a number of professional students who had been around for ten or fifteen years working on a thesis they were unlikely ever to finish.) After my first year of graduate school, in which I continued to work half-time on Wall Street, I realized I had a talent for economics and asked to be admitted to the doctoral program. The chairman of the department looked over my grades and pronounced that "my prognosis was good" and so I became a full time doctoral student.

Success in graduate school requires brains, sustained effort and hard work. Exceptional success at Columbia required a little luck as well. Luck to be plucked from the mass of students by a great economist and placed under his wing. I was lucky.

In the spring semester of my second year at graduate school, I audited Gary Becker's course on human capital, which covered his still unpublished manuscript on that subject. Since Becker had been on leave at the National Bureau of Economic

Research during my first year, I had not taken his "price theory" course or what is now more commonly termed microeconomics. In class, Becker called on me regularly (sometimes I thought "ruthlessly" for I was only an auditor) and referred to me as "an eager beaver." If I didn't come up with the answer at first, Becker would tease it out of me. Having been a member of a law school faculty for over twenty years, I am still struck by the difference between Becker's teaching style (unusual even in economics departments) and that of the typical law school professor. Like law classes, Becker called on students who did not volunteer. But Becker would work with the student for a few minutes until (hopefully) he came up with the right answer. In contrast, the law school professor practicing the Socratic method calls on different students in rapid succession, playing one off against another ("Ms. Y do you agree with. Mr. X's answer). To push the students to think more clearly, the professor will often vary the hypothetical until the reasoning behind the earlier answer collapses. A premium is placed on verbal agility and thinking quickly on one's feet. A series of questions may end without a definite answer and the teacher moves on to the next case. Indeed, the Socratic method impresses on the student that there are no right or easy answers in law. Yet the fact that the method survives (but in a somewhat gentler form today) is a tribute to its value in training students to become practicing lawyers.

Auditing Becker's course in human capital, marked the beginning of my training as a real economist. To be sure, I had already been in graduate school for over a year. Yet, for the first time, I began to appreciate that economics was more than just a set of formal tools but a way of thinking about interesting real world problems. I began to understand the advantages of simplifying and descriptively unrealistic assumptions, and how a person with imagination could develop a simple model to illuminate a real world problem. Such models provided an approach to thinking systematically about public policy and law. Instead of saying policy X was good or fair, one could use economic principles to spell out the consequences of that policy.

During my third year at graduate school, I completed my course requirements, audited Becker's price theory course, and passed my comprehensive oral examinations. For three or four months before the oral exams I was part of a small group of students (we called ourselves "Becker Bombers") who met regularly to review questions from Becker's prior exams and problems from Milton Friedman's soft cover textbook.[5] Working through this material made it clear to me the difference between knowing economics and thinking like an economist. The former comes from mastering the language and formal principles of economics that are found in graduate textbooks and articles in professional journals. The latter from applying these tools with varying degrees of sophistication to solving problems. The particular problem might be a conventional economic one (e.g., will a price ceiling on lumber lower the price of new construction) or a problem not ordinarily viewed as an economic one (e.g., do laws protecting privacy lead to more unconventional behavior). Any problem involving competing goals and choices constrained by limited resources and available opportunities is fair game for economics. The problem need not involve explicit markets or observable prices for one can derive shadow prices that function like market prices. Frequently, simple economic concepts applied in an imaginative way yield subtle insights. All this may sound commonplace today but thirty years ago it was not. It is a tribute to Gary Becker's pioneering efforts that we now take for granted that the domain of economics is not confined to explicit markets but is a "way of looking at life."[6]

My next stroke of good luck was quickly settling on a dissertation topic. Becker proposed that I study whether state fair employment laws improved the economic position of nonwhites in the United States.[7] I eagerly agreed both because I wanted to work with Becker and the topic was intrinsically interesting. To get me started, Becker gave me a copy of an unpublished paper by George Stigler and Claire Friedland which used regression analysis to estimate the effects of state utility regulation.[8] At that time, it was highly novel for an economist to employ multiple regression analysis to estimate empirically the actual effects of a law or regulation. The paper by Stigler and Friedland was one of the first. Before undertaking the empirical analysis, I set out to develop a model to explain the likely effects of fair employment laws. Here I added sanctions against firms that discriminated against nonwhites to Becker's theory of discrimination. I assumed that an employer violating a fair employment law faced a probability rather than a certainty of being caught and a sanction if caught. The greater that probability and the greater that sanction, the greater the cost of discriminating and the more likely the employer would increase its demand for nonwhite relative to white workers. Thus, I had a thesis that not only lent itself to imaginative modeling (by using the expected utility model to analyze law enforcement) but was capable of answering empirically an important public policy question.

Developing a model was the easy part compared to carrying out the empirical analysis. Acquiring empirical skills requires a good deal of "learning by doing." Graduate school had not prepared me for the many months I would have to spend meticulously gathering data state-by-state from census volumes, calculating state averages by race for earnings, years of schooling and other variables, fitting Pareto distributions to open ended Census intervals, and collecting data from state fair employment commissions on the number of prosecutions, enforcement expenditures, sanctions and so forth. I was my own research assistant and I carried out most of these calculations on a mechanical calculator that frequently jammed. Fortunately, computers make it possible today to avoid this kind of tedious work although I don't have the impression that this has increased the frequency of empirical dissertations in economics.

Getting started in law and economics

In its broadest sense, "law and economics" is coextensive with a large part of the field of industrial organization. Both cover, among other things, the study of the legal regulation of markets including economic analysis of the business practices described in antitrust cases. These cases provide a rich source of material on such practices as tie-in sales, exclusive dealing, vertical restrictions and information exchanges among competitors. Both fields also include research on the theoretical and empirical consequences of different types of government regulations and laws. Thus, the most recent issue of the Journal of Law & Economics (a leading journal in both industrial organization and law and economics) includes articles by economists on the anticompetitive effects of most-favored-nation clauses, the effects on stock prices of regulatory drug recalls, the performance of the airline industry under deregulation, and the impact of collective bargaining legislation on labor disputes in the public sector. For my purposes, however, I want to define law and economics more narrowly. I want to limit it to what is called the "new" law and economics, a field which essentially began with Ronald Coase's article on social cost over thirty years ago[9] and where most work has been carried on in law schools rather than economics departments.

The "new" law and economics applies the tools of economics to the legal system itself. It uses economics to explain and illuminate legal doctrines in all fields of law including the common law fields of torts, contracts and property, intellectual property, corporate law, bankruptcy law, criminal law and the legal process itself (e.g., the effects of fee shifting statutes, discovery rules and legal precedent on litigation). The "new" law and economics is not limited to areas of law that only impact explicit markets. It is a theory of both the legal rules themselves and their consequences for behavior. The former is the more controversial of the two. It treats legal rules and doctrines as "data" in order to test the hypothesis that the law is best explained as efforts by judges, often implicitly, to decide case as if they are trying to promote economic efficiency.

I got started in the "new" law and economics by chance rather than by any well thought out plan to work in this area.[10] Shortly after finishing my thesis on the effects of fair employment laws (the "old" law and economics) I came across a newspaper article on plea bargaining in criminal cases. The article pointed out that only a small fraction (probably less than five percent) of criminal defendants actually went to trial. The rest pleaded guilty, often to substantially reduced charges. Investigating a little further I learned similarly that only a small fraction of civil cases ended up in trial. Most were settled out-of-court before trial. Not only did these issues seem like a natural subject for economic analysis (an example of "seeing what is right in front of one's nose") but no one had previously examined it from the standpoint of economics—maybe because economists believed that people were more likely to behave emotionally than rationally in a litigation setting.

But as Becker's former student, I had no trouble assuming that parties behaved rationally in non-market settings. The ultimate test was whether rational behavior was a useful assumption not whether it was descriptively realistic. I reasoned (using Coase's theorem) that the prosecutor and defendant would reach a plea bargain on a sentence if both could be made better off compared to risking an uncertain trial outcome. Similarly, parties would prefer to settle a civil lawsuit out-of-court provided one could find a settlement that made both better off than their expected trial outcomes. Assuming that trials were more costly than plea bargains or settlements, I showed that if the parties agreed on the probabilities of winning and losing at trial, they would always settle (unless they had strong preferences for risk) because each party's utility from a settlement would be greater than his expected utility from a trial. Further, trials would be more likely to occur when the parties were mutually optimistic (i.e., each party believed he had a greater probability of winning a trial than his opponent believed), were risk preferrers, where the cost of trials were low relative to the cost of reaching a settlement, and where the stakes in litigation were greater (for that magnified the difference in expected outcomes for mutually optimistic parties). My paper also has implications for law enforcement for I showed that criminals as a class could be made worse off by plea bargains even though any particular offender was made better off by avoiding a trial (a true prisoner's dilemma) because settlements freed resources that enabled the prosecutor to pursue more criminals.

I presented a preliminary version of this paper[11] in 1967 to the labor workshop at the University of Chicago. At the time I was an assistant professor in the economics department at Chicago. My talk was not greeted with much enthusiasm. After, one of my senior colleagues in the department took me aside for some friendly advice. He said I was making a career mistake by doing research on problems like the courts that were only of marginal interest to other economists. Professional success, he emphasized, required working on problems of the latest interest to other economists. I asked him how one knew what was of the "latest interest." He replied that one could gauge interest by seeing what problems other economists were currently working on. In short, see what your colleagues are working on and try to take it a step further. I decided to ask Gary Becker what he thought (though I suspect I already knew what he would say). Becker had just finished his paper on the economics of crime, and one of Becker's students, Isaac Ehrlich, was completing a thesis at Columbia on the deterrent effects of conviction rates and sanctions on crime. Becker disagreed with my Chicago colleague. His advice was simple law enforcement and litigation are interesting and important social issues that can be illuminated by economics; don't worry so much about whether your work is part of the latest fad in economics; and ultimately good work will be recognized. Fortunately, I listened to Gary Becker.

In 1968 I moved from Chicago to New York City to accept a fellowship at the National Bureau of Economic Research, and a year later I joined the NBER's research staff. At that time, members of the NBER's staff resided almost entirely in New York City. Although I also had academic appointments in the economics departments at Columbia and later at the Graduate Center of the City University, my intellectual life centered on the NBER. The NBER offered me the freedom to choose projects interesting to me and to avoid the distractions associated with student turmoil at Columbia during this period. The Bureau had a professional and no-nonsense attitude toward research—projects were undertaken with the expectation that they would be completed, rough deadlines were imposed, progress reports were required, and research directors took a strong interest in the work under their direction. But there was also the give-and-take and informality of a university that I cherished. The Bureau was an ideal place for conducting serious empirical research.

When I joined the NBER it was best known for its empirical research in traditional economic subjects such as business cycles and national income accounting but it was beginning to branch out into other areas of economics. For example, Becker and Jacob Mincer ran projects on the economics of education and human capital, and Victor Fuchs directed a program in health economic. The Bureau formally established a program in law and economics in 1971 which was funded by a grant from the National Science Foundation. The program included Becker, myself, Isaac Ehrlich and Richard Posner (then professor at the University of Chicago Law School and now chief judge on the U.S. Court of Appeals of the Seventh Circuit). Adding Posner filled a critical hole in the program. In order to apply economics to areas of law other than crime and the courts we needed some expertise in law. Posner seemed ideal. He had a strong interest in economics, had already published several widely regarded papers in antitrust, and was starting to apply economics to torts and judicial administration.

It should be mentioned that the early applications of economics to law at the NBER (pre-Posner) and elsewhere required almost no knowledge of law. This was true of Becker's paper on crime, Ehrlich's pioneering studies of deterrence and law enforcement, and my own work on the courts, plea bargaining and the bail system. That this should be so is not surprising. We were economists applying the theoretical and empirical tools of economics to the systematic study of enforcement.[12] To be sure, we had to develop some basic understanding about the relevant legal terms and institutions under investigation, but that requires far less knowledge of law than becoming familiar and comfortable with legal rules and doctrines in order to analyze them from an economic standpoint.

An economist on a law school faculty

Although the Bureau provided a superb research environment, it could not match the intellectual excitement of the University of Chicago. Chicago was home to the economists I most admired—Becker, Coase, Friedman and Stigler. Plus it offered me the opportunity to work more closely with Posner. So in 1973 I eagerly accepted a tenured appointment at the University of Chicago Law School. The Law School had a long tradition of having an economist on its faculty starting with Henry Simons, Aaron Director and Ronald Coase. When I arrived Coase was still an active member of the faculty but taught only an occasional course. Still my appointment was somewhat unusual. I was genuinely interested in explaining legal rules and doctrines from an economic perspective. Coase was not. He believed that knowledge of institutions was valuable because it helped one understand how explicit markets truly worked. But Coase had little interest in showing, for example, that the various legal doctrines governing liability for accidents or contract damages had an implicit economic logic. It is one of the ironies of law and economics that the person whose pioneering work (cited by the Nobel committee) provided the foundation for the subject has been less than enthusiastic about its development. Coase believed that much of law and economics was outside the domain of economics and that, in any event, lawyers rather than economists were better suited for the enterprise. Most law professors went even further. They believed that lawyers would also fail in explaining law from an economic perspective.

At the few law schools with an economist on their faculty in the 1970s (as opposed to a law professor who happened to have a graduate degree in economics), the economist was hired to teach price theory, co-teach with a law professor a course on business regulation such as antitrust and serve as a resource to the few law professors who thought economics might have something to contribute to their particular area of law. The economist did not mess with law nor was he expected to do so. And even when he stuck to economics, the results could be unsettling. One only has to recall the often-told story of the antitrust course at Chicago in the 1950s co-taught by Professors Edward Levy, later Attorney General of the United States, and Aaron Director. During the first four classes of each week, Levy would carefully go over the cases and struggle to make sense of the judge's economic reasoning. On the fifth day, Director would explain why everything that went on during the previous four classes was wrong.

Research interests

Twenty years ago there were two options open to an economist who wanted to contribute to the "new" law and economics. He could collaborate with a law professor interested in economics or immerse himself in law and, given enough time and effort, become sufficiently comfortable with legal materials to work on his own. (Today there is a third way.

By studying the substantial law and economics literature, one may be able to find promising but often technical problems to work on.) I chose to do both. I collaborated with Posner and I immersed myself in the study of law. Not that I wanted to be a lawyer but I wanted to know enough about different areas of law to see where economics would be most useful. Unlike most other economists, I actually enjoyed reading law cases. I read them with an economist's eye, however. I looked for and often found an implicit economic logic in the outcome of a case. And if I didn't quite get the law right or misinterpreted what the judge said, neither of which was unusual, I always had Posner or one of my other colleagues at the law school to straighten me out.

My first paper with Posner started out as a theoretical comment on Becker's and Stigler's paper on private enforcement. We showed that private enforcement could lead to over enforcement relative to (optimal) public enforcement because a higher fine would lead private enforcers to step up rather than reduce their enforcement activity.[13] But the paper quickly developed into a more ambitious project. We tested the predictions of the analysis against real world observations. We explained why there is a greater reliance on private enforcement in contract, torts and other "private law" areas compared to criminal law; why victims rather than others have the exclusive rights to sue and redress violations; why the budgets of public enforcement agencies tend to be small relative to what private profit maximizing enforcers would spend; and why public enforcers nullify particular laws by declining to prosecute whereas private enforcers would not. We also applied the model to blackmail and bribery as forms of enforcement and the legal rules governing rewards for lost or stolen property—also a method of compensating private enforcers.

In an important sense the paper on private enforcement represented a sharp departure from my earlier work. It systematically applied economics to a large number of legal rules and showed how these rules promoted economic efficiency. Of course, this was mainly due to Posner for I lacked the necessary knowledge of law. But I was determined to remedy this deficiency by auditing law courses—particularly, basic first year courses such as civil procedure, contracts and torts—and by jointly teaching law courses and seminars with law professors

Over the next twenty years, Posner and I co-authored more than 25 articles and a book on tort law. Our work was truly a joint effort and continues to this day. I have had greater responsibility for the economic modeling and Posner for the law but each of us contributed substantially to both the economics and the law. True, there were substantial gains from trade because we each brought different skills to the enterprise but the final product greatly exceeded the sum of the individual parts. We each raised the marginal product of the other. Looking over the papers, it would be misleading to say "Posner did this" or "I did that" for the ideas, choice of topics, approaches to them and execution were always joint efforts. The topics we collaborated on covered a broad range of legal subjects including legal precedent, the resolution of legal disputes, laws governing rescue such as salvage in admiralty law, antitrust, torts, the role of an independent judiciary, trade secrets, trademarks and copyright. Our best known work, the book "The Economic Structure of Tort Law," showed how a relatively simple economic model of wealth maximization could explain and organize what at first appeared an incomprehensible array of unrelated rules and doctrines governing tort liability. We covered all the important areas of torts from simple problems such as the choice between negligence and strict liability rules for ordinary accidents, to more complicated questions involving defenses to liability, causation, joint torts (two or more injurers), catastrophic injuries (many victims), and intentional torts.

Although I have also worked on a number of projects on my own, including papers on litigation and copyright law, I continue to do collaborative work both with Posner and more recently with Larry Lessig, a recently appointed law professor at Chicago.[14] I am surprised that collaboration between lawyers and economists is not more common because the gains from trade seem so substantial. Aside from Posner and myself, the only other long term collaboration involves Charles Goetz, an economist, and Robert Scott, a law professor and now Dean, of the University of Virginia Law School.[15] On the other hand, an increasing phenomenon at law schools is the lawyer who also has a Ph.D. in economics. Most of these are recent law school graduates. Their work is a form of collaboration between a lawyer and economist but involves one person.

The changing role of the law school economist

Over the years I have become much more comfortable with law, and pretty much have become assimilated into the law school culture. That is also true for other economists who have full-time positions at law schools. We spend much more time with our colleagues at the law school than we do with economists in the economics department or business schools. Proximity is one reason but there are more fundamental forces at work.

One is that economics departments have become less interested in applied economics such as law and economics. Economics has become more formal and theoretical. Research is increasingly aimed at demonstrating technical skills and solving technical problems rather than at analyzing social problems. Consequently, the law school economist feels less comfortable intellectually on the other side of the campus. Fortunately, this is less true at Chicago, and I continue to attend economics and business school workshops with Becker, Sam Peltzman, Sherwin Rosen and others. But Chicago is unusual.

Another is that economists at law schools have more in common with law professors today than twenty years ago because economics has transformed legal scholarship in torts, contracts, securities, antitrust, corporations, environmental law, intellectual property and other business related areas. There are large numbers of law professors who consider themselves members of the law and economics movement.[16] Another indication of the growing importance of economics at law schools is the appointment of economists (but virtually no other nonlawyers) to full-time positions at all major and many other law schools. Twenty years ago, the economist at a law school was a peripheral figure. Today he occupies a central position.

A related factor is the increasing importance of economics in the teaching of law. Law schools are professional schools that view their primary mission as educating future practitioners. For economics to be more than of marginal importance, it must demonstrate its relevance to the education of future practicing lawyers. It has done this by making significant contributions to the practice of law. Economics has altered antitrust; plays a significant role in securities, pension, environmental, unfair competition and discrimination litigation; and is important in valuation and damage calculations in virtually all large scale commercial law suits. Law students are quick to recognize the value of economics in the practice of law. Knowing economics gives them an edge over their competitors. As a result, law and economics courses are increasingly popular at law schools as are our courses jointly taught by lawyers and economists in a variety of subjects. Moreover, it is not uncommon today for an economist to teach a law course alone, which was unheard of thirty years ago. Consider my teaching responsibilities. Although I run the law and economics workshop, I teach copyrights, trademarks and unfair competition and (my favorite) art law. These are not law and economics courses but regular law school courses. To be sure, I add a heavy dose of economics not only because I am an economist but because the cases explicitly discuss and recognize the importance of economic factors and because the use of economics (by lawyers) in private law subjects has become commonplace. Indeed, I have become so assimilated into the world of academic law that I am now a professor of law and economics not just a professor of economics (my original title at the law school).

The future

I have been struck by comments made to me on several occasions from young scholars starting out in law and economics today. The gist of their remarks is that "when you started out there were lots of areas of law open to economics but you and others have taken all the interesting problems so now there is nothing left." There is, of course, an element of truth to this but it is greatly exaggerated. Early on, an economist auditing a law school course in torts or contract was like a child in a candy store—there was an interesting topic to be discovered in almost every class. Indeed, the difficulty was not finding topics but deciding which ones to work on. My torts book with Posner is a good example. While auditing Posner's tort course, I worked up economic notes on the cases and doctrines discussed in class and in the casebook. Then I refined and expanded this material in connection with a course I taught in law and economics. These notes became the starting point for our tort book. But today economic analysis of common law fields like torts and contracts have been so picked over that it would be a mistake for a young scholar to concentrate on them. The same is probably true for litigation models though I am less confident here because recent applications of game theory to litigation has yielded some interesting new scholarship.

What is left? Law and economic scholars have only recently applied the tools of game theory to understanding how legal doctrines may overcome strategic behavior and asymmetrical information.[17] This remains a promising area for future work. Turning to particular fields of law, one observes that constitutional law has been barely touched by economic analysis. And family law, criminal law (as distinct from empirical studies of deterrence), legal procedure and intellectual property have been relatively neglected compared to torts, contracts and corporate law. These fields also remain promising for future work. But the most neglected side of law and economics is empirical. In most areas of law and economics there is a dearth of empirical studies that are surely worth doing. Recently, I surveyed all articles published in the Journal of Legal Studies (the leading "new" law and economics journal) during the last five years, and found that only about 20 percent had some empirical content. Contrast this with the Journal of Political Economy where more than 60 percent of articles published in the past year contained substantial empirical analysis.[18] This difference cannot be accounted for solely by differences in data availability. There are substantial bodies of data on the number and disposition of criminal and civil cases at both the trial and appellate levels, awards in civil cases, sentences in criminal cases, earnings of lawyers, accident rates and so forth. Moreover, computerized legal databases make it possible at relatively low cost to extract significant amounts of information from cases in order to develop data sets relevant to the problems at hand.

Finally, there are different approaches to research. One can work productively and imaginatively at either the intensive or extensive margin. The first approach is illustrated by Coase's work on problems such as marginal cost pricing, the organization of firms, social cost and durable goods monopolies. Before Coase, economists had worked on these problems for many years. Yet Coase was able to say something new and novel about these problems and ultimately to change the way economists think about them. Becker, on the other hand, works primarily at the extensive margin showing the relevance of economics to a wide range of social issues usually considered beyond economics. These include marriage, divorce, bringing up children, education, altruism, crime, addiction and preference formation. As Becker and Coase have shown, Nobel Prizes can be won at either margin. The fact that there now exists a substantial body of literature in law and economics makes it simultaneously more difficult to work at the extensive margin but easier to work at the intensive margin.

Consulting or law and economics in action

Describing my career in law and economics would be seriously incomplete without considering consulting or what I call "law and economics in action." In 1977, Posner, Andrew Rosenfield, then a third year student at the law school, and I founded the firm Lexecon Inc. Economics was just starting to catch on in antitrust litigation and regulatory proceedings. We were confident that it was going to play a bigger role in the future. At the same time, law firms and their clients often expressed dissatisfaction with the quality of economic consulting services they were receiving. Their main complaint was that, in the end, they weren't getting good value for their money. The economic analysis and empirical studies were costly and rarely provided much help. But part of the problem rested with the lawyers who had so little understanding of economics that they did not know how to deploy it effectively.

The idea behind Lexecon was a simple one. There existed a market niche for a firm that supplied high quality economic consulting services that would be relevant and helpful in litigation and regulatory matters. We brought unique qualities to this venture. Posner was a lawyer who knew economics, I was an economist who knew how to explain economics to lawyers, and Rosenfield, who had graduate training in economics to go along with his law degree, was willing to devote himself full time to building up Lexecon, as we were not. Together we could figure out what economic studies should be done, direct and supervise them efficiently, and, when needed, bring in other academic economists who had expertise and specialized knowledge in the areas being litigated.

Lexecon played an educational role as well. Many exceptionally talented and experience attorneys felt at sea when it came to economics and statistics. But they were fast and eager learners. We explained basic economics (and even econometrics) and showed them how they could use economics to help structure and strengthen legal arguments. With this panoply of services we were able to convince law firms to turn over to Lexecon the economic side of many large cases. We had another selling point. We did not pose an economic threat to law firms. We were not competing for their clients because we didn't practice law. Indeed, Lexecon became a competitive tool in the hands of law firms because it enabled them to offer their clients a superior product.

As they say the rest is history. Lexecon became enormously successful and spawned many imitators. It is a source of great personal satisfaction to me that I helped create and develop Lexecon. Today Lexecon has about 125 full-time employees in Chicago[19] (although Posner left in 1981 when he became a judge and I have significantly reduced my role in the past few years) including a large staff of extraordinarily able economists with Ph.D.'s, and affiliations with a number of leading academic economists including several Nobel Prize winners.[20]

Economic consulting has become an increasingly attractive option for some of the brightest Ph.D.'s in economics. It offers the prospect of considerably greater financial rewards than academics (but not the prospect of formal tenure) and a wide range of real world problems to work on because the role of economic evidence, once largely limited to antitrust cases and calculating damages in personal injury cases, has expanded to embrace virtually all kind of large scale commercial litigation. Economists are routinely employed in areas such as securities and corporate law, pension law, environmental and safety regulation, and discrimination litigation. Indeed, it would verge on legal malpractice not to use an economist in these areas.

There is, of course, an important difference between academics and consulting. An academic sets his own agenda. He has the luxury to choose whatever problem catches his fancy and the pace at which to pursue them. Not so in consulting. There, the problem is placed before you, and you face the press of time, the tension of litigation, long hours, and travel away from home. Moreover, millions of dollars may be at stake and your role may be crucial. Not surprising, one tends to get caught up in the excitement of litigation and relish the satisfaction from having done a first rate job. Rewards come more slowly, if at all, to the academic economist.

There is a common misconception about litigation among academic economists who have little or no consulting experience. They assume that the pressures of litigation compel an economist who testifies as an expert witness to slant his analysis, present only favorable results and massage the data in order to come up with the answers the client wants. The flaw in this argument is it ignores how litigation works. Both the data the expert relies on and his analysis are turned over to the opposing party way before any testimony in court is given. The opposition, armed with their own economists, will check the opposing expert's calculations, reestimate his equations, analyze the sensitivity of the estimates to alternative specifications, see how the results change if other variables are added, and so forth. The combination of high stakes and the workings of the adversary system means there is a very high probability that any mistakes, whether intentional or inadvertent, will be unmasked. The same holds for economic presentations before regulatory agencies such as the Antitrust Division of the Department of Justice or the Federal Trade Commission. They have their own professional staff of economists to analyze the expert's work. Contrast this with academic work. A well refereed journal will often catch theoretical mistakes.

But it is far easier to get away with sloppy and even intentionally misleading empirical analyses in academic studies than in litigation because it is rare that other economists will take the trouble to check the earlier work.

Concluding remarks

In describing his evolution as an economist, Ronald Coase wrote: "I came to realize where I had been going only after I arrived. The emergence of my ideas at each stage was not part of some grand scheme."[21] That phrase captures my journey as well. I had no particular career path in mind when I started graduate school. I chose economics rather than something else because I had taken a handful of economics courses as an undergraduate. I got started in law and economics by chance because I came across a newspaper article on plea bargaining. True, I wanted to apply economics to important social issues but law was just one of many possibilities. I worked on a wide range of topics in law that, on looking back, evidence a common approach but not an overall scheme to remake legal scholarship. I never thought I was part of a movement but now it is commonplace to hear about how the "law and economics movement" has transformed legal scholarship and teaching.

I was also extraordinarily fortunate to have worked with Becker and Posner. Becker opened my eyes as a student to the power of economics to illuminate social issues and has been a source of inspiration ever since. Posner is probably the most influential legal scholar and certainly the most prolific in this century. It is hard to imagine that law and economics would have been anywhere near as successful had he chosen another career.[22] I also had another extraordinary bit of luck. I married an economist more than twenty five years ago who has been my best critic and the source of countless ideas. I met Lisa when I was an assistant professor and she was a first year graduate student in the economics department at Chicago. Had the current rules and policies governing sexual harassment at universities and the like been in place in 1968, I would never have dated a graduate student. Many believe the benefits (e.g., reducing coercion by men) of sexual harassment policies exceed the transaction and other costs such policies may impose on the dating and marriage markets. In my case, however, I would have been a big loser. But the general subject of sexual harassment is a great topic for future work in law and economics.

Notes

1   As the reader will see, the term "art" in the title bears on the subject of the essay in several ways.
2   Paul Krugman, How I Work, 37 American Economist 25 (1993).
3   That friend, Charles Gwathmey, went on to become one of the leading architects in the United States today.
4   See "The Cunning Man" at 142. The doctor who speaks these words adds, however, that it is not so easy a task for the full quote reads "to learn to see what is right in front of one's nose; that is the task and a heavy task it is." Martha Nussbaum points out that Robertson Davies was not the first to make this point. It was made earlier

by Greek philosophers as well. For example, in an essay on Heraclitus, David Wiggins writes "But the power of Heraclitus—his claim to be the most adult thinker of his age and a grown man among infants and adolescents—precisely consisted in the capacity to speculate, in the theory of meaning, just as in physics, not where speculation lacked all useful observations, or where it need more going theory to bite on, but where the facts were as big and familiar as the sky and so obvious that it took actual genius to pay heed to them." See David Wiggins, "Heraclitus' Conceptions of Flux, Fire and Material Persistence" at p. 32 in Language and Logos: Studies in Ancient Greek Philosophy Presented to G.E.L. Owen, ed. M. Schofield and M. Nussbaum (Cambridge: Cambridge University Press, 1982).

5　The textbook, "Price Theory: A Provisional Textbook" was based on Friedman's graduate course at Chicago, and a number of problems in that book had been suggested by Aaron Director, an economics professor at the University of Chicago Law School.

6　See Becker's Nobel Lecture entitled "The Economic Way of Looking at Life."

7　In 1963 (when I started my dissertation) thirteen states had passed fair employment legislation. The major federal civil rights legislation was not enacted until 1964.

8　George Stigler and Claire Friedland, What Can Regulators Regulate? The Case of Electricity, 5 J. Law & Econ. 1 (1962).

9　R.H. Coase, "The Problem of Social Cost," 3 J. Law & Econ. 1 (1960).

10　Hereafter I use the phrase "law and economics" also to denote the "new" law and economics.

11　The paper was initially titled "Rationing the Services of Courts." A substantially revised version, which contained an empirical analysis of the frequency of both criminal and civil cases tried across different jurisdictions in the U.S. was eventually published in the Journal of Law & Economics in 1971. That paper plus papers by Richard Posner, Jack Gould and Steven Shavell have stimulated a voluminous law and economics literature on the resolution of legal disputes. In a somewhat dated survey article, Robert D. Cooter & Daniel L. Rubinfeld, Economic Analysis of Legal Disputes and Their Resolution, 27 J. Econ. Lit. 1067 (1989) discuss more than 100 such articles. I suspect that the number of articles has at least doubled since the year of the survey article.

12　Coase was an exception. He had taken some business law courses, and his social cost paper discusses a number of important early English nuisance cases.

13　Optimal enforcement (following Becker's earlier paper) typically involved a low probability of apprehension and conviction and a high fine which produced the same level of deterrence at lower costs.

14　Lessig and I are completely a large scale project estimating empirically the influence and reputation of federal court judges by counting citations to their opinions. Viewing citations as "output," we borrow from the human capital literature, and estimate equations of citations on experience and a variety of other variables. Not only do we rank judges but we examine factors that may explain differences in influence among judges (e.g., race, sex, quality of law school performance, prior experience, etc.).

15　As a rough measure of the benefits from collaboration, Landes and Goetz accounted for more than 45 percent of the citations in law journals to the articles and books of economists at the top fifteen law schools. (See Landes and Posner, The influence of Economics on Law: A Quantitative Study, 36 J. Law & Econ. 385 (1993))

16   A pretty good measure of this is that lawyers comprise about 50 percent of 400 or so members of the recently formed American Law & Economics Association.

17   For an excellent start in this direction see Douglas Baird, Robert Gertner and Randal Picker, Game Theory and the Law, Harv. Univ. Press (1994).

18   The reason there are relative few empirical articles in law and economics is an interesting question in itself. I recently addressed this issue in a presentation on law and economics at the annual meetings of the American Economics Association in 1994. I advanced several explanations including the fact that the initial success of law and economics at law schools came not from empirical studies but from the light that economics shed on legal doctrines; that the law school culture values verbal quickness and analytical skills but not painstaking empirical analysis; that law and economics has been centered at law schools rather than economics departments or business schools; and that Law professors, the major contributors to law and economics are selected for verbal not quantitative skills. Equally puzzling is why economists on law faculties also tend to avoid empirical analysis. But again this is related to both the reward structure at law schools and the kind of economists who have been attracted to law and economics.

19   I might add that Lexecon's offices were designed by Charles Gwathmey (see footnote 2).

20   Rosenfield is now President but is also a senior lecturer at the University of Chicago Law School where he teaches antitrust, securities and evidence.

21   R. H. Coase, My Evolution as an Economist (1994), unpublished version of a lecture in the "Lives of the Laureates" series, given at Trinity University, San Antonio, Texas on April 12. 1994.

22   It would be more accurate to say "had he not chosen economics as *one* of his careers." Posner is also a federal court of appeals judge (whose opinions are cited more frequently than any other appellate court judge) and a significant contributor to other fields such as law and literature and jurisprudence.

Chapter 5

Christine Jolls

BEHAVIORAL LAW AND ECONOMICS

1. Introduction

MANY TOPICS WITHIN ECONOMICS relate to law. A large body of work in public economics, for instance, examines the effects of legally-mandated government programs such as disability and unemployment insurance (Katz and Meyer 1990; Gruber 1994; Cutler and Gruber 1996; Autor and Duggan 2003); work on the labor market examines the effects of many types of antidiscrimination laws (Heckman and Payner 1989; Donohue and Heckman 1991; Acemoglu and Angrist 2001; Jolls 2004a); and recent corporate governance research studies the consequences of corporate and securities law on stock returns and volatility (Gompers, Ishii and Metrick 2003; Ferrell 2003; Greenstone, Oyer and Vissing-Jorgensen 2006). But, while all of these topics relate to law in some way, neither "law and economics" nor "behavioral law and economics" embraces them as genuinely central areas of inquiry. Thus an important threshold question for the present work involves how to characterize the domains of both "law and economics" and "behavioral law and economics."

Amid the broad span of economic topics relating to law in some way, a few distinctive features help to demarcate work that is typically regarded as within law and economics. One distinguishing feature is that much of this work focuses on various areas of law that were not much studied by economists prior to the advent of law and economics; these areas include tort law, contract law, property law, and rules governing the litigation process. A second feature of work within law and economics is that it often (controversially) employs the normative criterion of "wealth maximization" (R. Posner 1979) rather than that of social welfare maximization—not, for the most part, on the view that society should pursue the maximization of wealth rather than social welfare, but instead because law and economics generally favors addressing distributional issues that bear on social welfare solely through the tax system (Shavell 1981). Finally, a third distinguishing feature of much work within law and economics is its sustained interest in explaining and predicting the content, rather than just the effects, of legal rules. While a large body of work in economics studies the effects of law (as noted above), outside of work associated with law and economics only political economy has generally given central emphasis to analyzing the content of law, and then only from a particular perspective.[1]

Given this rough sketch of "law and economics," what then is "behavioral law and economics"? Behavioral law and economics involves both the development and the incorporation within law and economics of behavioral insights drawn from various fields of psychology. As has been widely recognized since the early work by Allais (1952) and Ellsberg (1961), some of the foundational assumptions of traditional economic analysis may reflect an unrealistic picture of human behavior. Not surprisingly, models based on these assumptions sometimes yield erroneous predictions. Behavioral law and economics attempts to improve the predictive power of law and economics by building in more realistic accounts of actors' behavior.

The present paper describes some of the central attributes and applications of behavioral law and economics to date; it also outlines an emerging focus in behavioral law and economics on prospects for "debiasing" individuals through the structure of legal rules (Jolls and Sunstein 2006). Through the vehicle of "debiasing through law," behavioral law and economics may open up a new space within law and economics between, on the one hand, unremitting adherence to traditional economic assumptions and, on the other hand, broad structuring or restructuring of legal regimes on the assumption that people are inevitably and permanently bound to deviate from traditional economic assumptions.

The paper proceeds as follows. Section 2 traces the development and refinement of one of the central insights of behavioral economics—that people frequently exhibit an endowment effect—both outside and within the field of behavioral law and economics. Section 3 moves to a general overview of the features of human decision making that have informed behavioral law and economics, emphasizing points of departure from work in other areas of behavioral economics. Section 4 describes a series of illustrative applications of behavioral law and economics analysis. Section 5 introduces the concept of debiasing through law, and section 6 concludes.

2. The endowment effect in behavioral economics and behavioral law and economics

Early on, law and economics had a central point of contact with behavioral economics. The point of contact was the foundational debate over the Coase theorem and the "endowment effect"—the tendency of people to refuse to give up entitlements they hold even though they would not have bought those entitlements initially (Thaler 1980:43–47). This early point of contact between law and economics and behavioral economics helped to lay the ground for a rich literature down the road on the endowment effect in both behavioral economics and behavioral law and economics.

2.1 The Coase theorem

An unquestioned centerpiece of law and economics is the Coase theorem (Coase 1960). This theorem posits that allocating legal rights to one party or another will not affect outcomes if transaction costs are sufficiently low; thus, for instance, whether the law gives a factory the right to emit pollution next to a laundry or, instead, says the laundry has a right to be free of pollution will not matter to the ultimate outcome (pollution or no pollution) as long as transaction costs are sufficiently low. The reason for this result is that, with low transaction costs, the parties should be expected to bargain for the efficient outcome under either legal regime. The Coase theorem is central to law and economics because of (among other things) the theorem's claim about the domain within which normative analysis of legal rules—whether rule A is preferable to rule B or the reverse—is actually relevant.

The Coase theorem has also played a central, albeit a rather different, role in the field of behavioral economics. More than fifteen years ago, Daniel Kahneman, Jack Knetsch and Richard Thaler (1990) reported the results of a set of experiments designed to provide a careful empirical assessment of the Coase theorem. In one round of experiments, each subject was given an assigned value for a "token" (the amount for which the subject could redeem the token for cash at the end of the experiment), and half of the subjects were awarded tokens. When subjects subsequently had the opportunity to trade tokens for money or (for those not awarded tokens) money for tokens, subjects behaved precisely in accordance with the Coase theorem. Exactly half of the tokens changed hands, as theory would predict (given random assignment of the tokens in relation to the specified values). The initial allocation of tokens proved irrelevant. These findings are a striking vindication of the Coase theorem.

Having thus established that transaction costs in the experimental setting were sufficiently low to vindicate the Coase theorem, Kahneman, Knetsch and Thaler went on to study subjects' behavior when the good to be traded was not tokens but, rather, Cornell University mugs that the subjects would retain after the experiment (rather than redeeming for an assigned amount of cash). In direct contravention of the Coase theorem, the initial assignment of entitlements to the mug mattered dramatically; those initially given mugs rarely sold them, while those not initially given mugs seldom bought them. Following Thaler (1980:44), Kahneman, Knetsch and Thaler referred to this effect as the "endowment effect"—the refusal to give up an entitlement one holds initially even though one would not have been willing to pay to acquire that entitlement had one not held it initially. [2] In the presence of the endowment effect, the Coase theorem's prediction of equivalent outcomes regardless of the initial entitlement no longer holds. This conclusion has obvious importance for the design of legal rules.

2.2 The endowment effect within law and economics

A central task of law and economics is to assess the desirability of actual and proposed legal rules. The endowment effect both preserves a larger scope for such normative economic analysis—because the Coase theorem and the associated claim of irrelevance of legal rules no longer hold—and profoundly unsettles the bases for such analysis.

The reason that the endowment effect so unsettles the bases for normative economic analysis of law is that in the presence of this effect the value attached to a legal entitlement will sometimes vary depending on the initial assignment of the entitlement. Normative analysis will then often become indeterminant, as multiple rules may maximize the desired objective (whether wealth or social welfare) depending on the starting allocation of entitlements (Kelman 1979:676–78). As Cass Sunstein and Richard Thaler (2003:1190) recently observed, in the presence of the endowment effect a "cost-benefit study cannot be based on willingness to pay (WTP), because WTP will be a function of the default rule." Thus, the cost-benefit study "must be a more open-ended (and inevitably somewhat subjective) assessment of the welfare consequences."[3] The conventional normative economic analysis feasible without the endowment effect often cannot survive in the presence of this effect.

One possible approach to normative analysis when the value of an entitlement varies depending on the initial assignment of the entitlement is to base legal policy choices not on the joint wealth or welfare of the parties directly in question—because the answer to the question of which rule maximizes their joint wealth or welfare may turn on the initial rule choice—but rather on the third-party effects of the competing rules. Thus, for instance, if it is unclear whether a particular workplace rule is or is not optimal for employers and employees (because employees will value the entitlement granted by the rule at more than its value with the rule in place but less than its value otherwise), but the rule will create important benefits for employees' families, then perhaps the rule should be adopted.

An alternative approach to normative analysis with varying entitlement values depending on the initial assignment of the entitlement is to make a judgment about which preferences—the ones with legal rule A or the ones with legal rule B—deserve greater deference. Sunstein and Thaler (2003:1190–91) offer some support for this view in the context of default terms in employee savings plans. Referring to research showing that employees are much more likely to enroll in a savings plan if enrollment is the default term and employees must affirmatively opt out to be excluded than if non-enrollment is the default term and employees must take affirmative steps to enroll, Sunstein and Thaler make the normative argument that the enrollment outcome is "highly likely" to be better under automatic enrollment than under a default term of non-enrollment because it turns out that very few employees drop out if automatically enrolled. They readily acknowledge that "[s]ome readers might think that our reliance on [employees'] behavior as an indication of welfare is inconsistent" with the basic point about indeterminacy of preferences, "[b]ut in fact, there is no inconsistency" because "it is reasonable to think that if, on reflection, workers realized that they had been 'tricked' into saving too much, they might take the effort to opt out." Sunstein and Thaler draw an analogy to rules calling for mandatory cooling-off periods before consumer purchases: "The premise of such rules is that people are more likely to make good choices when they have had time to think carefully and without a salesperson present." In other words, according to Sunstein and Thaler, we have reason to think that the revealed preferences of the automatically enrolled employee, or the consumer at the end of a cooling-off period, are a more appropriate basis for normative judgment than the revealed preferences of the employee who does not choose to enroll under a default term of non-enrollment, or the consumer before the cooling-off period. We will see similar issues, along with some prospect for avoiding the "inevitably subjective" determinations confronted by Sunstein and Thaler, in the discussion of bounded willpower in section 3.2 below.

2.3 The importance of context

Particularly in light of the central relevance of the endowment effect to normative economic analysis of law, it is appropriate to emphasize the important role of context in whether this effect occurs. An early literature in law and economics is responsible for helping to shape understandings of when the endowment effect will and will not occur.

Prior to the Cornell University "mugs experiments" described above, a series of law and economics articles had demonstrated a set of domains in which the Coase theorem was in fact empirically robust. Hoffman and Spitzer's (1982, 1986) experiments showed that in both large and small groups the predictions of the theorem were vindicated. Likewise, Schwab (1988) found that ultimate allocation of entitlements did not turn on their initial allocation.

All of these experiments, however, shared with the tokens experiment discussed above the feature that subjects' value of each possible outcome was directly specified in dollar terms by the experimenter. Thus, the law and economics work from the 1980s showed that if people are told specifically what each outcome is worth to them, they will generally find their way to a value-maximizing outcome, so long as transaction costs are sufficiently low. However, the later "mugs experiments" demonstrated that this result tends to collapse when actors are not instructed as to the value of outcomes to them. Viewed in light of the later work, the law and economics papers from the 1980s are best understood as showing some of the important limits on when the endowment effect will be observed and, more generally, the central role of context in influencing the occurrence or nonoccurrence of this effect. The work by Plott and Zeiler (2005) provides an important recent lens on the role of context in determining the existence and degree of the endowment effect.

Within behavioral law and economics, recent work has refined the basic point about the importance of context. Korobkin (1998), for instance, raised the important question of whether the endowment effect would obtain in the allocation to either prospective sellers or prospective buyers of contract law default rights, such as the right of sellers to withhold goods or services after unanticipated natural disasters or other similar events versus the right of buyers to demand goods or services in those circumstances. (For instance, if a theatre owner has promised to allow its theatre to be used by another party on a specific date, but the theatre then burns down before that date, does the theatre owner have the right not to provide the theatre, or does the other party have the right to collect damages for the harm it suffered because the theatre proved unavailable?) Such contact law entitlements do not attach—and indeed are irrelevant—until and unless a contract is ultimately agreed to, and thus Korobkin noted that it was unclear whether the initial allocation of the entitlements through contract law default rules would create the sort of sense of ownership or possession that in turn would generate an endowment effect.

Korobkin's experiments support the operation of the endowment effect in this context. He finds that if contract law allocates an entitlement to party A unless party A agrees to waive it, then a contract between that party and party B is more likely to award party A that entitlement than if contract law initially allocates the entitlement to party B—even with seemingly low transaction costs. Thus, Korobkin concludes, the endowment effect, and not the Coase theorem, provides the best account of the effects of contract law default rights. The deepening of knowledge about when the endowment effect does and does not occur—across contract settings and elsewhere—will help refine our understanding of the scope of this effect and, as a direct consequence, the validity of and limits on conventional normative economic analysis of law.

3. The modern domain of behavioral law and economics

Although the endowment effect has played a central role in behavioral law and economics, other features of behavioral economics are important as well. Following Thaler (1996), it is useful for purposes of behavioral law and economics analysis to view human actors as departing from traditional economic assumptions in three distinct ways: human actors exhibit *bounded rationality, bounded willpower,* and *bounded self-interest.* All three concepts are defined in the brief discussion below. As described below, bounded rationality consists in part of judgment errors, and along with the usual types of such errors discussed in the existing literature in behavioral economics, behavioral law and economics has recently emphasized a separate form of judgment error—implicit bias in how members of racial and other groups are perceived by individuals who consciously disavow any sort of prejudiced attitude; this form of judgment error provides the starting part for the discussion below.

3.1 Bounded rationality

Departures from traditional economic assumptions of unbounded rationality may be divided into two main categories, judgment errors and departures from expected utility theory.

3.1.1 Judgment errors

Across a wide range of contexts, actual judgments show systematic differences from unbiased forecasts. Within this category of judgment errors, behavioral law and economics has recently emphasized errors in the form of implicit bias in people's perceptions of racial and other group members.

Implicit Racial and Other Group-Based Bias. Perhaps the most elementary definition of the word "bias" is that a person believes, either consciously or implicitly, that members of a racial or other group are somehow less worthy than other individuals. An enormous literature in modern social psychology explores the cognitive, motivational, and other aspects of implicit, or unconscious, forms of racial or other group-based bias. This literature, however, has not featured significantly in most fields of behavioral economics. But a clear contrast is behavioral law and economics, which has recently given significant emphasis to the possibility and effects of implicit racial or other group-based bias.

The behavioral law and economics literature in this area has worked against the backdrop of a heavily Beckerian approach to discrimination. Seminal law and economics works on discrimination envision such behavior as in significant part a rational response to discriminatory "tastes" that disfavor association with particular group members (e.g. R. Posner 1989). The idea of implicit bias, by contrast, suggests that discriminatory behavior often stems not from taste-based preferences that individuals are consciously acting to satisfy, but instead from implicit attitudes afflicting individuals who seriously and sincerely disclaim all forms of prejudice, and who would regard their implicitly biased judgments as "errors." A number of recent works in behavioral law and economics have begun to explore the implications for the analysis of discrimination law of various types of implicit bias (e.g. Gulati and Yelnowsky 2006; Jolls and Sunstein 2006).

While social psychologists have identified diverse means of assessing and measuring implicit bias against members of racial and other groups (e.g., Gaertner and McLaughlin 1983; Greenwald, McGhee and Schwartz 1998), a particular measure, known as the Implicit Association Test (IAT), has had particular influence. In the IAT, individuals are asked to categorize words or pictures into four groups, two of which are racial or other groups (such as "black" and "white"), and the other two of which are the categories "pleasant" and "unpleasant." Groups are paired, so that respondents are instructed to press one key on the computer for either "black" or "unpleasant" and a different key for either "white" or "pleasant" (a stereotype consistent pairing); or are instructed instead to press one key on the computer for either "black" or "pleasant" and a different key for either "white" or "unpleasant" (a stereotype-inconsistent pairing). Implicit bias is defined as faster categorization when the "black" and "unpleasant" categories are paired than when the "black" and "pleasant" categories are paired. The IAT reveals significant evidence of implicit bias, including among those who assiduously deny any prejudice (Greenwald, McGhee and Schwartz 1998; Nosek, Banaji and Greenwald 2002).

An important question raised by the results on the IAT is whether implicit bias as measured by the test is correlated with individuals' actual behavior toward members of other groups. Studies including McConnell and Leibold (2001) and Dovidio, Kawakami and Gaertner (2002) find that scores on the IAT and similar tests show correlations with third parties' ratings of the degree of general friendliness shown by individuals toward members of other groups. Other connections between IAT scores and actual behavior are an active area of research.

Although implicit racial or other group-based bias is not conventionally grouped with other forms of bounded rationality within behavioral economics, the fit may be more natural than has typically been supposed. Such implicit bias may often result from the way in which the characteristic of race or other group membership operates as a sort of "heuristic"—a form of mental short-cut. (The concept of a heuristic is discussed more fully just below.) Indeed, recent psychology research emphasizes that heuristics often work through a process of "attribute substitution," in which people answer a hard question by substituting an easier one (Kahneman and Frederick 2002). For instance, people might resolve a question of probability not by investigating statistics, but by asking whether a relevant incident comes easily to mind (Tversky and Kahneman 1973). The same process can operate to produce implicit bias against racial or other groups. Section 5.1 below describes an example of how implicit bias has been analyzed within behavioral law and economics.

The "Heuristics and Biases" Literature. Judgment errors may arise not only from implicit bias against racial or other group members, but also from other biases studied within the so-called "heuristics and biases" literature within behavioral economics. Three types of judgment errors from this literature have received particularly sustained attention within behavioral law and economics.

One such judgment error is optimism bias, in which individuals believe that their own probability of facing a bad outcome is lower than it actually is. As a familiar illustration, most people think that their chances of having an auto accident are significantly lower than the average person's chances of experiencing this event (e.g., DeJoy 1989), although of course these beliefs cannot all be correct; if everyone were below "average," then the average would be lower.[4] There is also evidence that people underestimate their absolute as well as relative (to other individuals) probability of negative events such as auto accidents (Arnould and Grabowski 1981:34–35; Camerer and Kunreuther 1989:566). Optimism bias is probably highly adaptive as a general matter; by thinking that things will turn out well, people may often increase the chance that they will turn out well. Section 4.1 below describes an application of optimism bias in the behavioral law and economics literature.

A second judgment error prominent in behavioral law and economics is self-serving bias. Whenever there is room for disagreement about a matter to be decided by two or more parties and of course there often is in litigation as well as elsewhere—individuals will tend to interpret information in a direction that serves their own interests. In a compelling field study, Babcock, Wang and Loewenstein (1996) find that union and school board presidents asked to identify "comparable" school districts for purposes of labor negotiations identified different lists of districts depending on their respective self-interests. While the average teacher salary in districts viewed as comparable by union presidents was $27,633, the same average was $26,922 in districts viewed as comparable by school board presidents. As Babcock, Wang and Loewenstein observe, this difference was more than large enough to produce teacher strikes based on the size of past salary disagreements leading to strikes. Section 4.2 below discusses an application of self-serving bias in the behavioral law and economics literature.

A third judgment error extensively discussed in behavioral law and economics is the hindsight bias, in which decision makers attach excessively high probabilities to events simply because they ended up occurring. In one striking study, neuropsychologists were presented with a list of patient symptoms and then asked to assess the probability that the patient had each of three conditions (alcohol withdrawal, Alzheimer's disease, and brain damage secondary to alcohol abuse). While the mean probabilities for physicians who were not informed of the patient's actual condition were 37%, 26% and 37% respectively for the three conditions, physicians who were informed of the patient's actual condition routinely said they would have attached much higher probabilities to that condition (Arkes, Faust, Guilmette and Hart 1988). Even when, as in the study, people are specifically instructed to give the probabilities they would have assigned had they been the one making the diagnosis, people seem to have difficulty putting aside events they know to have occurred. As highlighted in section 4.3 below, the hindsight bias has clear relevance to the legal system because that system is pervasively in the business of adjudicating likelihoods and foreseeability after an accident or other event has occurred.

3.1.2 Departures from expected utility theory

Boundedly rational individuals not only make judgment errors but also deviate from the precepts of expected utility theory. While this theory is a foundational aspect of traditional economic analysis, Kahneman and Tversky's (1979) "prospect theory" offers a leading alternative to expected utility theory. Within behavioral law and economics, the feature of prospect theory that emphasizes the distinction between gains and losses relative to an endowment point has received by far the most attention; the relevant work on the endowment effect was discussed in some detail in section 2 above.

3.2 Bounded willpower

We often observe individuals choosing to spend rather than save, consume desserts over salads, and go to the movies instead of the gym despite all of their best intentions (Schelling 1984; Laibson 1997). Why do people fail to follow through on the plans they make? Behavioral economics has emphasized the concept of bounded willpower, which has a long pedigree in economics (Strotz 1955–56). This concept has featured in behavioral law and economics as well, as illustrated in section 4.4 below.

Much work in law and economics is normatively-oriented, and this feature of the work brings to the fore a set of normative questions about bounded willpower—much in the way that normative questions have been prominent in law and economics discussions of the endowment effect (pp. 72–74 above). With respect to bounded willpower, the central normative question concerns how to view a decision to spend rather than save, to consume desserts rather than salads, or to go to the gym rather than the movies. Why should (if they should) the preferences of the self who wishes to save, eat salad, or go to the gym rather than the self who wishes to spend, eat dessert, or watch movies be used as the benchmark in performing normative analysis?

One possible answer, partially reminiscent of a strand of the endowment effect discussion above, is that saving, eating salad, or going to the gym creates desirable third-party effects that are absent with spending, eating dessert, or watching movies. Another possible answer, also with an analogue in the earlier discussion, is that the preferences of the self who wishes to save, eat salad, or go to the gym reflect a considered judgment about the matter in question—the rightness of which, however, it is not possible always to keep before one's mind (Elster 1979:52). Of course, each of these two types of judgments about the relative merits of different preferences may be contentions in at least some settings.

3.3 Bounded self-interest

In principle, traditional economic analysis is capacious with respect to the range of admissible preferences. Preferences that give significant weight to fairness, for instance, can be included in the analysis (Kaplow and Shavell 2002:431–34). In practice, however, much of traditional law and economics posits a relatively narrow set of ends that individuals are imagined to pursue.

Contrary to this conventional approach, bounded self-interest within behavioral economics emphasizes that many people care about both giving and receiving fair treatment in a range of settings (Rabin 1993). As Thaler and Dawes (1992:19–20) observe:

> In the rural areas around Ithaca it is common for farmers to put some fresh produce on a table by the road. There is a cash box on the table, and customers are expected to put money in the box in return for the vegetables they take. The box has just a small slit, so money can only be put in, not taken out. Also, the box is attached to the table, so no one can (easily) make off with the money. We think that the farmers who use this system have just about the right model of human nature. They feel that enough

people will volunteer to pay for the fresh corn to make it worthwhile to put it out there.

Of course, a central question raised by bounded self-interest is what counts as "fair" treatment. Behavioral economics suggests that people will judge outcomes as unfair if they depart substantially from the terms of a "reference transaction"—a transaction that defines the benchmark for the parties' interactions (Kahneman, Knetsch and Thaler 1986a). In the basic version of the well-known ultimatum game, for instance, where parties divide a sum of money with no reason to think one party is particularly more deserving than the other, the "reference transaction" is something like an equal split; substantial departures from this benchmark are viewed as unfair and, accordingly, are punished by parties who receive offers of such treatment (Guth, Schmittberger and Schwarze 1982; Kahneman, Knetsch and Thaler 1986b). Section 4.5 below illustrates how this conception of bounded self-interest has been applied within behavioral law and economics.

4. Illustrative applications of behavioral law and economics

The present section offers a set of illustrative applications of behavioral law and economics. The discussion seeks to illustrate what has become essentially "normal science" within the literature in behavioral law and economics to date: identification of a departure from unbounded rationality, willpower or self-interest, followed by either an account of existing law or a proposed legal reform that takes as a fixed point the identified departure from unbounded rationality, willpower or self-interest. Section 5 shifts the focus to a new approach within behavioral law and economics, one that emphasizes the potential for responding to some bounds on human behavior not by taking people's natural tendencies as given and shaping law around them but, instead, by attempting to reduce or eliminate such human tendencies *through the legal structure*—the approach of "debiasing through law" (Jolls and Sunstein 2006a).

Recent surveys on behavioral law and economics by Guthrie (2003), Korobkin (2003), and Rachlinski (2003) have examined existing legally-oriented work on bounded rationality, devoting extensive attention to both judgment errors and departures from expected utility theory.[5] The present section, by contrast, focuses on a limited number of applications of bounded rationality, willpower and self-interest, attempting to give a fuller picture of some of the relevant work in these areas.

4.1 "Distributive legal rules"[6]

As noted in the introduction, one distinctive feature of law and economics is its frequent focus on wealth maximization—giving legal entitlements to those most willing to pay for them, without regard for distributional considerations—rather than social welfare maximization as the criterion for normative analysis. Many law and economics scholars object to "distributive legal rules"—non-wealth-maximizing legal rules chosen for their distributive consequences—because they believe that distributional issues are best left solely to the tax system (Kaplow and Shavell 1994).

A leading law and economics argument in favor of addressing distributional issues through the tax system rather than through non-tax legal rules is the argument that any desired distributional consequence can be achieved at lower cost through the tax system than through distributive legal rules. Of course, pursuit of distributional objectives through the tax system is not costless; higher taxes on the wealthy will tend to distort work incentives. But under traditional economic assumptions precisely the same is true of distributive legal rules: "[U]sing legal rules to redistribute income distorts work incentives fully as much as the income tax system—because the distortion is caused by the redistribution itself. . . ." (Kaplow and Shavell 1994:667–68). Thus, for example, under traditional economic analysis a thirty percent marginal tax rate, together with a non-wealth-maximizing legal rule that transfers an average of one percent of high earners' income to the poor, creates the same distortion in work incentives as a thirty-one percent marginal tax rate coupled with a wealth-maximizing legal rule. However, the former regime also entails costs due to the non-wealth-maximizing legal rule. (For instance, under a distributive legal rule governing accidents, potential defendants may be excessively cautious and thus may be discouraged from engaging in socially valuable activities.) Thus, whatever the desired distributive consequences, under traditional economic analysis they can always be achieved at lower cost by choosing the wealth-maximizing legal rule and adjusting distributive effects through the tax system than by choosing a non-wealth-maximizing rule because of its distributive properties (Shavell 1981).

A basic premise about human behavior underlies this analysis. Work incentives are assumed to be distorted by the same amount as a result of a probabilistic, non-tax mode of redistribution, such as the law governing accidents, as they are as a result of a tax. Thus, for example, if high-income individuals face a .02 probability of incurring tort liability for an accident, then a distributive legal rule that imposes $500,000 extra in damages (beyond what a wealth-maximizing rule would call for) would distort work incentives by the same amount as a tax of $10,000, assuming risk-neutrality.[7]

Why would distributive tort liability and taxes have the same effects on work incentives? "[W]hen an individual . . . contemplates earning additional income by working harder, his total marginal expected payments [out of that income] equal the sum of his marginal tax payment and the expected marginal cost on account of accidents." (Kaplow and Shavell 1994:671.) The expected costs of the two forms of redistribution are the same, and thus behavior is affected in the same way. At least that is the assumption that traditional economic analysis makes.

Is this assumption valid? From a behavioral economics perspective, it is not clear that an individual would typically experience the same disincentive to work as a result of a more generous (to victims) tort-law regime as would be experienced as a result of a higher level of taxation.[8] The discussion here will highlight one important reason, related to the phenomenon of optimism bias noted in section 3 above, that behavioral law and economics suggests work incentives may be distorted less by distributive tort liability—which operates probabilistically rather than deterministically—than by taxes. Other reasons for different effects of the two regimes, based on different contextual factors across the regimes, are discussed in Jolls (1998).

As just noted, a salient feature of distributive tort liability is the uncertainty of its application to any given actor. The effect of such liability "tends to be limited to those few who become parties to lawsuits" (Kaplow and Shavell 1994:675.) While one knows that one will have to pay taxes every year, one knows that one is quite likely not to become involved in an accident. To be sure, the possibility of uncertain or randomized taxation has received some discussion in the public finance literature. Even supporters of this approach, however, suggest that it is unrealistic from a practical perspective (Stiglitz 1987:1012–13).

Bounded rationality in the form of optimism bias—the tendency to think negative events are less likely to happen to oneself than they actually are—suggests that uncertain events are often processed systematically differently from certain events. Section 3.1.1 above referred to the general body of evidence suggesting the prevalence of optimism bias; there are also empirical studies suggesting that people offer unrealistically optimistic assessments in areas directly related to the effects of distributive tort liability. For instance, most people think that they are less likely than the average person to be sued (Weinstein 1980:810). Likewise, people think that they are less likely than the average person to cause an auto accident (Svenson, Fischhoff and MacGregor 1985; DeJoy 1989). They also think that their own probability of being caught and penalized for drunk driving is lower than the average driver's probability of being apprehended for such behavior (Guppy 1993).

What does optimism bias with respect to the probability of the negative event of tort liability imply for the distortionary effects of distributive tort liability as opposed to taxes? People will tend to underestimate the probability that they will be hit with liability under distributive tort liability; therefore, their perceived cost of the rule will be lower. As a result, their work incentives will tend to suffer a lesser degree of distortion than under a tax yielding the same amount of revenue for the government. For instance, in the numerical example from above, risk-neutral individuals may not attach an expected cost of $10,000 to a .02 (objective) probability of having to pay $500,000 extra in damages under distributive tort liability; they may tend to underestimate the probability that they will incur liability—and thus they may tend to underestimate the expected cost of liability—as a result of optimism bias.[9]

Of course, optimism bias is not the only phenomenon that affects how people assess the likelihood of uncertain events. In some cases people may tend to overestimate rather than underestimate the probability of a negative event because the risk in question is highly salient or otherwise available to them—for instance, contamination from a hazardous waste dump (Kuran and Sunstein 1999:691–97). However, the overestimation phenomenon seems relatively unlikely to affect the assessment of distributive tort liability, at least insofar as individuals rather than firms are concerned. Consider, for instance, the quintessential event that can expose an individual to tort liability: the auto accident. As noted above, people appear to underestimate the probability that they will be involved in an auto accident (relative to the actual probability); this presumably results from a combination of underestimation of the general probability of an accident (Lichtenstein, Slovic, Fischhoff, Layman and Combs 1978:564) and further underestimation of people's own probability relative to the average person's (Svenson, Fischhoff and MacGregor 1985; DeJoy 1989). The situation would probably be different, of course, for an event such as contamination from a hazardous waste dump, the probability of which might be overestimated due to its availability; but highly available events tend to involve firm, not individual, liability. It is difficult to come up with examples of events giving rise to individual liability the probability of which is likely to be overestimated rather than (as suggested above) underestimated. And with underestimation of the probability of liability, work incentives will typically be distorted less by distributive legal rules than by taxes.

4.2 Discovery rules in litigation

The introduction noted that an important aspect of work in law and economics is analysis of various areas of law that were not previously studied by economists. One such area concerns the rules governing the litigation process. When someone believes that a law has been violated, how does the legal system go about deciding the legitimacy of that claim? The American system relies centrally upon an adversary approach, under which competing sides are represented by legal counsel who argue in favor of their respective positions.

Of course, maximally effective advocacy for a position often requires one to obtain information under the control of one's opponent, and thus the American legal system contains a set of rules governing when and how one side in a legal dispute may obtain ("discover") information from the other side. Since 1993 these rules have required opposing parties to disclose significant information even without a request by the other party (Issacharoff and Loewenstein 1995). Under conventional economic analysis this approach should increase the convergence of parties' expectations and, thus, the rate at which they settle disputes out of court (e.g., Shavell 2004:427).

The phenomenon of self-serving bias described in section 3.1.1 above, however, suggests that individuals often interpret information differently depending on the direction of their own self-interest. Experimental work by Loewenstein, Issacharoff, Camerer and Babcock (1993), Babcock, Loewenstein, Issacharoff and Camerer (1995), and Loewenstein and Moore (2004) has examined self-serving bias in the specific context of litigation. In the first paper in the series, Loewenstein, Issacharoff, Camerer and Babcock found that parties assigned to the role of plaintiff or defendant interpreted the very same facts differently depending on their assigned role; subjects assigned to the plaintiff role offered higher estimates of the likely outcome at trial than subjects assigned to the defendant role even though they both received identical information about the case. Moreover, the authors found that subjects who exhibited the highest levels of self-serving bias were also least likely to succeed in negotiating out-of-court settlements. This work provided opening evidence of the role of self-serving bias in shaping the effect of information disclosure on the rate at which legal disputes are settled.

The initial study just described could not rule out the possibility that the relationship between the degree of self-serving bias and the frequency of settlement was non-causal, for it is possible that an unmeasured factor influenced both the degree of self-serving bias and the frequency of settlement. In a follow-up study, however, Babcock, Loewenstein, Issacharoff and Camerer (1995) provided strong evidence that the relationship was in fact causal. They found that parties who were not informed of their roles until after reading case materials and offering their estimates of the likely outcome at trial both failed to exhibit statistically significant degrees of self-serving bias *and* settled at significantly greater rates than parties who were informed of their roles before reading the case materials. The timing of exposure to the case materials matters because "[s]elf-serving interpretations are likely to occur at the point when information about roles is assimilated," for the simple reason that it "is easier to process information in a biased way than it is to change an unbiased estimate once it has been made" (Babcock, Loewenstein, Issacharoff and Camerer 1995:1339). The recent study by Loewenstein and Moore (2004) underlines the fact that self-serving bias will operate when there is some degree of ambiguity about the proper or best interpretation of a set of information, as will frequently be the case in litigation.

The prospect that litigants will interpret at least some information in a self-serving fashion means that the exchange of information in litigation may cause a divergence rather than convergence of parties' expectations. Relying in part on this argument, Issacharoff and Loewenstein (1995) suggest that mandatory disclosure rules in litigation may be undesirable. As they describe, self-serving bias undermines the conventional wisdom that "a full exchange of the information in the possession of the parties is likely to facilitate settlement by enabling each party to form a more accurate, and generally therefore a more convergent, estimate of the likely outcome of the case" (R. Posner 1992:557, quoted in Issacharoff and Loewenstein 1995:773). Consistent with Issacharoff and Loewenstein's argument, a set of amendments in 2000 significantly cut back—although they did not completely eliminate—the mandatory disclosure rules noted above (192 Federal Rules Decisions 340, 385–87).

4.3 The "business judgment" rule in corporate law

The third distinctive feature of law and economics discussed in the introduction concerned the field's interest in explaining and predicting the content of law—what the law allows and what it prohibits. First-generation law and economics scholars emphasized the idea that laws may be efficient solutions to the problems of organizing society; law and economics has also emphasized—as has the field of political economy— that laws may come about because of the rent-seeking activities of politically powerful actors (Stigler 1971).

Behavioral law and economics has extended this conventional account of the content of legal rules in two important ways. The first, which is the focus of the discussion in this section, is that in many cases incorporation of insights about bounded rationality, willpower and self-interest is needed for a satisfactory understanding of law's efficiency properties. A law may be efficient in part because of the way in which it accounts for one of the three bounds on human behavior, as the discussion below illustrates. The second extension of the conventional law and economics account of the content of law is the expansion of behavioral law and economics beyond the two familiar categories from the traditional account—the category of law-as-efficiency-enhancing and the category of law-as-the product-of-conventional-rent-seeking. Section 4.5 below discusses and illustrates this second extension developed by behavioral law and economics.

A prominent behavioral law and economics work seeking to understand and explain the efficiency of the content of law is Rachlinski (1998). Rachlinski examines a number of areas of law, including corporate law. A central rule of American corporate law is the "business judgment" rule, according to which corporate officers and directors who are informed about a corporation's activities and who approve or acquiesce in these activities have generally fulfilled their duties to the corporation as long as they have a rational belief that such activities are in the interests of the corporation.

This highly deferential standard of liability makes it difficult to find legal fault for the decisions of corporate officers and directors.

Rachlinski suggests that the business judgment rule may be corporate law's sensible response to the problem of hindsight bias. As described above, hindsight bias suggests that the sorts of decisions routinely made by the legal system, adjudicating likelihoods and foreseeability after a negative event has materialized, will often be biased toward excessively high estimates—and thus in favor of holding actors respon-sible—simply because the negative event materialized. But under the business judg-ment rule, officers and directors will not be held liable for decisions that turn out badly—"even if these decisions seem negligent in hindsight" (Rachlinski 1998:620). Hindsight bias suggests that things will often seem negligent in hindsight, once a negative outcome has materialized and is known, so the business judgment rule insu-lates officers and directors from the risk of such hindsight-influenced liability determinations. In the absence of the business judgment rule, Rachlinski argues, officers and directors would fail to make the risk-neutral business decisions desired by investors who can limit their overall investment risk through diversification; "[e]nsuring that managers effectively represent this concern and do not avoid business decisions that have a high expected payoff but also carry a high degree of risk is a central problem of corporate governance" (Rachlinski 1998:622). In this respect, hindsight bias can help to explain the efficiency of the content of law governing corporate officers and directors.

4.4 Rules governing contract renegotiation[10]

The behavioral law and economics applications discussed thus far have involved bounded rationality, but other applications have drawn on the other two bounds on human behavior. This subsection describes an application of the concept of bounded willpower within behavioral law and economics.

As discussed above, an individual with bounded willpower will often have diffi-culty sticking to even the best-laid plans. With respect to decisions about consump-tion versus saving, for instance, individuals who earnestly plan to save a substantial amount of next year's salary for retirement may tend, once next year arrives, to save far less than planned. If the failure to stick to the initial plan is understood in advance, then individuals may seek to precommit themselves to their initial plan. An obvious potential means of achieving such precommitment is a contract between the indi-vidual suffering from bounded willpower and a bank or other savings institution; but the efficacy of this approach from the standpoint of the individual at the time of con-templating such a contract depends critically on whether contracts are, or can be made, nonrenegotiable. Down the road it will always be in the parties' mutual inter-est to renegotiate the initial contract, for at later points the individual will be better off if the individual can consume more and save less than what the original contract called for, and thus at that point there is a surplus from renegotiation to be divided between the parties. Only if renegotiation is impossible can the parties avoid the effects of bounded willpower and achieve commitment to the initial plan.

The obvious question is then whether contract law allows nonrenegotiable contracts. Certainly the default rule of contract law is that renegotiated agreements are enforceable. The primary exception to enforcement of such agreements concerns renegotiated agreements coerced by one party's threat to breach the original contract if renegotiation does not occur.[11] But in the model discussed here, renegotiation is truly welfare-enhancing—at the time at which it occurs—for both parties relative to the original contract, so the coercion concern does not apply, and thus the default rule would allow enforcement of the renegotiated agreement.

Does contract law allow the parties to supplement the default rules governing renegotiation with additional terms of their own? Perhaps surprisingly, the answer to this question is generally "no." Justice Cardozo's 1919 opinion in Beatty v. Guggenheim Exploration Co. provides a classic example of the rule and its underlying rationale: "Those who make a contract, may unmake it. The clause which forbids a change, may be changed like any other. . . . 'Every such agreement is ended by the new one which contradicts it.' . . . What is excluded by one act, is restored by another. You may put it out by the door, it is back through the window. Whenever two men contract, no limitation self-imposed can destroy their power to contract again." (122 N.E. 378, 387–88.)

While existing contract law thus prohibits enforcement of contractual agreements not to renegotiate, a natural question is whether a contrary rule would be of any effect. Any clause limiting or prohibiting renegotiation will be effective only if some party to the contract has an incentive to enforce the clause. Jolls (1997) provides discussion of circumstances in which this will be the case. Consistent with the discussion here, the law has started to move away from the formalistic principle described above and in some instances now permits parties by contract to remove their future power to renegotiate their original contract *orally* (although written renegotiated agreements are still always enforceable) (Uniform Commercial Code sec. 2–209).

4.5 The content of consumer protection law[12]

A final illustration of behavioral law and economics reveals the way that work in this area has expanded upon the traditional law and economics notion that law's content reflects either efficiency or conventional rent-seeking. The notion that laws emerge from these two considerations would probably strike most citizens as odd. Instead, most members of society—which is to say most of the people who are entitled to elect legislators—believe that the primary purpose of the law is to codify "right" and "wrong." Can this idea be formalized, drawing in part on the notion of bounded self-interest from section 3.3 above?

Consider the case of consumer protection law, which imposes bans on certain market transactions including (in many jurisdictions) "usurious" lending and some forms of price gouging (see, e.g., Uniform Consumer Credit Code sec. 2.201). What accounts for these laws, which impose constraints on gain-producing transactions for ordinary commodities such as television sets and lumber? The bans seem difficult to justify on efficiency grounds; rules prohibiting mutually beneficial exchanges without obvious externalities are not generally thought to have a large claim to efficiency. The laws also do not generally seem well explained in terms of conventional rent seeking by a politically powerful faction.[13]

By contrast, laws banning usurious lending and price gouging when such activities are prevalent are a straightforward prediction of the theory of bounded self-interest described above. (The analysis here assumes that self-interested legislators are responsive to citizens' or other actors' fairness-based demands for the content of law.[14]) In the case of such bans, the transaction in question is a significant departure from the usual terms of trade in the market for the good in question—that is, a significant departure from the "reference transaction." The account above of bounded self-interest suggests that if trades are occurring frequently in a given jurisdiction at terms far from those of the reference transaction, there will be strong pressure for a law banning such trades. Note that the prediction is not that all high prices (ones that make it difficult or impossible for some people to afford things they might want) will be banned; the prediction is that transactions at terms far from the terms on which those transactions generally occur in the marketplace will be banned.

Consider this example:

> A store has been sold out of the popular Cabbage Patch dolls for a month. A week before Christmas a single doll is discovered in a store room. The managers know that many customers would like to buy the doll. They announce over the store's public address system that the doll will be sold by auction to the customer who offers to pay the most. (Kahneman, Knetsch and Thaler 1986a:735.)

Nearly three-quarters of the respondents judged this action to be either somewhat unfair or very unfair, though, of course, an economic analysis would judge the auction the most efficient method of assuring that the doll goes to the person who values it most. Although the auction is efficient, it represents a departure from the "reference transaction," under which the doll is sold at its usual price.

As in the doll example, if money is loaned to individuals at a rate of interest significantly greater than the rate at which similarly-sized loans are made to other customers, then the lender's behavior may be viewed as unfair. Likewise, because lumber generally tends to sell for a particular price, sales at far higher prices in the wake of (say) a hurricane, which drives demand sky high, are thought unfair. How then should popular items be rationed? Subjects in one study asked whether a football team should allocate its few remaining tickets to a key game through an auction thought that this approach would be unfair, while allocation based on who waited in line longest was the preferred solution (Kahneman, Knetsch and Thaler 1986b:S287-88). Of course, waiting in line for scarce goods is precisely what happens with laws against price gouging. Thus, pervasive fairness norms appear to shape attitudes (and hence possibly law) on both usury and price gouging. While "[c]onventional economic analyses assume as a matter of course that excess demand for a good creates an opportunity for suppliers to raise prices" and that "[t]he profit-seeking adjustments that clear the market are . . . as natural as water finding its level—and as ethically neutral," "[t]he lay public does not share this indifference" (Kahneman, Knetsch and Thaler 1986a:735).

Note that the behavioral law and economics analysis does not imply that these views of fairness are necessarily rational or compelling. Many of those who think "usurious" lenders are "unfair" might not have thought through the implications of their views (for example, that paying an outrageous price for a loan may be better than paying an infinite price, or that a loan to a riskier borrower is a product different in kind from a loan to a safer borrower). Still, if such views are widespread, they may underlie certain patterns in the content of law, such as the legal restrictions on usury and price gouging. The claim here is a positive one about the content of the law we observe, not a prescriptive or normative one about the shape practices or rules should take. As a positive matter, behavioral law and economics predicts that if trades are occurring with some frequency on terms far from those of the reference transaction, then legal rules will often ban trades on such terms.

Of course, further inquiry would be needed to offer a definitive explanation for the full pattern of usury and price gouging laws we observe. Usury seems to be broadly prohibited, so one is not faced with the question of why we observe bans in some states but not others. The same cannot be said of price gouging, which is prohibited only in certain states. Price gouging appears to be prohibited primarily by states that have recently experienced (or whose neighbors have recently experienced) natural disasters; but more in-depth research would be required to determine if this pattern comprehensively bears out.

5. Debiasing through law

The applications described in section 4 illustrate the usual approach in behavioral law and economics work to date: the analysis identifies a departure from unbounded rationality, willpower or self-interest and then offers either a proposed legal reform or an account of existing law that takes as a fixed point the identified departure from unbounded rationality, willpower or self-interest. This approach might be said to focus on designing legal rules and institutions so that legal outcomes do not fall prey to problems of bounded rationality, willpower or self-interest—a strategy of *insulation* of those outcomes from such bounds on human behavior.

A quite different possibility, focused most heavily on the case of judgment errors by boundedly rational actors, is that legal policy may respond best to such errors not by structuring rules and institutions to protect legal outcomes from the effects of the errors (which themselves are taken as a given), but instead by operating directly on the errors and attempting to help people either to reduce or to eliminate them. Legal policy in this category may be termed "debiasing through law"; the law is used to reduce the degree of biased behavior actors exhibit (Jolls and Sunstein 2006a). The primary emphasis is on judgment errors rather than either other aspects of bounded rationality or bounded willpower or self-interest, for the simple reason that those alternative forms of human behavior cannot uncontroversially be viewed as "biases" in need of debiasing. (Recall, for instance, the normative complexities discussed above in connection with both the endowment effect and bounded willpower. And clearly it would not generally be desirable to "debias" boundedly self-interested actors.) As described below, the basic promise of strategies for debiasing through law is that these strategies will often provide a middle ground between unyielding adherence to the assumptions of traditional economics, on the one hand, and the usual behavioral law and economics approach of accepting departures from those assumptions as a given, on the other.

5.1 Debiasing through substantive and procedural law

The idea of debiasing through law draws on a substantial existing psychology literature on the debiasing of individuals after a demonstration of the existence of a given judgment error (e.g., Fischhoff 1982; Weinstein and Klein 2002). Those who have investigated debiasing in experimental settings, however, have generally not explored the possibility of achieving debiasing through law. A few behavioral law and economics papers have examined the possibility of debiasing through the procedural rules governing adjudication by judges or juries; a well-known example builds on the studies described in section 4.2 above of self-serving bias in litigation and shows how requiring litigants to consider reasons the adjudicator might rule against them eliminates their self-serving bias (Babcock, Loewenstein and Issacharoff 1997). However, the potential promise of debiasing through law is far broader, for it is not only the procedures by which law is applied in adjudicative settings but the actual substance of law that may be employed to achieve debiasing.

Consider an example of debiasing through law developed by Jolls (2006), drawing on the work on implicit racial or other group-based bias described in 1.3.1.1 above. Might substantive rules governing employment discrimination play a role in debiasing individuals who exhibit such bias? Empirical studies suggest that implicit racial or other group-based bias is profoundly influenced by environmental stimuli. Individuals who view pictures of Tiger Woods and Timothy McVeigh before submitting to testing of implicit racial bias, for example, exhibit substantially less bias than individuals not exposed to the pictures of Woods and McVeigh (Dasgupta and Greenwald 2001). This study and, more broadly, the large social science literature on debiasing in response to implicit racial or other group-based bias (e.g., Macrae, Bodenhausen and Milne 1995; Dasgupta and Asgari 2004) have an intriguing practical counterpart in the ongoing controversies at many universities and the U.S. Capitol over the frequent pattern of largely or exclusively white, male portraits adorning classrooms and ceremonial spaces (Gewertz 2003; Stolberg 2003). In the employment context, it may not be irrelevant to the degree of implicit racial or other group-based bias found in employment decisionmakers whether, for instance, the walls of the workplace feature sexually explicit depictions of women—the source of frequent sexual harassment lawsuits—or instead feature more positive, affirming images of women. Employment discrimination law's policing of what can and cannot be featured in the workplace environment, described in detail in Jolls (2006), is thus an illustration of debiasing through substantive law.

It is important to emphasize the limits of the domain of this analysis of employment discrimination law as a mechanism for achieving "debiasing" in the sense in which the term is used here. In some cases racial or other group-based bias may reflect genuine tastes rather than, as discussed above, a divergence of implicit attitudes and behavior from non-discriminatory tastes. Of course, the features of employment discrimination law just referenced might still be desirable, and would certainly remain applicable, in the case of consciously discriminatory tastes, but they would no longer illustrate a form of debiasing through law in the sense used here because no form of judgment error would be under correction in the first place.[15]

5.2 General typology of strategies for debiasing through law

The example of debiasing through employment discrimination law and the earlier example from Babcock, Issacharoff and Loewenstein's work of debiasing through restructuring the adjudicative process together illustrate the basic distinction between debiasing through substantive law and debiasing through procedural rules.

		Type of Law	
		Procedural rules governing the adjudicative process	Substantive rules regulating actions taken outside of the adjudicative process
Role of Actor	Debiasing actors in their capacity as participants in the adjudicative process	Debiasing through procedural rules	"Hybrid" debiasing
	Debiasing actors in their capacity as decision makers outside of the adjudicative process		Debiasing through substantive law

Figure 5.1 Typology of strategies for debiasing through law

Figure 5.1 generalizes the point by mapping the terrain of strategies for debiasing through law more fully. The column division marks the line between procedural rules governing the adjudicative process and substantive rules regulating actions taken outside of the adjudicative process. The row division marks the line between debiasing actors in their capacity as participants in the adjudicative process and debiasing actors in their capacity as decision makers outside of the adjudicative process. The upper left box in this matrix represents the type of debiasing through law on which the prior work on such debiasing has focused: the rules in question are procedural rules governing the adjudicative process, and the actors targeted are individuals in their capacity as participants in the adjudicative process (Babcock, Loewenstein and Issacharoff 1997; Peters 1999).

Moving counterclockwise, the lower left box in the matrix is marked with an "X" because procedural rules governing the adjudicative process do not have any obvious role in debiasing actors outside of the adjudicative process—although these rules certainly may affect such actors' behavior in various ways by influencing what would happen in the event of future litigation. The lower right box in the matrix represents the category of debiasing through law emphasized in Jolls (2006) and Jolls and Sunstein (2006a, 2006b): the rules in question are substantive rules regulating actions taken outside of the adjudicative process, and the actors targeted are decision makers outside of the adjudicative process.

Finally, the upper right corner of the matrix represents a hybrid category that warrants brief discussion, in part to demarcate it from the category (just discussed) of debiasing through substantive law. In this hybrid category, it is substantive, rather than procedural, law that is structured to achieve debiasing, but the judgment error that this debiasing effort targets is one that arises within, rather than outside of, the adjudicative process. For example, Ward Farnsworth's (2003) work on self-serving bias suggests that such bias on the part of employment discrimination litigants (actors in their capacity as participants in an adjudicative process) might be reduced by restructuring employment discrimination standards (substantive rules regulating action outside of the adjudicative process) to increase the reliance of such standards on objective facts as opposed to subjective or normative judgments. This type of debiasing through law operates through reform of substantive law rather than procedural rules, but the actions to be debiased are those of litigants within the adjudicative process. In the case of debiasing through substantive law, by contrast, both the legal rules through which debiasing occurs and the capacities in which actors are targeted for debiasing are distinct from the context of the adjudicative process.

6. Conclusion

In Richard Thaler's view, the ultimate sign of success for behavioral economics will be that what is now behavioral economics will become simply "economics." The same observation applies to behavioral law and economics. But a potential barrier to reaching this outcome has been the frequency with which behavioral law and economics has recommended paternalistically overriding people's ability to make choices (Rachlinski 2003). For instance, as described in section 4.3 above, a prominent behavioral law and economics article praises the wisdom of the "business judgment" rule in corporate law notwithstanding the fact that this rule removes from the hands of judges and juries the power to hold corporate actors liable under the ordinary legal standard of negligence. Debiasing through law, discussed in section 5, holds the potential to be a path out of the perennial law and economics dilemma over paternalistic restrictions on choice because debiasing through law strategies can recognize human limitations while at the same time avoiding the step of removing choices from people's hands. Because debiasing through law cannot be applied in every context, however, future work in behavioral law and economics should also seek to refine and strengthen analyses concerned with structuring legal rules in light of the remaining (post-debiasing) departures from traditional economic assumptions of unbounded rationality, willpower and self-interest.

Notes

1   The three features of law and economics identified in the text are not meant to demarcate the intrinsic essence of the field; instead the claim is that these features characterize much of the existing work generally regarded as law and economics.

2   A recent article by Plott and Zeiler (2005) addresses the effect of experimental design on the existence and degree of the endowment effect.

3   Sunstein and Thaler's discussion is addressed to both the endowment effect and other factors that produce an effect of the law's structure on people's background preferences. The focus of the discussion here is the endowment effect.

4   As described in Jolls (1998), an interesting subtlety here is that if the question is whether one's probability of experiencing a bad event is below the average probability of experiencing that event (as distinguished from the average *person's* probability of experiencing that event), then it is possible for most people to be below average. To illustrate, suppose that for 80% of the population the probability of

being involved in an auto accident is 10%, and for 20% it is 60%. Then the average probability of being involved in an auto accident is 20% (. 1 × .8 .6 × .2 =.2). So for 80% of the population, the probability of being involved in an auto accident (10%) is below the average probability (20%). But the average person has a 10% chance of being involved in an auto accident, and it would be impossible for more than half of the population to have a probability below this. The natural interpretation of most studies of optimism bias would seem to be that they request a comparison with the average person's probability, rather than with the average probability; the average probability would often be quite difficult to compute and not within the grasp of most subjects. Moreover, at least one study has dealt explicitly with the issue raised here and has found significant evidence of optimism bias even using the average probability benchmark (Weinstein 1980:809–12).

5   While work on bounded willpower and bounded self-interest within behavioral law and economics has not recently been surveyed, examples of behavioral law and economics work on bounded willpower include Weiss (1991), Jolls (1997), and Camerer, Issacharoff, Loewenstein, O'Donoghue and Rabin (2003), while examples of behavioral law and economics work on bounded self-interest include Greenfield (2002), Jolls (2002), and Bar-Gill and Ben-Shahar (2003).

6   This subsection is an abridged version of Jolls (1998).

7   Of course, risk-averse actors may choose to purchase insurance against tort liability; see Jolls (1998) for a discussion of the role of insurance in this analysis.

8   However, as emphasized in Jolls (1998), only empirical evidence that we do not yet have can definitively resolve the question.

9   Note that underestimation of the probability of liability would affect not only the distortion of work incentives from a distributive (and thus, by the definition given above, non-wealth-maximizing) legal rule, but also the determination of what the wealth-maximizing legal rule would be. If potential tortfeasors underestimate the probability of liability, then optimal deterrence would require greater generosity to tort victims than the wealth-maximizing legal rule without underestimation of probabilities would involve. But the newly-generous rule would not be "distributive" in the relevant sense, since it would not be sacrificing wealth-maximization to achieve distributive goals. The focus of the present discussion, as stated above, is on legal rules that pursue distributive consequences at the expense of wealth-maximization.

10   This subsection is an abridged version of Jolls (1997).

11   As Richard Posner explained in a 1990 judicial opinion: "[T]here is often an interval in the life of a contract during which one party is at the mercy of the other. A may have ordered a machine from B that A wants to place in operation on a given date [and] may have made commitments to his customers that it would be costly to renege on. As the date of scheduled delivery approaches, B may be tempted to demand that A agree to renegotiate the contract price, knowing that A will incur heavy expenses if B fails to deliver on time. A can always refuse to renegotiate, relying instead on his right to sue B for breach of contract if B fails to make delivery by the agreed date. But legal remedies are always costly and uncertain." (United States v. Stump Home Specialties, Inc., 905 F.2d 1117, 1121–22.)

12   This subsection is an abridged version of section III of Jolls, Sunstein and Thaler (1998).

13   Although it may be possible to offer efficiency or conventional rent-seeking explanations for certain sorts of laws banning economic transactions (E. Posner 1995),

there does not seem to be a general theory or set of theories that can explain all or even most of these laws on traditional grounds.

14   Thus, like traditional economic analysis, the behavioral law and economics approach described here views legislators as maximizers interested in their own reelection; legislators interested in their own reelection will be responsive to the preferences and judgments of their constituents and those of powerful interest groups. If constituents believe that a certain practice is unfair, and should be banned, self-interested legislators will respond, even if they do not share these views. Likewise, if a mobilized group holds such views, then legislators' response will be affected, in much the same way as if the group sought legislation to serve a narrowly defined financial self-interest, as posited by the traditional economic account. "Fairness entrepreneurs" may play a role, mobilizing public judgments to serve their (selfish or nonselfish) interests. Of course, it is also possible that legislators themselves act on their own personal conceptions of fairness.

15   For further discussion of normative issues in debiasing through law, see Jolls and Sunstein (2006a, 2006b).

References

Acemoglu, Daron and Joshua D. Angrist. 2001. "Consequences of Employment Protection? The Case of the Americans with Disabilities Act," *Journal of Political Economy*, 109: 915–57.

Allais, Maurice. 1952. *Traite d'Economie Pure*. Paris: Impr. Nationale. Translated and edited by Maurice Allais and Ole Hagen as "The Foundations of a Positive Theory of Choice Involving Risk and a Criticism of the Postulates and Axioms of the American School," in *Expected Utility Hypotheses and the Allais Paradox: Contemporary Discussions of Decisions Under Uncertainty*, 27–145 (Dordrecht, Holland: D. Reidel Publishing, 1979).

Arkes, Hal R., David Faust, Thomas J. Guilmette and Kathleen Hart. 1988. "Eliminating the Hindsight Bias," *Journal of Applied Psychology*, 73: 305–07.

Arnould, Richard J. and Henry Grabowski. 1981. "Auto Safety Regulation: An Analysis of Market Failure," *Bell Journal of Economics*, 12: 27–48.

Autor, David and Mark Duggan. 2003. "The Rise in the Disability Rolls and the Decline in Unemployment," *Quarterly Journal of Economics*, 118: 157–206.

Babcock, Linda, George Loewenstein and Samuel Issacharoff. 1997. "Creating Convergence: Debiasing Biased Litigants," *Law and Social Inquiry*, 22: 913–26.

Babcock, Linda, George Loewenstein, Samuel Issacharoff and Colin Camerer. 1995. "Biased Judgments of Fairness in Bargaining," *American Economic Review*, 85: 1337–43.

Babcock, Linda, Xianghong Wang and George Loewenstein. 1996. "Choosing the Wrong Pond: Social Comparisons in Negotiations that Reflect a Self-Serving Bias," *Quarterly Journal of Economics*, 111: 1–19.

Bar-Gill, Oren and Omri Ben-Shahar. 2003. "Threatening an 'Irrational' Breach of Contract," *Supreme Court Economic Review*, 11: 143–70.

Camerer, Colin F., Samuel Issacharoff, George Loewenstein, Ted O'Donoghue and Matthew Rabin. 2003. "Regulation for Conservatives: Behavioral Economics and the Case for 'Asymmetric Paternalism,'" in Symposium: Preferences and Rational Choice: New Perspectives and Legal Implications, *University of Pennsylvania Law Review*, 151: 1211–54.

Camerer, Colin F. and Howard Kunreuther. 1989. "Decision Processes for Low Probability Events: Policy Implications," *Journal of Policy Analysis & Management*, 8: 565–92.

Coase, Ronald H. 1960. "The Problem of Social Cost," *Journal of Law and Economics*, 3: 1–44.

Cutler, David, M. and Jonathan Gruber. 1996. "Does Public Insurance Crowd Out Private Insurance?" *Quarterly Journal of Economics*, 111: 391–430.

Dasgupta, Nilanjana and Anthony G. Greenwald. 2001. "On the Malleability of Automatic Attitudes: Combating Automatic Prejudice With Images of Admired and Disliked Individuals," *Journal of Personality and Social Psychology*, 81: 800–14.

Dasgupta, Nilanjana and Shaki Asgari. 2004. "Seeing Is Believing: Exposure to Counterstereotypic Women Leaders and Its Effect on the Malleability of Automatic Gender Stereotypes," *Journal of Experimental Social Psychology*, 40: 642–58.

DeJoy, David M. 1989. "The Optimism Bias and Traffic Accident Risk Perception," *Accident Analysis and Prevention*, 21: 333–40.

Donohue, John J. III and James Heckman. 1991. "Continuous versus Episodic Change: The Impact of Civil Rights Policy on the Economic Status of Blacks," *Journal of Economic Literature*, 29: 1603–43.

Dovidio, John F., Kerry Kawakami and Samuel L. Gaertner. 2002. "Implicit and Explicit Prejudice and Interracial Interaction," *Journal of Personality and Social Psychology*, 82: 62–68.

Ellsberg, Daniel. 1961. "Risk, Ambiguity, and the Savage Axioms," *Quarterly Journal of Economics*, 75: 643–69.

Elster, Jon. 1979. *Ulysses and the Sirens: Studies in Rationality and Irrationality* (New York: Cambridge University Press).

Farnsworth, Ward. 2003. "The Legal Regulation of Self-Serving Bias," *U.C. Davis Law Review*, 37: 567–603.

Ferrell, Allen. 2003. "Mandated Disclosure and Stock Returns: Evidence from the Over-the-Counter Market" (mimeo).

Fischhoff, Baruch. 1982. "Debiasing," in *Judgment under Uncertainty: Heuristics and Biases*, ed. Daniel Kahneman, Paul Slovic and Amos Tversky, 422–44 (New York: Cambridge University Press).

Gaertner, Samuel L. and John P. McLaughlin. 1983. "Racial Stereotypes: Associations and Ascriptions of Positive and Negative Characteristics," *Social Psychology*, 46: 23–30.

Gewertz, Ken. 2003. "Adding Some Color to Harvard Portraits," *Harvard University Gazette* (May 1): 11.

Gompers, Paul A., Joy L. Ishii and Andrew Metrick. 2003. "Corporate Governance and Equity Prices," *Quarterly Journal of Economics*, 118: 107–55.

Greenfield, Kent. 2002. "Using Behavioral Economics to Show the Power and Efficiency of Corporate Law as Regulatory Tool," in Symposium: Corporations Theory and Corporate Governance Law, *U.C. Davis Law Review*, 25: 581–644.

Greenstone, Michael, Paul Oyer and Annette Vissing-Jorgensen. 2006. "Mandated Disclosure, Stock Returns, and the 1964 Securities Acts Amendments," *Quarterly Journal of Economics* (forthcoming).

Greenwald, Anthony G., Debbie E. McGhee and Jordan L.K. Schwartz. 1998. "Measuring Individual Differences in Implicit Cognition: The Implicit Association Test," *Journal of Personality and Social Psychology*, 74: 1464–80.

Gruber, Jonathan. 1994. "The Incidence of Mandated Maternity Benefits," *American Economic Review*, 84: 622–41.

Gulati, Mitu and Michael Yelnosky. 2006. *Behavioral Analyses of Workplace Discrimination* (Dordrecht, Holland: Kluwer Academic Publishers, forthcoming).

Guppy, Andrew. 1993. "Subjective Probability of Accident and Apprehension in Relation to Self-Other Bias, Age, and Reported Behavior," *Accident Analysis and Prevention*, 25: 375–82.

Guth, Werner, Rolf Schmittberger and Bernd Schwarze. 1982. "An Experimental Analysis of Ultimatum Bargaining," *Journal of Economic Behavior and Organization*, 3: 367–88.

Guthrie, Chris. 2003. "Prospect Theory, Risk Preference, and the Law," in Symposium: Empirical Legal Realism: A New Social Scientific Assessment of Law and Human Behavior, *Northwestern University Law Review*, 97: 1115–63.

Heckman, James J. and Brook S. Payner. 1989. "Determining the Impact of Federal Antidiscrimination Policy on the Economic Status of Blacks: A Study of South Carolina," *American Economic Review*, 79: 138–77.

Hoffman, Elizabeth and Matthew Spitzer. 1982. "The Coase Theorem: Some Experimental Tests," *Journal of Law and Economics*, 25: 73–98.

Hoffman, Elizabeth and Matthew Spitzer. 1986. "Experimental Tests of the Coase Theorem with Large Bargaining Groups," *Journal of Legal Studies*, 15: 149–71.

Issacharoff, Samuel and George Loewenstein. 1995. "Unintended Consequences of Mandatory Disclosure," *Texas Law Review*, 73: 753–86.

Jolls, Christine. 1997. "Contracts as Bilateral Commitments: A New Perspective on Contract Modification," *Journal of Legal Studies*, 26: 203–37.

Jolls, Christine. 1998. "Behavioral Economic Analysis of Redistributive Legal Rules," in Symposium: The Legal Implications of Psychology: Human Behavior, Behavioral Economics, and the Law, *Vanderbilt Law Review*, 51: 1653–77.

Jolls, Christine. 2002. "Fairness, Minimum Wage Law, and Employee Benefits," in Symposium: Research Conference on Behavioral Law and Economics in the Workplace, *New York University Law Review*, 77: 47–70.

Jolls, Christine. 2004. "Identifying the Effects of the Americans with Disabilities Act Using State-Law Variation: Preliminary Evidence on Educational Participation Effects," *American Economic Review* (Papers and Proceedings), 94: 447–53.

Jolls, Christine. 2006. "Antidiscrimination Law's Effects on Implicit Bias," in *Behavioral Analyses of Workplace Discrimination*, ed. Mitu Gulati and Michael Yelnosky (Dordrecht, Holland: Kluwer Academic Publishers, forthcoming).

Jolls, Christine, Cass R. Sunstein and Richard Thaler. 1998. "A Behavioral Approach to Law and Economics," *Stanford Law Review*, 50: 1471–1550.

Jolls, Christine and Cass R. Sunstein. 2006a. "Debiasing Through Law," *Journal of Legal Studies*, 35: 199–241.

Jolls, Christine and Cass R. Sunstein. 2006b. "The Law of Implicit Bias," *California Law Review* (forthcoming).

Kahneman, Daniel and Shane Frederick. 2002. "Representativeness Revisited: Attribute Substitution in Intuitive Judgment," in *Heuristics and Biases: The Psychology of Intuitive Judgment*, ed. Thomas Gilovich, Dale Griffin and Daniel Kahneman, 49–81 (New York: Cambridge University Press).

Kahneman, Daniel, Jack L. Knetsch and Richard H. Thaler. 1986a. "Fairness as a Constraint on Profit Seeking: Entitlements in the Market," *American Economic Review*, 76: 728–41.

Kahneman, Daniel, Jack L. Knetsch and Richard H. Thaler. 1986b. "Fairness and the Assumptions of Economics," *Journal of Business*, 59: S285–300.

Kahneman, Daniel, Jack L. Knetsch and Richard H. Thaler. 1990. "Experimental Tests of the Endowment Effect and the Coase Theorem," *Journal of Political Economy*, 98: 1325–48.

Kahneman, Daniel and Amos Tversky. 1979. "Prospect Theory: An Analysis of Decision Under Risk," *Econometrica*, 47: 263–91.

Kaplow, Louis and Steven Shavell. 1994. "Why the Legal System is Less Efficient Than the Income Tax in Redistributing Income," *Journal of Legal Studies*, 23: 667–81.

Kaplow, Louis and Steven Shavell. 2002. *Fairness versus Welfare* (Cambridge, Mass.: Harvard University Press).

Katz, Lawrence F. and Bruce Meyer. 1990. "Unemployment Insurance, Recall Expectations, and Unemployment Outcomes," *Quarterly Journal of Economics*, 105: 973–1002.

Kelman, Mark. 1979. "Consumption Theory, Production Theory, and Ideology in the Coase Theorem," *Southern California Law Review*, 52: 669–98.

Korobkin, Russell. 1998. "The Status Quo Bias and Contract Default Rules," *Cornell Law Review*, 83: 608–87.

Korobkin, Russell. 2003. "The Endowment Effect and Legal Analysis," in Symposium: Empirical Legal Realism: A New Social Scientific Assessment of Law and Human Behavior, *Northwestern University Law Review*, 97: 1227–93.

Kuran, Timur and Cass Sunstein. 1999. "Availability Cascades and Risk Regulation," *Stanford Law Review*, 51: 683–768.

Laibson, David. 1997. "Golden Eggs and Hyperbolic Discounting," *Quarterly Journal of Economics*, 112: 443–77.

Lichtenstein, Sarah, Paul Slovic, Baruch Fischhoff, Mark Layman and Barbara Combs. 1978. "Judged Frequency of Lethal Events," *Journal of Experimental Psychology: Human Learning and Memory*, 4: 551–78.

Loewenstein, George and Don A. Moore. 2004. "When Ignorance Is Bliss: Information Exchange and Inefficiency in Bargaining," *Journal of Legal Studies*, 33: 37–58.

Loewenstein, George, Samuel Issacharoff, Colin Camerer and Linda Babcock. 1993. "Self-Serving Assessments of Fairness and Pretrial Bargaining," *Journal of Legal Studies*, 22: 135–59.

Macrae, C. Neil, Galen V. Bodenhausen and Alan B. Milne. 1995. "The Dissection of Selection in Person Perception: Inhibitory Processes in Social Stereotyping," *Journal of Personality and Social Psychology*, 69: 397–407.

McConnell, Allen R. and Jill M. Leibold. 2001. "Relations Among the Implicit Association Test, Discriminatory Behavior, and Explicit Measure of Racial Attitudes," *Journal of Experimental Social Psychology*, 37: 435–42.

Nosek, Brian A., Mahzarin R. Banaji & Anthony G. Greenwald. 2002. "Harvesting Implicit Group Attitudes and Beliefs from a Demonstration Website," *Group Dynamics: Theory, Research, and Practice*, 6: 101–15.

Plott, Charles R. and Kathryn Zeiler. 2005. "The Willingness to Pay – Willingness to Accept Gap, the 'Endowment Effect,' Subject Misconceptions, and Experimental Procedures for Eliciting Valuations," *American Economic Review*, 95: 530–45.

Posner, Eric. A. 1995. "Contract Law in the Welfare State: A Defense of the Unconscionability Doctrine, Usury Laws, and Related Limitations on the Freedom to Contract," *Journal of Legal Studies*, 24: 283–319.

Posner, Richard A. 1979. "Utilitarianism, Economics, and Legal Theory," *Journal of Legal Studies*, 8: 103–40.

Posner, Richard A. 1989. "An Economic Analysis of Sex Discrimination Laws," *University of Chicago Law Review*, 56: 1311–36.

Posner, Richard A. 1992. *Economic Analysis of Law*, 4th ed. (Boston: Little Brown).

Rabin, Matthew. 1993. "Incorporating Fairness into Game Theory and Economics," *American Economic Review*, 83: 1281–1302.

Rachlinski, Jeffrey J. 1998. "A Positive Psychological Theory of Judging in Hindsight," *University of Chicago Law Review*, 65: 571–625.

Rachlinski, Jeffrey J. 2003. "The Uncertain Psychological Case for Paternalism," in Symposium: Empirical Legal Realism: A New Social Scientific Assessment of Law and Human Behavior, *Northwestern University Law Review*, 97: 1165–1225.

Schelling, Thomas C. 1984. "The Intimate Contest for Self-Command," in *Choice and Consequence* (Cambridge, MA: Harvard University Press).

Schwab, Stewart. 1988. "A Coasean Experiment on Contract Presumptions," *Journal of Legal Studies*, 17: 237–68.

Shavell, Steven. 1981. "A Note on Efficiency vs. Distributional Equity in Legal Rulemaking: Should Distributional Equity Matter Given Optimal Income Taxation?", *American Economic Review*, 71: 414–18.

Shavell, Steven. 2004. *Foundations of Economic Analysis of Law* (Cambridge, Mass.: Belknap Press of Harvard University Press).

Stigler, George J. 1971. "The Theory of Economic Regulation," *Bell Journal of Economics and Management Science*, 2: 3–21.

Stiglitz, Joseph E. 1987. "Pareto Efficient and Optimal Taxation and the New Welfare Economics", in *Handbook of Public Economics*, ed. Alan Auerbach and Martin Feldstein, 2: 991–1042 (Amsterdam: Elsevier Science Publishers).

Stolberg, Sheryl Gay. 2003. "Face Value at the Capitol: Senator Wants to 'Promote Some Diversity' in Congressional Artwork," *New York Times* (Aug. 13): E1.

Strotz, Robert H. 1955–56. "Myopia and Inconsistency in Dynamic Utility Maximization," *Review of Economic Studies*, 23: 165–80.

Sunstein, Cass R. and Richard H. Thaler. 2003. "Libertarian Paternalism Is Not an Oxymoron," *University of Chicago Law Review*, 70: 1159–1202.

Svenson, Ola, Baruch Fischhoff and Donald MacGregor. 1985. "Perceived Driving Safety and Seatbelt Usage," *Accident Analysis & Prevention*, 17: 119–33.

Thaler, Richard H. 1996. "Doing Economics Without *Homo Economicus*," in *Foundations of Research in Economics: How Do Economists Do Economics?*, ed. Steven G. Medema and Warren J. Samuels, 227–37 (Brookfield, VT: Edward Elgar Publishing Company).

Thaler, Richard H. 1980. "Toward A Positive Theory of Consumer Choice," *Journal of Economic Behavior and Organization*, 1: 39–60.

Thaler, Richard H. and Robyn M. Dawes. 1992. "Cooperation," in Richard H. Thaler, *The Winner's Curse: Paradoxes and Anomalies of Economic Life*, 6–20 (New York: The Free Press).

Tversky, Amos and Daniel Kahneman. 1973. "Availability: A Heuristic for Judging Frequency and Probability," *Cognitive Psychology* 5: 207–32.

Weinstein, Neil D. 1980. "Unrealistic Optimism About Future Life Events," *Journal of Personality and Social Psychology*, 39: 806–20.

Weinstein, Neil D. and William M. Klein. 2002. "Resistance of Personal Risk Perceptions to Debiasing Interventions," in *Heuristics and Biases: The Psychology of Intuitive Judgment*, ed. Thomas Gilovich, Dale Griffin and Daniel Kahneman, 313–23 (New York: Cambridge University Press).

Weiss, Deborah M. 1991. "Paternalistic Pension Policy: Psychological Evidence and Economic Theory," *University of Chicago Law Review*, 58: 1275–1319.

PART 3

The economics of the emergence and establishment of norms and customs

Why an analysis of norms and customary orders?

E CONOMISTS FIRST BECAME INTERESTED in social norms because of the role they play in the functioning of economic systems, i.e. from a "law and economics" perspective. In this regard, the first important paper devoted to this topic is Demsetz's 1964 article on *The Exchange and Enforcement of Property Rights*. Then, after Landes and Posner and others invented the "economic analysis of law", economists moved to the understanding of the mechanisms that explain the formation of norms – and then, as we shall see in the next section, their legal role or their role in the functioning of legal systems.

This link between "norms" or "customs" and the law represents the first important reason that explain why the topic – already analyzed by anthropologists and historians – attracted a lot of economists and scholars using economic tools. In effect, "law and economics" and the "economic analysis of law" developed in a country, the U.S.A., whose legal system supposedly is based on "customs". Now, as Ellickson notes in his article on *The Market for Social Norms* (emphasis added), "law is intimately intertwined with *custom*" (2001, p. 2; emphasis added), by which he not only suggests that norms, customs and the law are complementarily necessary to order societies but also because, in a system of Common law, the law emerges from customs which in turn grow out of norms. To understand the formation and role of norms amounts to an understanding of the basic unit of a Common law system.

A second point explains the development of economic analyses of the emergence and establishment of norms and customs: to show and to make clear that human beings are capable of developing their own rules in order to frame, organize and regulate their activities, to coordinate their plans of actions *without* a collective decision or *without* the intervention of a third player – that is, to be more precise, *without* the intervention of the State. There is no need for a centralized, public and state-sponsored provision of rules because there exists a spontaneous order in private actions. It is therefore no surprise then that there exists a close connection between the literature on the emergence of norms and the literature on private ordering or on "lawless" groups that will be discussed in the next chapter. From this perspective, the formation of norms and customs can thus be "analogized to a decentralized decision making process" (for instance, see Parisi, 2000, or Cooter, 1996) and likened to a "market process". Norms first emerge as the product of human actions and interactions – not of human design, to use the words of Cardinal de Retz, popularized by Hayek – between certain individuals and then generalize to the other members of the group. In effect, norms emerge and become established in small groups of friends and acquaintances with homogenous preferences.

Formally, and this is how a large part of the economic literature on norms formally represents the process, the emergence and establishment of norms is viewed as resulting from a repeated game. Norms are then assimilated as the Nash equilibrium in such games.

The emergence and establishment of norms

The first step in the process is the emergence of norms. These result from the frequent and repeated interactions that take place between individuals. When they repeatedly interact with each other, people tend to face the same problems, namely problems in coordinating their respective plans of action, eventually adopting the same solutions to the recurrent problems they faced. These can be described as conventions (in the sense given by Hume, Lewis or Schotter). More precisely, conventions emerge after a sequence of "trials" and "errors" through which they are tested and certain solutions are rejected, while others are chosen or selected. Individuals do not have to discuss the content of the rules; no explicit or formal agreement between the players is required to allow the emergence of conventions – these remain implicit. Similarly, one must note that these solutions are not explicitly and purposefully designed by one of the players to solve the problems they face. A sufficient condition is that individuals repeat interactions.

The second step, once adopted after a process of "trial and error", sees these conventions spread from the individuals who have initiated them to other individuals. Bandwagon or (either informational or reputation) "cascade" effects take place that explain this evolution and this dynamic development of norms. Let us nonetheless note that this latter part of the process, the imitation of other individuals, reveals the importance of another important element in the durable establishment of norms. In this process, it is not only sufficient that individuals repeat interactions. A necessary condition for the emergence and existence of norms is that enough individuals adopt the same ways of behavior, the same "solution" to the problem individuals face in order to have it transformed into a norm. In other words, it is necessary that the probability of meeting an individual that will accept the same kind of behavior or solution has to be above a threshold to insure that a convention becomes a norm or a custom (on this issue, see the works of Witt, for instance 1989 or more recently, Knudsen, 2002). Once again, no explicit agreement nor discussion is necessary.

A necessary condition: norms and small groups

That norms are directly and unintentionally produced by the individuals without the intervention of a third player means that they are not pure public goods. In effect, if rules are depicted as *pure* public goods, then this implies that their provision is affected by all the problems that affect the provision of any *pure* public good: individuals tend to free ride on others because they have no means to secure the benefit of their contribution; then no one contributes to the provision of the good. When this reasoning is applied to social order and rules, it means that no one will follow the rules that may exist. A third player is required to produce the rules and to guarantee their enforcement. The situation is chaotic. By contrast, the assumption that rules emerge from repeated interactions means that none of these problems arise.

In fact, norms are not pure but *local* public – or *club* – goods. Individuals contribute to their provision – i.e. they follow the same norms as others – precisely because others behave in the same way: that is, because of the homogeneity of preferences and the existence of shared (religious or social) beliefs and common knowledge or, eventually, because individuals simply belong to the same group. This is what most of the literature on spontaneous orders demonstrates and documents: norms emerge from the repeated interactions that take place *within* a given group (see the next chapter on "lawless groups" for references), with a corollary being that *inter*-groups interactions are another matter: spontaneous and decentralized processes are ineffective between groups because individuals do not have anything in common and also because there exists no inter-group means of control and punishment.

Counter-examples can nonetheless be put forward that show that norms emerge from interactions between strangers: soldiers from opposing camps in the trenches during World War I (Axelrod, 1984; Ashworth, 1980); bandits from different groups in the Anglo-Scottish borderlands in the 16th century (Leeson, forthcoming). It could then be said that norms emerge from interactions between heterogenous agents (Leeson, 2008; see also Leeson, 2006, 2005). A first explanation is that, in some cases, individuals signal their willingness to cooperate to strangers with whom they want to interact. A second explanation is that "social homogeneity is multidimensional" (Leeson, 2005, p. 243); as a consequence, even if individuals belong to different groups, they nonetheless have elements in common that explain their cooperation.

Therefore, from these examples of norms emerging in small groups and from these counter-examples, it appears that the necessary condition for the emergence of norms is a certain form of willingness to cooperate and that, in certain circumstances, it can transcend the boundaries of groups or give birth to other groups.

The normativity of norms

The normativity of customs does not come from the fact that rules are explicit and that individuals know them. It results from the fact that they have emerged from repeated interactions. Therefore, individuals follow them because they have participated in their "creation" and also because they anticipate that others will follow them. In fact, individuals use them because they know that others also use them and that each individual knows that others know them etc., i.e. because they form a "common knowledge" among the players (Josselin and Marciano, 1995 and 2005).

One may also understand the benefits of the individuals who adopt the same rules as others in terms of positive externalities or "network externalities": when one individual uses the same norms or conventions as a large number of others, he then belongs to a network of users and benefits from the positive external effects that can be associated with being a member of a network. In other words, it can be said that individuals expect a certain form of "benefit" or "reward" associated with following the rules; it can therefore be shown that individual reputation and the esteem of others are elements that play an important role in the attitude of individuals towards rules; following norms also allows individuals to send a signal to the other members of the group (Ellickson summarizes these explanations). But, following a rule is not only a matter of gains. Not to respect a rule may also be costly: one may be ostracised and rejected by the other members of the group if one does not follow the norm others have accepted. Therefore, these rules are self-enforcing and, once again, no external (and in particular public) and institutionalized system of enforcement is required.

The limits of norms

A first limit of norms comes precisely from the fact that they emerge from interactions between individuals and that, therefore, individuals learn them when and because they participate in their emergence and establishment. As a corollary, newcomers, strangers or non-group members, that is all those individuals who did not participate in interactions, may face difficulties or costs to learn norms. In effect, they have to participate in interactions without knowing the rules that order and regulate them. In somes cases, for instance a priority rule at crossroads, the costs may prove to be really high. As a consequence, emergent rules will be limited to the group of individuals among which they emerged but are unlikely to be exported to other groups. In other words, the rules that have emerged within a group cannot always be used in inter-group interactions.

The second consequence is that rules which have emerged have not been discussed. They are what they are, as the result of a process, and nothing can be said about their quality. This means that no one can know for sure that interactions between individuals spontaneously give birth to an "efficient" or a "good", i.e. just and moral, rule. Many are those who have stressed this twofold problem (see e.g. Nozick, 1974; or even Friedman, 1979). In other words, spontaneous coordination may fail and a "bad" or "inefficient" equilibrium can be selected.

Thirdly, a spontaneous or a customary order may be characterized by too much stability or by too much inertia. Therefore, societies or groups can remain in locked-in situations in certain institutional settings – this is worse when excess inertia characterizes a society in which a morally "bad" or an unjust norm exists; these two problems are different and complementary. Thus, not only can a population of individuals "choose" a "bad" or "inefficient" rule but they can also remain stuck at this point.

These "lock-in" effects have been studied by industrial economists in their analyses of the diffusion of technologies that exhibit network externalities; the phenomenon is exactly of the same nature as may happen with emerging norms.

Therefore, spontaneous norms can be limited. Solutions can be envisaged or proposed that solve these problems – for instance, the rules used in a given social group may be institutionalized to increase their domain of application and allow strangers to use them; a process of discussion may be created to evaluate the quality (efficiency or moral content) of rules; and also, individuals – opinion leaders or entrepreneurs – may be necessary to move societies out of locked-in situations. All these solutions reveal that it may be necessary to move from spontaneous norms to more constructed ones, as will be seen in the next sections.

References

Summary

The literature on the emergence of norms and their establishment as conventions and/or conventions date back to the origins of political economy, when Hume argued that *conventions* are a necessary cornerstone for the development of economic activities. It was not, however, until the end of the twentieth century that economists used their tools and theories, in particular game theory, to explain how and under which conditions repeated interactions could give birth to norms. One of the first economic analyses devoted to spontaneous coordination is certainly that of the 2005 Nobel prize laureate, Thomas Schelling (1960). Also among the first important works, one must mention Ullman-Margalit (1977), Axelrod (1981), and Sugden (1986). These works remain important because of their innovativeness and because of their focus on the concepts that are now at the core of economic theories on the emergence of norms.

More recently, economic analyses on the emergence and role of norms has incorporated the idea that the evolution of norms could not be a linear process. On the contrary, it has been shown that a "critical mass" of followers is required to guarantee that the norm will be used and then transformed into a custom and then into a legal rule: if the number of followers is not sufficient, then the process of propagation is blocked; on the contrary, the process of propagation is guaranteed just beyond the threshold. The literature on "cascade", "snowball" or "bandwagon" effects is huge in economics and in sociology (where it actually started with the works of Mark Granovetter, 1978, for instance; see also, among others, Kuran, 1995; Banerjee, 1992, 1993; Bikhchandani, Hirshleifer, and Welch, 1992; Welch, 1992). Most of the works published in this domain are highly technical. We have rather chosen two non-technical articles to illustrate these analyses (Young and Witt).

The third paper (Ellickson) included in this volume perfectly summarizes the recent economic theories of norms – explanations of the demand and of the supply side of the *market for norms*. This article is interesting not only because this is a clear survey of the literature. It is also important because it shows that no single and general economic theory of the existence and evolution of norms exists. On the contrary,

economists tend to use many different concepts and therefore propose various complementary – but also to some extent rival – explanations.

Further reading

Axelrod, Robert. 1981. "The Emergence of Cooperation among Egoists", *American Political Science Review*, 75 (2), pp. 306–318.

Axelrod, Robert. 1984. *The Evolution of Cooperation*. New York: Basic Books.

Ashworth, Tony. 1980 *Trench Warfare 1914–1918: The Live and Let Live System*. New York: Holmes and Maier.

Banerjee, Abhijit V. 1992. "A Simple Model of Herd Behavior", *Quarterly Journal of Economics*, 107(3), pp. 797–817.

Banerjee, Abhijit V. 1993. "The Economics of Rumours", *Review of Economic Studies*, 60(2), pp. 309–327.

Bikhchandani, Sushil, David Hirshleifer, and Ivo Welch. 1992. "A Theory of Fads, Fashion, Custom and Cultural Change as Informational Cascades", *Journal of Political Economy*, 100, pp. 992–1026.

Cooter, Robert D. 1996. "Decentralized Law for a Complex Economy: The Structural Approach to Adjudicating the New Law Merchant", *University of Pennsylvania Law Review*, 144 (5), pp. 1643–1696.

Elster, Jon. 1989. "Social Norms and Economics", *Journal of Economic Perspectives*, 3 (3), 99–117.

Friedman, David. 1979. "Private Creation and Enforcement of Law: A Historical Case", *Journal of Legal Studies*, 8 (2), pp. 399–415.

Granovetter, Mark. 1978. "Threshold Models of Collective Behavior", *American Journal of Sociology*, 83, pp. 1420–1443.

Josselin, Jean-Michel and Alain Marciano. 1995. "Constitutionalism and Common Knowledge: Assessment and Application to a Future European Constitution", *Public Choice*, 85(1–2), October, 173–188.

Josselin, Jean-Michel and Alain Marciano. 2005. "General Norms and Customs", in Jurgen C. Backhaus (ed.), *The Elgar Companion to Law and Economics* (second revised edition), Cheltenham: Edward Elgar, pp. 424–432.

Knudsen, Thorbjørn. 2002. The Evolution of Cooperation in Structured Populations, *Constitutional Political Economy*, 13 (2), pp. 129–148.

Kuran, Timur. 1995. *Private Truths, Public Lies: The Social Consequences of Preference Falsification*. Cambridge, MA: Harvard University Press.

Leeson, Peter. 2005. "Self-enforcing arrangements in African political economy", *Journal of Economic Behavior & Organization*, 57, pp. 241–244.

Leeson, Peter. 2006. "Cooperation and Conflict: Evidence on Self-Enforcing Arrangements and Heterogeneous Groups", *American Journal of Economics and Sociology*, 65 (4), pp. 891–907.

Leeson, Peter. 2008. "Social Distance and Self-Enforcing Exchange", *Journal of Legal Studies*, 37 (1), pp. 161–188.

Leeson, Peter. Forthcoming. "The Law of Lawlessness", *Journal of Legal Studies*.

Nozick, Robert. 1974. *Anarchy, State and Utopia*. New York: Basic Books.

Parisi, Franceso. 2000. "Spontaneous Emergence of Law: Customary Law", in *Encyclopedia of Law and Economics*, edited by Bouckaert, Boudewijn and De Geest, Gerrit, Cheltenham: Edward Elgar.

Peyton Young, H. 1996. "The Economics of Conventions", *Journal of Economic Perspectives*, 10 (2), pp. 105–122.

Posner, Eric A. 1996. "Law, Economics, and Inefficient Norms", *University of Pennsylvania Law Review*, 144 (5), pp. 1697–1744.

Schelling, Thomas. 1960. *The Strategy of Conflict*. Cambridge, MA: Harvard University Press.

Sugden, Robert. 1986. *The Evolution of Rights, Cooperation, and Welfare*. New York: Basil Blackwell.

Sugden, Robert. 1989. "Spontaneous Order", *Journal of Economic Perspectives*, 3 (3), pp. 85–97.

Ullman-Margalit, Edna. 1977. *The Emergence of Norms*. Oxford: Oxford University Press.

Welch, Ivo. 1992. "Sequential Sales, Learning, and Cascades", *Journal of Finance*, 47 (2), pp. 695–732.

Welch, Ivo. 2000. "Herding among Security Analysts", *Journal of Financial Economics*, 58(3), pp. 369–96.

Witt, U. 1989. "The Evolution of Economic Institutions as a Propagation Process", *Public Choice*, 62 (2), pp. 155–172.

Chapter 6

Robert C. Ellickson

THE MARKET FOR SOCIAL NORMS

M Y TITLE SEEMS AN OXYMORON. Conventionally conceived, markets generate goods and services, not informal rules of conduct. Nonetheless, my thesis is that the basic tools of microeconomics can illuminate social phenomena that traditionally have not been subjects of economic inquiry. Economists have developed analytic tools of unmatched power for dealing with the consequences of differences among individuals (and firms).

Consider the conventional graph portraying a market for widgets. Because suppliers vary in skills and other endowments, the supply curve slopes upward to the right. Because consumers vary in wealth, preferences, and other attributes, the demand curve slopes downward and intersects the supply curve. What generates widgets? The actions not of everyone, but of only the inframarginal individuals: the suppliers who face relatively low costs and the consumers willing to bid particularly high for the commodity.

I suggest that a new social norm arises through a process much like the market for widgets.[1] A norm is not the product of "diffuse social forces," as a sociologists might put it, but rather of the purposive actions of discrete individuals, especially those who are particularly suited to providing the new rule and those who are particularly eager to have it adopted.[2] To be fruitful, the analogy between markets and norm making must surmount some major difficulties. While money is the medium through which consumers compensate the suppliers of widgets, what currency might supporters of a social change use to reward the avant garde who lead the way? I address this question, and a host of others, in the pages that follow.

Because law is intimately intertwined with custom, policy makers would benefit greatly from an understanding of how social norms arise. Nevertheless, scholars influenced by the law-and-economics approach traditionally have paid scant attention to the topic. For example, in a classic article that helped launch the field of law and economics, Harold Demsetz (1967) depicted how members of a tribe of Labradorian

Indians had privatized their hunting territories in order to exploit new opportunities to sell fur pelts to Europeans. Demsetz offered no explanation, however, of how the Labradorians had succeeded in altering their ways. In effect, he relegated the inner workings of the tribe to a black box. By the mid-1990s, however, dozens of law-and-economics scholars had begun contributing to a boomlet of interest in norms. In this article, I build on the contributions of Richard McAdams, Eric Posner, and others of the "new norms scholars" whose writings are relevant to the question of norm creation.[3]

Although the new norms scholars differ on many points, they generally share a common conception of norms and a common methodological approach. They regard a social norm as a rule governing an individual's behavior that third parties other than state agents diffusely enforce by means of social sanctions.[4] A person who violates a norm risks becoming the target of punishments such as negative gossip and ostracism. Conversely, someone who honors a norm may reap informal rewards such as enhanced esteem and greater future opportunities for beneficial exchanges. A person who has *internalized* a norm as a result of socialization enforces the norm against himself, perhaps by feeling guilt after violating it or a warm glow after complying with it (especially if the norm is burdensome to honor).[5] A norm can exist even if no one has internalized it, however, so long as third parties provide an adequate level of informal enforcement.[6]

An understanding of social norms can illuminate an issue at the core of both political theory and public economics. According to the view classically associated with Thomas Hobbes, people are unable to coordinate with one another without significant assistance from a coercive central authority. According to this Hobbesian conception, the basic problem is that public order is a public good. Each individual seemingly has an incentive to free-ride on the efforts of anyone who volunteers to serve as a member of the social police.[7] According to the standard theory of public goods, only a Leviathan able to tax and regulate can succeed in countering this free-rider tendency. Echoes of this Hobbesian view surface in the work of the new norms scholars associated with the "New Chicago School" (Lessig, 1998).[8] Recognizing the centrality of norms, they advocate intentional governmental interventions to manipulate the norm-making process. By contrast, some Burkean and libertarian theorists insist that a social group commonly can succeed in using informal methods to deter crime and provide other sorts of public goods.[9] According to this alternative perspective, social traditions winnowed through natural selection tend to be wiser than the ratiocinated policies of the most brilliant policy makers.[10] All commentators, whether they aim to shrink or expand the role of the state, can benefit from a better understanding of how norms arise, persist, and change.

What follows is a modest step toward this end. Section 1 presents some stylized assumptions about individuals and their motivations. Section 2 explores the supply side of the norms market, in particular the role of change agents, such as norm entrepreneurs and opinion leaders, who either act in new ways or provide new patterns of social sanctions. Turning to the demand side of the market, section 3 stresses the roles of members of the social audience, the most detached evaluators of others' social behaviors. In brief, members of the audience can compensate worthy suppliers of new norms by conferring esteem (or, in the alternative, trading opportunities) upon them. Section 4 analyzes two events that may trigger a change in norms: an alteration in the economic conditions that a stably constituted social group faces, or an external event that reconfigures who belongs to a group. After either sort of event, the model suggests how a cascade toward a new norm might occur. Section 5 investigates social failures—that is, potential defects in the market for norms. Section 6 explores the comparative advantages that an organization, particularly the state, may have when it participates in the norm-making process.

I develop the theory at an intermediate level of rigor. Although the market analogy is strained in some respects, it does reveal how individuals have varying incentives to participate in norm making. Given prevailing academic norms, my inclusion of various simplifying assumptions is likely to offend humanists, and my failure to include a formal mathematical model is likely to disappoint some theorists. But, as the theory itself explains, a would-be change agent has to expect to take some heat.

Norm makers' roles and attributes

Roles: actors, enforcers, and members of the audience

In the model, an individual may belong to one or more social groups, which may vary in size. An individual qualifies as a member of a group if he is situated in a way that enables him (1) to learn about what the other members do when they interact (that is, to obtain historical information), and (2) to bestow punishments and rewards on other members by means of gossip, ostracism, adjustment of exchange relationships, and other self-help methods.

At various times each member assumes three distinct roles within the group: as an *actor*, as an *enforcer*, and as a *member of the audience*. A person is an *actor* when engaging in behavior unrelated to norm enforcement—for example, lighting a cigar, driving a car, or giving a lecture on mathematics. This sort of *primary behavior* may affect the welfare of the group's other members for better or worse. Smoke from a cigar at a dinner party, for instance, may be injurious to other guests. In the model, the demand for norms springs primarily from the desires of the members of a group to have informal rules designed to make an actor take into account the external costs and benefits of primary behavior (Coleman, 1990, pp. 249–57).[11]

An *enforcer* is on the front line of the system of informal social control. Enforcers observe what actors do and respond by meting out calibrated social rewards and punishments. These social sanctions can range from (usually) minor ones such as making a facial gesture or a responsive comment, to weightier ones such as a gift or a punch in the nose. A host who chastises a guest who smokes at a dinner party is acting as an enforcer, as is a student who openly compliments a mathematics professor after a guest lecture, as is a parent who grounds a teenager for using drugs.

Although further tiers of participants may well exist in an actual system of norms, for simplicity the model adds only one more, the *members of the audience*. Each member of the audience observes what both actors and enforcers do, but can respond only by conferring esteem or opprobrium (negative esteem) on enforcers.[12] (As will be explained, in this instance and others, devotees of Eric Posner's signaling theory of norms are invited to substitute *future exchange opportunities* for *esteem*.)[13] In the illustrative situations presented in the prior paragraph, the audiences would consist of, at minimum, the other dinner guests, the other attendees at the lecture, and the parent's friends and neighbors. In brief, norms arise when enforcers, to please their audiences, administer informal sanctions to influence the behavior of actors. A central task is to explain why rational and self-interested actors might choose to participate in all three roles.

Assumed homogeneous attributes of individuals

To keep the analysis tractable, the model makes some simplifying assumptions about a person's knowledge, desires, and capabilities. In some respects individuals are assumed to be homogeneous.

Perfect historical knowledge. As noted, all members of a group are assumed to know, either by direct observation or receipt of gossip, what all members previously have done in their various roles.

Power to levy social sanctions. Each member is assumed to be capable of rendering rewards and punishments. An enforcer may choose among an unlimited panoply of sanctions, including material and violent ones. A member of the audience, however, can confer only esteem (positive or negative). As explained in section 3, a member incurs no net personal costs when rendering an esteem sanction.

Utilitarian bias. A model of norm change presupposes an understanding of participants' objectives. These determine not only who contributes to norm reform but also what events provoke reformers to act. Because human affairs are complex and conflict-ridden, a simplifying heuristic about participants' objectives can help reveal processes of norm change that otherwise would remain obscure. To that end, I reductively assume that each member of a social group, *when acting in the role of a member of the audience*, has a *utilitarian bias*—that is, a selfless preference for norm changes that satisfy the criteria of Kaldor-Hicks efficiency.[14] This means that each member of the audience would favor a norm change if the members who would be beneficiaries of the change would gain enough to be potentially able to compensate the members who would lose from the change. So long as members of the group would gain in the aggregate, no audience member would object to an emerging norm on the ground that it would disadvantage him or others. Audience members, in other words, would not insist on Pareto superiority. According to the assumption of a utilitarian bias, a new antismoking norm, for example, would win unanimous support from the audience if it would be cost-effective for the group in the aggregate, even though it might be detrimental to individuals who smoked.[15]

   If a reductive assumption is to be made about human motivation, why should it be utilitarianism? The choice has a number of things to commend it. First, anthropologists and other investigators commonly have induced from field studies that human groups indeed tend to make cost-effective improvements in rules (Ellickson, 1991, pp. 184–264; see also Sober and Wilson, 1998). Second, a number of evolutionary game theorists predict, at least in the contexts they model, a drift toward more efficient norms (Bendor and Swistak, unpublished; Kandori, Mailath, and Rob, 1993).

   Third, in the long run, pursuit of utilitarian outcomes need not aggravate distributive injustices, a central concern of skeptics of utilitarianism.[16] Because of the transaction costs of securing unanimity, a group can increase its aggregate wealth if it can force selected members to bear isolated losses for the good of the whole. If, conversely, every member had the power to veto a change, a group would either have to forgo many reforms that would satisfy Kaldor-Hicks criteria, or incur the onerous administrative costs involved in compensating the myriad potential losers from reforms. Given this unappealing choice, a rational person should see that it is generally in his long-run interest to entitle his group to follow Kaldor-Hicks (as opposed to Paretian) criteria in norm making—that is, to refrain from compensating losers from an efficient change.[17] Over the long haul the member gains from this utilitarian ethic so long as his share of the transaction-cost savings that it generates is sufficient to offset the losses he incurs when reforms do disserve his interests. In sum, in a group in which the fabric of social interactions is thick, a rational member should be able to see the advantage of having a utilitarian bias when appraising a proposed norm change.

That said, I should reemphasize that I assume a utilitarian bias only to have a simplifying heuristic. In reality, most individuals no doubt pursue messy amalgams of objectives. Moreover, to assume as I do that audience members apply Kaldor-Hicks criteria is to assume that they transcend self-interest when performing in that role. This is optimistic, to put it gently. It is necessary, however, to stipulate *some* substantive objective that members seek in order to predict how they will act. One of the model's central results is that the audience tends to get what it wants, whatever that happens to be. If audience members were to prefer norms consistent with Rawlsian justice, congruent with their religion, or causing them to be poorer, they would be able to use esteem rewards to induce norm suppliers to serve these alternative ends.

Assumed heterogeneous attributes of individuals

On the other hand, in order to unlock the black box concealing the process of norm change, individuals are assumed to differ along several dimensions other than those just listed. As a result some members of a group have sharper incentives to lead the process of norm change.

Variable endowments. Individuals are assumed to differ in endowments such as physique, wealth, and human capital.[18] As a result, they may obtain different levels of *tangible benefits* when a new norm is adopted. For example, a person suffering from emphysema receives more benefits than most when an antismoking norm is put into effect.

Variable discount rates. Some group members are more future-oriented than others.

Variable technical intelligence. Although members observe everything (have perfect historical knowledge), they differ in their abilities to assess the costs and benefits that an act or enforcement effort generates for group members in the aggregate. For example, some individuals know more than others about the dangers of secondhand smoke or about the topic of a lecture on mathematics.

Variable social intelligence. Apart from differences in technical intelligence, individuals vary in their abilities to forecast group social dynamics. Some are as astute as Thomas Schelling and know when existing social conditions are ripe for a cascade to a new norm (Schelling, 1960, 1978). Others are deficient in social intelligence and have a relatively poor sense of how one person's decision can influence another's.

Variable leadership skills. People vary in their ease of organizing and inspiring those around them.[19] As a result of these variations, as well as differences in technical and social intelligence, some individuals can work for social innovations more effortlessly than others can. These low-cost suppliers can be expected to be disproportionately successful in the market for norms.

The supply side of the market for norms: change agents

A traditional sociological designation for an individual who promotes a change in norms is *moral entrepreneur*.[20] In 1996 Cass Sunstein devised the notion of a *norm entrepreneur* (Sunstein, 1996b, p. 909), a phrase that many legal scholars since have embraced (e.g., E. Posner, 2000).[21] In this section, I aspire to develop a richer vocabulary that distinguishes among a variety of specialists who supply new norms.

A new norm wins acceptance only when most actors conform to it and enforcers routinely levy sanctions to support it. Therefore both actors and enforcers are involved in the supply of norms. Actors participate when they adopt new patterns of primary behavior. An example is a smoker who tests the limits of propriety at a dinner party. Enforcers serve as suppliers when they react in new ways to the behaviors of actors. An example is a dinner guest who creatively responds to smoking by another guest, perhaps either by lauding the smoker's courage or, conversely, by throwing a glassful of wine to extinguish the smoker's cigarette. Those on the demand side of the market for norms then react to these stimuli.

Figure 6.1 depicts the operation of both the supply and demand sides of the market for norms. The supply side is indicated by the solid arrows pointing to the right; these identify flows of evidence of behavior on the part of both actors and enforcers.[22] The demand side of the market is indicated by the solid arrows in Figure 6.1 that point to the left; these indicate the responses of enforcers and members of the audience to the social evidence they receive from norm suppliers. (In this

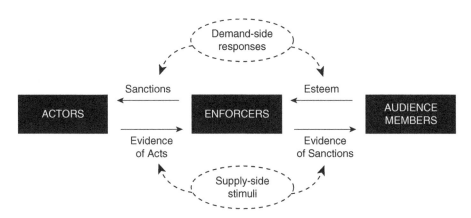

Figure 6.1 The market for norms.

model, it must be stressed, an enforcer's behavior simultaneously expresses demand to actors and supplies a norm to audience members.)[23]

I refer to an actor or enforcer who is relatively early in supplying a new norm as a *change agent*. According to the rational-actor perspective, a change agent offers a new norm because he anticipates that over time he will receive a flow of benefits that will outweigh (in present value terms) the various costs he will incur while acting in that role. A change agent moves earlier than others because his expected net benefits from his course of conduct are unusually large. This may be so either because his expected costs are uncommonly low, his expected benefits uncommonly high, or both.[24]

Change agents tend to have attributes that make them relatively low-cost suppliers of new norms. In general, they possess superior technical intelligence, social intelligence, and leadership skills. These attributes reduce the opportunity costs they incur when they work for norm reform.

Change agents also tend to face favorable conditions on the benefit side of the ledger. Successful promoters of a new norm receive two distinguishable sorts of benefits. First, each garners a personal share of the *tangible benefits* that the new norm creates for the group. As illustrated below, change agents tend to have special personal endowments conducive to their receipt of above-normal tangible benefits. Second, as a special reward for helping bring about social reform, change agents receive *esteem* and other social rewards when group members widely accept a new norm. Individuals embedded in social subnetworks consisting of persons prone to esteem them are prime candidates to become change agents.

These factors help explain the prominence of black religious leaders in the civil rights movement. Because they were black, they had much to gain from dismantling racial segregation. Because they were religious leaders, they were ideally positioned to receive early esteem from members of their immediate social groups (that is, members of their congregations), and relatively immune to social opprobrium, economic retaliation, and physical violence on the part of racist whites.

A change agent also is likely to have either a relatively low, or an extraordinarily high, discount rate. The stigma and other personal costs of attempting to change a norm generally are incurred early, whereas the esteem and tangible benefits generally cannot be reaped until the norm has won the day. Therefore, the more future-oriented a person is, the more rational it is to pursue social reform. At the other extreme, an individual who is utterly present-oriented has no fear of reputational sanctions that might be levied to deter deviance from accepted practice.

In an effort to clarify the dynamics of norm change (but at the admitted risk of a surfeit of jargon), I distinguish among three subcategories of change agents: self-motivated leaders, norm entrepreneurs, and opinion leaders.[25] Although all three types respond relatively early to a shift in cost-benefit opportunities, they lead for different reasons. Figure 6.2 depicts in a general way the chronological sequence in which a series of successful change agents participate in supplying a new norm.[26]

Self-motivated leaders

A self-motivated leader moves early to change a norm because, on account of his special endowments (and perhaps unusually low discount rates), he anticipates receiving an unusually high level of net tangible benefits from challenging the existing norm.[27]

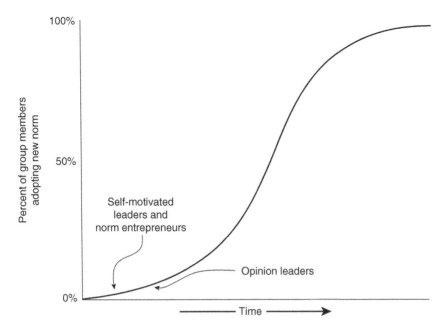

Figure 6.2 The involvement of change agents in the supply of a new norm.

Indeed, these net tangible benefits are sufficiently large to motivate him to favor change even in the absence of potential esteem rewards. Hence the adjective *self-motivated*.[28] To illustrate: A charismatic person faces lower costs of working for social change. A lessening of smoke especially benefits persons with emphysema or other lung disease. Therefore a charismatic person suffering from emphysema would be an ideal candidate to become a self-motivated leader of an antismoking campaign.

Self-motivated leaders commonly spark changes in the network norms that facilitate communication and coordination. For example, in 1833 Augustine Taylor invented in Chicago the balloon-frame method of wood construction, a system more lightweight and flexible than the traditional post-and-beam system. Other builders rapidly switched to the balloon frame and it remains the dominant system of light construction in the United States (Davis, Easterlin, and Parker, 1972, p. 621).[29] The self-motivated change agents in this instance were Taylor (the actor), and the head of the St. Mary's Roman Catholic Church (the enforcer), who snubbed traditional mores and permitted Taylor to proceed with his unorthodox design. Both parties likely possessed superior technical intelligence and anticipated unusually large tangible benefits, given the nature of their current and future building projects.

When a new norm suddenly becomes manifestly advantageous for a group, many self-motivated individuals with unexceptional leadership abilities may supply it simultaneously. When this happens, historians will have difficulty attributing the new norm to particular change agents. For instance, dueling fast became extinct in the South once the Civil War had shattered the social networks of the Southern aristocracy. Although antidueling societies had been active in the South before the war (Picker, 1997, p. 1285, n. 88), esteem rewards apparently were not needed to motivate the rejection of dueling after Appomattox.

A technical innovation may diffuse across space from its place of invention as neighbors copy the best practices of those around them. A momentous historical example is the slow diffusion of agriculture outward from its birthplace in the Fertile Crescent 10,000 years ago (Diamond, 1997, pp. 180–91).[30] The earliest inventors and copiers in this instance are likely to have had endowments that gave them special tangible benefits from engaging in farming. Many millennia later, Griliches (1957) found that the American farmers who pioneered the planting of hybrid corn tended to be the ones who would profit most from that innovation. In the late 1970s in China, the rapid repudiation of Maoist communal agriculture was partly triggered by a successful (and illegal) return to family farming by residents of the village of Xiaogang (Eckholm, 1998). Although these villagers later were esteemed in China for having helped provoke Deng to adopt legal reforms, their original motivation likely was their relatively high levels of tangible benefits from privatizing their fields.

Norm entrepreneurs

For the remaining two types of change agents—norm entrepreneurs and opinion leaders—external rewards provide an essential carrot. Although leaders of both types are likely to garner some tangible benefits from a norm change, they also need esteem to cover their full costs of supplying a new norm. *Norm entrepreneurs* are specialists who campaign to change particular norms, whereas *opinion leaders* are generalists. Ward Connerly, Martin Luther King, Jr., Catharine MacKinnon, Joseph McCarthy, and Carry Nation are norm entrepreneurs. Jimmy Carter, Walter Cronkite, Doris Kearns Goodwin, and Billy Graham are opinion leaders. Both types tend to be endowed with personal attributes, such as charisma and skill in communication, that reduce their costs of serving in these capacities.

What special traits distinguish a successful norm entrepreneur in particular? A norm entrepreneur tends to possess a relatively high level of technical knowledge relevant to the norms within his specialty. This knowledge enables the entrepreneur to respond early to a change in cost-benefit conditions. Entrepreneurs who favor antismoking norms tend to know much about lung diseases. Joseph McCarthy ascended when he appeared to have inside information about communist infiltration of government, and then foundered when it seemed that much of his specific information was bogus.

Opinion leaders

Unlike a self-motivated leader and a norm entrepreneur, an opinion leader is not at the forefront of norm change but instead is located one position back from the front (see Figure 6.2).[31] An opinion leader evaluates the initiatives of these other change agents (the true catalysts) and then decides which of their causes to endorse. Opinion leaders therefore play a pivotal role in determining whether change agents succeed in triggering a cascade toward a new norm (Rogers, 1983, pp. 27–28 and 281–88).[32]

A successful opinion leader tends to have two exceptional characteristics. The first is an usually high level of social intelligence, which helps the opinion leader anticipate better than most which social innovations will end up attracting bandwagon support. An adept opinion leader, for example, may be aware that many have been disguising their true opinions about the merits of current norms (Sunstein, 1996b, pp. 929–30). Opinion leaders involved in the Velvet Revolutions in Eastern Europe, for instance, best sensed that support for communism was less genuine than it seemed. Second, an opinion leader is likely to be a person to whom other members of the group are unusually prone to defer in order to avoid being socially out of step.[33] An opinion leader may have earned this trust through prior accomplishments in the arena of norm enforcement and change. A village elder is a generic example. The costs of supplying a new norm fall when someone expects to be followed.

A norm entrepreneur who commands little trust is wise to recruit to his crusade an opinion leader whom the audience regards as more credible. Thus, in 1786–87 James Madison, the political entrepreneur spearheading the nascent movement to replace the Articles of Confederation, recognized the monumental advantage of enlisting George Washington in the cause.[34]

The demand side of the market for norms: the role of a social audience

Individuals indicate their demand for various norms by levying informal rewards (or punishments) to indicate their approval (or disapproval) of what norm suppliers are doing. I refer to persons who provide early support to suppliers of a new norm as *appreciative observers*. Enforcers function as appreciative observers when they reward actors who are engaging in new forms of primary behavior. Members of the audience function as appreciative observers when they confer esteem on innovative enforcers. These relationships are portrayed by the leftward pointing solid arrows in Figure 6.1. Note that the same individuals can be, and commonly are, involved on both the supply and demand sides when a norm changes. An activist for gay rights is likely to provide encouragement to allies in the same cause. Nevertheless, the supply and demand sides are conceptually distinct. For example, a gay person who remains in the closet might choose to participate on only the demand side of social change.

The special attributes of appreciative observers

As the previous section explained, the change agents who supply new norms tend to possess either special endowments or special information. This also is true of their counterparts on the demand side, the appreciative observers who are early supporters of a social change.

Some appreciative observers, like the hypothetical gay person in the closet, have attributes that make them anticipate special benefits from the adoption of a new norm. They can be expected to be among the first enforcers to reward those who are supplying it. Other appreciative observers, apart from their prospective personal tangible benefits, have unusually good technical intelligence about the cost-benefit tradeoffs that competing norms pose.[35] They can be expected to be among the first enforcers and audience members to recognize when the supplier of a cost-effective new norm is doing something worthy of group reward. For instance, in the late 1950s, the observers most aware of the high costs of Jim Crow policies to African Americans would likely be among the first to esteem the civil rights activists astir at the time.

Finally, persons with an extraordinary level of social intelligence (like the opinion leaders on the supply side) tend to be key providers of positive reinforcement to proponents of a new norm. For example, once enough technically knowledgeable observers had begun to support the demise of Jim Crow policies in the South, the most socially aware members of the Southern audience would be among the first both to realize that the old regime was doomed and to join the bandwagon of rewarding the change agents who were hastening its end.

How costlessly conferred rewards can induce costly sanctioning: partial solutions to the second-order collective-action problem

It is easy to understand why an actor would choose to conform to a norm that is systematically enforced. If it is gauche to smoke at a dinner party, lighting a cigar would damage the cigar smoker's reputation. But it is harder to understand why an onlooker rationally would make the effort to administer punishments on wrongdoers and rewards on rightdoers.[36] Why would a host care to enforce an antismoking norm? One reason, possibly, would be tangible benefits: if secondhand smoke is either carcinogenic or unpleasant, the host obtains environmental benefits by suppressing it. But the host's enforcement also would help the other guests and to that extent would be a public good. Much norm enforcement, say against acts such as littering or giving birth out of wedlock, generates mainly public benefits, not benefits to the enforcer personally. When the private costs of enforcement seem to exceed the tangible benefits, what might motivate an enforcer to act as a member of the social police instead of as a free-rider? Although many legal scholars intuitively reject the Hobbesian view that order is never possible without a central authority, they have struggled to come up with a plausible explanation of how people ever are able to solve this second-order collective-action problem.

In the late 1990s, however, two of the new norms scholars—Richard McAdams and Eric Posner—independently proposed rival theories that suggest how members of an audience could, in some contexts, costlessly confer rewards to spur enforcers to function as informal police officers.[37]

Richard McAdams's esteem theory of norms

McAdams (1997, pp. 355–75) postulates that an individual values the esteem of others for its own sake.[38] Just as eating a tasty dessert is a source of pleasure, so is receiving kudos. Esteem sanctions, either positive or negative, therefore can influence the behavior of a change agent.

McAdams's more provocative idea is that an individual incurs no net costs when conferring esteem on another.[39] This assumption of zero esteeming-costs is plausible in some contexts. The historical information needed to accord esteem tends to be readily at hand. A dinner guest with adequate technical and social knowledge instantaneously can evaluate the propriety of a host's enforcement actions against a smoker. In many contexts conferring esteem also is virtually effortless. To smile or to frown, to salute or to snub, to praise or to rebuke—all require little more effort than taking a breath.

To be sure, conferring negative esteem can be costly if the target can retaliate in some way. McAdams (1995, pp. 1024–25) notes, however, that a member actually may reap offsetting benefits by participating as a member of the social police. For instance, an audience member who had internalized norms governing performance in that role might feel a warm glow after performing well in this capacity.[40] Indeed, appreciative members of live audiences at entertainment events appear to enjoy conferring applause. Any benefits derived from esteeming would reduce, and perhaps outweigh, an audience member's conceivable costs.

McAdams's conception of the demand side for norms suggests a scenario for a group with a utilitarian bias. Members of the audience survey the behaviors that various norm suppliers are offering. Audience members then costlessly confer positive esteem on enforcers who are serving the aggregate welfare of the members of the group, and negative esteem on other enforcers. Because enforcers value receiving esteem, they are induced to supply efficient norms. Some historical episodes indicate that this scenario is not far-fetched. Diffusely situated observers did confer esteem to reward change agents who had incurred high risks during the civil rights movement in the South (Chong, 1991, pp. 100–01, 191–92).

Eric Posner's signaling theory of norms

In an article (1998) and book (2000) Eric Posner has developed a more limited, but potentially more testable, theory of norms. Drawing on the work of Michael Spence (1974), Posner views norms as conventions that govern the behaviors that a person employs to signal that he is a "good type" to deal with. By wearing the "right" clothes, for instance, an actor advertizes that he is likely to be a good person to hire or marry. Transported into the present model, Posner's analysis suggests that an enforcer would be tempted to function as a member of the social police in situations where that service would signal his general trustworthiness to the members of the audience. To an audience with a utilitarian bias, the more efficient the norm that an enforcer supplies, the more favorable the signal. Audience members later would reward a meritorious enforcer by entering into additional cooperative exchanges with him. To illustrate, the host of a dinner party signals that he is a "good type" by enforcing a norm against smoking; a week later, an appreciative attendee invites the host to serve as a trustee for a trust, an exchange that will benefit the attendee because he now is more confident than before that the host is a "good type."

Posner's theory is similar to McAdams's in important respects. First, both theories anticipate a strong correlation between social rewards and an enforcer's net private costs. Posner asserts that the favorability of an audience's response to a signal increases with the cost of the signal to the signaler. An audience that confers esteem similarly is likely to correlate its aggregate reward with the size of an enforcer's sacrifice. Superheroes win more plaudits than ordinary heroes do.

Second and more important, under both theories *members of a social audience at no net cost can provide valuable carrots to the enforcers who create norms.* McAdams views esteem as costlessly conveyed. When a signal results in additional exchanges, as Posner anticipates, the members of an audience similarly incur no net costs. A consensual trade normally generates gains for all involved. In this context, audience members benefit from receiving and responding to signals because they are able to make more discerning choices among trading partners.[41]

In sum, under ideal conditions both theories anticipate that audience members would have no incentive to free-ride on the efforts of others to reward an enforcer who had supplied a public good. In developing my model, I adopt only this common denominator of the two theories and have no need to endorse either of them as such.[42] Throughout this article I consistently refer to audience rewards as "esteem," but only to keep the exposition compact. Whenever "esteem" appears, a reader who prefers Posner's theory to McAdams's is invited to mentally substitute "enhanced opportunities for cooperative interactions" and to ponder whether the analysis still holds.

Differences between McAdams's and Posner's theories

The two theories also vary in important respects. First, Posner's theory promises to be more testable than McAdams's.[43] In most contexts, it is easier to observe an exchange transaction than a conferral of esteem.

Second, Posner's theory is more compatible with traditional economic analysis. In his conception, audience members act prosocially in order to obtain the tangible benefits of better future trades, not because they are innately public-spirited, have internalized norms of public-regardingness, or can esteem at zero cost.

Third, the two theories have different implications about the timing of a merito-rious enforcer's rewards from an audience. McAdams seems to envisage an immediate conferral of esteem. Posner, by contrast, foresees rewards as delayed until subsequent periods of play, when mutually favorable transactions are executed. Posner's theory therefore more strongly implies that a person with a high discount rate or a person in end game would perform unreliably in the role of enforcer. For instance, Posner's theory suggests that the contemporary jury is an ill-advised legal institution, at least if the major function of a jury is to bring contemporary social norms to bear in a legal proceeding. In an urban setting today, jurors are strangers with scant prospects of further interaction once the group has disbanded. Posner's theory predicts jurors therefore have weak incentives to signal that they are good types by enforcing prevailing norms. If jurors in fact perform well, they either must bring internalized norms of civic duty into the jury room or (as McAdams supposes) must hunger for esteem from fellow jurors.

Fourth, as section 5.2 explains, an audience must appropriately aggregate its total rewards to get enforcers' incentives right. Both McAdams's and Posner's theo-ries suggest difficulties of proper aggregation, but of different sorts.[44]

How norms change

The model rests on the reductive assumption that members of a group have a utilitar-ian bias. An upshot of this assumption is that norms can be expected to evolve when underlying supply and demand conditions change. What kinds of events might pro-voke shifts in economic conditions? What sorts of change agents and appreciative observers are likely to respond first when an old norm is under stress? This section explores these questions first in general terms and then in the context of a particular example: the rise of norms against smoking.

Events that can trigger a change in norms

An exogenous shock creates new economic conditions within a stable group

In a social group with static membership, a new trading opportunity, technology, or environmental event may alter cost-benefit conditions.[45] As mentioned at the outset, Demsetz (1967) has described the response of a tribe of Labradorian Indians to the arrival of Europeans eager to exchange goods for pelts. In earlier times, the tribe's norms had supported communal hunting rights within its forests, a system that creates few incentives for an individual hunter to conserve the stock of game. Once the European traders came on the scene the tribe shifted to a system of exclusive hunting territories.[46] This system is more efficient when game is scarce, because the sole owner of a territory inhabited by nonmigratory wild animals has a much sharper incentive than a communal owner does to avoid overhunting.[47]

New scientific or technical information similarly can alter social practices.[48] Rain dancing is apt to become less common after members of a tribe have encountered the science of meteorology. In the 1940s, pediatricians routinely prescribed tonsillectomies; they later dropped this norm after wholesale use of the procedure was shown to be inadvisable.[49] In the 1950s in the U.S., the increasing military threat posed by the Soviet Union helped support the rise of norms against associating with communists (E. Posner, 1998, p. 775).

An environmental shock also can alter endowments and hence cost-benefit conditions. A drought, for example, may give rise to norms supporting conservation of water. The devastation of a war or natural disaster is apt to trigger norms of mutual support in part because people who have lost wealth see more benefit in having an informal system of social insurance. Relatedly, a stable group that migrates may vary its norms as it confronts changing environmental conditions. High-seas whalers, for example, efficiently adapted their informal rules of capture to the characteristics of the species of whales present in a fishery (Ellickson, 1991, pp. 191–206).

A group adds or loses members

Because individuals vary in their endowments, a change in group composition can alter internal cost-benefit conditions.[50] New blood is likely to be a source of new informal arrangements. A university can reinvigorate a fading academic department by hiring a cluster of established but youthful scholars; because their time horizons are longer, these young scholars have more to gain from the emergence of norms of scholarly output that would enhance the department's reputation. The subtraction of certain members from a group similarly may affect what norms are cost-justified in the aggregate.[51] The exclusion of children from an apartment building, for example, would lessen the costs of a norm against noise making because fewer children would have to bear the burden of suppressing their high spirits.

A war or natural disaster may shatter the outer boundaries of a group and change its norms as a result. Defeat in the Civil War ended the insulation and cohesion of the Southern aristocracy, thereby decimating the aristocrats' gains from the constitutive ritual of dueling. The events of World War II helped break down ethnic and (to a lesser degree) racial barriers in American life. Conversely, the destruction of a group's unifying forces may lead to a balkanization of norms. Indeed, the passing of Tito weakened pan-Slavic nationalism in Yugoslavia and enabled more parochial ethnic groups to reassert their norms.

A government may provide the exogenous shock that alters group composition. Before the 1960s, Southern whites and blacks were socially (if not necessarily physically) segregated. In that environment, whites were likely not only to tolerate racist jokes, but even to encourage that form of humor in order to enhance the status of whites as a group (McAdams, 1995). The Civil Rights Acts of the 1960s helped bring about significant integration of workplaces and schools in the South, with the result that many whites there began to belong to reference groups that included significant numbers of blacks. Blacks now had leverage to administer informal sanctions and confer esteem. After these changes in social structure, whites became far less likely to engage in racist humor.

Innovations in transportation and communication technologies make new concatenations of human interactions possible. In general, these tend to widen social relations and erode parochial norms. The expansion of trade, for example, fosters cooperation by expanding the compass of merchants' reputational stakes.[52] On the other hand, innovations such as web pages, e-mail, and cheap long-distance flights can enable geographically scattered persons with common narrow interests to maintain a group that previously could not have been sustained. For instance, these new technologies may help both a university to unite its alumni and an international terrorist group to knit together its sympathizers.

The process of norm change: responses of change agents and appreciative observers

Either sort of exogenous shock—a shift in internal cost-benefit conditions or an alteration of group membership—can spur a group to change its informal rules. But groups do not act as such, individuals do. As previously discussed, individuals possess different attributes that incline them to play specialized roles in the process of norm change.

Norm cascades: in general

Recent commentators on the dynamics of norm change have borrowed from game theory, evolutionary biology, and the economics of information. According to the new norms scholars, in the paradigm case an upstart norm starts slowly, gains momentum, and culminates in a triumphant rush. Various authors refer to a tipping point being passed (Cooter, 1998; McAdams, 1997, pp. 365–72), to an equilibrium changing not gradually but in punctuated fashion (Roe, 1996, pp. 663–65), or to a cascade being triggered (Sunstein, 1996b, p. 909).[53]

The literature on cascades suggests why people follow leaders. Works in this genre distinguish between two relevant phenomena: informational cascades and reputational cascades. According to the foundational article, "An informational cascade occurs when it is optimal for an individual, having observed the actions of those ahead of him, to follow the behavior of the preceding individual without regard to his own information" (Bikhchandani, Hirshleifer, and Welch, 1992, p. 994).[54] One goes along

with the crowd on the ground that the crowd is probably right. A person joins a reputational cascade, by contrast, to avoid the social disapproval that may be visited on
those who are out of step (Kuran, 1998; Kuran and Sunstein, 1999, pp. 685–87). One
goes along with the crowd to be with the crowd, even if one knows that the crowd is
wrong.

Cascade theory helps reveal how change agents and appreciative observers
become so influential. The basic scenario of a successful bandwagon is this: an exogenous change creates new cost-benefit conditions that favor a switch to a new norm.
Various change agents, employing advocacy or exemplary acts or enforcements, offer
up competing norms to govern the new conditions. The first change agents to supply
new norms are self-motivated leaders who will attain net tangible benefits from a
shift, and norm entrepreneurs who have the best technical information about the
aggregate advantages of possible changes.[55] Over time members of the audience assess
these competing offerings and confer esteem on worthy change agents. Because the
first change agents to move are challenging traditional ways, for a time ordinary
members of the audience may accord them less esteem than previously. Norm entrepreneurs' early losses tend to be mitigated, however, by their relatively low supply
costs (arising from their special knowledge and skill), their social proximity to appreciative observers who soon will be according them *higher* esteem, and their (typically)
low discount rates. Opinion leaders—those with the best social intelligence—then
play a key role. They notice that the technical experts have been gravitating toward
the new norm, a sign that it is one that other audience members eventually will learn
to appreciate. Hopping on the bandwagon, the opinion leaders begin to supply the
new norm and to esteem the actors who have been pushing it. An ordinary member
of the group observes all these moves and for a number of reasons eventually infers
that it would be prudent to join the cascade. First, because technical experts are
approving the change, it is likely to be good for the group. Second, social experts,
those who best understand where the crowd will end up, also are on board, and it is
socially risky not to follow them. The mass of ordinary members ultimately conforms
to what its respected leaders have been doing. The informational and reputational
cascades both crash to completion.

The speed of norm evolution is influenced by the magnitude of the gains from
change and the rate at which the members of the group acquire the technical and
social knowledge necessary to appreciate that the new norm is more utilitarian than
the old one. The entire process may proceed briskly. Sunstein gives as examples the
rise of feminism, the abandonment of communism in Eastern Europe and of Apartheid
in South Africa, and the collapse of reflexive political correctness on American cam-
puses (1996b, pp. 929–30).

An application: the rise of the norm against smoking

In North America informal pressure against smoking in a social setting increased
markedly during the last third of the twentieth century.[56] My theory suggests the
following stylized historical account.[57]

The triggering event is the gradual amassing of new scientific information about
health risks associated with first- and secondhand smoke.[58] Medical researchers and
public health officials, who have a superior command of this technical information,

soon emerge as the norm entrepreneurs in the antismoking cause. Nonsmokers who suffer from lung diseases join in as self-motivated leaders. These early change agents receive plaudits from appreciative medical experts. Key opinion leaders then increasingly join the cause. Although Edward R. Murrow smoked conspicuously on camera, television executives make sure that successor news anchors do not.[59] The general public takes its cues from these leaders and starts directing opprobrium at smokers and their suppliers. As the bandwagon grows, social hosts increasingly decline to set out ashtrays for guests. Everett Koop, David Kessler, and the other norm entrepreneurs in the antismoking cause come to be broadly esteemed.[60]

The actual story, of course, is more complex. The norm against public smoking has diffused at different rates within different demographic groups. In the U.S., college graduates are much less likely than high school dropouts to smoke (Kagan and Vogel, 1993, pp. 22, 47 n. 20, 48 n. 25). College graduates are likely to have lower discount rates, somewhat better technical information about the risks of smoking, and a lower likelihood of belonging to an oppositional subculture in which smoking is fashionable *because* mainstream norms have been shifting against it (Gusfield, 1993, p. 66).

A man in France is considerably more likely to smoke than is a man in North America.[61] It is implausible to chalk this up to differences in technical information in the hands of the health experts in the two nations. Legal variations may account for some of the difference. Although France heavily taxes tobacco products and tightly controls their advertizing, it has relatively lax laws on smoking in workplaces and public accommodations (Kagan and Vogel, 1993). But differences in norms may matter as well. Partly because opinion leaders in France have been somewhat slower than their counterparts in North America to quit smoking, the French public seems less supportive of antismoking norms.[62] But why would French opinion leaders be relatively slow to act? Some observers might be tempted to resort to an ad hoc cultural explanation, such as that smoking serves as a more potent signal of sophistication in France than it does in North America.[63] Data on trends in smoking in France, Canada, and the U.S., however, suggest that the direction and pace of norm change actually has been rather similar in the three nations. In each of the three, about 20% fewer members of the total adult male population were smoking in the early 1980s than were in the mid-1960s.[64] This suggests the main reason that France has more smokers and weaker antismoking norms today is that a larger fraction of its population happened to be smoking when the new information about the dangers of tobacco surfaced. Cultural variations among the three nations may have affected their baseline smoking rates, but not the basic thrust of their social responses to the new medical evidence.

Social failures: the limitations of norms

Up to this point, I have been generally upbeat about the ability of members of a social group to adapt their norms to new conditions. This tone is generally consistent with my prior work (Ellickson, 1991) and the views of Cooter (1996, pp. 1677–78), Demsetz (1967), and the other "optimists" about norms.[65] But there also are many "pessimists" among the scholars, including Eric Posner (2000, pp. 171–79) and, in important respects, McAdams (1997, pp. 409–24).[66] The pessimists repeatedly indicate how the norm-making process may fail to serve utilitarian ends. In this section, I suggest that the scholars in these opposing camps may disagree less about the nature of norm making than about the likelihood that government officials can outperform norm makers.

Conventional transaction-cost economics helps lay bare how social processes may fail. In Coase's (1960) hypothetical world of zero transaction costs, a norm could not be the source of a deadweight loss because, if it were, all affected persons instantly would contract to reform it. Nonutilitarian norms therefore can arise only in contexts where transaction costs are high.[67] The details of social contexts, such as the number of members involved, thus matter a great deal. Transaction costs are especially likely to impede correction of an inefficient norm when (1) the costs of the norms are mostly deflected to outsiders, (2) a group has difficulty coordinating the aggregate amounts of its rewards to worthy change agents, (3) a group's esteem awards are likely to be insufficient to overcome various forms of inertia favoring the status quo, and (4) social conditions make a group vulnerable to reputational cascades toward inefficient fashions. I treat these in turn.

The slighting of outsiders' interests

All the new norms scholars, even the optimists, agree that a closely knit group may generate a norm that injures outsiders more than it helps insiders.[68] McAdams's (1995, pp. 1033–82) analysis of Southern traditions of racial segregation, for example, indicates how the norms that Southern whites developed to enhance their own status had horrific effects on blacks. A legislature therefore may be wise to enact a statute, such as a Civil Rights Act, that attends to the external costs that a parochial norm has been inflicting. For the same reason, a common-law judge should not elevate a custom of an industry to the status of law in a context where the custom affects the welfare of outsiders who have no practical capacity to bargain.[69] The customs of the tugboat industry, for example, which may well serve the needs of shippers, cannot be expected to serve the interests of owners of oceanfront improvements that a wayward barge might strike.[70]

The difficulty of coordinating aggregate rewards to worthy change agents

To get the incentives of enforcers right, an audience must dispense its rewards in the appropriate total amounts. If all your other neighbors already have praised you for chastising a smoker, perhaps I should refrain from adding yet more praise, so that you do not start devoting too much time to antismoking campaigns. More precisely, in present-value terms, an audience's expected aggregate rewards ideally should equal the value of the social benefits that an enforcer produces. Coordinating total laurels to accomplish that equivalency is a collective-action problem of the highest degree of difficulty.

Although neither McAdams's nor Eric Posner's theory provides much hope that a group can aggregate its rewards well, McAdams's is somewhat more encouraging. Esteem rewards in practice do seem to be intentionally gradated. Newspapers vary the lengths of obituaries, writers vary the heartiness of congratulatory messages, and live audiences vary the enthusiasm of their applause.[71] Rosa Parks, who challenged the segregation of public facilities in the South, and Joseph Welch, who took on Joseph McCarthy at his height, were seen as particularly heroic and accordingly received especially high levels of esteem.

If rewards take the form of future exchanges, however, as Posner's theory supposes, an enforcer's aggregate rewards invariably will be poorly calibrated to induce behavior that serves the group in the aggregate. Although accomplishing a *great* deed is likely to signal that one is a "good type" better than merely accomplishing a *good* deed, trading partners still have little or no incentive to appropriately aggregate their bestowals on signalers. They act as seekers of gains from trade, not as rewarders of producers of public goods.

Under both McAdams's and Posner's theories, then, audiences are capable only of creating crude aggregate incentives. Whether this crudeness would result in too much norm change, or too little, would depend on the social context.

Sources of inertia: why custom may "lag"

For a variety of other reasons, however, aggregate audience rewards to worthy change agents generally are likely to be too low, not too high. As a result, inefficient social norms tend to be weeded out too slowly.

Cognitive biases in favor of the status quo

An individual tends to regard the prospective loss of a given amount as more momentous than the prospective gain of an equivalent amount.[72] This loss aversion would incline audience members to withhold esteem from a challenger of the status quo even when they might later find they were pleased that the norm had been challenged. Other forces, however, may work to soften this effect. For instance, a person might earn the status of an opinion leader by showing skill in helping others overcome their status quo biases.

The costliness of displacing internalized norms

Internalization of a norm reduces a person's receptiveness to new technical information that indicates that the norm has become obsolete. As a result, enforcers and audience members who have internalized an old norm take a longer time to appreciate the deeds of a supplier of a new and better norm.[73] When the audience has been socialized to favor the status quo, would-be change agents are more cautious about challenging it.

Southern norms of dueling can serve to illustrate this point. Before the end of the Civil War, an upper-class Southerner male was honor-bound to follow dueling rituals to resolve a dispute over a dignitary slight.[74] Rich white Southerners, fearing that black slaves might rebel against them, had more need than Northerners to maintain their solidarity. Dueling rituals were constitutive norms that generally served that end.[75] The freeing of slaves after the South's loss in the Civil War eliminated many of the benefits of maintaining upper-class solidarity. This profound change triggered a norm cascade that quickly obliterated the ritual of dueling (Schwartz, Baker, and

Ryan, 1984, p. 349). It is likely, however, that dueling had become obsolete long before but that high transaction costs had prevented members of the Southern elite from coordinating to eliminate the practice (McAdams, 1997, pp. 423–24; Schwartz, Baker, and Ryan, 1984, pp. 328–29). One reason may have been that most members of older generations had internalized dueling norms and therefore resisted the sporadic efforts of reform-minded legislators and members of antidueling societies to extirpate the custom (Hasen, 1996, p. 2150).

The costliness of moving away from a local optimum

The new norms scholars seem to be most concerned about another potential source of inertia. Game theorists have established that a group may settle on an equilibrium that is less utilitarian than another because it is not in the interest of any person to be the first to move away from it.[76] In more technical language, a group may become stuck at a local optimum as opposed to the global optimum.[77] When members of a group are aware that they have a bad norm, they may be able to coordinate a move to a better norm if they can cheaply communicate and contract with one another.[78] But transaction costs, which presumably grow with group size, can keep a group glued to an inefficient norm.[79] In particular, if there are too few appreciative observers with the technical knowledge to recognize that the time for change has arrived, change agents may not have adequate esteem incentives to embark on the hard work of triggering a cascade from the status quo.

Perverse reputational cascades (rat-race norms)

To complicate matters further, another body of theory suggests that in some social circumstances norms governing fashions may not only shift too quickly but also produce poor outcomes. The variabilities of the length of skirts and the width of neckties are standard examples. Eric Posner (2000, pp. 174–77) and others who view norms as signals contend that people can succumb to a negative-sum game when they jockey for status. When individuals are unable to coordinate a truce, norms may push them to engage in conspicuous consumption, to undergo cosmetic surgery, and to excessively manicure their front lawns. In these instances, change agents pursuing ephemeral personal gains promote a new fashion, and others are prompted to join the bandwagon to avoid being out of step. These sorts of reputational cascades not only consume resources but also may result in fashions that are less efficient than the ones they replace.[80]

The debate between norm pessimists and norm optimists

Drawing on these potential sources of social failure, pessimistic scholars delight in putting forward examples of norms that support seemingly wasteful practices such as dueling, footbinding, and female circumcision. None of the optimistic scholars appears to deny the possibility of social failure, but they instead stress the presence of corrective forces, such as the market for norms, that tend to spring into action after a social group has gone off track.[81] An optimist might point out that all the wasteful norms listed in the first sentence of this paragraph are either defunct or in decline.[82]

The debates over the efficiency of prevailing network norms further illuminate the differences between the camps. Pessimistic economists assert the obsolescence of the QWERTY keyboard, which originally was designed in part to prevent typewriter keys from colliding (David, 1985). Optimistic economists, by contrast, claim that QWERTY's disadvantages are slight and that it has survived in the face of powerful corrective pressures (Liebowitz and Margolis, 1990).[83] Pessimists may point to the persistence of the English system of weights and measures in the U.S.; optimists, to the widespread inroads of the metric system in scientific laboratories and other venues where its advantages are greatest.

I sense that the differences between the pessimists and optimists are not as profound as they first appear. Optimists should admit that transaction costs can immunize an inefficient norm from change and that a reputational cascade at times will generate an inefficient norm. For their part, pessimists should admit that corrective social forces such as the market for norms generally tend to erode norms that are suboptimal for a group's insiders. Indeed, the more inefficient a current norm, the greater the incentives of change agents to attack it.[84]

In the end, the key difference between the two camps appears to be that the optimists have less confidence than the pessimists that a government can outperform social forces in reforming inefficient norms. And it is worth reemphasizing that both optimists and pessimists generally applaud a government that uses its laws to counter group norms that are injurious to outsiders.

Organizations and governments as change agents

An individual concerned about norms need not act singly, but instead can coordinate on either the supply or demand side through an organization such as a household, private association, or government.[85] This section analyzes the comparative advantages of these sorts of institutions in the field of norm making.

An organization can exploit scale economies. It also can spread risks, for example, by coordinating a number of early moves simultaneously in order to lower the amount of opprobrium heaped on a first mover. In addition, by shortening lines of communication between the organization's members who are appreciative observers and those who are change agents, it can help assure the change agents that they will receive some esteem from the outset of their campaigns. A norm-change organization with prior successes may earn a reputation as a credible source of technical and social information, strengthening its social power. These advantages, taken together, may explain why organizations such as the NAACP, SCLC, and SNCC were central in the fight against norms of racial segregation in the South.[86]

Organizations have disadvantages as well. There is the familiar risk that an agent may pursue personal, not organizational, interests. An individual's incentives when acting through an organization are especially likely to be dulled when the external rewards for successful norm innovation are uniformly spread among all organization members. An organization that pushes new norms therefore is likely to provide internal incentives to reward the agents who have done the most work. These might take the form of promotions, higher compensation, or internal esteem.[87]

Nongovernmental organizations as change agents

Many nonprofit organizations devote themselves to norm change. In one dramatic instance, sects of Christian missionaries played a central role in triggering the decline of footbinding, a custom that Chinese parents once followed in order to make their daughters more desirable marriage partners. In 1889, 99% of parents in Tinghsien were still honoring this practice. The missionaries helped create self-sustaining anti-footbinding societies, whose ideas spread so rapidly that footbinding had practically ceased by 1919 (Picker, 1997, pp. 1284–85). Two different kinds of nongovernmental organizations were active in the process: the Western missionary organizations and the Chinese antifootbinding societies.

For-profit organizations generally are less involved in the production of public goods such as norms. Nevertheless, a business may influence informal rules when it spreads technical or social information through its advertizing. An ad for a nicotine skin-patch helps communicate that smoking is addictive; an ad for Virginia Slims signals that smoking is "in" among young women. Corporate measures also may influence the identity of social groups to which employees belong. A firm may sponsor a softball team and resist organization of a union. Or it may pay for an executive's fee to join a local country club, a membership that would help bind the executive to local commercial society and its attendant norms.

Governments as change agents

According to the Hobbesian conception, a government exercises its unrivaled power to coerce in order to quell free-riding. This enables it not only to administer punishments that other institutions cannot but also to bestow rewards financed by compulsory taxes. These tools enable a government to provide public goods, including a legal system that enhances social order. Legal scholars traditionally have focused on how specialized government agents produce and enforce legal rules. The new norms scholars reject this legal centralism, however, and emphasize that a state commonly also seeks to influence the norm-making process at work in civil society. At times government agents may do this directly, as various Surgeons General did when they served as norm entrepreneurs in the campaign against smoking. Or a government may act indirectly, perhaps by altering the incentives of private norm-makers.[88]

Kahan (1997), Lessig (1998), Sunstein (1996b), and the other members of the New Chicago School warm to the possibilities of government norm-shaping.[89] Although cognizant of the risks of totalitarianism (Lessig, 1995, pp. 949–50 n. 19, 1016–19, 1034–44; Sunstein, 1996b, pp. 965–67), they believe that in a pluralistic society government interventions readily can be cabined to prevent excesses. The agenda of the New Chicago School invites a preliminary examination of the comparative advantages of governments in the norm-making process. It is implausible that government agents inherently possess better technical intelligence than do members of "civil society."[90] Rather, the case for state involvement must rest either on the state's special capabilities as a moral educator, or on its unmatched capacity to exercise force. How plausible are these grounds for government norm-shaping?

A government's comparative advantages in changing norms

A normative statement by a government agent or institution might carry more inherent weight than an equivalent statement by a nongovernmental change agent. Nancy Reagan used to urge teenagers to "Just Say No" to drugs. Is there reason to believe that her views were more influential than an equivalent statement by an equally famous celebrity would have been? Do citizens give any deference to merely hortatory language in a statute? The new norms scholars have begun to investigate this cluster of questions—conventionally dubbed whether law can serve an "expressive function" when it is not backed by sanctions.[91]

Cooter (1996, p. 1675) offers a scenario in which he anticipates that a legislature's embrace of a norm would carry special expressive weight. He supposes that a municipality has enacted a pooper-scooper ordinance that no one expects it to enforce. He argues the ordinance nevertheless might embolden a pedestrian to chastise an irresponsible dog owner, because the pedestrian now could say, "Clean up. It's the law."

Members of a group are likely to follow norm makers who they think possess better information than they do. On what dimensions of the pooper-scooper issue might a city resident perceive that members of city council have superior information? It is implausible that citizens would especially respect the *moral intelligence* of city politicians. Indeed, opinion polls indicate that the public has a relatively low opinion of public officials' ethics.[92]

In some contexts, an ordinary person might defer to a government official's hortatory statement on the ground that the official has superior *technical knowledge*. A Surgeon General therefore is better positioned to speak out on the dangers of cigarettes than a First Lady is to speak out on the dangers of drugs. But informational asymmetries hardly are present when the issue at hand is the removal of canine wastes.

Nevertheless, Cooter's scenario is plausible because a city resident is apt to sense that local elected officials possess better *social knowledge* than ordinary citizens do. As McAdams (1997, pp. 397–407) ably explains, a person who knows that a norm enjoys widespread social acceptance is more willing to support it.[93] Politicians specialize in discerning public opinion. A democratic legislature is a superior—indeed, on many issues an unsurpassed—forum for revealing the presence or absence of a social consensus. The enactment of a pooper-scooper ordinance therefore strongly signals that there has been a norm cascade in favor of cleaning up after dogs, and this signal may embolden a pedestrian to join the bandwagon. It follows that a law that citizens perceive to be the product of special-interest lobbying (say a ban on ticket-scalping) will *not* influence the evolution of norms because it will not convey credible evidence of an underlying social consensus.

Citizens relatively indifferent toward their standing with most other members of the public are likely to disregard a democratic government's exhortations. For instance, a teenager is apt to be less responsive to Nancy Reagan's opinions about drugs than to a rock star's. A president's spouse caters to the entire national electorate, whereas a rock star caters to anti-establishment youth, a more potent reference group for most teenagers.

How a government can use its coercive powers to influence norm making

A government's basic norm-shaping tools are readily discerned.[94] First, it can augment the payoffs of private change agents who share its agenda, and lessen the payoffs of those who do not. For instance, a government can use subsidies or tax benefits to financially boost antismoking activists. Conversely, to deter cigarette advertizing, it could impose a ban or a time-place-manner regulation backed by criminal or civil sanctions.[95] By altering the level of tangible benefits that change agents expect to receive, these sorts of policies influence change agents' willingness to supply new norms.

Second, to speed the rate of norm change, a government can subsidize the provision of favorable technical and social information in order to influence opinion leaders and appreciative observers. Notable instances are the Surgeon General's Reports of 1964 and 1986, which reported, respectively, scientific evidence on the dangers of first- and secondhand smoke (Gusfield, 1993, pp. 54–60, 79).

Third, government can attempt to regulate groups as such.[96] For example, it can attempt to lessen the efficacy of an existing group, such as a youth gang, whose norm-making activity it generally disfavors. This might involve an attack on the constitutive norms (such as gang symbols) that maintain the solidarity of the group, rewarding informers who divulge group strategies, enforcing legal rights of privacy that impede a group's ability to monitor its members (McAdams, 1997, pp. 424–32), and conditioning other government benefits on nonmembership in the group.[97] Conversely, a government can strengthen a group whose norms it generally favors, say by funneling subsidies to individuals through the group. The social influence of a religious institution grows when a government gives grants to its soup kitchens.

Finally, instead of passively accepting the boundaries of existing groups, a government can attempt to alter those boundaries in order to achieve its goals. As noted earlier, the enactment of the Civil Rights Acts of the 1960s lessened the parochialism of Southern whites and changed their norms. A government that engages in ethnic cleansing, by contrast, enhances both the homogeneity of its demographic groups and the parochialism of their norms.

The ethnic cleansing example should serve as a caution to the members of the New Chicago School. Even if informal norm making is vulnerable to the social failures described in Section 5, it does not follow that an activist government would improve matters. Government actions commonly have unanticipated consequences. The Bolsheviks aggressively attempted to inculcate norms of selflessness and ended up dissipating Russia's scarce social capital. As Robert Clark (1989, p. 1732) has noted, a society that relies on norms encounters fewer risks than a society that empowers technocrats to rule by force. The basic point is that a narrow interest group cannot capture the diffuse forces of "civil society" as easily as it can the state.[98] The most serious atrocities of the Nazis, Bolsheviks, and Balkan ethnic cleansers began only after those groups had attained political power. Although the state does have some special capabilities in norm making, it is also by far the most dangerous participant in that process.[99]

Conclusion

A new social norm typically emerges not from a collective decision by the members of an informal group but from the purposive decisions of members acting as individuals. The basic tools of microeconomics can help illuminate this process. This article has presented a semirigorous model in which a new norm arises out of the workings of a market for norms. Change is triggered by a shift in either cost-benefit conditions or group composition. Because individuals are heterogeneous in important respects, they respond differently to these triggering events. The first persons to supply new norms generally have either special endowments that provide them with unusually high tangible benefits from norm reform, superior technical knowledge of cost-benefit conditions, or superior social knowledge of group dynamics. Members of the social audience observe the competing efforts of these norm suppliers and reward the most meritorious by conferring on them either esteem or, according to a rival theory, new exchange opportunities. Under ideal conditions, members of the audience—key participants in the demand side of the market for norms—have no incentive to free-ride in rewarding a worthy norm-innovator because they incur no net costs when bestowing their rewards.

The model incorporates numerous simplifying assumptions in order to render complex social phenomena more tractable. Two of the most heroic assumptions are that members of a social audience selflessly prefer utilitarian outcomes and that they can successfully coordinate the aggregate rewards that they confer. Critics are invited to exploit these and other weaknesses. More fundamentally, it is not obvious that modeling norm making as a market process enlightens more than it distorts. I am firmly convinced, however, of the value of a theory that links norm changes with heterogeneities among individuals.

Some (perhaps many) portions of my analysis may seem obvious. The reason is simple. Because we each spend much of our days swimming in social waters, we all have deep intuitive understandings of social phenomena. Common law judges similarly appear to have had a good understanding of microeconomics before the time of Adam Smith. But just as economic theory has served to deepen economic understandings, a more powerful theory of social norms should serve to sharpen social intelligence.

In particular, theory can stimulate valuable empirical work. As Ronald Coase (1960, pp. 18–19) stressed in his foundational article, a better understanding of the human condition ultimately depends on study of actual practices. Despite this advice, law-and-economics scholars, while eager to draw on *others'* studies of norms governing smoking, dueling, footbinding, and so on, themselves rarely undertake primary research on norms. I esteem the few, such as Lisa Bernstein, who have broken the mold, and I urge you to do the same.[100]

Notes

1   There is a large literature, much of it by sociologists, on the diffusion of new ideas and practices. See Rogers (1983) for a review of the field. Although the scholars who contributed to this literature developed many of the terms that I employ (*change agent*, *opinion leader*, and so on), they seldom envisage norm creation as a process involving interaction between a supply side and a demand side. But compare Chong (1991, pp. 141–64) (developing a supply-and-demand model of collective action) and Coleman (1990, pp. 241–99) (moving toward a similar conception).

2   Sociologists traditionally have employed a methodological wholism that views aggregations such as cultures and social classes as operative agents in the generation of norms.

Many legal scholars who have examined cultural evolution have declined to focus on the incentives and decisions of discrete individuals. See, for example, Cover (1983). Economists, by contrast, are noted for their methodological individualism.

3   For a concise overview of the new norms scholarship, see McAdams (1997).

4   This article focuses on norms that constrain actions of single individuals. No attention is given to norms that bear on the conduct of organizations of individuals— for instance, customary international law and the norms governing the internal labor markets of corporations. On these complex issues, see, for example, Goldsmith and Posner (1999) and Rock and Wachter (1996). The dynamics of organizational behavior of course may differ from the dynamics of individual behavior. See, for example, McAdams (1995, p. 1014), which marshals evidence that a team of individuals is more likely than a single individual to defect in iterated prisoner's dilemma games.

5   For a hypothesis that might lead to a neurobiological account of the internalization process, see Damasio (1994, pp. 173–80).

6   In my view, these patterns of external sanctions are the best evidence of the existence of a norm (Ellickson, 1991, pp. 128–30). But compare Cooter (1996, pp. 1661–66), which views internalization as a necessary condition for the existence of a norm.

7   A classic analysis is Olson (1965).

8   Representative contributions are Kahan (1997), Lessig (1998), and Sunstein (1996b).

9   See, for example, Morriss (1998).

10 See Clark (1989, p. 1729 n. 58), which associates Cicero, Burke, and Hayek with this view.

11 Norms appear in as many varieties as legal rules do (Ellickson, 1991, pp. 132–36, 184–264). This article focuses mainly on *substantive norms*, the informal rules that govern the primary behavior of actors. *Procedural*, *remedial*, and *controller-selecting* (jurisdictional) *norms* govern how enforcers carry out the process of informal sanctioning. Particularly intriguing are the *constitutive norms* that govern the obligations of members of a group to communicate with one another and to engage in ritual activities. Members may especially esteem persons adept at supplying their group with an ideology, that is, an account that justifies its system of norms and thereby enhances group solidarity (McAdams, 1995, pp. 1059–62).

12 Someone who confers esteem or opprobrium directly upon an actor is playing the role of an enforcer, not audience member.

13 See text accompanying notes 41–42.

14 By forcing an actor to take externalities into account, an enforcer may reduce the deadweight losses (unexploited gains from trade) that a group's members incur. A new norm, however, is likely to entail different transaction costs than the one it replaces. An audience with a utilitarian bias therefore would esteem only enforcers who had supplied norms that would serve to minimize the sum of deadweight losses and transaction costs that all members would incur. For evidence that individuals are inclined to don public-spirited hats under conducive circumstances, see Lewinsohn-Zamir (1998) and sources cited therein. See also Margolis (1982), which hypothesizes that an individual has preferences for group outcomes that are distinct from the individual's preferences for personal outcomes.

15 See Dau-Schmidt (1990, pp. 19–22) (arguing that norm shapers can pursue only Kaldor-Hicks efficiency) and Ellickson (1991, pp. 170–74) (inducing a hypothesis

that norms tend to advance Kaldor-Hicks efficiency). See also Coleman (1990, pp. 260–65) (assessing the problem) and Sunstein (1996b, pp. 955–56) (analyzing situations where some gain and some lose).

16 Many norms that appear to have a distributive thrust (Lessig, 1995, pp. 1004–07) are reconcilable with utilitarian ethics. For example, norms that support selective giving of alms to the poor create an informal social-insurance system that can enhance efficiency in an environment where people are risk-averse. See Binmore (1998, pp. 285–98), a model that supports sharing by preliterate hunters, and Ridley (1996, pp. 85–102), which describes the universal hunter-gatherer custom of sharing meat after successful pursuit of large game.

17 The seminal analysis is Michelman (1967). But compare Libecap (1989, pp. 4–28), which assumes that losers from a socially beneficial change in rules invariably would seek compensation before consenting to it.

18 I have declined to allow for variations in tastes as such. But compare Bernheim (1994, p. 844), which views nonconformists as people with extreme preferences.

19 Scholars from many disciplines have striven to develop theories of leadership. See, for example, Gardner (1995) in psychology, Gouldner (1950) in sociology, Hermalin (1998) in economics, and Schneider, Teske, and Mintrom (1995) in political science.

20 See, for example, H. Becker (1963, pp. 147–48); see also R. Posner (1998, pp. 1638, 1664–68).

21 Jolls, Sunstein, and Thaler (1998, pp. 1519–22) introduce the notion of an *availability entrepreneur* who seizes upon a recent event (such as toxic wastes at Love Canal) to mobilize support for a cause (such as enactment of Superfund legislation dealing with toxic wastes).

22 If a fourth tier—or any further tier—of participants were added to the model, the arrows connecting that tier would be characterized in the same fashion.

23 To illustrate: a dinner guest who has upbraided another for smoking has both expressed demand to that smoker and also supplied a norm for the other guests at the dinner table to appraise.

24 I ignore special psychological attributes and developmental histories that change agents are likely to possess. On that front, see, for example, Sulloway (1996), which asserts that later-born children tend to challenge the status quo more than firstborns do.

25 For a sampling of others' efforts to distinguish among change agents, see Lionberger (1960, pp. 52–66), which distinguishes among "innovators," "communicators," and "influentials"; and Rogers (1983, pp. 241–346), which distinguishes among contributors according to both timing ("innovators," "early adopters," etc.) and function ("opinion leaders," "change agents," etc.).

26 Figure 6.2 mimics the structure of a graph appearing in Rogers (1983, p. 11).

27 My taxonomy of change agents can be applied to both actors and enforcers. For instance, a norm entrepreneur can pioneer either a new pattern of primary behavior or a new pattern of sanctioning.

28 Compare the notion of a *passive leader*, developed in Kuran (1998, p. 654).

29 Business customs, such as this one, are shaped not only by informal exchanges but also by explicit contracts.

30 See also Picker (1997), which presents a model in which actors are influenced by events in their "information neighborhoods."

31 *Opinion leader* apparently derives from Berelson, Lazarsfeld, and McPhee (1954, pp. 109–14). These authors define the phrase more broadly than I do.

Compare Bikhchandani, Hirshleifer, and Welch (1992, pp. 1002–03), which stresses the role of opinion leaders in triggering changes in social practices, and McAdams (1997, p. 416).

32   See text accompanying notes 53–64.

33   See also Clark (1989, p. 1730 nn. 59–60), which discusses the possibility that humans have an evolved biological instinct to conform to the behavior of others, particularly persons of high status.

34   See Wills (1984, pp. 147–58), which describes Madison's recruitment efforts. Washington was not only the paramount opinion leader of the post-Revolutionary era, but also, because of his wide-ranging experiences, something of a technical expert in the field of governmental structure.

35   Their role in many respects is similar to that of a writer of newspaper editorials, a critic in the arts, or a peer reviewer in academic life.

36   It is frequently argued that norms tend to be undersupplied because enforcers are unable to capture all the benefits of enforcement activity. See, for example, Katz (1996, pp. 1749–50) and E. Posner (1998, pp. 792–95).

37   Audience is my term, not McAdams's or Posner's.

38   See also McAdams (1995) and compare Smith ([1759] 1982, p. 116). See also Ridley (1996, pp. 109–14), which describes debate among anthropologists over whether a hunter-gatherer gives food to others to obtain esteem or reciprocal gifts.

39   Apparently a number of scholars hatched this idea independently. Besides McAdams, see Pettit (1990, pp. 738–42) and Sober and Wilson (1998, pp. 144–46, 151, 166–68). Compare Cooter (1996, pp. 1668–69), which asserts that enforcers can cheaply engage in negative gossip and ostracism.

40   Social psychologists find that most people believe that rewards should be apportioned according to the merit of individuals—so-called "equity theory." See Binmore (1998, pp. 277–78). If equity theory is sound, an audience member, in order to maintain his self-conception as a moral person, would have to esteem others who have been conferring public goods. Some scholars have explored how socialization or evolutionary processes might generate internationalized norms that would induce a meritorious enforcer to reward himself after he had served the public weal. See, for example, Bowles and Gintis (unpublished), a model in which an enforcer obtains utility simply by enforcing a norm. See also the sources cited in note 14.

41   This statement assumes that signals in fact convey valuable information, which under Spence's theory they do only when there are separating (as opposed to pooling) equilibria. It also assumes that most transactions take place in markets where the elasticities of supply and demand enable both producers and consumers to garner some surplus.

42   Indeed, I regard both theories as highly reductive, as a beginning theory has to be.

43   See also E. Posner (1998, pp. 786 n. 32, 797–98).

44   See text accompanying note 71.

45   An economic change can affect the costs and benefits associated not only with primary behavior but also with the operation of the system of social control itself. Advent of the Internet, for example, might enhance an enforcer's capacity to obtain social information and an audience member's capacity to confer esteem.

46   But compare E. Posner (1996a, pp. 1712–13), which asserts that the Labradorian Indians may have taken two centuries to adjust their land tenure norms.

47   In a related vein, economic historians partly attribute the enclosure (parcelization) of medieval open fields to improvements in farm technologies and to increased demand for labor and wool. See sources cited in Ellickson (1993, pp. 1388–92). Most enclosures cannot be characterized as pure instances of norm change, however, because they were backed by governmental force.

48   Because norms themselves can affect the rate of innovation, in a more ambitious model technological change would be endogenous. But any model must keep some variables independent. For a succinct analysis of this methodological point, see Basu, Jones and Schlicht (1987, p. 3).

49   See also Bikhchandani, Hirshleifer, and Welch (1992, pp. 1011–12), which puts the tonsillectomy example to somewhat different use.

50   I treat a change in group composition as an exogenous event. In reality, concerns about norms may affect the make-up of groups. See Sunstein (1996b, pp. 919–20), which discusses how disgruntled persons may use the power of exit to form their own norm communities.

51   In an influential empirical study of commercial practices, Lisa Bernstein (1996) found that merchants apply "end-game norms" when they do not foresee the possibility of further interactions, but apply more cooperative "relationship-preserving norms" to resolve midgame disputes.

52   See Bernstein (1992, pp. 140, 143–44), which reports how advances in communications can broaden the domain in which a person has reputational stakes, and Hirschman (1982), which describes the seventeenth-century view that commerce is a civilizing agent.

53   See also Picker (1997, pp. 1250–51) (illustrating the possibility of rapid norm change).

54   See also Bikhchandani, Hirshleifer, and Welch (1998), which updates the theory.

55   Although all the characters in this scenario are presented as if they were distinct individuals, a person with the requisite attributes could assume a number of these roles simultaneously.

56   Statistics on declines in the adult smoking population can serve as a rough proxy for the rise of the antismoking norm. The percentage of American adults smoking fell from 42% in 1955 to 26% in 1991 (McAdams, 1997, p. 404 n. 219).

57   Legal scholars have devoted extensive attention to the evolution of norms governing smoking. See, for example, Lessig (1995, pp. 1025–34), McAdams (1997, pp. 404–07), and Rabin and Sugarman (1993).

58   There is broad agreement that the new information about health risks arising from smoking precipitated the decline in the number of smokers. See, for example, Gusfield (1993, pp. 54–60), and Zimring (1993, pp. 96–99). On the history of the diffusion of scientific information about the risks of smoking, see Hanson and Logue (1998, pp. 1181–1223), which asserts, among other things, that consumers still underestimate the risks of addiction to tobacco.

59   See Kagan and Skolnick (1993, p. 79), which describes how "visible elites" in the U.S. dropped smoking.

60   In this instance public officials were prominent among the key change agents. On the role of government in norm change, see text accompanying notes 88–99.

61   In the early- to mid-1980s, about two-thirds of men in Japan smoked, one-half in France did, and one-third in Canada and the United States did (Zimring, 1993, p. 98).

62   See Kagan and Vogel (1993, p. 34) (comparing smoking behavior of elites in France, Canada, and the U.S.).

63   Compare Lessig (1995, p. 1030) (downplaying the impact of new scientific information on smoking norms, on the ground that smoking has a different "social meaning" in Europe than in North America).

64   See Zimring (1993, p. 98) for a graph depicting a drop in France from 72% to 50%; in the U.S., from 53% to 35%; and in Canada, from 54% to 32%.

65   See also Schwartz, Baker, and Ryan (1984, pp. 330–31), which argues that a convention survives only if it serves a group's instrumental and symbolic goals. Sober and Wilson (1998, pp. 10–11, 170–73) refer to this perspective, with which they largely agree, as group functionalist.

66   See also Basu, Jones, and Schlicht (1987, pp. 8–12), Kraus (1997), and Roe (1996, pp. 651–52).

67   See generally McAdams (1997, pp. 355–75, 393–94) (analyzing how changes in information and enforcement costs would affect the evolution of norms).

68   See, for example, Cooter (1996, pp. 1684–85).

69   Cooter (1996, p. 1655) argues, more generally, that the law's willingness to defer to a group's custom should depend on the soundness, from a lawmaker's perspective, of the incentive structures that the group's members face.

70   The tugboat example is drawn from Judge Learned Hand's famous decision in *The T.J. Hooper*, which held that evidence that a firm had complied with industry custom did not conclusively prove that it had not been negligent. On the possibility that maritime customs will disserve outsiders, see Judge Richard Posner's opinion in *Rodi Yachts, Inc. v. National Marine, Inc.* (p. 888). See also Epstein (1992, p. 4) and Landes and Posner (1987, pp. 132–33), which articulates the more general proposition that custom is apt to be efficient where transaction costs are low but not where transactions costs are high.

71   If esteem is costless to confer, as McAdams supposes, an audience conceivably could provide it in infinite quantities, which would make its receipt valueless. Any esteem theory of norms therefore has to include a conception of how members of an audience budget esteem.

72   See Rabin (1998) for a review of evidence on this point.

73   As McAdams (1995, pp. 394–97) points out, a rapid cascade toward a new norm indicates that the old norm was not effectively internalized. Cascades thus are hard to square with the notion, mentioned in note 6, that internalization is a necessary condition for the existence of a norm.

74   Many of the new norms scholars discuss dueling. Besides the sources cited in this paragraph, see, for example, Lessig (1995, pp. 968–72) and E. Posner (1996a, pp. 1736–40).

75   This resembles the theory developed in Schwartz, Baker, and Ryan (1984). But compare Cohen and Vandello (1998, p. 570), which attributes the white South's enduring "culture of honor" (which excuses self-help violence to remedy an insult) to its origins as a herding society remote from law enforcers.

76   Game theorists use folk theorem to refer to the proposition that virtually any outcome is a Nash Equilibrium under conditions of repeat play. On the possibility of multiple stable equilibria in the context of norms, see Akerlof (1976) and Kuran (1998, pp. 641–46).

77   This possibility commands a wide consensus. See, for example, Cooter (1996, pp. 1687–88); McAdams (1997, pp. 409–24); E. Posner (1996a, pp. 1711–25), which discusses a variety of reasons why norms may lag behind technological

change; and R. Posner (1997, p. 366). For an elegant demonstration of this risk when automatons engage in repeat play, see Picker (1997, p. 1248).

78   On the potentially useful role of a government in coordinating a simultaneous switch to a new norm, see Posner and Rasmusen (1999, pp. 377–78).

79   A global optimum is more efficient than the status quo only if the reduction in deadweight losses attained by getting to the global optimum would exceed the incremental transaction costs incurred in making the move. See note 14.

80   See also Kahan (1997, pp. 352–61) on risks of herd behavior toward tax cheating, juvenile delinquency, and the like; Kraus (1997, p. 403), which draws on Boyd and Richerson's (1985) theory of the evolution of norms; McAdams (1997, pp. 412–24) on this and other varieties of inefficient norms; and Pesendorfer (1995), which develops a model in which cycling of fashions is wasteful.

81   See generally Cooter (1994, pp. 224–26) and McAdams (1997, p. 410) (describing how self-interest, voice, and exit all create pressures toward norm efficiency).

82   On the decline of female circumcision, see Crossette (1998).

83   As an optimist, I point to the rapid evolution of the network norms in the recorded music industry—from 78-RPM records to 33-RPM records, to tapes, to compact discs, to whatever the future will bring.

84   My analysis implies that the sum of a change agent's tangible benefits and esteem rewards would be positively correlated with his contributions to aggregate efficiency. As noted in Cooter (1996, pp. 1649, 1690–94), the notion that change agents disproportionately attack inefficient norms brings to mind the hypothesis, familiar to law-and-economics scholars, that litigants disproportionately challenge inefficient common law rules.

85   See also G. Becker (1996, pp. 225–30), which develops a model in which members of the upper class of a society instigate norm change and compensate those disadvantaged by the change.

86   In his stimulating article on norm evolution, Randal Picker (1997, pp. 1284–85) envisions institutions as having a special role in "seeding" experimental norms. This conclusion, however, flows entirely from the stylized structure of Picker's computerized tournament, not from any demonstrated advantages of institutions as change agents. In Picker's tournament, enforcers are unable to invent new norms but instead simply mimic the best strategy that they observe at work in their "information neighborhoods." Therefore, Picker's recommendation that institutions have a special role in seeding norms derives solely from his artificial assumption that individuals are incapable of supplying new norms. Compare the same at p. 1235, where Picker agrees that he has not provided a theory of the generation of new norms.

87   Rohacek (1998) analyzes how a private organization that generates public goods can provide material incentives to its activists.

88   Because my focus is on norm making, I do not discuss the use of governmental powers to supplant norms with law.

89   Members of the school share other common characteristics, notably an appreciation of the practical significance of norms and an interest in behavioral economics, the approach outlined in Jolls, Sunstein, and Thaler (1998).

90   For example, when externalities are not present, tugboat operators and their shippers are better than judges and jurors at determining the safety equipment that a tug should carry. See sources cited in note 70.

91   See, for example, Dau-Schmidt (1990), which primarily discusses how legal expressions can assist internalization of norms; and Sunstein (1996a), which

primarily explores the influence of law on the behavior of actors and enforcers. See also E. Posner(1998, pp. 793–97).

92   See "Opinion Pulse" (The American Enterprise, 1999), which reports that in 1998 about 20% of Gallup Poll respondents regarded the honesty and ethical standardsof elected officials at all levels of government as "high" or "very high"; these ratings were above those for lawyers (14%) but well below those for, say, bankers (30%), policemen (49%), and college instructors (53%). Tyler (1990, pp. 45–46) asserts that people tend to respect the law as such, even when they disagree with the morality that underlies it. Tyler's respondents, however, made highly favorable moral assessments of all six laws featured in his survey instrument (Tyler 1990, p. 44). If Tyler had included several immoral laws his findings might have changed.

93   See also text accompanying note 54 (sources on informational and reputational cascades).

94   For a variety of views on the appropriate scope of state regulation of norms, see McAdams (1997, pp. 351–432), E. Posner (1996a, pp. 1725–36), Posner and Rasmusen (1999, pp. 380–82), and Sunstein (1996b, pp. 948–50).

95   Some commentators urge governmental action to prevent wasteful arms races in signaling behavior. See Pesendorfer (1995, p. 786) (asserting that sumptuary legislation regulating clothing styles may enhance efficiency). But compare E. Posner (2000, p. 176) (skeptically assessing proposals to tax consumption of positional goods).

96   The definitive discussion is E. Posner (1996b); see also Picker (1997, pp. 1265–81, 1285–86).

97   See Kahan (1998, pp. 612–15) (recommending curfews and antiloitering laws that would make it harder for a gang to signal power to teenagers) and Kuran (1998) (discussing production of norms that sustain ethnic groups).

98   Some observers suppose that powerful factions can manipulate social norms in their favor. Marx saw the "ruling class" as able to inculcate a false consciousness in the masses. Some feminist scholars see males as having dominated the norm-making process to the detriment of women. On the possibility of interest-group capture of norms, see McAdams (1997, p. 416) and E. Posner (1996a, p. 1719).

99   Most law-and-economics scholars seem not to share the New Chicago School's relative confidence in the state. See, for example, Bernstein (1996, p. 157) (concluding that merchants' norms are superior to legal rules); Macey (1997, pp. 1137–49); Picker (1997, pp. 1284–88) (favoring government seeding of experimental norms, but not grander governmental interventions); E. Posner (1998, pp. 795–98) (seemingly retreating from a rosier view of state intervention expressed in E. Posner [1996a]); and Roe (1996, pp. 665–66). Compare Tushnet (1998, pp. 587–88) (stating that "culture is rather resistant to conscious manipulation, particularly by law").

100   See Bernstein (1992, 1996, 1999) and West (1997).

References

Akerlof, George. 1976. "The Economics of Caste and of the Rat Race and Other Woeful Tales," 90 Quarterly Journal of Economics 599–617.

Basu, Kaushik, Eric Jones, and Ekkehart Schlicht. 1987. "The Growth and Decay of Custom: The Role of the New Institutional Economics in Economic History," 24 Explorations in Economic History 1–21.

Becker, Gary S. 1996. *Accounting for Tastes*. Cambridge, MA: Harvard University Press.

Becker, Howard S. 1963. *Outsiders: Studies in the Sociology of Deviance*. New York: Free Press.

Bendor, Jonathan, and Piotr Swistak. Unpublished. "The Evolution of Norms," Stanford University.

Berelson, Bernard R., Paul F. Lazarsfeld, and William N. McPhee. 1954. *Voting*. Chicago: University of Chicago Press.

Bernheim, B. Douglas. 1994. "A Theory of Conformity," 102 *Journal of Political Economy* 841–77.

Bernstein, Lisa. 1992. "Opting Out of the Legal System: Extralegal Contractual Relations in the Diamond Industry," 21 *Journal of Legal Studies* 115–57.

—. 1996. "Merchant Law in a Merchant Court," 144 *University of Pennsylvania Law Review* 1796–1821.

—. 1999. "The Questionable Empirical Basis of Article 2's Incorporation Strategy: A Preliminary Study," 66 *University of Chicago Law Review* 710–80.

Bikhchandani, Sushil, David Hirshleifer, and Ivo Welch. 1992. A Theory of Fads, Fashions, Custom, and Cultural Change as Informational Cascades," 100 *Journal of Political Economy* 992–1026.

—. 1998. "Learning from the Behavior of Others: Conformity, Fads, and Informational Cascades," 12 *Journal of Economic Perspectives* 151–70.

Binmore, Ken G. 1998. "The Evolution of Fairness Norms," 10 *Rationality and Society* 275–301.

Bowles, Samuel, and Herbert Gintis. Unpublished. "The Evolution of Strong Reciprocity," University of Massachusetts, Amherst.

Boyd, Robert, and Peter J. Richerson. 1985. *Culture and the Evolutionary Process*. Chicago: University of Chicago Press.

Chong, Dennis. 1991. *Collective Action and the Civil Rights Movement*. Chicago: University of Chicago Press.

Clark, Robert C. 1989. "Contracts, Elites, and Traditions in the Making of Corporate Law," 89 *Columbia Law Review* 1703–47.

Coase, Ronald H. 1960. "The Problem of Social Cost" 3 *Journal of Law and Economics* 1–44.

Cohen, Dov, and Joe Vandello. 1998. "Meanings of Violence," 27 *Journal of Legal Studies* 567–84.

Coleman, James S. 1990. *Foundations of Social Theory*. Cambridge, MA: Harvard University Press.

Cooter, Robert D. 1994. "Structural Adjudication and the New Law Merchant: A Model of Decentralized Law," 14 *International Review of Law and Economics* 215–31.

—. 1996. "Decentralized Law for a Complex Economy: The Structural Approach to Adjudicating the New Law Merchant," 144 *University of Pennsylvania Law Review* 1643–96.

—. 1998. "Expressive Law and Economics," 27 *Journal of Legal Studies* 585–608.

Cover, Robert M. 1983. "The Supreme Court, 1982 Term—Foreword: *Nomos* and Narrative," 97 *Harvard Law Review* 4–68.

Crossette, Barbara. 1998. "A Uganda Tribe Fights Genital Cutting," *New York Times*, July 16, 1998, A8.

Damasio, Antonio R. 1994. *Descartes' Error: Emotion, Reason, and the Human Brain*. New York: G.P. Putnam.

Dau-Schmidt, Kenneth G. 1990. "An Economic Analysis of Criminal Law as a Preference-Shaping Policy," 1990 *Duke Law Journal* 1–38.

David, Paul A. 1985. "Clio and the Economics of QWERTY," 75 *American Economic Review* 332–37.

Davis, Lance E., Richard A. Easterlin, and William N. Parker. 1972. *American Economic Growth*. New York: Harper & Row.

Demsetz, Harold. 1967. "Toward a Theory of Property Rights," 57 *American Economic Review* 347–59.

Diamond, Jared. 1997. *Guns, Germs, and Steel*. New York: W. W. Norton.

Eckholm, Erik. 1998. "Village of Small Farmers Marks Own Great Leap," *New York Times*, September 19, A4.

Ellickson, Robert C. 1991. *Order Without Law*. Cambridge, MA: Harvard University Press.

——. 1993. "Property in Land," 102 *Yale Law Journal* 1315–1400.

Epstein, Richard A. 1992. "The Path to *The T. J. Hooper*: The Theory and History of Custom in the Law of Tort," 21 *Journal of Legal Studies* 1–38.

Gardner, Howard. 1995. *Leading Minds: An Anatomy of Leadership*. New York: BasicBooks.

Goldsmith, Jack L., and Eric A. Posner. 1999. "A Theory of Customary International Law," 66 *University of Chicago Law Review* 1113–77.

Gouldner, Alvin W., ed. 1950. *Studies in Leadership: Leadership and Democratic Action*. New York: Harper.

Griliches, Zvi. 1957. "Hybrid Corn: An Exploration in the Economics of Technological Change," 25 *Econometrica* 501–22.

Gusfield, Joseph R. 1993. "The Social Symbolism of Smoking and Health" in Robert L. Rabin and Stephen D. Sugarman, eds., *Smoking Policy: Law, Politics, and Culture*. New York: Oxford University Press.

Hanson, John D., and Kyle D. Logue. 1998. "The Costs of Cigarettes: The Economic Case for Ex Post Incentive Regulation," 107 *Yale Law Journal* 1163–1361.

Hasen, Richard L. 1996. "Voting Without Law," 144 *University of Pennsylvania Law Review* 2135–79.

Hermalin, Benjamin E. 1998. "Toward an Economic Theory of Leadership: Leading by Example," 88 *American Economic Review* 1188–1206.

Hirschman, Albert O. 1982. "Rival Interpretations of Market Society: Civilizing, Destructive, or Feeble?" 20 *Journal of Economic Literature* 1463–84.

Jolls, Christine, Cass R. Sunstein, and Richard Thaler. 1998. "A Behavioral Approach to Law and Economics," 50 *Stanford Law Review* 1471–1550.

Kagan, Robert A., and Jerome H. Skolnick. 1993. "Banning Smoking: Compliance Without Enforcement," in Robert L. Rabin and Stephen D. Sugarman, eds., *Smoking Policy: Law, Politics, and Culture*. New York: Oxford University Press.

Kagan, Robert A., and David Vogel. 1993. "The Politics of Smoking Regulation: Canada, France, the United States," in Robert L. Rabin and Stephen D. Sugarman, eds., *Smoking Policy: Law, Politics, and Culture*. New York: Oxford University Press.

Kahan, Dan M. 1997. "Social Influence, Social Meaning, and Deterrence," 83 *Virginia Law Review* 349–95.

——. 1998. "Social Meaning and the Economic Analysis of Crime," 27 *Journal of Legal Studies* 609–22.

Kandori, Michihiro, George J. Mailath, and Rafael Rob. 1993. "Learning, Mutation, and Long Run Equilibria in Games," 61 *Econometrica* 29–56.

Katz, Avery. 1996. "Taking Private Ordering Seriously," 144 *University of Pennsylvania Law Review* 1745–63.

Kraus, Jody S. 1997. "Legal Design and the Evolution of Commercial Norms," 26 *Journal of Legal Studies* 377–411.

Kuran, Timur. 1998. "Ethnic Norms and Their Transformation Through Reputational Cascades," 27 *Journal of Legal Studies* 623–59.

Kuran, Timur, and Cass R. Sunstein. 1999. "Availability Cascades and Risk Regulation," 51 *Stanford Law Review* 683–768.

Landes, William M., and Richard A. Posner. 1987. *The Economic Structure of Tort Law.* Cambridge, MA: Harvard University Press.

Lessig, Lawrence. 1995. "The Regulation of Social Meaning," 62 *University of Chicago Law Review* 943–1045.

—. 1998. "The New Chicago School," 27 *Journal of Legal Studies* 661–91.

Lewinsohn-Zamir, Daphna. 1998. "Consumer Preferences, Citizen Preferences, and the Provision of Public Goods," 108 *Yale Law Journal* 377–105.

Libecap, Gary D. 1989. *Contracting for Property Rights.* Cambridge: Cambridge University Press.

Liebowitz, S.J., and Stephen E. Margolis. 1990. "The Fable of the Keys," 33 *Journal of Law and Economics* 1–25.

Lionberger, Herbert F. 1960. *Adoption of New Ideas and Practices.* Ames: Iowa State University Press.

Macey, Jonathon R. 1997. "Public and Private Ordering and the Production of Legitimate and Illegitimate Rules," 82 *Cornell Law Review* 1123–49.

Margolis, Howard. 1982. *Selfishness, Altruism and Rationality.* New York: Cambridge University Press.

McAdams, Richard H. 1995. "Cooperation and Conflict: The Economics of Group Status Production and Race Discrimination," 108 *Harvard Law Review* 1003–84.

—. 1997. "The Origin, Development, and Regulation of Norms," 96 *Michigan Law Review* 3388–433.

Michelman, Frank I. 1967. "Property, Utility and Fairness: Comments on the Ethical Foundations of 'Just Compensation' Law," 80 *Harvard Law Review* 1165–1258.

Morriss, Andrew P. 1998. "Miners, Vigilantes and Cattlemen: Overcoming Free Rider Problems in the Private Provision of Law," 33 *Land and Water Law Review* 581–696.

Olson, Mancur. 1965. *The Logic of Collective Action.* Cambridge, MA: Harvard University Press.

"Opinion Pulse," 1999. *The American Enterprise.* (March/April) 90.

Pesendorfer, Wolfgang. 1995. "Design Innovations and Fashion Cycles," 85 *American Economic Review* 771–92.

Pettit, Philip. 1990. *"Virtus Normative.* Rational Choice Perspectives," 100 *Ethics* 725–55.

Picker, Randal C. 1997. "Simple Games in a Complex World: A Generative Approach to the Adoption of Norms," 64 *University of Chicago Law Review* 1225–88.

Posner, Eric A. 1996a. "Law, Economics, and Inefficient Norms" 144 *University of Pennsylvania Law Review* 1697–1744.

—. 1996b. "The Regulation of Groups: The Influence of Legal and Non-Legal Sanctions on Collective Action," 63 *University of Chicago Law Review* 133–97.

—. 1998. "Symbols, Signals and Social Norms in Politics and the Law," 27 *Journal of Legal Studies* 765–98.

—. 2000. *Law and Social Norms.* Cambridge, MA: Harvard University Press.

Posner, Richard A. 1997. "Social Norms and the Law: An Economic Approach," 87 *American Economic Review* 365–69.

—. 1998. "The Problematics of Moral and Legal Theory," 111 *Harvard Law Review* 1637–1717.

Posner, Richard A., and Eric B. Rasmusen. 1999. "Creating and Enforcing Norms, with Special Reference to Sanctions," 19 *International Review of Law and Economics* 369–82.

Rabin, Matthew. 1998. "Psychology and Economics," 36 *Journal of Economic Literature* 11–46.

Rabin, Robert L., and Stephen D. Sugarman, eds. 1993. *Smoking Policy: Law, Politics, and Culture.* New York: Oxford University Press.

Ridley, Matt. 1996. *The Origins of Virtue.* London: Viking.

Rock, Edward B., and Michael L. Wachter. 1996. "The Enforceability of Norms and the Employment Relationship," 144 *University of Pennsylvania Law Review* 1913–52.

Rodi Yachts, Inc. v. National Marine, Inc., 984 F. 2d 880 (7th Cir. 1993).

Roe, Mark J. 1996. "Chaos and Evolution in Law and Economics," 109 *Harvard Law Review* 641–68.

Rogers, Everett M. 1983. *Diffusion of Innovations*, 3rd ed. New York: Free Press.

Rohacek, Jerry K. 1998. "Revolutionary Armies, Labor Unions, and Free-Riders: Organization, Power, and In-Kind Benefits," 3 *Independent Review* 229–41.

Schelling, Thomas C. 1960. *The Strategy of Conflict.* Cambridge, MA: Harvard University Press.

—. 1978. *Micromotives and Macrobehavior.* New York: W. W. Norton.

Schneider, Mark, Paul Teske, and Michael Mintrom. 1995. *Public Entrepreneurs: Agents for Change in American Government.* Princeton, NJ: Princeton University Press.

Schwartz, Warren F., Keith Baker, and David Ryan. 1984. "The Duel: Can These Gentlemen Be Acting Efficiently?" 13 *Journal of Legal Studies* 321–55.

Smith, Adam [1759] 1982. *The Theory of Moral Sentiments.* D. D. Raphael and A. L. Macfie, eds. New York: Oxford University Press.

Sober, Eiliott, and David Sloan Wilson. 1998. *Unto Others: The Evolution and Psychology of Unselfish Behavior.* Cambridge, MA: Harvard University Press.

Spence, A. M. 1974. *Market Signaling.* Cambridge, MA: Harvard University Press.

Sulloway, Frank J. 1996. *Born to Rebel: Birth Order, Family Dynamics and Creative Lives.* New York: Pantheon Books.

Sunstein, Cass R. 1996a. "On the Expressive Function of Law," 144 *University of Pennsylvania Law Review* 2021–53.

—. 1996b. "Social Norms and Social Roles," 96 *Columbia Law Review* 903–68.

The T. J. Hooper, 60 F. 2d 737 (2d Cir. 1932).

Tushnet, Mark. 1998. "'Everything Old Is New Again': Early Reflections on the 'New Chicago School,'" 1998 *Wisconsin Law Review* 579–90.

Tyler, Tom R. 1990. *Why People Obey the Law.* New Haven: Yale University Press.

West, Mark D. 1997. "Legal Rules and Social Norms in Japan's Secret World of Sumo," 26 *Journal of Legal Studies* 165–201.

Wills, Garry. 1984. *Cincinnatus: George Washington and the Enlightenment.* Garden City, NY: Doubleday.

Zimring, Franklin E. 1993. "Comparing Cigarette Policy and Illicit Drug and Alcohol Control," in Robert L. Rabin and Stephen D. Sugarman, eds., *Smoking Policy: Law, Politics, and Culture.* New York: Oxford University Press.

Chapter 7

H. Peyton Young

THE ECONOMICS OF CONVENTION

C ONVENTIONS REGULATE much of economic and social life, yet
they have received surprisingly little attention from economists.[1] By a *convention*,
we mean a pattern of behavior that is customary, expected and self-enforcing. Everyone
conforms, everyone expects others to conform, and everyone has good reason to
conform because conforming is in each person's best interest when everyone else
plans to conform (Lewis, 1969). Familiar examples include following rules of the
road, adhering to conventional codes of dress and using words with their conventional
meanings. Conventions with direct economic implications include species of money
and credit, industrial and technological standards, accounting rules and forms of economic contracts. Indeed, it would scarcely be an exaggeration to say that almost all
economic and social institutions are governed to some extent by convention.

The main feature of a convention is that, out of a host of conceivable choices, only
one is actually used. This fact also explains why conventions are needed: they resolve
problems of indeterminacy in interactions that have multiple equilibria. Indeed, from
a formal point of view, we may *define* a convention as an equilibrium that everyone
expects in interactions that have more than one equilibrium.

The economic significance of conventions is that they reduce transaction costs.
Imagine the inconvenience if, whenever two vehicles approached one another, the
drivers had to get out and negotiate which side of the road to take. Or consider the
cost of having to switch freight from one type of railroad car to another whenever
a journey involves both a wide-gauge and a narrow-gauge railroad line. This was
a common circumstance in the nineteenth century and not unknown in the late
twentieth: until recently, Australia had different rail gauges in the states of New South
Wales and Victoria, forcing a mechanical switch for all trains bound between Sydney
and Melbourne.

Conventions are also a notable feature of legal contracts. People rely on standard
leases, wills, purchasing agreements, construction contracts and the like, because it is

less costly to fill in the blanks of a standard contract than to create one from scratch. Even more important, such agreements are backed up by legal precedent, so the signatories have greater confidence that their terms are enforceable.

We may discern two ways in which conventions become established. One is by central authority. Following the French Revolution, for example, it was decreed that horse-drawn carriages in Paris should keep to the right. The previous custom had been for carriages to keep left and for pedestrians to keep right, facing the oncoming traffic. Changing the custom was symbolic of the new order: going on the left had become politically incorrect because it was identified with the privileged classes; going on the right was the habit of the common man and therefore more "democratic."[2]

In Britain, by contrast, there seems to have been no single defining event that gave rise to the dominant convention of left-hand driving. Rather, it grew up by local custom, spreading from one region to another. This is the second mechanism by which conventions become established: the gradual accretion of precedent.

The two mechanisms are not mutually exclusive, of course. Society often converges on a convention first by an informal process of accretion; later it is codified into law. In many countries, rules of the road were not legislated until the nineteenth century, but by this time the law was merely reiterating what had already become established custom.

This paper examines the process by which conventions emerge through the second mechanism—the accumulation of precedent. The intuitive idea is that, as an interaction is repeated over and over by many different individuals, one particular way of resolving the interaction gains an edge through chance. This lends it greater prominence, which means that more people hear about it, which leads to more people using it, and so forth. A positive feedback loop is created. Eventually one way of doing things drives out the others, not because it is inherently better, but because historical circumstances gave it an early lead that allowed it to pull ahead of the rest.[3]

In this paper I propose to analyze the process of forming conventions by an evolutionary "bottom up" model. The paper begins with a game-theoretic description of how individuals make choices at the micro level. Unlike traditional game theory, however, we will not assume that people have unlimited powers of calculation and foresight. Instead we shall be dealing with people who are boundedly rational and take the world around them as given. Over time their dispersed and uncoordinated decisions interact in ways that they do not necessarily foresee. The question is whether these interactions eventually converge to a convention. If so, how long does it take? Can similar societies converge to different conventions? Are some conventions more likely to be observed than others? We shall sketch out a model that can be used to answer these questions and then offer some applications.

Right or left

Let's begin with a simple example. It is the middle of the eighteenth century, the place is the English countryside, and two horse-drawn carriages are rapidly approaching one other from opposite directions. (Since the roads are bad, both are probably hogging the middle.) The choices for the coachmen are to pass on the left or on the right.

Assume for the moment that there is no established convention or law to help them decide what to do. This interaction can be viewed as a one-shot game with payoffs of the following form:

	L	R
L	1,1	0,0
R	0,0	1,1

This game has three equilibria: both go left, both go right or both randomize with 50–50 probability between left and right.

Classical game theory does not give a coherent account of how people would play a game like this. The problem is that there is nothing in the structure of the game itself that allows the players—even purely rational players—to deduce what they ought to do. How then do people (rational or otherwise) actually play such games? The answer is that they rely on contextual cues that lie outside the game per se that allow them to coordinate on a particular equilibrium. Schelling (1960) called these cues *focal points*. The relevant focal points cannot be defined a priori; they depend on the coordination problem at hand and on the culture in which the players are embedded. Schelling observed that people are usually remarkably good at knowing what the salient focal points are even though they may be quite idiosyncratic to a given situation. However, he did not explain how they come into being. This is the problem that this paper seeks to address.

In the case of our two coachmen, it is reasonable to suppose that the relevant focal points are provided by precedent. They know from personal experience (and from talking with others) whether coaches tend to pass on the left or on the right. If their information is that coaches usually pass on the left, then it makes sense to go left; if they usually pass on the right, it makes sense to go right. Note that this reasoning does not require them to be especially rational. Each operates on the assumption that the world around them is going to continue today much as it did yesterday, which makes information about precedents relevant. Nor do they need to conjecture *why* people are doing what they are doing. They simply assume that others are going to follow previous patterns. Note also that they are typically making their decisions on the basis of very incomplete information. A coachman cannot know in practice what happened in all previous encounters between two coaches; he knows about a few cases, which lead him to develop expectations about what the oncoming coach is going to do.

An evolutionary model of convention formation

Let us now step back from this example and consider the problem of convention formation more generally. A number of individuals face a one-shot game that is played repeatedly by different players drawn from a large population. The payoffs may depend on who is playing, but the rules and strategies of the game are fixed. We assume that the players are boundedly rational and only partially informed. They do not have perfect foresight, they do not know in detail the structure of the process they are engaged in, and they do not know why other players are acting the way they are. Instead, they use simple rules of thumb to adjust their behavior based on their information about what other players are currently doing or have done in previous periods. Furthermore, there are unexplained variations in their behavior that play a role analogous to mutations in biological evolution. These three elements—local interaction between individuals, boundedly rational responses to the perceived environment, and random perturbations—define an "evolutionary game dynamic."

To be concrete, we shall describe the evolutionary process in terms of a two-person coordination game, though in fact the model extends easily to general n-person games (Young, 1993a). In each time period, one pair of players is drawn at random from the population to play the game. We shall assume for simplicity that all pairs are equally likely to be drawn, though this is not essential. (Later we shall consider variations in which players only meet their neighbors.) The expectations of the players are governed by the history of the process up to that time, where the "history" is simply a list of all pairs of agents who have played so far and the actions that they took.

Players obtain information about the history in two ways—from their personal experiences and from information they pick up from others. For example, a coachman, in talking with his friends at the local inn, hears about encounters they had with oncoming carriages in the recent past. In addition, he may have had some encounters himself, but let's assume for the moment that he has not been driving for awhile or is new on the job. He also may hear about incidents that occurred years ago, but disregards these as being outdated.

Among the encounters he knows about, suppose that more than half the carriages attempted to take the right side of the road. Our coachman then predicts that, when he next meets a carriage on the road, the probability is better than 50–50 that it will go right. Given this expectation, it is best for him to go right also (assuming that the payoffs are symmetric between left and right).

This behavioral rule can be generalized as follows. Let m (memory) be the maximum number of time periods that an agent looks back into the past. Assume for simplicity that in each period there is exactly one encounter and that each person hears about a certain number of prior encounters through word of mouth. A convenient way to model this way of acquiring information is to suppose that the agent draws a random sample from the last m encounters. The sample size s reflects the size of the agent's informational network and is an inherent property of the agent, not a result of an optimal search. Based on this information, he calculates the observed frequency distribution of left and right, and uses this to predict the probability that the next carriage he meets will go left or right. He then chooses a best reply. We shall call this behavioral rule "best reply to recent sample evidence."

While this rule seems reasonable enough, it does not seem likely that agents would always follow it (or any other) rule exactly. There will always be unexplained variation in their behavior—ways in which our predictions fail to capture what agents actually do. We model this unexplained behavior by a random variable. Let's say that with some small probability ε an agent chooses randomly between left and right, while with probability $1-\varepsilon$ he adopts a best reply to recent sample evidence. In reality, of course, there will almost always be a specific reason why an agent acts the way he does. But this is like saying there is always a reason why a coin lands heads instead of tails—air currents, initial spin, height of throw and so forth. Since these effects cannot be known or predicted in advance, it is appropriate to model their aggregate impact as a random variable.

To illustrate concretely how such an evolutionary process works, let people's potential memory reach back 10 periods *(m* = 10), and suppose that each agent knows about only three of the past 10 encounters *(s* = 3). Finally, let's assume that there is one chance in a hundred that an agent chooses randomly, so that $\varepsilon = 1/100$. Suppose that people managed to coordinate on left for each of the last 10 periods. Then we have the following situation, where decisions of one player are on the top row and decisions of the other are on the bottom row, and time is moving from left to right:

LLLLLLLLLL

LLLLLLLLLL

This pattern represents a convention because it perpetuates itself when agents always choose best replies given their information. The reason is that, no matter what agents arrive on the scene next period, and no matter what particular precedents they know about from the above history, left is necessarily a best reply. It is an "absorbing state" in the sense that, once reached, the process never leaves it.

When the possibility of mistakes is introduced, however, the process has no absorbing states; there is always a chance that someone will take an unconventional action. For example, if society is in the left convention, several agents may nevertheless try to go right (with possibly disastrous results). If enough instances of right accumulate through random variation, the process will tip into the basin of attraction of the right convention, which then gains ground purely by best-reply dynamics. In this particular example, it suffices that three agents choose right in order to tip the process into the right convention. For example, we might obtain the following configuration by chance:

LLLLLLLLRR

LLLLLLLLLR

Now suppose a newcomer enters the scene in the next period and samples three of the previous encounters at random. By chance these might include the two most recent encounters and one other. Thus, out of the six carriages he has heard about, three went to the right. This leads him to conclude that left and right driving are equally popular. (As a newcomer, he has no experience of his own to modify this conclusion.) This leaves him indifferent between going left and right, so we can say that there is a 50–50 probability he will choose right the next time he meets an oncoming coach. However, the same reasoning holds for the agent who is driving toward him: there is a positive probability that he will also sample the last two encounters and choose right in response. Note that neither is making a mistake in doing so; both are acting rationally based on their information. Thus with positive probability we obtain the following situation in the next period:

LLLLLLLRRR

LLLLLLLLRR

Observe that the left-most pair L, L has been deleted because each record disappears after it is more than 10 periods old. At this point it should be clear that, within eight more periods, there is a positive probability of reaching a situation where for the preceding 10 periods that lie within memory, both players have always chosen the right side. This is the right-hand convention. In other words, three idiosyncratic choices ("mistakes") were sufficient to create a situation in which rational choices after that point could, with positive probability, tip the process out of the left convention and into the right convention. The crucial point is that, when the probability ε of making a mistake is small, and mistakes are made independently, the probability of tipping out of one convention and into the other is on the order of ε^3. This is because all the subsequent events needed to reach the opposite convention have much higher probability than the original three mistakes when ε is sufficiently small.

Simplified as this account may be compared to the decision situations that people actually face, it does capture three crucial elements of such decisions: they are based on limited information, the decision makers are boundedly rational, and there is unexplained variation in their behavior.

Moreover, the model yields several important qualitative predictions. It says that even if we know the initial state of society, we cannot predict what the prevailing convention will be at each future date. To put the matter differently, if two societies start off under similar initial conditions, there is a positive probability that at any given future time they will be operating different conventions. Such a process is said to be *path dependent*.

Unlike some of the path-dependent processes hypothesized in the literature on technological adoption, however, this model does not exhibit lock-in. It is path dependent in the short run but not in the long run. The reason is that, in our model, past decisions are eventually forgotten. This reduces the inertia to change and means that every so often society "flips" from one convention to another.[4] These incidents are triggered by repeated stochastic shocks to the system that we have modeled as unexplained behaviors. Over a long period of time, these shocks generate an ergodic process; in other words, there is statistical regularity in the frequency with which different states are observed *independent of the initial conditions*.

It can be shown that, if all agents have a positive probability of interacting, if they have sufficiently incomplete information and if random deviations have sufficiently low probability, then most of the time most of the population will be using the same convention (Young, 1993a; Kandori, Mailath and Rob, 1993).[5] We call this the *local conformity effect*. It does not say that the world is in equilibrium *all* of the time, but within a community of interacting agents it is close to equilibrium *most* of the time.

Now compare several communities that are alike in every way except that they do not interact with one another (for example they might be located on separate islands). If we run the process in each starting from similar initial conditions, then at any sufficiently distant future time there is a positive probability that they will be using different conventions. This is the *global diversity effect*.

While a convention tends to remain in place for a long period of time once it is established, it will eventually be dislodged by a series of random shocks. Society then careens toward a new convention, which also tends to remain in force for a long time. Similar dynamics are observed in biological evolution where random mutations occasionally give rise to new species that displace the old ones in a rush. This is known as the *punctuated equilibrium effect*.

Is there any evidence that conventions actually do follow a dynamic process characterized by these three effects? In the remainder of the paper we shall consider evidence from two quite different sources—the evolution of rules of the road and norms in distributive bargaining.

Rules of the road

Before about 1750, there was relatively little vehicular traffic on the roadways of Europe, and what traffic there was tended to keep to the center to avoid falling into the ditch.[6] To the extent that left-right conventions existed at all, they appear to have been highly localized. The earliest mention of definite rules is for major bridges. In the year 1300, for example, Pope Boniface VIII issued an edict that pilgrims to Rome should keep to the left when crossing the Ponte Sant'Angelo. In 1736, Saxony decreed that traffic should keep to the right on a new bridge over the River Elbe. In 1756, the English Parliament passed a law requiring vehicles on London Bridge to keep left.

Whether seeded by such local decrees, or arrived at by a process of individual trial and error, these local rules gradually diffused more widely, until they were established at the regional and then national level. At this point we can think of nations, rather than individuals, as the principal actors in the convention game. If a nation is surrounded by countries who are following a different convention, it may have an incentive to switch to a rule that conforms with its neighbors.

The surprising fact is, however, that until the end of the eighteenth century, the dominant convention in much of western Europe was for horse-drawn carriages to keep *left*. Great Britain, France, Sweden, Portugal, Austria, Hungary, Bohemia and parts of Italy and Germany drove left, and some continued to do so until well into this century. How then did continental Europe evolve to mostly right-hand driving today?

The answer is through a chain of historical accidents that gradually tipped the balance in favor of right. As we have already mentioned, France switched to right-hand driving after the Revolution for symbolic reasons. Napoleon then adopted this convention for his armies and imposed it in some of the countries he occupied. This set a train of events in motion that eventually caused other countries to switch. Portugal, which shares a border with right-driving Spain, converted after the First World War. The western-most provinces of Austria (Vorarlberg and Tyrol, which are sandwiched in between Germany, Switzerland and Italy) adopted the right-hand rule in the nineteenth century. The rest of Austria followed suit province by province in the 1920s, though the changeover was not completed until the *Anschluss* with Germany in 1938. (Hungary and Czechoslovakia also switched to the right-hand rule under German occupation.) Historically, Italy was a jumble of conflicting customs, with traffic in some cities keeping to the left, and traffic in much of the countryside keeping to the right. This situation was not straightened out until the 1930s. By the 1960s, only Sweden (among continental European countries) was driving on the left, and it switched over in 1967. While each of these cases has its particular explanation, the general impetus for change is clear: the more countries who adopt the same convention, the more likely it is that the others will follow suit.

One way to think about this process is to introduce a neighborhood structure into our earlier model.[7] The players in the game are now countries which have specific geographical locations. Let us represent each country by a point and draw an edge between two countries if they share a common border (see Figure 7.1). On each edge there is cross-border traffic, and a cost is incurred by the two countries on either side of the border if they have conflicting rules of the road. Suppose that in each time period one country is drawn at random, and it asks itself whether it should switch.

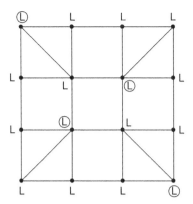

Figure 7.1 A schematic map of countries (nodes) and border crossings (edges)

Let's assume that it does switch provided that its total costs, summed over all the edges adjacent to it, would go down. (We ignore the cost of switching due to the need for new infrastructure; this changes the details of the following discussion but not its substance.)

What are the equilibrium configurations of such an adjustment process? One is the situation in which all countries are using the same convention, as in Figure 7.1. But this is not the only possibility. For example, one could have an equilibrium in which two different conventions hold sway in regions that are weakly connected, as shown in Figure 7.2. It is also possible for two conventions to coexist even if the interconnections are quite dense. This situation is shown in Figure 7.3, where the countries form two blocks—one driving left, the other going right. If we assume there is an equal amount of traffic on each edge, there is no incentive for any one country to switch, because each is adjacent to more countries using the same convention than to countries using the opposite one. This shows how conflicting conventions can exist side by side.

The story changes, though, if we suppose that countries occasionally switch convention at random, that is, for reasons outside the model. (The French Revolution is an example.) In this case the process exhibits punctuated equilibrium behavior: an established configuration can give way to another when enough random changes accumulate to push the process out of the basin of attraction of one equilibrium and into the basin of attraction of another. In Figure 7.3, for example, it takes at least two switches to destabilize the equilibrium: if the circled countries shift to right-hand

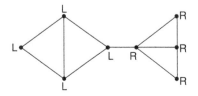

Figure 7.2 A bottleneck separating two regions using different conventions

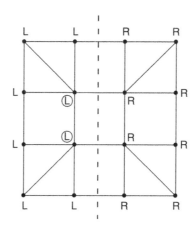

Figure 7.3 The left convention changes to right when the circled countries switch

driving, then it is rational for the countries above and below it to switch to right-hand driving also, and the right convention eventually spreads across the board.

Compare this to the situation in which, at first, *all* countries are using the left convention and then a few switch to the right. The reader may check that it takes at least four switches (for example, the circled ones in Figure 7.1) to drive the left convention off the board.

This argument suggests the general proposition that it is easier to destabilize side-by-side conventions than to destabilize a uniform convention; hence a uniform convention will be more stable over the long run. With some additional hypotheses, this assertion can be proved rigorously using techniques borrowed from statistical mechanics (Blume, 1993). Suppose that the probability of a country switching to a new convention is proportional to ε^p, where p equals the difference in cost between the new convention and what the country is doing now, and "cost" is proportional to the amount of traffic crossing into neighboring countries with conflicting conventions. A country is therefore less likely to switch if the cost of doing so is high, but there is some probability it will switch anyway for idiosyncratic reasons. Finally, let us assume that the graph is connected, that is, one can drive from any country to any other. It can be shown that when ε is small, the probability that all countries are following the same convention is substantially higher over the long run than the probability of a side-by-side equilibrium in which some use one convention and some the other. Moreover, this result holds for any two competing conventions (not just left-right driving) when the agents' decisions are governed only by what their neighbors are doing (An and Kiefer, 1993). Of course this result addresses only the long-run behavior of the adjustment process; in the short to medium run, less stable transient patterns may well be observed.

While the model described above is quite simple, the evolutionary pattern of rules of the road is consistent with the qualitative effects it predicts. First, local communities and regions usually have a single, well-established convention (local conformity). Second, communities that do not interact may operate under different conventions (global diversity). Third, an established convention is not locked in forever; if we wait long enough, it will eventually be displaced by chance events that tip the process into a new regime (punctuated equilibrium). Indeed, prompted by the French Revolution, we have probably been witnessing just such a shift from left to right driving over the last couple of hundred years.

Norms in distributive bargaining

We turn now to distributive bargaining, a different arena in which conventions play an important role. When two people bargain over their shares of a common "pie," in what proportions do they divide it? In this case, the evolutionary model predicts quantitative as well as qualitative outcomes.

Let us first recall what classical theory has to say about the problem. In the model advanced by Nash (1950, 1953), the outcome of a distributive bargain depends principally on the alternatives of the parties and their aversion to risk. A person who is risk neutral and has a good fallback position will tend to get a better deal than someone who is risk averse and has unattractive alternatives, all else being equal.[8] To the extent that people vary in their opportunities and preferences, the theory predicts that we can expect to see considerable variation in the shares that they negotiate.

However, this is often not what we see in practice. What is missing from the above account are social norms and customs that point the bargainers toward particular solutions. By a *distributive bargaining norm* we mean shares that are customary and expected for the parties in a given bargaining situation. The effect of these norms is to lend greater uniformity and predictability to bargaining outcomes than classical theory predicts. For example, if two people are given a sum of money to divide in a laboratory setting, they almost invariably divide it 50–50 (Nydegger and Owen, 1974). But if they earn it by contributing different amounts of effort or skill, they may divide according to some other norm (for example, in proportion to their contributions).[9]

More generally, experimental evidence shows that bargainers can be conditioned by the experimental setup to expect a particular outcome, which is then reinforced as it is played over and over again. This solution becomes a norm that the subjects rationalize afterwards as being "fair," even though it may be idiosyncratic to the particular history of play experienced by a particular group (Roth, 1987; Binmore, 1991; Binmore, Swierzbinski, Hsu and Proulx, 1993).

The same holds in real-world bargaining situations: norms condition the parties to expect certain outcomes that depend on the bargaining context. In the United States, for example, a lawyer who takes a malpractice suit on a contingency basis conventionally gets one-third of the award, and the client gets two-thirds. Real-estate agents customarily get 6 percent of the sale price of a house. Of course, people use such sharing contracts because they give agents an incentive to work diligently on behalf of their clients. But there seems to be no economic justification for the *particular* shares that we observe. If there were, we would expect the shares to fluctuate like prices under changing supply and demand conditions, but this is not the case. Rather, the shares appear to be conventions that got an early start through chance events and remain in place because they succeed in conditioning the parties' expectations. (There may also be implicit collusion in some of these markets that helps keep the norm in place.)

A particularly telling example occurs in sharecropping. A sharecropping contract specifies the fractions of the harvest for the landowner and the laborer who works his land. Such contracts are widely used in agricultural societies, both primitive and advanced, and they have been extensively studied by agricultural economists. One of the reasons why the parties favor sharecropping contracts is that they divide the risk of crop failure more evenly than a pure wage or rental contract would (Stiglitz, 1974). However, the issue that concerns us here is not the *form* of the contract but its *terms*. A striking feature of sharecropping is how little variation there is in contracts involving different bargainers, different soil qualities, different sizes of plots, and even different crops. For example, Bardhan (1984) analyzes extensive survey data on sharecropping practices in certain regions of India for paddy and wheat. He finds that, in a sample of over 300 villages, more than two-thirds had a single type of contract within the village, and over 95 percent had at most two forms of contract within the village. While some differences exist in the terms of individual contracts, he concludes (p. 115) that there is little evidence that the outcome is very sensitive to the relative bargaining power between tenants and landowners, their degrees of risk aversion or even the size of the farm.

A second significant feature of sharecropping contracts is that the terms vary substantially from one village to another, even between villages that are similar in other respects like soil type, rainfall, scale of land holdings, and so on. Thus in village *A* the rule may be one-third for the landlord and two-thirds for the laborer, while in village *B* some distance away it is half-half, and for village *C* it is two-thirds for the landlord and one-third for the tenant. Moreover, substantial differences between villages hold up when one looks at the real incomes of tenants and landlords instead of the shares themselves (Bardhan, 1984, ch. 4; Bardhan and Rudra, 1986). Of course, such disparities can persist only if labor is relatively immobile, but this appears to be the case: personal connections, local credit arrangements, and differences in dialect and culture substantially limit the mobility of laborers outside of a small area.

Perhaps the most striking feature of the data, however, is the prevalence of equal split between labor and land. In over two-thirds of the villages Bardhan surveyed, 50–50 was the dominant form of contract, and in most of these cases it was the only form of contract (Bardhan, 1984, Table 9.3). There is nothing in classical bargaining theory—or for that matter in classical economic theory—that would predict these results.[10] It is not even clear why 50–50 would be a prominent focal point when the parties are in such obviously asymmetric positions.

We can shed some light on these matters by adopting an evolutionary point of view. Imagine that the agents in each village are boundedly rational and myopic. They do the sensible thing most of the time—that is, they optimize up to a point—but their information is limited, and they have little ability to anticipate how future events are going to unfold. Assume now that when two agents come to the bargaining table their expectations are shaped by precedent, that is, by what they and others like them have received in recent bargains. If almost all landlords in the area get three-fifths, for example, then it is reasonable to expect that the landlord in this case will insist on three-fifths. Similarly, the laborer (knowing the landlord's expectations) will find it reasonable to insist on no more than two-fifths. Thus a positive feedback loop is created—precedents affect present expectations, which determine current actions, which in turn become future precedents. All of this is subject to random perturbations that arise from misperceptions, miscalculations, changing economic circumstances and other unpredictable forces that buffet the process about.

As we have already seen, this kind of dynamic process exhibits the following qualitative behavior. First, within a given village where interactions are frequent, we can expect that most people will be using the same rule most of the time (local conformity). Second, in villages that do not interact, the prevailing conventions may differ—depending on the historical path the process follows—even though they have similar resource endowments (global diversity). Third, every so often the local convention may suddenly shift in response to accumulated stochastic shocks (punctuated equilibrium). The data on India do not cover a long enough period to test this last prediction, but they certainly are consistent with the first two effects.

Moreover, the evolutionary model predicts something else. It says that when the perturbations are fairly small, one particular equilibrium (or one class of equilibria) will be observed more often than the others. These equilibria are *stochastically stable*, that is, they are robust under small, persistent random shocks (Foster and Young, 1990).[11] In discussing rules of the road, for instance, we saw that a globally uniform convention is more stable over the long run than two opposing conventions side by side, even though both are equilibria in a static sense. In the bargaining problem, it turns out that an even more striking result holds, namely, one division of the pie is more stable than the others. To understand why, let us focus on a particular village and suppose that in each period one landlord and one tenant must negotiate a contract. We model the one-shot bargaining game as follows. The landlord demands x, and the tenant demands y. If their demands are mutually compatible $(x + y \leq 1)$, each side gets what it asked for. If the demands are incompatible $(x + y > 1)$, the negotiation breaks down, and they get nothing. This is known as the Nash demand game (Nash, 1953). Notice that for every value of x strictly between zero and one, the outcome in which the landlord demands x and the tenant demands $1 - x$ is a strict Nash equilibrium of this game.

To simplify the argument, assume that each side has only three possible demands—high (3/4), medium (1/2) and low (1/4). Assume further that the payoff to each bargainer is proportional to the share of the crop he gets, that is, the parties are risk neutral. Then the payoff matrix is as follows:

		Tenants		
		H	M	L
	H	0, 0	0, 0	75, 25
Landlords	M	0, 0	50, 50	50, 25
	L	25, 75	25, 50	25, 25

There are three possible conventions: 1/4 : 3/4, 3/4 : 1/4, and 1/2 : 1/2, where we list the landlord's share first and the tenant's second.

To determine the stochastically stable convention, we must compute the probability that enough stochastic shocks accumulate to push the community out of one convention and into another, and we must do this for every pair of conventions. As before, we assume that agents make their choices based on information acquired by word of mouth and personal experience. Occasionally they make idiosyncratic, unexplained choices that function like mutations. Assume for simplicity that each bargainer knows the demands that were made in *s* out of the previous *m* bargains (whether these demands were compatible or not). He uses this information to predict how much the other side is likely to demand and chooses a best reply with probability $1 - \varepsilon$. However, with probability ε he demands 3/4, 1/2, or 1/4 at random. (When an agent chooses randomly, we may assume that all actions are chosen with equal probability, though the analysis does not depend on this assumption.)

To illustrate, suppose that the sample size is $s = 12$, $\varepsilon = .01$, and the current convention is 3/4 : 1/4. No matter which of the precedents appear in an agent's sample, the best reply is to choose 3/4 if the agent is a landlord and 1/4 if he is a tenant. To destabilize this convention requires that some agents choose something unconventional. Suppose that four tenants in succession demand 1/2 instead of 1/4. If the next landlord samples the most recent data, he may be led to believe that tenants demand 1/2 one-third of the time (because his sample has four out of 12 instances of this), and that they demand 1/4 two-thirds of the time. A best reply to this situation is 1/2. The same decision could be made by the next landlord, and the next after that and so forth. After enough landlords have demanded 1/2, tenants who sample this information will rationally demand 1/2. Thus the original four mistakes (whose probability is ε^4) can tip the process from the 3/4: 1/4 regime to the 1/2:1/2 regime.

It can be checked, however, that it takes at least six mistakes to go the other way, that is, to tip out of the 1/2: 1/2 convention into either of the others. Figure 7.4 shows the transition probabilities as a function of ε and s between every two conventions (when $s/2$ or $s/3$ are fractional, they are rounded to the next higher integer). When ε is small the probability of getting out of 1/2: 1/2 is substantially lower than the probability of getting in. It follows that, when ε is sufficiently small (and s is sufficiently large), the process is much more likely to be in the 1/2: 1/2 convention than in either of the others.[12]

This result generalizes as follows. Suppose that i) all agents are risk neutral or risk averse; ii) for every landlord with a given utility function there is a positive probability that the laborer against whom he is matched has the same utility function and vice versa; iii) all agents have the same amount of information s, which is sufficiently large and sufficiently incomplete $(s/m \leq .5)$; and iv) the agents can demand any decimal fraction of the pie, where the demands are rounded to some fixed number of decimal places to keep the state space finite. Then a 1/2: 1/2 split is the unique stochastically stable convention (Young, 1993b).

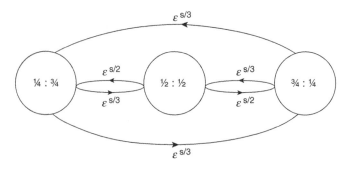

Figure 7.4 Transition probabilities between conventions

Concretely, this means the following. Suppose the evolutionary process is run in each of 100 villages starting from arbitrary initial conditions and with no communication between the villages. Then after a sufficiently long period of time, 50–50 will be the dominant mode of division in most (though not necessarily all) of the villages. This is quite consistent with the pattern we see in the data.

Of course other explanations for the prevalence of 50–50 are possible. The parties may simply consider 50–50 to be the "fairest" solution. Or they may select it because it is ' "focal" (Schelling, 1960). On reflection, however, it is not clear why anyone would consider equal division to be either fair or focal when the bargainers contribute such different inputs to the production process. Nor would one expect focal points to play such an important role when the stakes are so high. Yet it appears that they do.

We can make sense of these facts by viewing focal points as the outcome of an evolutionary process of expectations formation. Something comes to be focal; it is not necessarily focal in itself. Using a relatively simple model, we have shown that some norms are more likely to be observed than others—not because they are more prominent, or more natural, or more ethical *a priori*, but simply because they are more *stable* in the long run. We may even conjecture that long-run stable solutions, like equal division, acquire some of their ethical force *because* of their inherent stability.

These results do not hinge on unrealistically strong assumptions about rationality and common knowledge; nor do they presuppose that individuals can foresee all the results of their (and others') actions. At the same time, we do not dispense with rationality altogether. Instead, we think of society as groping its way through the uncoordinated actions of individuals doing the best they can with limited information. In spite of this rather untidy state of affairs (and in part because of it), the resulting evolutionary dynamic has both qualitative and quantitative features that seem to be broadly in keeping with empirical evidence.

Notes

1   Important exceptions are Sugden (1986) and Ullman-Margalit (1977). The interested reader might also refer to the symposium on social norms that appeared in the Fall 1989 issue of this journal, with articles by Sugden (1989) and Elster (1989).

2   See Hopper (1982), Hamer (1986) and Lay (1992, pp. 199–200).

3   A similar process has been proposed for the diffusion of technologies that exhibit networking externalities (Katz and Shapiro, 1985; David, 1985; Arthur, Ermoliev and Kaniovski, 1987; Arthur, 1989). The more people who choose IBM-compatible personal computers over Macintoshes, for example, the more likely it is that software will be developed for IBMs as compared to Macintoshes, and thus the more worthwhile it becomes to own an IBM. A similar story can be told for the layout of typewriter keyboards, VHS versus Beta for videocassette recorders, cassettes versus compact discs for prerecorded music and so forth. When the diffusion of such technologies occurs through many individual, decentralized decisions, the process can be modelled in much the same way as the adoption of conventions. When diffusion is governed by the strategic choices of a few large firms, however, the process must

be analyzed differently. See the symposium on network externalities that appeared in the Spring 1994 issue of this journal, with articles by Katz and Shapiro (1994), Besen and Farrell (1994) and Liebowitz and Margolis (1994).

4   In some models of technological adoption, it is assumed that products never wear out and adoption decisions are once and for all (Arthur, Ermoliev and Kaniovski, 1987; Arthur, 1989). Under this assumption, perturbations in the process ultimately cannot overcome the weight of the past (which grows indefinitely over time), and it locks into an outcome in which one product takes all of the market with probability one. In our case, finite memory corresponds to the idea that products have a finite life. Under this assumption, persistent stochastic shocks prevent lock-in over the long run.

5   The Kandori, Mailath and Rob (1993) model is similar to the one presented here except that agents in their model do not have partial information or a long memory. They choose a best reply to the frequency distribution of all actions in the preceding period with high probability and choose randomly among actions with low probability. The qualitative dynamics of this process are very similar to those described in the text.

6   This account is based on Lay (1992). See also Hopper (1982), Kincaid (1986) and Hamer (1986). I am indebted to Jean-Marcel Goger and Arnulf Gruebler for historical information on France and Austria, respectively.

7   The first spatial model of an evolutionary type was proposed by Schelling (1971) to describe neighborhood segregation patterns. For recent work on spatial evolutionary game dynamics see Blume (1993), Ellison (1993), Anderlini and Ianni (1993), Berninghaus and Schwalbe (1992), Goyal and Jenssen (1993) and An and Kiefer (1993).

8   For a detailed discussion of the Nash model and variations on it, see Luce and Raiffa (1957), Binmore and Dasgupta (1987) and Osborne and Rubinstein (1990).

9   For experimental setups that elicit a variety of norms, see Yaari and Bar-Hillel (1981).

10   As Stiglitz (1989, p. 22) puts it: "[T]he range of contract forms [in sharecropping] seems far more restricted than theory would suggest. . . . Although there have been several attempts to explain this uniformity, none has gained general acceptance."

11   This concept was introduced by Foster and Young as an alternative to the notion of evolutionary stable strategy (ESS) due to Maynard-Smith and Price (1973). The drawback of an ESS is that it is only stable against a small one-time shock, whereas most evolutionary processes are subjected to *persistent* shocks. For applications of this concept not mentioned in the text, see Young and Foster (1991), Nöldeke and Samuelson (1993), Samuelson (1994) and Kandori and Rob (1995).

12   The argument uses techniques from the theory of perturbed dynamical systems (Freidlin and Wentzell, 1984; Foster and Young, 1990; Young, 1993a; Kandori, Mailath and Rob, 1993).

References

An, Mark Y., and Nicholas M. Kiefer, "Evolution and Equilibrium Selection in Repeated Lattice Games," preprint, Cornell University, 1993.

Anderlini, Luca, and Antonella Ianni, "Local Learning on a Torus," preprint, Cambridge University, 1993.

Arthur, W. Brian, "Competing Technologies, Increasing Returns, and Lock-in by Historical Events," *Economic Journal*, March 1989, *99*, 116–31.

Arthur, W. Brian, Yuri Ermoliev, and Yuri Kaniovski, "Strong Laws for a Class of Path-Dependent Stochastic Processes." In Arkin, V., A. Shiryaev, and R. Wets, eds., *Proceedings of the International Conference on Stochastic Optimization*. Berlin: Springer Lecture Notes in Control and Information Sciences, 1986, *81*, 287–300.

Arthur, W. Brian, Yuri Ermoliev, and Yuri Kaniovski, "Path-Dependent Processes and the Emergence of Macrostructure," *European Journal of Operational Research*, 1987, *30*, 294–303.

Bardhan, Pranab, *Land, Labor, and Rural Poverty*. New York: Columbia University Press, 1984.

Bardhan, Pranab, and Ashok Rudra, "Labour Mobility and the Boundaries of the Village Moral Economy," *Journal of Peasant Studies*, 1986, *13*, 90–115.

Berninghaus, Siegfried K., and Ulrich Schwalbe, "Learning and Adaptation Processes in Games with Local Interaction Structures," preprint, University of Mannheim, 1992.

Besen, Stanley M., and Joseph Farrell, "Choosing How to Compete: Strategies and Tactics in Standardization," *Journal of Economic Perspectives*, Spring 1994, *8*, 116–31.

Binmore, Ken, "Do People Exploit their Bargaining Power: An Experimental Study," *Games and Economic Behavior*, 1991, *3*, 295–322.

Binmore, Ken, and Partha Dasgupta, eds., *The Economics of Bargaining*. Oxford: Blackwell, 1987.

Binmore, Ken, J. Swierzbinski, S. Hsu, and C. Proulx, "Focal Points and Bargaining," *International Journal of Game Theory*, 1993, *22*, 381–409.

Blume, Larry, "The Statistical Mechanics of Strategic Interaction," *Games and Economic Behavior*, 1993, *4*, 387–424.

David, Paul, "Clio and the Economics of QWERTY," *American Economic Review*, May 1985, *75*, 332–37.

Ellison, Glenn, "Learning, Local Interaction, and Coordination," *Econometrica*, September 1993, *61*, 1047–71.

Elster, Jon, "Social Norms and Economics," *Journal of Economic Perspectives*, Fall 1989, *3*, 99–117.

Foster, Dean, and H. Peyton Young, "Stochastic Evolutionary Game Dynamics," *Theoretical Population Biology*, 1990, *38*, 219–32.

Freidlin, Mark, and Alexander Wentzeil, *Random Perturbations of Dynamical Systems*. Berlin: Springer Verlag, 1984.

Hamer, Mick, "Left is Right on the Road: The History of Road Traffic Regulations," *New Scientist*, December 25, 1986, *112*.

Hopper, R. H., "Left-Right: Why Driving Rules Differ," *Transportation Quarterly*, 1982, *36*, 541–48.

Goyal, Sanjeev, and Maarten Janssen, "Interaction Structure and the Stability of Conventions," preprint, Erasmus University, 1993.

Kandori, Michihiro, and Rafael Rob, "Evolution of Equilibria in the Long Run: A General Theory and Applications," *Journal of Economic Theory*, 1995, *65*, 383–415.

Kandori, Michihiro, George Mailath, and Rafael Rob, "Learning, Mutation, and Long-Run Equilibria in Games," *Econometrica*, January 1993, *61*, 29–56.

Kaniovski, Yuri, and H. Peyton Young,'" Learning Dynamics in Games with Stochastic Perturbations," *Games and Economic Behavior*, 1995, *11:2*, 330–63.

Katz, Michael, and Carl Shapiro, "Network Externalities, Competition, and Compatibility," *American Economic Review*, June 1985, *75*, 424–40.

Katz, Michael, and Carl Shapiro, "Technology Adoption in the Presence of Network Externalities," *Journal of Political Economy*, August 1986, *94*, 822–41.

Katz, Michael, and Carl Shapiro, "Systems Competition and Network Effects,"*Journal of Economic Perspectives*, Spring 1994, *8*, 93–115.

Kincaid, P., *The Rule of the Road*. New York: Greenwood, 1986.

Lay, Maxwell G., *Ways of the World*. New Brunswick NJ.: Rutgers University Press, 1992.

Lewis, David, *Convention: A Philosophical Study*. Cambridge, Mass.: Harvard University Press, 1969.

Liebowitz, S. J., and Stephen E. Margolis, "Network Externality: An Uncommon Tragedy, "*Journal of Economic Perspectives*, Spring 1994, *8*, 133–50.

Luce, R. Duncan, and Howard Raiffa, *Games and Decisions*. New York: Wiley, 1957.

Maynard-Smith, John, and George R. Price, "The Logic of Animal Conflict," *Nature*, 1973, *246*, 15–18.

Nash, John, "The Bargaining Problem," *Econometrica*, April 1950, *18*, 155–62.

Nash, John, "Two-Person Cooperative Games," *Econometrica*, January 1953, *21*, 128–40.

Nöldeke, Georg, and Larry Samuelson, "An Evolutionary Analysis of Backward and Forward Induction," *Games and Economic Behavior*, 1993, *5*, 425–54.

Nydegger, R. V., and Guillermo Owen, "Two-Person Bargaining: An Experimental Test of the Nash Axioms," *International Journal of Game Theory*, 1974, *3*, 239–49.

Osborne, Martin, and Ariel Rubinstein, *Bargaining and Markets*. New York: Academic Press, 1990.

Roth, Alvin, ed., *Laboratory Experimentation in Economics*. Cambridge, U.K: Cambridge University Press, 1987.

Rudra, Ashok, and Pranab Bardhan, *Agrarian Relations in West Bengal: Results of Two Surveys*. Bombay: Somaiya, 1986.

Samuelson, Larry, "Stochastic Stability in Games with Alternative Best Replies," *Journal of Economic Theory*, 1994, *64*, 35–65.

Schelling, Thomas C., *The Strategy of Conflict*. Cambridge, Mass.: Harvard University Press, 1960.

Schelling, Thomas C., "Dynamic Models of Segregation," *Journal of Mathematical Sociology*, 1971, *1*, 143–86.

Stiglitz, Joseph E., "Incentives and Risk Sharing in Sharecropping," *Review of Economic Studies*, April 1974, *41*, 219–55.

Stiglitz, Joseph E., "Rational Peasants, Efficient Institutions, and a Theory of Rural Organization: Methodological Remarks for Development Economics." In Bardhan, P., ed., *The Economic Theory of Agrarian Institutions*. Oxford: Clarendon Press, 1989, pp. 18–29.

Sugden, Robert, *The Evolution of Rights, Cooperation, and Welfare*. New York: Basil Blackwell, 1986.

Sugden, Robert, "Spontaneous Order," *Journal of Economic Perspectives*, Fall 1989, *3*, 85–97.

Ullman-Margalit, Edna, *The Emergence of Norms*. Oxford: Oxford University Press, 1977.

Yaari, Menachem, and Maya Bar-Hillel, "On Dividing Justly," *Social Choice and Welfare*, 1981, *1*, 1–24.

Young, H. Peyton, "The Evolution of Conventions," *Econometrica*, January 1993a, *61*, 57–84.

Young, H. Peyton, "An Evolutionary Model of Bargaining," *Journal of Economic Theory*, February 1993b, *59*, 145–68.

Young, H. Peyton, and Dean Foster, "Cooperation in the Short and in the Long Run," *Games and Economic Behavior*, 1991, *3*, 145–156.

Chapter 8

Ulrich Witt

THE EVOLUTION OF ECONOMIC INSTITUTIONS AS A PROPAGATION PROCESS

1. Introduction

T HE FOCUS OF THE PRESENT paper is on general, abstract regularities in the evolution of socioeconomic institutions. In its orientation, the paper follows recent contributions by Taylor (1976), Ullmann-Margalit (1978), Thompson and Faith (1981), Schotter (1981, 1986) that have been inspired by game theory. Although they differ in method, these recent contributions all follow more or less explicitly the tradition of what will be labeled here the *Smith-Menger-Hayek conjecture* of a 'spontaneous', i.e., unintended and unplanned, emergence of institutions. Adam Smith's notion of the "invisible hand" and Adam Ferguson's conjecture that institutions are "the result of human action but not of human design" express the basic idea. It has been restated independently by Menger (1883) and, more recently, has been extensively elaborated by Hayek (e.g. 1967, for a survey see Vanberg, 1986).

In what follows, an attempt is made to generalize the recent, game-theory-oriented debate in two directions. First, the theoretical background is extended so that cases where there is no strategic interaction at the basis of socioeconomic institutions can also be covered. This is achieved by interpreting the evolution as a diffusion process. It turns out that, in this process, the crucial, general regularies are interdependency effects between the decisions of the individuals involved. They take on systematically varying forms for different institutions. Second, on this basis an effort is made to subsume what may be labeled the *Olson-Buchanan-Tullock conjecture* on the emergence of institutions. According to this, certain institutions cannot be expected to emerge in the way assumed by the alternative conjecture: the interests pursued by the individuals involved do not necessarily lead them to 'spontaneously' create or support an institution. In this case, for the institution to actually emerge, some kind of collective action would be required. The basic idea has been outlined in the influential book of Olson (1965) and it also figures prominently in the Virginia School of economic thought (see, e.g., Buchanan 1965 and 1975; Tullock 1974).

The paper proceeds as follows. In Section 2 the propagation of an institution is modeled on the basis of some simple assumptions and the notion of the frequency-dependency effect is explained. Section 3 discusses the case of 'spontaneous' emergence of institutions where strategic interaction is absent. In Section 4, situations with strategic interaction are shown to be special cases of the suggested model. Section 5 is devoted to discussing the class of institutions whose propagation requires special forms of collective action. In the concluding section the results are used for a straightforward interpretation of institutional change.

2. Propagation of institutions and the frequency-dependency effect

The approach chosen in this paper is individualistic, that is, an attempt is made to reconstruct the theory of institutions from decision-making or, more generally, behavior at the level of the individual agent. Since the approach is intended as a general one, including both situations in which institutions result from strategic interaction and those where the individuals involved do not notice that their own decisions affect those of others, institutions are broadly defined as follows.

> *Definition:* An institution is a unique behavioral regularity spread out among individuals or a pattern of diverse, but coinciding, possibly even mutually dependent, behavioral regularities. It is displayed whenever the involved individuals are faced with the same constituent situation of choice.

Under this definition, many different forms of institutions can be imagined: those in the realm of markets (division of labor, exchange, use of money, and more specific organizational forms such as e.g., department stores, supermarkets, etc.); those in the realm of non-market behavior (e.g., rules and mores, education, family conduct, hierarchical division of labor as in corporations, etc.); or those based on explicit agreements and regulations (e.g., interaction rules, traffic regulation, laws, standing orders, etc.). In any case, the fact that the regularities may be more or less spread out in a population of individuals (or of groups of interacting individuals) points to a crucial feature of institutions, their varying degree of propagation or relative frequency of adoption. For expository convenience assume that the decision to adopt (a) or not to adopt (n) is fully informed with respect to what kind of behavior is required, be it a unique and independent regularity or one that has, in a division of activities, to contribute to a pattern of coinciding regularities. The respective behavior may be adopted by none, some, or all of the involved individuals. Accordingly, if F(a) indicates the relative frequency of adoption, the propagation of an institution can be measured by F(a) on the unit interval.

The emergence and propagation of institutions are interpreted in this paper similarly to those of ordinary behavioral innovations, possibly ones that require coincident innovations on the part of other individuals. Since the focus is on the propagation rather than on the emergence of novelty, let us assume that the idea of a new behavioral regularity, the nucleus of a new institution, has somehow emerged. Its actual propagation depends, then, first on the particular communication processes by which the knowledge of the new form of behavior (new option of choice) is diffused throughout the population. Second, it depends on whether the new option is in fact chosen, i.e., the regularity is individually adopted (the institution supported, complied to, etc.).

The first process may be a spontaneous, unguided diffusion along established communication networks between the individuals, or it may result from the activities of one or more "diffusion agents" (Brown, 1981) who, for self-interested motives, try to convince the potential adopters of the benefits of adopting the respective regularity. An obvious difference between the two cases is that, in the former, in contrast to the latter, the decisions on the part of potential adopters can be viewed as independent in the sense that no suasion, negotiations, or organizational measures take place. Let us start here by assuming the former situation (the 'independent' choice; we will come back to the latter in Section 5).

With respect to the question of whether the new behavioral regularity is actually adopted or not, an individualistic approach suggests to assume that an individual is more likely to decide in favor of the new option (rather than not conforming) the more he can expect to improve his position by doing so, given his current preferences, his perception of the choice set, and, where relevant, his assessment of the extent to what others contribute/comply to. More precisely:

> *Assumption 1*: The individual probability of adopting a new behavioral regularity f(a) is the larger, the larger the individual net benefit from choosing a rather than n is assessed provided the net benefit is positive; otherwise f(a) = 0.

This hypothesis can be considered as a statistical reformulation of the standard (deterministic) opportunity cost theory according to which individuals always choose the best available alternative, no matter how much better it is compared to the next best alternative(s). A second hypothesis, crucial for the argument in this paper is:

> *Assumption 2*: The extent to which an individual is able to improve his position by adopting a behavioral regularity depends on the relative frequency F(a) with which other individuals in the population have already adopted (or in certain cases can be expected to adopt) the respective regularity or regularities.

This assumption is quite evidently satisfied wherever there are interdependencies among decision-makers.[1] Obviously, this is the case where the individuals have to contribute to a pattern of coinciding, mutually dependent behavioral regularities in order to successfully establish the institution. But even where a division of activities is not required, where, in fact, purely stereotypic behavior is concerned, there seem to be reasons why frequency-dependency may matter. For instance, whether a business man opens the first or the tenth supermarket in a small town makes a difference to the benefits he receives; but joining a production cooperative may be more beneficial if it has already a significant number of members. Furthermore, adopting *new* modes of behavior, i.e., behavior that deviates from previously established forms, may, as such, induce disapproving or even hostile (sometimes possibly also sympathetic) reactions from the environment. These reactions tend to fade away the more common the new mode becomes, that is, the more frequently it is adopted by the population.

If, for expository convenience, agents are assumed to behave identically, the probability f(a) of adopting a new behavioral regularity thus depends for each individual on the extent to what the respective regularity (or the pattern of regularities) is already represented in the population, i.e., on F(a). Written as a function:

$$f(a) = \phi\,[F(a)]. \tag{8.1}$$

For population as a whole, however, each individual decision in favor of option a changes the composition of adopters and non-adopters. Since the outcome of each individual decision is assumed to be f(a) we have

$$\Delta F(a) = \psi\,(f(a) - F(a)) \tag{8.2}$$

where $\Delta F(a)$ is the change of the composition of adopters and non-adopters in the population and ψ some monotonous, sign-preserving function such that the change of the composition is a function of the composition itself.

3. Frequency-dependency under non-strategic behavior

The assumptions in the previous section imply that the propagation of an institution is governed by the utility or the benefits to the potential adopters from taking on the constituent behavioral regularities. The utility has been argued to depend on the relative frequency of adopters in the population. It will now be shown that the kind of dependency may vary strongly between institutions so that they differ systematically with respect to the way and the extent to which they propagate. The exposition starts with the more easily handled situation where the agents do not strategically interact.

Assumptions 1 and 2 together imply the adoption function (8.1). Since, by the first assumption, f(a) monotonically varies with the individual net benefit from choosing a over n, various cases can be plausibly imagined as characterized by the following alternative assumptions:

> *Assumption 3a:* $\phi\,[F(a)] > 0$ for $F(a) = 0$ and in the entire interval $[0,1]$
>
> (i) $\phi' > 0$, or
> (ii) $\phi' < 0$, or
> (iii) $\phi' = 0$.

> *Assumption 3b:* $\phi\,[F(a)] = 0$ for $F(a) = 0$ and $0 \le \phi' < 1$ in the neighborhood of $F(a) = 0$ such that the graph of $\phi\,[F(a)]$
> (iv) remains below the 45°-line in the interval $[0,1]$ or
> (v) intersects the 45°-line from below at a point F^{**}, $0 < F^{**} \le 1$.

The different cases can be illustrated by diagrams in which the graph of (8.1) is depicted for the different specifications such as in Figures 8.1–8.3. For expository

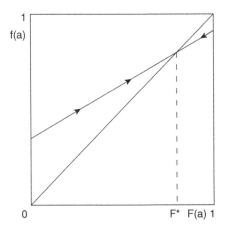

Figure 8.1 Propagation of an institution in case (i)

convenience let us assume that the composition of the population changes continuously so that (2.2) becomes $dF(a)/dt = f(a) - F(a)$. Figures 8.1–8.3 can then be interpreted analogously to the phase diagram of this first-order differential equation. Accordingly, all points on the $45°$-line represent situations in which, in the mean, the prevailing relative frequency $F(a)$ is just maintained by the individual decision, i.e., propagation equilibria $F*$ of an institution. At all points on a graph above (below) the $45°$-line the individual adoption probability is greater (smaller) than the already existing relative frequency of a, so that the latter in the mean increases (decreases) by the individual's decision. These tendencies are indicated by arrows on the graphs that have been depicted for exemplary purposes in the diagrams.

Consider Figure 8.1, where case (i) is exemplified. Adopting the behavioral regularity yields a net benefit to everybody from the very beginning. The further the institution propagates the more attractive it becomes, e.g., because of increasing reputation or some positive scale effects. As an example for this case, think of education or the use of some particular exchange medium (money). Depending on the absolute magnitudes the behavior constituent for the institution is, as shown in the figure, not necessarily adopted by the entire population. It is possible that a share $1-F*$ of the individuals finds alternative n more attractive after a share $F*$ of the population has already chosen a. For instance, education might be a case in point. A differentiation of the educational system would have to be expected.

In Figure 8.2, representing case (ii), the net benefits develop differently in the propagation process: they steadily decline from an initially high value so that the individual probability of adoption is decreasing the more adopters there are already. Many market institutions seem to fall under this case as increasing adoption may mean increasing competition if the population is made up of the individuals on one side of the market. Department stores (on the supply side) or joint stock companies (on the demand side of the capital market) may be given as examples. The implication is, in general, only a partial propagation of the institution. The same holds true for the limiting case (iii) which is not depicted here. Taken together we obtain:

Proposition 1: Given the cases of assumption 3a, an institution spontaneously propagates without any measures being taken and establishes itself

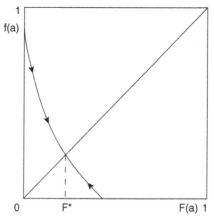

Figure 8.2 Propagation of an institution in case (ii)

in the population in the sense that any random deviation from F* resulting, e.g., from fluctuations in the population will be compensated for, i.e. F* ≤ 1 is a stable propagation equilibrium.

Now consider Figure 8.3 where a dotted graph is depicted for case (iv). The individual net benefit from adoption would still be increasing with the number of adopters but ϕ [F(a)] < F(a) for all F(a) > 0. The obvious consequence is that such an institution cannot gain a foothold in the population. By contrast, the solid curve, representing case (v), shows values of ϕ [F(a)] > F(a) for all F(a) > F**, F** therefore indicates a 'critical mass' or critical relative frequency: once F(a) happens to exceed F** it will propagate completely. (If the function is bounded from above such that it intersects the 45°-line at some F*, F** < F* < 1, from above, the relative frequency may also settle at an equilibrium level smaller than 1.)[2]

Clearly differing from the cases (i)–(iii) we now find:

Proposition 2: Given the cases of assumption 3b an institution will not spontaneously propagate unless the critical frequency F** is somehow

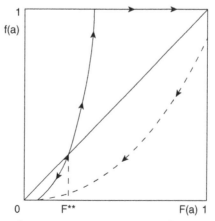

Figure 8.3 Propagation of an institution in case (iv) and (v)

exceeded. F** is an unstable propagation equilibrium which is not restored once F(a) deviates because of fluctuations in the population. The direction of deviation determines whether the institution will be established at a stable equilibrium F* ≤ 1 or will not gain a foothold at all.

4. Frequency-dependency under strategic behavior

Where an institution is constituted by the adoption of a pattern of coinciding, possibly mutually dependent, but divers behavioral regularities on the part of a group of agents, as in cases where a division of activities is required, it is most likely that the potential adopters strategically interact. Situations in which individuals decide on whether or not to adopt a behavioral regularity in view of the possible choices of the other individuals in the population are slightly more complicated. With some simplifications, it is not difficult to show, however, that systematically differing types of institutions as characterized by the various cases in the previous section are implied here, too. Consider a population of m agents involved in the m-person non-zero sum game

$$\Gamma = \{(1, \ldots, i, \ldots, m), (S_1, \ldots, S_i, \ldots, S_m), (\Pi_1, \ldots, \Pi_i, \ldots, \Pi_m)\} \quad (8.3)$$

in which agent i has a strategy set

$$S_i = \{a, n\}, \quad i = 1, \ldots, m, \quad (8.4)$$

and his pay-off, if he chooses strategy $s_i \in \{a, n\}$, is

$$\Pi_i = \Pi_i \{S_1, \ldots, S_j, \ldots, S_m\}. \quad (8.5)$$

As a simplification underlying the following considerations assume (8.5) is identical for all i = 1, . . ., m, that is, Γ is a symmetrical game. For any two agents i and j in the population, i ≠ j, the game situation can then partially be represented in normal form by the 2 × 2 matrix

		j	
		a	n
i	a	$\Pi(a, a)$ $\Pi(a, a)$	$\Pi(a, n)$ $\Pi(a, n)$
	n	$\Pi(n, a)$ $\Pi(n, a)$	$\Pi(n, n)$ $\Pi(n, n)$

Assuming random pairing for expository convenience, the expected pay-offs of the two strategies a (adopting the behavioral regularity constituent for the institution)

and n (not adopting) are conditional on the relative frequency with which the strategies will elsewhere be adopted in the population:

$$E\left[\Pi_i\left(s_i = a \mid F(a)\right)\right] = F(a)\Pi(a, a) + [1 - F(a)]\Pi(a, n) \qquad (8.6)$$

and

$$E\left[\Pi_i\left(S_i = n \mid F(a)\right)\right] = F(a)\Pi(n, a) + [1 - F(a)]\Pi(n, n) \qquad (8.7)$$

Analogously to assumption 1, agent i is supposed the more likely to decide in favor of strategy a the higher the (positive) net benefit from choosing a rather than n. Hence the difference between (8.6) and (8.7) can be used as a criterion function that determines the individual probability of adoption $f(a)$. Setting $\Pi_i(a, a) - \Pi_i(n, a) = D_a$ and $\Pi_i(a, n) - H_i(n, n) = D_n$ we obtain:

$$f(a) \begin{cases} = \min\left[D_n + (D_a - D_n)F(a), 1\right] & \text{as long as } f(a) > 0, \\ = 0 & \text{otherwise.} \end{cases} \qquad (8.8)$$

This is a special, piecewise linear form of (8.1).

On the basis of (8.8) we are now in the position to investigate the propagation of a certain strategy in symmetrical m-person games as a special case of the propagation of an institution. The analysis is similar to recent adaptations of game theory to the context of biology (see Maynard Smith, 1982, for an introduction) though the interpretation differs. In fact, for the symmetrical situation chosen here, any stable propagation equilibrium $F^* > 0$ represents what is labeled an evolutionary stable strategy (see Maynard Smith, 1982: 10–20; and Selten, 1983, for the latter) in pure strategies in the context of biological game theory.

In order to substantiate the above claim that institutions show similar differences with respect to their propagation conditions under non-strategic as well as strategic behavior let us now briefly review some numerical examples of well-known prototype

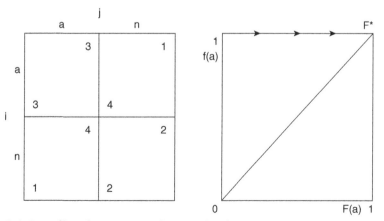

Figure 8.4 Pay-offs and propagation function for the convergence game

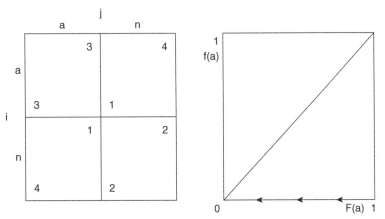

Figure 8.5 Pay-offs and propagation function for prisoners' dilemma game

games (see Ullmann-Margalit, 1978; Schotter, 1981, or the elementary text by Hamburger, 1979, for the taxonomy of games). Inserting the specification of the *convergence game* illustrated below (strategy a may, e.g., be product innovation, strategy n no product innovation) into (8.8)[3] yields the graph in Figure 8.4 and, thus, in almost trivial form, a stable propagation equilibrium F* = 1 corresponding to the unique equilibrium in the underlying game.

The *prisoners' dilemma game* with strategies a: cooperate, n: not cooperate, is represented in Figure 8.5 which exemplifies that, as expected, the cooperative strategy a cannot propagate in the population. Again, the equilibrium of the underlying game obtains in trivial form. For both games, covering case (iii) in the previous section, the frequency-dependency does not play a role.

More interesting insights can be gained from investigating games with less clear-cut equilibrium features as, for example, the *'chicken' game* (Figure 8.6) where strategy a might mean following some new form of honest trade convention as opposed to keeping to an established but somewhat corrupted form n. The game has two equilibria in pure strategies off the principal diagonal. As can easily be reconstructed,

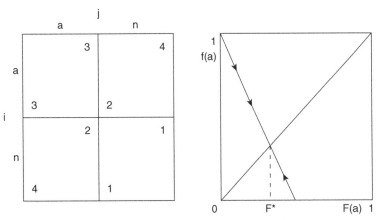

Figure 8.6 Pay-offs and propagation function for the 'chicken' game

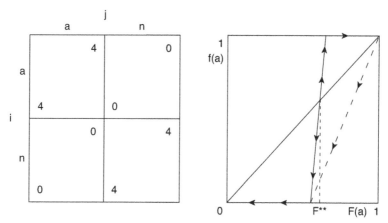

Figure 8.7 Pay-offs and propagation function for the pure coordination game

the propagation function $f(a) = 1 - 2F(a)$ intersects the 45°-line at a stable propagation equilibrium F*, $0 < F* < .5$, a situation similar to case (ii) in the previous section.

The *'pure' coordination game* where a may represent some set of conventions (weights and measures, language, manners, traffic, etc.) and n another has no dominant strategies but two equilibria in pure strategies. The corresponding propagation function $f(a) = -4 + 8F(a)$ yields a positive branch which intersects the 45°-line from below in an unstable propagation equilibrium F**, a critical frequency point, as depicted in Figure 8.7. Two stable equilibria situations prevail in $F(a) = 0$ and the stable propagation equilibrium F* = 1. Note that the numerical specification is crucial for the existence of the critical frequency phenomenon. If 1 is inserted instead of 4, the propagation function remains below the 45°-line except in the unstable equilibrium point at $F(a) = 1$ (the dotted graph in Figure 8.7). This means that convention a cannot gain a foothold. With its varying specification, the game provides a piecewise linear analog to the cases (iv) and (v) discussed in the previous section.

As demonstrated, in the propagation of institutions under conditions of strategic interaction, two different modes can be distinguished analogously to the propositions 1 and 2 in Section 3: institutions may spontaneously establish themselves without further preconditions or they may do so only if it happens that a critical adoption frequency is somehow exceeded.

5. Agents of collective action and the propagation of institutions

The preceding discussions showed that the relationships between individual utility or benefits and the relative adoption frequency of an institution imply differing propagation patterns. Put into the perspective of the long-standing debate on how institutions emerge, this result has some interesting implications. As is well known, in this debate there are two competing positions. On one side, the *Smith-Menger-Hayek conjecture* of a spontaneous emergence of institutions holds that they are "the result of human action but not of human design". On the other side, it has traditionally been maintained, in particular in sociology and law theory, that institutions are a kind of created, shaped structure or corpus. Individuals are seen as joining in order to constitute an institution in a purposeful, organized action. As Vanberg (1983) has nicely pointed out, this interpretation becomes, in a specific economic and somewhat pessimistic blending, what might be labeled the *Olson-Buchanan-Tullock conjecture* underlying the theory of collective action.

The considerations in the previous sections indicate that the two forms of institutional evolution may be complementary, each occurring under different conditions. In fact, the *Smith-Menger-Hayek conjecture* seems perfectly covered by the cases in assumption 3a as summarized in proposition 1, and some examples used above have already been mentioned by Menger (1883) as cases in point. In this section it remains to be explained how the cases in assumption 3b and their properties as given in proposition 2 are indeed dependent on collective action and to which extent the rather pessimistic *Olson-Buchanan-Tullock conjecture*, which predicts an insufficient development of such institutions, applies.

The last sections have offered little which can explain the actual process of how institutions come about under the conditions of assumption 3b. From the graphs of the propagation functions in the Figures 8.3 and 8.7 it is clear, however, that it would be advantageous to all or most of the agents in the population if they adopted the new institution once the critical frequency F^{**} is exceeded, an advantage that would induce them to support and maintain the institution in their own interest. (In the game version, this is equivalent to saying that the propagation equilibrium F^* is an equilibrium point of the game from which nobody has an incentive to deviate.) Up to that point there is, however, a problem. For a new institution to be successful, it has first to reach F^{**}, despite the fact that, up to this point, self-interest dictates that the new institution should not be adopted or supported. How is this problem overcome?

The answer suggested here is simple: by a special form of collective action being organized. The outlook for future self-reinforcement may attract organizers, leaders, agitators, moralists, intriguers, political entrepreneurs, in short agents who, for the most diverse motives, specialize in eliciting and arousing interest, producing agreements, and arranging alliances. They operate as "diffusion agents", engaged in the propagation of a new institution which, in effect, means doing away with the independence and isolation of the individual adoption decision (which has so far been assumed, see Section 2). All that these agents have to achieve is to induce a sufficient number of other agents to expect that collective adoption will come about, so that the expectation becomes self-fulfilling: just a little more than the critical mass.

Unlike those institutions covered by the *Smith-Menger-Hayek conjecture*, organized, intentional pursuit of a collective action by at least some agents is thus a prerequisite for an institution of the second kind to be established. If this is true, it seems straightforward, of course, to apply the *Olson-Buchanan-Tullock conjecture* to this kind of collective action. This is to argue that, at least in large populations, such an action does not (sufficiently) occur, since it requires the agents of collective action to provide a public good. Since the path-breaking book by Olson (1965), this is a corner-stone in the theory of collective action (for a more recent summary see Hardin, 1982). And, indeed, although the agents of collective action in the present context intervene only for the limited transition phase, and although it is not unlikely that their individual motives for acting are less oriented to material cost/benefit considerations than in Olson's examples, the validity of his argument cannot wholly be denied.

Once F** is exceeded, all agents may profit without incurring the costs of attaining this. Free-riding is possible and, if the costs are substantial, there may be no or not enough agents of collective action who are willing to provide the public good of organizing the transition. Confirming Olson's original thesis, this is more likely to happen in large populations if the costs of organizing increase with the number of agents. In larger populations it is then more 'expensive' to reach F** than in smaller ones, as the absolute number of agents who have to be convinced is greater. Increasing costs may, *ceteris paribus*, curb the individual willingness to act as agent of collective action.

What is not entirely clear is the question of how the costs and benefits of the various agents are actually structured in the situation before F** is reached (i.e., in a situation supposed to require the provision of a public good). It may be argued that, even in large groups, it is, in fact, best described as a 'chicken game' (see Fogarty, 1981; Lipnowski and Maital, 1983) with strategies engage (a) or not engage (n) as has been discussed in the previous section. In that case, there may be fewer agents of collective action than desirable, but—viewed as an evolving institution itself—it can be concluded from the example of Figure 8.6 that a significant number of them may appear: a stable propagation equilibrium may exist, which implies that in a population of potential agents of collective action, a positive share of them will in fact adopt the attitude and help in establishing institutions of the second kind.

Even under the *Olson-Buchanan-Tullock conjecture*, institutions involving some kind of organizational initiative can thus under certain conditions be expected to emerge. In a broader sense their evolution may as well be interpreted as a spontaneous one, since it depends on some individuals adopting the role of an agent of collective action which is itself a behavioral regularity of the first kind. Looking at the game-theoretic background of the institutions subsumed here under the second category, it becomes clear, however, that they consist basically of the class of coordination games (games with multiple equilibria in pure strategies in the principal diagonal of the pay-off matrix). Examples that are often given are all sorts of conventions, statutes, traffic regulations, standing orders, language rules, manners, etc.

Not included are all those institutions that require a cooperative solution in a prisoners' dilemma game. This is a very large class which, certainly, is of utmost importance in the framework of the theory of collective action (see, e.g., Nabli and Nugent, 1989). Unfortunately, it is not as easily accessible with the frequency-dependency approach suggested above as the other cases that have been discussed. As shown in Figure 8.5, there is no critical frequency involved in the p.d.-game that would leave room for an immediate intervention of agents of collective action. The shape of the propagation function flatly turns down any hope of success, given the original pay-offs. Nevertheless, many such institutions can be empirically observed to exist. Any explanation for this (based on the assumption of individually rational behavior), it appears, has to include hypotheses that, in effect, transform the pay-off structure to make the dilemma vanish.

In this way, some more differentiated activities on the part of agents of collective action must be assumed. Imagine, e.g., an attempt is made, in a first step, to propagate retaliatory measures in case that, in a prisoners' dilemma, somebody offering cooperation has been cheated. If the attempt were successful, retaliation would reduce the offender's temptation pay-off. But, the costs of retaliatory action would have to be incurred by the victim reducing the sucker's pay-off still further compared to the original game. If the original (partial) pay-off matrix (Figure 8.5) were thus changed as follows:

$\Pi(a, a) = 3$	$\Pi(a, n) = 1$
$\Pi(a, a) = 3$	$\Pi(a, n) = 0$
$\Pi(n, a) = 0$	$\Pi(n, n) = 2$
$\Pi(n, a) = 1$	$\Pi(n, n) = 2$

agitation would have transformed the p.d.-game into a coordination game with a propagation function similar to the solid line in Figure 8.7. A critical frequency F^{**}, $0 < F^{**} < 1$, would occur that allowed room for organizing collective action in the sense above discussed.

Unfortunately, however, the attempt to overcome the prisoners' dilemma by convincing the people of the necessity of retaliatory action may itself induce a prisoners' dilemma and, thus, simply a regress. Chances for arriving at the above coordination game when starting from a p.d.-game seem bad, unless recourse to additional arguments can be made. It has been argued elsewhere that possibly genetically caused variance in individual preferences together with social learning (which is itself frequency-dependent) may ensure the transformation (Witt, 1986). Another, historical, conjecture might be that agents in command of measures of coercion that have otherwise come into existence tend to assume the role of agents of collective action. Since they often are able to extend the measures to new areas, they may be able to punish free-riding and thus to transform a prisoners' dilemma situation into a pure coordination game.

6. Conclusions: regularities in institutional change

By interpreting the evolution of institutions as a diffusion process in which frequency dependency effects govern the adoption patterns, some characteristic differences between institutions emerging according to the *Smith-Menger-Hayek conjecture* and those resulting from collective action along the lines of the *Olson-Buchanan-Tullock conjecture* have been outlined. The discussion can easily be extended to explain regularities in institutional change. The propagation of an institution often not only means adopting or not adopting a new behavior but at the same time may imply turning away or not turning away from a previous behavioral regularity. Where this happens, an established institution n is declining according to the relation $F(a) = 1 - F(n)$ to the extent that a new institution a is propagating.

Decline, break-down, death of institutions is an almost trivial historical experience. (In fact, explaining the viability of larger economic systems may be an intricate theoretical problem; see Day, 1987.) The exposition above suggests the following: If new institutions spontaneously propagate according to case (ii) there will always be institutional pluralism (in biology this is called polymorphism). The established institution finds a niche for survival. In the cases (i), (iii), and (v) the extent to which this is possible depends on the numerical values. If, as in Figure 8.3 (solid curve), the critical mass phenomenon is associated with stable situations $F^* = 0$ or 1, the two institutions are mutually exclusive. A dramatic supersession can be expected to take place once the agents of collective action succeed in inducing slightly more than the critical mass to adopt the new institution.

Besides such dramatic forms of change there are, of course, the various possibilities for a creeping decline in which institutions prevailing in former times may be driven out of the population as a consequence of slow shifts in the parameter values. As a consequence of changing relative prices, redistributions, technical progress, but also of changing tastes and changing attention, the propagation functions may shift in such a way that niches for the old institutions are eliminated. As far as the cases (iv) and (v) are concerned, some of the activity of agents of collective action may indeed aim at redirecting attention, providing the 'right' information, and shaping tastes in such a way that the situation (iv) is gradually shifted into a situation (v). The dotted curve in Figure 8.3 then rotates upwards and F^{**} moves to the left until the costs of convincing the critical mass are sufficiently low and F^{**} can be passed.

The present paper has exclusively focussed on propagation processes. A theory of evolution is somewhat incomplete, however, without also considering the process of emergence of novelty. Where the ideas for possible new behavioral regularities come from, how they are selected, and who will be motivated to try them where—as a novelty—their implications cannot fully be anticipated is left open here. Needless to say, these questions may be of considerable importance in providing a full understanding of the regularities of institutional change as such change involves more than the adaptation process modeled above.[4] Future research should thus also focus on answering these additional questions.

Notes

1   Such interdependencies can be more generally expected than they are in economics, particularly in price theory, where they are usually interpreted as being perfectly mediated by the market, i.e., prices (except in the case of 'true', i.e., non-pecuniary, externalities). Note that the outcome of individual interactions is no longer determined by the individual choices alone if there are interdependencies. The assertion that "the whole (i.e., aggregate behavior) is more than the sum of its parts" has something to it as the particular form and the sequence of interactions in historical time may shape the choices of the individuals in different ways.

2   Critical mass models have recently been given attention in various areas of economics, e.g., in the context of speculation about other individuals' behavior (Schelling, 1978), of the development of technical regimes (David, 1987), of interdependencies in consumption behavior (Granovetter and Soong, 1986), of solutions to the prisoners' dilemma by collective learning (Witt, 1986), of the stabilization of conservative attitudes against revolutionary ones (Kuran, 1987).

3   In principle, the pay-offs may be interpreted as utility indices in the usual way. In order to determine (8.8) numerically, they are, however, treated here like cardinal values. Note that the position and shape of the resulting propagation functions may change with the numerical specification of the pay-offs.

4   A discussion of the questions requires extensions at the foundations of economic theory and, thus, goes far beyond the present paper. The interested reader may be referred to Witt (1987) and (1989).

References

Brown, L.A. (1981). *Innovations-diffusion – A new perspective*. London: Methuen.

Buchanan, J.M. (1965). Ethical rules, expected values, and large numbers. *Ethics* 76: 1–13.

Buchanan, J.M. (1975). *The limits of liberty*. Chicago: Chicago University Press.

David, P. (1987). Some new standards for the economics of standardization in the information age. In P. Dasgupta and P.L. Stoneman (Eds.), *Economic policy and technological performance*. London: Cambridge University Press.

Day, R.H. (1987). The evolving economy. *European Journal of Operations Research* 30: 251–257.

Fogarty, T.M. (1981). Prisoner's dilemma and other public good games. *Conflict Management and Piece Science* 5: 111–120.

Granovetter, M., and Soong, R. (1986). Threshold models of interpersonal effects in consumer demand. *Journal of Economic Behavior and Organization* 7: 83–99.

Hamburger, H. (1979). *Games as models of social phenomena*. San Francisco: Freeman.

Hardin, R. (1982). *Collective action*. Washington: Resources for the Future.

Hayek, F.A. (1967). Notes on the evolution of systems of rules and conduct. In F.A. Hayek, *Studies in philosophy, politics, and economics*, 66-81. London: Kegan Paul.

Kuran, T. (1987). Preference falsification, policy continuity, and collective conservatism. *Economic Journal* 97: 642–665.

Lipnowski, I., and Maital, S. (1983). Voluntary provision of pure public good as the game of 'chicken'. *Journal of Public Economics* 20: 381–386.

Maynard Smith, J. (1982). *Evolution and the theory of games*. Cambridge: Cambridge University Press.

Menger, C. (1883). *Untersuchungen über die Methode der Sozialwissenschaften und der politischen Ökonomie insbesondere*. Wien: Braumüller.

Nabli, M.K., and Nugent, J.B. (1989). *The new institutional economics and development:Theory and applications to Tunisia*. Amsterdam: North-Holland.

Olson, M. (1965). *The logic of collective action*. Harvard: Harvard University Press.

Schelling, T. (1978). *Micromotives and macrobehavior*. New York: Norton.

Schotter, A. (1981). *The economic theory of social institutions*. Cambridge: Cambridge University Press.

Schotter, A. (1986). The evolution of rules. In R. Langlois (Ed.), *Economics as a process*, 117-133. Cambridge: Cambridge University Press.

Selten, R. (1983). Evolutionary stability in extensive two-person games. *Mathematical Social Sciences* 5: 269–363.

Taylor, M. (1976). *Anarchy and cooperation*. London: Wiley.

Thompson, E.A., and Faith, R.L. (1981). A pure theory of strategic behavior and social institutions. *American Economic Review* 71: 366–380.

Tullock, G. (1974). *The social dilemma*. Blacksburg: Center for the Study of Public Choice.

Ullmann-Margalit, E. (1978). *The emergence of norms*. New York: Oxford University Press.

Vanberg, V. (1983). Der individualistische Ansatz zu einer Theorie der Entstehung und Entwick-lung von Institutionen. *Jahrbuch für Neue Politische Ökonomie 2*: 50–69.

Vanberg, V. (1986). Spontaneous market order and social rules. *Economics and Philosophy* 2: 75–100.

Witt, U. (1986). Evolution and stability of cooperation without enforceable contracts. *Kyklos* 39: 245–266.

Witt, U. (1987). How transaction rights are shaped to channel innovativeness. *Journal of Institutional and Theoretical Economics* 143: 180–195.

Witt, U. (1989). *Individualistic foundations of evolutionary economics*. Cambridge: Cambridge University Press.

PART 4

The economics of legal systems

Introduction

THE ECONOMIC LITERATURE devoted to the analysis of legal systems quite commonly distinguishes "orders" or "societies" according to the nature of the legal means that are used to coordinate individual interactions and to regulate their actions or control their behaviors; that is, to distinguish them according to the *origins* of legal rules. Three forms or "families" of legal orders are then identified: lawless orders or groups or societies, customary-common law societies, and statute law societies.

To identify different families of legal systems, and to present them in a specific order, has no implications in terms of a hierarchy that exists among them. Nor does this imply that they correspond to precise and realistic descriptions of actual legal systems. The word "family" that is frequently used in comparative law reveals that we are not dealing with specific legal systems. In other words, the three families of legal orders presented above are idealized representations of legal orders.

Lawless societies, groups or orders

Certain groups of individuals or social orders or societies are described as "lawless" (Benson, 1989). A rather provocative term, "lawless" is not employed to designate groups and social orders in which there are no rules but rather those in which no specific, centralized and public, legal system exists, i.e. where there are no legal institutions and legal structures in charge of the provision of rules. To put it differently, these groups do not function with rules imposed on individuals by an agency external to the game and in a monopolist position through a top-down process. In those groups, the only rules used are the norms and customs that have emerged through repeated interactions among group members, and, since norms are supposedly the result of a market-based and decentralized process, "lawless" groups are viewed as *private* orders, functioning through decentralized and bottom-up processes.

A lot of empirical evidence has then been provided, showing that tribes (in primitive societies) or business communities (traders or merchants, either in ancient or more recent times) are "lawless" groups and function as private orders. This shows that norms and customs, as defined and described in the preceding section, play the role of legal rules.

The question then concerns the capacity of (emergent) norms to regulate and order the functioning of large societies. In other words, under which conditions can norms play the role of legal rules and be sufficient to order societies and, complementarily, to prevent disorder and chaos? A first answer is that emergent norms can function as legal rules, i.e. they promote order and prevent disorder because individuals accept and use them. One must then recall, as has been stressed in the preceding section, that norms are local public goods. A (relatively) small number of individuals therefore accept contributing to their provision, i.e. accept the norm as a legal rule, use it, and respect it. In other words, norms are self-enforcing *within* the limits of the group within which they emerged.

This perspective has two complementary consequences. First, this means that lawless groups are necessarily limited in size and, accordingly, that spontaneous or emergent norms can indeed serve as legal rules but only in small groups. This is precisely what the empirical evidence gathered in this literature on private ordering tells us. Second, "lawless" groups, groups relying exclusively on norms, should be socially more coherent than larger groups and therefore characterized by few – or fewer, compared to larger groups – conflicts. This is what has been argued by the defenders of this conception of social order.

However, "few" or fewer conflicts does not mean no conflict at all. Problems may arise within the group mainly because of the way individuals acquire knowledge about the rules. In effect, knowledge comes from their participation in interactions. The individuals who did not take part in these interactions may not be aware of the precise content of the rule: they will not acquire knowledge of this information spontaneously. Mechanisms have then to be devised that explicitly ensure the publicity of norms. Most of the time in "lawless" groups, an individual or a group of individuals is granted the responsibility to communicate the norms to all the members of the group, but this may not be sufficient and problems of interpretation may arise, both within the group as well as in regard to individuals coming from other groups, i.e. with individuals following different norms. It is therefore strictly impossible to make conflict totally disappear. Mechanisms have to be devised to *solve* or *settle* these conflicts.

Two features of these mechanisms must be emphasized. First, they are temporary, in the sense that they exist but are triggered or put into use only when and if a conflict arises. Second, enforcement remains strictly and exclusively *private*, in the twofold sense that cases are always brought up by the victims and are then settled by arbitration by "private" courts – i.e. assemblies of arbitrators chosen by the plaintiff and the defendants. Most of the cases, even the important ones stressed by Friedman (1979, p. 406), are settled by arbitration. When arbitration does not function, higher courts are involved in the process and the intervention of judges is required. Judges may then, as is the case in Iceland (see Friedman), be appointed by the subgroups that compose the population. Furthermore, they are chosen to play the role of an arbitrator or a mediator – even at a higher level. This means that they have to ground their decisions in the norms that exist and have emerged via voluntary interactions. In certain circumstances, for instance with groups of traders or merchants, an appeal to state sponsored courts, where they exist, remains possible to solve conflicts that private enforcement means have not been able to settle. However, these procedures are almost never used. Conflicts are usually settled within the groups with spontaneous means.

Common law and judge-*made* law legal systems

Common law systems – that exist in countries which follow the English legal traditions, like the UK, the USA, and ex-British colonies – supposedly function like customary legal systems do: these are bottom-up decentralized and spontaneous legal orders, i.e. based on rules, either customs or norms, that emerge from repeated interactions between individuals. Therefore, common law systems can be characterized as having the same advantages – rules are not created by a monopolist producer and are self-enforcing, but they also have the same limits: norms can play the role of legal rules only within small groups – as "lawless" orders.

However, one should not make the mistake of considering the two systems as equivalent. There exists a *logical*, and therefore decisively important, difference between customary and common law legal systems. Common law systems include a specific legal apparatus, a state-backed organization made of courts which use codes and statutes, which are absent from customary legal orders, "lawless" and private as they are. Thus, the judges of the common law belong to a body of "public" enforcement and common law courts are state-sponsored courts. In other words, common law systems are a first instance of centralized, top-down legal systems. To grasp the difference between the two systems, one may refer to the progressive transformation of the English legal system from a customary decentralized legal order into a common law system, in which the King or Queen and the royal judiciary occupy a central and significant position.

Judges of the Common law can then be – and sometimes are – described as "impartial spectators", in the sense that their role consists of clarifying and making explicit the norms that individuals use when they are insufficiently clear to allow a peaceful coordination among individuals. In other words, judges are not supposed to create or invent the law in a top-down process but have to base their decisions on the customs that exist in the society. Certainly, in common law systems, the law and custom often take the form of general guiding principles that have to be interpreted by judges and who then benefit from a certain discretionary power. However, it can also be argued that the discretionary power of judges is limited and determined by the rules and practices which prevail in a society because individuals often view them by the decisions made by other judges. Common law judges make their decisions by using rules that no one has explicitly and intentionally created. This explains that common law systems are assumed to be ruled by "the law" rather than by "men"; from this perspective, they are not different from competitive markets that are ruled by prices rather than regulated by monopolist price-makers (on the "rule of law", see for instance Boettke and Oprea, 2003).

One should nonetheless note that this perspective on common law systems as decentralized and market-like is too optimistic and idealistic (see Tullock, 1997, ch. 2). To be more precise, common law systems differ from customary legal orders: the very existence of a state-sponsored legal apparatus makes all the difference. No surprise then if common law systems are far more centralized not only than customary legal orders but also than what their defenders assume. These are systems in which judges benefit from a non negligible discretionary power because their task not only consists in discovering legal rules but also in "creating" them. Furthermore, many instances can be found that show how those in power in common law countries – such as Canada, England, or the USA – have succeeded in escaping the law and excluded themselves from the control of the law. As Gordon Tullock said, "Many of the public institutions of the U.S. legal system were developed to facilitate the monarchy's efforts to centralize and consolidate their power" (1977). Then, common law systems appear to be closer to statute law ones than to "lawless" orders.

Statute or civil law systems

As a third "family" of legal systems, used in France, ex-French colonies, and continental Europe, statute or civil law systems share one (fundamental) element in common with the preceding "family" of legal systems: the existence of a legal apparatus and a state-sponsored legal organization. But these two families of systems differ with regard to the nature of rules, that is, to be more precise, they differ with regard to the role of judges and of the legal organization in the *creation* of rules. Firstly, there is a larger proportion of statutes, that is rules enacted by legislators, in statute law than in common law systems and, as a consequence, the role of judges and that of customs and norms are less important.

A central feature of common law systems is that judges are supposedly constrained by customs and by jurisprudential norms that they have to take into account in their decisions. By contrast, in statute law systems, the decisions taken by judges are less dependent on past decisions or on decisions made by other judges than in common law systems. There exist jurisprudential rules that judges may choose to follow but, at least theoretically, these are not the most important rules in the hierarchy of norms upon which the legal order rests. The most important, higher rules in the legal hierarchy are those gathered in various legal codes. This is not to say that there are no codes in common law systems. But their nature and the process through which they are established differs from one system to the other. The statute law codes are not based on customs, as is the case in common law countries. They are made of rules explicitly devised and created by a monopolist provider and then imposed on the individuals and statute law codes are established through a top-down process.

From an economic perspective, these systems are compared to and analyzed as monopolist legal systems, or as systems in which there exists a "central planner" (Cooter, 1996, op. cit.; Leoni, 1961 [1991], p. 19) in charge of the provision of legal rules. Therefore, these systems are criticized for suffering from exactly the same problems as those that also affect monopolies and centralized economic systems. In particular, legislators or codifiers have no incentives to devise efficient rules. On the contrary, they are vulnerable to the pressures of rent-seeking groups. It can be the case that centralized legal systems create uncertainty and instability because rules can change without rhyme or reason. Also, those central legal planners cannot gather the relevant information on individual practices and are therefore unable to devise rules that can be easily accepted by individuals. As a consequence, statute law systems are "inferior" to common law systems: not only less efficient in economic terms – this will be discussed later – but also in terms of order because they generate instability and uncertainty.

These analyses are developed by defenders of common law systems that rest on the misleading assumption that there are no differences between common law systems and customary legal orders, which we have noted earlier are two different legal systems. Then, statute law and common law systems may share the same disadvantages. Furthermore, in terms of advantages, it appears centralized statute law systems do not face the problems of harmonization that affect common law orders. All the more that, as it has been shown in the case of the French Code Napoleon (see Merryman, 1985; Josselin and Marciano, 2002) and of the German civil Code (Merryman, 1985), legal rules are not created with total arbitrariness. Codification appears to consist in mixing existing emergent customs with explicitly constructed rules.

These observations confirm that the differences between statute law and common law systems are less actual than is often theoretically assumed in particular, as comparative legal scholars have insisted, in a global era such as ours. This certainly does not mean that analyses based on "legal families" or "legal origins", such as those summarized in this introduction, are useless. Instead, it rather implies that the categories presented in this section can best be viewed as ideal-types or models or as ideal representations of actual systems; these models are necessary for scientific analysis.

References

Summary

The literature on the different legal systems is huge, especially on customary legal systems and common law systems. We can explain this by the fact that economists and legal scholars are interested in systems of rules capable of coordinating individuals' plans of action without the necessary intervention of a third, external player – that is, without the intervention of the State. When deciding which articles to include in this volume, it was particularly difficult to choose one out of dozens of articles published on the virtues (or vices) of spontaneous coordination. Hence, a list of important papers that provide interesting theoretical analysis illustrated with case studies has been provided. Among the key articles, we have chosen to include David Friedman's "Private Creation and Enforcement of Law". This is one of the earlier works of the issue of spontaneous orders and their legal systems – the case of Iceland. Also of interest is the fact that Friedman's analysis reveals some limits and problems which such lawless orders must try and solve.

With regard to the systems of common law, it is at the same time more difficult and easier to find general articles devoted to the economics of those legal systems. The explanation is that most of the research done in this domain refers to specific legal or to aspects that will be discussed in the next sections (the role of judges, the *stare decisis* principle and the efficiency of spontaneous orders). It is nonetheless informative to refer to the works of F. A. Hayek (in particular, "Rules and Order", the first volume of *Law, Legislation and Liberty*) when providing a philosophical explanation or justification of why common law systems are perfect illustrations of spontaneous orders (which is probably not the case) – one can find a critical review of Hayek's definition of "common law as custom" in Posner's *Economic Analysis of Law* (2007, pp. 259–260).

I have chosen to reproduce in this volume two more related articles. The first one, by Peter Aranson, is a study of Bruno Leoni and his *Freedom and the Law*. This is an interesting paper because it is written by a defender of common law systems writing about another defender and promoter of common law systems. It provides a good summary of the advantages of the common law and of the disadvantages of centralized legal systems, as viewed by the promoters of common law systems. Complementarily, another paper is proposed, in which Richard Wagner demonstrates why comparisons between these two kinds of systems is impossible because, Wagner claims, "there is no such thing as the common law or statute law process".

Finally, a fourth article is reprinted that is devoted to the German civil code. As its author Jürgen Backhaus notes, the German civil code was "passed with the explicit input of the leading economists of their time in Germany, and based on explicit economic reasoning" (1999, p. 9). It therefore provides a good illustration of the use of economics in a process of explicitly designing a legal code.

Further reading

Aranson, Peter A. 1988. "Bruno Leoni in Retrospect", *Harvard Journal of Law and Public Policy*, 11 (3), pp. 661–711.

Backhaus, Juergen. 1999. "The German Civil Code of 1896: An Economic Interpretation", *European Journal of Law and Economics*, 7 (1), 5–14.

Benson, Bruce. 1989. "Enforcement of Private Property Rights in Primitive Societies: Law Without Government", *Journal of Libertarian Studies*, 9 (1), pp. 1–26.

Benson, Bruce L. 1991. "An Evolutionary Contractarian View of Primitive Law: The Institutions and Incentives Arising under Indian Law", *Review of Austrian Economics*, 5 (1), pp. 41–65.

Benson, Bruce L. 1999. "An Economic Theory of the Evolution of Governance and the Emergence of the State", *Review of Austrian Economics*, 12 (2), pp. 131–160.

Bernstein, Lisa. 1992. "Opting Out of the Legal System: Extralegal Contractual Relations in the Diamond Industry", *Journal of Legal Studies*, 21 (1), pp. 115–157.

Boettke, Peter and Ryan Oprea. 2003. "Rule of law", in *The Encyclopedia of Public Choice*, edited by Charles Rowley and Friedrich Schneider. Boston: Kluwer Academic Publishing, Vol. 2, pp. 507–510.

Cooter, Robert D. 1991. "Inventing Market Property: The Land Courts of Papua New Guinea", *Law and Society Review*, 25 (4), pp. 759–801.

Cooter, Robert D. 1996. "Decentralized Law for a Complex Economy: The Structural Approach to Adjudicating the New Law Merchant", *University of Pennsylvania Law Review*, 144 (5), pp. 1643–1696.

Ellickson, Robert. 1991. *Order Without Law: How Neighbors Settle Disputes*. Cambridge, Mass: Harvard University Press.

Friedman, David. 1979. "Private Creation and Enforcement of Law: A Historical Case", *Journal of Legal Studies*, 8 (2), pp. 399–415, reprinted in this volume.

Greif, Avner. 1989. "Reputation and Coalitions in Medieval Trade: Evidence on the Maghribi Traders", *Journal of Economic History*, 49 (4), pp. 857–882.

Greif, Avner, Paul Milgrom and Barry R. Weingast. 1994. "Coordination, Commitment, and Enforcement: The Case of the Merchant Guild", *Journal of Political Economy*, 102 (4), 745–776.

Hayek, Friedrich. 1973. *Law, Legislation and Liberty, Vol. 1: Rules and Order*. London: Kegan Paul.

Josselin, Jean-Michel and Alain Marciano. 2002. "The Making of the French Civil Code: An Economic Interpretation", *European Journal of Law and Economics*, 14 (3), pp. 193–203.

Landa, Janet T. 1981. "The Political Economy of The Ethnically Homogenous Chinese Middleman Group in Southeast Asia: Ethnicity and Entrepreneurship in a Plural Society", in *The Chinese in Southeast Asia: Ethnicity and Economic Activity*, Peter Goslong and Linda Y. C. Lim (eds). Singapore: Maruzen Asia, for Economic Research Centre and Centre for South and Southeast Asian Studies, pp. 86–101.

Landa, Janet T. 1983. "A Theory of The Ethnically Homogenous Middleman Group: An Institutional Alternative to Contract Law", *Journal of Legal Studies*, 10 (2), pp. 349–362.

Landes, William and Richard A. Posner. 1975. "The Private Enforcement of Law", *Journal of Legal Studies*, 4 (1), pp. 1–46.

Leeson, Peter. 2007. "An-arrgh-chy: The Law and Economics of Pirate Organization", *Journal of Political Economy*, 115 (6), pp. 1049–1094.

Leoni, Bruno. 1961 [1991]. *Freedom and the Law*. Indianapolis: Liberty Fund.

Merryman, John Henry. 1985. *The Civil Law Tradition: An Introduction to the Legal Systems of Western Europe and Latin America*, Stanford, CA: Stanford University Press.

Milgrom, Paul R., Douglass North and Barry R. Weingast. 1990. "The Role of Institutions in the Revival of Trade: The Medieval Merchant Law, Private Judges and the Champagne Fairs", *Economics and Politics*, 2 (1), 1–23.

Parisi, Franceso. 2000. "Spontaneous Emergence of Law: Customary Law", in *Encyclopedia of Law and Economics*, edited by Bouckaert, Boudewijn and De Geest, Gerrit (eds). Cheltenham, Edward Elgar.

Ogus, Anthony. 1999. "Self Regulation", in *Encyclopedia of Law and Economics*, Boudewijn Bouckaert and Gerrit De Geest (eds). Cheltenham: Edward Elgar.

Schwartz, Alan and Robert E. Scott. 1995. "The Political Economy of Private Legislatures", *University of Pennsylvania Law Review*, 143 (3), pp. 595–654.

Tullock, Gordon. 1971. *The Logic of Law*. New York and London: Basic Books.

Tullock, Gordon. 1980. *Trials on Trial: The Pure Theory of Legal Procedure*. New York: Columbia University Press.

Tullock, Gordon. 1997. *The Case Against the Common Law, The Blackstone Commentaries*. Fairfax: Locke Institute.

Chapter 9

David Friedman

PRIVATE CREATION AND ENFORCEMENT OF LAW

A historical case

Introduction[1]

T HE PURPOSE OF THIS paper is to examine the legal and political institutions of Iceland from the tenth to the thirteenth centuries. They are of interest for two reasons. First, they are relatively well documented; the sagas were written by people who had lived under that set of institutions[2] and provide a detailed inside view of their workings. Legal conflicts were of great interest to the medieval Icelanders; Njal, the eponymous hero of the most famous of the sagas,[3] is not a warrior but a lawyer—"so skilled in law that no one was considered his equal." In the action of the sagas, law cases play as central a role as battles.

Second, medieval Icelandic institutions have several peculiar and interesting characteristics; they might almost have been invented by a mad economist to test the lengths to which market systems could supplant government in its most fundamental functions. Killing was a civil offense resulting in a fine paid to the survivors of the victim. Laws were made by a "parliament," seats in which were a marketable commodity. Enforcement of law was entirely a private affair. And yet these extraordinary institutions survived for over three hundred years, and the society in which they survived appears to have been in many ways an attractive one. Its citizens were, by medieval standards, free; differences in status based on rank or sex were relatively small;[4] and its literary output in relation to its size has been compared, with some justice, to that of Athens.[5]

While these characteristics of the Icelandic legal system may seem peculiar, they are not unique to medieval Iceland. The wergeld—the fine for killing a man—was an essential part of the legal system of Anglo-Saxon England, and still exists in New Guinea.[6] The sale of legislative seats has been alleged in many societies and existed openly in some. Private enforcement existed both in the American West[7] and in pre-nineteenth-century Britain; a famous character of eighteenth-century fiction,

Mr. Peachum in Gay's "Beggar's Opera," was based on Jonathan Wild, self-titled "Thief-Taker General," who profitably combined the professions of thief-taker, recoverer of stolen property, and large-scale employer of thieves for eleven years, until he was finally hanged in 1725.[8] The idea that law is primarily private, that most offenses are offenses against specific individuals or families, and that punishment of the crime is primarily the business of the injured party seems to be common to many early systems of law and has been discussed at some length by Maine with special reference to the early history of Roman law.[9]

Medieval Iceland, however, presents institutions of private enforcement of law in a purer form than any other well-recorded society of which I am aware. Even early Roman law recognized the existence of crimes, offenses against society rather than against any individual, and dealt with them, in effect, by using the legislature as a special court.[10] Under Anglo-Saxon law killing was an offense against the victim's family, his lord, and the lord of the place whose peace had been broken; wergeld was paid to the family, manbote to the crown, and fightwite to the respective lords.[11] British thief-takers in the eighteenth century were motivated by a public reward of £40 per thief.[12] All of these systems involved some combination of private and public enforcement. The Icelandic system developed without any central authority comparable to the Anglo-Saxon king;[13] as a result, even where the Icelandic legal system recognized an essentially "public" offense, it dealt with it by giving some individual (in some cases chosen by lot from those affected) the right to pursue the case and collect the resulting fine, thus fitting it into an essentially private system.

In the structure of its legislature, Iceland again presents an almost pure form of an institution, elements of which exist elsewhere. British pocket boroughs, like Icelandic *goðorð*, represented marketable seats in the legislature, but Parliament did not consist entirely of representatives from pocket boroughs. All *goðorð* were marketable and (with the exception, after Iceland's conversion to Christianity, of the two Icelandic bishops) all seats in the *lögrétta* were held by the owners of *goðorð*, or men chosen by them.

The early history of Iceland thus gives us a well-recorded picture of the workings of particularly pure forms of private enforcement and creation of law, and of the interaction between the two. Such a picture is especially interesting because elements of both have existed, and continue to exist, in many other societies, including our own.

There are three questions in the economics of law which I believe this history may illuminate. The first is the feasibility of private enforcement.[14] The second is the question of whether political institutions can and do generate "efficient" law. The third is the question of what laws are in fact efficient. All three involve formidable theoretical difficulties; in the body of this paper I limit myself to sketching the arguments, describing how the Icelandic institutions worked, and attempting to draw some tentative conclusions. Appendix A gives some numerical information on the scale of punishments in Iceland, and Appendix B suggests how the Icelandic system might be adapted to modern society.

The modern literature

Some years ago, Becker and Stigler pointed out that a system of private enforcement of law, in which the person who caught a criminal received the fine paid by the offender, would have certain attractive characteristics;[15] in particular, there would be no incentive for bribery of the enforcer by the criminal, since any bribe that it paid the criminal to offer it would pay the enforcer to refuse.[16] The argument was criticized by Landes and Posner; they argued that since the level of fine determined both the "price" of criminal activities to the criminal and the "price" of enforcement activities, it could not in general be set at a level which would optimize both criminal and enforcement activities.[17] They further argued that enforcement had a positive externality (raising the probability of catching a criminal, hence lowering total crime) which would not be internalized by the enforcer; this effect by itself would tend to lead to suboptimal enforcement.

The first argument may well be correct; since government enforcement also provides no guarantee of optimality, it leaves open the question of which system is superior, as Landes and Posner pointed out. This is an empirical question and one on which the Icelandic case may provide some evidence. Landes and Posner's second argument shows insufficient ingenuity in constructing hypothetical institutions. If "enforcers" contract in advance to pursue those who perpetrate crimes against particular people, and so notify the criminals (by a notice on the door of their customers), the deterrent effect of catching criminals is internalized; the enforcers can charge their customers for the service. Such arrangements are used by private guard firms and the American Automobile Association, among others. The AAA provides its members with decals stating that, if the car is stolen, a reward will be paid for information leading to its recovery. Such decals serve both as an offer to potential informants and as a warning to potential thieves. Under medieval Icelandic institutions, who was protected by whom was to a considerable degree known in advance.

Another difficulty with private enforcement is that some means must be found to allocate rights to catch criminals—otherwise one enforcer may expend resources gathering evidence only to have the criminal arrested at the last minute by someone else. This corresponds to the familiar "commons" problem. One solution in the literature[18] is to let the right to prosecute a criminal be the private property of the victim; by selling it to the highest bidder he receives some compensation for the cost of the crime. This describes precisely the Icelandic arrangements.

Posner has asserted at some length[19] that current common law institutions have produced economically efficient law. I will argue that while that may or may not be true of those institutions, there are reasons why the Icelandic institutions might be expected to produce such law. Two specific features of "efficient" law in the Icelandic system which I will discuss are efficient punishment and the distinction between civil and criminal offenses.

History and institutions

In the latter half of the ninth century, King Harald Fairhair unified Norway under his rule. A substantial part of the population left;[20] many went either directly to Iceland, which had been discovered a few years before, or indirectly via Norse colonies in England, Ireland, Orkney, the Hebrides, and the Shetland Islands. The political system which they developed there was based on Norwegian (or possibly Danish[21]) traditions but with one important innovation—the King was replaced by an assembly of local chieftains. As in Norway (before Harald) there was nothing corresponding to a strictly feudal bond. The relationship between the Icelandic *goði* and his thingmen (*þingmenn*) was contractual, as in early feudal relationships, but it was not territorial; the *goði* had no claim to the thingman's land and the thingman was free to transfer his allegiance.

At the base of the system stood the *goði* (pl. *goðar*) and the *goðorð* (pl. *goðorð*). A *goði* was a local chief who built a (pagan) temple and served as its priest; the *goðorð* was the congregation. The *goði* received temple dues and provided in exchange both religious and political services.

Under the system of laws established in A.D. 930 and modified somewhat thereafter, these local leaders were combined into a national system. Iceland was divided into four quarters, and each quarter into nine *goðorð*.[22] Within each quarter the *goðorð* were clustered in groups of three called things. Only the *goðar* owning these *goðorð* had any special status within the legal system, although it seems that others might continue to call themselves *goði* (in the sense of priest) and have a *goðorð* (in the sense of congregation); to avoid confusion, I will hereafter use the terms *goði* and *goðorð* only to refer to those having a special status under the legal system.

The one permanent official of this system was the *lögsögumaðr* or law-speaker; he was elected every three years by the inhabitants of one quarter (which quarter it was being chosen by lot). His job was to memorize the laws, to recite them through once during his term in office, to provide advice on difficult legal points, and to preside over the *lögrétta*, the "legislature."

The members of the *lögrétta* were the *goðar*, plus one additional man from each thing, plus for each of these two advisors. Decisions in the *lögrétta* were made, at least after the reforms attributed to Njal, by majority vote, subject apparently to attempts to first achieve unanimity.[23]

The laws passed by the *lögrétta* were applied by a system of courts, also resting on the *goðar*. At the lowest level were private courts, the members being chosen after the conflict arose, half by the plaintiff and half by the defendant—essentially a system of arbitration. Above this was the thing court or "Varthing", the judges[24] in which were chosen twelve each by the *goðar* of the thing, making thirty-six in all. Next came the quarter-thing for disputes between members of different things within the same quarter; these seem to have been little used and not much is known about them.[25] Above them were the four quarter courts of the Althing (*Alþingi*) or national assembly—an annual meeting of all the *goðar* each bringing with him at least one-ninth of his thingmen. Above them, after Njal's reforms, was the fifth court. Cases undecided at any level of the court system went to the next level; at every level (except the private courts) the judges were appointed by the *goðar*, each quarter court and the fifth court having judges appointed by the *goðar* from all over Iceland.[26] The fifth court reached its decision by majority vote; the other courts seem to have required that there be at most six (out of thirty-six) dissenting votes in order for a verdict to be given.[27]

The *goðorð* itself was in effect two different things. It was a group of men—the particular men who had agreed to follow *that goði,* to be members of that *goðorð.* Any man could be challenged to name his *goðorð* and was required to do so, but he was free to choose any *goði* within his quarter and to change to a different *goðorð* at will.[28] It was also a bundle of rights—the right to sit in the *lögrétta*, appoint judges for certain courts, etc. The *goðorð* in this second sense was marketable property. It could be given away, sold, held by a partnership, inherited, or whatever.[29] Thus seats in the law-making body were quite literally for sale.

I have described the legislative and judicial branches of "government" but have omitted the executive. So did the Icelanders. The function of the courts was to deliver verdicts on cases brought to them. That done, the court was finished. If the verdict went against the defendant, it was up to him to pay the assigned punishment—almost always a fine. If he did not, the plaintiff could go to court again and have the defendant declared an outlaw. The killer of an outlaw could not himself be prosecuted for the act; in addition, anyone who gave shelter to an outlaw could be prosecuted for doing so.

Prosecution was up to the victim (or his survivors). If they and the offender agreed on a settlement, the matter was settled.[30] Many cases were settled by arbitration, including the two most serious conflicts that arose prior to the final period of breakdown in the thirteenth century. If the case went to a court, the judgment, in case of conviction, would be a fine to be paid by the defendant to the plaintiff.

In modern law the distinction between civil and criminal law depends on whether prosecution is private or public; in this sense all Icelandic law was civil. But another distinction is that civil remedies usually involve a transfer (of money, goods, or services) from the defendant to the plaintiff, whereas criminal remedies often involve some sort of "punishment." In this sense the distinction existed in Icelandic law, but its basis was different.

Killing was made up for by a fine. For murder a man could be outlawed, even if he was willing to pay a fine instead. In our system, the difference between murder and killing (manslaughter) depends on intent; for the Icelanders it depended on something more easily judged. After killing a man, one was obliged to announce the fact immediately; as one law code puts it: "The slayer shall not ride past any three houses, on the day he committed the deed, without avowing the deed, unless the kinsmen of the slain man, or enemies of the slayer lived there, who would put his life in danger."[31] A man who tried to hide the body, or otherwise conceal his responsibility, was guilty of murder.[32]

Analysis

One obvious objection to a system of private enforcement is that the poor (or weak) would be defenseless. The Icelandic system dealt with this problem by giving the victim a property right—the right to be reimbursed by the criminal—and making that right transferable. The victim could turn over his case to someone else, either gratis or in return for a consideration.[33] A man who did not have sufficient resources to prosecute a case or enforce a verdict could sell it to another who did and who expected to make a profit in both money and reputation by winning the case and collecting the fine. This meant that an attack on even the poorest victim could lead to eventual punishment.

A second objection is that the rich (or powerful) could commit crimes with impunity, since nobody would be able to enforce judgment against them. Where power is sufficiently concentrated this might be true; this was one of the problems which led to the eventual breakdown of the Icelandic legal system in the thirteenth century.[34] But so long as power was reasonably dispersed, as it seems to have been for the first two centuries after the system was established, this was a less serious problem. A man who refused to pay his fines was outlawed and would probably not be supported by as many of his friends as the plaintiff seeking to enforce judgment, since in case of violent conflict his defenders would find themselves legally in the wrong. If the lawbreaker defended himself by force, every injury inflicted on the partisans of the other side would result in another suit, and every refusal to pay another fine would pull more people into the coalition against him.

There is a scene in *Njal's Saga* that provides striking evidence of the stability of this system. Conflict between two groups has become so intense that open fighting threatens to break out in the middle of the court. A leader of one faction asks a benevolent neutral what he will do for them in case of a fight. He replies that if they are losing he will help them, and if they are winning he will break up the fight before they kill more men than they can afford![35] Even when the system seems so near to breaking down, it is still assumed that every enemy killed must eventually be paid for. The reason is obvious enough; each man killed will have friends and relations who are still neutral—and will remain neutral if and only if the killing is made up for by an appropriate wergeld.

I suggested earlier that one solution to the externality problem raised by Landes and Posner was to identify in advance the enforcer who would deal with crimes committed against a potential victim. In Iceland this was done by a system of existing coalitions—some of them *goðorð,* some clearly defined groups of friends and relatives. If a member of such a coalition was killed, it was in the interest of the other members to collect wergeld for him even if the cost was more than the amount that would be collected; their own safety depended partly on their reputation for doing so. This corresponds precisely to the solution to the problem of deterrence externality described above.

How well do the Icelandic laws fit the ideas of "economically efficient" law in the modern literature?[36] In Appendix A, I give some quantitative calculations on the value of various fines. Here I will discuss two qualitative features of Icelandic law which seem to correspond closely to the prescriptions of modern analysis.

The first is the prevalence of fines. A fine is a costless punishment; the cost to the payer is balanced by a benefit to the recipient. It is in this respect superior to punishments such as execution, which imposes cost but no corresponding benefit, or imprisonment, which imposes costs on both the criminal and the taxpayers.[37]

The difficulty with using fines as punishments is that many criminals may be unable to pay a fine large enough to provide adequate deterrence. The Icelandic system dealt with this in three ways. First, the offenses for which fines were assessed were offenses for which the chance of detection was unity, as explained below; it was thus sufficient for the fine to correspond to the cost of the crime, without any additional factor to compensate for the chance of not being caught.[38] Second, the society provided effective credit arrangements. The same coalitions mentioned above provided their members with money to pay large fines. Third, a person unable to discharge his financial obligation could apparently be reduced to a state of temporary slavery until he had worked off his debt.[39]

The second feature is the distinction between what I have called civil and criminal offenses. Since civil offenses were offenses in which the criminal made no attempt to hide his guilt, a reasonably low punishment was sufficient to deter most of them. High punishments were reserved for crimes whose detection was uncertain because the criminal tried to conceal his guilt. A high punishment was therefore necessary to keep the expected punishment (at the time the crime was committed) from being very low.[40] Further, the difference between the two sorts of offenses provided a high "differential punishment" for the "offense" of concealing one's crime, an offense which imposed serious costs—both costs of detection and the punishment costs resulting from the need to use an inefficient punishment (since no payable fine, multiplied by a low probability of being caught, would provide a sufficiently high deterrent).

Generating efficient law

Is there any reason to expect the Icelandic system to generate efficient law? I believe the answer is a qualified yes. If some change in laws produced net benefits, it would in principle be possible for those who supported such a change to outbid its opponents, buy up a considerable number of goðorð, and legislate the change. A similar potential exists in any political system; one may think of it as the application of the Coase theorem to law. The effect is limited by transaction costs—which were probably large even in the Icelandic system but, because the goðorð was legally marketable, smaller than under other political arrangements.[41]

A second reason is that inefficient laws provided, in some cases, incentives for individual responses which could in turn make changes in the laws Pareto desirable (without side payments). Suppose, for example, that the wergeld for killing was too low—substantially below the point at which the cost of an increase to an individual (involving the possibility that he might be convicted of a killing and have to pay) balanced the advantages of increased security and higher payments if a relative were killed. The individual, functioning through the coalition of which he was a member, could then unilaterally "raise" the wergeld by announcing that if any member of the coalition were killed, the others would kill the killer (or some other member of his coalition, if he were not accessible) and let the two wergelds cancel. This is essentially what happens in the famous "killing match" in *Njal's Saga,* where Hallgerd and Bergthora alternately arrange revenge killings while their husbands, Njal and Gunnar, pass the same purse of silver back and forth between them.[42] Once such policies became widespread, it would be in the interest of everyone, potential killers, potential victims, and potential avengers, to raise the legal wergeld. And even before the legal wergeld was raised, killers would begin offering higher payments (as part of "out-of-court" settlements) to prevent revenge killings.[43]

Conclusion

It is difficult to draw any conclusion from the Icelandic experience concerning the viability of systems of private enforcement in the twentieth century. Even if Icelandic institutions worked well then, they might not work in a larger and more interdependent society. And whether the Icelandic institutions did work well is a matter of controversy; the sagas are perceived by many as portraying an essentially violent and unjust society, tormented by constant feuding. It is difficult to tell whether such judgments are correct. Most of the sagas were written down during or after the Sturlung period, the final violent breakdown of the Icelandic system in the thirteenth century. Their authors may have projected elements of what they saw around them on the earlier periods they described. Also, violence has always been good entertainment, and the saga writers may have selected their material accordingly. Even in a small and peaceful society novelists might be able to find, over the course of three hundred years, enough conflict for a considerable body of literature.

The quality of violence, in contrast to other medieval literature, is small in scale, intensely personal (every casualty is named), and relatively straightforward. Rape and torture are uncommon, the killing of women almost unheard of; in the very rare cases when an attacker burns the defender's home, women, children, and servants are first offered an opportunity to leave.[44] One indication that the total amount of violence may have been relatively small is a calculation based on the Sturlung sagas. During more than fifty years of what the Icelanders themselves perceived as intolerably violent civil war, leading to the collapse of the traditional system, the average number of people killed or executed each year appears, on a per capita basis, to be roughly equal to the current rate of murder and nonnegligent manslaughter in the United States.[45]

Whatever the correct judgment on the Icelandic legal system, we do know one thing: it worked—sufficiently well to survive for over three hundred years. In order to work, it had to solve, within its own institutional structure, the problems implicit in a system of private enforcement. Those solutions may or may not be still applicable, but they are certainly still of interest.

Appendix A: *Wages and Wergelds*

Two different monies were in common use in medieval Iceland. One was silver, the other wadmal *(vaðmál)*, a woolen cloth. Silver was measured in ounces *(aurar)* and in marks; the mark contained eight ounces. Wadmal was of a standard width of about a meter, and was measured in Icelandic ells *(alnar)* of about 56 centimeters.[46] The value of an ounce *(eyrir)* of silver varied, during the twelfth and thirteenth centuries, between 6 and 7 ½ ells.[47] The "law ounce" was set at 6 ells;[48] this appears to have been a money of account, not an attempt at price fixing.

Grágás, the earliest book of Icelandic written law, contains a passage setting maximum wages—presumably an attempt to enforce a monopsonistic cartel agreement by the landowning thingmen against their employees.[49] The passage is unclear; Þorkell Jóhannesson estimates from it that the farm laborer's wage, net of room and board, amounted to about one mark of silver a year and cites another writer who estimates it at about three-quarters of a mark.[50] Þorkell Jóhannesson also states that wages (net of room and board) seem to have been low or zero at the time of settlement but to have risen somewhat by the second half of the tenth century. He dates *Grágás* to the second half of the twelfth century, or perhaps earlier; Conybeare gives its date as 1117.

These figures give us only a very approximate idea of Icelandic wages. The existence of maximum wage legislation suggests that the equilibrium wage was higher than the legislated wage.[51] But wages, as Þorkell Jóhannesson points out, must have varied considerably with good and bad years; the legislation might be an attempt to hold wages in good years to a level below equilibrium but above the average wage.

I have attempted another and independent estimate of wages, based on the fact that one of the two monetary commodities was woolen cloth, a material which is highly labor intensive. If we knew how many hours went into spinning and weaving an ell of wadmal, we could estimate the market wage rate; if it takes y hours to produce one ell, then the wage of the women making cloth (including the value of any payment in kind they receive) should be about $1/y$.

I have estimated y in two ways—from figures given by Hoffman for the productivity of Icelandic weavers using the same technology at later periods,[52] and from estimates given me by Geraldine Duncan, who has herself worked with a warp-weighted loom and a drop spindle, the tools used by medieval Icelandic weavers.[53] Both methods lead to imprecise results: the first because reports disagree and also because the sources are vague whether the time given is for weaving only or for both weaving and spinning, the second because Mrs. Duncan did not know the precise characteristics of wadmal, or precisely how the skill of medieval Icelandic weavers compared with her own. My conclusion is that it took about a day to spin and weave an ell of wadmal; this estimate could easily be off by a factor of two in either direction. If we assume that, in a relatively poor society such as Iceland, a considerable portion of the income of an ordinary worker went for room and board, this figure is consistent with that given in *Grágás*.

A rough check on these estimates of wages is provided by the fact that the *lögsögumaðr* received an annual salary of 200 ells of wadmal, plus a part of the fines for certain minor offenses. While his position was not a full-time one, it involved more than just the two weeks of the Althing; he was required to give information on the law to all comers. Since the man chosen for the post was an unusually talented individual, it does not seem unreasonable that the fixed part of his salary (which, unlike the wages discussed before, did *not* include room and board) amounted to five year's wages, or an amount of wadmal which would have taken about ten months to produce. Thus, this figure is not inconsistent with my previous estimate of wages.

It is interesting to note that during the Sturlung period, when wealth had become relatively concentrated, the richest men had a net worth of about three to four hundred year's production of wadmal—or about a thousand cows. The former figure would correspond today to about six million dollars, but the latter to only a few hundred thousand—wages having risen considerably more, over the last millenium, than the price of cattle.

Table 9.1 gives values for a number of things in ounces, ells, years of production of wadmal, and years of wages. The ounce is assumed to be worth six ells, the year's production of wadmal to be three hundred ells (three hundred days at one ell/day) and the year's wage to be one mark of forty-eight ells.

Wergeld for a thrall, the price of a thrall, and the manumission price of a thrall were all equal, as might be expected. The price of a thrall presumably represents the capitalized value of his production net of room and board. It seems at first surprising that this should amount to only a year and a half of wages (also net of room and board), but we must remember that wages, according to Þorkell Jóhanneson, were lower in the early period, when thralldom was common; thralldom disappeared in Iceland by the early twelfth century, about when *Grágás* was being written.

It is worth noting that the wergeld for a thrall was considerably lower than for a free man. This is to be expected. The wergeld for a thrall was paid to his master and

Table 9.1

	Ounces	Ells	Years Production of Wadmal	Years Wages	Source
Normal price of male thrall	12	72	.24	1.5	Carl O. Williams, *supra* note 4, at 29
Manumission price of thrall	12	72	.24	1.5	Sveinbjorn Johnson, *supra* note 4, at 225
Wergeld for thrall	12	72	.24	1.5	*Id.*
Wergeld for free man	100	600	2	12.5	Njal's saga, *supra* note 3, at 108
Wergeld for free man[a]	400	2400	8	50	*Id.*
Wergeld for important man	200	1200	4	25	*Id.* at 255 ns.
Wergeld for important man[a]	800	4800	16	100	*Id.*
Law-speaker Salary		200+	.8+	5 +	Vigfusson & Powell, *supra* note 1, at 348
Wealth of very rich man (Sturlung period)		120,000	400	2500	Einar Ólafur Sveinsson, *supra* note 44, 45
Wealth of very rich man (Sturlung period)		96,000	320	2000	*Id.*
Price of cow (c. A.D. 1200)		90–96	.3–.32	1.9–2	*Id.* at 56.

[a] Magnusson and Palsson (Njal's Saga, *supra* note 3, at 63, trans., n.) interpret the ounce by which compensations are measured as probably meaning "an ounce of unrefined silver . . . worth four legal ounces." Williams, *supra* note 4, at 31, interprets it as the legal ounce.

it was his master, not the thrall, who had some part in the political bargaining process by which, I have argued, wergelds were set. The value of a thrall to his master would be the capitalized value of his net product. But the value of a free man to himself and his family includes not only his net product but also the value to him of being alive. Food and board, in other words, are expenses to the owner of a thrall but consumption to a free man. Furthermore, one would expect that the costs of the thrall to the owner would include costs of guarding and supervision that would not apply to the free man's calculation of his own value.

If we interpret the "ounce" of *Njal's Saga* as a legal ounce, the usual wergelds for free men again seem somewhat low, ranging from 12½ year's wages for an ordinary man to twice that for a man of some importance.[54] Here again, we must remember that there is considerable uncertainty in our wage figures. Twelve and a half years' wages might be a reasonable estimate of the value of a man to his family, assuming a market interest rate of between 5 and 10 percent, but it hardly seems to include much allowance for his value to himself. If we accept the interpretation in Magnusson and Palsson[55] of the ounce in which the wergelds of *Njal's Saga* are paid as an ounce of unrefined silver, worth four legal ounces, the figures seem more reasonable.

Appendix B

The first step in applying the Icelandic system of private enforcement to a modern society would be to convert all criminal offenses into civil offenses, making the offender liable to pay an appropriate fine to the victim. In some cases, it might not be obvious who the victim was, but that could be specified by legislation. The Icelanders had the same problem and took care to specify who had the right to pursue each case, even for procedural offenses.[56] For some minor offenses anyone could sue; presumably, whoever submitted his case first would be entitled to the fine. It must be remembered that specifying the victim has the practical function of giving someone an incentive to pursue the case.

The second step would be to make the victim's claim marketable, so that he could sell it to someone willing to catch and convict the offender. The amount of the claim would correspond approximately to the damage caused by the crime divided by the probability of catching the criminal.[57] In many cases it would be substantial.

Once these steps were taken, a body of professional "thief-takers" (as they were once called in England) would presumably develop and gradually replace our present governmental police forces.

One serious problem with such institutions is that most criminals are judgment proof: their resources are insufficient to pay any large fine. The obvious way to deal with this would be some variation on Icelandic debt-thralldom. An arrangement which protects the convicted criminal against the most obvious abuses would be for every sentence to take the form of "so many years or so many dollars." The criminal would then have the choice of serving out the sentence in years or accepting bids for his services. The employer making such a bid would offer the criminal some specified working conditions (possibly inside a private prison, possibly not) and a specified rate at which the employer would pay off the fine. In order to get custody of the criminal, the employer would have to obtain his consent and post bond with the court for the amount of the fine. In order for the private-enforcement system to work, it would be necessary for most criminals to choose to work off their sentences instead of sitting them out (since their fines provide the enforcer's incentive). This could be arranged by appropriately adjusting the ratio between the number of years and the number of dollars in the sentence.

There might be some crimes, such as murder, for which the appropriate fine would be so high that the convicted killer would be unable to work it off, however unattractive the alternative. For such cases the system would break down and would have to be supplemented by some alternative arrangement—perhaps a large bounty paid by the state for the apprehension and conviction of murderers.

It would be beyond the scope of this article to argue the advantages and disadvantages of such a system, or to compare at length its potential abuses with those of our present system of enforcement and punishment; it would be beyond my competence to discuss the legal problems, and in particular the constitutional objections, that might be raised to its introduction.

Notes

1   I have been hampered in this work by my unfortunate ignorance of Old Norse. In particular *Grágás,* the earliest compilation of Icelandic law, seems never to have been translated into English, save for a few fragments in Origines Icelandicae (Gudbrand Vigfusson & F. York Powell trans. 1905) [hereinafter cited as Vigfusson & Powell]. A Norse scholar willing to correct that lack would do a considerable service to those interested in the legal institutions of this extraordinary society.

2   Most of the principal sagas were written down in the second half of the thirteenth century or, at the latest, the first half of the fourteenth. Prior to 1262 the institutions seem to have been relatively close to those established in the tenth century, although their workings may have been substantially different as a result of the increased concentration of wealth and power which led to their final collapse.

3   Magnus Magnusson & Hermann Palsson trans., Njal's Saga (Penguin ed. 1960) [hereinafter cited as Njal's Saga].

4   Sveinbjorn Johnson, Pioneers of Freedom (1930). A partial exception is the status of thralls, although even they seem freer than one might expect; in one saga a thrall owns a famous sword, and his master must ask his permission to borrow it. Carl O. Williams, in Thraldom in Ancient Iceland 36 (1937), estimates that there were no more than 2000 thralls in Iceland at any one time, which would be about 3% of the population. Williams believes they were very badly treated, but this may reflect his biases; for example, he repeatedly asserts that thralls were not permitted weapons despite numerous instances to the contrary in the sagas. Stefansson estimates the average period of servitude before manumission at only five years but does not state his evidence. Vilhjalmur Stefansson, Icelandic Independence, Foreign Affairs, January 1929, at 2 70.

5   C. A. Vansittart Conybeare, The Place of Iceland in the History of European Institutions 6–8 (1877).

6   New York Times, Feb. 16, 1972, at 17, col. 6. For an extensive survey of wergeld in Anglo-Saxon and other early societies, see Frederic Seebohm, Tribal Custom in Anglo-Saxon Law (1911).

7   Terry L. Anderson & P. J. Hill, An American Experiment in Anarcho-Capitalism: The *Not* So Wild, Wild West (1978) (staff paper in Economics, Montana State Univ. at Bozeman, Ag. Econ. & Econ. Dept.).

8   Marilyn E. Walsh, The Fence 17–23 (1977).

9   H. S. Maine, Ancient Law 355–71 (1963).

10   *Id*. at 360–61.

11   Seebohm, *supra* note 6, at 330–335; and Naomi D. Hurnard, The King's Pardon for Homicide before A.D. 1307, at 1–5 (1969).

12   Walsh, *supra* note 8, at 18–19.

13   "In no part of Anglo-Saxon England and at no time in its history is any trace to be found of a system of government knowing nothing of the rule of kings." P. H. Blair, An Introduction to Anglo-Saxon England 194 (2nd ed. 1977).

14   This question is discussed at some length in modern libertarian or anarcho-capitalist writings. See David Friedman, The Machinery of Freedom (1973); and Murray N. Rothbard, For a New Liberty (1973).

15   Gary Becker & George Stigler, Law Enforcement, Malfeasance, and Compensation of Enforcers, 3 J. Legal Stud. 1 (1974).

16   This is not quite true. Since the trial process might impose costs on the criminal, such as uncertainty and unreimbursed time, he might be willing to pay the enforcer more than the expected value of the fine. In this case, bribery is an efficient substitute for the court process.

17   William M. Landes & Richard A. Posner, The Private Enforcement of Law, 4 J. Legal Stud. 1 (1975).

18   *Id*. at 34.

19   Richard A. Posner, Economic Analysis of Law (2nd ed. 1977).

20   Some estimates put it at about 10%.

21   Barthi Guthmundsson, The Origin of the Icelanders (Lee M. Hollander trans. 1967), argues that the settlers were in large part Danes who had colonized in Norway and thus brought Danish institutions with them to Iceland.

22   In the northern quarter there were twelve *goðorð*; the rules for membership in the *lögrétta* and the appointment of judges were modified to compensate for this fact, so that the northern quarter had the same number of seats as each of the other three quarters. I shall ignore the resulting complications (and some other details of the system) in the remainder of the description. I shall also ignore the disputed question of which features were in the original system and which were added by modifications occurring between A.D. 930 and *c*. A.D. 1000.

23   Conybeare, supra note 5, at 95 ns.; and 1 Vigfusson & Powell, *supra* note 1, bk. 2, § 3, at 343–344.

24   The Icelandic judges correspond more nearly to the jurymen of our system than to the judge, since it was up to them to determine guilt or innocence. Conybeare, *supra* note 5, at 146. There was no equivalent of our judge; individual experts in the law could be consulted by the court. According to Sigurdur A. Magnusson, Northern Sphinx 14 (1977), "Since every breach of the law had a fixed fine, the judges merely had to decide whether the culprit was guilty or innocent." The *lögrétta* had the power to reduce sentences.

25   Conybeare, *supra* note 5, at 48.

26   *Id*. at 50–51. But Sveinbjorn Johnson, *supra* note 4, at 64; and James Bryce, Studies in History and Jurisprudence 274 (1901), state that the judges of the quarter court were appointed only by the *goðar* of that quarter.

27 Magnusson *supra* note 24, at 14; and Conybeare, *supra* note 5, at 95 ns., both interpret the requirement for the lower courts as no more than six dissenting votes. If
this was not achieved, the case was undecided and could be taken to a higher court.
While there does not seem to have been anything strictly equivalent to our system
of appeals, claims that a case had been handled illegally in one court could be
resolved in a higher court. In a famous case in *Njálssaga* the defendant tricks the
prosecution into prosecuting him in the wrong court (by secretly changing his
goðorð, and hence his quarter) in order to be able to sue the prosecutors in the fifth
court for doing so. *Id*. at 93–94; Njal's Saga, *supra* note 3, at 309–310. Similarly, if
a private court was unable to reach a verdict, or in cases of "contempt of court,
disturbance of the proceedings by violence, brawling, crowding, etc.," or if the
plaintiff was unwilling to submit the case to a private court, it went to the appropriate public court instead. Conybeare, *supra* note 5, at 77.

28 *Id*. at 33–34, 47; Bryce, *supra* note 26, at 268–69.

29 Conybeare, *supra* note 5, at 28.

30 But according to Johnson, *supra* note 4, at 112, for certain serious offenses
the plaintiff was liable to a fine if he compromised his suit after it had been
commenced.

31 Quoted by Conybeare, *supra* note 5, at 78 ns., from the *Gulaþing Code*.

32 For a discussion of the contrast between Icelandic and (modern) English ideas of
murder, see *id*. at 78–81.

33 For examples, see Njal's Saga, *supra* note 3, at 75, 151.

34 The question of why the system eventually broke down is both interesting and difficult. I believe that two of the proximate causes were increased concentration of
wealth, and hence power, and the introduction into Iceland of a foreign ideology—
kingship. The former meant that in many areas all or most of the *goðorð* were held
by one family and the latter that by the end of the Sturlung period the chieftains
were no longer fighting over the traditional quarrels of who owed what to whom,
but over who should eventually rule Iceland. The ultimate reasons for those changes
are beyond the scope of this paper.

35 "But if you are forced to give ground, you had better retreat in this direction, for I
shall have my men drawn up here in battle array ready to come to your help. If on
the other hand your opponents retreat, I expect they will try to reach the natural
stronghold of Almanna Gorge . . . I shall take it upon myself to bar their way to this
vantage ground with my men, but we shall not pursue them if they retreat north or
south along the river. And as soon as I estimate that you have killed off as many as
you can afford to pay compensation for without exile or loss of your chieftaincies,
I shall intervene with all my men to stop the fighting; and you must then obey my
orders, if I do all this for you." Njal's Saga, *supra* note 3, at 296–97. A similar passage
occurs *id*. at 162–63.

36 See especially Posner, *supra* note 19; and Gary Becker, Crime and Punishment: An
Economic Approach, 76 J. Pol. Econ. 169 (1968). Also, Gordon Tullock, The Logic
of the Law (1971).

37 I am here comparing the direct costs and benefits of different sorts of
punishment. Both execution and fine have the additional indirect "benefit" of
deterrence. Execution has the further indirect benefit of preventing repetition of
the crime.

38 Some additional punishment might be required to compensate for the chance
that a guilty person would be acquitted on a technicality, as sometimes happened.

The advantage of private enforcement for acts where detection is easy is discussed by Landes & Posner, *supra* note 17, at 31–35, in the context of modern law.

39   My only source for this is Williams, *supra* note 4, at 117–121. The system seems to have differed from the later English imprisonment for debt, which served as an incentive to pay debts but not as a means of doing so.

40   This may be only an approximate statement. The sagas describe many miscarriages of justice, including outlawry based on relatively minor offenses. Here as elsewhere I am trying to distinguish what the rules were from how they may sometimes have been applied, partly because I believe that misapplications probably became common only in the later years, as part of the general collapse of the system described in the Sturlung sagas. Since most of the sagas were written during or shortly after the Sturlung period, I regard their description of that period as accurate and their description of the earlier "saga" period as somewhat exaggerating the resemblance between the two periods. They portray the Sturlung period as one in which justice was less common than in the saga period, and much less common than in the period between the two.

41   For a description of a very different system of private production of law (by lawyers), see Maine, *supra* note 9, at 32–41. There seems no obvious reason to expect the Roman system he describes to generate efficient law.

42   Njal's Saga, chs. 36–45, at 98–119.

43   One common procedure was for the defendant to offer the plaintiff "self-judgment"—the right to set the fine himself.

44   Einar Ólafur Sveinsson, The Age of the Sturlungs 68, 73 (Jóhann S. Hannesson trans. 1953) (Islandica vol. 36); Njal's Saga 266.

45   *Id*. at 72 gives an estimate of three hundred and fifty killed in battle or executed during a fifty-two-year period (1208–1260). The population of Iceland was about seventy thousand. For the U.S. figures, see Michael S. Hindelang *et. al.*, Sourcebook of Criminal Justice Statistics—1976, at 443 (1977).

46   Marta Hoffman, The Warp-Weighted Loom 213 (1964).

47   Knut Gjerset, History of Iceland 206 (1924).

48   Njal's Saga 41, trans, n. Also Þorkell Jóhannesson, Die Stellung der Freien Arbeiter in Island 37 (1933).

49   *Id*. at 207–208.

50   *Id*. at 211.

51   The existence of maximum wage legislation raises a problem for my thesis that the Icelandic system generated efficient law. The simplest answer is that I do not expect to see perfectly efficient law. Maximum wage legislation can most naturally be interpreted as a cartel arrangement among the landowners; such an arrangement may well be in their interest, provided that the farm workers are unable, for organizational reasons connected with the public-good problem, to combine in order to bribe the landowners to repeal the legislation or, within the Icelandic system, to buy sufficient *goðorð* to repeal it themselves.

52   Hoffman, *supra* note 46, at 215–16.

53   Private communication.

54   In comparing this figure with current sentencing levels for murder or manslaughter, one must remember that killing, in Icelandic law, was distinguished from murder by the fact that the killer "turned himself in." Thus even if the average sentence served by the convicted killers in our society were as high as 12½ years—which it

surely is not—the corresponding *expected* punishment would be much higher in the Icelandic case.

55   Njal's Saga, *supra* note 3, at 63.

56   Vigfusson & Powell, *supra* note 1, bk. 2, at 340, 356, 358–59.

57   This is only a first approximation; the optimal fine must make allowance for enforcement costs—part of the cost of a crime is the cost of catching the criminal—and for the net cost of collecting the fine. This is a complicated subject and beyond the scope of this paper.

Chapter 10

Peter H. Aranson

BRUNO LEONI IN RETROSPECT

Introduction

THREE DECADES HAVE PASSED since Bruno Leoni delivered his Claremont Men's College (now Claremont-McKenna College) lectures, on which his volume, *Freedom and the Law*,[1] was based. That volume was first published in 1961, and Leoni died in 1967. Since the early 1960s, while Leoni's book lay dormant, two new intellectual disciplines have emerged that have reordered our thinking about man and social life: public choice, and law and economics. The first consists of the application of microeconomic analysis to political and governmental action. The second consists of the same application to the substance and procedures of law.

Each discipline has gone through a roughly comparable development.[2] Early works tried to model decision making in political and legal processes, respectively.[3] Eventually, neoclassical concerns for efficiency emerged. Today both disciplines grapple with the subjectivity of preferences and costs, and with the decentralized character of knowledge.[4]

What is striking to the reader who comes fresh to Leoni's writings is not just that he anticipated, nay, urged[5] the development of both disciplines. He also drew a straight line from the initial interdisciplinary connections between economics and politics and law, to the most contemporary information-related concerns of these newly-merged disciplines. Modern social scientists might not have followed his lead even had they been aware of his work. Had they done so, however, today they might be much further along in grasping the nature of and connections among, the previously intellectually separated domains of markets, law, and politics.

Surely, some of the intervening work seems useful and at times necessary. We can appreciate its usefulness in contemplating some of Leoni's "mistakes," errors that reflect the state of knowledge during his lifetime. For example, in his attack on Duncan Black's monograph,[6] Leoni did not grasp the importance of political disequilibrium as a tool for analysis and criticism of electoral and legislative processes.[7] Both processes exhibit a fundamental chaos[8] and sometimes give way to dictatorial agenda control[9] and manipulation through strategic voting.[10] Electoral and legislative processes thus reflect no necessary connection between citizens' preferences and public-policy outcomes, unlike markets, which can reflect a parallel connection between consumers' preferences (marginal valuations) and prices and output.

Nor did Leoni have available to him important intervening work on the theory of the publicly traded corporation. At one point in his book[11] he cites approvingly writings that identify a problem in the separation of ownership and control in large, publicly traded corporations. At another point[12] he defends legislated disclosure laws governing new stock issues. In his view, legislation had merely incorporated older common law rules.[13] But our current understanding of markets for corporate control[14] and of the publicly traded firm as a nexus of contracts, based on comparative advantage and efficient risk-shifting,[15] could have supported Leoni's more basic arguments in his comparisons of private and public choice.

Finally, although Leoni seems far more circumspect than do most other writers concerning the proper domain of legislation, he accepts its generic public-goods justification. That argument remains subject to severe theoretical restrictions, based on a comparison of the costs and benefits of public action, on a study of the appropriate methods of that action, on a regard for correct jurisdictional arrangements, and on the potential inventiveness of the private sector in solving (or ignoring) the problem of appropriability.[16] Leoni also did not fully grasp the implications of the economic-calculation problem, with respect to the legislature's ability correctly to identify public goods.[17] He subscribed to the idea that government should supply lighthouse services,[18] as did most theorists before Coase's demonstration by way of historical record, that private supply is possible, and that public supply may grow out of private persons' legislative rent-seeking.[19] But Leoni did anticipate the development of cable television[20] as a response to the appropriability problem. And he also anticipated Demsetz[21] by nearly a decade on the importance of scarcity in the development of property rights beyond common pool arrangements.[22]

These problems, and a few others as well,[23] pale in comparison to Leoni's insights and contributions. His errors were not errors in his day, although those who persist in making the same mistakes merit appropriate criticism.

This retrospective reviews Leoni's insights and contributions and then brings them "up to date," by tracing out various developments since 1961. Part II recapitulates Leoni's views on three issues: freedom, law, and legislation. Part III then reports on subsequent related developments in these areas. Part IV concludes this retrospective.

Leoni on freedom, law, and legislation

Freedom

Bruno Leoni, like Hume,[24] Hayek,[25] and other liberal theorists, understands "freedom . . . as the absence of constraint exercised by other people, including the authorities, over the private life and business of each individual."[26] Here, we emphasize five aspects of Leoni's view of freedom: that it has a negative (liberal) and not a positive character; that it implies certain kinds of constraints; that negative and positive freedom remain irreconcilable; that liberal freedom reflects unanimous consent; and that its nature is both primary and instrumental.

Negative freedom and positive freedom

Freedom for Leoni is the absence of constraint,[27] or perhaps the greatest possible absence of constraint consistent with the absence of constraints on others. It is the Golden Rule in negative form: "Do not do unto others what you would not wish others to do unto you."[28] This formulation differs sharply from the positive injunction to "do unto others." Instead, it requires merely that people do not intrude in the choices of others.

Freedom and constraint

Negative freedom, liberal freedom, as our discussion of common law systems reveals,[29] cannot exist apart from some kind of constraint. But that constraint is consistent with the idea of maximizing liberal freedom, the absence of constraint, for in certain "cases . . . people have to be constrained if one wants to preserve the freedom of other people."[30] That is, "the constraint that is linked inevitably to freedom is only a negative constraint . . . imposed solely . . . to make other people renounce constraining in their turn."[31] Leoni has in mind constraints on those engaged in "misproductive" work, including "beggars, blackmailers, robbers, and thieves,"[32] but the purpose of such constraints must be to minimize the constraints that such persons would impose on others. "A free market," for example, allows "those engaged in market transactions [to] have some power to constrain the enemies of a free market."[33]

Negative and positive freedom irreconcilable

The idea of positive freedom is inconsistent with that of negative freedom. "Economic security" or "freedom from want," for example, is not within the compass of negative freedom, because it requires constraints on others.[34] Hence, an irreconcilable conflict remains between liberal freedom and socialist "freedom," because socialist freedom creates legal obligations, and therefore constraints on others that they would not accept *ex ante*.[35]

Freedom and consent

An institution that maximizes freedom must rest on consent, which Leoni believes must be unanimous.[36] Positive freedom never can obtain unanimity, because it creates rights for some but obligations for others. But liberal freedom, because it imposes only those obligations that people *individually* agree to, reflects unanimous consent. In this sense Leoni finds himself concurring with Rousseau[37] in claiming that institutions based on negative freedom will express the "common will."

Again, such institutions must constrain their enemies. But the laws that constrain would be agreed to *ex ante*, even by murderers and thieves, provided that they did not know that they would be murderers or thieves at the time the law is "discovered." Just as surely, these people would not consent to particularistic laws that allowed murder and theft by specific persons other than themselves.[38]

Freedom as an instrumental and primary value

Though he describes both aspects of freedom, Leoni does not say explicitly whether he embraces freedom as a primary or instrumental goal. But Leoni implies that freedom is a primary goal, to be valued for itself. For example, he approvingly cites the words of Democritus, that "poverty under a democracy is as much to be preferred above what an oligarchy calls prosperity as is liberty above bondage."[39] That is, "(l)iberty and democracy come first in this scale of values; prosperity comes after."[40]

Freedom also may engender tolerance. With the institutions that emerge under, and to protect, freedom, "all the members of the community appear to agree in principle that feelings, actions, forms of behavior, and so on . . . are perfectly admissible and permissible without disturbing anybody, regardless of the number of individuals who feel like behaving or acting in these ways."[41] And as Leoni quotes from the Funeral Oration of Pericles,

> The freedom which we enjoy in our government extends also to our ordinary life. There, far from exercising a jealous surveillance over each other, we do not feel called upon to be angry with our neighbor for doing what he likes, or even to indulge in those injurious looks which cannot fail to be offensive, although they inflict no penalty.[42]

But liberal freedom, Leoni finds, along with tolerance, is instrumental. Again from Pericles we learn that the soldiers of Athens, "judging happiness to be the fruit of freedom and freedom of valor, never would decline the dangers of war."[43] Freedom in its institutional embodiments thus leads to happiness, perhaps as judged by standards of material wealth. Leoni finds evidence for "the strict connection between the free market and the free law-making process," in the observation "that the free market was at its height in the English-speaking countries when the common law was practically the only law of the land relating to private life and business."[44] And more to the point, "the socialistic solution of the so-called social problem" cannot "promot[e] public welfare and eliminat[e], as far as possible, poverty, ignorance, and squalor, for this end is not only perfectly compatible with individual freedom, but may also be considered as complementary to it."[45]

Law and other spontaneous orders

The Austrian school of economics (and especially the writings of Hayek) provides the strongest intellectual influence Leoni's thought. The freedom that Leoni proposes embraces the right to engage in the widest possible variety of personal and economic actions and choices. The result of this freedom is the development of spontaneous orders in human institutions—science, fashions, taste, language, economic organization, and law.[46] From there, the entire corpus of Austrian economics becomes available as argument for the virtues of liberal freedom and for the proposition that any legislation or government regulation that resembles central economic planning must fail, with a consequent decline in the governed population's welfare.[47]

But Leoni is no anarchist.[48] He acknowledges the occasional desirability of legislation and the virtues of judge-made, unwritten law. Four of Leoni's arguments concerning the common law process remain central: that it is a spontaneous process resulting in a spontaneous order that parallels the unconstrained market relation; that it rests on rights, and therefore protects liberal freedom; that it creates long-run certainty; and that nevertheless judges sometimes go astray.

Law as a spontaneous order

By "law" Leoni means judge-made law, as in a common law process. He reports that much of Roman law, early continental (pre-codified) law, as well as Anglo-Saxon law was of this variety.[49] Law is "a sort of vast, continuous, and chiefly spontaneous collaboration between the judges and the judged . . . to discover what the people's will is in a series of definite instances—a collaboration that in many respects may be compared to that existing among all the participants in a free market."[50]

Of Roman law Leoni writes that "[t]o a certain extent, it put juridicial relations among citizens on a plane very similar to that on which the free market put their economic relations. Law, as a whole, was no less free from constraint than the market itself."[51] Comparing law-making to the development of language, economic transactions, and fashions, Leoni notes that "all of these processes . . . are performed through the voluntary collaboration of an enormous number of individuals each of whom has a share in the process itself according to his willingness and ability to maintain or even to modify the present condition . . ."[52]

As in the market relation, so in law: "Common citizens were the real actors in this respect, just as they still are the real actors in the formation of the language and, at least partially, in economic transactions in the countries of the West."[53] In "discovering" what the law is, judges at common law are thus like "grammarians who epitomize the rules of a language or . . . statisticians who make records of prices or of quantities of goods exchanged in the market," because they are merely "simple spectators of what is happening around them," not "rulers of their fellow citizens as far as the language of the economy is concerned."[54]

Freedom and the law

Leoni's insights[55] into how the common law process is consonant with, and indeed supports freedom is extraordinary, not the least because he was writing nearly three decades before the full flowering of law and economics. First, legal action begins not with judges but with the instant parties to a dispute, who have failed to settle the matter between them. The implied limitation on the initiating power of judges at least partly constrains the law's domain.[56]

Second, the judge's decision is "effective mainly in regard to the parties to the dispute, only occasionally in regard to third persons, and practically never in regard to people who have no connection with the parties concerned."[57] With respect to some common law cases, Leoni here is clearly wrong. Judges sometimes do consider third-party interests,[58] and one contemporary view of law and economics would have them do so explicitly.[59] But the common law process puts high transaction-cost barriers in the way of assembling such interests, thus making "vote-trading" or analogous activities among a variety of interests very difficult in the courts. Even if a judge's decision changes a preexisting rule, that was not its overt intent, and in large bodies of law (for example, contract law), subsequent parities sometimes may contract away from any provision in a new rule that they find unsatisfactory.[60]

Third, change in the common law is a slow incremental process, which makes use of the accumulated wisdom in the body of precedents.[61] Hence, the judge's "power is further limited by the unavoidable reference of every decision to decisions issued in similar cases by other judges."[62] The common law process, strictly construed, thus provides few judicial opportunities for the wholesale rearrangement of rights and obligations; and because of the decentralized nature of the process at the trial level, the common law may not be a potent source of nonconsensual redistributions.

There is more to Leoni's claims for the common law than this list attributes to it. But other virtues of the common law remain implicit in the text of *Freedom and the Law*. Leoni understands the nature of legal conflict in "classical" common law to be thus. One party, the plaintiff, claims that an adverse nonconsensual rearrangement of rights (freedoms) has occurred because of the defendant's act of ommission or commision. In property law he might allege a trespass, nuisance, or faulty conveyance. In contract law he might argue that the defendant has breached an agreement, the elements of which form a binding contract. In tort law he might state that another's actions have damaged his person or property.

Each claim's central element is the defendant's asserted failure to perform a generally (in tort law) or specifically (in contract law) cognizable and previously accepted obligation, to the plaintiff's (nonconsenting) detriment. In other words, the defendant has abridged the plaintiff's freedom. The plaintiff, then, asks the court to restore that freedom with an appropriate remedy.

That is all! There is no sense in this description that the judge must then "create" law that will apply to all parties in the future, in similar circumstances. That "creation" might seem to accompany the judge's decision. But that was not the judge's intent.[63] He merely sought to "discover" what the parties' rights and obligations had been, to confirm their legitimate expectations. Judges may engage in folly,[64] but their central mission remains solely to discover preexisting rights and obligations.

> Usages, tacit rules, the implications of conventions, general criteria relating to the suitable solutions of particular legal problems also with reference to possible changes in the opinions of people at any given time and in the material background of those opinions—all these are yet to discovered. One may well say that this is an undeniably difficult, sometimes painful, and very often long process. It always was. According to the experience of our ancestors, the usual way of meeting this difficulty . . . not only in Anglo-Saxon countries but everywhere in the West, was to entrust the process to specially trained persons like lawyers or judges.[65]

This search for pre-existing expectations of rights and obligations tales place against the vast background of previously discovered law (precedent) and a specific, limited dispute. Grand social or economic theory has no place in this search. It is not the judge's object of inquiry. As Leoni cites Sir Matthew Hale, "It is a reason for me to preferre a law by which a kingdome hath been happily governed four or five hundred years than to adventure the happiness and peace of a kingdome upon some new theory of my own."[66] Indeed, Neratius proscribes the search for such a theory itself: "*Rationes eorum quae constituuntur inquiri non oportet, alioquin multa quae ceria sunt subvertuntur.*"[67]

We close the circle by observing that if there be no law but common law, then that law applies to all people equally and judges discover it behind a veil of ignorance.[68] There can be no special pleaders for the creation of special rights and obligations beyond those that already exist in law or remain to be discovered as (unanimously) preferred, *ex ante*, in the practice and expectations of the people.[69] Hence, the obligation that one person's "freedom from want" would impose on another would find no hearing at common law,[70] just as similar claims for special, previously unrecognized rights would fall on deaf ears.[71] For such demands find no place in a consensual order.

Certainty and law

Leoni understands that freedom, and therefore prosperity, requires an irreducible core of institutional certainty.[72] The common law provides for certainty in the same manner that it undergirds freedom. Its goal is to express a particular, limited aspect of the preexisting consensual order. Leoni describes at length the difference between written (legislated) codes and unwritten law. Legislation provides instantaneously certain language, but the process of its adoption makes real, long-run certainty a chimera. "All these rules are precisely worded in written formulae that . . . interpreters cannot change at their will. Nevertheless, all of them may go as soon and as abruptly as they came. The result is that . . . we are *never certain* that tomorrow we shall still have the rules we have today."[73]

The unwritten law's certainty, by contrast, grows out of its appeal to precedent and its limits on the judge's decisions, which we previously have reviewd.[74] Change may occur in the common law, but it is always at the margin and often subject to private contractual revision. The body of unwritten law stands largely unchanged. The common law merely confirms ongoing expectations. "[P]rivate Roman law [for example] was something to be described or to be discovered, not something to be enacted—a world of things that were there, forming part of the common heritage of all Roman citizens."[75] Stated differently, "law is simply a complex of rules relating to the behavior of the common people."[76] The principles of that law appeared to Hale to be such that "one age and one tribunal may speake the same thinges and carry on the same thred of the law in one uniforme rule as neare as possible. . . ."[77]

Errant judges

Leoni acknowledges "that judiciary law may undergo some deviations the effect of which may be the reintroduction of the legislative process under a judiciary guise."[78]

Judges in supreme courts especially, "may be in a position to impose their own personal will upon a great number of dissenters,"[79] which would disorder the common law foundation of liberal freedom. To the extent that supreme courts follow common law procedures, the limitations that Leoni identifies would confine them as well.[80] But if supreme courts exceed common law bounds, then Leoni would favor their use of super-majorities to change "long-established precedents" or "previous interpretations of the constitution."[81] His principal concern, though, is with judicial acquiescence in administrative determinations. Bureaucrats enjoy broad delegated powers. So bureaus may impose capricious, arbitrary, freedom-destroying, and therefore lawless constraints.[82]

Legislation

If one insight stands out *in Freedom and the Law,* it is that *"there is more than an analogy between the market economy and a judiciary or lawyers' law, just as there is much more than an analogy between a planned economy and legislation."*[83] For everything that the market economy and the common law represent, central economic planning and legislation represent their opposites. Here, we examine Bruno Leoni's analysis of legislation with respect to six characteristics. Like central economic planning, legislation does not fully allow a spontaneous order to emerge in private action; faces severe informa-tion problems; grows out of rent-seeking; imposes coercion beyond the legitimate constraints of the common law; creates long-run uncertainty; and possibly originated in an early (but perhaps innocent) intent to shift from unwritten to written law.

Legislation subverts the spontaneous order

Legislation "may be too quick to be efficacious" and "too unpredictably far-reaching to be wholly beneficial. . . ."[84] It is "the terminal point of a process in which authority always prevails, possibly against individual initiative and freedom."[85] Legislation is "incompatible with individual initiative and decision when it reaches a limit that con-temporary society seems already to have gone far beyond."[86]

Contrasted with a spontaneous order, in which law is "a result of a secular process," legislation expresses "what the law *should be* as a result of a completely new approach and of unprecedented decisions."[87] Arguing for restrictions on legislative action, Leoni recalls that under the liberal freedom of the common law, "all individual choices adjust themselves to one another and no individual choice is ever overruled."[88] But because of legislation's widening domain, "the area in which spontaneous individual adjustments have been deemed necessary or suitable has been far more severely circumscribed"[89] than is compatible with liberal freedom. Legislation saps the social order of spontaneity. As Matthew Hale argues:

> [T]hey that please themselves with a persuasion that they can with as much evidence and congruitie make out an unerring system of laws and politiques [that is, we would say, written constitutions and legislation equally applicable to all states [i.e., conditions] as Euclide demonstrates his conclusions, deceive themselves with notions which prove ineffectual *when they come to particular application.*[90]

Legislation, central planning, and economic calculation

Leoni discerns that early writers understood the tradition of liberal freedom, spontaneous order, and judge-"discovered" law, as well as the legislative threat to these institutions. This threat is severe, because legislation itself, written law, suffers from the socialist-calculation problem: legislators cannot collect the requisite information, under any reasonable assumptions about its distribution, fragmentary nature, and often undiscovered importance. This problem grows directly from the decentralized, fragmentary character of knowledge.[91] As Cicero paraphrased Cato, "there never was . . . a man so clever as to foresee everything and . . . even if we could concentrate all brains into . . . one man, [he could not] . . . provide for everything at one time without having the experience that comes from practice through a long period of history."[92]

Leoni recognizes that legislation shares in the inability of central economic planning to solve the economic-calculation problem. "*[A] legal system centered on legislation resembles . . . a centralized economy in which all the relevant decisions are made by a handful of directors, whose knowledge of the whole situation is fatally limited and whose respect, if any, for the people's wishes is subject to that limitation.*"[93]

The legislative process thus suppresses the spontaneous order in private choice. Politics is not devoid of a spontaneous order growing out of the actions of those so engaged.[94] But the political process creates positive rights and obligations that distort and restrain the spontaneous orders of market and common law that otherwise would emerge.

In particular, "the more numerous the people are whom [legislators] . . . tr[y] to 'represent,' . . . and the more numerous the matters in which one tries to represent them, the less the word 'representation' has a meaning referable to the actual will of actual people other than that of the persons named as their 'representatives.'"[95] No real contract emerges between representatives and citizens, as "a consequence of the very extension of representation to as many individuals as possible in a political community."[96]

The voter himself has no way to connect his vote to public-policy outcomes.[97] And "the issues at stake . . . are too many and too complicated and . . . very many of them are actually unknown both to the representatives and the people represented. . . . [N]o instructions could be given in most cases."[98] Representatives cast their legislative votes under the same disadvantage, "since they vote without knowing the results of their vote until the group decision has been made."[99]

Majority rule also contributes to the legislature's inability to reflect citizens' preferences, even if all of these information problems were to disappear. In the limit, says Leoni, quoting John Stuart Mill, the preferences of one-half of the population remain ignored as a consequence of the general election. The preferences of the remaining one-half are cleft in twain as a consequence of majority rule in the legislature.[100] Hence, legislation mirrors at best "the contingent views and interests of a handful of people ([one-half] the legislators), whoever they may be, . . .[as] a remedy for all concerned."[101] Or worse, it "always reflects the will of a contingent majority within a committee of legislators . . . ."[102]

Legislative uncertainty, in turn, makes it "impossible for the authorities to make any calculation regarding the real needs and the real potentialities of the citizens," and "[t]he authorities can never be certain that what they do is actually what people would like them to do. . . ."[103] Therefore, "the authorities are [not] better qualified to discover and even to satisfy individual 'needs' that private citizens would not be able or even might not want to satisfy if they were free to choose."[104]

In a passage that finds unmistakable reflection in modern public-choice theory, Leoni ties together the incapacity of democratic legislatures and other social-choice mechanisms to reveal citizens' preferences for public goods, with the theoretical reason for a legislature's existence, to produce such goods. He thereby restores a symmetry of evaluation between public and private sectors that is often lacking in economic thought.

> To contend that legislation is "necessary" whenever other means fail to "discover" the opinion of the people concerned would only be another way of evading the solution of the problem. If other means fail, this is no reason to infer that legislation does not. Either we assume that a "social opinion" on the matter concerned does not exist or that it exists but is very difficult to discover. In the first case, introducing legislation implies that this is a good alternative to the lack of a "social opinion"; in the latter case, introducing legislation implies that the legislators know how to discover the otherwise undiscoverable "social opinion."[105]

Rent-seeking

Because of its majoritarian character, along with most voters' and many legislators' ignorance about many issues and the preferences of those whom their political actions might affect, people with special interests in particular issues can pursue benefits from the political process that they cannot secure under conditions of unanimity and perfect information, which is to say, in the market. That is, legislation remains "the expression of the particular will of certain individuals and groups who [are] lucky enough to have a contingent majority of legislators on their side at a given moment."[106] The political process thus provides an opportunity for persons and groups to demand, and representatives to supply, rents through legislation.[107]

Legislation thereby expresses the preferences of "vested interests," which are "ready to defend the inflation of the legislative process. . . ."[108] But because most citizens remain unconsulted and unconsenting in this process, the result is "a potential *legal war of all against all*, carried on by way of legislation and representation."[109] As small, contingent majorities pursue positive rights,[110] an implicit-prisoners' dilemma forms in the political process, since "[e]veryone probably has more to gain from a system in which his decisions would not be interfered with by the decisions of other people than he has to lose . . . [if] he could not interfere in turn with other people's decisions."[111]

Consequently, a multiplicity of laws emerges, "one for landlords, one for tenants, one for employers, one for employees, etc.," which destroys the consensual basis of "equality before the law."[112] The manipulation of the money supply also becomes a means for establishing the positive freedom of special classes of persons, namely debtors.[113] Even the formerly spontaneous order of language becomes politicized, as various groups seek its debasement, to assert their positive claims on others.[114]

Leoni is uncommonly modern in his appreciation of the mechanisms of political rent-seeking. For example, he refers to research on vote-trading, logrolling, which he interprets as the means by which small minorities coalesce to form legislative majorities.[115] Similarly, he discerns a difference between European and American variants of rent-seeking. In European polities, social and economic "cleavages" tend not to "crosscut,"[116] but instead are mutually reinforcing, so that two large, fairly permanent coalitions form on the left and right. But in the United States, cleavages tend to cross-cut, so each small group is on its own.

Those who bear the costs of legislatively enacted positive freedoms ordinarily suffer because of their pervasive lack of knowledge. Small groups, therefore, can press their legislative claims without fear of opposition.[117] Temporary legislative minorities then merely wait their turn and "adjust themselves to defeat only because they hope to become sooner or later a winning majority . . ."[118]

Legislation, coercion, and constraint

Groups that assert their claims to positive rights need not do so because they oppose those whom those rights would obligate. The information and majoritarian problems alone might ensure that the preferences of those obligated remain unconsulted. The enactment of positive freedoms nevertheless implies a correlative imposition of obligations, constraints on others, which freedoms are inconsistent with liberal freedom. That is "Legislation always implies a kind of coercion and unavoidable constraint of the individuals who are subject to it."[119]

For example, consider the positive "freedom from want." A person may choose within the market relation to become a supplier of goods. His choice remains entirely voluntary, and he accepts within the market relation the principle that other people have a liberal freedom from constraint. They can buy his goods or not, as they see fit.[120] If the supplier fails, he has no recourse and expected none within the liberal freedom of market and common law. But legislation differs, "because the very attempt to introduce 'freedom from want' has to be made . . . through legislation and therefore through decisions on the basis of majority rule,"[121] not unanimous consent.

Legislation also imposes uniformity, perhaps in prices or in enforced consumption.[122] And "group decisions imply procedures like majority rule which are not compatible with individual freedom of choice of the type that any individual buyer or seller in the market enjoys as well as in any other choice he makes in his private life."[123] Paradoxically, then, the enforced consumption[124] produced by "[l]egislation may have and actually has in many cases today a negative effect on the very efficacy of the rules and on the homogeneity of the feelings and convictions *already prevailing* in a given society."[125] That is, "legislation may . . . deliberately or accidentally disrupt homogeneity by destroying established rules and by nullifying existing conventions and agreements *that have hitherto been voluntarily accepted.* . . ."[126]

For Leoni, "majority will is not the "common will,' "[127] "the people" are not the individual, and individual freedom is not democracy.[128] Therefore, because of legislation's "violent empirical operation on the body politic,"[129] as Leoni quotes Pollock, its use should be limited.

> [W]e should . . . reject the resort to legislation *whenever it is used merely as a means of subjecting minorities in order to treat them as losers in the field.* . . .

[W]e should reject the legislative process *whenever it is possible for the individuals involved to attain their objectives without depending upon the decision of a group and without actually constraining any other people to do what they would never do without constraint*. [And] . . . *whenever* [there exists] *any doubt . . . about the advisability of the legislative process as compared with some other kind of process having for its objects the determination of the rules of our behavior, the adoption of the legislative process ought to be the result of a very accurate assessment*.[130]

Legislation and uncertainty

We have reviewed Leoni's argument that unwritten law provides long-run certainty while written law does not.[131] Because written law is the explicit product of legislation,[132] we may carry forward the burden of that argument here. The "law" of legislation remains uncertain over time, which creates two related effects.

First, private calculating becomes very difficult, especially for those persons "who must plan for the future and who . . . [must] know, therefore, what the legal consequences of . . . decisions will be."[133] Private planning becomes tenuous under a legislative regime, because "[t]he legal system centered on legislation, while involving the possibility that other people (the legislators) may interfere with our actions every day, also involves the possibility that they may change their way of interfering every day.[134] Because of the instability of legislative coalitions, reflecting shifting contingent majorities,[135] "we are *never certain* that tomorrow we shall still have the rules we have today."[136]

Second, this uncertainty, growing out of a continual process of rent-seeking, makes private contractual reliance risky. "[T]he very possibility of nullifying agreements and conventions through supervening legislation tends in the long run to induce people to fail to rely on any existing conventions or to keep any accepted agreements."[137] Hence, contractual exchanges requiring temporally separated future performance become less attractive, leading the parties to develop costly alternatives, such as contractual hostages (if that is possible at all under the statute), otherwise unwarranted vertical integration of production processes,[138] or the foregoing of such exchanges entirely.

These two effects grow with the domain and frequency of appeals to legislation. "The more intense and accelerated is the process of law-making, the more uncertain will it be that present legislation will last for any length of time," because "there is nothing to prevent a law, certain [in its written form] . . . , from being unpredictably changed by another law no less 'certain' than the previous one."[139]

The early origins of legislation

How did the legislative process come to subvert the common law's liberal freedom, to become a source of rent-seeking and uncertainty? The historical process that Leoni traces out suggests a model of legislative aggrandizement. The process began with a simple desire and "very modest idea of reassessing and restating lawyers' law by *rewriting* it afresh in the codes, but not in the least by *subverting* it through them."[140] This activity "was intended chiefly as a compilation of past rulings, and its

advocates . . . stress[ed] precisely its advantages as an unequivocal and clear-cut abridge-
ment as compared with the rather chaotic mass of individual legal works on the part of
lawyers."[141]

But legislative compilation turned an open system based on a spontaneous order
into a closed system[142] based on centralized control. Interested parties would consult
the stark outlines of the code, instead of the richly detailed *and explained* fabric of case
law.[143] One imagines that this change shifted comparative advantage away from those
whose advocacy reflected the discipline of legal scholarship and toward those whose
advocacy was merely imaginative and politically entrepreneurial. But for whatever
reason, legal scholarship declined, and the force of common law diminished apace.[144]
Soon it became natural "to conceiv[e] of the whole of the law as *written law* . . . as a single
series of enactments on the part of legislative bodies according to majority rule."[145]

We do not know when rent-seeking entered the picture. More than likely it was
there from the beginning.[146] Or, perhaps rent-seeking was the natural consequence of
majority rule and the restricted information and partial preference revelation that
accompany legislative processes.[147] It matters not. What does matter is the present
substitution of the constraining results of the legislative process for the liberal consequences of the common law.

Recent developments

This review of *Freedom and the Law*, except for a brief initial cataloging of some
"mistakes" and an occasional footnote, takes Bruno Leoni's writing on its own terms.
While prior references to subsequent contributions are few, the form of this review
accommodates a recounting of later works, a matter to which we now turn.

Freedom

Many problems and misunderstandings result because most social scientists remain
unprepared to reason about freedom and leave the subject to the philosophers. But
neither philosophy nor any particular social science alone can capture freedom's full
meaning and importance. Indeed, we require an analysis of freedom that combines
both economics and philosophy, which analysis Leoni begins to sketch out.

Liberal freedom versus positive freedom

That economists and other social scientists commonly leave the study of freedom
to the philosophers seems apparent in the recent proliferation of "great works" of
political philosophy such as: Rawls's *A Theory of Justice*,[148] Nozick's *Anarchy, State, and
Utopia*,[149] and a spate of writings by Marxists[150] and legal philosophers.[151] But with
the exception of the Austrians[152] and of James M. Buchanan's[153] constant and faithful
attention to freedom, there are few writings on freedom itself by non-Marxist
economists.

The philosophers have dominated the field in a manner that recapitulates Leoni's[154]
(and Hayek's[155]) reflections on the distinction between negative and positive freedom.
On one side we find arrayed philosophers such as Nozick, who views property as the

embodiment of freedom.[156] On the other we find political philosophers such as Christian Bay[157] and G. A. Cohen,[158] who deem the positive freedom of Marxism to be logically compelling but the negative freedom of classical liberalism to be empirically empty.

Economists do write about freedom, and their work in this area is of great importance. But it lacks a concern for, not to say rejects, "doctrinaire" appeals to distinctly philosophical considerations. For example, economists might identify price controls or regulatory barriers to entry as reductions in (liberal) freedom. These policies then stand as proximate causes of reductions in human welfare. Economists have gone far in arguing the *case* for freedom with just such demonstrations.

But these examples do not build a compelling *theory* of freedom or its absence. Instead, they compile evidence about the *effects* of freedom or its absence. Without a theory of freedom, however, one cannot distinguish between freedom's presence and its effects. Indeed, economists sometimes call the effects by the name "freedom." And this confusion has been disabling for both theory and practice.

Stigler exemplifies this confusion by rejecting the Hayek-Leoni claimed difference between liberal and positive freedom.[159] He "share[s] Hayek's opposition to a host of modern public policies."[160] But he claims that they cannot be attacked on grounds that rely on this difference, which he regards as merely "moral," and therefore beyond the economist's compass. Indeed, one person's assertion of such grounds, for Stigler, is the moral equivalent of another's claim to the contrary.

Instead, Stigler identifies wealth-maximizing public policies with liberty. If such policies increase a person's earnings, then his opportunity set expands and he has more freedom than otherwise; but if his earnings decline, then he is less free. Accordingly, Stigler believes that economists *qua* economists cannot distinguish between liberal and positive freedom.

> [W]hether the state forbids me (by a rationing system) to use more than ten gallons of gasoline a week, or whether I am prevented from doing so by its (gasoline's) high price (not including taxes) is of little direct significance to me: in either case my driving is limited by decisions (to ration or to buy gas) of my fellow citizens.[161]

Hence, we cannot "distinguish coercion by other men from other [market] limitations on our choice,"[162] so "the purpose of a distinction between wealth and liberty is . . . elusive."[163]

As a consequence of this reasoning, "[o]ne may [only] derive normative conclusions on public policy by recourse to [the] . . . criterion of individual utility maximization," because "[t]he concept of wealth is both broad and specific: it is the wealth of individual men, as judged by themselves, which measures their capacity to choose [their liberty]."[164]

Then comes Stigler's necessary argument. "If a policy is demonstrably inefficient in achieving its goals, the more efficient policy ought to be preferred by members of the society," and "[u]nless the superior efficiency of a policy is shown, the prospects of influencing a rational society are negligible."[165] But, "if the society is irrational (it does not seek to maximize its members' utilities), then the source of influence over the society's policies—and knowledge of economic laws[—]will have no relevance to that influence."[166] Therefore, "[p]erhaps these policies cannot be effectively opposed on *any* ground, but surely that of efficiency offers more promise."[167]

This asserted equivalence between political and market constraints, which argues for an equivalence between liberal and positive freedom, remains fully consistent with, and indeed identical to, the contemporary Marxist argument of alienation resulting from the market relation.[168] Alienation in Marxist interpretation views people—both workers *and* capitalists—as losing control over their lives and choices because of others' decisions. They cannot plan, they cannot achieve self-actualization, and their actions hold no meaning for them.

It is difficult to discern where Stigler's asserted identity between market- and collectivity-imposed constraints differs from this interpretation. But there is more here than the unpersuasive objection that Stigler's thought mirrors contemporary Marxist thought. That "something" is Stigler's (and the Marxists') studied ignoring of the rest of the Austrian argument, as well as Stigler's specific rejection of recent contributions in public-choice theory.

Stigler claims that restrictions on both liberal and positive freedom may reduce the domain of choice, which thereby diminishes wealth. (The opposite relation also can occur, in that some constraints may increase wealth.) And a reduction in wealth may reduce (undifferentiated) freedom in its turn. So wealth and freedom become equivalent. But suppose, with Leoni,[169] that we can assign particular freedoms to the category of "liberal" or "positive." Some difficult assignment problems might remain. But we ignore them, because Stigler's argument is not that; it is just that the distinction, even if clear, would make no difference.

Stigler would argue that sometimes there is a happy coincidence between a liberal freedom and increased wealth. In such cases Stigler and the Austrians do not differ in their policy *preferences*. Still, a positive freedom might coincide with Stigler's goal of increased wealth. At this point the issue is joined.

The Austrian argument, reflecting the economic-calculation problem, is that Stigler cannot know that *any* policy that enacts a positive freedom indeed will increase wealth. The policy certainly will subvert the spontaneous orders of market and common law, and there will be far less economized use of information. Stigler thus has claimed that economists can do an impossible thing. And even if the positive-freedom policy "maximizes" wealth in strict neoclassical and static terms, there can be no claim for a more nearly global, dynamic wealth maximization growing out of invention and entrepreneurship. An expansion of liberal freedom may increase wealth. But policies designed solely to increase wealth may not increase liberal or even positive freedom.[170]

The immediate attractiveness of public policies based on (wealth-maximizing) calculations alone threatens the broader "institutional efficiency"[171] derived from the spontaneous orders of market and common law. Stigler thus ignores the function of rules that undergird liberal freedom. As Hayek notes:

> The preservation of a free system is so difficult precisely because it requires a constant rejection of measures which appear to be required to secure particular results, on no stronger grounds than that they conflict with a general rule, and frequently without our knowing what will be the costs of not observing the rule in the particular instance. A successful

defence of freedom must therefore be dogmatic and make no concessions to expediency, even where it is not possible to show that besides the known beneficial effects, some particular harmful result would also follow from its infringement. Freedom will prevail only if it is accepted as a general principle whose application to particular instances requires no justification. . . .[172]

Stigler's argument, of course, is much simpler to dismiss. Suppose that both his budget and relative prices, on the one hand, and a government rationing scheme, on the other, would lead the consumer to purchase exactly the same amounts of gasoline. Negative freedom, though, concerns the *right* to change. So now suppose that the consumer discovers a new opportunity requiring considerably greater travel by automobile. A market relation allows the consumer to react to his now greater marginal valuation of travel by increasing his gasoline use. The government-imposed rationing system does not. Hence, the rationing system fails to incorporate altered decisions (except by trading off less-preferred travel), while rationing by market prices does not. Liberal freedom thus entails the ability to pursue unforseen opportunities, a matter that Stigler wholly ignores.

Machlup, in precisely these terms, anticipates the Austrian argument against Stigler's asserted identity of negative and positive freedom.[173] He begins by criticizing "[t]his fusion of the idea of non-interference," a concept fully compatible with Leoni and Hayek's notion of liberal, negative freedom, "with the idea of effective power (which often means buying power),"[174] In Machlup's view, this combining "could not but spread confusion."[175] In particular:

> A definition of freedom which negates the difference between non-interference and effective power (or welfare or want satisfaction) destroys the essential meaning of the word "freedom." If it is defined as the capacity or opportunity to get what one wants, we are barred from analyzing the important question whether the development of this capacity or opportunity is better served by restrictionism or by non-interference, by collective control or by individual freedom.[176]

With respect to the claim that a concatenation of these two views of freedom cannot hold good in a dynamic economy with changing opportunities, Machlup points out that "certain freedoms may be of great importance for individuals and for society when no knowledge, no opportunity, and no power exist as yet to make use of presumably 'empty' freedoms."[177] The constrained-consumer example is but a simplified instance of such opportunities. For, "[t]heir importance lies in the aspirations and ambitions which they arouse and which may lead to the search for the knowledge, opportunity, and power that are required to exercise the previously unused freedoms. In short, 'ineffective' freedoms can be highly effective."[178]

Implicit in Stigler's argument is a second claim, which he presses elsewhere.[179] Many of his writings develop a "black-box" model of the political process, characterizing politics as a kind of market, in which people maximize wealth. The model does contribute to an understanding of the political process, and I have used it in arguing that constitutional sea changes, such as the American reapportionment revolution, have few public-policy consequences.[180] A kind of "constitutional Coase theorem" thus emerges, in which the only consequences of changes in rules are wealth effects, provided that transaction costs are low under alternative rules.

But this model proves too much. The structure of rules and rights does matter.[181] The majority-rule relation is not a market relation, *even* under conditions of perfect information and low transaction costs. For example, Ordeshook and I have constructed a model of an n-person legislature, in which majority rule leads to unstable (disequilibrium) redistributions toward the (equally unstable) majority coalition, through the use of cost-benefit inefficient programs, even under conditions of zero transaction costs, perfect information, and a market for votes.[182] Such redistributions rest on assertions of positive freedom, and not on the liberal freedom of the (unanimous) market relation. But the model applied to the market rule—unanimity—shows neoclassical efficiency.

Such models reveal a vast difference between individual rationality and "social rationality," even within a neoclassical structure. Individual rationality under majority rule can and does lead to "social irrationality,"[183] meaning at least incoherence (instransitivity) and probably Pareto-inferior policies. Adding imperfect information and high transaction costs to the model then recaptures the essence of Leoni's argument about legislation, his application of the economic-calculation problem, with its implications for the distinction between liberal and positive freedom.[184]

Liberal freedom, positive freedom, and constitutional choice

A second body of literature seems more difficult to counter, because it claims that people might opt for positive freedom (and obligation) under a market-like, unanimous-decision rule, one designed to set the terms of a constitution.[185]

The constitutional claim for positive freedom follows these lines. First, suppose that at the level of constitutional choice, only unanimous consent can express or be compatible with liberal freedom.[186] Second, assume that a veil of ignorance[187] deprives constitution choosers of information about their post-constitutional positions. Third, suppose that the choosers unanimously decide to adopt a constitution providing for either any kind of wealth redistribution or particular kinds of wealth redistributions (for example, following an insurance principle[188]) in subsequent decisions by a majority-rule institution. That is, they constitutionally and unanimously recognize the legitimacy of legislative enactments of positive freedoms. Are these people then less free?

I cannot satisfactorily answer this question. Nor am I certain that others can do so. A response to the first possibility—unanimously consenting to any kind of majority-preferred wealth redistribution—must rely on a prior theory of whether freedom always should be inalienable. The Declaration of Independence declares "liberty" to be so, as it does "life" and the "pursuit of happiness." This, then, is an issue that is too lengthy and too complex to pursue here, although it is the subject of extensive legal commentary.[189]

The second possibility—unanimously consenting, say, to majority-preferred wealth redistributions based on an insurance principle—remains subject to some clarification. For example, if private-sector agents can make a market in insurance, should a constitution prohibit public-sector agents from doing so? And if the constitution allows public-sector insurance, does that work a restriction on liberal freedom, with a concomitant growth in positive freedom and obligation? Is Stigler then right, that the supplier's legal identity may be a difference that makes no difference?

Deciding that these redistributions promote positive freedom returns us to the question of the alienability of liberal freedom. But suppose that these redistributions do not really create positive freedoms. Does our inquiry end? I think not. The question then becomes whether any majority-rule legislature is *able* to develop the kinds of programs that the unanimously chosen constitution intended. Leoni would argue that the task cannot be done.[190] Instead, the resulting legislation would resemble other legislation in its more general redistributionist, uncertain, and rent-seeking aspects. Legislators, voters, interest groups, and bureaucrats, after all, are not rational by parts.

Can further constitutional provisions constrain legislators to do what the constitution writers intended? Probably not. For such provisions, as we shall find,[191] have offered but a weak defense against the very kinds of actions that Leoni and others complain of.[192] Perhaps other forms of constraints on legislators might work better, but this possibility seems unlikely.[193]

Law

Current literature in law and economics, especially with respect to common law, often recapitulates the debate between Stigler and the Austrians. There is another view in this debate, however, with distinctly ideological roots in claims for positive rights and obligations, of the sort referred to earlier under the category of "errant judges."[194] The three views of the legal process, then, can take three explanatory or predictive forms:

1   Leoni—judges at common law (will) decide cases before them according to precedent and common law processes of legal reasoning and "discovery," with the intent of preserving the liberal freedom of the parties to the dispute;

2   Posner[195]—judges at common law (will) decide cases before them with the intent of increasing the wealth of society;

3   Wright[196] and Dworkin[197]—judges at common law (will) decide cases before them with the intent of incorporating their personal ideologies into law.

Each of these positive forms has an associated normative form, in which the words "ought to" substitute for the word "will." We label these normative forms as $1'$, $2'$ and $3'$, respectively. Judges under 2 or $2'$ and 3 or $3'$ act like legislators, except that the first (operating under 2 or $2'$) might claim to be "instructed" delegates, while the second (operating under 3 or $3'$) do not necessarily do so.

Within the law and economics community today, the debate is between those who take positions 1 or $1'$ and 2 or $2'$. Those who assert position 3 or $3'$ generally oppose any economic analysis of law—Austrian or neoclassical—because they view law as apart from the market relation. But in asserting ideologically devised, rights-based theories, their claims sometimes resemble those of scholars at positions 1 or $1'$. This resemblance, of course, is more apparent than real.

In extending the review of legal scholarship beyond Leoni's day, it is useful to follow historical order. With important exceptions, there came first an attention to the development of rules by examining actual case law and changes in precedent. Next, several scholars turned their attention to creating mathematical models of the common law process, with some specialized work on the incentive effects of particular rules. Finally, because both of these bodies of research ordinarily claim that the common law process tends to converge on wealth-maximizing rules, the present stage of the debate emerged, concerning whether judges explicitly should try to adopt such rules.

Empirical work

Judge Posner dominates the first two stages of this development. His early work on negligence,[198] followed by his compilation across all areas of law, in *Economic Analysis of Law*,[199] set the prevailing research agenda. Posner's work, and that of scholars who follow in this tradition,[200] adopts this format. First, the writer describes an area of common law and the alternative rules that judges might apply in it. Second, he provides a verbal economic model, discerning the efficient (wealth-maximizing) rule. Third, he reviews cases to decide whether judges choose as the model predicts (form 2). Finally, he sometimes exhorts judges to adopt such rules (form 2').

Posner's early study of the rule of negligence provides a good example of this research.[201] From an implicit economic model, he reasons that in tort law such a rule would be wealth-maximizing under greater industrialization, while a strict-liability rule would not. He then examines nineteenth century appellate decisions in the United States and finds the pervasive adoption of the negligence standard, which his model had predicted. Posner then advocates the negligence rule.[202]

Goetz's remarks on landlord-tenant law provide a second example.[203] When most residential rental property consisted of single-family dwellings, imposing liability in tort on the tenant (and not on the landlord) for injuries to visitors made sense, because the (relatively permanent) tenant was better able to detect potentially dangerous conditions. But with today's large apartment developments and rapid tenant turnover, the landlord is better able to detect such conditions. So it makes sense (minimizes information costs) to shift liability to him.[204]

Dynamic models of the common law process[205]

Before Posner's early work, there had been attempts to discern some economic characteristics of the legal process. Coase's essay, *The Problem of Social Cost*,[206] first alerted scholars that precedent—rules of rights and obligations—might have *allocative* consequences, the stuff of neoclassical microeconomic analysis. Coase showed that in the absence of transaction costs, and under conditions allowing for the alienability of a prior common law right, subsequent contracting would allow the parties to assign the right to its highest valued use. That is, the prevailing common law rule itself would have no allocative consequences. Coase then examined several nuisance cases where transaction costs were high, and he found (mistakenly, I believe), in the manner of Posner's later work, that judges tend to adopt wealth-maximizing rules.

Calabresi and Melamed,[207] at about the same time that Posner's essay on negligence appeared (1972), then sought to distinguish conditions under which courts would adopt property rules or liability rules. Property rules give one party a defensible right to be secure in his person, property, or contractual expectations, and courts ordinarily (though not always) protect them with injunctive relief if possible, along with whatever damages are due from the defendant's actions before the injunction has issued. Within the structure of the Calabresi-Melamed theory, courts tend to adopt such rules under low transaction-cost conditions. But they tend to impose liability rules, awarding damages only, under high transaction-cost conditions.

If there was agreement all around (which, in truth, there was not) that judges adopt wealth-maximizing rules (as measured by the standards of neoclassical theory), it was not clear how they could do so. Classical common law courts approach the cases before them more nearly in the manner that Leoni describes (form 1) and far less in the manner of economists (form 2).

The solution to this puzzle appeared at hand with some general models of the common law process, beginning with the work of Rubin.[208] His model, building on Gould's earlier work,[209] is the essence of simplicity. Suppose that an accident occurs, that tortfeasor and victim both have continuing interests in precedent, that the law of the case clearly places liability on one of them, and that both parties agree on the stakes and on the probability that the plaintiff (defendant) will prevail at trial. Rubin shows that if the rule is efficient, then the parties prefer settlement to suit; but if it is inefficient, then they may go to trial, depending on the level of legal costs. Each time a trial occurs under a putatively inefficient rule, there is a nonzero probability that the court will reverse the rule, so each subsequent trial gives a court the opportunity to adopt the efficient rule. Hence, under the assumptions stated the law of the case tends toward efficiency over time.

This model, and others like it,[210] does not rely on judges' motivations to reach efficient rules. Rubin's "invisible-hand" theorem thereby comports with Leoni's description of the common law process as creating a spontaneous order.[211] Indeed, Rubin later defends his theory of the common law's efficiency thus: because common law rules tend toward efficiency, each person can take any action that appears "reasonable," with little fear that he has placed himself in danger of a suit. He need not know the law, but only what is "reasonable" (customary). If the prevailing rule is inefficient, then "reasonable" actions will animate the legal process until the rule changes to embrace the "reasonable" (that is, "efficient") form.[212]

Elsewhere,[213] I survey these models, and the burden of that review is less sanguine for efficiency claims than Rubin at first argued. First, the models reflect only modest agreement about the appropriateness of various assumptions. One counts among the models literally millions of possible combinations and permutations of systems of assumptions about conditions under which the common law operates. A few lead to efficiency; many do not; and the vast majority remain unexplored.

Second, Rubin[214] argues more recently that, because of today's litigants' increasingly asymmetric interests and high transaction costs, the common law process has become subject to the same forces as the legislative process. He then provides several examples showing judges acting more in accord with form 3 than with form 1 or 2.

Third, even if these models predict an efficiency-seeking common law process, it remains unclear whether that result implies a choice of form 1′ or 2′, or even of form 1 or 2. Here, we close this circle by considering the common law battlefield between the Austrians and the neoclassical economists.

The common law and economic calculation

Some things that people do naturally, they might not do as well, or would not do at all, if they thought about how or why they do them.[215] I recall once speaking with a former construction worker who had made his living by riveting I-beams on sky-scrapers. One day, while standing on a naked girder forty stories above the ground, he suddenly thought about his peril, had to be carried from the girder, and became a clothing salesman.[216]

The parallel between this worker's predicament and that of a judge at common law trying to adopt wealth-maximizing rules seems far from exact, but it will do. A classical common law judge, like Leoni's "grammarian" or "statistician,"[217] by searching to discover the parties' liberal freedoms, may simply replicate the wisdom of the market and thus adopt rules that, by postdiction, might be deemed efficient. That is, a judge acting in accordance with form 1 appears in retrospect to have acted in accordance with form 2. Perhaps Rubin's description of what Leoni interprets to be a spontaneous order is a central part of this process, though surely it is not the only part.

But could it go the other way? Could a judge who adopts form 2 do as well at maximizing wealth as could a judge who adopts form I? Manifestly, it is far from apparent that a "Posnerian" judge, operating under form 2 rather than form 1, could replicate the classical judge's product.

All of Leoni's (and the Austrians') observations on law and legislation combine to deny that such a replication is possible.[218] But today we can say far more. In analyzing the ordinary common law case in the traditional areas of contract, property, and tort, efficiency theorists base their models on a simple equation: Total cost = Damage costs + Avoidance costs. "Damage costs" in a tort case, for instance, refer to the expected number of accidents that would occur under a particular rule times the expected cost of each accident; avoidance costs refer to the cost of avoidance itself (added safety measures, for example), as well as to the reduction in beneficial activities that avoidance might imply. Suppose that under any particular rule each party maximizes his utility subject to the rule. An "efficient" rule, compared with its alternatives, minimizes the sum of these two costs.

Here, the economic-calculation problem reappears.[219] If the judge seeks to impose a wealth-maximizing rule, how will he gain a knowledge of these costs? Recall that Leoni's judge is concerned *at most* only with the *expectations* of these costs as they *should have* appeared to the instant litigants *at the penultimate moment of choice.* The "Posnerian" judge, by contrast, must form a prediction of how these costs (or expectations of them) will appear to all subsequent parties who might possibly find themselves in the same positions as did the instant litigants.

These costs, however, existed only at the penultimate moment of choice and only for the instant litigants. Knowledge of such costs, then, exists only *ex hypothesis* for future parties, and that knowledge, at best, would be widely disseminated in fragmentary form throughout the economy. Hence, the judge who would pursue the explicit imposition of efficient rules *perforce* simultaneously would face the same information problems as a central economic planner.[220] What is worse, such a judge's span of knowledge must be less than a legislator's, because the judge's knowledge at most reflects only the information that the two litigants are willing and able to provide.

Freedom, and the choice of legal rules

The debate over wealth-maximizing *versus* classical judges crystalizes in the choice of legal rules. As a general proposition, Austrians prefer property rules to liability rules; and if they must choose a liability rule (as in most tort law), then they prefer strict liability to negligence.[221]

These preferences grow out of a high regard for the rights-based, spontaneous order of the market. But such an order works best, and sometimes may only be possible, if rights are defined and defended. The Austrians' economy, then, relies on a rights-based consensus, as Leoni describes it.[222] It is not merely that the economic-calculation problem makes it impossible for a judge operating under a liability rule to assess damages, say, to "make the plaintiff whole." More important, a liability rule makes rights at least contingent on the forbearance (or care) of others. But a property rule sends decisions back to the market, where the information resides, while it simultaneously uncouples rights from a judicially contingent liability determination.[223]

A similar reasoning applies to the choice of strict liability over negligence, once one adopts a liability rule in a particular area of law. The judge's problem seems almost entirely informational. He would face insuperable difficulties in discerning, say, the values of the variables that go into the "Hand formula" or into any of its modern variants, because the costs, benefits, and probabilities involved in the determination of negligence seem beyond *ex post* recapture (or *ex ante* prediction).[224] Hence, Austrians would prefer to approach the problem of harm as they would any other external cost, by shifting that cost back to its source.

The difference between Austrians and neoclassical "Posnerians" appears here in stark outline, with few details. The comparison doubtless is unfair when applied to individual scholars. Posner himself remains acutely aware of the information problem, and he has so stated in his preference to return disputes to the market if transaction costs are low,[225] Epstein, by contrast, whose writings place him within the Austrian tradition,[226] does not recommend applying property rules uniformly to all claims of nuisance.[227]

But the difference between Austrians and Posnerians[228] remains very real, as a 1981 Louisiana case might illustrate, In *J.Weingarten, Inc. v. Northgate Mall, Inc.*,[229] the plaintiff Weingarten had subleased from the defendant space in a mall, to operate a grocery store. The lease provided that Northgate would not "erect any additional buildings in the parking area . . . except within the space shown on a plat. . . ."[230] Northgate "also promised to maintain a ratio of six car parking spaces for each 1,000 [square] feet of floor space. . . ."[231] The lease granted plaintiff an "'irrevocable non-exclusive easement' over all parking areas shown on the plat, [and it gave him] 'the right to obtain an injunction specifically enforcing such rights and interests without the necessity of proving inadequacy of legal remedies or irreparable harm.'"[232]

Defendant Northgate breached by building an addition to the mall exceeding in square feet that allowed by the lease. Plaintiff sued for specific performance. The trial court, notwithstanding the terms of the lease, awarded damages but not specific performance, on the grounds, *inter alia*, of a potential $4 million loss to defendant (from destroying much of the added building). The Louisiana Court of Appeal reversed and issued an injunction calling for specific performance within six months.[233]

The Supreme Court of Louisiana, on a liberal reading of the Louisiana statutes, then reversed the Court of Appeal and remanded the case to the trial court for assessment of damages against Northgate.[234]

It seems beyond peradventure that an "Austrian" judge faced with these facts would adopt a property rule and award specific performance. A "Posnerian" judge might not do so but instead might rely on a liability rule and award money damages. The wealth-maximizing judge surely would be aware of the suppression of contractual reliance that his decision would foster. (If you want to breach a contract, do it in a big way![235]) But he would balance that cost against the waste of a building, along with defendant's claim that his mall's (and therefore Weingarten's) competitive position would decline without the addition.[236]

The *Weingarten* decision involves a myopic appeal to wealth-maximizing, as compared with an appeal to common law principle. The Louisiana Supreme Court denied the plaintiff its right to enforce the contract, which the defendant voluntarily had entered into. Therefore, the court denied plaintiff its rights under the contract, and *inter alia* diminished the efficacy of similar future contractual exchanges. But the court also denied this defendant and all subsequent persons in similar situations their right to alienate property under contractual guarantees.[237]

Stated differently, in Hayek's language the court substituted "expediency" (a judgment based on cost/benefit comparisons) for principle (a judgment based on long standing legal principles, which would have sent the plaintiff and defendant's decisions back to the market, where correct information resides).

> [W]hen we decide each issue solely on what appear to be its individual merits, we always over-estimate the advantages of central direction [now in the hands of the court]. Our choice will regularly appear to be one between a certain known and tangible gain [the $4 million building] and the mere probability of the prevention of some unknown beneficial action by unknown persons [the decline of contractual reliance]. If the choice between freedom and coercion is thus treated as a matter of expediency, freedom is bound to be sacrificed in almost every instance.[238]

Legislation

Three approaches to legislation

Beyond the contributions of Leoni[239] and the Austrians,[240] research over the last quarter century into the legislative process reflects three overlapping and reinforcing traditions. There is, first, the work on rent-seeking, growing out of Tullock's[241] and Krueger's[242] writing, which is a principal concern of scholars at the Center for Study of Public Choice.[243] This work explores the origins and characteristics of, and incentives for, rent-seeking.[244]

The second research tradition, centered in the law and economics faculties of the University of Chicago, reflects Stigler's "black-box" model of the political process.[245] This work's central concern is the demand for regulation (as a source of rents) among regulated firms. In places this work blends into the first tradition, although it is far less concerned with rights and inefficiency. In most respects it has formalized and translated into economics some much older contributions of political scientists.[246]

This second approach also complements the third, an institution-by-institution study of rules and incentives. Its practitioners, economists and political scientists, are mostly graduates of the doctoral programs at the University of Rochester and California Institute of Technology. Here, I review developments in this third area, not to disparage the other two, but because its concentration on institutions parallels Leoni's concerns.

Rational ignorance

Many of the models developed with this third approach do not rely on imperfect information, as does Leoni's critique of legislation.[247] The condition of imperfect information nevertheless requires explanation, because it remains central to the rest of these models, and at least partly central to their initial development. Downs[248] was the first systematically to explore the citizen's information problem. In a large electorate, he observed, the citizen's expected utility from voting, minus that from abstaining, is probably negative. The citizen's instrumental reason for allocating time and other scarce resources to acquiring more information about public-policy issues or candidates' positions on those issues would be to increase the likelihood of casting a vote in his own interest. But because the value of the vote is nil, allocating additional resources to acquire more information would not be rational. Hence, most citizens remain (rationally) ignorant about most public-policy issues, most of the time.

There are two exceptions to this prediction. First, and not of great importance, some citizens collect political information because of the activity's entertainment (consumption) value. Second, and of greater importance, some citizens have paid a sunk cost of acquiring information about specific public policies in connection with an activity that directly affects them.

Those old enough to collect Social Security payments provide a good example of this exception. Such persons may receive several hundred dollars monthly, and each had to go through the process of qualifying for these payments. In doing so each acquired substantial information about the program and thereby can assess any proposal for a change in the system. Such changes may affect a young nonrecipient's monthly payments into the system by a few dollars. But the effect lies below his perceptual threshold both because the additional amount of money involved is relatively small and because he has not yet acquired enough information to assess the post-retirement impact of these changes on him.

From this informational asymmetry, it is but a modest step to infer that legislators will be able to assemble and represent the preferences of recipients and their interest-group intermediaries far better than the preferences of those who now pay into the system. Even "altruistic" recipients or "welfare-regarding" legislators would find it difficult to know the preferences of non-recipients and probably impossible to vote on or represent their interests.

Downs hypothesized that people in their specialized roles as producers will have more information about, and would be better able to express their preferences concerning, associated public-policy issues than they will in their more general role as consumers.

The Social-Security example leads one to broaden Downs's proposition, because consumer groups may be specialized as well.

Interest-group politics

Interest groups reinforce these informational asymmetries. Compared with unorganized citizens, group members have substantial political advantages. Groups enjoy large scale economies in collecting, processing, and disseminating political information to their specialized memberships. And they face significantly lower costs of bargaining with legislators, and in monitoring, sanctioning, and enforcing any bargain struck.[249]

Olson[250] points out that an interest group may confront a serious free-rider problem. But the resolution of this problem conditions the nature of the groups that succeed in forming and in maintaining their existence.[251] First, groups formed for other purposes will capture the full benefits of their political activities, *provided that those benefits are appropriable*. Such groups include government agencies themselves with respect to the legislatures that fund them; lower levels of government (for example, cities, counties, and states) with respect to legislatures at higher levels (for example, the federal government); and monopolies or industries with dominant firms. Such groups allocate resources for political activities just as they do private-sector expenditures, setting each expenditure where another dollar in each category would produce the same marginal benefit.

For groups without an independent existence, which might experience free-rider problems, the legislature can provide such statutory terms as compulsory union membership or regulatory cartelizarion.[252] Direct government grants in the form of "research contracts" with high overhead payments often provide the required funds.[253] As we shall discover,[254] legislators provide these benefits to groups, because the value added to each group's income stream allows the legislator a part of the rent created.

Given (asymmetric) rational ignorance and group dominance in assembling and conveying citizens' preferences to legislators, one might conclude that Leoni's view of the legislative process has been confirmed. But the demonstration requires additional steps. First, we must investigate the nature of interest groups' political demands. Under rational ignorance the problem is straightforward. If a group member (and therefore a legislator) does not know about anyone else's preferences save his own, then he cannot enter those preferences into his calculations, no matter what his intentions might be.

But suppose that both group members and legislators do have this kind of information about others' preferences. Ordeshook and I have modeled the resulting game.[255] We found that with or without the possibility of coalitions among interest groups, and provided only that the equivalent of roughly equal additional tax shares will be imposed on the members of all groups, each group will pursue politically a program that provides its members with a private, divisible (among groups) good, and not for a program that provides all citizens wih a public good. We also discovered that groups will tend to use their budgets to buy cost-benefit "efficient" programs in the private sector but will seek to purchase "inefficient" programs in the public sector, by using the fisc as a "common pool."[256] "Political services" such as legislators provide, moreover, often may be inferior goods.[257] Finally, if the costs or "tax shares" of the demanded programs are concentrated in one or a few other groups, then each legislator will prefer to grant each such group its publicly supplied benefit in the form of regulation.[258] Restoring asymmetric information to the model merely serves to make the analysis of coalition possibilities (the cooperative game) unnecessary.

The legislative process

Most of the findings about interest-group decision making carry forward into a consideration of the legislative process.[259] Thus, our discussion can be far briefer than the subject would seem to require. Ordeshook and I have extended these interest-group models to examine legislatures.[260] We find that legislators' incentives coincide with those of interest groups. (We ignore legislator shirking[261] and the problem of dividing rents between legislator and constituent.[262])

Simply stated, there are few obvious and reasonable ways for legislators to "make a market" in the political supply of public goods. Legislators thus face the same problem of public-goods production as do private-sector decision makers. So, "market failure" and "political failure" are the same phenomenon, occurring in different institutional settings. Empirical research reinforces these conclusions.[263] Theoretical and empirical work, in sum, reveals that legislatures are complex organizations (in both their leadership and committee structures[264]) for creating private benefits at collective cost.

The executive and the electoral process

Can a popularly elected chief executive understand (register) and correct the welfare-degrading nature of the legislature's public-policy game? To explore this possibility Ordeshook and I[265] developed an election model in which candidates for office or incumbents seeking re-election might campaign on a platform promising to add or delete the private-benefit programs that various groups demand or now receive. The model predicts occasional net declines in public-sector size (that is, more programs deleted than added) under very unusual conditions (citizens with perfect information about, and sensitivity to, changes in their wealth, *and* incremental choice—deciding on programs to add or delete one at a time—among candidates). But under more plausible conditions (citizens with asymmetric information and incremental choice by candidates), the model predicts net additions of private-benefit programs.

The bureaucracy

Earlier, we cast bureaus and agencies as interest groups.[266] Indeed, one model of bureaucracy—the monopoly-bureau model—suggests the appropriateness of that formulation.[267] It hypothesizes that bureaus merely add themselves to the set of interest groups. An alternative view casts bureaus and agencies as more or less perfect agents of their legislative oversight committees.[268] The results of that formulation obviously are not more promising for the character of legislation or of its execution.

The courts

Finally we consider the role of the courts. We suggest earlier that constitutional provisions appear not to constrain the output of the political process in the manner that the constitution writers intended.[269] There is considerable legal writing on this subject. Epstein, for example, has decried the decline in the courts of the Contract Clause,[270] of the Fifth Amendment's Takings Clause,[271] and of other provisions in the United States Constitution[272] whose purpose it was to limit the use of government for rent-seeking ends. I have reviewed elsewhere[273] the recent Supreme Court history of cases challenging governmental attacks on patently obvious constitutional rights in economic areas. I found the Supreme Court to be no friend of liberal freedom.

Sunstein,[274] Easterbrook,[275] and Macey[276] acknowledge the presence of these protective (against rent-seeking) purposes and goals in the Constitution's language. But Sunstein believes that all rights are governmental creations, contingent on the legislature's decisions; Easterbrook encourages the judiciary to enforce whatever bargains interest groups have struck with the legislature (but nothing more); and Macey would have judicial review assume a public-regarding purpose for all legislation.

Most judicially eschewed constitutional provisions are *substantive* limitations on governmental actions. Certainly, the United States Supreme Court jealously has guarded the lawmaking *process*, as specified in Article One of the Constitution.[277] But it has blinked at the broadest delegations of lawmaking power to the administrative agencies[278] and has done little to confine congressional enactments or agency activities, even when they trample on constitutionally protected rights.[279]

Landes and Posner[280] have developed a model to explain judicial acquiescence in legislative action. In their view, both legislators and interest groups prefer private-benefit programs whose "payments" flow in perpetuity, to those programs covering only one or a few years. Long-run programs reduce transaction costs and allow the successful initiating legislator to capitalize immediately his share of the rents, even if he retires at the end of the session.

This structure places all legislators in a prisoners' dilemma. A single legislator might prefer to kill a long-term program, but such action would (expectationally) diminish the value of inperpetuity grants for all other legislators (and interest groups). The entire legislature "solves" this dilemma by creating institutional rules and practices (the committee structure[281] and the filibuster, for example) that make passing new (including rescinding) legislation difficult. The legislature then passes fewer bills, but those passed enjoy far greater permanence.

The courts could threaten this "solution," because a legislator might use them to make an "end run" around the legislative process, to rescind a long-term program adopted earlier. In Landes and Posner's view, the accommodation struck between the legislature and the courts provides that the legislature will defend the judiciary's independence, while the courts will avoid overturning the legislature's enactments.[282]

The problem of judicial control of the political branches confronts us with both discerning the interactions between and among institutions and the problem of judicial review in a democracy. My own view on this subject, which I press elsewhere,[283] is that Attorney General Meese[284] and others who adopt his highly specialized position of original intent (or original meaning) have not developed an argument that can withstand close scrutiny.

A reading of the preceding pages might lead one to conclude that my preference for "judicial activism" grows not out of a concern for the Constitution's plain meaning, but out of a results-oriented approach not grounded in principled legal reasoning. That reading, however, would be superficial. Leoni's work, and that of other authors cited here, suggests the presence of rent-seeking, a profound failure of representative democracy. Landes and Posner,[285] indeed, invoke the presence of that failure to help explain judicial acquiesence in legislative determinations. It seems apparent, then, that the political system does not "self-correct" through judicial control. But is that result constitutionally infirm?

I believe that it is, Rent-seeking remains such a strong force, with so profound theoretical and empirical credentials, that it seems plain that the Framers were aware of it and crafted the Constitution to suppress it. Indeed, a reading of the *Federalist Papers*[286] not to mention the Constitution itself, in strong clauses such as the contracts clause,[287] the takings clause,[288] and the privileges and immunities clauses[289] leaves little doubt that the Constitution requires a principled judicial activism to control the political branches.

Where original-intent theorists go wrong, I believe, is in discerning that *all* judicial activism is unprincipled. A closer reading of the constitutional history and the Constitution itself helps to clarify the matter. Surely, the self-animating judicial process in the production of positive freedom appears to be constitutionally infirm. But a judiciary responsive to the constitutional protection of negative freedom remains on far firmer ground.

Further reflections

Earlier, in exploring positive and normative models of judges' decision making, I pointed out that some would have judges decide cases according to their own ideologies.[290] Present judicial activity provides several examples of this phenomenon, but none better reflects its essence than Judge J. Skelly Wright's explanation for his decision in *Javins v. First National Realty Corp.*,[291] in which he "read into" all residential lease contracts in the District of Columbia an "implied warrant of habitability," which the reader will recognize, with Leoni, as a positive freedom that the common law had not provided. Judge Wright said of *Javins*:

> Why the revolution in landlord tenant law is traceable to the 1960's rather than the decades before I really cannot say with any degree of certainty.
>
> Unquestionably the Vietnam War and the civil rights movement of the 1960's did cause people to question existing institutions and authorities. And perhaps this inquisition reached the judiciary itself. Obviously, judges cannot be unaware of what all people know and feel. . . .
>
> I was indeed influenced by the fact that, during the nationwide racial turmoil of the sixties and the unrest caused by the injustice of racially selective service in Vietnam, most of the tenants in Washington, D.C. slums were poor and black and most of the landlords were rich and white. There is no doubt in my mind that these conditions played a subconscious role in influencing my landlord and tenant decisions. . . .

[Javins] was my first exposure to landlord and tenant cases. . . . I didn't like what I saw, and I did what I could to ameliorate, if not eliminate, the injustice involved in the way many of the poor were required to live in the nation's capital.

I offer no apology for not following more closely the legal precedents which had cooperated in creating the conditions that I found unjust.[292]

Perhaps Professor Stigler would try to explain to Judge Wright, that such a ruling as that in *Javins* would reduce the housing stock available to poor people, black and white. Both Bruno Leoni and Professor Hayek certainly would concur, but they would go on to explain the nature of the market process and point out that Judge Wright's admittedly limited information did not allow him to rearrange rights with any confidence in the outcome. I doubt that either claim alone would sway the author of *Javins*.

But Judge Wright's comments also reveal that while the debate between liberal freedom and the economist's version of utilitarianism has gone on, another player, ideologically driven to impose his view of a "just" society, has taken the field and appears to be winning the day. We appreciate Bruno Leoni partly because he bequeathed to our "new" understanding a very old pedigree. But we appreciate him all the more because his work now directs us toward the task of constructing an economic theory of freedom, not wealth. I can appropriately close with Leoni's own words: "I think there is a lesson in this. But I have finished mine."[293]

Notes

1   B. Leoni, Freedom and the Law (2d ed. 1972).
     Little has been written about Leoni, and my discussions with certain of his friends and colleagues have revealed little more than what Arthur Kemp stated in his Foreword to the second edition of *Freedom and the Law* (*id*. at *vi–vii*):
     Born April 26. 1913, Bruno Leoni lived a dynamic, intense, vigorous and complex life as a scholar, lawyer, merchant, amateur architect, musician, art connoisseur linguist and—above all else—as a defender of the principles of individual freedom in which he so passionately believed. He was Professor of Legal Theory and the Theory of the State at the University of Pavia where he also served as Chairman of the Faculty of Political Science, as Director of the Institute of Political Science, and as founder-editor of the quarterly journal, *Il Politico*. As a distinguished visiting scholar, he traveled all over the world, delivering lectures at the Universities of Oxford and Manchester (in England), Virginia and Yale (in the United States), to mention only a few. As a practicing attorney, he maintained both his law office and his residence in Turin where he was also active in the Center of Methodological Studies. He found time, on occasion, to contribute columns to the economic and financial newspaper of Milan, *24 ore*. His successful efforts in saving the lives of many allied military personnel during the German occupation of northern Italy (1944) gained him not only a gold watch inscribed "To Bruno Leoni for Gallant Service to the Allies, 1945," but also the eternal gratitude of too many persons to mention. In September, 1967, he was elected President of The Mont

Pèlerin Society at the Congress of that Society held in Vichy, France—the culmination of long years of service as Secretary of the Society to which he devoted a major portion of his time and energies.

Bruno Leoni died tragically on the night of November 21, 1967 . . .

A memorial volume of some of Leoni's works and testimonials, Ommagio a Bruno Leoni (P. Scaramozzino ed. 1969), is available, but has not been consulted in writing this article.

2   Aranson, Economic Explorers on Continents without Property Rights: Economics in Political Science and Law (1985) (paper prepared for the Annual Meeting of the American Economic Association, New York City) (on file at the JLPP office).

3   The public choice literature is reviewed in P. Aranson, American Government: Strategy and Choice (1981); A. Feldman, Welfare Economics and Social Choice Theory (1984); D. Mueller, Public Choice (1979); P. Ordeshook, Game Theory and Political Theory (1986); W. Riker & P. Ordeshook, An Introduction to Positive Political Theory (1972). For reviews of law and economics, see C. Goetz, Law and Economics: Cases and Materials (1984); A. Polinsky, An Introduction to Law and Economics (1983); R. Posner, Economic Analysis of Law (3d ed. 1986). The Economics of Legal Relationships: Readings in the Theory of Property Rights (H. Manne ed. 1975), provides a good early compilation of writings in this area.

4   For public choice, see McKelvey & Ordeshook, *Elections with Limited Information: A Fulfilled Expectations Model Using Contemporary Poll and Endorsement Data as Information Sources*, 36 J. Econ. Theory 55 (1985); McKlvey & Ordeshook, *Information, Electoral Equilibria, and the Democratic Ideal*, 48 J. Pol. 909 (1986). *See also* P. Aranson, Risk, Uncertainty, and Retrospective Voting (1981) (paper prepared for the Annual Meeting of the American Political Science Association, New York City). A much earlier and more general discussion within the Austrian and London School of Economics framework is available in J. Buchanan, Cost and Choice (1969). *See also* L.S.E. Essays on Cost (J. Buchanan & G. Thirlby eds. 1973). For relevant contributions in law and economics, see Epstein, *The Static Conception of the Common Law*, 9 J. Legal Stud, 253 (1980); Rizzo. *Law Amid Flux: The Economics of Negligence and Strict Liability in Tort*, 9 J. Legal Stud. 291 (1980); P. Aranson, The Common Law as Central Economic Planning (1986) (paper prepared for a Liberty Fund, Inc., Conference on the Problems of Economic Calculation under Socialism, New York City). *See also* Muris, *Cost of Completion or Diminution in Value: The Relevance of Subjective Value*, 12 J, Legal Stud. 379 (1983).

5   B. Leoni, *supra* note 1, at 27, 50–51.

6   D. Black, The Theory of Committees and Elections (1963).

7   B. Leoni, *supra* note 1, at 108–10. For a fuller exposition of the problems that political disequilibrium poses for governmental decision making, see W. Riker, Liberalism against Populism: A Confrontation Between the Theory of Democracy and the Theory of Social Choice (1982). *See generally* K. Arrow, Social Choice and Individual Values (2d ed. 1963); Plott, *Axiomatic Social Choice Theory: An Overview and Interpretation*, 20 Am. J. Pol. Sci. 511 (1976).

8   *See, e.g.*, W. RIKER, *supra* note 7; McKelvey, *General Conditions for Global Intransitivities in Formal Voting Models*, 47 Econometrica 1085 (1979); Riker, *Implications from the Disequilibrium of Majority Rule for the Study of Institutions*, 74 Am. Pol. Sci. Rev. 432 (1980); Schofield, *Instability of Simple Dynamic Games*, 45 R. Econ. Stud. 575 (1978).

9   *See, e.g.*, R, Farquharson, Theory of Voting (1969); Levine & Plott, *Agenda Influence and Its Implications*, 63 Va. L. Rev. 561 (1977); McKelvey, *Intransitivities in*

Multidimensional Voting Models and Some Implications for Agenda Control, 12 J. Econ.
Theory 472 (1976); Niemi, Bjurulf & Blewis, *The Power of the Chairman*, 40 Pub.
Choice 295 (1983).

10   *See, e.g.*, Denzau, Riker & Shepsle, *Farquharson and Fenna: Sophisticated Voting and
Home Style*, 79 Am. Pol. Sci. Rev. 1117 (1985); Gibbard, *Manipulation of Voting
Schemes: A General Result*, 41 Econometrica 587 (1973); Kramer, *Sophisticated Voting
over Multidimensional Choice Spaces*, 2 J. Math. Soc. 165 (1972); McKelvey & Niemi,
A Multistage Game Representation of Sophisticated Voting for Binary Procedures, 18 J. Econ.
Theory I (1978); Satterthwaite *Strategy Proofness and Arrow's Conditions: Existence
and Corresponding Theorems for Voting Procedures and Social Choice*, 10 J. Econ. Theory
187 (1975).

11   B. Leoni, *supra* note 1, at 123. For the principal statement of this orthodox position,
sec A. Berle & G. Means, The Modern Corporation and Private Property (rev. ed.
1968).

12   B. Leoni, *supra* note 1, at 146.

13   On the common law background of disclosure laws, see H. Manne, Insider Trading
and the Stock Market, ch. 2 (1966).

14   *See* Easterbrook & Fischel, *Voting in Corporate Law*, 26 J. L. & Econ. 395 (1983);
Fama, *Agency Problems and the Theory of the Firm*, 88 J. Pol. Econ. 288 (1980); Manne,
Mergers and the Market for Corporate Control, 73 J. Pol. Econ. 110 (1965); Manne, *Our
Two Corporate Systems: Law and Economics*, 53 Va. L. Rev. 259 (1967); Manne, *Some
Theoretical Aspects of Share Voting*, 64 Colum. L. Rev. 1427 (1964).

15   A good summary is available in Wolfson, *A Critique of Corporate Law*, 34 U. Miami L.
Rev. 959 (1980). *See also* Jensen & Meckling, *Theory of the Firm: Management Behavior,
Agency Costs, and Ownership Structure*, 3 J. Fin. Econ. 305 (1976).

16   For a review of these restrictions, see Aranson & Ordeshook, *Public Interest, Private
Interest, and the Democratic Policy*, in The Democratic State 87, 98–106 (R. Benjamin
& Elkin eds.1985).

17   *See* J. Buchanan, *supra* note 4. *See also* I. Kirzner, Discovery and the Capitalist
Process (1985); Buchanan, *Positive Economics, Welfare Economics, and Political Economy*,
2 J. L. & Econ. 124 (1959).

18   B. Leoni, *supra* note 1, at 171.

19   Coase, *The Lighthouse in Economics*, 17 J. L. Econ. 357 (1974). For related research
concerning the private supply of fire-fighting services and education, see McChesney,
*Government Prohibitions on Volunteer Fire Fighting in Nineteenth-Century America:
A Property Rights Perspective*, 15 J. Legal Stud. 69 (1986); West, *The Political Economy of
American Public School Legislation*, 10 J. L. & Econ. 101 (1967).

20   B. Leoni, *supra* note 1, at 172.

21   Demsetz, *Toward a Theory of Property Rights*, 57 Am. Econ. Rev.: Papers & Proc. 347
(1967).

22   B. Leoni, *supra* note 1. at 54.

23   *See* Leoni's (*id.* at 160–67) lengthy attack on the expert billiard-player analogy that
Milton Friedman uses to motivate the *as if*, metaphorical nature of microeconomic
models. *See* M. Friedman, Essays in Positive Economics II (1953). Leoni's criticism
aimed at showing that an agent's choice set has an infinity of points (as does any
segment of the real line), and therefore prediction remains impossible. While it
represents a simple misunderstanding of the theoretical enterprise, Leoni's criticism of Friedman is more telling in its claim that economists cannot know what an
agent is about to discover, and therefore they can predict only those choices that

occur within a closed system. Of course, postdiction—that is, explanation—is another matter, for then some of the agent's new information has been revealed to the researcher.

24   D. Hume, An Enquiry Concerning the Principles of Morals (C. Hendel ed. 1957).
25   F. Hayek, Law, Legislation, and Liberty (3 vols. 1973, 1976, 1979); F. Hayek, The Constitution of Liberty (1972) (hereinafter Constitution of Liberty).
26   B. Leoni, *supra* note 1, at 90.
27   *Id*. at 3.
28   *Id*. at 14.
29   *See infra* at 669–72.
30   B. Leoni, *supra* note 1, at 3.
31   *Id*. at 49.
32   *Id*. at 50.
33   *Id*. at 49.
34   *Id*. at 4.
35   *Id*. at 104.
36   *Id*. at 138.
37   *Id. See* J. Rousseau, Du Contrat Social (1943).
38   B. Leoni, *supra* note 1, at 63, 139.
39   *Id*. at 79.
40   *Id*.
41   *Id*. at 137.
42   *Id*. at 78.
43   *Id*. at 79.
44   *Id*. at 91.
45   *Id*. at 177.
46   *Id*. at 154–55.
47   On the resemblance between regulation and central planning, see I. Kirzner, *supra* note 17, at 119–49.
48   B. Leoni, *supra* note 1, at 131–32.
49   *Id*. at 20–21 J. *See* Epstein, *supra* note 4 (developing the similarity between Roman private law and common law).
50   B. Leoni, *supra* note 1, at 21.
51   *Id*. at 85.
52   *Id*. at 149.
53   *Id*. at 87–88.
54   *Id*. at 88.
55   *Id*. at 21.
56   Considering the large backlog of cases that confronts most American jurists today, the absence of formal initiating powers may not constrain them. They can choose almost at will the issues they want to consider. Inconsistent rulings and increasing amounts of legislation doubtless worsen the caseload problem. As most contemporary models of the common law process explain, *see infra* at 695–96, if potential litigants agree on the probability that each will prevail at trial, then they are more likely to settle than sue. Thus, increased caseloads and judicial discretion at least partly grow out of ambiguous legal precedents. *See* Adams, *Would We Rather Fight Than Settle?*, 51 Fla. B.J. 496 (1977) and references cited *infra* notes 208–10. The Supreme Court has decided to reconsider Runyon v. McCrary, 427 U.S. 160 (1976), a landmark case interpreting the extension of liability to private contracts

under 42 U.S.C. § 1981 (1982), in light of these problems. *See* Patterson v. McLean Credit Union, 805 F.2d 1143 (4th Cir. 1986). *cert. granted*, 108 S. Ct. 65 (1987), *reargument ordered per curiam*, 108 S. Ct. 1419 (1988).

57   B. Leoni, *supra* note 1, at 21.

58   *See, e.g.*, Boomer v. Atlantic Cement Co., 26 N.Y.2d 219, 257 N.E.2d 870 (1970).

59   *See, e.g.*, R. Posner, *supra* note 3, at 343–46. *But cf.* Jensen. Meckling & Holderness, *Analysis of Alternative Standing Doctrines*, 6 Int. Rev. L. & Econ. 205 (1966).

60   *See infra* note 204.

61   B. Leoni, *supra* note 1, at 21.

62   *Id.*

63   Even if the judge sought a wider effect, his ruling need not have a pervasive influence in the manner of legislation or regulation. For example, in United Stales v. Carroll Towing Co., 159 F.2d 169 (2d Cir. 1947). Judge Learned Hand "defined" in algebraic terms the "reasonable man" standard that a potential tortfeasor must follow to avoid a finding of negligence against him. But Judge Hand did not intend to define negligence anew; he merely wrote down its preexisting elements as found in prior cases.

64   *See infra* at 673–74.

65   B. Leoni, *supra* note 1, at 20.

66   *Id.* at 94.

67   Leoni's translation: "[W]e must avoid making inquiry about the rationale of our institutions, lest their certainty be lost and they be overthrown." *Id.*

68   *Id.* at 63.

69   *Id.* at 137.

70   *Id.*

71   *Id.* at 106.

72   *Id.* at 97.

73   *Id.* at 76 (emphasis in original).

74   *Id.* at 93. *See supra* at 669–72.

75   *Id.* at 84.

76   *Id.* at 88.

77   *Id.* at 93.

78   *Id.* at 184.

79   *Id.*

80   *Id.* at 185.

81   *Id.* at 186.

82   *Id.* at 72–73, 97–103.

83   *Id.* at 22 (emphasis in original).

84   *Id.* at 5.

85   *Id.* at 6.

86   *Id.* al 9.

87   *Id.* at 11 (emphasis in original).

88   *Id.* at 132.

89   *Id.*

90   *Id.* at 93 (Leoni's words in brackets) (emphasis added).

91   *See* J. Buchanan, *supra* note 4; Hayek, *The Use of Knowledge in Society*, 35 Am. Econ. Rev. 519 (1945); I. Kirzner, Perception, Opportunity, and Profit (1979).

92   B. Leoni, *supra* note 1, at 89.

93   *Id.* at 21–22 (emphasis in original).

94 *See* F. Hayek, The Road to Serfdom (1944). *See also* Riker, *The Heresthetics of Constitution-Making: The Presidency in 1787, with Comments on Determinism and Rational Choice*, 78 Am. Pol. Sci. Rev. 1 (1984).

95 B. Leoni, *supra* note 1, at 18.

96 *Id*. at 123.

97 *Cf. id*. at 110.

98 *Id*. at 124.

99 *Id*. at 112.

100 *Cf. id*. at 125.

101 *Id*. at 5.

102 *Id*. at 6.

103 *Id*. at 90.

104 *Id*. at 171.

105 *Id*. at 16.

106 *Id*. at 11.

107 A "rent" is a payment to the supplier of a good or service greater than that required to bring the good or service into existence. For a fuller discussion of rent-seeking, *see infra* at 703–05.

108 B. Leoni, *supra* note 1, at 14.

109 *Id*. at 20 (emphasis in original).

110 *Id*. at 136.

111 *Id*. at 167.

112 *Id*. at 69. This multiplicity of laws characterizes both statute and common law today. This practice is ancient, however, and Leoni may not have interpreted it correctly. Its common law forms might even be welfare-regarding. For example, some differentiation would occur between common law rules governing disputes arising from agricultural and residential leases when residential leases became unattached from leases on plots of agricultural land. Particular rules—for instance, that in the calculation of damage, if a tenant breaches a lease agreement the landlord has a duty to mitigate damages by trying to find another tenant—might be appropriate for residences, but not for agricultural plots. This is because there could be no mitigation if planting season passed, or if the landlord expected to receive payment in a share of the crops. *See* Rabin, *The Revolution in Landlord-Tenant Law: Causes and Consequences*, 69 Cornell L. Rev. 517 (1984). This example suggests that common law particularized to specific activities might reflect appropriate concerns, and is not merely the result of rent-seeking.

113 B. Leoni, *supra* note 1, at 144.

114 *Id*. at 88.

115 *Id*. at 11–12.

116 Social and political cleavages may either "reinforce" or "cross-cut." For example, suppose that voters are either Catholic or Protestant, and are workers or capitalists. If all workers are Catholics, while all capitalists are Protestants, then these religious and economic cleavages are reinforcing. But if one-half of workers belong to each faith, and so too for capitalists, then the cleavages are cross-cutting. Cross-cutting cleavages are said to moderate political conflict, while reinforcing cleavages are said to identify it. *See* W. Kornhauser, The Politics of Mass Society (1959); A. Lijphart, Democracy in Plural Societies (1977); S. Lipset, Political Man: The Social Bases of Politics (1960); E. Schattschneider, Party Government (1942); D. Truman, The Governmental Process: Political Interests and Public Opinion (1951).

117 B. Leoni, *supra* note 1, at 11–12, 140.

118   *Id*. at 11.

119   *Id*. at 12.

120   *Id*. at 54–55.

121   *Id*. at 105.

122   *Id*. at 121.

123   *Id*. at 124.

124   *Id*. at 13.

125   *Id*. at 17 (emphasis in original).

126   *Id*. (emphasis added).

127   *Id*. at 138.

128   *Id*. at 103.

129   *Id*. at 56.

130   *Id*. at 13–14 (emphasis in original).

131   *See supra* at 672–73.

132   The continental codes even today have very definite common law-like, judge-determined origins. *See* Aranson, *Economic Efficiency and the Common Law: A Critical Survey*, in Law and Economics and the Economics of Legal Regulation 51 (G. Skogh & M. von Schulenberg eds. 1986).

133   B. Leoni. *supra* note 1. at 8.

134   *Id*.

135   *Id*. at 11–12.

136   *Id*. at 76 (emphasis in original).

137   *Id*. at 17.

138   *See* Klein, Crawford & Alchian, *Vertical integration, Appropriable Rents, and the Competitive Contracting Process*, 21 J.L. & Econ. 297 (1978).

139   B. Leoni, *supra* note 1, at 81.

140   *Id*. at 10 (emphasis in original).

141   *Id*.

142   *Id*. at 145.

143   *Id*. at 148.

144   *Id*.

145   *Id*. (emphasis in original).

146   Claims persist in legal history that the early common law treatise writers were less than disinterested in the particular substance of their compilations.

147   *See supra* at 675–79.

148   J. Rawls, A Theory of Justice (1971).

149   R. Nozick, Anarchy, State, and Utopia (1974).

150   *See, e.g.*, Cohen, *Capitalism, Freedom, and the Proletariat*, in The Idea of Freedom 9 (A. Ryan ed. 1979).

151   For an excellent review, see Terrell, *Liberty; The Concept and its Constitutional Context*, 1 Notre Dame J.L. Ethics & Pub, Pol'y 545 (1985).

152   *See, e.g.*, F. Hayek, *supra* note 25; Constitution of Liberty, *supra* note 25.

153   J. Buchanan, The Limits of Liberty: Between Anarchy and Utopia (1975).

154   *See supra* at 665–66.

155   Constitution of Liberty. *supra* note 25, at 12.

156   R. Nozick, *supra* note 149. I here rely on John Gray's assessment of what Nozick means to say. *See* Cray, *Marxian Freedom, Individual Liberty, and the End of Alienation*, 3 Soc. Phil. & Pol'y 160 (1986).

157   C. Bay, The Structure of Freedom (1965).

158   Cohen, *supra* note 150.

159   Stigler, *Wealth, and Possibly Liberty*, 7 J. Legal Stud. 213 (1978). Stigler's argument appears in a more general and less combative form in Moore, *An Economic Analysis of the Concept of freedom*, in H. Manne, *supra* note 3, at 108.

160   Stigler. *supra* note 159. at 217.

161   *Id.* at 216.

162   *Id.* at 215.

163   *Id.* at 215–16.

164   *Id.* at 216–17.

165   *Id.* at 217.

166   *Id.*

167   *Id.* (emphasis in original).

168   *See* Gray, *supra* note 156, at 163–64.

169   *See supra* at 665–6.

170   For example, a 1982 Supreme Court case overturned the California Supreme Court's judicial application of statutory language that nullified due-on-sale clauses in home-mortgage contracts. *See* Fidelity Fed. Sav. & Loan Ass'n v. de la Cuesta, 458 U.S. 141 (1982). Present mortgagors might benefit from the nullification, but future mortgagors, their right to alienate this provision thereby restricted, would not benefit. Thus, attempts to aid a class often produce only transitional gains for its pre-existing members. On *de la Cuesta*, see Haddock & Hall, *The Impact of Making Rights Inalienable*, 2 Sup. Ct. Econ. Rev. 1 (1983). On the problem of transitional gains, see Tullock, *The Transitional Gains Trap*, 6 Bell J. Econ. 671 (1975).

171   The term derives from Rizzo, *supra* note 4.

172   F. Hayer, *supra* note 25, at 61.

173   Machlup, *Liberalism and the Choice of Freedoms*, in Roads to Freedom: Essays in Honour of Friedrich A. von Hayek 117 (E. Streissler ed. 1960). I thank Israel Kirzner for informing me of this important essay.

174   *Id.* at 120.

175   *Id.*

176   *Id.* at 126.

177   *Id.* at 130.

178   *Id.*

179   *See, e.g.*, Stigler, *Economic Competition and Political Competition*, 13 Pub. Choice 91 (1972); Stigler, *The Theory of Economic Regulation*, 2 Bell J. Econ. & Mgmt. Sci. 3 (1971).

180   Aranson, *Political Inequality: An Economic Approach*, in Political Equilibrium: A Delicate Balance, Essays in Honor of William H. Riker 133 (P. Ordeshook & K. Shepsle eds. 1982). *See* Riker, *Democracy and Representation: A Reconciliation of* Ball v. James *and* Reynolds v. Sims, 1 Sup. Ct. Econ. Rev. 39 (1982).

181   *See* McKelvey & Ordeshook, *An Experimental Study of the Effects of Procedural Rules on Committee Behavior*, 46 J. Pot. 182 (1984); Shepsle & Weingast, *When Do Rules of Procedure Matter*, 46 J. Pol. 206 (1984), The correlative law-and-economics contributions are Coase, *The Problem of Social Cost*, 3 J. L. & Econ. 1 (1960), and Demsetz, *When Does the Rule of Liability Matter?*, I J. Legal Stud. 13 (1972).

182   The results are reported in Aranson & Ordeshook, The Political Bases of Public-Sector Growth in a Representative Democracy (1978) (paper prepared for the Annual Meeting of the American Political Science Association, New York City) (on file at the JLPP office). *See also* Aranson and Ordeshook, *supra* note 16, at 131–37.

183   *See* references cited *supra* notes 6–10.

184   *See supra* at 675–77.

185   I have in mind Rawls's second principle of justice. *See* J. Rawls, *supra* note 148.

186   *See, e.g.,* J. Buchanan & G. Tullock, The Calculus of Consent: Logical Foundations of Constitutional Democracy ch. 7 (1962); J. Buchanan, *supra* note 153.

187   *See* J. Buchanan & G. Tullock, *supra* note 186; J. Rawls, *supra* note 148.

188   *See, e.g.,* E. Browning & J. Browning, Public Finance and the Price System 226–27 (2d ed, 1983).

189   *See, e.g.,* Calabresi & Melamed, *Property Rules, Liability Rules, and Inalienability: One View of the Cathedral*, 85 Harv. L Rev. 1089 (1972). An excellent recent treatment is available in Rose-Ackerman, *Inalienability and the Theory of Property Rights*, 85 Colum. L. Rev.931 (1985). *See also* Haddock & Hall, *supra* note 170; Holderness, *A Legal Foundation for Exchange*, 14 J. Legal Stud. 321 (1985); Radin, *Market-Inalienability*, 100 Harv. L.Rev. 1849 (1987). For a discussion of alienability in con-stitutional argument, see Aranson, *Calculus and Consent*, in Democracy and Public Choice 60 (C. Rowley ed. 1987).

190   *See supra* at 674–81; Aranson, *supra* note 189.

191   *See infra* at 706–09.

192   *See, e.g.,* Aranson, *Procedural and Substantive Constitutional Protection of Economic Liberties*, 7 Cato J. 345 (1987); Aranson, *Judicial Control of the Political Branches: Public Purpose and Public Law*, 4 Cato J. 719 (1985); Epstein, *Toward a Revitilization of the Contract Clause*, 51 U. Chi. L. Rev. 703 (1984).

193   Aranson, *Public Deficits in Normative Economics and Positive Political Theory*, in The Economic Consequences of Government Deficits 157 (L. Meyer ed. 1983): Aranson & Ordeshook, *Alternative Theories of the Growth of Government and Their Implications for Constitutional Tax and Spending Limits*, in Tax and Expenditure Limitations 143 (H. Ladd & T. Tideman eds. 1981); Shepsle, *Overgrazing the Budgetary Commons: Incentive-Compatible Solutions to the Problem of Deficits*, in The Economic Consequences of Government Deficits 211 (L. Meyer ed. 1983).

194   *See supra* at 673–74.

195   *See* R. Posner, *supra* note 3.

196   *See* letter of judge J. Skelly Wright, *infra* at 710, as quoted in Rabin, *supra* note 112, at 549.

197   *See* R. Dworkin, Taking Rights Seriously (1978).

198   Posner, *A Theory of Negligence*, 1 J. Legal. Stud. 24 (1972).

199   R. Posner, *supra* note 3.

200   *See, e.g.,* Epstein, *The Temporal Dimension in Tort Law*, 53 U. Chi. L. Rev. 1175 (1986); Holderness, *supra* note 189.

201   Posner, *supra* note 198.

202   The incentive effects of a negligence rule subsequently were shown to be equiva-lent to those of a rule of strict liability with contributory negligence, a result that Posner recognizes. *See* Brown, *Toward an Economic Theory of Liability*, 2 J. Legal. Stud. 323 (1973).

203   Goetz, *Wherefore the Landlord-Tenant Law "Revolution" ? Some Comments*, 69 Cornell L. Rev. 592 (1984).

204   And in any event, the landlord and tenant's ability to contract away from such a rule should be sufficient to reduce the costs of imposing it. *See* Coase, *supra* note 181. *See also* Aranson, *supra* notes 4, 132.

205   This section relies in large part on Aranson, *supra* note 132.

206   Coase, *supra* note 181.

207   Calabresi & Melamed, *supra* note 189.

208   Rubin, *Why Is the Common Law Efficient?*. 6 J. Legal Stud. 51 (1977).

209   Gould, *The Economics of Legal Conflicts*, 2 J. Legal Stud. 279 (1973).

210   *See, e,g.*, Cooter & Kornhauser, *Can Litigation Improve the Law Without the Help of Judges?*, 9 J. Legal Stud. 139 (1980); Goodman, *An Economic Theory of the Evolution of the Common Law*, 7 J. Legal Stud. 393 (1978); Landes & Posner, *Adjudication as a Private Good*, 8 J. Legal Stud. 235 (1979); Priest, *The Common Law Process and the Selection of Efficient Rules*, 6 J. Legal Stud. 65 (1977); Terrebonne, *A Strictly Evolutionary Model of Common Law*, 10 J. Legal Stud. 397 (1981).

211   *See supra* at 668–89.

212   Rubin. *Predictability and the Economic Approach to Law: A Comment on Rizzo*, 9 J. Legal Stud. 319, 329 (1980).

213   *See* Aranson, *supra* note 132.

214   Rubin. *Common Law and Statute Law*, 11 J. Legal Stud. 205, 216–19 (1982).

215   *See* B. Leoni, *supra* note 1, at 94.

216   F. Hayek, *supra* note 25, at 74, states the matter in a different connection: "[I]ndividuals had learned to observe (and enforce) rules of conduct long before such rules could be expressed in words . . . ." Heiner has pursued the connection between imperfect information and the emergence of rules in an important series of papers. *See* Heiner, *Imperfect Decisions and the Law: On the Evolution of Legal Precedent and Rules*, 15 / Legal Stud. 227 (1966); Heiner, *The Origins of Predictable Behavior*, 73 Am. Econ. Rev. 560 (1983).

217   *See supra* at 669.

218   *See. e.g., supra* at 674–77.

219   For a full discussion of the problem, see Aranson, *supra* note 4.

220   *id.* For the intellectual source of this criticism, see J. Buchanan, *supra* note 4: *see also* J. Buchanan & G. Thirlby, *supra* note 4.

221   *See, e.g.*, Epstein, *supra* note 4; Rizzo, *supra* note 4.

222   *See supra* at 666–67; 669–72.

223   *See* Epstein, *supra* note 4.

224   *See, e.g., supra* note 63; Brown, *supra* note 202 (developing modern variant of the Hand formula); Rizzo, *supra* note 4.

225   *See, e.g.*, R. Posner, *supra* note 3, *See also* Judge Posner's "Solomonic" but much maligned and incorrectly reported decision returning a dispute to the parties' private forum, in Menora v. Illinois High School Ass'n, 685 F.2d 1030 (7th Cir. 1982).

226   *See* Epstein, *A Theory of Strict Liability*, 2 J. Legal Stud. 151 (1973); Epstein, *supra* note 4.

227   Epstein, *Nuisance Law: Corrective Justice and Its Utilitarian Constraints*, 8 J. Legal Stud. 49 (1979). *See also* Epstein, *supra* note 200.

228   The set of "Posnerians" need not include Judge Posner in all matters. Charles J. Goetz has informed me, for example, that Judge Posner regards the case reviewed here as wrongly decided. *See also supra* note 225.

229   404 So. 2d 896 (La. 1981).

230   *Id.* at 898.

231   *Id.*

232   *Id.*

233   J. Weingarten Inc. v. Northgate Mall, 390 So. 2d 527, 538 (La. App. 1980).

234   *Weingarten*, 404 So. 2d at 902.

235   *See Weingarten*, 590 So. 2d at 535.

236   *Weingarten*, 404 So. 2d at 901. *See also* Muris, *supra* note 4.

237   *See* Haddock & Hall, *supra* note 170.

238   F. Hayek, *supra* note 25, at 57.

239   *See supra* at 674–83.

240   *See* F. Hayek, supra note 25: Constitution of Liberty, *supra* note 25.

241   Tullock, *The Welfare Costs of Tariffs, Monopoly, and Theft*, 5 West. Econ. J. 224 (1967).

242   Krueger, *The Political Economy of the Rent-Seeking Society*, 64 Am. Econ. Rev. 291 (1974).

243   *See* The Theory of the Rent-Seeking Society (J. Buchanan, R. Tollison & G. Tullock eds. 1980), which provides a good survey of this tradition.

244   For a good review of recent problems, see Tullock, *Back to the Bog (Efficient Rents 3)*, 46 Pub. Choice 259 (1986).

245   *See* Stigler, *supra* note 179, and more recently Jordan, *Producer Protection, Prior Market Structure, and the Effects of Government Regulation*, 15 J. L. & Econ. 151 (1972); Peltzman. *Toward a More General Theory of Regulation*, 19 J. L. & Econ. 211 (1976); Posner, *Taxation by Regulation*, 39 Bell J. Econ. & Mgmt. Sci. 22 (1971); Posner, *Theories of Economic Regulation*, 5 Bell J. Econ. & Mgmt. Sci. 335 (1974).

246   *See, e.g.*, A. Bentley, The Process of Government (1908); E. Schattschneider, Politics, Pressures, and the Tariff (1935); T. Lowi, The End of Liberalism: The Second Republic of the United States (2d ed. 1979).

247   *See supra* at 675–77.

248   A. Downs, An Economic Theory of Democracy (1957). *See also* Buchanan, Individual Choice in Voting and the Market, 62 J. Pol. Econ. 334 (1954); P. Aranson. Rational Ignorance in Politics, Economics, and Law (1987) (paper prepared for l'Universite' d'Ete' de la Nouvelle Economic, l'Universite' d'Aix-en-Provence).

249   Aranson & Ordeshook, *supra* note 16, at 118–21.

250   M. Olson, The Logic of Collective Action (2d ed. 1971).

251   *See* Aranson & Ordeshook. *supra* note 16, at 118–22, 135–37.

252   *See* Wagner, *Pressure Groups and Political Entrepreneurs: A Review Essay*, I Papers on Non-Market Decision Making 161 (1969); *see also* N. Frohlich, J. Oppenheimer & O. Young, Political Leadership and Collective Goods (1971).

253   *See* J. Berry, Lobbying for the People: The Political Behavior of Public Interest Groups (1977); Downing & Brady, *Constrained Self Interest and the Formation of Public Policy*, 54 Pub. Choice 15 (1979).

254   *See infra* at 705.

255   Aranson and Ordeshook, *supra* notes 16, 182. *See also* Aranson & Ordeshook, *A Prolegomenon to a Theory of the Failure of Representative Democracy*, in American Re-evolution: Papers and Proceedings 23 (R. Auster & B. Sears eds. 1977).

256   Aranson & Ordeshook, *supra* note 182.

257   Aranson & Ordeshook, *supra* note 193.

258   *See* Aranson, Gellhorn & Robinson, *A Theory of Legislative Delegation*, 68 Cornell L. Rev. 1 (1982); Fiorina. *Legislative Choice of Regulatory forms: Legal Process or Administrative Process*, 39 Pub. Choice 33 (1982).

259   *See* Shepsle & Weingast, *Political Solutions to Market Problems*, 78 Am. Pol. Sci. Rev. 417 (1984); Shepsle & Weingast, *Political Preference for the Pork Barrel*, 25 Am. J. Pol. Sci. 96 (1981); Weingast, Shepsle & Johnsen, *The Political Economy of Benefits and Casts: A Neoclassical Approach to Distributive Politics*, 89 J. Pol. Econ. 642 (1981).

260   Aranson & Ordeshook, *supra* notes 16, 182.

261   Nelson and Silberberg, *Ideology and Legislator Shirking*, 25 Econ. Inquiry 15 (1987).

262   Tullock, *supra* note 244.

263   *See, e.g.*, J. Ferejohn, Pork Barrel Politics (1974); M. Fiorina, Congress: Keystone of the Washington Establishment (1977); D. Mayhew, Congress: The Electoral Connection (1974).

264   *See, e.g.*, Shepsle & Weingast, *The Institutional Foundations of Committee Power*, 81 Am. Pol. Sci. Rev. 85 (1987); Weingast and Marshall, *The Industrial Organization of Congress; or, Why Legislatures, Like Firms, are Not Organized as Markets*, 96 J. Pol. Econ. 132 (1988).

265   Aranson & Ordeshook, Incrementalism, the Fiscal Illusion, and the Growth of Government in Representative Democracies (1977) (paper prepared for the Annual Meeting of the Southern Economic Association, New Orleans). The results are reported in Aranson & Ordeshook, *supra* note 16, at 149–64.

266   *See supra* at 703.

267   W. Niskanen, Bureaucracy and Representative Government (1971). For a critical but constructive review of this literature, see Orzechowski, *Economic Models of Bureaucracy*, in Budgets and Bureaucrats: The Sources of Government Growth 229 (T. Borcherding ed. 1917).

268   *See* Weingast & Moran, *Bureaucratic Discretion or Congressional Control? Regulatory Policymaking by the Federal Trade Commission*, 91 J. Pol. Econ. 765 (1983); Weingast, *Regulation, Reregulation, and Deregulation: The Political Foundations of Agency Clientele Relations*, 44 Law & Contemp. Probs. 247 (1981); Weingast, *The Congressional-Bureaucratic System: A Principal-Agent Perspective (With Applications to the SEC)*, 44 Pub. Choice 147 (1984). *Cf.* Jarrell, *Change at the Exchange: The Causes and Effects of Deregulation*, 27 J.L. & Econ. 273 (1984). *See also* Wood, *Principals, Bureaucrats, and Responsiveness in Clean Air Enforcements*, 82 Am. Pol. Sci. Rev. 213 (1988).

269   *See supra* at 691.

270   Epstein, *supra* note 192.

271   R. Epstein, Takings: Private Property and the Power of Eminent Domain (1985).

272   Epstein, *Taxation, Regulation, and Confiscation*, 20 Osgoode Hall L.J. 433 (1982).

273   Aranson, *supra* note 192.

274   Sunstein, *Naked Preferences and the Constitution*, 84 Colum. L. Rev. 1689 (1984).

275   Easterbrook, *Foreword: The Court and the Economic System*, 98 Harv. L. Rev. 4 (1984).

276   Macey, *Promoting Public-Regarding Legislation through Statutory Interpretation: An Interest Group Model*, 86 Colum. L. Rev. 223 (1986).

277   U.S. Const. art. I. § 7, cls. 2–3. *See, e.g.*, I.N.S. v. Chadha, 462 U.S. 919 (1983) (invalidating the "legislative veto"); Bowsher v. Synar, 106 S. Ct. 3181 (1986) (over-turning that part of Gramm-Rudman-Hollings Act providing for congressional appointment of executive-branch personnel).

278   Aranson, Gellhorn & Robinson, *supra* note 258.

279   *See* citations *supra* notes 192, 271–72.

280   Landes & Posner, *The Independent Judiciary in an Interest-group Perspective*, 18 J.L. & Econ. 875 (1975). *But see* Macey, *supra* note 276; Aranson, *supra* note 192.

281   *See* Shepsle & Weingast, *supra* note 264; Weingast and Marshall, *supra* note 264; Weingast, *A Rational Choice Perspective on Congressional Norms*, 23 Am. J. Pol. Sci. 245 (1979).

282   *See, e.g.*, National Cable Television Ass'n v. United States, 415 U.S. 336 (1974); Kent v. Dulles, 357 U.S. 116 (1958). Easterbrook takes this positive model and enshrines it as a normative one for judicial decision making. *See supra* note 275.

283   *See* Aranson, *supra* note 192.

284   *See. e.g.*, Speech by Edwin W. Meese, III, before the American Bar Association (July 9, 1985), in The Great Debate: Interpreting our Written Constitution 1 (1986).

285   Landes & Posner, *supra* note 280.

286   *See* The Federalist Nos. 10, 62 (J. Madison).

287   U.S. Const, art. I, § 10, cl. 1. *See* R. Epstein, *supra* note 192.

288   U.S. Const. amend. V. *See* R. Epstein, *supra* note 271.

289   U.S. Const. art. IV, § II, cl. 1; *id.* at amend XIV, § 1. *See* Aranson, *supra* note 192.

290   *See supra* at 692, *passim*.

291   Javins v. First Nat'l Realty Corp., 428 F.2d 1071 (D.C. Cir.), *cert. denied*, 400 U.S. 925 (1970).

292   Rabin, *supra* note 112, at 549.

293   B. Leoni, *supra* note 1, at 175.

Chapter 11

Richard E. Wagner

CRAFTING SOCIAL RULES

Common law vs. statute law, once again

Introduction

A MARKET ECONOMY is a self-ordered network of economic activities that results from people pursuing their interests within a framework of rules represented primarily by the principles of property, contract, and tort. Those rules, and the processes by which they are adopted and revised, provide the foundation upon which a market economy rests. Just as a substantial economic literature has explored the efficiency properties of a market economy, a more recent literature has sought to explore the efficiency properties of the legal order that governs market processes. In so doing, a contrast has been developed between common law, which emerges out of the activities of judges, juries, and lawyers, and statute law, which emerges out of the activities of legislators and bureaucrats.

It seems hardly surprising that scholars of law and economics would inquire about the economic efficiency of common law and statute law as alternative processes for producing the rules that govern a market economy, for such inquiry seems a natural extension of an economic assessment of alternative institutional arrangements. Much, though not all, of this literature accords common law processes higher standing with respect to economic efficiency than statute law. Indeed, some of this literature argues that the tendency toward efficiency within common law processes is quite strong, though it is fully possible to weaken those efficiency claims while still according a general advantage to common law over statute law.

The bulk of this literature notwithstanding, there would seem to be no universal statement that can be asserted about the comparative efficiency properties of common law and statute law. Primarily this is because any reference to common law and statute law invokes an excessive aggregation that ignores the wide variety of particular institutional formats that are possible. While it is always possible to deal with generic representations of common law and statute law processes, these representations are of little use in assessing particular institutional illustrations of either category, because their comparative properties will depend on particular institutional details pertaining to those processes. In exploring this theme, I shall first review the efforts to assess common law and statute law with respect to economic efficiency. Then I shall explain why generic comparisons cannot serve as substitutes for particular institutional comparisons. Following this, I shall explore some aspects of a widespread confusion between formal and substantive arguments.

Common law and economic efficiency

In his 1973 treatise on the *Economic Analysis of Law,* Richard Posner advanced the thesis that common law rules tend to promote economic efficiency while statute law rules do not. Most of that book consisted of arguments seeking to reconcile a vast array of common law rulings and doctrines with notions of economic efficiency interpreted as aggregate wealth maximization. Similarly, in their detailed examination of tort law, William Landes and Richard Posner (1987) argue that "the common law of torts is best explained as if the judges who created the law through decisions operating as precedents in later cases were trying to promote efficient resource allocation."[1]

To be sure, no one claims that judges truly possess the knowledge necessary to promote economic efficiency, even should they have an interest in doing so. As for their interests it seems clear that these are highly variegated. Some judges might well be efficiency zealots, but there are many who seem to delight in striking down capitalist practices they find repugnant, as in overturning contracts on grounds of unconscionability, regardless of the subsequent economic consequences. Many hypotheses have been advanced about judicial motivation, and many different motives are doubtlessly at work in the judiciary. Judges hardly constitute a homogeneous group, and there is surely no reason to think that the pursuit of economic efficiency should be an object of judicial fetishism.

Whether judges might promote a network of efficient rules through some invisible hand process, regardless of their motivation, is a different matter. Paul Rubin (1977) and George Priest (1977) sought to develop such an explanation for common law efficiency, with efficiency resulting not from the intent of judges but from the self-interested actions of litigants. With respect to two-person accidents, efficiency requires that liability rest on the person for whom the sum of accident costs and prevention costs are lower. If the prevailing rule allocates liability to the higher cost avoider, that party will have a stronger incentive to litigate the case as the stakes involved become higher relative to litigation costs. In situations where both parties have a *continuing* interest in the precedent or rule, inefficient rules will invite litigation when efficient rules will not. The greater the inefficiency, the stronger the likelihood of litigation. Even should a judicial decision to overturn a precedent be purely a random event, inefficient rules will tend to be replaced by efficient rules.[2]

The papers by Rubin and Priest inspired a considerable literature. For instance, Goodman (1978), Landes and Posner (1979), Terrebonne (1981), and Heiner (1986) developed arguments generally supportive of the Rubin and Priest arguments about the efficiency features of common law processes. Cooter and Kornhauser (1980), however, developed a model with no tendency toward efficiency, unless a presumption were imposed to the effect that judges had a personal interest in promoting economic efficiency. And Rubin (1982) subsequently argued that while common law and statute law were both economically efficient in the 19th century, both had become economically inefficient by the early 20th century.[3]

The argument about common law efficiency is based on an analogy between litigation and bidding in auctions. A trial is viewed as a process by which a rule is put up for bid, with the parties bidding through their expenditures on litigation. The typical presumption is that the party that spends more is more likely to win, with the result being that legal rules tend to reflect the desires of highest bidders. However, as De Alessi and Staaf (1991) explain, the effort to use such a framework to characterize the economic efficiency of the common law involves an insoluble aggregation problem. For the litigation process involves two people only, with the rule subsequently applying to everyone. A statement about efficiency cannot be made without invoking some presumption about the preferences of those people who were not represented in the litigation. Without some way of aggregating those absent preferences, there is no way to determine whether the rules that emerge from a process of two-party litigation would be the same as those that would emerge from a process of collective choice operating under a rule of unanimity.

It should also be noted that the claim of common law efficiency arises from a setting where both parties have a continuing interest in the rule being litigated. If only one party has a continuing interest, with the other party concerned only with the particular case, the rule will tend to become that which is desired by the party with the continuing interest, regardless of the efficiency of the rule. The reason for this is that the party without the continuing interest will have a weaker incentive to litigate, because most of the gains from successful litigation will redound to people who will find themselves in the same position in the future. Without some ability to link those future interests to the present litigation, the party with the continuing interest will tend to spend more and to win. The persistence of an inefficient rule in this setting is explained on the same grounds as inefficiency is explained in the literature on rent seeking: concentrated interests dominate diffuse interests, because the latter cannot overcome the high cost of organizing for concerted action.

To be sure, the claim about possible inefficiency in this instance is not free from challenge. It may be readily acknowledged that in the absence of a continuing interest, the rule will tend to become that which is desired by the party with the continuing interest. Let it be granted that among the set of all such instances, there will be some cases where the rule is efficient and other cases where it is not. Even so, there is no way to determine which of those rules are the inefficient ones. One can always make claims about what would happen if transaction costs were zero, but without omniscience there is no way to test such a claim.[4] It is always possible to assert the opposing claim, but there is no procedure for testing that claim. A higher bid is not offered, and there is no external vantage point from which it is possible to distinguish between cases where this is because there is no source of higher valuation and those cases where such a source does exist, but high transaction cost prevents its revelation. Transaction costs are ubiquitous, and there is no way to determine what people would have done had those costs been different from what they are.

Statute law and economic efficiency

What about the economic efficiency of statute law? Much of the literature stemming from the theory of rent seeking views statute law as economically inefficient, as illustrated by the Tullockian rectangles (Tullock 1967; Tollison 1982; Rowley, Tollison, and Tullock 1988). The central claims about inefficiency are well known. People invest resources in seeking special legislative favors that otherwise could have been devoted to genuine production. They also invest resources in seeking to avoid being on the losing end of other people's rent seeking activities, as well as in striving to maintain present positions from erosion through future legislation (Tollison and Wagner 1991).

It may be granted that such resources, considered as the cost of rent seeking, could be devoted to other uses were it not for the various incentives that propel rent seeking. But it is similarly true that resources devoted to such uses as locks, firearms, and karate lessons could be put to other uses, if only people would genuinely respect each other's rights of person and property. The necessity for such expenditures might well be regretted, but such a sentiment of regret would not warrant the claim that they were inefficient, because, given human nature as we know it, there might not be a better alternative that can be attained, even if there might be many that can be imagined. Rights will not be respected just because the world would be nicer if they were; conflict is endemic to the human condition. As a purely formal matter, people can be modeled as apportioning their resources between market production, defending against the predatory activities of others, and seeking to prey on others through offensive rent seeking, according to their individual values, talents, and capacities (Buchanan 1975). Pursuit of such a perspective would surely lead to a conclusion that statute law would, as a purely formal proposition, contain similar efficiency properties as common law, as Becker (1983) points toward and Wittman (1989) argues explicitly.

This claim is essentially a matter of the arithmetic of gains from trade. For if statute law is economically inefficient, dominant political support could be organized to change the law in the direction of efficiency. Should it turn out that a change is not made, the failure to change could always be attributed to high transaction costs, just as it could be with respect to common law. But such an attribution would be but one possible hypothesis. An alternative hypothesis would involve the contrary argument that the change is not prevented by high transaction cost, but rather is prevented by the inferiority of the proposed change. There is no external vantage point from which these hypotheses can be tested. Absent unanimous consent to make a change, there is no cognitive basis for asserting a claim of Pareto inefficiency (Buchanan 1959). It would thus seem equally plausible to give an account of economic efficiency under statute law as under common law, or at least to assert that the efficiency properties of such processes might seem generally to be similar.

Complaint, judgment, and rule formation

Common law and statute law are commonly portrayed as sharply contrasting processes. Yet what strikes me as most notable about both processes is their essential similarity. While these processes might differ in particular details, they possess the same formal structure. For both processes are activated by a complaint or petition.

That complaint is then heard before some body, either a judge and jury or a legislative assembly, and that body subsequently renders a judgment. In a common law proceeding, a farmer might bring a complaint against a rancher because of the damage done to the farmer's crops by the rancher's cattle. If so, the case would be heard by a jury selected from among the people who live in the area, and the Court would eventually render some judgment. The statute law process would follow essentially the same form. The farmer's complaint about the damage done by wandering cattle would now be addressed to a legislative assembly. The remedy requested could vary greatly, covering such wide-ranging possibilities as a specific tax break or subsidy for the petitioner to the articulation of a rule requiring ranchers to fence their cattle.

To be sure, this similarity of form can hide many substantive differences that influence the particular operation of either process. These differences limit, if not eliminate, the ability to speak generically of differences between common law and statute law processes. Once it is recognized that there are many *particular* formats for common law and statute law processes, in the absence of some proof that the least efficient form of common law process will be superior to the most efficient form of statute law process it becomes impossible to assert any conclusive argument based on a comparison of generic alternatives.

There are numerous ways in which common law and statute law processes could be made more or less similar. For instance, juries are typically empaneled for short periods of time whereas legislators can serve for long periods, depending on their success in future elections. But there is no reason why the period for which jurors serve could not be extended, which would make juries more like legislatures. Alternatively, the period of time for which legislators serve could be shortened, as through term limits, or even through selection by lot, which would make legislators more like jurors. Moreover, judges could be made more, or less, like legislatures, depending on whether they are elected, selected by the legislature with lifetime tenure, or selected by lot with lifetime tenure (or with fixed tenure, for that matter). In any case, the characteristics of those who issue common law rulings could be made very similar to those who issue statute law rulings, or they could be made very disparate, depending on particular institutional details governing those processes.

In the common law setting, the complaint must be lodged against some specific person or set of persons, for it is these people who will be asked to provide a remedy. In the statute law setting, however, the complaint is typically more general, and is not addressed against particular defendants who will be asked to provide the remedy. Hence, the common law process marshals automatically the opposition of the defendant; the process itself enlists an opponent to the plaintiff's claim. This is generally not so with the legislative process. Opposition will be provoked only to the extent that the proposed legislative remedy threatens to reduce the net worth of some well organized interest group.

In the simple farmer-rancher setting, a farmer's proposal that the legislature initiate mandatory fencing at rancher's expense, and at standards that might even slow down a buffalo, would evoke strong opposition from the ranchers. But in a complex society, legislation would often have a diffuse pattern of costs. Consider, for instance, legislation to require buildings to be accessible to people in wheel chairs. Opponents of such legislation are less likely to provide resistance than they would under a common law process, because the common law process would involve a single case and a named defendant. The legislative process names no defendant who will have to pay a successful plaintiff, and, moreover, the organization of group interests in opposition may often be difficult because some producers may gain while others lose.

So long as legal processes are merely a reflection of the use of knowledge in society (Hayek 1945), this distinction between common law and statute law would seem to be inessential. But if to some extent legal processes of rule articulation are educational, the differences between the two processes may be more significant, because they can influence the very pattern of knowledge within a society. In particular, common law and statute law would seem to differ substantially in what it is they have to teach about individual liberty and responsibility in society. The common law process would seem to involve a basic presumption that people are responsible for their own circumstances. Individual unhappiness is a personal matter, to be dealt with by the individual as he sees best. A desire for a higher standard of living, then, would tell that person to find ways to produce services more highly valued by others. This presumption that people are responsible for their well being is to be challenged only when a plaintiff can identify particular people who have violated his rights, a situation that in turn undermines the presumption that people are responsible for their circumstances.

The statutory process, for the most part, involves the starkly different presumption that people are not responsible for their own circumstances. Unhappiness with one's standard of living thus leads neither to a focus on possible activities that would lead to the production of services more highly valued by others nor to an identification of particular people who have violated the complainant's rights. Rather, the statutory process inspires a claim that the complainant's unsatisfactory situation is attributable to society in general, and not to anyone in particular. The problem resides with social structures, patterns, institutions, and the like, and not with the individuals who are seeking some improvement in their position.

Bruno Leoni (1991: 78f.) notes that the Athenian constitution of the 5th century B.C. was reformed to make the legislative process somewhat similar to the common law process in this regard. Any proposed legislation was submitted to a committee of magistrates who were charged with defending the existing body of statutes against the revisions that the proposed legislation would entail. Furthermore, a sponsor of legislation apparently could be sued by another legislator on the grounds that the legislation was defective or in conflict with other valid laws. In this manner, proposed legislation operated much like common law in automatically enlisting a strongly interested opponent. Without some such process, the existing body of rules is in much the position of a commons, when compared with proposed legislation, save to the extent that proposed legislation galvanizes the opposition of strong interest groups.

To be sure, juries are like legislatures, in that their decisions involve the expenditure of other people's money. Neither faces a budget constraint, although it is possible to envision legislative processes that do involve such a budget constraint. For instance, the Wicksellian system, with its emphasis on proportional representation and approximate unanimity, seeks to create a setting where representative assemblies would be more a reflection of fiscal sobriety than would seem to be possible for a jury, unless the jurors were to finance their verdicts from their own pockets.[5]

Form, substance, and claims of common law efficiency

One of the most notable things about the literature on common law efficiency is its concentration on the *formal* structure of the argument to the neglect of issues *of substantive* conduct. Efficiency is a concept derived from the logic of comparative statics, and it has no ready applicability to historical processes independently of some prior evaluation that distinguishes what is good or desirable from what is not. Even Pareto efficiency is highly value laden (Rowley and Peacock 1975), and characterization of its value judgment as being minimal and innocuous is really a reflection of its typically formal and not substantive usage. And rather than enter into controversial discussions of value that would be required by any substantive treatment of efficiency, the discussion has stayed at the purely formal level. Nonetheless, it is surely the case that people think of efficiency as a substantive concept, as denoting something good. A statement that common law rules promote efficiency is thus regarded not simply as a statement about the formal structure of an argument, but as a substantive statement about the quality of legal rules and the economic well-being they promote. What this means, however, is that formal arguments are used to support substantive conclusions that they cannot possibly substantiate.

Consider the formal structure of tort argument concerning efficiency, as represented by Judge Learned Hand's formulation in *United States v. Carroll Towing Co.*[6] A barge that had been left unattended in New York Harbor broke loose from her moorings, causing damage. Hand declared that any judgment about negligence "is a function of three variables: (1) The probability that she will break away; (2) the gravity of the resulting injury, if she does; (3) the burden of adequate precautions." Hand continued, "Possibly it serves to bring this notion into relief to state it in algebraic terms: if the probability be called P; the injury, L; and the burden, B; liability depends upon whether . . . B<PL." Hand went on to note that even in a crowded harbor during wartime it would be unreasonable to expect the barge to be attended around the clock. But he also noted that it had been left unattended for 21 hours, which he declared to be excessive under the circumstances.

While *Carroll Towing* is not cited often, this is not to deny that it summarizes the economic content of tort law. This is certainly the claim of Landes and Posner (1987), though they note that the relationship should be expressed in terms of marginal magnitudes and activity changes, as against the total magnitudes that Judge Hand used in his illustration. Consider just the first two of the 14 cases Landes and Posner (1987) examine in their section on "Judicial Applications of the Hand Formula" (96–107). In *Hendricks v. Peabody Coal Co.,*[7] an abandoned strip mine that had filled with water was used as a swimming hole. A 16-year-old boy was injured upon diving into the water, because he hit a submerged shelf. The court ruled for the plaintiff, noting that "the entire body of water could have been closed off with a steel fence for between $12,000 and $14,000. The cost was slight compared to the risk to the children involved." The burden to the defendant of taking precautions, B, was low relative to the anticipated damage to the plaintiff, PL. Landes and Posner state that "the court was on safe ground in concluding that the defendant had failed to use due care" (97).

By contrast, *Adams v. Bullock*[8] illustrates, according to Landes and Posner, a "situation where the cost of care is disproportionate to the expected accident cost, so that the failure to take care is not negligent" (97). A 12-year-old boy was swinging an eight-foot-long wire over the side of a bridge he was crossing, when the wire touched the defendant's trolley wire beneath the bridge, burning the boy. In this case the court ruled that the accident was an "extraordinary casualty, not fairly within the area of ordinary prevision." In terms of the Landes and Posner interpretation of the Hand Formula, P was so small indeed that B>PL would have to hold.

To be sure, no suggestion is made that such computations are made explicitly. Rather the suggestion is that in any effort to make sense of the stock of rulings, where sometimes the plaintiff wins and sometimes the defendant does, the categories represented by B, P, and L, and the relationship represented by the Hand Formula, can provide illumination as to the pattern of outcomes of the cases. Perhaps so, but the law and economics literature surely errs when it treats such categories as B, P, and L as solid, concrete facts, more akin to eternal needs for food and water than to ephemeral fashions for particular types of cuisine. For the opposite is surely the case.

Consider again the *Hendricks* and *Adams* cases. In *Adams* the plaintiff was ruled liable, but in *Hendricks* the liability was placed on the defendant. Landes and Posner attribute this difference to the illuminating power of economic reasoning, as represented by the Hand Formula. And it would surely seem that B was higher in *Adams* while P was lower. As for L, it is difficult to tell, probably more so for the 12-year-old in *Adams* than for the 16-year old in *Hendricks*. But there is no objective ground whatsoever for concluding that PL>B in *Hendricks* while PL<B in *Adams*. *Hendricks* was decided in 1969, *Adams* in 1919. An alternative possibility would be that in 1919 liability would have been placed on the plaintiff in both cases, while in 1969 (or 1992) the defendant would have been liable in both cases. This would be because of a growing sentimentality nurtured by the dominance of legislation over law, and of the Samaritan's Dilemma that this has fostered (Buchanan 1977).

For further amplification, consider five of the many cases discussed in Peter Huber (1988), where plaintiffs received judgments in their favor. One case involved a man trying to mount a 16.5 inch tire on a 16 inch rim. Understandably, the man had difficulty in doing so, and had to inflate the tire to 48 pounds to get it to hold to the rim. With such high pressure, the tire subsequently exploded, the car crashed, and the man was injured. He sued the manufacturer for failing to warn him explicitly against the danger of over-inflating a tire and putting it on the wrong sized rim. He won his case. In a second case, a teenager was burning a candle in a room. Wishing to give the room a more pleasing aroma, the teenager poured cologne over the candle, and engulfed himself in flames. When the trial was over, the cologne manufacturer was ruled liable for the teenager's burns, for failing to issue a warning about the cologne's flammability. In a third case, a man who deliberately jumped in front of a subway train in New York City was mutilated. For this act he was awarded $650,000, based on his claim that the driver should have stopped more quickly. Fourth, two men went sailing in a hot air balloon, which apparently got wet from a storm. The men later stuffed the balloon into a dryer in a laundermat. For their shrapnel wounds from the exploding dryer, the men were awarded $885,000 from the manufacturer. Finally, a man entered a road race in southern California. Apparently not being fast enough to get attention, he strapped a refrigerator to his back. He got quite a bit of attention when his refrigerator slipped, sending him crashing to the ground. He also received $1 million from the manufacturers of the refrigerator and the belt.

It would certainly be possible to place these five cases into the formal structure of the Hand Formula. For the terms in that formulation appear to be precise and objective, and yet are subjectively grounded in people's beliefs and values. Consider P, the objective-sounding probability of an accident. In the case of the blown-out tire, it could well be admitted that it would be exceedingly unlikely that someone would try to mount a 16 inch tire on a 16.5 inch rim. Nonetheless, it would always be possible to imagine a situation where someone would try to do such a thing. And if that person were successful, the severity of a resulting accident might be so calamitous that the cost to the manufacturer of warning against such an activity would be less than the expected value of the accident loss. As a matter of pure form, this possibility would have to be admitted–just as no one has been able to refute the compelling quality of Pascal's wager.

But as a matter of substantive conduct, it might reasonably be wondered whether economic well-being is promoted by forcing a manufacturer into anticipating some-one else's negligence and inattention, if not outright stupidity, as well as, perhaps, parental culpability through neglect in their bringing their children to adulthood in such an unfit condition.[9] People will do stupid things, some people apparently quite often. However regrettable this might be, the cultivation of institutional processes and ideological beliefs that support the proposition that people are not responsible for their actions will surely intensify the prevalence of stupidity. Law, whether common or statute, is more or less a reflection of community values. These, and not some naturally occurring magnitudes, are reflected in the Bs, Ps, and Ls of the Hand formulation. The extent to which those values are good is a separate matter. The form of the economic argument will hold in any case, but the formal argument does not address concerns of substance.

Efficiency, order, and social rules

It is quite possible to reject the meaningfulness of Pareto efficiency as a substantive concept, while nonetheless recognizing that social processes regarding the formation of rules can be assessed in terms of their ability to provide a framework of stable rules within which people can plan their economic activities. Those activities do get coordinated, even if it is admitted that substantive claims about efficiency cannot be made without importing values into the judgment. As Hayek (1973) explains, it is the order of rules governing economic relationships that generates the observed order of actions. Relatedly, Lachmann (1971) argues that social institutions supply points of orientation around which people pursue their plans and projects. And in similar fashion, De Alessi and Staaf (1991) argue that what is important about the common law is its stability and certainty, its slowly changing nature, which provides a framework of stability within which people can undertake their economic activities.[10] The ability of the common law to provide such orientation would be understandable, even if any claim about Paretian efficiency would be judged problematical.

It seems to be widely presumed that statute law changes more rapidly than common law, thereby producing less stability than common law. The plausibility of such an argument is probably reinforced by notions arising out of the public choice literature on voting cycles, for which any existing outcome can be defeated by some alternative proposal. Yet the point of the literature on structure-induced equilibrium is that stability is provided not by the structure of preferences but by the structure of rights and expectations created by political institutions (Shepsle and Weingast 1981; Ordeshook 1992). Even though any statute can be defeated by some alternative, that alternative typically will be blocked from the agenda by virtue of the structure of rights created within a particular constitutional framework. Hence, stability and order would seem to be a dominant feature of statute law as well as common law. To be sure, there might well be differences in the expected durabilities of common law and statute law. But in the absence of evidence on this point, common law and statute law would both seem to provide some combination of stability and change.[11]

The inconclusive character of any assessment of common law and statute law processes calls attention to the possibility that the very distinction between common law and statute law is overdrawn, at least within the contemporary nation-state where the reach of the secular authority is ubiquitous. Before the emergence of the nation-state, social rules were crafted within a process involving multiple sources of authority with overlapping jurisdictions. The two primary sources of authority were the ecclesiastical and secular authorities, with each possessing spheres of autonomy that were characterized by jurisdictional conflict along various boundaries. Civil order in this setting required some modicum of mutual respect and tolerance. The common law articulated by secular judges was surely constrained by the existence of a competing, ecclesiastical source of authority.[12] Law could transcend politics in this setting, because neither the secular nor the ecclesiastical authority commanded anyone's full allegiance. Unconstitutionality was synonymous with illegality. But with the Church evolving into just one among many voluntary associations within the state, as against transcending the state, the state became the sole or residual source of authority. Competing sources of authority no longer exist, or rather exist only with the forbearance of the nation-state, so we should not be surprised that the substance of common law rules differs as a result. The dichotomy between statutory and common law is largely irrelevant in the contemporary nation-state, because both derive from the same source in a setting where there no longer exist polycentric sources of competing authority. This is not to deny that different processes for generating social rules can have significant implications for economic well-being, but rather is to deny that the distinction between common law and statute law is of any categorical significance within the contemporary nation-state which has the capacity to absorb all alternative sources of authority into itself.

Notes

1   Along similar lines see Steven Shavell (1987). In contrast, Peter Huber (1988) is resoundingly critical of tort law.
2   To be sure, the speed at which this process operates will depend on the likelihood that precedents will be overturned. If this random process were one where a precedent were overturned only if a Jack of Diamonds were drawn from a deck of cards, inefficient rules would have stronger persistence than if a head on a single flip of a coin were sufficient to overturn a precedent.

3   These efficiency claims are surveyed in Rowley (1989), as well as in several of the essays in Mercuro (ed) (1989).

4   Margolis (1987) makes a similar point in his comparison of two approaches to the efficiency of the common law, where he argues the superiority of the approach that takes transaction costs as given over the one that speculates over what things would be like if transaction costs were zero.

5   The Wicksellian system characterized here is examined in Wagner (1988).

6   159 F.2d 169 (2d Cir. 1947).

7   115 [1]. App. 2d 35, 253 N.E.2d 56 (1969).

8   227 N.Y. 208, 125 N.E. 93 (1919).

9   In light of such scholarship as that presented in Charles Murray (1984), which shows the impact of welfare state programs in promoting parental neglect of children along many dimensions, such culpability would perhaps extend to the legislative sponsors of such programs as well. This would certainly be an implication of the Athenian process noted by Bruno Leoni, and discussed above.

10   Similar outlooks are developed in Epstein (1980) and Rizzo (1980). To be sure, stability of rules is not sufficient independently of some substantive consideration of working properties. For Stalin's constitution surely provided a framework that offered relative stability and predictibility.

11   Huber (1988) explains that the revolution in tort law over the past generation, which overturned a wide variety of long-standing practices and expectations, largely occurred through common law processes.

12   For a valuable examination of this see Harold Berman (1983, esp. pp. 255–69).

References

Becker, G. S. (1983) "A Theory of Competition Among Pressure Groups for Political Influence." *Quarterly Journal of Economics* 98: 371–99.

Berman, H. J. (1983) *Law and Revolution: The Formation of the Western Legal Tradition.* Cambridge: Harvard University Press.

Buchanan, J. M. (1959) "Positive Economics, Welfare Economics, and Political Economy." *Journal of Law and Economics* 2: 124–38.

Buchanan, J. M. (1975) *The Limits of Liberty.* Chicago: University of Chicago Press.

Buchanan, J. M. (1977) "The Samaritan's Dilemma." In: J. M. Buchanan (ed) *Freedom in Constitutional Contract.* College Station: Texas A & M Press: 169–85.

Cooter, R. and Kornhauser, L. (1980) "Can Litigation Improve the Law without the Help of Judges?" *Journal of Legal Studies* 9: 139–63.

De Alessi, L. and Staaf, R. J. (1991) "The Common Law Process: Efficiency or Order?" *Constitutional Political Economy* 2: 107–26.

Epstein, R. A. (1980) "The Static Conception of the Common Law." *Journal of Legal Studies* 9: 253–75.

Goodman, J. C. (1978) "An Economic Theory of the Evolution of the Common Law." *Journal of Legal Studies* 7: 393–406.

Hayek, F. A. (1945) "The Use of Knowledge in Society." *American Economic Review* 35: 519–30.

Hayek, F. A. (1973) *Rules and Order.* Chicago: University of Chicago Press.

Heiner, R. A. (1986) "Imperfect Decision and the Law: On the Evolution of Legal Precedent and Rules." *Journal of Legal Studies* 15: 227–61.

Huber, P. W. (1988) *Liability: The Legal Revolution and Its Consequences.* New York: Basic Books.

Lachmann, L. M. (1971) *The Legacy of Max Weber.* Berkeley, CA: The Glendessary Press.

Landes, W. M. and Posner, R. A. (1979) "Adjudication as a Private Good." *Journal of Legal Studies* 8: 235–84.

Landes, W. M. and Posner, R. A. (1987) *The Economic Structure of Tort Law.* Cambridge: Harvard University Press.

Leoni, B. (1991) *Freedom and the Law.* 3rd ed. Indianapolis, IN: Liberty Press.

Margolis, S. E. (1987) "Two Definitions of Efficiency in Law and Economics." *Journal of Legal Studies* 16: 471–82.

Mercuro, N. (ed) (1989) *Law and Economics.* Boston: Kluwer Academic Publishers.

Murray, C. (1984) *Losing Ground.* New York: Basic Books.

Ordeshook, P. C. (1992) "Constitutional Stability." *Constitutional Political Economy* 3: 137–75.

Posner, R. A. (1973) *Economic Analysis of Law.* Boston: Little, Brown.

Priest, G. (1977) "The Common Law Process and the Selection of Efficient Rules." *Journal of Legal Studies* 6: 65–82.

Rizzo, M. J. (1980) "Law Amid Flux: The Economics of Negligence and Strict Liability in Tort." *Journal of Legal Studies* 9: 291–318.

Rowley, C. K. (1989) "The Common Law in Public Choice Perspective: A Theoretical and Institutional Critique." *Hamline Law Review* 12: 355–83.

Rowley, C. K. and Peacock, A. T. (1975) *Welfare Economics: A Liberal Restatement.* New York: John Wiley & Sons.

Rowley, C. K., Tollison, R. D., and Tullock, G. (1988) *The Political Economy of Rent-Seeking.* Boston: Kluwer Academic Publishers.

Rubin, P. (1977) "Why is the Common Law Efficient?" *Journal of Legal Studies* 6: 51–63.

Rubin, P. H. (1982) "Common Law and Statute Law." *Journal of Legal Studies* 11: 205–23.

Shavell, S. (1987) *Economic Analysis of Accident Law.* Cambridge: Harvard University Press.

Terrebonne, R. P. (1981) "A Strictly Evolutionary Model of Common Law." *Journal of Legal Studies* 10: 397–407.

Tollison, R. D. (1982) "Rent Seeking: A Survey." *Kyklos* 35: 575–602.

Tollison, R. D. and Wagner, R. E. (1991) "Romance, Realism, and Economic Reform." *Kyklos* 44: 57–70.

Tullock, G. (1967) "The Welfare Costs of Tariffs, Monopolies, and Theft." *Economic Inquiry* 5: 224–32.

Wagner, R. E. (1988) *"The Calculus of Consent:* A Wicksellian Retrospective." *Public Choice* 56: 153–66.

Wittman, D. (1989) "Why Democracies Produce Efficient Results." *Journal of Political Economy* 97: 1395–1424.

Chapter 12

Jürgen G. Backhaus

THE GERMAN CIVIL CODE OF 1896

An economic interpretation

Introduction

O N AUGUST 12, Napoleon Bonaparte as First Consul promulgated a decree appointing a Code Commission of four and instructed them to have the Code ready by the ensuing November. After a carefully designed process of revisions, the Code Civil was promulgated on March 21, 1804. Again in August, on August 18, 1896, the German Emperor ratified the German Civil Code, which took effect on January 1, 1900. Between these dates, there was a century of civil codification, well known to the historians of law yet less well known to students of law and economics. In fact, the great codifications were inspired by far sighted rulers and legal scholars already before the French revolution. The Code Fredéric or Prussian Gesetzbuch of 1751, later became the *Landrecht* of 1794 and, although not purporting to be complete, was actually favoured by Savigny over the Code Civil. A table gives the chronology of codification relevant to the German civil law.[1]

A Chronology of the German Civil Code

Year	Event
1683	Danske lof: proclaimed by King Christian V of Denmark
1686	Swedish Codification Commission
1734	Swedish Code
1751	Code Fredéric or Prussian Gesetzbuch (later Landrecht of 1794)
1756	Codex Maximilianeus Bavaricus Civilis
1770	Sardinian Code (based on *Roman* called *common* law)

A Chronology of the German Civil Code (cont'd)

Year	Event
1794	General Landrecht (common law) for the Prussian States
1800	French Code Commission
1804	Code Civil des Français or Code Napoleon
1811	General Civil Code for all Austrian States
1813	Napoleon's defeat in Leipzig
1814	Dispute on codification in Germany.
	A.J.F. Thibaut: The Need for a General Civil Code (pro)
	Fr. Carl v. Savigny: The Needs (Beruf) for our Time in Legislation and Jurisprudence (contra)
1815	N. Th. Gönner: On Legislation and Jurisprudence in Our Time (pro)
1816	P.J.A. (von) Feuerbach: A Few Words about Historical Jurisprudence (pro)
1820	German federation (Bund) remains pure confederation without common codification
1842–	Draft civil codifications in Hesse, Bavaria, Saxony and others
1847	Conventions of German law scholars in Frankfurt and Lübeck (pro)
1849	Frankfurt constitution of the Church of Saint Paul (pro, article 64)
1850	Failure due to the nullifications of its laws
1866	Dresden draft for the Northern Federation (law of obligations)
1871–1873	German constitution
	Change of the constitution to provide for common codification (Lex Lasker of December 20, 1873)
1874	Pre-commission
1874–1888	First commission
1879–1884	Pre-drafts
1881–1888	Plenary meetings, result is the first draft and the motivations
1889–1893	Deliberations of the ministerial commission
1889–1896	Second commission
1896	Revisions of the third draft in the imperial council
1896	Deliberations in the parliament during 53 sessions
1896	First of July: of 393 members, 288 present, 222 pro, 48 contra, 18 abstentiants
1900	From the 1st of January of this year, the German Civil Code is and remains in force

From a law and economics point of view, it is immediately apparent that the great codifications occur when a large political entity also allows for larger markets to emerge. It is this more expansive market exchange which calls for better and more predictable legal rules, since the local customs can no longer be regarded as the only or main source of the law. The central question in this context is, of course, whether an efficient law will emerge as a consequence of a codification, or whether it is more likely to emerge through a competition of rules that will absorb the relevant knowledge and generate the most efficient one as the pre-dominant precedent. Today, we refer to this set of questions as the "efficiency of the common law debate".[2]

This debate, however, did not originate with modern law and economics. It had its early peak in the so-called codification dispute of 1814–1816. The debate was opened by Friedrich Thibaut (1772–1840) Professor first at Jena and then at Heidelberg and a leading teacher of the Pandektenrecht or a German Common Law. In his "Need of a Common Civil Law in Germany",[3] he first describes the miserable condition of legal disharmony prevailing in Germany at that time, and then presents a plan for the codification of German Civil Law. This plan was immediately countered and ultimately deferred by the criticism of Friedrich Carl von Savigny,[4] Savigny's main point being that Germany's legal problems could not be resolved by implementing a grandiose systematically conceived plan, rather meticulous and systematically organized empirical (in his case historical) research was first "called for" (Beruf).

II

Almost two generations later, the so-called historical school in German jurisprudence had, indeed, done a lot of this ground work, and the economic exigencies of the new political and economic unity in Germany proved stronger than the provisions of the constitution conceived only three years earlier. However, by now codification had also become a political issue, and the different political parties pitted their hopes on the codification work in order to further their program, ably assisted by academics representing the different camps.

A case in point is the Austrian lawyer Anton Menger (1841–1906) who in 1890 published his critique of the draft of the German Civil Code of 1888 under the title *The Civil Law and the Property Less Classes.*[5] He represented those who wished to make the codification simultaneously an instrument of legislation aimed at social policy.[6]

Anton Menger's book is written from the point of view of a theory of private law based on socialist but not Marxist principles. Of the two different basic instincts he identifies as driving individual behaviour, self interest and common interest (Gemeinnutz), he wants to support institutions that allow common interest to prevail over self-interest. He feels that the institutions of private law in allowing a full realization of self-interest unnecessarily compromise common interest and thereby harm the less advantaged. Therefore, he wants to restrict the ability of private individuals to give up rights in contractual relationships such as when entering into a labour contract, into a residential lease or—in his particular case into marriage, as he sees the labourer, the tenant, and the wife regularly as the disadvantaged party to the contract.[7] From this vantage point, he is also critical of the historical approach to legislation which was to form the other major force of criticism of the draft code. In emphasizing the historically grown contractual forms over theoretically and deductively conceived rules to be codified, he argues, the historically working lawyers necessarily and unwittingly translate the historically grown imbalances into the new Code and thereby perpetuate these imbalances.[8] Accordingly, Anton Menger and his critique first makes his basic point of view clear and adds on to this his criticism of on the one hand the historical approach and on the other hand the passivity of the judge in the civil procedure (p. 29–32), then deals with family law, notably the law of marriage and divorce, the imbalance in the law of marital possessions, and the treatment of illegitimate children; in the third part he discusses the law of things (notably property) and in the fourth part the law of obligatory relations, notably the labour contract and the lease. The fifth part is devoted to the law of inheritance.

Anton Menger's critique of the German Civil Code in its draft form was later going to be rather important in the parliamentary debates during 1896 when the social democrats, in particular, took up many of his arguments. His extensive study of some 230 pages had first appeared in the journal *Archives for Social Legislation and Statistics (Archiv für Soziale Gesetzgebung und Statistik)* edited by Heinrich Braun, in issues 1 and 3 of 1889 and 1 of 1890.[9]

In order to provide the proper intellectual context, it should perhaps be noted that Menger continued his work and expanded his framework steadily. In 1903, he published a general theory of the state containing four books: 1) the state and the law in general, 2) the order of economic life and of re-production in the popular labour state, 3) the organization of the popular labour state and 4) the transition to the popular labour state, his socialist utopia. This popular labour state is, generally described, one with very little economic inequality, and the issues discussed in book two again are property in relation to marriage, in relation to the labour contract, in relation to the means of production, in relation to consumer decisions and in relation to inheritance, with substantial room being devoted to illegitimate children but also aspects of procedural law, including penal law. Virtually the entire activist agenda of modern contemporary American legal discourse can be found in this book.[10] The theoretical back drop of this work is Menger's *The Right to the Full Fruit of Labour*[11] which builds on the triple rights to have the full fruits of labour, to exist, and to have a right to work (droit au travail). And thirdly—but by no means completely, the whole system is complemented by a manual of economic policy covering the same institutions and basic world view, but seeing the whole program now as one to be realized by economic policy or, in modern terms, as the progressive agenda.[12]

While in Vienna, Braun's Archive published Menger's powerful critique of the draft code from the point of view of a socialist theory of law, in Berlin the "historical" position was forcefully formulated by Otto von Gierke and published equally first in several installments in the leading journal, then in revised form as a book.[13]

Otto von Gierke (1841–1921) was born in Stettin as the son of a Prussian official. He studied law at the University of Berlin and held professorships at the universities of Breslau (1872–1884), Heidelberg (1884–1887) and Berlin (1887 until his death).

Gierke is generally described as having formulated, based on the writings of Jacob Grimm (1785–1863), a specific Germanist school of law as opposed to the Romanists.

> "At the beginning of Gierke's carreer, German legal scholarship was dominated by the Romanist school of Savigny; but Gierke began and remained a strong Germanist. The Germanists, like the Romanists, were historically minded; their research, however, did not take them back to the Roman empire, Justinian's code, and the reception, but followed the path marked out by Jacob Grimm to the law of the ancient German *Mark* and the *Gemeinde* (local community) to feudal records, town charters, the rules of guilds in search of 'truly German' and legal principles. The first

volume of Gierke's *Das deutsche Genossenschaftsrecht* (1868–1913) ... was the first product of his self-imposed task of broadening the foundation for a German theory of associations by a detailed study of successive types of organizations in German history."[14]

From an economic point of view, the emphasis should not be on the specific nationality of the German law. The emphasis of this empirical research is rather on the law as it has developed by itself, instead of the law as it has been imposed by church or state, both drawing on Roman law which is thereby transported through time without recognition of the immediate history where it is to be applied. The working hypothesis is that the law can be empirically found in the customs, charters, contracts and the like of identifiable associations of men, be these commercial, political, charitable, professional or other associations. In establishing contractual relationships one with the other, persons actually create a new legal entity, such as a corporation. Here, the view is distinct from the Roman tradition which has to create the fiction of a legal identity being granted by the state through *fiat*. Hence, the research is firmly embedded into identifiable economic practices.

> "Gierke's concept of 'social law' enables him to construe the internal rules of churches, trade unions, business corporations, etc., as independent of state determination and to put such bodies on an equal basis with human persons in claiming areas of freedom into which the state cannot intrude." (Lewis, 1968, p. 180)

This specific approach to legal research was similar enough to economic research into history of the time that it could be merged with the economic research into a powerful critique of legislation.

The German Civil Code

The economists have a long tradition of influencing legislation. Schmoller called his journal the "Annual of Legislation, Administration and Political Economy in Germany". Hence, it is no surprise that economists would intervene into the debates about large legislative projects. Outstanding examples are the great codifications, such as the "Code Civil de Napoleon" and the German Civil Code. The German Civil Code can actually even be considered an explicit attempt at efficient legislation. The Civil Code was, in its ultimate form, passed with the explicit input of the leading economists of their time in Germany, and based on explicit economic reasoning. Otto von Gierke played an important role in this process. How this came about is worth recounting briefly.

In 1848, when the first German democratic parliament convened in the Church of St. Paul in Frankfurt, there were no less than 56 different legal systems governing bills of exchange. This exceeded by far the number of Member States of the German Federation at that time. It is obvious that such splintering of the legal system stood in the way of the rapidly developing market economy, and there was therefore already an initiative of the Frankfurt parliament to pass a common German Civil and also Commercial Code. However, the parliament had a short life span, and it dissolved before it had even seriously started the task. There were new initiatives in

1866 and 1869 in the northern German Federation, the pre-cursor of the Reich, but only after the unification of the German states as a confederation of principalities in 1871 could the task be resumed, and this happened with initiatives in 1873 in both the imperial parliament and the imperial council (the representation of the confederated princes). In 1874 the pre-commission of five members was established, and in the same year in 1874 a commission of eleven was established under the chairmanship of Pape. This commission issued a report in 1887, and the "act of introduction" with various drafts of by-laws was also issued in 1887 and 1889 in order to provide for a broad discussion. However, the editor of the leading economics journal in Germany at the time, the *Jahrbücher für Gesetzgebung, Verwaltung und Volkwirtschaft im deutschen Reich* (Annals of Legislation, Administration and Political Economy in Germany), Gustav (von) Schmoller with his colleagues in the German Economic Association (Verein für Socialpolitik), agreed that the draft was impractical because it did not build on established economic practices and their respective legal counterparts, rather providing a deductively reasoned set of norms based on the Roman law tradition, and hence not corresponding to the economic practices of a developed industrialized market economy. Entire issues of the journal were devoted to critiques of the draft act, with the articles by Otto (von) Gierke having the strongest influence.[15] This unsolicited advice led to the establishment of a second commission in 1890 which provided a completely revised draft Code in 1895 which was duly passed, after stormy discussions in the imperial parliament, on July 1, 1896 with 222 votes in favour and 48 against, on July 14 in the imperial council, and ratified by the Emperor on August 18. The Code took effect on January 1, 1900. And, with numerous smaller revisions, it has remained the same since. This episode illustrates again that efficient legislation is possible, although it also illustrates that, had the economics profession not intervened, legislation would probably have been imposed that would have burdened the German economy with high and persisting transactions costs. The Code would not have become the export article it actually proved to become, still today. Gierke's approach proved to be important well after the Civil Code had been passed. In building on his criticism of the first draft of the Code, he further developed his criticism into a full theory of German private law, consisting of the three pillars of the law of persons 1895, the law of things 1905 and the law of obligatory relations 1917. It was this coherent body of legal theory, based on empirical research, which allowed for consistent interpretations of the Code in the vicissitudes of the different economic and social environments of first the empire, second the war economy of 1914–1918, the challenge of the hyper-inflation that it posed to private contracts, the corporatist economy established by the national socialists, the war economy again, and finally the reconstruction period in Germany after the currency reform of 1948.

III

In his extensive criticism, Gierke had identified essentially three main problems he saw with the Code. First, there was the reversal of purpose. Instead of creating a unified law for a unified political entity, the unified law was seen as a way to create a more unified entity. For this reason, in order not to compromise the legislative authority of the constituent states, the Commission had avoided important areas of the law, in particular those where there is an overlap between private law and public law, the distinction being somewhat artificial in a rapidly growing economy with a strongly participating state. (p. 63)

Secondly, the law was seen as being not only written in an obscure language, and not readily available to the educated lay person, if with great difficulty this educated lay person had mastered the obscure language, in Gierke's view he would often find strange solutions to his problems, and many times even those that squarely contradicted his own sense of the law. (p. 66)

Thirdly, and relatedly, this was due to the completely unempirical posture of the drafters of the act, with the further implication that a highly rational public law was confronted with an ineffective and inadequately researched private law, a situation which in practice would lead to high costs imposed on the economy when public law by virtue of the application of good lawyering would prevail over private law. (p. 68)

Again, it is not difficult to recognize the position of modern law and economics in these writings.

Gierke was by no means the only author featured in Schmoller's *Annual of Legislation, Administration and Political Economy in Germany*.[16] The Code proved to be important for other legislative enterprises as well, and hence we have a very extensive coverage of the Swiss Civil Code several years later.[17]

In the legislative session, two issues that had already been focussed on by Menger almost de-railed the entire process. The socialists wished to make the family and the law of private associations a major focus of their legislative effort. The conservatives and the Catholic Centre Party likewise focussed on the family, but in the opposite direction. In the law of associations, a coalition between the Catholic Centre Party, the liberals and the socialists was technically possible. Yet, both changes would in all likelihood not have passed the imperial council. Hence, instead of arranging for a dual majority on the one side in the family issue with the conservatives and on the other side in the associations issue with the liberals and the socialists, the Centre Party proved to be the rock on which the entire legislative effort could be founded. This was difficult because attendance during the deliberations turned out to be low. When the legislation was introduced, attendance stood at between forty and fifty members of parliament, and as the legislation drew on, the conservatives, annoyed by a provision to compensate for crop damage caused by wild hares, threatened to return to their estates for the early summer harvest. Ultimately, the early summer proved to be wet and the crop damage due to wild hares clause was struck out. 200 Imperial messengers had to stay only barely into the month of July, since the act was passed on July 1 in 1896, with 222 votes in favour, 48 votes against and 18 abstentions.[16]

Notes

1   I owe this table to German lecture notes by my Frankfurt colleague Joachim Rückert, "Materialien zur Vorlesung: Einführung in das Zivilrecht und Zivilrecht I", Frankfurt: Johann-Wolfgang-Goethe Universität, 1994. The chronology has not only been translated from German but also substantially been adapted.

2   By way of introduction, see section II of the first volume of Richard A. Posner and Francesco Parisi, "Law and Economics: Theoretical and Methodological Foundations" (The International Library of Critical Writings in Economics). Cheltenham: Edward Elgar, 1997.

3   "Über die Notwendigkeit eines allgemeinen bürgerlichen Rechts für Deutschland", Heidelberg: 1814–1840(2).

4   "Vom Beruf unserer Zeit für Gesetzgebung und Rechtswissenschaft", Heidelberg: 1815; the debate has been documented well in Jacques Stern (ed.) *A.F.J. Thibaut and F.C. von Savigny: zum hundertjährigen Gedächtnis des Kampfes um ein einheitliches bürgerliches Recht für Deutschland,* Berlin: 1914.

5   Anton Menger, *Das bürgerliche Recht und die besitzlosen Klassen: eine Kritik des Entwurfes eines bürgerlichen Gesetzbuches für das deutsche Reich,* Tübingen: Laupp, 1890.

6   From 1877–1989, Anton Menger was a professor of Austrian law of civil procedure at the University of Vienna. He was the brother of Carl (1840–1921), who from 1879–1903 taught political economy at the same university and held sharply different (conservative) views. The full spectrum of the political orbit was present in their family, as a third brother, Max, held Marxist views. All three brothers played respectively different important roles in imperial Vienna.

7   It should be noted that similar views were also held by Max Weber, not, however by Werner Sombart, who combined a socialist perspective with historical research methods.

8   Similar arguments are today levelled against the Chicago School of Law and Economics. See for instance, Robert Paul Malloy, *Law and Economics: a Comparative Approach to Theory and Practice,* Saint Paul: Minnesota West Publishing, 1990; for a review see Jürgen Backhaus, *Business Library Review,* 18(1), 1992, p. 21–25.

9   This was an important journal privately financed by its editor. Later, Sombart who was also a friend of Heinrich and his wife Lilly Braun, would buy the journal in order to continue its publication.

10   A modern statement can be found in Susan Rose Ackermann, *Re-Thinking the Progressive Agenda: The Reform of the American Regulatory State,* New York: The Free Press, 1992. Note that Susan Rose Ackermann sees not codification but regulation as the primary means of realizing this agenda.

11   Anton Menger, *Das Recht auf den vollen Arbeitsertrag in geschichtlicher Darstellung,* Stuttgart: Cotta, 1886 (1), 1904 (3).

12   Anton Menger, *Volkspolitik,* Jena: Gustav Fischer, 1906.

13   This classic is still in print. See Otto von Gierke, *Personen, Gemeinschaften und Vermögensbegriffe in dem Entwurfe eines bürgerlichen Gesetzbuches für das deutsche Reich,* Leipzig: Duncker & Humblot, 1889, reprinted in E.I. Bekker and O. Fischer, *Beiträge zur Erläuterung und Beurteilung des Entwurfes eines bürgerlichen Gesetzbuches für das deutsche Reich (2),* Glashütten im Taunus: Verlag Detlev Auvermann, 1974, vol. 2, part 18.

14   John D. Lewis, "Otto von Gierke", *International Encyclopedea of the Social Sciences,* 6, 1968, pp. 177–181.

15   See *e.g.* his "Der Entwurf eines bürgerlichen Gesetzbuches und das deutsche Recht" [The draft of a Civil Code and German Law]. *Jahrbücher für Gesetzgebung, Verwaltung und Volkswritschaft,* 12 (3,4), 1888, pp. 842–904; 1179–1264; 13 (1) 1889, 183–322.

16   On the approach in general:
    —Henry C. Adams, "Volkswritschaft und Rechtsordnung: Grössnungsrede auf der Jahresversammlung der 'American Economic Association' am 29. Dezember 1896", in: Gustav Schmoller, *Jahrbuch für Gesetzgebung, Verwaltung und Volkswritschaft im deutschen Reich,* drittes Heft, Leipzig: Duncker & Humblot, 1898, pp. 271–298.

—G.J. Better and D. Zischer, *Beiträge zur Erläuterung und Beurtheilung des Entwurfs eines Bürgerlichen Gesetzbuches für das deutsche Reich,* Berlin und Leipzig: Verlag von I. Guttentag, 1888.

—F. Bierhaus, *Die Entstehungsgeschichte des Entwurfs eines Bürgerlichen Gesetzbuches für das deutsche Reich,* Berlin und Leipzig: Verlag von I. Guttentag, 1888.

—Paul Stolterfoth, *Beiträge zur Beurtheilung des Entwurfs eines Bürgerlichen Gesetzbuches für das deutsche Reich,* Leipzig: Verlag von Beit & Comp., 1890

—Otto Gierke, "Personengemeinschaften und Vermögensinbegriffe", in: E.I. Bekker and O. Fischer, *Beiträge zur Erläuterung und Beurteilung des Entwurfes eines Bürgerlichen Gesetzbuches für das Deutsche Reich, 2,* Glashütten im Taunus: Verlag Detlev Auvermann KG, 1974.

—Paul Oertmann, "Neuere Litteratur zum Bürgerlichen Gesetzbuche", in: Gustav Schmoller (ed.), *Jahrbuch für Gesetzgebung, Verwaltung und Volkswritschaft im Deutschen Reich,* Leipzig: Duncker & Humblot, 1902, pp. 369–390.

—K. Schneider, "Über die demnächstige Gestaltung des Grundbesitzrechtes in Deutschland, insbesondere die Verwirflichung eines Heimstättenrechtes: Eine Studie zum Entwurfe des deutschen bürgerlichen Gesetzbuches", in: Gustav Schmoller (ed.), *Jahrbuch für Gesetzgebung, Verwaltung und Volkswirtschaft im Deutschen Reich,* Leipzig: Duncker & Humblot, 1890, pp. 125–164.

17   See Max Rümelin, "Der Vorentwurf zu einem Schweizerischen Civilgesetzbuches" (The Draft of a Swiss Civil Code), in: Gustav Schmoller, *Jahrbuch für Gesetzgebung, Verwaltung und Volkswritschaft im Deutschen Reich,* (25) 3, Leipzig: Duncker & Humblot, 1901, pp. 835–917 (part I) and 1523–1601 (part II). See also on the Code generally:

—Michael John, *Politics and the Law in Late Nineteenth-Century Germany: The Origins of the Civil Code,* Oxford: Clarendon Press, 1989.

And the feminist perspective:

—Christiane Berneike, *Die Frauenfrage ist Rechtsfrage: Die Juristinnen der deutschen Frauenbewegung und das Bürgerliche Gesetzbuch,* Baden-Baden: Nomos Verlagsgesellschaft, 1995.

Bibliography

Adams, Henry C. (1898). "Volkswirtschaft und Rechtsordnung: Grössnungsrede auf der Jahresversammlung der 'American Economic Association' am 29. Dezember 1896." In: Gustav Schmoller, *Jahrbuch für Gesetzgebung, Verwaltung und Volkswirtschaft im deutschen Reich,* drittes Heft, Leipzig: Duncker & Humblot, pp. 271–298.

Backhaus, Jürgen. (1990). Review of: Robert Paul Malloy, *Law and Economics; a Comparative Approach to Theory and Practice,* Saint Paul: Minnesota West Publishing. *Business Library Review,* 18 (1), 1992, p. 21–25.

Berneike, Christiane. (1995). *Die Frauenfrage ist Rechtsfrage: Die Juristinnen der deutschen Frauenbewegung und das Bürgerliche Gesetzbuch,* Baden-Baden: Nomos Verlagsgesellschaft.

Better, G.J. and Zischer, D. (1888). *Beiträge zur Erläuterung und Beurtheilung des Entwurfs eines Bürgerlichen Gesetzbuches für das deutsche Reich,* Berlin und Leipzig: Verlag von I. Guttentag.

Bierhaus, F. (1888). *Die Entstehungsgeschichte des Entwurfs eines Bürgerlichen Gesetzbuches für das deutsche Reich,* Berlin und Leipzig: Verlag von I. Guttentag.

von Gierke, Otto. (1889). "Der Entwurf eines bürgerlichen Gesetzbuches und das deutsche Recht" [The draft of a Civil Code and German Law]. Jahrbücher für Gesetzgebung, Verwaltung und Volkswirtschaft, 12 (3,4), 1888, pp. 842–904; 1179–1264; 13 (1) 1889, 183–322.

von Gierke, Otto. (1895). *Deutsches Privatrecht,* 3 volumes, Münich and Leipzig: Duncker & Humblot. Volume 1, *Allgemeiner Teil und Personenrecht.* Volume 2, *Sachenrecht,* 1905. Volume 3, *Schuldrecht,* 1917.

von Gierke, Otto. (1974). *Personen, Gemeinschaften und Vermögensbegriffe in dem Entwurfe eines bürgerlichen Gesetzbuches für das deutsche Reich,* Leipzig: Duncker & Humblot, 1889 reprinted in E.I. Bekker and O. Fischer, *Beiträge zur Erläuterung und Beurteilung des Entwurfes eines bürgerlichen Gesetzbuches für das deutsche Reich* (2), Glasfütten im Taunus: Verlag Detlev Auvermann, vol. 2, part 18.

von Gierke, Otto. (1888). "Der Entwurf eines bürgerlichen Gesetzbuches und das deutsche Recht" [The draft of a Civil Code and German Law]. *Jahrbücher für Gesetzgebung, Verwaltung und Volkswirtschaft,* 12 (3,4), pp. 842–904; 1179–1264; 13 (1) 1889, 183–322.

Gierke, Otto. (1974). "Personengemeinschaften und Vermögensinbegriffe." In: E.I. Bekker and O. Fischer, *Beiträge zur Erläuterung und Beurteilung des Entwurfes eines Bürgerlichen Gesetzbuches für das Deutsche Reich,* 2, Glashütten im Taunus: Verlag Detlev Auvermann KG.

John, Michael. (1989). *Politics and the Law in Late Nineteenth-Century Germany: The Origins of the Civil Code,* Oxford: Clarendon Press.

Lewis, John D. (1968). "Otto von Gierke," *International Encyclopedea of the Social Sciences,* 6, 177–181.

Malloy, Robert Paul. (1900). *Law and Economics; a Comparative Approach to Theory and Practice,* Saint Paul: Minnesota West Publishing.

Menger, Anton. (1890). *Das bürgerliche Recht und die besitzlosen Klassen: eine Kritik des Entwurfes eines bürgerlichen Gesetzbuches für das deutsche Reich,* Tübingen: Laupp.

Menger, Anton. *Das Recht auf den vollen Arbeitsertrag in geschichtlicher Darstellung,* Stuttgart: Cotta, 1886 (1), 1904 (3).

Menger, Anton. (1906). *Volkspolitik,* Jena: Gustav Fischer.

Oertmann, Paul. (1902). "Neuere Litteratur zum Bürgerlichen Gesetzbuche." In: Gustav Schmoller (ed.), *Jahrbuch für Gesetzgebung, Verwaltung und Volkswirtschaft im Deutschen Reich,* Leipzig: Duncker & Humblot, pp. 369–390.

Pearson, Heath. (1997). *Origins of Law and Economics: The Economist's New Science of Law 1830–1930,* Cambridge: Cambridge University Press.

Posner, Richard A. and Parisi, Francesco. (1997). "Law and Economics: Theoretical and Methodological Foundations" (the international library of critical writings in economics). Cheltenham: Edward Elgar.

Rose Ackermann, Susan. (1992). *Re-Thinking the Progressive Agenda; The Reform of the American Regulatory State,* New York: The Free Press.

Rückert, Joachim. (1994). "Materialien zur Vorlesung: Einführung in das Zivilrecht und Zivilrecht I," Frankfurt: Johann-Wolfgang-Goethe Universität.

Rümelin, Max. (1901). "Der Vorentwurf zu einem Schweizerischen Civilgesetzbuches." In: Gustav Schmoller, *Jahrbuch für Gesetzgebung, Verwaltung und Volkswirtschaft im Deutschen Reich,* Leipzig: Duncker & Humblot, pp. 835–917 (part I) and 1523–1601 (part II).

Savigny, Carl von. (1815). "Vom Beruf unserer Zeit für Gesetzgebung und Rechtswissenschaft," Heidelberg.

Schneider, K. (1890). "Über die demnächstige Gestaltung des Grundbesitzrechtes in Deutschland, insbesondere die Verwirflichung eines Heimstättenrechtes: Eine Studie zum Entwurfe des deutschen bürgerlichen Gesetzbuches." In: Gustav Schmoller (ed.), *Jahrbuch für Gesetzgebung, Verwaltung und Volkswirtschaft im Deutschen Reich,* Leipzig: Duncker & Humblot, pp. 125–164.

Stern, Jacques. (1914). (ed.) *A.F.J. Thibaut and F.C. von Savigny: zum hundertjährigen Gedächtnis des Kampfes um ein einheitliches bürgerliches Recht für Deutschland,* Berlin.

Stolterfoth, Paul. (1890). *Beiträge zur Beurtheilung des Entwurfs eines Bürgerlichen Gesetzbuches für das deutsche Reich,* Leipzig: Verlag von Beit & Comp.

Thibaut, Friedrich. "Über die Notwendigkeit eines allgemeinen bürgerlichen Rechts für Deutschland," Heidelberg: 1814–1840 (2).

PART 5

The economics of judicial decision making

Judges as rational decision makers

I N 1972, Posner closed the first volume of the *Journal of Legal Studies* with an Afterword in which he remarks that an "important theme of this volume is the quest for a theory of legal decision-making" (p. 439). The word "quest" is evidence that, at that time, judges' behavior and judicial decision making remained outside of "law and economics". Economic analyses of judicial decision making began to emerge only in the early seventies, with the birth of an "economic analysis of law".

From this perspective, the lack of work on the supply of legal rules and on the behavior of the central actors in common law systems can be viewed as surprising. After all, there already existed economic analyses of the behavior of the demand side of legal markets (including that of criminals) and also public choice analyses of the behavior of suppliers of rules such as elected officials and bureaucrats. It may be that scholars were reluctant to analyze the behavior of judges within the framework of the standard economic model. In effect, it would have meant that judges, as with any other individuals, could be supposed to be rational and therefore modeled as acting out of self-interested motives.

This is the assumption that Posner (1973, 1993) and Landes and Posner (1976) made in the first attempts to incorporate legal decision making within the frame of the rational choice model of human behavior. Judges, adds Posner, can even be viewed as rational utility maximizers (1993). However, not all economic analyses of judges' behavior equate rationality with the maximization of a utility function. Most of the time, a more simple definition of rationality is used and it is assumed that legal decision making results from a comparison between costs and benefits. Let us not assume that an explanation of judicial decision making in terms of costs and benefits is not contradictory with the idea that judgements depend on the notion of justice or the policy preferences of judges. Undoubtedly, policy preferences and justice do enter the calculation of judges, as we will see in this section, where we present some of the analyses of judicial decision making as rational choice.

Once again, there exist a large amount of economic works devoted to legal decision making (see Rubin, 2000, for an exhaustive analysis). Let us focus on an issue that has attracted a lot of interest these last years, namely the question of why judges follow past cases or, more broadly, decisions made by other judges especially when – and this is the most frequent situation – there is no obligation to do so? Reciprocally, what are the reasons that lead them to innovate and depart from the precedent? This is a relatively complex twofold question, to which many complementary answers have been proposed.

The importance of costs in legal decision making

The costs associated with a legal decision, as they are modeled in economic analyses, can be either private or collective. The latter are those that result from the consequences of a legal decision on society; from this perspective, legal decisions can obviously be characterized, to use the words of Kirchgässner and Pommerehne (1993), as "low cost decisions": judges do not have to personally bear the costs implied by the consequences of his or her decisions, but other individuals – the rest of the society – do have to. However, this certainly does not mean that judges have no interest in collective issues. Judges do have policy preferences and a sense of justice, there is no doubt about it, and we emphasize this to show that these preferences enter the calculation of judges. When using precedents or decisions made by other judges, they may be obliged to enforce rules with which they disagree. This represents a first kind of personal or private cost, even if linked to collective issues. Furthermore, judges cannot avoid spending time and energy and money carrying out their work and reaching a decision. Then, since they are rational, judges may be interested in decreasing the costs of decision making; this implies a decrease in their individual workload and an increase in their spare or leisure time: utility then increases. To reach this goal, an obvious and efficient solution consists of making decisions based on the decisions made by other judges in different but similar cases. It enables judges "to avoid having to rethink the merits of particular legal doctrine" (Macey, 1998, p. 71). Complementarily, judges may adopt the decisions made by other judges because they believe that the other judges are, or were, better informed than they are (see Banerjee, op. cit; Bikhchandani, Hirshleifer, and Welch, op. cit; Welch, op. cit.; Daughety and Reiganum, 1999 or, more recently, Levy, 2005, for applications to judicial decision-making). They thus use the information gathered by other judges and crystallized in precedent rather than their own information. It is less costly and also more reliable. In both cases, be it to increase their spare time or be it because they trust others, judges may have a strong tendency to use decisions made in the past.

To use precedent to avoid or to reduce the costs associated with decision making is also interesting because the benefits that result from a legal decision are mostly psychological and difficult to ascertain. Thus, a legal decision generates gains in utility that result from having made a choice in accordance with his or her private preferences; therefore, judges will use past cases or adopt decisions made by others if and only if those decisions correspond to their preferences and/or if the costs of not following their private preferences are not too high.

How to secure the benefits of legal decision making

Furthermore, and this is another problem, legal decisions are (almost pure) public goods. Once made, they can *freely* be used again and again by others because of the difficulty in preventing others from using them, it being as difficult as it always is to exclude individuals from the consumption of any pure public good. Indeed, the difficulty is even greater than with market goods, for which it is always possible to establish property rights. What would property rights mean in the case of legal decisions? How could they be established? As a form of "intellectual" property right (on this see Harnay and Marciano, 2006)? No straightforward answer can be proposed for such questions because such means do not exist. Accordingly, it is therefore not surprising that judges tend to follow decisions made by others: there are no genuine incentives to innovate – the lack of incentives is all the more important given that, as noted above, judges do not suffer from the collective costs implied by their decisions. In other words, the tendency to follow precedent can be explained within the limits of the self-interested economic model.

The tendency to follow past cases can also be explained by using the concept of a network. Judges do form a network of users of legal cases and the value of each of these cases depends on the number of its users: the more judges use it, the greater its value. In other words, there are positive network externalities resulting from the fact that many judges refer to the same decisions. From this perspective, judges have no interest in innovating: this would decrease the amount of externalities they gain as members of a network. More precisely, as long as the adoption externalities associated with the precedent are larger than those associated with the new rule, it is more beneficial to follow the precedent than to create a new rule.

So far, we have provided explanations for the "conservative" behavior of judges, but there are also those who depart from existing rules and innovate. This kind of behavior can appear as paradoxical for judges modeled as rational players, but the paradox disappears if one takes into account additional factors influencing the behavior of judges and judicial decision making, namely reputation, popularity, and prestige (Landes and Posner, 1976; Levy, 2005; Miceli and Cosgel, 1994; Whitman, 2000). These works assume that judges pay attention to other judges and take care of how other judges, legal scholars and lawyers will receive their decisions. Furthermore, it is assumed that judges benefit from an increase in utility when their decisions are quoted or mentioned by others and, conversely, if a decision is rejected or overturned, a judge suffers from a loss of utility. As a consequence, a judge who uses past decisions or decisions made by others will not be quoted and will accordingly not receive any reputational gain – no gain in terms of utility. Hence, there is an incentive to innovate. Judges therefore face a dilemma: to follow a precedent (it is less costly than to innovate but it generates no benefits in terms of reputation) or to depart from the existing rule and to innovate (the behavior is more costly and risky than the preceding one, because the innovation can be rejected, but also more rewarding if the decision is accepted and quoted).

Obviously, the way judges solve the dilemma depends on their personal preferences, with regard to a specific case but also with regard to the functioning of the legal system in a broader sense, and also with regard to social justice. It also depends on their abilities. It can then be shown that judges tend to imitate the behavior of others: they follow the precedent or innovate depending on what other judges do (in a world of imitators, the probability of innovation being rejected is important; in a world of innovators, the probability of precedent cases being overturned is also high). But, as shown by Levy (2005), the attitude of "careerist" judges depends on their ability: judges who perceive themselves as having a strong incentive to innovate and depart from the precedent see it as an opportunity to show their ability; by contrast, less able judges have an incentive to follow the precedent.

Such varied behavior patterns will have important consequences for the functioning of a legal system. In effect, if judges do not want to depart from precedent because they do not want to have their decisions rejected, the system will not only be stable but too stable. This corresponds to a phenomenon of "excessive inertia". By contrast, a system populated by innovators may be unstable (Whitman, 2000) and exhibit too much innovation.

References

Summary

Judicial decision making represents an important share of the "law and economics" literature. The works that are then produced are mainly based on the assumption that judges are rational decision-makers – see Rubin's survey on *Judge Made Law*. From this perspective, following (or departing) from non-binding precedents is not always easy to understand, hence, the important number of works devoted to this question. Among them, we have chosen to reproduce papers in which the role of reputation is emphasized as crucial.

Assuming that judges are rational decision makers does not imply that they are interested in monetary rewards only. On the contrary, non-monetary gains – and, therefore, reputation – seems to play a decisive role in the decisions made by judges. Miceli and Cosgel have proposed one of the first economic models to explain the role of reputation. Whitman (2000) extends their model by showing that the search for reputation may generate stability rather than instability. And Posner (2000) proposes an empirical analysis of the practice of judicial quotation that indeed confirms the role of reputation.

Further reading

Banerjee, Abhijit V. 1992. "A Simple Model of Herd Behavior", *Quarterly Journal of Economics*, 107(3), pp. 797–817.

Banerjee, Abhijit V. 1993. "The Economics of Rumours", *Review of Economic Studies*, 60(2), pp. 309–327.

Bikhchandani, Sushil, David Hirshleifer, and Ivo Welch. 1992. "A Theory of Fads, Fashion, Custom and Cultural Change as Informational Cascades", *Journal of Political Economy*, 100, pp. 992–1026.

Daughety, A. F. and Jennifer E. Reinganum. 1999. "Stampede to Judgment: Persuasive Influence and Herding Behavior by Courts", *American Law and Economics Review*, 1 (2), pp. 158–189.

Harnay, Sophie and Alain Marciano. 2004. "Judicial conformity versus dissidence: an economic analysis of judicial precedent", *International Review of Law and Economics*, 23, pp. 405–420.

Harnay, Sophie and Alain Marciano. 2006. "Intellectual property rights and judge-made law. An economic analysis of the production and diffusion of precedent", in *Property Rights Dynamics in the Third Millenium: A Law and Economics Perspective*, edited by D. Porrini and G. Ramello, London: Routledge.

Kirchgässner, Gebhard and Werner Pommerehne. 1993. "Low-cost decisions as a challenge to public choice", *Public Choice*, 77 (1), pp. 107–115.

Kornhauser, Lewis A. 1989. "An economic perspective on stare decisis", *Chicago-Kent Law Review*, 65(1), pp. 63–92.

Landes, William M. and Richard A. Posner. 1976. "Legal Precedent: A Theoretical and Empirical Analysis", *Journal of Law and Economics*, pp. 249–307.

Levy, Gilat. 2005. "Careerist Judges and the Appeals Process", *RAND Journal of Economics, 36* (2), pp. 275–297.

Macey, Jonathan. 1989. The internal and external costs and benefits of stare decisis, *Chicago-Kent Law Review*, 65 (1), pp. 93–113.

Macey, Jonathan. 1998. "Precedent", in P. Newman (Ed.), *The New Palgrave Dictionary of Law and Economics*. Palgrave-MacMillan, pp. 71–76.

Miceli, Thomas J. and Metin M. Cosgel, "Reputation and Judicial Decision-Making", *Journal of Economic Behavior and Organization*, 23 (1), pp. 31–51, reprinted in this volume.

Posner, Richard A. 1973. "An Economic Approach to Legal Procedure and Judicial Administration", *Journal of Legal Studies*, 2 (2) pp. 399–458

Posner, Richard A. 1993. "What Do Judges and Justices Maximize? (The Same Thing Everybody Else Does)", *Supreme Court Economic Review*, 3, pp. 1–41.

Posner, Richard A. 2000. "An Economic Analysis of the Use of Citations in the Law," *American Law and Economics Review*, 2 (2), pp. 381–406, reprinted in this volume.

Rubin, Paul. 2000. "Judge-Made Law", in Boudewijn Bouckaert and Gerrit De Geest (eds.), *Encyclopedia of Law and Economics*. Cheltenham: Edward Elgar.

Talley, E. 1999. "Precedential cascades: An appraisal", *Southern California Law Review*, 73(1), pp. 87–137.

Welch, Ivo. 1992, "Sequential Sales, Learning, and Cascades", *Journal of Finance*, 47(2), pp. 695–732.

Welch, Ivo. 2000. "Herding among Security Analysts", *Journal of Financial Economics*, 58(3), pp. 369–96.

Whitman, Douglas. G. 2000. "Evolution of the Common Law and the Emergence of Compromise", *Journal of Legal Studies*, 29(2), pp. 753–781.

Chapter 13

Thomas J. Miceli and Metin M. Cosgel

REPUTATION AND JUDICIAL DECISION-MAKING

1. Introduction

ECONOMIC MODELS of the common law have generally relied on rational behavior by litigants and invisible hand-type arguments to explain the evolution of the law [Rubin (1977) and Priest (1977)]. In these models, the behavior of the judges has been either ignored, or treated in an unsatisfactory or ad hoc manner.[1] Similarly, recent interest among economists in the judicial practice of *stare decisis*, or decision by precedent, has focused on the efficiency of the practice without trying to explain why judges rationally follow it [Blume and Rubinfeld (1982), Heiner (1986), and Kornhauser (1989)]. This neglect of judicial motivation in models of the law is like explaining equilibrium in ordinary markets by modeling only the demand side and treating the supply side as exogenous. The model of the judicial decision-making developed in this paper represents an initial attempt to explicitly model the "supply" of legal precedents by seriously examining the incentives of judges.

The difficulty economists have had in developing satisfactory models of judicial behavior apparently stems from the absence of a well-defined objective function that self-interested judges can be viewed as maximizing [e.g., Posner (1986, pp. 505–506), Kornhauser (1989, pp. 63–64)]. Analogies to other economic agents are unsatisfactory in this regard, given that the compensation of judges is not dependent on their decisions,[2] and that they are not generally subject to electoral control. One notable attempt to explain judicial decision-making based on judicial self-interest is by Landes and Posner (1976), who posit that judges derive utility by imparting their own ideology to the law through their rulings, which other judges perpetuate as precedent.[3] The reason judges are willing to follow the decisions of other judges, Landes and Posner argue, is to avoid the disutility of being overruled by a higher court. This concern suggests more generally the role of reputation in judicial decision-making; the importance of how a judge is viewed by his or her colleagues, by law professors, law students, and the general public. Indeed, the close public scrutiny recent Supreme Court nominees have undergone highlights the importance of their past record, especially on pivotal issues. If judges care about their reputation, for its own sake or for its effect on their future prospects, then their opinions will reflect more than simply the desire to make the "right" decision in a case, or to adhere strictly to the dictates of formalism. They will also serve as "exercise[s] in self-advertisement and self-aggrandizement" for the judge [Posner (1990b, p. 147)]. The concern with reputation underscores the role of interdependence among judges in judicial decision making.

The practice of decision by precedent implies a view of judges as producers of precedents, and current and future litigants as consumers of precedents. In this sense, precedents serve as rules that guide people's behavior. However, a judge's concern with reputation implies a further set of consumers, or audience, for his decisions; namely, judges and other members of the judicial community, both present and future. Precedent in this regard acts as a signal of the authoring judge's stature within the legal community. A satisfactory model of judicial behavior has to account for this sort of communication among judges and other legal observers by means of signed judicial opinions.

In this paper, we examine the role that reputation might play in judicial decision-making. We begin with a general discussion of the importance of interdependence among judges, or more generally, between a judge and his "audience," that is implied by the above notion of reputation. Posner argues in his recent study of Judge Benjamin Cardozo that reputation is conferred on the judge rather than being produced by him [Posner (1990b, p. 59)]. At the same time, the above argument suggests that a judge's decisions are inputs into his reputation. With this in mind, we develop a simple model of judicial decision-making based on self-interest which captures the essential features of reputation. Specifically, the model highlights the importance of history through the force of precedent, and the future through a judge's desire to create new precedent. In general, we show that reputation can both restrain judicial discretion (the Landes and Posner argument), but also inspire it if future judges are expected to be persuaded by a decision and follow it, thereby enhancing the authoring judge's reputation.

2. Judicial interdependence and reputation

Views of the principle of decision by precedent have been based on metaphors from economics (capital stock), communications theory (redundancy), or literary theory (interpretation).[4] While these metaphors have been useful in understanding the practice of *stare decisis*, they provide little insight into the motivation of judges as to why they follow a precedent or deviate from it. Consequently, the evolution of a precedent over time and the relationship between decision by precedent and the efficiency of the law remain largely open questions.

An examination of decision by precedent must capture the interdependence among judges in their decision making. A judge might have his own private views on a particular case, but in deciding the case he is constrained by the existence of a judicial community and precedents applicable to like cases. In the extreme, a judge must follow a precedent set by a higher court if the case at hand is sufficiently similar. More generally, a precedent serves as a guide to current decisions, and is not necessarily binding. When it is not, the force of a precedent depends on its reception by judges as an input to decision making, as determined, for example, by the extent to which judges reason from analogy [Eisenberg (1988) and Posner (1990a)]. The analysis of precedent here thus applies to situations where it is not necessarily binding (e.g., courts of last resort, or cases that can be distinguished from previous cases).

The interdependence among judges implicit in decision by analogy takes the decision problem faced by a judge beyond his private views and preferences; it implies a "social interpretation" of legal rules as embodied in precedent. This does not mean, of course, that a judge's autonomy is suppressed. It simply means that his choice of whether to follow a precedent or to try to change it depends on the previous decisions of judges (the force of precedent) and their expected future behavior (attitudes towards new precedent). That all judges are subject to the same consideration and part of the same judicial community suggests that the decision problem confronting a judge in each case can be quite a complicated matter.

Setting a new precedent is a costly and risky activity. The extensive research and writing required to present an argument and the ever present risk of being overturned by higher courts or not being followed by equal courts would presumably make deviation from a precedent a questionable undertaking for rational judges with valuable time and resources. Yet it is a fact that precedents are regularly challenged, and not always because of changing social and political environments. It is also the case that judges follow precedent much of the time, even when they are not in total agreement with it. The question then becomes the respective costs and benefits of following and deviating from precedent.

Economists' silence on questions related to judicial incentives and behavior is well known because of the difficulty of specifying the objectives of public judges.[5] For example, the compensation of judges does not depend on their rulings, and precedents set by a particular judge do not yield any direct pecuniary benefits.[6] Similarly, there are no monetary costs or benefits of following a previously set precedent.

Costs and benefits do not have to be monetary, of course. Landes and Posner (1976, p. 272), for instance, approach precedent setting behavior with a presumption that a judge "derives utility by imposing his policy preferences on the community." Such behavior, however, might lead to excessive disregard for existing precedent which, according to Landes and Posner, is kept in check by the appellate review process.[7] Their approach overcomes the difficulty with judicial incentives by postulating non-monetary costs and benefits, which in turn internalize the externalities created by the existence of precedents. But this approach says little about the selection of those cases in which the judge should follow precedent (instead of deviating) and the private and social costs and benefits, if any, of doing so.

At the private level, the presumption that a judge might have views on a case suggests a likely source of personal conflict. A judge has to take a precedent into consideration, but at the same time has autonomy in decision when the precedent is not binding. In each case under consideration, a conflict between the personal view of the judge and those expressed by precedent implies a possible inclination to move away from precedent in order to avoid the disutility of deviating from his personal views. A unique example of this sort of internal conflict is found in the following explanation by Judge Skelly Wright of his precedent setting decision in *Javins v. First National Realty Corp.*[8]:

> I didn't like what I saw and I did what I could to ameliorate, if not eliminate, the injustice involved in the way the poor were required to live in the nation's capital.
>
> I offer no apology for not following more closely the legal precedent which had cooperated in creating the condition I found unjust.[9]

The judge's decision of whether to deviate or not from precedent, however, might involve other considerations. The costs and benefits of a deviation include elements beyond the judge's personal valuation of different alternatives. The non-pecuniary costs and benefits of action (follow or deviate) in the presence of a precedent arise out of interactions within the legal system and accrue to the decision making judge as attributed by others. What possible benefits could a judge expect from influencing the decisions of judges in the future by setting a new precedent?

The key to understanding the interdependence among judges is the nature of interaction and communication among them. Communication in the legal sphere takes place for the most part through the written opinions of judges on cases they decide. As Shapiro (1972, p. 134) argues, the judicial opinion "is the principal mode of communication." A court's opinion regarding a case aims to justify the grounds for reaching a decision, in line with precedent or not. In following a precedent a judge has to establish the link between his case and the precedent. And in deviating from precedent, he has to establish why the previous decisions should not rule the present case, why his ruling is the more appropriate one, and why it should guide similar cases in the future. Alternatively, he may attempt to portray a decision as being in line with precedent even though it actually effects a substantial change in a legal rule.[10]

If the opinion presented by a judge appeals to others, the precedent set by him may be followed. The citations (explicit or implicit) received by the judge will in turn enhance his reputation and increase prestige within the legal community.[11] Conversely, a failed attempt at setting a precedent is likely to take away from the reputation of a judge. A reasonable objective of a judge therefore might be to choose actions that will increase his reputation positively.[12] Although economists have paid little attention to the role of reputation as a motive [but see Kuran (1990)], historically its importance was recognized by the likes of Smith and Veblen.

The "prediction theory" of the law proposed by Holmes provides a basis for this view of judicial decision making.[13] In this view, the law is nothing more than how judges will decide a particular case. Thus, if potential litigants (Holmes' so called "bad men") want to discover the law, they must predict how a judge would decide a dispute which might arise from their behavior. Judges interested in reputation must similarly predict how later judges will decide a particular case in order to gauge the chances of reversal or citation in the future. For example, the threat of reversal is described by Posner (1990a, p. 224) as follows: "Weak sanctions can operate powerfully on judges. One is criticism, and reversal is a form of criticism … Most judges try to avoid being reversed, and this commits them to the prediction theory." An example of how reversal can impact a judge's decision-making is Judge Learned Hand's decision in *Agwilines, Inc. v. Eagle Oil & Shipping Co.*[14] In this case, Judge Hand followed a precedent set two decades earlier in a case that had overturned Hand's own decision at the appeals court level.[15] Hand's opinion in *Agwilines* reflects both the sting of the earlier reversal and his reluctant acceptance of the Supreme Court's ruling. Specifically, after summarizing his decision in the earlier case, Judge Hand wrote:

> To all of this the Supreme Court said "no."... Perhaps it was not necessary... to consider our argument...; but the court did so and definitely repudiated it.... In the face of this decision we cannot see how we can do otherwise than affirm the decree at bar; if any change is to be made the Supreme Court must make it.[16]

On the other hand, Posner's (1990b) analysis of Judge Cardozo's reputation relies heavily on his analysis of the citations of Cardozo's opinions and scholarly writings by other judges and legal scholars as a measure of his reputation. Thus, a judge seeking reputation faces a trade-off — in order to be cited he must initiate new precedents, but this opens the possibility of reversal of his decisions by a higher court or simply neglect of his decisions by future judges.[17] The formal model developed below highlights this trade-off.

The emphasis on reputation immediately raises the question of the audience among whom the reputation is sought. In the writing of any text one aims at an audience. What is the relevant audience faced by a judge in writing an opinion? Put differently, the question is one of specifying where the costs and benefits of reputation count most for a judge. In answering this question, Landes and Posner emphasize a judge's fear of being overturned by a higher court, while Cooter sees the relevant audience as "consist[ing] of the lawyers and litigants who bring cases before the judges."[18] In either formulation the parties thought relevant for reputation are those that are or might be directly involved in cases decided by this judge: namely, future disputants and higher courts. Taking a closer look at the purposes of writing opinions, however, we realize that there must be other parties involved in one's reputation. Otherwise why would judges write detailed opinions justifying their decisions, and then sign them? It could not be for the benefit of the parties involved only, since the opinion could be revealed to them privately in court, while the implied legal rule could be made public for the benefit of future litigants. Nor could it be for higher courts only, since the opinion could be expressed privately in a written statement to be kept in the case file to be used when necessary.

There must surely be other reasons for writing opinions aimed for public disclosure. An obvious one is that they enable a judge "to cultivate an admiring audience outside of ... his judicial colleagues" [Posner (1990b, p. 147)]. The relevant audience of a judge consists of other judges who might act upon the opinion by following a new precedent if there has been a deviation from the old one, as well as legal scholars and students who study the production and evolution of laws. Thus, in addition to providing reasons for a decision and defending its merits, signed opinions allow judges to establish individual reputations among their audience. In the model of judicial self-interest to be developed in the next section, the non-pecuniary benefits of reputation will play a crucial role in judicial decision-making.

3. A simple model of judicial self-interest

In this section we develop a simple model of judicial decision-making that captures the essential aspects of the foregoing discussion. The model is highly stylized, and thus abstracts from many of the subtleties of actual judicial decision making. This enables us, however, to focus attention on the issue of primary interest—how judicial self-interest translates into the broad patterns of judicial decision-making that we observe. Of particular interest is why judges follow the decisions of past judges when those decisions are not binding (e.g. when the decisions are those of parallel or lower courts). In examining this issue, a prior problem we ignore is the determination of the relevant precedent for a particular case. This often is a difficult task given that no two cases are identical. We sidestep this problem by assuming that similar cases arise periodically, and that the judge faced with such a case immediately recognizes it and knows with certainty what the previous decisions have been. Our model thus tracks the decision made in a particular type of case over time as it is decided by a sequence of judges chosen at random.[19]

Judges will thus be indexed by t, the time at which they confront the case in question. Each judge t decides the case to maximize his utility, which depends, first, on the judge's private preferences over the outcome of the case. This reflects the judge's personal view of how the case should be decided, based, for example, on his sense of justice, his political views, and perhaps his theory of the law (with one possible component of the latter being his commitment to decision by precedent). Let the private utility function for judge t be denoted $V_t(x)$, where x indicates the outcome of the case. Assume that the judge's privately optimal outcome for the case is unique, and is denoted x_t^*. For reasons to be discussed below, the judge's actual decision in the case, x_t, may be something other than x_t^*. When x_t does not coincide with x_t^*, however, the judge suffers a utility loss as a result of what Kuran (1990) calls *preference falsification*.[20] This utility loss is given by:

$$V_t(x_t) \equiv V_t(x_t^*) - V_t(x_t). \tag{13.1}$$

In our model, a judge fails to decide a case in accordance with his private optimum in order to reduce the loss of utility from some other source. As discussed above, this source is the reputation he establishes among his peers, notably, other judges, lawyers, law professors, and law students. Kuran (1990) refers to this as one's reputational utility. Our discussion in the previous section suggests that a measure of a judge's reputation is his record of citations and rate of reversal—how often other judges cite his opinions and how often his opinion is overturned. Such a measure captures the extent to which judges can extend their influence beyond the case at hand, any increases in expected wealth resulting from a greater chance of promotion [Higgins and Rubin (1980)], and generally judges' disdain for being reversed. Note, for example, that the disutility of reversal is what may prompt a judge to follow a previous judge's decision; if he incurs relatively high disutility from being reversed, he may opt for precedent to avoid that possibility. On the other hand, following precedent forecloses the chance of being cited in the future for those judges who place high value on expanding their influence, and involves potential costs from preference falsification.[21] This is the fundamental trade-off of the model.

Formally, a judge's reputational utility is modelled as follows. Consider judge t deciding a case for which the existing ruling is z_{t-1}. The judge can either follow precedent ($x_t = z_{t-1}$), or depart from precedent ($x_t \neq z_{t-1}$). If he follows precedent, he receives no reputational utility (i.e., he can be neither cited nor reversed),[22] whereas if he departs from precedent, he has a chance of being followed or reversed by subsequent judges. For simplicity, we assume that only the next judge's decision matters for a judge's reputation. That is, judge t cares only what judge $t + 1$ does. This obviously understates the potential value of a reputation, as in the case of a judge who initiates a decision that remains in force for several periods. We show in the Appendix, however, that allowing this possibility has only quantitative, not qualitative, effects on the model. Moreover, the fact that future citations yield only discounted benefits reduces their impact on current decisions, especially if the case in question arises infrequently.

Given these caveats, we let u be the utility judge t receives if judge $t + 1$ follows his decision and d be the disutility if judge $t + 1$ departs from his decision. Both are assumed to be constant, time invariant, and the same for all judges. Also define q_t as judge t's assessment of the probability that judge $t + 1$ will *depart* from his decision (q_t will be derived in detail below). This makes judge t's expected reputational utility $(1 - q_t)u - q_t d = u - q_t(u + d)$. But recall that this utility can be received only if judge t departs from the existing precedent; following precedent does not enhance or detract from his reputation. Consequently, we write judge t's reputational utility more generally as

$$R_t(x_t) = \begin{cases} u - q_t(u+d), & \text{if } x_t \neq z_{t-1} \\ 0, & \text{if } x_t = z_{t-1.} \end{cases} \qquad (13.2)$$

Combining this with (13.1) yields judge t's overall expected utility as[23]

$$U_t(x_t) = V_t(x_t) + R_t(x_t). \qquad (13.3)$$

(Note that, for simplicity, $R_t(x_t)$ is not discounted though it is only realized in the future. In the Appendix, future utility is discounted.)

Judge t's optimal decision, x_t, is found by maximizing (13.3). If he chooses to follow precedent, $x_t = z_{t-1}$ and his utility is

$$U_t(z_{t-1}) = V(z_{t-1}). \qquad (13.4)$$

If, however, he chooses to depart from precedent, his utility depends on the particular decision he makes. An obvious candidate for the latter is x_t^*, the judge's private optimum (we assume that $x_t^* \neq z_{t-1}$). This decision yields utility of

$$U_t(x_t') = V_t(x_t') + u - q_t(u + d). \qquad (13.5)$$

In fact, we will show that x_t^* maximizes judge t's utility of departing from precedent provided that q_t is independent of his decision; that is, provided he does not believe that his decision affects the likelihood of its being followed by the next judge. The conditions under which this assumption is satisfied will be discussed below. Its implication is that, when judge t departs from precedent, he will always choose his private optimum, x_t^*.

The foregoing therefore implies that judge t chooses between two options, z_{t-1} and x_t^*, depending on which yields a higher expected utility. He thus chooses to depart from precedent in favor of his private optimum if (13.5) is greater than (13.4); that is, if [24]

$$V_t(x_t^*) + u - q_t(u+d) - V_t(z_{t-1}) > 0.$$

Rearranging and substituting from (13.1), this condition becomes

$$v_t(z_{t-1}) + u - q_t(u+d) > 0, \tag{13.6}$$

where, recall, $v_t(z_{t-1})$ is defined as the disutility the judge suffers when he makes a decision different from his private optimum (i.e. his disutility from preference falsification). Note that if $q_t = 1$, (13.6) becomes $v_t(z_{t-1}) > d$. This implies that, even if a judge is certain to be reversed by the next judge, he may still depart from precedent if the disutility from preference falsification exceeds the disutility of being reversed. We assume that this is not true for at least some judges to insure some adherence to precedent in equilibrium.

Given that u and d are parameters, note that judge t's decision depends on $v_t(\cdot)$ and q_t. The function $v_t(\cdot)$ captures the influence of the past on the judge in that it represents a comparison of his private preference with the prevailing precedent. We assume that $v_t(\cdot)$ differs across judges, possibly capturing differences in private preferences as well as different degrees of respect for precedent. For instance, a judge with a larger value of $v_t(\cdot)$ might feel more strongly about asserting his personal view of a case as compared to a judge with a smaller $v_t(\cdot)$ who feels greater respect for precedent. And as we would expect, condition (13.6) implies that for a given q_t, the former judge is more likely than the latter to depart from precedent.

We now make an important simplifying assumption: we assume that $v_t(\cdot)$ does not depend on the "distance" between judge t's private optimum, x_t^*, and the existing precedent, z_{t-1} (given that these two differ), but only on the fact that they differ. That is,

$$v_t(x_t) = \begin{cases} v_t, & \text{if } x_t \neq z_{t-1.} \\ 0, & \text{if } x_t = z_{t-1}, \end{cases} \tag{13.7}$$

where v_t is a constant for any judge t.[25] Differences in v_t thus reflect only differing commitments by judges to their own view of the best outcome of a case versus that dictated by precedent; for instance, their taste for discretion versus self-restraint. This assumption is made primarily to allow derivation of a stationary equilibrium (in a sense that will be clear shortly).

The implication of (13.7) is that no judge believes he can influence the decision of the next judge by strategically deciding his case (given that $x_t \neq z_{t-1}$). To see this, suppose that $v_t(\cdot)$ does depend on distance (that is, it depends on x_t). Then a judge could increase the likelihood that the next judge will follow his decision by strategically choosing x_t so as to reduce the chance that (13.6) will be satisfied for that judge (assuming the latter is similarly motivated). This is possible because whatever decision judge t makes becomes the precedent for judge $t + 1$. Thus, for judge $t + 1$, if $v_{t+1}(\cdot)$ depends on a comparison of x_{t+1}^* to the prevailing precedent (z_t), then judge t could manipulate the choice of judge $t + 1$. As a result, judge t would not necessarily choose x_t^* when departing from precedent (as we assumed above), since some other x_t might increase his reputational utility enough (by making it more likely that judge $t + 1$ will follow his decision) to compensate for the loss of private utility. The specification in (13.7) allows us to ignore this sort of strategic decision-making, which would greatly complicate the model. The simplification is not entirely without cost, however, given that judicial rhetoric often aims at persuasion, though it is not clear how the desire to persuade would affect the decision itself.

We do assume, however, that judges can form an *expectation* of what the next judge facing a similar case will do. Forming such an expectation requires that all judges have the same motivation (i.e., they decide cases according to (13.6)), and that v_t be regarded as a random variable with a known distribution. The latter assumption follows from the independence of v_t across judges, and the random arrival of like cases.

Given these assumptions, let us reconsider the decision by judge t of whether or not to follow precedent. First, we rewrite the condition for judge t to depart (condition (13.6)) as follows

$$\frac{v_t + u}{u + d} > q_t.$$

(13.8)

Next, we consider the determination of q_t, the probability that the next judge deciding a similar case, judge $t + 1$, will depart from judge t's decision. Our assumption that judge $t + 1$ is a random draw from the known population of judges, and the fact that he also will decide cases according to (13.8), implies the following condition:

$$q_t = \Pr\left[(v_{t+1} + u)/(u + d) > q_{t+1}\right],$$

(13.9)

where $(v_{t+1} + u)/(u + d)$ is a function of the random variable v_{t+1}, and hence is a random variable itself. Defining $F(\cdot)$ as the distribution function of $(v + u)/(u + d)$, (13.9) further implies

$$q_t = 1 - F(q_{t+1}).$$

(13.10)

We consider only stationary equilibria such that $q_t = q_{t+1} = q$ for all t. Thus, assuming that $F(\cdot)$ is time invariant,[26] the equilibrium q is defined by the equation

$$q = 1 - F(q).$$

(13.11)

Existence of an equilibrium follows by a simple fixed point argument,[27] and is illustrated in Figure 13.1. In this equilibrium, those judges for whom $(v + u)/(u + d) > q$ depart from precedent, while those for whom $(v + u)/(u + d) < q$ follow precedent, and (13.11) insures that the expectations of judges about what other judges will do are fulfilled on average.

4. An example: two types of judges

In this section we illustrate the above equilibrium for the case of two types of judges. Specifically, suppose a fraction α of judges have a high v, v_2, and the remainder $(1 - \alpha)$

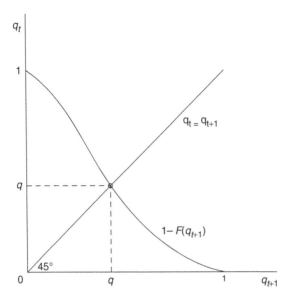

Figure 13.1

have a low v, v_1, where $v_2 > v_1$. For instance, one might think of the v_2s as "activist" judges and the v_1s as "restrained" judges. u and d are defined as above, and are the same for both types of judges. Also, assume that $v_i < d$, $i = 1,2$; that is, both types of judges receive greater disutility from being overturned than from falsifying their preferences. As noted above, this insures that both types will follow precedent under some circumstances. This assumption implies that the following inequalities hold:

$$\frac{v_1 + u}{u + d} < \frac{v_2 + u}{u + d} < 1.$$
(13.12)

To derive the equilibrium defined by (13.11), it is first necessary to derive $1 - F(q)$, the probability that a randomly chosen judge will depart from precedent for a given value of q. From (13.12), it follows that when $q < (v_1 + u)/(u + d)$, both types of judges will depart, so $1 - F(q) = 1$; when $(v_1 + u)/(u + d) < q < (v_2 + u)/(u + d)$, only type v_2s will depart, so $1 - F(q) = \alpha$; and when $(v_2 + u)/(u + d) < q$, neither type will depart, so $1 - F(q) = 0$. The resulting function is shown in Figure 13.2. According to (13.11) (and Figure 13.1), the equilibrium occurs where the $45°$ line intersects $1 - F(q)$. As drawn, this occurs at $q = \alpha$, which implies that $(v_1 + u)/(u + d) < \alpha < (v_2 + u)/(u + d)$. Thus, in equilibrium, all activist judges depart from precedent, and all restrained judges follow precedent.

The equilibrium need not separate judges strictly according to their type, however. As an example, consider Figure 13.3, which shows the case where $\alpha < (v_1 + u)/(u + d)$. Notice that setting $q = \alpha$ here implies that both types of judges will depart from precedent, in which case $q = 1$ in equilibrium. Thus, (13.11) is not satisfied. As an alternative, we conjecture an equilibrium in which $q = (v_1 + u)/(u + d)$. This implies that all type v_2 judges will depart from precedent, as in the previous case, whereas type v_1 judges will be indifferent between following precedent and departing from it. In order to support

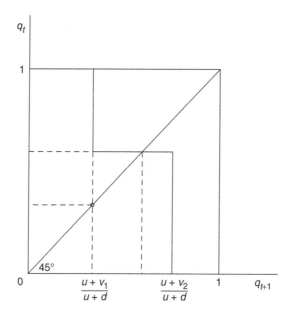

Figure 13.2

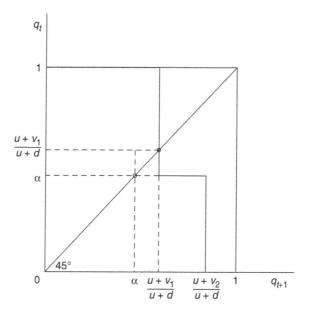

Figure 13.3

an equilibrium, we therefore assume that the latter adopt a mixed strategy. That is, they randomize between their two options (following and departing) in such a way that the conjectured equilibrium satisfies (13.11) and the beliefs of judges are fulfilled.[28]

To derive such a mixed strategy for type v_1 judges, we first define p_1 as the probability that a type v_1 judge will depart from precedent when indifferent (she will thus follow precedent with probability $1 - p_1$). The resulting fraction of judges (of both types) expected to depart from precedent is therefore $\alpha + (1 - \alpha)p_1$. Given the conjectured equilibrium, we have

$$q = \frac{v_1 + u}{u + d} = \alpha + (1 - \alpha)p_1. \tag{13.13}$$

Solving the second equality for p_1 yields its equilibrium value

$$p_1 = \frac{v_t + u}{(1 - \alpha)(u + d)} - \frac{\alpha}{(1 - \alpha)}. \tag{13.14}$$

It is easily verified from (13.14) that $p_1 > 0$ provided $(v_1 + u)/(u + d) > \alpha$, which holds by assumption in this case; and that $p_1 < 1$ provided $(v_1 + u)/(u + d) < 1$, which holds by (13.12).

A similar mixed strategy equilibrium can be derived for the case where $(v_2 + u)/(u + d) < \alpha$. In this case, all type v_1 judges follow precedent, and type v_2 judges are indifferent between following and departing. Defining p_2 as the probability that a type v_2 judge will depart from precedent when indifferent, we can employ the above procedure to derive the equilibrium value of p_2 as

$$p_2 = \frac{v_2 + u}{\alpha(u + d)}. \tag{13.15}$$

We have thus identified three different types of equilibria in the two judge example: (i) an equilibrium in which all high v judges depart from precedent and all low v judges follow precedent; (ii) and equilibrium in which all high v and some low v judges depart from precedent, while the remaining low v judges follow precedent; and (iii) an equilibrium in which some high v judges depart from precedent, while the remaining high v and all low v judges follow precedent. Given the parameters u and d, the particular equilibrium that arises depends on the fraction of each type of judge in the population. This relationship is shown in Figure 13.4, which graphs the equilibrium fraction of judges departing from precedent, q, as a function of α, the fraction of high v judges.

As shown, q is constant for low α, increases linearly with α for intermediate values, then becomes constant again for high α. This relationship reflects the interaction of two effects. First, as α increases, there are more high v judges in the population; i.e., those who, all else equal, are more likely to depart from precedent. This tends to increase q. But, as more judges are expected to abandon precedent, the expected return from doing so declines, given that a judge's reputational utility is decreasing in q (see (13.6)). This second effect tends to increase reliance on precedent.[29] Figure 13.4 shows that for both very low and very high values of α, these two effects just offset each other, whereas for intermediate values, the first effect dominates.

5. The strength of precedent matters

In this section we consider how a judge's decision of whether or not to follow precedent is affected by the strength of the precedent. We measure strength here by the

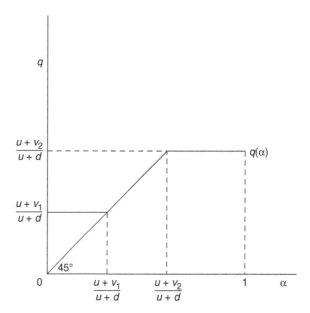

Figure 13.4

number of periods that a decision has been in place. The conventional view is that the longer a precedent has been in place, the more authority it acquires, and hence the more deferential judges should be towards it [Posner (1990a, p. 90)]. We will show that, in the context of our model, if judges internalize this view, it can have a significant impact on the expected life span of legal rules, independently of their social utility.

To develop this argument formally, let n be the number of periods a given decision has been in place, where $n \geq 1$. To capture the effect of n on judicial decision-making, we assume that $v = v(n)$, with $v' < 0$. That is, judges feel less disutility from preference falsification when they follow a precedent that has been in place longer. This reflects the fact that judges, no matter how activist, place some weight on precedent, where that weight is increasing in the latter's strength. Perhaps judges believe that following entrenched precedents enhances the integrity of the judicial process, thereby adding to their public image as judges, or they simply have been indoctrinated to think this way [See, e.g., Posner (1990b, p. 22)].

To see how concern for n affects a judge's decision, consider condition (13.8). While the left-hand side is decreasing in n, q turns out to be independent of n. This follows, first, from our assumption above that a judge cares only about the probability of the next judge departing from precedent if he (the deciding judge) departs herself; and second, from the fact that when a judge departs, $n = 1$ in the next period. Thus, by definition, the q in condition (8) is the probability of the next judge departing *given that $n = 1$.*

Based on this result, consider again the two judge example from the previous section. Let $v_i = v_i(n)$, where $v_i'<0$, $i = 1, 2$, and $v_2(n) > v_1(n)$ for all n. Also, assume that the equilibrium is such that $q = \alpha$; that is, $(v_1(1) + u)/(u + d) < \alpha < (v_2(1) + u)/(u + d)$

(the case shown in Figure 13.2). Finally, define n' as the solution to the following equation:

$$\frac{v_2(n^*)+u}{u+d} = \alpha, \qquad (13.16)$$

where $n^* > 1$ by construction. Consider first $n < n^*$. In this case, $(v_2(n) + u)/(u + d) > q > (v_1(n) + u)/(u + d)$ and the equilibrium is identical to that derived in the previous section: all v_1 judges follow precedent, and all v_2 judges depart from precedent.

Now consider $n > n^*$. In this case, (13.16) implies that neither type of judge will depart from precedent since $(v_i(n) + u)/(u + d) < \alpha$ ($i = 1,2$). And since n only becomes larger in subsequent periods, it follows that the precedent will *never* be overturned. In this example, n^* therefore represents a threshold in that any precedent enduring for this number of periods will subsequently be followed by all judges.[30] Figure 13.5 illustrates this result.[31]

It is possible to calculate the probability that a given decision will attain the threshold necessary to render it impregnable. Beginning with $n = 1$, recall that v_1 judges will follow the decision and v_2 judges will overturn it as long as $n < n^*$. Thus, for n to reach n^*, there must be a string of $n^* - 1$ consecutive type v_1 judges. Since judges are paired with cases randomly, and the fraction of v_1 judges is $1 - \alpha$, the probability of this occurring is simply

$$(1 - \alpha)^{n^* - 1}. \qquad (13.17)$$

However, if a type v_2 judge gets to decide this case anytime before n reaches n^*, the prevailing decision will be reversed and n is reset to 1, starting the process again. More generally, if there is a continuum of judge types, as in the general model

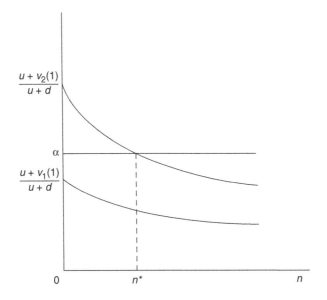

Figure 13.5

in section 3, there may not exist a finite n^* beyond which the probability of reversal of a decision falls to zero. Rather, the probability would simply decline over time, perhaps approaching zero in the limit.

6. Summary and conclusion

This paper has examined the role of judicial self-interest in the production of legal precedents. In the model, the preferences of judges were represented by a utility function with two components: private utility and reputational utility. The judge's private utility arose from his personal view of how a case should be decided, while his reputational utility depended on his expectation of how his decision would be viewed by observers of the legal process: other judges, lawyers, litigants and the public. Thus, the judge's decision to follow a given precedent involved a trade-off between these two sources of utility. For example, he might deviate from precedent if he expected other judges to regard his decision as a new precedent, which would then enhance his reputation. On the other hand, he might follow a precedent he disagreed with if, after overturning it, he expected a high probability of reversal. The equilibrium rate at which judges followed precedent thus depended on the distribution of judicial preferences across the population of judges.

The model contributes to the economic theory of the law an explicit characterization of the decision-making of judges based purely on their self-interest. Previous models have viewed the law as a product solely of rational litigant behavior, filtered through some exogenous decision structure. What remains is to pair a model of rational litigant behavior with the model of rational judicial behavior to determine the equilibrium rate of legal change. Only then will we have a complete picture of the economic structure of the legal process.

Appendix

This appendix considers the case where a judge's reputational utility depends on all future citations of his decision for as long as it remains the precedent. The judge thus receives utility u for each citation and disutility d for a reversal. Also, in this version of the model, future utility or disutility is discounted by the factor $\delta \equiv 1/(1 + r)$. We continue to focus only on stationary equilibria where q is the probability of reversal of a decision in any period.

Consider a decision initiated by judge t. In period $t + 1$ it will be followed with probability $1 - q$ and reversed with probability q. If the decision is followed, in the next period, $t + 2$, there again is a probability $1 - q$ that it will be followed and q that it will be reversed. This continues in periods $t + 3, t + 4,\ldots$, and for as long as the decision was followed in the previous period. Once a reversal occurs, however, we assume the process stops (i.e., no further reputational utility will be received). The present value of expected utility for judge t that results from this process is given by

$$\sum_{t=1}^{\infty} \delta^t \left(1-q\right)^{t-1} \left[u - q(u+d)\right]$$

(A1)

where, notice, the term in square brackets is identical to the one period (undiscounted) reputational utility employed in the text. Since this term, along with δ and q, are constant over time (by assumption), (A1) equals

$$[\delta/(1-\delta(1-q))][u-q(u + d)] \qquad\qquad (A2)$$

Notice that (A2) differs from the expression in the text (the first line of (13.2)) only by the first bracketed term.

Notes

1   For example, judges are modelled as explicitly promoting efficiency [Cooter, Kornhauser, and Lane (1979)]; as favoring the party spending the most on litigation [Goodman (1978) and Katz (1988)]; or as random decision makers [Priest (1977); Cooter and Kornhauser (1980)]. Also see Kornhauser (1989, p. 64).

2   See, however, Greenberg and Haley (1986) for a model of judicial compensation in which judges are seen as self-selecting appointments to the bench in part to consume its non-pecuniary benefits. Such self-selection, the authors argue, tends to attract self-restrained judges.

3   Also see Posner (1986, pp. 505–5, 511–2). Higgins and Rubin (1980) and Cohen (1991) develop empirical tests of the Landes and Posner model. While Higgins and Rubin's results are largely negative, Cohen finds general support for the theory.

4   See, for example, Landes and Posner (1979), Shapiro (1972), and Posner (1988).

5   This is in contrast to private judges (e.g., commercial arbitrators), who provide an alternative dispute resolution mechanism to public courts. Since these judges have to attract business, they can be viewed as profit maximizers. See, for example, Cooter (1983) and Landes and Posner (1979) for discussions of adjudication as a private good.

6   But see Higgins and Rubin (1980).

7   Macey (1989) portrays this as a prisoner's dilemma problem, where individual judges have an incentive to disregard all but their own precedents. In fact, we argue below that the structure of the game is not that of a prisoner's dilemma (see note 29).

8   428 F. 2d 1071 Cert. denied, 400 U.S. 925 (1970). This was one of the earliest cases to find an implicit warranty of habitability in rental leases.

9   Quoted in Rabin (1984).

10   An example of this strategy may be Cardozo's famous decision in *MacPherson v. Buick Motor Co.*, 217 N.Y. 382, 111 N.E. 1050 (1916), which marked a clear change in product liability law, but which Cardozo portrayed as simply a restatement of existing law. See Posner (1990b, p. 109). Eisenberg (1988, p. 132–35) refers to this technique as transformation.

11   See Posner (1990b, Ch. 5) for a citation analysis of the reputation of Judge Cardozo.

12   See, for example, Landes and Posner (1976) and Cooter (1983).

13   See Holmes (1897) and Posner (1990a, pp. 221–28). Hart (1961) offers a critique of the prediction theory.

14   153 F.2d 869, 873 (2d Cir. 1946).

15   *Robins Dry Dock and Repair Co. v. Flint*, 275 U.S. 303 (1927).

16   *Agwilines*, pp. 871–72, as quoted in Goldberg (1991, p. 269). We thank a referee for bringing this case to our attention.

17   The latter case is relevant for judges in courts of last resort, as Cardozo usually was (thanks to a referee for this point).

18   Cooter (1983, p. 129). Notice, however, the context of his argument, which is based on the hypothesis that public judges behave much like private judges in attempting to maximize the demand for their services.

19   The random pairing of judges with cases is a combination of the random occurrence of similar cases and the random assignment of judges to cases in most courts [Posner (1990b, pp. 145–47)].

20   Also see Posner (1990b, Chapter 5), on the internal conflicts that shape a judge's decision.

21   Posner's (1990b) data suggest that most judges are rarely cited. Thus, the cost of preference falsification will provide the stronger push to deviate from precedent for most judges.

22   Of course, a subsequent judge might cite judge t as one of a collection of cases all supporting a given precedent, but we assume that such a citation does not enhance judge t's reputation.

23   See Wittman (1983) for a model where politicians have similar utility functions, combining their private preference in the policy space and their probability of reelection.

24   For now, we ignore the case where judges are indifferent. See section 4 below.

25   Kuran (1987, pp. 60–61) adopts a similar specification in the context of the utility certain decision-makers receive from points along a policy interval.

26   For example, assume that as old judges leave the system, they are replaced by identical judges at a constant rate.

27   We assume that $F(\cdot)$ has the usual properties; namely, $F(0) = 0$, $F(1) = 1$, and $F' > 0$.

28   See Hirshleifer (1987) for a discussion of mixed strategies in a law and economics context.

29   These two effects show why the game does not have the structure of a prisoner's dilemma. In the latter, all parties choose the dominant strategy (depart) regardless of what others do. In contrast, if a large fraction of judges depart in our model, following becomes the preferred strategy. Thus, the situation more closely resembles the game of "chicken."

30   Kuran (1991) examines a similar threshold effect in the context of social decision-making and Cohen (1991) notes its impact on judicial decisions. The result also resembles the type of "bandwagon" effects studied by Granovetter and Soong (1986) and Iannaccone (1989).

31   The rule in *Hadley v. Baxendale*, 9 Exch. 341 (Exch. 1854), which limits damages in breach of contract cases to those reasonably foreseen by the promisor, may be an example of a precedent that has attained this status.

References

Cohen, Mark, 1991, Explaining Judicial Behavior or What's 'Unconstitutional' about the Sentencing Commission? *Journal of Law, Economics, and Organization* **7**, 183–99.

Cooter, Robert D., 1983, The Objectives of Private and Public Judges, *Public Choice* **41**, 107–132.

Cooter, Robert D. and Lewis Kornhauser, 1980, Can Litigation Improve the Law without the Help of Judges? *Journal of Legal Studies* **9**, 139–163.

Cooter, Robert D., Lewis Kornhauser, and David Lane, 1979, Liability Rules, Limited Information, and the Role of Precedent, *Bell Journal of Economics* **10**, 366–373.

Eisenberg, Melvin, 1988, *The Nature of the Common Law* (Harvard University Press, Cambridge).

Goldberg, Victor, 1991, Recovery for Pure Economic Loss in Tort: Another Look at Robins Dry Dock v. Flint, *Journal of Legal Studies* **20**, 249–75.

Goodman, John, 1978, An Economic Theory of the Evolution of the Common Law, *Journal of Legal Studies* **7**, 393–406.

Granovetter, Mark and Roland Soong, 1986, Threshold Models of Interpersonal Effects in Consumer Demand, *Journal of Economic Behavior and Organization* **7**, 83–99.

Greenberg, Paul and James Haley, 1986, The Role of the Compensation Structure in Enhancing Judicial Quality, *Journal of Legal Studies* **15**, 417–426.

Hart, H. L. A., 1961, *The Concept of Law* (Oxford University Press, Oxford).

Heiner, Ronald A., 1986, Imperfect Decisions and the Law: On the Evolution of Legal Precedent and Rules, *Journal of Legal Studies* **15**, 227–261.

Higgins, Richard and Paul Rubin, 1980, Judicial Discretion, *Journal of Legal Studies* **9**, 129–38.

Hirshleifer, Jack, 1987, *Economic Behavior in Adversity* (University of Chicago Press, Chicago).

Holmes, Oliver W., 1897, The Path of the Law, *Harvard Law Review* **10**, 457–78.

Iannaccone, Laurence R., 1989, Bandwagons, and the Threat of Chaos, *Journal of Economic Behavior and Organization* **11**, 431–42.

Katz, Avery, 1988, Judicial Decisionmaking and Litigation Expenditure, *International Review of Law and Economics* **8**, 127–143.

Kornhauser, Lewis, 1989, An Economic Perspective on Stare Decisis, *Chicago Kent Law Review* **65**, 63–92.

Kuran, Timur, 1987, Chameleon Voters and Public Choice, *Public Choice* **53**, 53–78.

Kuran, Timur, 1990, Private and Public Preferences, *Economics and Philosophy* **6**, 1–26.

Kuran, Timur, 1991, Cognitive Limitations and Preference Evolution, *Journal of Institutional and Theoretical Economics* **147**, 241–273.

Landes, William M. and Richard A. Posner, 1976, Legal Precedent: A Theoretical and Empirical Analysis, *Journal of Law and Economics* **19**, 249–307.

Landes, William M. and Richard A. Posner, 1979, Adjudication as a Private Good, *Journal of Legal Studies* **19**, 249–307.

Macey, Jonathan, 1989, Internal and External Costs and Benefits of Stare Decisis, *Chicago Kent Law Review* **65**, 93–113.

Posner, Richard A., 1988, *Law and Literature* (Harvard University Press, Cambridge).

Posner, Richard A., 1990a, *The Problems of Jurisprudence* (Harvard University Press, Cambridge).

Posner, Richard A., 1990b, Cardozo: A Study in Reputation (University of Chicago Press, Chicago).

Priest, George, 1977, The Common Law Process and the Selection of Efficient Rules, *Journal of Legal Studies* **6**, 65–82.

Rabin, Edward, 1984, The Revolution of Landlord-Tenant Law: Causes and Consequences, *Cornell Law Review* **69**, 517–84.

Rubin, Paul, 1977, Why is the Common Law Efficient? *Journal of Legal Studies* **6**, 51–63.

Shapiro, Martin, 1972, Toward a Theory of Stare Decisis, *Journal of Legal Studies* **1**, 125–134.

Wittman, Donald, 1983, Candidate Motivation: A Synthesis of Alternative Theories, *American Political Science Review* **77**, 142–57.

Chapter 14

Douglas Glen Whitman

EVOLUTION OF THE COMMON LAW AND THE EMERGENCE OF COMPROMISE

Precedent, *n*. In Law, a previous decision, rule or practice which, in the absence of a definite statute, has whatever force and authority a Judge may choose to give it, thereby greatly simplifying his task of doing as he pleases. As there are precedents for everything, he has only to ignore those that make against his interest and accentuate those in the line of his desire.

Lawful, *adj*. Compatible with the will of a judge having jurisdiction.

[AMBROSE BIERCE, *The Devil's Dictionary*]

UNDER WHAT circumstances will a common-law process yield legal rules that people can reliably assume judges will follow? In a system of judge-made law, judges are nominally bound to follow precedent whenever deciding cases, but in actual fact judges do depart from precedent from time to time. Sometimes the new rule pronounced by a judge who parts from precedent will be upheld and become the new precedent, while other times the new rule will be repudiated by other judges in subsequent cases. If such departures from precedent were never allowed, the law could never evolve over time to deal with new problems and circumstances; but if such departures are allowed, the constancy and reliability of the common law seem to be in jeopardy. In a system where any given judge can in principle depart from an existing rule, why (and when) does it make sense for people to rely on any particular legal rule in making their plans and decisions about how to act?

The answer to this question has a number of serious implications for the legitimacy of the legal system. The ideal of the rule of law depends upon the principle that people should know in advance when they will and when they will not be punished for their actions—or, at least, they should be able to make reasonably reliable predictions. The rule of law also depends on the principle that like cases should be decided in a like manner, so that the citizens who live under the law will be treated equitably, not discriminatorily. But if judges cannot be counted on to pronounce the same rules in similar cases, at least most of the time, these principles cannot be upheld, and the ideal of the rule of law suffers as a result.[1]

The indeterminacy problem also bears upon the issue of the efficiency of the common law. A number of economists analyzing the law have argued that the common law tends to evolve, over time, toward efficient (that is, wealth-maximizing) rules. In general, the models that support this conclusion assume that, when a given rule is the precedent, agents will adjust their behavior to fit the precedent. A prominent example is the model of George Priest,[2] in which inefficient rules cause agents to behave in a manner that produces more cases with higher stakes, so that inefficient rules get relitigated and overturned more often than efficient rules.[3] But what if agents have no expectation that an inefficient (or efficient) precedent will actually be upheld in their own case? If there is a substantial possibility that a rule other than the current precedent will be pronounced, then the characteristics of the current rule may be irrelevant to the agents' choices.

This paper addresses the question of reliability in the legal system via a model of self-interested judicial behavior. The legal process is treated as a sequence of cases, each of which is decided by a single judge randomly selected from the judge pool. Each time a judge faces a case, she must decide whether to follow precedent or instead announce an alternative rule. In doing so, she will have to consider both reputational concerns and her personal preferences over rules in order to make the optimal choice. The interaction of all judges' choices determines whether or not the process will ultimately lead to convergence on a single legal rule.

In Section I, I outline the paper's basic model. I then derive implications for legal reliability, under the assumption of two rules competing for the attention of judges. Specifically, I conclude that if division of opinion among judges is low relative to the strength of judges' activist tendencies, then the system will converge on a single rule. This is because even activist judges who disagree with whichever rule is the precedent will follow precedent anyway, for fear of having their opinions rejected by subsequent judges. On the other hand, if division of opinion among judges is high, oscillation between the two rules will take place, thereby depriving potential litigants of the ability to predict what rule will be pronounced in their cases.

In Section II, I revise the model by adding a third rule into the mix. This third rule will be a potential compromise, in that no judge considers it the best rule but all judges consider it better than the alternative. I then derive conditions under which convergence on the compromise rule can occur. It turns out that a compromise is most likely to be viable when division of opinion among judges is highest—in other words, just when oscillation would be most common in the absence of a compromise rule.

In Section III, I consider the relationship between this and other models of the evolution of the common law, discuss two real-world illustrations of the model's conclusions, and make some concluding remarks.

I. Two competing rules

A. The two-rule model

What is the mechanism through which the doctrine of stare decisis[4] operates? Suppose that a judge faces a precedent with which she disagrees. On the one hand, she may choose to follow precedent, and most likely her peers will not blame her for doing so, since following precedent is supposed to be the norm. But in sticking with precedent, she must affirm a rule that offends her in some way, perhaps for ideological reasons, or perhaps because the precedent just does not seem right in this particular case. She will experience some amount of cognitive dissonance, or to use a term coined by Timur Kuran, "preference falsification."[5] On the other hand, she may break with precedent and pronounce a rule she finds more acceptable. By doing so, she experiences "preference satisfaction" (the converse of preference falsification) from making what she considers the right decision, and she also takes part in a kind of gamble. If subsequent judges uphold her decision, then she will experience the gain in reputation associated with pioneering a successful new rule. But if subsequent judges return to the precedent she rejected, a corresponding loss in reputation will result. A judge who cares about the esteem of her peers in the legal community, as well as the possibility of promotion to higher benches, will surely wish to avoid having her decisions repudiated.

These factors, preferences over rules and reputational utility, provide the basis for the following model of self-interested decision making by judges. The model's basic framework, which I have borrowed in large part from the model of Thomas J. Miceli and Metin M. Cosgel,[6] is as follows: Imagine there exists a well-defined area of law. Within this area of law, an endless line of cases arise in sequence. Each time a new case occurs, a judge is selected randomly from a pool of judges to decide the case. This judge will take the rule announced by the last judge to decide such a case as the relevant precedent. In deciding the case, the judge announces a legal rule—possibly the precedent announced by the last judge, possibly an alternative. Whichever rule she chooses will constitute the precedent faced by the next judge.

I will assume (for now) that there are only two rules competing for the attention of judges, designated rule 1 and rule 2. Let γ equal the proportion of judges who favor rule 1 and $(1 - \gamma)$ the proportion who favor rule 2. I will refer to judges in the first group as 1-preferrers and judges in the second group as 2-preferrers. The parameter γ will sometimes be used as a measure of division of opinion among judges in the judge pool. When γ is close to zero or one, a substantial majority of judges favor one rule over the other, so division of opinion is low. On the other hand, when γ is close to one-half, there is greater division of opinion, because the two rules command approximately equal support among judges.

If a judge chooses to break from precedent, she takes a risk with her reputation, because it matters to her whether subsequent judges affirm or reject her judgments. For the sake of simplicity, in this model only the very next judge's decision will make a difference in this regard. If a judge announces a new precedent and the next judge affirms it, the current judge will reap a reputational gain of u. If, on the other hand, the next judge rejects the new precedent, the current judge will suffer a reputational loss of d. (Both of these quantities are utility valued, constant, time invariant, and identical for all judges.) Again, these factors come into play only when a judge breaks from precedent; a judge who follows precedent is perceived as the norm.

When a judge chooses to follow precedent, she will feel neither a positive nor a negative impact on her reputation. She will, however, fail to experience the satisfaction associated with announcing a rule she agrees with. Let $V_i(x)$ denote a judge's private utility from pronouncing rule x. Let x_t^p denote the judge's preferred legal rule, and let x^n_i denote the judge's nonpreferred rule. If the judge pronounces her nonpreferred rule instead of her preferred rule, she will experience the following loss in utility:

$$v_i = V_i(x^p_i) - V_i(x^n_i) .$$
(14.1)

This is the cost of reaffirming a precedent that one disagrees with—or, alternatively, it is the guaranteed benefit (aside from any reputational effect) of breaking from precedent and asserting one's preferred rule instead. I will call v_i the judge's preference satisfaction value.[7] As implied by the i subscript, this term need not be the same for all judges; some judges may care more about announcing their preferred rules than others.

A judge's v_i value can be interpreted as a measure of her propensity toward activism, since judges with higher v_i values are more concerned with implementing their own preferences over rules, and such judges will (other things equal) be more inclined to break from precedent than judges with lower v_i values. (I should point out that this is a functional definition of activism that may differ from others' use of the term.) I assume there is some known distribution of v_i values in the judge pool. I also assume that judges' preference satisfaction values are bounded below by $\underline{v}$ and above by $\bar{v} < d$. The purpose of this last assumption is to guarantee that there are no judges who will break from a precedent they disagree with *no matter what;* clearly, if a judge's gain from pronouncing her preferred rule outweighs the worst possible loss from doing so, this judge will always pronounce her preferred rule. The significance of this assumption will become apparent later.

All judges are taken to be expected utility maximizers. In deciding whether to follow precedent or break from it, a judge will compare the expected sum of private and reputational utility from each course of action and pick the action with the higher expected total. Suppose that a judge faces precedent x^n_i, and if she breaks from precedent in favor of rule x^p_i, she believes there is a probability p that the next judge will reject the rule and announce x^n_i and a corresponding probability $(1 - p)$ that the next judge will affirm the new precedent. The current judge therefore faces an expected utility of

$$V_i(x^p_i) + (1 - p)u - pd \text{ or } V_i(x^p_i) + u - p(u + d)$$
(14.2)

from pronouncing her preferred rule, which she will compare to a guaranteed utility of $V_i(x^n)$ from following precedent. She will break from precedent if

$$V_i(x^p_i) + u - p(u + d) > V_i(x^n_i)$$
(14.3)

or, after rearranging terms and applying the definition of v_i,

$$p < \frac{v_i + u}{u + d}$$
(14.4)

In other words, if she believes the probability of the next judge rejecting a new precedent is sufficiently low, then the current judge will go ahead and pronounce her preferred rule. But if the probability of rejection is too high (if the inequality above is reversed), she will stick with precedent.[8]

Of course, the value of p will depend on what rule is pronounced. It could be that rule 1 is more likely than rule 2 to be rejected by the next judge, or vice versa. I will therefore let p equal the probability that the next judge, given a precedent of rule 2, will reject it in favor of rule 1. In addition, let q equal the probability that the next judge, given a precedent of rule 1, will reject it in favor of rule 2. Given these definitions, inequality (14.4) actually represents the condition for 2-preferrers to depart from a precedent of rule 1 in favor of rule 2, since p is the chance that the next judge will reject the new precedent of rule 2. The equivalent condition for 1-preferrers to depart from a precedent of rule 2 in favor of rule 1 is

$$q < \frac{v_i + u}{u + d}, \tag{14.5}$$

which is identical to (14.4), except that p has been replaced by q.

For the remainder of the paper, I will employ the following shorthand notation,

$$y_i \equiv \frac{v_i + u}{u + d},$$

and similarly for other expressions of the general form $(v + u)/(u + d)$. (For example, $\bar{y}$ corresponds to y_i when $v_i = \bar{v}$.) This expression appears often and has an intuitive explanation: it is the ratio of the greatest potential gain from breaking precedent $(v_i + u)$ to the total utility at stake in the gamble that results from doing so $(u + d)$. Like v_i, y_i can be treated as a measure of the strength of a judge's activist impulses: The larger is y_i, the more likely is the judge to break precedent. We can think of v_i as a judge's *absolute* propensity to be activist and y_i as a judge's *relative* propensity to be activist.

The analysis so far has implicitly assumed that only a judge who disagrees with the current precedent will break from it. It is conceivable, however, that a judge might depart from precedent purely for reputational purposes. Specifically, a 1-preferring judge who faces a precedent of rule 1 will break precedent in favor of rule 2 if

$$V_i(x_i^n) + u - p(u + d) > V_i(x_i^r), \tag{14.6}$$

which reduces to

$$p < \frac{u - v_i}{u + d}. \tag{14.7}$$

And similarly, a 2-preferring judge who faces a precedent of rule 2 will break precedent in favor of rule 1 if

$$q < \frac{u - v_i}{u + d}. \tag{14.8}$$

Clearly, these conditions will always fail if we assume $u < v_i$ for all judges. This assumption means that the reputational gain from pronouncing a successful new rule is always less than the loss due to pronouncing a rule one dislikes. This assumption will be made later for simplicity, but it is not crucial to the analysis.

In each of the four breaking conditions just stated, observe that a judge thinking of departing from precedent needs to consider the probability that the next judge will depart from the new precedent she has just announced. This probability has two components: first, the probability that the next judge will *disagree* with the new rule and subsequently break from it and, second, the probability that the next judge will *agree* with the new rule and subsequently break from it. The sum of these two components is the total probability of a new rule being overturned by the next judge.

Let us consider the case of a current judge who is considering breaking from a precedent of rule 1 in favor of rule 2. The probability that the next judge will disagree with the new precedent and break from it (that is, the first component described above) is equal to the probability that the next judge will disagree, multiplied by the probability that this judge's appropriate condition for breaking precedent is satisfied. The first part—the probability the next judge will disagree—is simply equal to γ, the fraction of judges in the judge pool who disagree with rule 2. The second part—the probability that this judge's condition (14.5) will be satisfied—is determined by the distribution of v_i values. Hence,

$$\text{Pr (next judge disagrees and breaks)} = \gamma \Pr\left(q < \frac{v_i + u}{u + d} \right) \qquad (14.9)$$

Similar reasoning applied to the probability of the next judge *agreeing* with the new precedent and nonetheless breaking from it (that is, the second component described above) will show that if the current judge breaks from a precedent of rule 1 in favor of rule 2, then

$$\text{Pr(next judge agrees and breaks)} = (1 - \gamma) \Pr\left(q < \frac{u - v_i}{u + d} \right) \qquad (14.10)$$

The sum of these two expressions is the total probability that the next judge, randomly chosen from the judge pool, will break from a precedent of rule 2:

$$p(q) = \gamma \Pr\left(q < \frac{v_i + u}{u + d} \right) + (1 - \gamma) \Pr\left(q < \frac{u - v_i}{u + d} \right) \qquad (14.11)$$

Here we have an expression for p, the probability of a random judge breaking from a precedent of rule 2, in terms of q, the probability of a random judge breaking from a precedent of rule 1. Why the interdependence? The reason is that whether the next judge will decide to go back to rule 1 will depend on the likelihood q of the next judge *plus one* going back to rule 2 again.

By analogous reasoning, we can derive a similar expression for q in terms of p:

$$q(p) = (1 - \gamma) \Pr\left(p < \frac{v_i + u}{u + d} \right) + \gamma \Pr\left(q < \frac{u + v_i}{u + d} \right) \qquad (14.12)$$

The two equations (14.11) and (14.12) are very much like reaction functions: Given the probability q of a precedent of 1 being replaced by 2, judges who face a precedent of 1 will react by breaking from a precedent of 2 (in favor of 1) some fraction p of the time.

Likewise, given the probability p of a precedent of 2 being replaced by 1, judges who face a precedent of 2 will react by breaking from a precedent of 1 some fraction q of the time.[9]

An equilibrium (specifically, a stationary perfect Bayesian equilibrium) of this system occurs when there exists a pair of values $p*$ and $q*$ that satisfy both equations (14.11) and (14.12). Any such equilibrium is self-reinforcing, in the sense that $p*$ will induce judges to take actions that lead to $q*$, and vice versa. At least one equilibrium is guaranteed to exist for any γ (between zero and one) and any distribution of v_i values satisfying the assumptions above.[10]

In what follows, I will make the simplifying assumption that $u < v_i$ for all judges. When this is the case, no judge will depart from a precedent she agrees with. The reaction functions (14.11) and (14.12) become

$$p(q) = \gamma \Pr(q < y_i) \qquad\qquad (14.13)$$

and

$$q(p) = (1 - \gamma) \Pr(p < y_i), \qquad\qquad (14.14)$$

respectively. Adopting this assumption simplifies the analysis but does not change any qualitative conclusions.[11]

Implications

The equilibrium probabilities $p*$ and $q*$ will determine the evolution of the area of law in question. Each represents the probability of transition from one rule to another rule in a single case. Suppose, for instance, that the current precedent is rule 2. Then there is a $(1 - p*)$ probability that rule 2 will remain the precedent for at least one more case and a $p*$ probability that it will be replaced as precedent by rule 1 in the next case. Likewise, if the current precedent is rule 1, then there is a $(1 - q*)$ chance that rule 1 will remain the precedent for at least one more case and a $q*$ probability that it will be replaced by rule 2 in the next case.

How the legal system will evolve depends on the relative sizes of the transition probabilities $p*$ and $q*$. Robert Cooter and Lewis Kornhauser[12] examine the properties of a legal system in which they are always positive. In their approach, the transition probabilities are taken as exogenous, rather than derived from a model of judicial behavior as in this paper. They conclude, among other things, that such a system will not converge on any particular rule; instead, the system will oscillate among the rules, with each rule spending a certain percentage of the time as precedent.[13] Specifically, rule 1 will in the long run spend $p*/(p* + q*)$ of the time as precedent, while rule 2 will spend $q*/(p* + q*)$ of the time as precedent.[14] Hence, the relative sizes of the transition probabilities affect how often each rule is on top, but they will not cause the system to pick one rule and stick with it. But what if the transition probabilities are not strictly positive? If one probability is equal to zero, then the system will converge on a single rule. Suppose, for instance, that $p* = 0$ and $q* > 0$. Then if rule 2 is ever announced as precedent, it will forever remain as precedent, because the chance of a judge rejecting a precedent of rule 2 in favor of rule 1 is nil. And since the probability of a precedent of rule 1 being rejected in favor of rule 2 is positive, it is certain that rule 2 will eventually be announced as precedent. Therefore, the system will converge on rule 2.

A necessary condition for the system to converge on a single rule is as follows:

$$\gamma < (1-\bar{y}) \ \text{ or } \ \gamma > \bar{y} \tag{14.15}$$

As long as this condition holds, there exists an equilibrium in which one of the transition probabilities is equal to zero.

For instance, suppose $\gamma > \bar{y}$ and $p = \gamma$, so that $p > \bar{y}$. Consequently, no 2-preferring judge would ever depart from a precedent of 1. According to equation (14.14), it must be the case that $q = 0$. And when $q = 0$, we can see from equation (14.13) that $p = \gamma$. Thus, $q^* = 0$ and $p^* = \gamma$ are mutually reinforcing and constitute an equilibrium of the system. This equilibrium would lead to convergence on rule I.[15] Similar reasoning shows that if $\gamma < (1 - y)$, then $q^* = (1 - \gamma)$ and $p^* = 0$ constitute an equilibrium that leads to convergence on rule 2. Figure 14.1 shows a convergent equilibrium, under the assumption that v_i is uniformly distributed over the interval $[v, \bar{v}]$. (This distribution is only an example, and it is not necessary for the general result.)

If condition (14.15) does not hold, both transition probabilities will be positive and oscillation between rules will result. Figure 14.2 shows an oscillating equilibrium, again under the (unnecessary) assumption of a uniform distribution. In short, we can see from condition (14.15) that whether or not convergence is possible depends on the *most* activist judge's propensity toward activism, $\bar{y}$. This is because there must be enough supporters of a rule to deter even the most activist advocate of the other rule from breaking precedent.

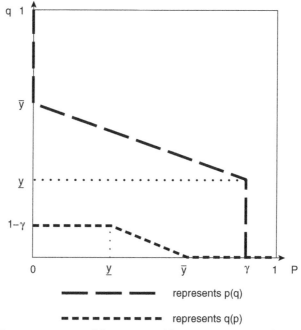

Figure 14.1 A convergent equilibrium. Equilibrium is $p^* = \gamma$ and $q^* = 0$. Parameter values used are $\gamma = .875, \underline{y} = .3125, \bar{y} = .625$, with a uniform distribution.

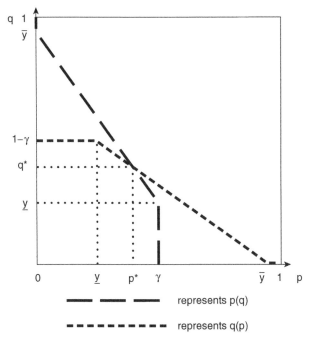

Figure 14.2 An oscillating equilibrium. Equilibrium is $p* = q* = .3947$. Parameter values used are $\gamma = .5$, $\underline{y} = .25$, $\overline{y} = .9$, with a uniform distribution.

There is more to the story, however, because even if a convergent equilibrium is possible, other equilibria may be possible as well. Figure 14.3 shows an example (again using a uniform distribution of preference satisfaction values) of a situation in which there is more than one equilibrium that could occur. In this type of situation, the parameters of the situation—the fraction of judges who support each rule, the degree of activism among judges, and so on—do not uniquely determine the outcome of the system. Which equilibrium actually occurs depends crucially upon the expectations of judges and the history of the system. Convergence on a single rule is possible, but not guaranteed.

To eliminate any chance of oscillation, we need the following *sufficient* condition for convergence on a single rule:

$$\gamma < \underline{y} \text{ or } \gamma > (1 - \underline{y}) \tag{14.16}$$

This condition (jointly with the necessary condition (14.15)) assures that any equilibrium *must* be convergent. Suppose, for example, that $\gamma > (1 - y)$. Since q cannot be larger than $(1 - \gamma)$, we have $q < y$, and thus equation (14.13) reveals that $p* = \gamma$. In other words, 1-preferring judges will break from a precedent of rule 2 in favor of rule 1, even if they know that *all* 2-preferring judges will go right back to 2. And then, since $p* = \gamma$ and the necessary condition holds, $q* = 0$. Similar reasoning shows that if $\gamma < y$ (and the necessary condition holds), then the equilibrium is $p* = 0$, $q* = (1 - \gamma)$. In other words, whether or not convergence is guaranteed depends on the *least* activist judge's propensity toward activism, y. This is because there must be few enough supporters of one rule that even the least zealous advocate of the other rule is willing to break precedent.

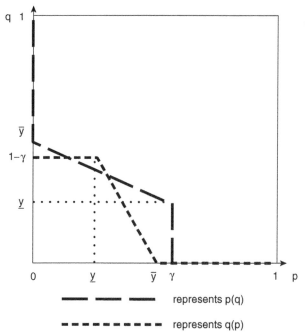

Figure 14.3 A convergent equilibrium. Equilibria occur at $p^* = \gamma$, $q^* = 0$; $p^* = .2872$, $q^* = .3724$; and $p^* = .1406$, $q^* = 1 - \gamma$. Parameter values used are $\gamma = .55$, $\underline{y} = .25$, $\bar{y} = .5$, with a uniform distribution.

The foregoing results imply a picture like Figure 14.4. This figure displays a unit interval representing all possible values of γ. As the figure shows, for high division of opinion (in the center of the interval), convergence is impossible; for medium division of opinion, convergence is possible but not guaranteed; and for low division of opinion (near the endpoints of the interval), convergence on a single rule is guaranteed.[16] In summary, convergence on one rule is most likely when division of opinion among judges is low and least likely when division of opinion among judges is high. Conversely, oscillation between rules is *least* likely when division of opinion is low and *most* likely when division of opinion is high. This fact will take on added importance in Section II, once we have discovered the circumstances under which convergence on a third, "compromise" rule is most likely to occur: when division of opinion is high.

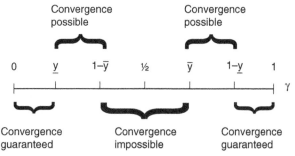

Figure 14.4 Necessary and sufficient conditions for convergence.

II. Appearance of a third rule

A. The three-rule model

Despite the existence of circumstances in which the legal system can be expected to converge on a single rule within an area of law, there remain many other circumstances in which that is not the case. In these circumstances, the system will instead oscillate between the two competing legal rules. Such oscillation robs potential litigants of the ability to anticipate the actions of the courts and adjust their behavior accordingly. Short of widespread changes in the preferences and beliefs of judges, is there anything that can obviate these unfortunate results?

In this section, I will argue that the answer is yes, at least sometimes. One solution to the dilemma emerges when we include a third rule—a potential compromise—among the alternatives available to judges. If this third rule has certain properties (to be discussed shortly), it can act as an "attractor" from which a judge is less willing to depart than her nonpreferred rule, even though she would rather announce her preferred rule. As a result, the third rule may emerge as the dominant rule in the system, from which no judge will deviate. This can even occur if no judge thinks the third rule is the best!

Where would this third rule come from? This question lies outside the model presented here, which treats the appearance of a third alternative as exogenous. In the real world, the conception of a new rule could result from a creative act on the part of a judge or legal scholar. The new rule might be introduced into the legal process by a judge who disagrees with the current precedent but who does not wish to take the risk of rejecting it entirely. She might therefore introduce a compromise, knowing (or suspecting) that it will be sufficiently agreeable to other judges that it will stick as the new precedent and thereby augment her reputation. Alternately, there might be a single judge who introduces the compromise rule because she actually considers it *better* than both existing rules. (This is, of course, contrary to the assumption above that the new rule is no one's first choice. But admitting judges who like the new rule best would only strengthen the model's conclusions, which hold even if no one actually prefers the new rule.)

The structure of the model duplicates the one used in Section I, with no changes but a few additions. As before, γ represents the fraction of judges who favor rule 1, $(1 - \gamma)$ the fraction who favor rule 2. There is now a third rule, rule 3, available to judges, but no judge considers it inherently the best, so there are still only two major factions of judges.

Rule 3 does have a special feature, however: it is every judge's *second* preference. This assumption is operationalized by letting the amount of preference satisfaction from announcing rule 3 be less than the amount of preference satisfaction from announcing one's preferred rule. Or, from the perspective of a judge announcing a precedent she disagrees with, it is less "painful" to announce the compromise rule than to announce the rule she disagrees with most. To be more precise, let

$$v_i' = V_i(3) - V_i(x_i^n)$$

(14.17)

and

$$v_i'' = V_i(x_i^p) - V_i(3),$$

(14.18)

where, as before, x_i^p is the judge's preferred rule and x_i^n her nonpreferred rule, and 3 is the compromise rule. The value v_i' represents the preference satisfaction from picking the compromise rule rather than one's least preferred rule. The value v_i'' represents the preference satisfaction from picking one's preferred rule rather than the compromise rule. The sum of v_i' and v_i'' is v_i. As before, I assume there exists a known distribution of preference satisfaction values in the judge pool and that the range of possible values is bounded above and below (that is, v_i' has a maximum of $\bar{v}'$ and a minimum of $\underline{v}'$, and v_i'' has a maximum of $\bar{v}''$ and a minimum of $\underline{v}''$). Since there are now three rules, any equilibrium must consist of six transition probabilities. Specifically, let

p = probability of transition from rule 2 to rule 1,
q = probability of transition from rule 1 to rule 2,
p_c = probability of transition from rule 2 to rule 3,
q_c = probability of transition from rule 1 to rule 3,
p_b = probability of transition from rule 3 to rule 1, and
q_b = probability of transition from rule 3 to rule 2.

In the two-rule world, I assumed for simplicity that $v_i > u$, which assured that judges would not depart to their nonpreferred rules purely for reputational purposes. I will make two equivalent assumptions here: first, $v_i' > u$, which assures that judges will not depart from the compromise rule to their nonpreferred rules; second, $v_i'' > u$, which assures that judges will not depart from their preferred rules to the compromise rule. Together, these three assumptions guarantee that whenever a judge breaks from precedent, she always moves to a rule she prefers to the precedent, though not necessarily to her most preferred rule. Again, these assumptions are made for simplicity.[17]

Under these assumptions, it turns out that p, p_c, and p_b represent the actions of 1-preferrers (since none of them involves a transition away from rule 1 or toward rule 2), while q, q_c, and q_b represent the actions of 2-preferrers (since none of them involves a transition away from rule 2 or toward rule 1).

The next task is to derive the judges' conditions for breaking precedent. In order for a judge to depart from a precedent to another rule, two conditions must be satisfied: first, defecting to that rule must be better than following precedent; second, defecting to that rule must be better than defecting to a different rule. For example, consider a 1-preferring judge. If she faces a precedent of rule 2, she can depart to either rule 1 or 3. In order for her to depart to rule 1, doing so must be better than following precedent and better than departing to rule 3. In all of what follows, I will use the word "willingness" to indicate that a judge considers departing to a given rule better than following precedent, without necessarily implying that it is better than departing to the other possible rule. I will use the word "superiority" to indicate that defecting to a given rule is better than defecting to the other rule. Thus, in order for a judge to defect to a particular rule, both the "willingness condition" and the "superiority condition" must be satisfied.

Take the case of a 2-preferrer facing a precedent of rule 1. In order for this judge to be willing to defect to rule 2 (that is, for defecting to rule 2 to be better than following precedent), it must be the true that

$$V_i(x_i^p) + u - (p + p_c)(u + d) > V_i(x_i^n).$$

(14.19)

Notice that this inequality is almost identical to condition (3), which was the condition for a 1-preferring judge to defect from rule 1 to rule 2 in the two-rule model. The only difference is that now the chance of the next judge repudiating the new precedent is not just p, but $(p + p_c)$, since the next judge may go to rule 1 (with probability p) or to rule 3 (with probability p_c). The above condition reduces to

$$(p+p_c) < \frac{v_i + u}{u+d}. \tag{14.20}$$

This is the willingness condition for 2-preferrers to defect from rule 1 to rule 2. By analogous reasoning, the willingness condition for 1-preferrers to defect from rule 2 to rule 1 is

$$(q+q_c) < \frac{v_i + u}{u+d}. \tag{14.21}$$

The satisfaction of condition (14.20) or (14.21) does not indicate that a judge will, in fact, defect to her preferred rule from her nonpreferred rule, because we have yet to consider the possibility of her defecting to rule 3 instead.

In order for any judge to be willing to defect from her nonpreferred rule to rule 3, it must be true that

$$V_i(3)+u-(q_b + p_b)(u+d) > V_i(x_i^n). \tag{14.22}$$

which follows from the fact that $(q_b + p_b)$ is the probability that the next judge will depart from a precedent of rule 3. This condition reduces to

$$(q_b + p_b) < \frac{v_i' + u}{u+d}. \tag{14.23}$$

This condition for willingness to defect to rule 3 is the same for both 1-preferrers and 2-preferrers, because both groups face the same probability that the next judge will depart from rule 3.

All of the conditions stated so far are willingness, not superiority, conditions. Suppose that both conditions (14.20) and (14.23) hold for some judge; then this 2-preferrer considers defection to either rule 2 or 3 to be preferable to following a precedent of rule 1. But to which will she actually choose to defect? In order for a 2-preferring judge to depart from a precedent of rule 1 to 2 rather than to rule 3, it must be true that

$$V_i(x_i^p)+u-(p+p_c)(u+d) > V_i(3)+u-(q_b + p_b)(u+d), \tag{14.24}$$

which reduces to

$$v_i'' > (p+p_c - q_b - p_b)(u+d) \tag{14.25}$$

This condition has a natural interpretation. Since departing to one's preferred rule and departing to the compromise rule both involve breaking from precedent, both create potential reputational effects. What matters, then, is the *difference* between the probability of one's preferred rule being left by the next judge, $(p + p_c)$, and the probability of the compromise rule being left by the next judge, $(q_b + p_b)$. The cost of defecting to one's preferred rule rather than to the compromise rule is the expected difference in reputational utility attributable to the compromise rule being less likely to be left by the next judge, $(p + p_c - q_b - p_b)(u + d)$. The benefit of defecting to one's preferred rule rather than the compromise is avoiding a preference falsification loss of v_i''. A comparison of the two determines which course of action is preferable.

The equivalent condition for a 1-preferrer to depart to rule 1 rather than rule 3 is

$$v_i'' > (q + q_c - q_b - p_b)(u + d). \tag{14.26}$$

The interpretation is exactly the same as condition (14.25), except the probability of the next judge leaving one's preferred rule is $(q + q_c)$ instead of $(p + p_c)$

Finally, we need conditions for judges to leave rule 3 in favor of another rule. In order for a 2-preferring judge to leave rule 3 in favor of rule 2, it must be that

$$(p + p_c) < \frac{v_i'' + u}{u + d}. \tag{14.27}$$

And in order for a 1-preferring judge to leave rule 3 in favor of rule 1, it must be that

$$(q + q_c) < \frac{v_i'' + u}{u + d}. \tag{14.28}$$

(These conditions are derived via the same logic as the previous willingness conditions; no superiority conditions are necessary, since I have assured that no judge will depart from the compromise in favor of her nonpreferred rule.)

The seven conditions just derived—(14.20), (14.21), (14.23), (14.25), (14.26), (14.27), and (14.28)—define the three-rule legal system. They can be combined into six equations or "reaction functions," each of which states one of the six transition probabilities as a function of the other five. These six equations would define the three-rule system in the same manner that equations (14.13) and (14.14) define the two-rule system: specifically, any $(p^*, q^*, p_c^*, q_c^*, p_b^*)$ sextuplet that satisfies all six equations constitutes an equilibrium. I will omit the statement of the six equations, since they will not be necessary in what follows, and instead I will simply note that, once again, at least one equilibrium of the system is guaranteed to exist.[18]

B. Implications

Within this framework, there are many kinds of conceivable equilibria, and exploring them all would be beyond the scope of this paper. Instead, I will focus on the equilibrium that produces convergence on the compromise rule, since only this type of equilibrium can obviate a situation of oscillation that would occur in the absence of a compromise rule. But first I will make a few brief comments about the other equilibria. Not surprisingly, the appearance of a "compromise" rule does not always guarantee a compromise will actually occur. As we will see, a rule must possess some very specific properties for it to be a viable compromise. If a third rule is introduced that does not have these properties, the outcome could be very different. Some equilibria, for instance, involve oscillation among all three rules; thus, the compromise may not only fail to produce convergence on a single rule, but in fact add an additional source of uncertainty.[19] In other equilibria, there ends up being oscillation between the third rule and one of the other rules, leaving either rule 1 or rule 2 out in the cold. And in still other equilibria, the third rule ends up being completely irrelevant, because there is convergence on one of the original two rules, or oscillation between the original two rules that excludes the third rule.

Under what circumstances, then, will there be an equilibrium that involves convergence on the compromise rule? Clearly, such equilibrium must have $q_b = 0$ and $p_b = 0$; otherwise, there would be a positive probability of the compromise rule being left, and hence no convergence. This fact has a couple of implications. First, since $q_b + P_b = 0$, condition (14.23) is automatically satisfied, meaning that every judge is willing to depart from her nonpreferred rule in favor of the compromise rule. Thus, every judge who faces her nonpreferred rule as a precedent will depart to something, either her preferred rule or the compromise rule (as we will see in a moment, it will definitely be the compromise). Therefore, $p + p_c = \gamma$, since all 1-preferrers depart from a precedent of rule 2, and $q + q_c = (1 - \gamma)$, since all 2-preferrers depart from a precedent of 1.

A second implication follows from this conclusion. To justify $q_b = 0$ and $p_b = 0$, all judges must be deterred from leaving the compromise rule in favor of their preferred rules; that is, conditions (14.27) and (14.28) must fail to hold for all judges. So we need to have $(p + p_c) > \bar{y}''$ and $(q + q_c) > y$. And we already know that $(p + p_c) = \gamma$ and $(q + q_c) = (1 - \gamma)$, so we have

$$\gamma > \bar{y}'' \text{ and } (1-\gamma) > \bar{y}'' \tag{14.29}$$

(In keeping with the previously adopted shorthand, $\bar{y}'' = (\bar{v}'' + u)/(u + d)$.) This condition has a natural interpretation: the proportion of judges who oppose any judge's preferred rule must be large enough to deter her from leaving the compromise in favor of that rule.

It turns out that any judge who is unwilling to defect from the compromise would, when facing her nonpreferred rule as precedent, rather depart to the compromise than depart to her preferred rule. Suppose, on the contrary, that a judge preferred to depart to her preferred rule rather than to the compromise rule; then condition (14.25) or (14.26), whichever is appropriate to the judge's type, must hold. Since $q_b + p_b = 0$, $(p + p_c) = \gamma$, and $(q + q_c) = (1 - \gamma)$, for condition (14.25) or (14.26) to hold we need

$$v_i'' > \gamma(u + d) \text{ or } v_i'' > (1-\gamma)(u + d) \tag{14.30}$$

But these conditions imply

$$\frac{v_i''}{(u + d)} > \gamma \text{ or } \frac{v_i''}{u + d} > (1 - \gamma) \tag{14.31}$$

Since $\bar{y}_i'' = (v_i'' + u)/(u + d) > v_i'' (u + d)$, we can conclude that $y_i'' > \gamma$ or $y_i'' > (1 - \gamma)$. But either of these statements would contradict condition (14.29); therefore, in order for an equilibrium to involve convergence on the compromise rule, every judge must choose to depart to the compromise rather than her preferred rule. Hence, $p = 0$, $q = 0$, $p_c = \gamma$, and $q_c = (1 - \gamma)$. Intuitively, this is true because any judge who is unwilling to leave the compromise for her own preferred rule would also depart to the compromise rather than to her preferred rule. This conclusion follows from the fact that, when no one will leave the compromise, anyone who goes to the compromise is guaranteed a reputational gain.[20]

There is therefore only one possible equilibrium that involves convergence on the compromise rule: $p^* = 0$, $q^* = 0$, $p_c^* = \gamma$, $q_c^* = (1-\gamma)$, $p_b^* = 0$, $q_b^* = 0$. This equilibrium corresponds to a single overarching condition (14.29), that must be satisfied in order for an equilibrium that involves convergence on the compromise rule to occur.[21]

This condition has an intriguing implication: *a compromise should be easier to find when there is greater division of opinion among judges*. This becomes evident if we rewrite condition (14.29) as $\bar{y}'' < \min\{\gamma, 1 - \gamma\}$. Since γ and $(1 - \gamma)$ always lie on opposite sides of and equidistant from one-half, lower division of opinion—that is, γ closer to zero or one—pushes down the ceiling on viable values of $\bar{y}''$. The smallness of $\bar{y}''$ can be thought of as a measure of how "good" the compromise is; the smaller it is, the less preference falsification judges experience from adopting the compromise. A less satisfactory compromise (one with high $\bar{y}''$ rerequires greater division of opinion for it to work, while a better compromise (one with low $\bar{y}''$) can succeed when division of opinion is not as severe.

To some extent, this result is an artifact of the model's construction. It might seem implausible to assume that a potential compromise rule always produces the same amount of preference satisfaction (v_i'') for preferrers of both of the original rules. It is perhaps more plausible to think that a compromise would tend to "lean" toward either rule 1 or rule 2, so that members of one group will be more satisfied with the compromise and members of the other group less satisfied. In effect, the assumption of a single preference satisfaction value restricts the analysis to compromise rules that exactly "split the difference" between the two original rules, in some sense. To correct this problem, it would be necessary to allow there to be two different values of $\bar{v}''$ for 1-preferrers and 2-preferrers. This would complicate the analysis but not substantially change the conclusions. Suppose that $\bar{v}''$ takes on the value $\bar{v}_1''$ for 1-preferrers and $\bar{v}_i''$ for 2-preferrers. Presumably, these values stand in an inverse relationship to each other, since a rule that 1-preferrers like more is probably a rule the 2-preferrers like less, and vice versa. Let $\bar{y}_1''$ and $\bar{y}_2''$ be defined in the usual fashion. Then condition (14.29) becomes

$$\gamma > \bar{y}_2'' \text{ and } (1-\gamma) > \bar{y}_1''$$

(14.32)

The implications of this condition differ only slightly from those stated earlier. In general, the farther apart are $\bar{y}_1''$ and $\bar{y}_2''$—that is, the more lopsided is the compromise rule—the more lopsided must be the support for the rules if the compromise is to work. For example, if 1-preferrers suffer greater preference falsification from the compromise rule[22] (larger $\bar{y}_1''$, than $\bar{y}_2''$), there need to be enough 2-preferrers $(1 - \gamma)$ to deter the 1-preferrers from leaving the compromise.

This might seem to contradict the earlier conclusion that greater division of opinion assists the emergence of a compromise, but that is not quite true. The question is, how large is the space of potential compromise rules? Since any potential compromise rule is characterized by the two values $\bar{y}_1''$ and $\bar{y}_2''$, the space of potential compromise rules can be represented as a two-dimensional area, as in Figure 14.5. In this figure, $\bar{y}_1''$, is measured along the left-hand axis and $\bar{y}_2''$ is measured along the right-hand axis. The conditions of (14.32) demarcate the viable subset of the space of potential compromise rules. When $\gamma = 1/2$, the set of viable compromise rules is given by the shaded square. If γ changed to something else, such as γ' in the figure, some potential compromises would be ruled out while others would become viable. Specifically, the area labeled L would be lost, and the area labeled G would be gained. Note that the area L is greater than the area G. This is a general feature of any shift away from even division of opinion: the total area of potential compromises shrinks. Conversely, a movement toward greater division of opinion will increase the total area of potential compromises.[23] Of course, the effect this has in a particular area of law depends on where the compromise rules that are actually conceivable lie in the area of all potential compromises. For example, if for some reason there were no conceivable compromise rule in the southeast quadrant of Figure 14.5, a movement in the direction of a smaller γ could increase the likelihood of finding a viable compromise.

In conjunction with the results of the two-rule model in Section I, these conclusions have a significant implication: a viable compromise rule is most likely to be found in exactly those situations in which convergence on rule 1 or rule 2 is least

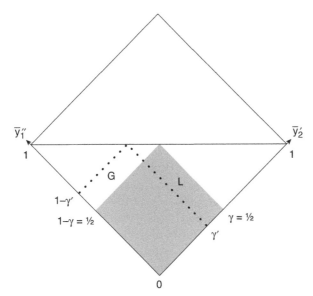

Figure 14.5 Area of viable compromises. Shaded area is area of viable compromises when $\gamma = 1/2$. L is the area lost when γ shifts to γ'. G is the area gained from the same shift.

likely to occur! When division of opinion is low, meaning that γ is close to zero or one, convergence on one of the two original rules is possible and, when division of opinion is lower still, guaranteed—and this is just when a compromise is least likely to be reached. On the other hand, when division of opinion is high, meaning that γ is close to one-half, convergence on one of the two original rules is impossible—and that is also when a compromise is most likely to be viable. In a sense, the option of compromise provides a means (albeit not an infallible one) of obviating the problem of oscillation that afflicts the two-rule world, by providing a third alternative in situations wherein judges' opinions are too evenly divided for the legal system to settle on one of two competing rules.

III. Commentary

A. Related literature

Much of the existing literature on the evolution of the common law can be classified into one of two approaches, which I will call "demand side" and "supply side." The demand-side models explain the evolution of legal rules primarily in terms of the behavior of potential litigants, whose actions are driven in part by the efficiency and other properties of the legal rules that affect them. The behavior of judges is generally taken as random or exogenous in these models. Supply-side models, on the other hand, explain the evolution of legal rules primarily in terms of the preferences and behavior of the makers of law, judges.

The model employed in this paper falls into the supply-side camp. In treating judges as individuals who desire to implement their own legal preferences but who are constrained by the need to preserve their reputations, I have followed the lead of several other authors, including William Landes and Richard Posner, Georg von Wangenheim, and Miceli and Cosgel,[24] whose approach I have adapted. But the most popular models of legal evolution have come from the demand-side camp, whose canonical contributions include those by Paul Rubin, Priest, John Goodman, and a separate paper by Landes and Posner.[25] These authors all address their analysis to the question of whether the common law evolves toward more efficient (that is, wealth-maximizing) rules over time. The natural question is how, if at all, the present model could incorporate the insights of these authors.

The answer is tricky, for it depends crucially upon how those authors are interpreted. At least three of these models (Rubin's, Priest's, and Landes and Posner's) make predictions about the proportion of areas of law that will have efficient precedents, not about whether any particular area of law will have an efficient precedent. The present model, on the other hand, deals with a single area of law, making it difficult to integrate their approaches with my own. Fortunately, Cooter and Kornhauser[26] have outlined a useful framework for evaluating these models, which I will adapt for my purposes. For simplicity, I will limit myself to an analysis of the two-rule world.

The statement in Section I that a (p^*, q^*) equilibrium would result in rule 1 spending $p^*/(p^* + q^*)$ of the time, and rule 2 $q^*/(p^* + q^*)$ of the time, as precedent was based on the implicit assumption that new cases arrive at a constant rate. Cooter and

Kornhauser allow for the possibility that different rules will have different likelihoods of being challenged like so: Let r_1 equal the probability that a precedent of rule 1 will be challenged in a given period, and let r_2 equal the probability that a precedent of rule 2 will be challenged in a given period. The probability that a given precedent will be overturned in 1 period is equal to the probability that it will be challenged, multiplied by the chance that the challenged precedent will be overturned. Thus, if rule 1 is the precedent, the chance of it being replaced by rule 2 within 1 period is r_1q^*, and if rule 2 is the precedent, the chance of it being replaced by rule 1 within 1 period is r_2p^*. These probabilities replace q^* and p^* in determining how much time each rule spends as precedent; thus, rule 1 will spend $r_2p^*/(r_2p^* + r_1q^*)$ of the time as precedent, while rule 2 will spend $r_1q^*/(r_2p^* + r_1q^*)$ of the time as precedent.

This conclusion is useful because three of the canonical models (those of Rubin, Priest, and Landes and Posner) rely on the assumption that inefficient rules will generate either more or less litigation than efficient rules— in other words, that r_1 and r_2 will differ. Let us suppose that rule 1 is more efficient than rule 2. Rubin essentially argues that potential litigants will choose to settle suits when the precedent is efficient but go to court when the precedent is inefficient, so that $r_1 = 0$ while $r_2 > 0$.[27] The result is that rule 1 would, in the long run, spend 100 percent of the time as precedent. Priest argues that inefficient rules generate greater stakes than efficient rules and that (other things equal) greater stakes cause more disputants to go to court rather than settling; thus, $r_1 < r_2$. While this would not cause the system to converge on the efficient rule, it would cause the efficient rule to spend more time as precedent than it would if the rules were litigated at the same rate, because $r_2p^*/(r_2p^* + r_1q^*) > p^*/(p^* + q^*)$ when $r_1 < r_2$. Finally, Landes and Posner argue, against Priest, that inefficient rules might get litigated at a lower rate than efficient rules, because in many areas of law it is possible for potential litigants to contract around an inefficient rule, while they will avoid contracting costs by going to court under an efficient rule. Thus, $r_1 > r_2$, an assumption that yields the conclusion that an inefficient rule would spend more time as precedent than it would under identical litigation rates.[28]

But all three models, at least as interpreted here, founder on a problem foreshadowed in this paper's introduction: If the system oscillates among two or more rules, only myopic agents will assume that the standing precedent will be applied. Rational agents will instead base their behavior on the expectation that each rule will be applied with a certain probability. This argument implies that agents will base their behavior—before a dispute arises as well as when choosing whether or not to settle—on the percentage of time that each rule spends as precedent. It is therefore implausible to assume that r_1 and r_2 will differ. Instead, a single probability $r = r(p^*, q^*)$ will actually determine whether a dispute arises in a given period. In consequence, rule 1 will spend $rp^*/(rp^* + rq^*) = p^*/(p^* + q^*)$ of the time as precedent (and similarly for rule 2). That is, *the actions of potential litigants will exert no pressure on precedent to move toward one rule or the other*. They may, however, affect the speed at which oscillation takes place, because when r is larger, transitions from one rule to the other will take place more often.[29]

Goodman does not rely on differential rates of litigation to reach the conclusion that the legal system will lean toward efficiency. Instead, he argues that judges are most likely to rule in favor of the party to a dispute who has invested the most in the litigation process. Since an inefficient rule by definition generates greater losses for some parties than gains for others, those who benefit from having an inefficient rule overturned will invest more than those who benefit from keeping it in place.[30] Hence, judges will be more likely to overturn an inefficient rule than an efficient rule. In terms of the present model, Goodman's argument implies that if rule 1 is the efficient rule, $p^* > q^*$ (the inefficient rule is more likely to be overturned than the efficient rule). While the model does not explicitly allow for differential investment in litigation, it could possibly be incorporated into a broader interpretation of the term γ. While γ has been treated as the proportion of judges who always favor rule 1 over rule 2, it could also be interpreted as the likelihood that a random judge will consider rule 1 more appropriate than rule 2 *in the dispute at hand*. If it is indeed the case that those who gain from overturning an inefficient precedent will spend more on litigation, then γ should be larger than it would be if differential expenditures were ruled out, since more judges will perceive rule 1 to be "right" in a random dispute.

Whether or not this affects the equilibrium values of p and q depends crucially on the initial γ (unmodified by differential investment) and the magnitude of the investment effect. If the investment effect were small, γ might not change enough to alter the equilibrium in any substantial way. On the other hand, if the investment effect were large, or if the initial γ were close to the threshold between one type of equilibrium and another, then a significant shift could take place, in which case the efficient rule would be the precedent for a larger percentage of the time than otherwise. If the investment effect pushed γ past one of the thresholds identified in this paper, it could make convergence possible where it was not before or guaranteed where it was only possible before.

B. Illustrations

The evolutionary picture suggested by this article's model seems to comport well with the actual development of certain areas of law. While some areas of law tend to change little over time, others display an ongoing struggle between doctrines or approaches. One example of the latter is the well-known tension between strict liability and negligence in the law of tort. As Mario Rizzo[31] has argued, that tension seems to have been resolved, in part, by the emergence of doctrines like "assumption of risk" and "negligence per se" that represent the importation of strict-liability notions into a negligence-based structure. The combined doctrine constitutes a compromise of sorts between the two approaches.

Similarly, the law of nuisance, in cases where the plaintiff voluntarily settles nearby an already existing nuisance, has been torn between two alternative doctrines: the coming-to-the-nuisance doctrine (which says the plaintiff should lose in these cases) and the balancing doctrine (which decides such cases by weighing a variety of economic costs and benefits of allowing the nuisance). As I have argued elsewhere,[32] the case law in this area has historically exhibited an oscillation between the two approaches, followed by the emergence of de facto court-enforced zoning as a compromise between them. In the law of both tort and nuisance, one can observe the kind of oscillation and compromise predicted by the model presented here. Whether other areas of law exhibit a similar evolution remains a subject for further research.

C. Concluding remarks

The modeling strategy employed here is, of course, abstract, and a number of objections might be raised against it. First, the model does not account for the hierarchical nature of most court systems, in which higher courts may review the decisions of lower courts. Second, the model does not account for the existence of cases that do not clearly fall within one area of the law or another; such cases may muddy the waters, since it might be unclear whether a previous decision is the ruling precedent in a current case or not. Third, the model does not allow for there to be more than three rules. If more than one potential compromise rule began to compete for the attention of judges, it is conceivable that a compromise rule that would otherwise be viable might no longer be able to hold its dominant position. All of these objections are valid, and incorporating these factors into the model would lead to a more complete (and much more complex) analysis of the issue.

Nonetheless, the model addresses, if in rudimentary fashion, a significant question that haunts the common law. In any given area of the common law, one can often find more than one rule competing for the attention of judges. Even when one rule is nominally the standing precedent, another rule is often waiting in the wings to take its place when a judge sees fit to announce it. This presents a problem: the legal system may flip-flop from one rule to another indefinitely. But is this actually a serious problem, and if so, when? The conclusion of this paper is that oscillation among legal rules is in fact possible, but it is not as serious a problem as it might at first appear. In a number of situations, the legal system will instead produce convergence on a single rule upon which agents can rely when choosing their plans and behavior.

When there are only two rules competing for hegemony, convergence on one rule occurs when division of opinion among judges is low, relative to the strength of judges' activist impulses. If there are enough judges who support one rule, even activist judges who oppose that rule will nonetheless follow it as a precedent rather than risk having their decisions repudiated by subsequent judges. On the other hand, if the judge pool is more evenly divided in support of the two rules, oscillation between the two rules becomes a serious possibility and (for sufficiently divided opinion) a certainty.

When a third "compromise" rule is introduced to the situation, the legal system is most likely to converge on that compromise when opinion is divided—in other words, precisely when oscillation is most common in a world of only two rules. Of course, in any situation of disagreement, from bargaining over goods to political negotiations, it is not surprising to find that compromises get struck from time to time. What is intriguing is the manner in which a compromise might emerge in the context of the evolution of law. The judges in the system need not agree, in any explicit sense, to announce only the compromise rule; nor is any external enforcement mechanism required. Instead, the compromise could conceivably be introduced by a single judge in a single case, and other judges would follow suit based on their self-interested calculation of reputational effects, weighed against their desire to implement their personal preferences over legal rules. The compromise emerges out of a decentralized process of judge-by-judge decision making.

The fact that multiple equilibria are possible under some circumstances emphasizes that the parameters of a legal situation, such as the number of supporters of a given rule, the degree of activism among judges, the aversion of judges to being overturned, and so on, do not always uniquely determine the outcome produced by the system. The history of the system and, more important, the expectations judges have about each other can substantially affect the behavior of the system; in fact, these factors can even decide whether the system does or does not converge on a single rule.

Finally, this paper's model emphasizes the role of judicial opinion in shaping the evolution of the system. That judges' opinions and beliefs affect the development of law might seem obvious, but in light of models of the evolution of law that emphasize the capacity of law to develop independently of or even in spite of judges' opinions, it is important to recognize that such "demand-side" approaches can only explain so much. The present model confirms our intuition that trends in judicial thinking do indeed strongly influence the direction of legal change, though not so strongly that current legal doctrine can be explained exclusively in terms of the opinions of the present pool of judges. History, expectations, and judicial preferences all interact to determine the course of legal change.

Notes

1   For more on the indeterminacy problem as it relates to the rule of law, see Jason Scott Johnston, Uncertainty, Chaos, and the Torts Process: An Economic Analysis of Legal Form, 76 Cornell L. Rev. 341 (1991); and Christopher L. Kutz, Just Disagreement: Indeterminacy and Rationality in the Rule of Law, 103 Yale L. J. 997 (1994).

2   George L. Priest, The Common Law and the Selection of Efficient Rules, 6 J. Legal Stud. 65 (1977).

3   Other models of legal evolution include Paul H. Rubin, Why Is the Common Law Efficient? 6 J. Legal Stud. 51 (1977); John C. Goodman, An Economic Theory of the Evolution of the Common Law, 7 J. Legal Stud. 393 (1978); and William M. Landes & Richard A. Posner, Adjudication as a Private Good, 18 J. Legal Stud. 235 (1979), which will be addressed in Section III.

4   "To stand on a decision," that is, the legal doctrine that precedents ought to be followed.

5   Timur Kuran, Private and Public Preferences, 6 Econ. & Phil. 1 (1990); cited in Thomas J. Miceli & Metin M. Cosgel, Reputation and Judicial Decision-Making, 23 J. Econ. Behav. & Org. 31 (1994).

6   Miceli & Cosgel, *supra* note 5. The most important difference between this paper's model and Miceli and Cosgel's is that Miceli and Cosgel assume a judge will never face a precedent she agrees with. The upshot of this assumption is that Miceli and Cosgel's model produces a single probability value that represents the chance that any judge will break from any precedent, rather than the two probability values produced by this paper's model. It is not clear why Miceli and Cosgel assume judges always disagree with precedents they face. It appears to have been a provisional assumption, but the assumption is never dropped later.

7   Miceli and Cosgel, *id.*, call this the judge's preference falsification value. I have adopted the term preference satisfaction to emphasize that it is not just the relative loss from making a "bad" decision, but also the relative gain from making a "good" decision.

8   If $p = (v_i + u)/(u + d)$, the judge will be indifferent between following and breaking precedent. An indifferent judge could take either action, or even adopt a mixed strategy (randomizing between following and breaking). This is true of all the other decision rules (yet to come) as well.

9   In writing these "reaction functions," I have assumed for ease of exposition that the distribution of v_i values is continuous, so that the functions are in fact functions rather than correspondences. (This assumption is not crucial, and it is dropped in the proof of the existence of equilibrium.) If noncontinuous distributions—particularly distributions with mass points—are allowed, then a positive mass of judges may be indifferent between following and breaking precedent at some values of p and q. Indifferent judges may take either action, or even adopt a mixed strategy. For any q such that some judges are indifferent, $p(q)$ can take on two values—one equal to the proportion of judges who break precedent if all indifferent judges choose to break, and one equal to the proportion of judges who break if all indifferent judges choose to follow. In addition, since indifferent judges can adopt mixed strategies (randomizing over whether to break or follow), $p(q)$ can also take on all values in between these extremes.

10   A proof of the existence of an equilibrium is available from the author upon request. The key element of the proof is a fixed-point theorem (along with a demonstration of the upper hemicontinuity of the reaction functions) used to show that the "reaction functions" must cross at least once.

11   A proof of the following results that does not employ the assumption $u < v_i$ is available from the author upon request.

12   Robert Cooter & Lewis Kornhauser, Can Litigation Improve the Law without the Help of Judges? 9 J. Legal Stud. 139 (1980).

13   Actually, Cooter and Kornhauser's results are broader: they show that the system will oscillate among all rules that can be reached with positive probability. It is not necessary that every 1-period transition probability be positive, so long as there is a positive chance of each rule being reached eventually. For instance, if there were a 50 percent chance of transition from A to B and a 20 percent chance of transition from B to C, then C could be reached in 2 periods with positive probability even if the chance of transition from A to C in 1 period were zero. Obviously, this possibility is irrelevant when there are only two rules.

14   These fractions are derived by finding the limiting distribution (over rule 1 and rule 2) that results from iterating the stochastic process indefinitely.

15   As we will see below, however, this is not necessarily the only equilibrium.

16   In some cases, incidentally, the medium range will not occur. This happens when $\bar{y} > 1 - \underline{y}$, so that satisfaction of the necessary condition for convergence immediately implies satisfaction of the sufficient condition for convergence. In such circumstances, convergence is either impossible or guaranteed. Also, the range wherein convergence is impossible fails to exist when $\bar{y} < 1/2$, since either $\gamma > \bar{y}$ or $(1 - \gamma) > \bar{y}$ (or both) must hold.

17   A proof of the following results that does not rely on the assumptions just stated is available from the author upon request.

18   Proof is available from the author upon request.

19   One factor that mitigates this possibility is the fact that, as suggested earlier, a judge would be most inclined to introduce a third rule if she thought the system would converge on it. Otherwise, she could suffer a reputational loss for even introducing it. There is, however, no guarantee that a judge will not introduce a rule that does not lead to convergence.

20   To be more specific: when no one will leave the compromise, anyone who goes to the compromise from another rule is guaranteed a reputational benefit of u. Yet when someone is faced with the compromise as a precedent, no such benefit is available. Meanwhile, the potential preference satisfaction is the same in both situations, since both choices are between the preferred rule and the compromise. Thus, anyone who will stay on the compromise (rather than go to her preferred rule) will certainly depart to the compromise (rather than go to her preferred rule).

21   Satisfaction of this condition guarantees the satisfaction of any other conditions for the equilibrium in question to be possible.

22   Recall that v_i'' represents the utility difference between the preferred rule and the compromise rule. Announcing the compromise rather than one's preferred rule therefore yields a loss in utility (preference falsification) of v_i''.

23   The total area of potential compromises is equal to $\gamma(1 - \gamma)$, which reaches a maximum at $\gamma = \frac{1}{2}$.

24   William M. Landes & Richard A. Posner, Legal Precedent: A Theoretical and Empirical Analysis, 19 J. Law & Econ. 249 (1976); Georg von Wangenheim, The Evolution of Judge-Made Law, 13 Int'l Rev. L. & Econ. 381 (1993); Miceli & Cosgel, *supra* note 5.

25   Rubin, *supra* note 3; Priest, *supra* note 2; Goodman, *supra* note 3; Landes & Posner, *supra* note 3.

26   Cooter & Kornhauser, *supra* note 12.

27   Cooter and Kornhauser argue that this is an implausible assumption, because it relies on the "group rationality" assumption that disputants will always choose to settle if doing so minimizes their joint costs.

28   Cooter and Kornhauser's interpretation of Landes and Posner (Cooter & Kornhauser, *supra* note 12; Landes & Posner, *supra* note 3) does not capture all the subtleties of that model. Much of Landes and Posner's analysis relies on treating precedent as the stock of all previous decisions, rather than just the last decision. Incorporating this insight in the present model would require a much more extensive revision than I will attempt here.

29   This analysis depends on potential litigants knowing the percentage of time each rule spends as precedent, but not knowing what the current precedent is. If they know the current precedent, they will employ transition probabilities instead. If, for example, the precedent is rule 1, they will base their actions on the belief that rule 1 will be applied with probability $(1 - q^*)$ and rule 2 with probability q^*. This is implausible, however, because potential litigants often choose their behavior long before a dispute occurs and the case goes to court, and in the meantime the precedent could change. The further in the future dispute and trial are likely to occur, the more agents will rely on the percentage of time each rule spends as precedent instead of transition probabilities.

30   One problem with this analysis is that an inefficient rule could create dispersed costs for some and concentrated benefits for others. So even if the costs are greater than the benefits in total, collective action problems may prevent those who benefit from changing the rule from investing enough in litigation relative to those who benefit from keeping the rule in place.

31   Mario J. Rizzo, Rules versus Cost-Benefit Analysis in the Common Law, 4 Cato J. 865 (1985).

32   Douglas G. Whitman, Economic Efficiency of the Coming to the Nuisance Doctrine: A Reappraisal (unpublished manuscript, New York Univ. 1997).

Chapter 15

Richard A. Posner

AN ECONOMIC ANALYSIS OF THE USE OF CITATIONS IN THE LAW

Introduction

S CARCITY OF QUANTITATIVE scholarship has been a serious shortcoming of legal research, including economic analysis of law. When hypotheses cannot be tested by means of experiments, whether contrived or natural, and the results assessed rigorously by reference to the conventions of statistical inference, speculation is rampant and knowledge meager. The situation can be improved, I shall argue, by making greater use of citations analysis, guided by economic theory, as a methodology of quantitative empirical research. Both adjudication, a central practical activity of the legal system, and legal research are citation-heavy activities. Judges, lawyers who brief and argue cases, and law professors and students engaged in traditional legal-doctrinal research could all be thought, with only slight exaggeration, to make their living in part by careful citation both of judicial decisions and of law-review articles and other secondary materials. The seriousness with which the legal profession takes citations suggests that the analysis of citations in law is likely to uncover more systematic features, a more consistent practice, of citing than would a similar analysis in fields for which citing is of less consequence. Counting citations is already a well-established method of empirical research in law, economics, sociology (especially the sociology of science), and academic administration. It is being used increasingly in law[1]—mainly in economic analysis of law—yet it remains limited in relation to potential topics. Statistical analysis of citations practices has become fast and cheap as a result of faster, more powerful computers, and of computerized citations indexes.[2] The cost of citations analysis thus is falling. But the fact that a particular kind of research is feasible, even easy to do, cannot explain why anyone wants to do it. Low cost is not enough; there have to be benefits—and anyway the opportunity costs of adopting one research method over another are not low. Citations analysis is

growing mainly because it enables rigorous quantitative analysis of elusive but important social phenomena such as reputation, influence, prestige, celebrity, the diffusion
of knowledge, the rise and decline of schools of thought, *stare decisis* (that is, the basing
of judicial decision on previous decisions—precedents), the quality of scholarly
output, the quality of journals, and the productivity of scholars, judges, courts, and
law schools.[3]

Citations analysis is not an inherently economic methodology; most of it has been
conducted without any use of the theories or characteristic empirical techniques of
economists. It is an empirical methodology usable by a wide range of disciplines. But
I shall argue that an economic framework fosters precision in its use. Indeed, the
human capital model developed by economists may actually be essential to using
citations analysis to compare and evaluate individual performance, whether by judges
or by scholars.

The reasons—and the motives—for citing

Citations (that is, mentions of a previous work, published or unpublished, or simply
of an author's or other person's name) figure prominently in many forms of
documentation (electronic as well as printed), including patents, newspaper and
magazine articles, scholarly journals, and books. In case-law systems, such as those of
the United States and England, citations, mainly but not only to previous decisions,
are a conspicuous feature of most judicial opinions. It does not follow from the
commonness of citing that citing is an activity worth studying. That depends on why a
work or author is cited. If there were no reason—if citations were random—this
would be an interesting finding but there would be little point in studying citation
practice further; indeed, there would be no practice of citing to study. But, if only
because citing is not costless—there is the bother of finding the citation, and the
possibility of criticism for misciting or failing to cite—it would be surprising if
citations were random, and there is evidence that they are not, even in fields less committed to precedent and therefore to citation than law is. Notably, citation counts
have been consistent predictors of the receipt of high academic honors, such as the
Nobel prizes in the sciences (Cronin, 1984; Feist, 1997; cf. McAllister, Anderson, and
Narin, 1980; So, 1998). As I note later, citation studies of eminent judges yield results
consistent with the more common, qualitative indicia of judicial distinction.

Several reasons for citing come to mind. The first, which is dominant in
historiography, is simply to identify a source of information, so that the reader of the
citing work can verify the accuracy of statements of fact made in it. "Historical
footnotes list not the great writers who sanction a given statement or whose words
an author has creatively adapted, but the documents, many or most of them not literary texts at all, which provided its substantive ingredients" (Grafton, 1997, p. 33).
The second reason for citing, which is closely related, is to incorporate a body of
information by reference, that is, to guide the reader to a place where he can find the
information if interested in it. Let me merge these two reasons for citing into one—
"information"—which is to be understood broadly, as taking in ideas and
arguments as well as facts. The motive for the informational citation is simply to
respond to a demand for information.

The next reason for citing, which I'll call "priority," is to demonstrate compliance with any applicable norm against plagiarism by acknowledging the authorship of ideas, arguments, or (in the case of citations to "prior art" in patent applications) technology used in the citing work. In scientific and social scientific fields, with the partial exception of law, most citations are "priority" citations. Strictly, priority citations are a subset of informational citations; the priority is in making an argument, discovering an idea, or inventing a product or process. But whereas a writer will make informational citations without prodding, simply in order to make his work more valuable to the reader, he will make priority citations (except to himself!) reluctantly, under the constraint of the antiplagiarism norm.

Most self-citations are designed either to incorporate by reference information contained in other works by the citer, to establish the priority of some earlier work of his over work done by others since then, or to advertise his previous work in the hope that more people will read it. One of the worries about citations analysis is that as it becomes more familiar, citation behavior will become strategic, and authors thus will cite themselves more in order to increase their citations count. That is, the gains from self-advertising will be greater and so the number of such citations will increase because the cost of additional self-citations is low. But actually this gambit is unlikely to succeed, because it is so easy to subtract out self-citations in counting citations to a person's work. Reciprocal citing may be a more serious problem. One can imagine informal deals between academic allies to jack up each other's reputations by citing each other heavily, although they will encounter the usual problems of holding a cartel together. There is some evidence that journal editors receive citations in the journals they edit that they would not receive if they were not editors—citations designed to increase the likelihood that the citing article will be accepted for publication (Lange and Frensch, 1999; Wright, 1994).

Another common reason for citing is to identify works or persons with which or with whom the author of the citing work disagrees. These citations ("negative citations") are motivated not by antiplagiarism norms but by the need to establish the context of the citer's work. Not to cite one's opponent would be like reviewing a book without naming the book or its author.

Still another reason for citing, one particularly important in law and other "authoritarian" institutions such as hierarchical churches and totalitarian states (consider the reason for citations to *Mein Kampf* in Nazi Germany or for citations to the works of Marx and Engels in communist societies), is to provide an authoritative basis for a statement in the citing work. I'll call this "authority" citing. In a system of case law, previously decided cases provide a reason independent of analytical power for reaching a particular outcome in the current case, and the citation of such a case is an invocation of that authority. This is true even when the citation seeks to distinguish or overrule the previous case. The citation is motivated by the authority of the previous case, which may have to be deflected or destroyed in order to enable the desired outcome of the current case. But many judicial decisions have an informational rather than an authority-related role; they are cited as shorthand for legal doctrines, cogent arguments, or forceful articulations of relevant ideas or policies. Few judicial citations are "priority" citations, however, because there is no antiplagiarism norm in adjudication. In this respect the situation in law resembles that in literature before creativity became defined as originality (Posner, 1998, pp. 389–405).

A final reason for citing, call it the "celebratory," is midway between informational citing and authority citing. The feature of the cited work that induces the citation is the work's prestige or reputation.[4] By associating it with his own work, the citer enhances the credibility of his work. Because this is a common reason for citing, there is added uncertainty about the meaning to be ascribed to a citation. It can signify an acknowledgement of priority or influence, a useful source of information, a focus of disagreement, an acknowledgment of controlling authority, or the prestige of the cited work or its author. All of these are forms of influence, in a broad sense, and that may be enough to justify lumping them together for purposes of citations studies concerned with measuring influence. But they differ as proxies for quality, and measuring quality is the focus of some citations studies.

This problem, the interpretive problem presented by citation behavior, is related to another problem, the problem of responsible citation behavior, which arises from the distinction between a reason for citing and a motive for citing.[5] Many self-citations, for example, are motivated by a desire for self-aggrandizement, or by sheer laziness—the cost of finding one's own work to cite is less than the cost of finding someone else's. Not all are, though. Indeed, self- and other citations to a person's work might well turn out to be positively correlated at least for heavily cited authors, because the previous work of a productive and influential scholar may be a large part of the knowledge base of his current work. In the case of judicial citations, the Landes study, discussed later, finds a positive correlation between self- and other citations and explains that a judge who writes his own opinions is more likely both to be an influential judge and to cite himself a lot, because he is more familiar with his previous decisions than his law clerks would be if they were writing his opinions.

Resuming the catalog of "impure" motives for citing, I point out that some citations reflect a desire to flatter the author of the cited work, who may be in a position to assist the citer's career or may be a likely journal referee of the cited work. And some scholarly citations are motivated by piety or gratitude, or by a desire to make a display of erudition. I have mentioned the possibility of reciprocal citing. It is even conceivable that in highly competitive fields of scholarship, young scholars especially might be reluctant to cite their peers, and prefer to cite the dead, who are no longer competitors. Most important, because the cost of inaccurate citing usually is low (primarily the cost is being subjected to criticism for miscitation or for failing to find the most apt work to cite), there is much careless citing, and so quantitative studies of citations are bound to contain a lot of "noise." But imperfection of data is nothing new—nor, as we shall see, does it disable useful statistical analysis—and there is some competitive constraint on irresponsible citing because rival scholars have an incentive to expose such practices, unless the irresponsibility merely takes the form of citing to excess.

The heterogeneity problem

Even if all citers were scrupulous and accurate, the heterogeneity of citations would make simple aggregation prone to mislead, even after such obvious sources of distortion as self-citations were removed. Suppose, for example, that an academic department relied on the number of citations to an academic's scholarly writing as a factor in deciding whether to give him tenure. Suppose further that the principal criterion for tenure was originality. The writings of the individual under consideration might have garnered a great many citations, but if they were mostly informational in character—perhaps he had written a series of review articles that provided convenient summaries of previous work—the count of his citations would give a misleading impression of whether he deserved tenure.

This is a greater source of distortion than the possibility that many of the citations to the individual's work are negative. Negligible work is more likely to be ignored than to be cited. A negative citation often indicates that a work has gotten under the skin of the critic, perhaps because it mounts a powerful challenge to established positions or ways of thinking.

The signal, or information, conveyed by a citation, or by a count of citations, varies for still other reasons as well. A newspaper citation to a scholar's work is a better indication of the popular appeal of his work than is a citation in a scholarly journal to that work, but the latter is a better indication of the work's scholarly character. A citation made by a distinguished scholar or appearing in a high-quality journal is better evidence of the quality of the cited work than a citation by an undistinguished scholar or in an undistinguished journal. A citation by the same or a lower court, for which the cited case is authoritative, is a weaker signal of respect or regard for the cited case or its author than a citation by a higher or coequal court, which is not required as a matter of *stare decisis* to follow, distinguish, or otherwise refer to the cited case.

The number of citations to a scholarly work or a judicial opinion may, moreover, reflect adventitious factors, in particular the size of the population of potential citers and the citation conventions of particular disciplines. "The erudite scholar (rightly or wrongly associated with an older Germanic tradition) who displays his learning in his footnotes is hardly recording the strong intellectual influences which have acted upon him. The ostensibly casual scholar (surely trained at Oxbridge) considers citation beyond a name, preferably misspelled, to be a pedantical display" (Stigler and Friedland, 1975, p. 485). Comparisons across fields and, because of growth in the number of journals, over time are therefore difficult to make. Even within a single field differences in specialization can confound citation comparisons; other things being equal, more specialized, applied work is cited less often than more general work (such as a survey article or a theoretical article)—the potential audience is smaller for the former than for the latter. Similarly, theoretical journals tend to be more frequently cited than applied journals, and in particular the "balance of trade"— citations of a journal versus citations by the journal— runs in favor of theoretical and against applied journals (Stigler, 1994). Also, methodological articles, and judicial opinions dealing with procedural issues, tend to be cited more frequently than substantive works because they have a broader domain of applicability.

Differences in the vintages of cited works also make comparison difficult. The older the work, the more time it has had to accumulate citations, but the number of citations is apt to be depressed by shifts in interest away from the topic of the cited work or by the appearance of up-to-date substitutes for it. In economic terms, the stock of knowledge capital created by scholarly or judicial activity, just like a stock of physical capital, both is durable and depreciates. A further problem in interpreting the number of citations to a work is that it may be difficult to distinguish empirically between a work that is no longer cited because it has been totally depreciated and a work that has been so influential that the ideas in it are now referred to without citation to the work and often without mention of the author's name (e.g., the theory of relativity, or the theory of evolution, or the concept of consumer surplus). "An innovator's work is accepted and used by others. The influence may be most powerful when we simply do not cite at all" (Stigler and Friedland, 1975, p. 486). For example, counting citations to the writings of Adam Smith or Jeremy Bentham would be certain to produce an underestimation of their influence—and in Bentham's case for the additional reason that he published little during his lifetime and much of his influence was through personal contact with people who became his followers and transmitted his influence through their own writings.[6]

A point closely related to the last is that differences in citation rates may be magnified because of the information costs of citers, which may fall with the number of times a work is cited (cf. Adler, 1985). The more often the work is cited, the more familiar it becomes, reducing the cost of recalling and locating the work relative to the cost of recalling and locating a less cited and hence less familiar work. This is a kind of network externality, akin to that which makes telephone service more valuable the more subscribers it has or a new word more valuable the more people know its meaning.

Another way to see this is to think of the citer as a shopper among competing "brands." Because no citation royalty is paid to the author of the cited work, the more familiar the brand the cheaper it is to cite it rather than to cite a substitute. John Rawls is thus the standard citation for the concepts of the original position and the veil of ignorance, even though those concepts were explained earlier by John Harsanyi;[7] Harsanyi is less well known than Rawls and so it is "costlier" to cite him. The cost of citing the better-known work is lower not only to the citer, but also to his audience, to which a citation to a familiar work may convey more information. A raw comparison of the number of citations to Rawls and to Harsanyi would thus exaggerate the relative quality, originality, or even influence of the two theorists.

For all the reasons that I have been discussing in this and the preceding section, and for other reasons as well,[8] the use of counts of citations for purposes of evaluation or hypothesis-testing must be approached with caution. But it is equally important to realize that the existence of "noise" in data does not invalidate quantitative analysis. Critics of citations analysis often fail to note that if errors in data are randomly distributed with respect to the variable of interest (such as research quality or impact), they are unlikely to invalidate the conclusions of the study, provided that the data sample is large (Stigler, 1987). A related point is that errors that equally bias both sets of data being compared do not bias the comparison (id., p. 333), and so if, for example, the question is whether a particular scholar or journal was more heavily cited in 1999 than in 1989, many of the errors that might distort the number in each year can be ignored as not affecting the comparison. But, equally clearly, responsible citations analysis requires great care in methods of aggregation, correction, and interpretation. I shall give illustrations of the necessary adjustments in the course of explaining the two main uses of citations analysis that have emerged to date—as a tool of management and as a means of hypothesis testing.[9]

Citations analysis as a management tool

When an enterprise produces goods that are sold in an explicit market, the valuation of its output is straightforward, and generally it is also feasible to determine the contribution of the enterprise's employees and other suppliers to that output. But not all enterprises are of this kind. Two notable exceptions are research universities and appellate courts. A principal output of both types of enterprise is published work that is not sold. This has been thought in some quarters to preclude analyzing the outputs of these institutions in market terms (O'Neill, 1998, pp. 155–57). An economist would be inclined to question this conclusion. Academics and judges, economists are prone to believe, are not much different in basic tastes and drives from other people, and universities and courts are subject to budget constraints that require economizing activity. Academic and judicial productivity is much discussed, and comparisons (across academics, academic departments, courts, judges) are attempted. The problem is one of measurement rather than of fundamental incentives and constraints. If that problem can be solved, the market for professors and judges can be assimilated to normal labor markets. Citations analysis can make a significant contribution to the solution, and this is important for operating in these markets as well as for understanding their operation.

For example, the federal government has for the last 15 years been encouraging its research laboratories to focus more on research having commercial applications. Has the change in policy been effective? A study of government patents found that government research is indeed being cited more frequently in private patents (Jaffe, Fogarty, and Banks, 1998). The Patent Office has strict requirements about citing the "prior art," as it is called, and this provides a basis for believing that counting citations in patents provides meaningful, though not wholly reliable, information about the utility of the cited inventions.[10] The application of this methodology to the evaluation of research programs, academic or otherwise, is straightforward (Brown, 1996; Nederhof and Van Wijk, 1999; Oppenheim, 1997).

In my own work on judicial administration, I have suggested that weighting the number of decisions of a federal court of appeals by the number of citations to those decisions by other courts of appeals, which is to say courts not bound as a matter of *stare decisis* to follow the cited court's decisions, yields a meaningful measure of judicial output. This measure can be used to compare the productivity of the different courts (Gulati and McCauliff, 1998, pp. 198–200; Posner, 1996a, p. 234). It cannot be the complete measure, if only because it implicitly weights unpublished decisions, which are not citable as precedents, at zero, even though they are an important part of the output of modern appellate courts. An unpublished decision resolves a dispute, which is a useful thing to do even though it does not create a citable precedent. Some adjustment should be feasible, however, to yield a total productivity figure. And when productivity is regressed on the different production functions of the different courts, it becomes possible to suggest improvements, as I'll note later.

An even more audacious use of citations as a judicial management tool is to "grade" appellate judges by the number of other-court citations to their opinions. Landes, Lessig, and Solimine, in an ambitious study that I'll call "the Landes study" for the sake of brevity, rank federal appellate judges in just this way (Landes, Lessig, and

Solimine, 1998).[11] There are comparability problems: the judges are appointed at different times and to courts that have different caseloads, and the number of judges as well as the number of cases is changing over time. The authors seek to overcome these problems by regressing other-court citations on variables that include—besides the judge himself—the judge's length of service, his court's caseload, the date on which he was appointed, and other factors that are expected to influence the number of citations that the judge would receive were he of average quality. The coefficient on the judge variable thus indicates how many other-court citations are due to his personal characteristics rather than to the factors that are not judge-specific which influence citations. Since those factors cannot be controlled for perfectly, the ranking that the Landes study produced is at best a rough guide to the relative quality (or influence, or reputation—it is not altogether clear which is being measured) of the judges in the sample. Still, it may well be an improvement over purely qualitative efforts to evaluate appellate judges.

Entire courts can be evaluated similarly. In view of current criticisms that the U.S. Court of Appeals for the Ninth Circuit is weak, perhaps because of its large size (it is almost twice as large as the next largest federal court of appeals), and should be split up or otherwise revamped or reformed, it is natural to inquire how that court fares when this method of evaluation is used. The answer is, not very well. It ranks eleventh out of the 13 federal courts of appeals and the low ranking of the Federal Circuit (which is number 13) is probably due to that court's highly specialized jurisdiction. Among the generalist circuits, the Ninth ranks eleventh out of 12 (the twelfth being the Sixth Circuit). Even the D.C. Circuit, which is also specialized, though less so than the Federal Circuit, outranks the Ninth Circuit (at 10).[12]

Citations analysis is more commonly used to rank scholars than judges (Gordon and Purvis, 1991; Medoff, 1989; Shapiro, 2000; Sen, 1998) and as such is now widely used as a management tool in connection with the hiring and promotion of faculty in research universities (Gray, 1983). This is a natural use of citations analysis because the principal output of the faculty of such universities is published research and the more heavily a research paper is cited, the more influential and important it is likely to be. Again, comparability problems must be overcome; it would be ridiculous to count citations of rival candidates of very different length of service and think that one had made a meaningful comparison, unless perhaps the younger (not necessarily in age, but in length of time in academia) had more citations than the older. But adjustments similar to those made in the Landes study in order to compare the output of different judges should be feasible, and with these adjustments citations analysis becomes a reasonably objective (though it should not be the only) basis for making decisions on hiring, promotion, and salary. The need for an objective basis for such decisions is particularly important in an era in which academic administrators can be forced to defend their personnel decisions in the courts against charges of racial, sexual, or other invidious discrimination.

Citations analysis can similarly be used to evaluate the scholarly impact (presumably correlated with the quality) of scholarly journals and academic presses. This has been in fact one of the most common applications of such analysis (Hodgson and Rothman, 1999; Leibowitz and Palmer, 1984; Tahai and Kelly, 1996). A journal's "impact factor" (conventionally, the number of citations in year t to articles published in the journal in years $t - 1$ and $t - 2$ divided by the number of those articles) can in turn be used to weight a scholar's citations by multiplying the number of citations to his work by the impact factor of the journals in which those citations appear.[13] The aim is to correct objectively for differences in journal, and hence citation, quality. The method only seems to involve double counting. Citations are used to weight the journal, and if it is heavily cited this might seem to imply that articles cited in it will be cited by later journals as well. But that is not necessarily so. Suppose an article by A is cited in an article by B published in heavily cited (hence imputed to be high-quality) journal X. B's article can be expected to be cited more frequently than if it had been published in a lower-quality journal, but articles citing B's article will not necessarily cite articles cited by B, such as A's article. Nevertheless the fact that B cited A is, given that B's article appeared in a high-quality journal, a mark in A's favor.

The impact-factor measure has been criticized as "entirely miss [ing] the archival impact of the journals and giv[ing] much greater weight to those publications of a more ephemeral nature or to those publications more concerned with debates about current issues than with research" (Stigler, 1994, p. 98).[14] So impact-adjusted citations must themselves be adjusted, but with this qualification, they can be used to rank both individual scholars and entire departments more objectively than by raw citation scores (Dusansky and Vernon, 1998, p. 157; Fish, 1998, p. 1077).

The practical utility of citations ranking of scholars is not limited to academic administration, As I have already intimated, in cases in which academics claim to have been discriminated against by the university that employs them, citations analysis can be used to help determine whether the alleged discrimination was invidious or was instead based on the plaintiff's lack of scholarly distinction.[15]

Hypothesis testing with citations

The use of citations analysis in academic research is conceptually distinct from its use in academic or judicial administration but overlaps as a matter of practice. The patent study I cited earlier can be used to evaluate the government's research policy but also to test hypotheses about the economics of technology transfer (Jaffe, Fogarty, and Banks, 1998, pp. 202–3; Jaffe, Trajtenberg, and Henderson, 1993). We have seen that studies of judicial citation practices can be used both to evaluate courts and judges and to test hypotheses about judicial behavior and explain differences in productivity across courts and judges. They can be used to identify and trace academic networks and to chart the rise and decline of rival schools of thought within a discipline (Landes and Posner, 1993).

There are three closely related economic models that can be used to guide research that employs citations analysis: a human capital model, a reputation model, and an information model. All are closely related to the discussion in the first section of this paper of the motives for citation. The motives are assumed to be self-interested, and economic models tease out the implications of assuming rational self-interested action.

I will emphasize the human capital model, which is the most important for reasons that will become clear, and discuss the other two very briefly. In a reputation model (Posner, 1990), emphasis is laid on the fact that reputation is something accorded by the "reputers" to advance their own self-interest, for example their interest in economizing on information costs. This can produce, as I hinted earlier, a "superstar" effect, in which small differences in quality generate huge differences in income, or, in this case, in citations (cf. Rosen, 1981). The sociologist Robert K. Merton argued in this vein that scholars would use an author's reputation as a screening device, and hence tend to cite better-known authors more frequently than was warranted by any actual difference between the quality of their work and that of less well-known authors (Merton, 1968). He called this phenomenon the "Matthew Effect" after the statement in the Gospel according to St. Matthew that to he who has more will be given. Merton's conjecture is supported by a study which finds that journals that use "blind" refereeing (that is, that do not disclose the author's name to the referee) are cited more frequently, after correction for other differences, than nonblind-refereed journals (Laband, 1994).

In a recent paper that compares Web "hits" and newspaper citations to leading legal scholars with citations to these scholars in scholarly journals, Landes and I found a greater superstar effect for celebrities than for scholars (Landes and Posner, 2000). We conjectured that this is a function of the extent of the market. The general public's interest in law is quite limited, and the public demand for the output of legal scholars is therefore easily satisfied by a handful of high-profile figures. The scholarly community has a much broader interest in legal scholarship and therefore values the output of a much larger number of scholars.

In the information model, citations are conceived of as creating a stock of information. The analyst can use the model to illuminate such issues as the geographic diffusion of information, as in the patent study that I cited earlier, and the rate at which the stock depreciates, for example as a function of the generality, and hence adaptability to changing circumstances, of the cited work. A related approach, sociological rather than economic in character, seeks to demarcate schools of thought by identifying patterns of cross-citation (Stigler and Friedland, 1975).

In the standard human capital model used in labor economics, earnings are modeled as a function of the investment in the worker's human capital (that is, his earning capacity). His stock of human capital grows in the initial stages of his working career as a result of on-the-job training and experience. But like other capital, human capital depreciates, and eventually the worker's total stock of human capital declines when new investment falls below the replacement level as the worker approaches retirement. The reason new investment falls eventually is that the shorter the worker's remaining working life, the less time he and his employer have to recover the cost of any new investment.

Earnings (E) and years worked (time, t) are thus related as in

$$E(t) = a + b_1 t_1 - b_2 t_2 \tag{15.1}$$

where $E(t)$ is annual earnings as a function of time (years worked from first job to retirement), a is an earnings component that is independent of investment in human capital and is assumed to be constant over time, b_1 represents an annual increase in earnings brought about by investments in human capital, and $-b_2$ represents an annual reduction in earnings caused by depreciation of the individual's stock of human capital. The peak year of earnings ($t*$) is found by differentiating $E(t)$ with respect to t and setting the result equal to zero (satisfaction of the other conditions for a maximum can be assumed), yielding $t* = b_1/b_2$. An individual reaches his peak year of earnings later the more his earnings are raised by investments in human capital (b_1) and the smaller the effect of length of service (hence imminence of retirement) in reducing his earnings by causing him to invest less in replacing human capital as it depreciates (b_2). If $E(t)$ is replaced by the natural log of $E(t)$, then the coefficients (b_1 and b_2) can be interpreted as rates of growth.

The twist that human capital citations analysis gives to the standard model is to replace earnings with citations. This is an appropriate adjustment in the case of activities in which earnings are not well correlated with output. The federal judiciary provides an excellent example. All judges of the same rank (district judges, circuit judges, and so forth) are paid the same salary, regardless of years of service, reversal rate, number of opinions published, or any other factor that might be used by a private employer to determine a worker's marginal product.

In many universities, too, faculty compensation is on a lockstep basis, and even when it is not, salary differentials are invariably far smaller than any reasonable estimate of differences in the academic output of different members of the faculty.[16] A possible explanation is that an academic's full income includes fame (Stephan, 1996) and so varies across academics in accordance with differences in the quality of their work.[17] This point has been made in distinguishing between science and technology. "Science aims at increasing the stock of knowledge, while the goal of technology is to obtain the private rents that can be earned from this knowledge" (Dasgupta and David, 1987, p. 529). Because the achievement of the scientist's goal depends on complete disclosure, and complete disclosure impedes the obtaining of rents, science must devise an alternative method of compensation. "The rule of priority is a particular form of payment to scientists" (id., p. 531). This can help us understand why the acknowledgment of priority is a norm of scholarship. And the usual form of acknowledgement of priority is citation. However, citations acknowledge other forms of scholarly contribution as well.

The economic model of citations as an earnings substitute recognizes that variance in earnings is not a function just of length of service and investments in human capital. The variable that I labeled *a* represents the other factors that influence output, including quality variables such as intelligence, judgment, and writing skill that are only loosely (and sometimes not at all) related to training or other forms of investment in human capital. Recall that in the Landes study the human capital model was used to predict differences in the output of court of appeals judges, and the residual (unexplained) differences were then used to rank the judges, that is, to determine their relative endowments of *a*.

An alternative method of getting at *a* is to limit the comparison of citations to judges serving on the same court in the same period of time, thus obviating the need to make adjustments for differences in caseload composition and in the dates of the cited works, or to scholars of the same approximate age or length of service. I have used this cruder method of adjustment to verify the superior quality or influence of Benjamin Cardozo and Learned Hand relative to their colleagues on the New York Court of Appeals and U.S. Supreme Court (for Cardozo) and the U.S. Court of Appeals for the Second Circuit (for Hand) (Posner, 1990, pp. 83–90; 1995, pp. 188–92; see also Greely, 1996, pp. 133–50). For broader comparisons, however, the human capital model is indispensable, as it enables correction for differences in the location of a judge or scholar in the life cycle.

We need not view *a* as a black box; the Landes study sought to explain the rankings of federal court of appeals judges by such factors as self-citation, the degree to which the judge's court has a specialized jurisdiction (which would tend to reduce the number of citations by other courts), and whether the judge had attended an elite law school, received a good rating from the American Bar Association when he was evaluated for appointment, or had previous judicial experience (Landes, Lessig, and Solimine, 1998, pp. 320–24). All the factors but the last were found to have a statistically significant relation to the judge's rank, and in the predicted direction.

The study did not find any effect of race or sex on the number of judicial citations. In contrast, a recent study of citations in scholarly journals to legal academics finds that being female or a member of a minority is associated with being cited less frequently after correction for other factors, such as field and length of service. The implication is that affirmative action, which is common in law schools' faculty hiring, leads, as opponents contend, to the hiring of less-qualified minority and female candidates, as measured by their scholarly output once hired. Indeed, the author finds significant discrimination against Jewish males, who other things being equal are cited much more frequently than other legal academics (Merritt, 2000).[18] Of course, the Jewish males might just be better than the other groups. The acid test for discrimination would be to compare the number of citations to marginal Jewish males to the number of citations to the marginal members of other groups; if the first number were higher, implying that the hiring of more Jews would raise the total number of citations to the faculty, this would be evidence of discrimination.

Another recent study of the legal academy finds a negative relation between research output as measured by citations and hiring one's own graduates as distinct from hiring graduates of other law schools (Eisenberg and Wells, 2000). Still another recent study contributes to our knowledge of the legal-academic production function by finding (though on the basis of a very small sample) that scholarship and teaching are net complements rather than substitutes in the production of scholarship (Lindgren and Nagelberg, 2000). My study of the citations output of the federal courts of appeals (Posner, 1996a, pp. 234–36) similarly casts light on the production function of appellate courts, showing for example that the greater the number and length of a court's majority opinions, and the fewer the number of footnotes and of dissenting opinions, the greater will be the number of citations to that court by other courts. Footnotes in judicial opinions tend to confuse the reader, and a dissenting opinion undermines the majority opinion not only by indicating a lack of unanimity but also by expressing criticisms of the outcome that the majority would have preferred to pass over in silence.

The study also found that citation-weighted output fell as the number of judges on the court rose, which is consistent with the evidence mentioned earlier regarding the Ninth Circuit. Further light is cast on this issue by regressing the other-court citations data in the Landes study on the number of judgeships per circuit. The result is a negative correlation that barely misses statistical significance at the conventional 5% level. (The *t* statistic is -2.091, and the r^2 is .33.) This is additional evidence that increasing the number of judges of an appellate court reduces the quality of the court's decisions.

The Landes study was limited to judges of the same court system (allowing for some differences in specialization), and my studies have been limited to judges of the same court or to courts of the same system (the federal courts of appeals, again). When citations to heterogeneous courts are aggregated, citation totals may still be meaningful as measures of influence, but they cease to be meaningful as measures of quality. The same is true of studies of scholarly citations. Comparing total scholarly citations across all legal scholars (Shapiro, 2000) may be a valid measure of influence, but it cannot be a valid measure of quality, since differences in citations across fields may reflect differences in the size of fields and in the number of journals in different fields, and even citation conventions, rather than differences in perceived quality. But aggregating scholarly citations by field over time is a valid method of charting the rise and fall of different fields, for example (in law) economic analysis, feminist jurisprudence, and doctrinal analysis.[19] For that matter, comparison of citations across fields is meaningful if what one is interested in is the relative size of different fields; the amount of citation activity is one measure of the amount of research in or knowledge produced by a field.

Treating a body of judicial opinions as a capital stock invites attention to the depreciation of precedent, a topic that Landes and I addressed in the first economic study of legal citations (Landes and Posner, 1976). The analogy to physical capital is here quite close. A specialized machine can be expected to obsolesce more quickly than one that can be adapted to different tasks, since the former is less adaptable to change. Similarly, the more general a precedent is, the less rapidly it is likely to depreciate. And just as a sturdy machine can be expected to depreciate less rapidly (other things being equal) than a fragile one, so the more authoritative the court (for example, the Supreme Court relative to a lower federal court), the more slowly the precedents it produces are likely to depreciate, as our study indeed found. We can also expect the depreciation rate to be higher, the greater the rate of legal change—and so I found in a comparison of English and American cases (Posner, 1996b). And a big change in law, such as the abolition of the general federal common law by the *Erie* decision,[20] can have a dramatic effect in obsoleting precedent (Landes and Posner, 1980).

The age profile of citations is relevant to the study of scholarship, including legal scholarship, as well as judicial behavior. Other things being equal, the half-life (or other measure of decay) of citations to scholarly work and scholarly journals is shorter the more progressive the discipline (or subdiscipline, such as economic analysis of law, critical legal studies, or feminist jurisprudence) in the sense that it is continuously generating new research that yields findings that supersede earlier findings. But citation half-life is longer the more rapidly the number and size of the discipline's publication outlets are growing. The reason for the latter, less obvious effect is that a rapid expansion of outlets creates more opportunities for older articles to be cited, assuming there is some citation lag (in part because of the Matthew Effect—the new journal is not as heavily cited as the old until it accrues a reputation) so that the articles in the new outlets will not be cited immediately (Abt, 1998).

The net depreciation of human capital is a function not only of the depreciation rate but also of the rate of new investment. That rate falls off not only because the expected return is truncated by retirement but also because of the aging process. Judging is a famously geriatric profession, especially in the common law countries, such as England and the United States. In part this is an artifact of the lateral-entry method of filling judgeships in these countries: the older the average age of entry, the older the average age of the profession is bound to be. But another possibility is that in a judicial system which relies heavily on precedent—a backward-looking mode of decision making—aging will take a lesser toll on ability than in a profession such as mathematics that emphasizes the manipulation of abstract models.[21] This hypothesis can be tested by relating citations to the age of the judge whose decision is being cited; I have done this and found little evidence of a negative aging effect before the age of 80 (Posner, 1995, pp. 182–96).

Conclusion

To summarize, citations analysis guided by economic theory offers substantial promise of improving our knowledge of the legal system, in particular its academic and judicial subsystems. Much has been done already, as I have tried to show; much remains to be done, if I am correct that citations analysis is a versatile, rigorous, practical—and, increasingly, an inexpensive—tool of empirical research.

Notes

1   Many of the legal citations studies are cited in this paper. Several appear in the conference volume "Interpreting Legal Citations" (*Journal of Legal Studies*, supplement, 2000). The papers given at the conference covered a wide range of topics, including law school rankings, whether lateral hires to law school faculties are better scholars than faculty members promoted from within, the growth of nonlegal citations in judicial opinions, and the application of fractal analysis to citations.

2   These are primarily the indexes for the natural sciences (Science Citation Index), social sciences (Social Sciences Citation Index), and the arts and humanities (Arts and Humanities Citation Index) published by the Institute for Scientific Information. In addition, for law—which has a long and rich history of citation counting; see Shapiro (1992)—the West Publishing Company has excellent computerized databases of both judicial opinions and legal articles. The original legal citations service, Shepard's Citations, was in fact the inspiration for the ISI indexes (Baird and Oppenheim, 1994, pp. 2, 3). The World Wide Web is also usable for citations analysis; search engines such as AltaVista can be used to count "hits" to named individuals, books, or articles. For uses of the Web in this way, see Landes and Posner (2000) and Neth (1998).

3   The literature of citations analysis is by now vast, and I will not attempt exhaustive citation. The pioneers were sociologists of science. See, for example, Merton (1973). For a book-length discussion, now unfortunately rather out of date, by the founder of the ISI, see Garfield (1979); it is somewhat updated, however, in Garfield (1998). Baird and Oppenheim (1994) give a good overview of the field; for reference to science citations, see Schoonbaert and Roelants (1996).

4   There is an analogy to celebrity endorsements of products. See Agrawal and Kamakura (1995).

5   For a rare study of the motives for citing, see Wang and White (1995).

6   The problems of using citations analysis to gauge intellectual influence are well discussed in Zuckerman (1987).

7 As acknowledged, somewhat grudgingly as it seems to me, in Rawls (1971, p. 137, n. 11), citing Harsanyi (1953, p. 434).

8 Chapman (1989, pp. 336, 339–41) lists 25 problems with using citation data published by the ISI (see note 3 above) to estimate the quality or impact of research. I have discussed the principal ones in the text, but it may be useful to list all 25 to give the flavor of the critical literature. In Chapman's words, "Some journals not considered"; "Exclusion of citations in books"; "Bias toward applied research"; "Psychology is in [both] the SCI [Science Citation Index] and SSCI [Social Sciences Citation Index]"; "Referencing [i.e., citing] conventions"; "Inclusion of letters, abstracts, book reviews"; "Prestige of publication outlets"; "One 'citation' even if there is repeated reference to the work"; "First-authors only [i.e., only the name of the first-listed author to a coauthored work is indexed]"; "Cross-disciplinary comparisons; and psychology's multi-dimensionality"; "Comparisons of individuals; and 'straight' versus 'complete' counts"; "Social factors influence choice"; " 'Stars' are overwhelming"; "Name-initial homographs"; "Bias against some married women [if they have published under more than one name]"; "Bias against newcomers"; "Few to cite in a narrow specialty; and self-citations"; "One person—several alphabetical entries"; "Human errors at ISI"; "Obliteration by incorporation"; "Methods/recipe papers—spuriously inflated citations?"; "Citation does not necessarily denote approval"; "Citation without knowledge"; "Quantity is not quality"; "Citations reflect existing recognition." See also Cronin (1984, pp. 63–73), and MacRoberts and MacRoberts (1986). Chapman (1989, p. 342) acknowledges that some of the criticism of citations analysis may be due to sour grapes on the part of scholars who discover that they are not heavily cited.

9 I do not, however, discuss efforts to develop objective measures of citation content analysis. See, for example, Swales (1986).

10 The authors tried to verify the accuracy of the citations, and found that 75% were meaningful, the rest essentially noise (Jaffe, Fogarty, and Banks, 1998, p. 202). Baird and Oppenheim (1994, p. 7) estimate that at least 20% of citations are erroneous.

11 This is not the only focus of their study; I discuss other aspects of it later. For a somewhat similar study, but of Supreme Court Justices, see Kosma (1998).

12 Landes, Lessig, and Solimine (1998, p. 318 [Table 5], p. 277 [Table 1], p. 332). Using a somewhat different sample, however, the Landes study shows the Ninth Circuit receiving an average number of other-court citations (Landes, Lessig, and Solimine, 1998, p. 331 [Table A4]). Other quantitative measures of judicial performance support a negative evaluation of the Ninth Circuit. See Posner (2000).

13 See, for a critical discussion of this procedure, Anonymous (1998).

14 For a striking example, see Perdew and Tipler (1996, pp. 15, 97).

15 Cases in which citations analysis has been used for this purpose include *Tagatz v. Marquette University,* 861 F2d 1040, 1042 (7th Cir, 1988); *Weinstein v. University of Illinois,* 811 F.2d 1091, 1093 (7th Cir., 1987); *Demuren v. Old Dominion University,* 33 F. Supp. 2d 469, 481 (E.D. Va., 1999), and *Fisher v. Vassar College,* 852 F. Supp. 1193, 1199-2001 (S.D.N.Y., 1992), overruled on other grounds, 70 F.3d 1420 (2d Cir., 1995), modified, 114 F.3d 1332 (2d Cir., 1997) (en banc).

16 Nevertheless, there is evidence that number of citations to an academic's work is a significant predictor of his salary. See, for example, Sauer (1988) and Diamond (1986). This is presumably because scholarly fame is positively correlated with the value of the scholar's output.

17   Empirical evidence for this conjecture in the case of economists is presented in Levy (1988).

18   That is not, however, Merritt's interpretation of her data. A different study (Kolpin and Singell, 1996), also employing citations as a proxy for quality, finds discrimination against women by economics departments.

19   In Landes and Posner (1993, p. 424), we concluded that

> the influence of economics on law was growing at least through the 1980s (it is too early [in 1993] to speak about the 1990s), though the rate of growth may have slowed beginning in the mid-1980s; that the growth in the influence of economics on law exceeded that of any other interdisciplinary or untraditional approach to law; and that the traditional approach [of legal scholarship]—what we call "doctrinal analysis"—was in decline over this period relative to interdisciplinary approaches in general and the economic approach in particular.

20   *Erie R.R. v. Tompkins,* 304 U.S. 64 (1938).

21   Psychologists distinguish between "fluid intelligence," the ability to manipulate abstract symbols, and "crystallized intelligence," the ability to work from a long-established knowledge base, such as knowledge of one's language.

References

Abt, Helmut A. 1998. "Why Some Papers Have Long Citation Lifetimes," 395 *Nature* 756–57.

Adler, Moshe. 1985. "Stardom and Talent," 75 *American Economic Review* 208–12.

Agrawal, Jagdish, and Wagner A. Kamakura. 1995. "The Economic Worth of Celebrity Endorsers: An Event Study Analysis," 59 *Journal of Marketing* 56–62.

Anonymous. 1998. "Citation Data: The Wrong impact?" 1 *Nature Neuroscience* 641–42.

Baird, Laura M., and Charles Oppenheim. 1994. "Do Citations Matter?" 20 *Journal of Information Science* 1–15.

Brown, Lawrence D. 1996. "Influential Accounting Articles, Individuals, Ph.D. Granting Institutions and Faculties: A Citational Analysis," 21 *Accounting, Organizations and Society* 723–54.

Chapman, Anthony J. 1989. "Assessing Research: Citation-Count Shortcomings," 2 *The Psychologist: Bulletin of the British Psychological Society* 336–44.

Cronin, Blaise. 1984. *The Citation Process: The Role and Significance of Citations in Scientific Communication.* London: Taylor Graham.

Dasgupta, Partha, and Paul A. David. 1987. "Information Disclosure and the Economics of Technology," in George R. Feiwel, ed., *Arrow and the Ascent of Modern Economic Theory.* New York: New York University Press.

Diamond, Arthur M., Jr. 1986. "What Is a Citation Worth?" 21 *Journal of Human Resources* 200–15.

Dusansky, Richard, and Clayton J. Vernon. 1998. "Rankings of U.S. Economics Departments," 12 *Journal of Economic Perspectives* 157–70.

Eisenberg, Theodore, and Martin T. Wells. 2000. "Inbreeding in Law School Hiring: Assessing the Performance of Faculty Hired from Within," 29 *Journal of Legal Studies* 369–88.

Feist, Gregory J. 1997. "Quantity, Quality, and Depth of Research as Influences on Scientific Eminence: Is Quantity Most Important?" 10 *Creativity Research Journal* 325–35.

Fish, Raymond P. H. 1998. "What Are the Research Standards for Full Professor of Finance?" 63 *Journal of Finance* 1073–79.

Garfield, Eugene. 1979. *Citation Indexing—Its Theory and Application in Science, Technology, and Humanities.* New York: Wiley.

———. 1998. "From Citation Indexes to Informetrics: Is the Tail Now Wagging the Dog?" 48 *Libri* 67–80.

Gordon, Michael E., and Julia E. Purvis. 1991. "Journal Publication Records as a Measure of Research Performance in Industrial Relations," 45 *Industrial and Labor Relations Review* 194–201.

Grafton, Anthony. 1997. *The Footnote: A Curious History.* Cambridge, MA: Harvard University Press.

Gray, Philip Howard. 1983. "Using Science Citation Analysis to Evaluate Administrative Accountability in Salary Variance," 38 *American Psychologist* 116–17.

Greely, Henry T. 1996. "Quantitative Analysis of a Judicial Career: A Case Study of Judge John Minor Wisdom," 53 *Washington and Lee Law Review* 99, 133–50.

Gulati, Mitu, and C. M. A. McCauliff. 1998. "On Not Making Law," 61 *Law and Contemporary Problems* 157–227.

Harsanyi, John C. 1953. "Cardinal Utility in Welfare Economics and in the Theory of Risk-Taking," 61 *Journal of Political Economy* 434–35.

Hodgson, Geoffrey M., and Harry Rothman. 1999. "The Editors and Authors of Economics Journals: A Case of Institutional Oligopoly?" 109 *Economic Journal* F165–F186.

Jaffe, Adam B., Michael S. Fogarty, and Bruce A. Banks. 1998. "Evidence from Patents and Patent Citations on the Impact of NASA and Other Federal Labs on Commercial Innovation," 46 *Journal of Industrial Economics* 183–205.

Jaffe, Adam B., Manuel Trajtenberg, and Rebecca Henderson. 1993. "Geographic Localization of Knowledge Spillovers as Evidenced by Patent Citations," 108 *Quarterly Journal of Economics* 577–98.

Kolpin, Van W., and Larry D. Singell, Jr. 1996. "The Gender Composition and Scholarly Performance of Economics Departments: A Test for Employment Discrimination," 49 *Industrial and Labor Relations Review* 408–23.

Kosma, Montgomery N. 1998. "Measuring the Influence of Supreme Court Justices," 27 *Journal of Legal Studies* 333–72.

Laband, David N. 1994. "A Citation Analysis of the Impact of Blinded Peer Review," 272 *JAMA (Journal of the American Medical Association)* 147–49.

Landes, William M., Lawrence Lessig, and Michael E. Solimine. 1998. "Judicial Influence: A Citation Analysis of Federal Courts of Appeals Judges" 27 *Journal of Legal Studies* 271–332.

Landes, William M., and Richard A. Posner. 1976. "Legal Precedent: A Theoretical and Empirical Analysis," 19 *Journal of Law and Economics* 249–307.

———. 1980. "Legal Change, Judicial Behavior, and the Diversity Jurisdiction," 9 *Journal of Legal Studies* 367–86.

———. 1993. "The Influence of Economics on Law: A Quantitative Study," 36 *Journal of Law and Economics* 385–424.

———. 2000. "Citations, Age, Fame, and the Web," 29 *Journal of Legal Studies* 319–44.

Lange, Lydia L., and P. A. Frensch. 1999. "Gaining Scientific Recognition by Position: Does Editorship Increase Citation Rates?" 44 *Scientometrics* 459–86.

Leibowitz, S. J., and J. P. Palmer. 1984. "Assessing the Relative Impacts of Economics Journals," 22 *Journal of Economic Literature* 77–88.

Levy, David M. 1988. "The Market for Fame and Fortune," 20 *History of Political Economy* 615–25.

Lindgren, James, and Allison Nagelberg. 2000. "The False Conflict between Scholarship and Teaching," Unpublished, Northwestern University School of Law.

MacRoberts, Michael H., and Barbara R. MacRoberts. 1986. "Quantitative Measures of Communication in Science: A Study of the Formal Level," 16 *Social Studies of Science* 151–72.

McAllister, Paul R., Richard C. Anderson, and Francis Narin. 1980. "Comparison of Peer and Citation Assessment of the Influence of Scientific Journals," 31 *Journal of the American Society for Information Science* 147–152.

Medoff, Marshall H. 1989. "The Ranking of Economists," 20 *Journal of Economic Education* 405–15.

Merritt, Deborah Jones. 2000. "Scholarly Influence in a Diverse Legal Academy: Race, Sex, and Citation Counts," 29 *Journal of Legal Studies* 345–68.

Merton, Robert K. 1968. "The Matthew Effect in Science," 159 *Science* 56–63.

———. 1973. *The Sociology of Science: Theoretical and Empirical Investigations.* Norman W. Storer, ed. Chicago: University of Chicago Press.

Nederhof, J., and E. Van Wijk. 1999. "Profiling Institutes: Identifying High Research Performance and Social Relevance in the Social and Behavioral Sciences," 44 *Scientometrics* 487–506.

Neth, Marcy. 1998. "Citation Analysis and the Web," 17 *Art Documentation* 29–33.

O'Neill, John. 1998. *The Market: Ethics, Knowledge and Politics.* New York: Routledge.

Oppenheim, Charles. 1997. "The Correlation between Citation Counts and the 1992 Research Assessment Exercise Ratings for British Research in Genetics, Anatomy and Archeology," 53 *Journal of Documentation* 477–87.

Perdew, John P., and Frank J. Tipler. 1996. "Ranking the Physics Departments: Use Citation Analysis," *Physics Today,* October, 15.

Posner, Richard A. 1990. *Cardozo: A Study in Reputation.* Chicago: University of Chicago Press.

Posner, Richard A. 1995. *Aging and Old Age.* Chicago: University of Chicago Press.

———. 1996a. *The Federal Courts: Challenge and Reform.* Cambridge, MA: Harvard University Press.

———. 1996b. *Law and Legal Theory in England and America.* New York: Oxford University Press.

———. 1998. *Law and Literature.* Cambridge, MA: Harvard University Press.

———. 2000. "Is the Ninth Circuit Too Large? A Statistical Study of Judicial Quality," 29 *Journal of Legal Studies* 711–19.

Rawls, John. 1971. *A Theory of Justice.* Cambridge, MA: Belknap Press of Harvard University Press.

Rosen, Sherwin. 1981. "The Economics of Superstars," 71 *American Economic Review* 845–58.

Sauer, Raymond D. 1988. "Estimates of the Returns to Quality and Coauthorship in Economic Academia," 96 *Journal of Political Economy* 855–66.

Schoonbaert, Dirk, and Gilbert Roelants. 1996. "Citation Analysis for Measuring the Value of Scientific Publications: Quality Assessment Tool or Comedy of Errors?" 1 *Tropical Medicine and International Health* 739–52.

Sen, B. K. 1998. "Ranking of Scientists—A New Approach," 54 *Journal of Documentation* 622–28.

Shapiro, Fred R. 1992. "Origins of Bibliometrics, Citation Indexing, and Citation Analysis: The Neglected Legal Literature," 43 *Journal of American Society for Information Science* 337–39.

———. 2000. "The Most-Cited Legal Scholars," 29 *Journal of Legal Studies* 409–26.

So, C.Y. K. 1998. "Citation Rankings versus Expert Judgment in Evaluating Communication Scholars: Effects of Research Specialty Size and Individual Prominence," 41 *Scientometrics* 325–33.

Stephan, Paula E. 1996. "The Economics of Science," 34 *Journal of Economic Literature* 1199–1235.

Stigler, George J., and Claire Friedland. 1975. "The Citation Practices of Doctorates in Economics," 83 *Journal of Political Economy* 477–507.

Stigler, Stephen M. 1987. "Precise Measurement in the Face of Error: A Comment on MacRoberts and MacRoberts," 17 *Social Studies of Science* 332–34.

———. 1994. "Citation Patterns in the Journals of Statistics and Probability," 9 *Statistical Science* 94–108.

Swales, John. 1986. "Citation Analysis and Discourse Analysis," 7 *Applied Linguistics* 39–56.

Tahai, Alireza, and G. Wayne Kelly. 1996. "An Alternative View of Citation Patterns of Quantitative Literature Cited by Business and Economic Researchers," 27 *Journal of Economic Education* 263.

Wang, Pei Ling, and Marilyn Domas White. 1995. "A Qualitative Study of Scholars' Citation Behavior," 33 *Proceedings of the 59th ASIS Annual Meeting* 255–61.

Wright, Richard A. 1994. "The Effect of Editorial Appointments on the Citations of Sociology Journal Editors, 1970–1989," 25 *American Sociologist* 40–45.

Zuckerman, Harriet. 1987. "Citation Analysis and the Complex Problem of Intellectual Influence," 12 *Scientometrics* 329–38.

PART 6

Efficiency of the common law: myth or reality

Introduction

T HE CLAIM that common law systems are efficient, that they generate efficient outcomes either directly or indirectly, either consciously or unconsciously, is an old one – as old as law and economics itself, Coase having mentioned it as early as 1960. However, one should not conclude that there is no need to dwell on what could be past and out-dated issues. The question of the efficiency of legal systems remains an issue of debate: new models are proposed or old ones revised and refined and empirical tests produced. It seems difficult to find definite answers. Thus, on the one hand, one finds claims of a "mirage" (Rizzo, 1980) of efficiency and an assertion that the available evidence in favor of efficiency is "porous" at best (Webster, 2004, p. 40). On the other hand, there are those who have faith in efficiency and trust the empirical evidence that shows it. The question is far from settled and is an important part of law and economics/the economic analysis of law, it being necessary to present the models developed on this topic. In order to do this, let us refer to the distinction proposed by one of the first to contribute to the debate, Paul Rubin (2005). Rubin distinguishes between micro- and macro-efficiency (or systemic efficiency): micro-efficiency can be measured at the level of specific rules while macro-efficiency is evaluated at a more general level, the level of the entire economy.

Micro-efficiency

Supply side models

Supply side models insist on the role of judges in the tendency of common law systems to be efficient. The argument Posner made in this regard is that judges behave as any other economic agents – as we have noted earlier, they are rational utility maximizers. Therefore, Posner assumes, judges have a "taste" or a "preference" for efficiency. They tend to promote it in each of their decisions. In addition, the tendency towards efficiency can be reinforced, especially in common law systems, by the role of precedent. Given this, the judges of the common law behave "impartially" and "neutrally" – the rules they produce are not biased towards the interests of litigants or towards those of rent-seeking groups; in addition, they are also neutral in terms of redistribution because they cannot redistribute wealth through their decisions.

That judges have a preference for efficiency could be admitted, at least in certain cases, but it remains hard to prove systematically, even through empirical studies. This would imply a systematic analysis of past cases to see whether or not judges made an efficient decision, and would require a definition of efficiency and a way to measure it for each decision. No judge can pride himself on being a central planner: the required knowledge to select the most efficient rules and, after that, to evaluate the consequences of his choices, exceed his capacities. At the end of this section, we will see that efficiency of the legal system can be measured but *globally* and therefore *indirectly* as the efficiency of an economic system. It is far more difficult to measure efficiency at the individual level. In order to be more efficient, judges have to be capable of anticipating and evaluating the consequences of their decision for the whole of society and to implement this in their decisions: a highly improbable scenario (Aranson, 1992).

Furthermore, the impartiality of judicial decision making can be questioned. It can be shown that the influence of pressure groups on rule making is a reality, with the recent literature on anti-trust laws illustrating the problem. Similarly, in contrast to what Posner assumed, judges in the common law do have "strong tastes for distributional goals" (Zywicki, 2003, p. 14). In other words, Posner's supply side model does not convincingly justify the claim that common law *is* efficient or *should* promote efficiency. This result can be complemented by the results obtained in the models based on "cascades" or "bandwagon" effects: because judges use past cases, there exists a path-dependency in legal decision making that may create too much stability or inertia. A legal system may then remain locked in a situation in which inefficient rules prevail (see Ogus, 2002; Harnay and Marciano, 2004).

Demand side models

In order to save the efficiency argument, one may first envisage demand side models. This is the avenue chosen in the late 1970s by Rubin (1977) and Priest (1977) who develop models based on the assumption of "selective litigation". This means that the evolution of the common law depends on or results from the selective actions of private litigants. Thus, according to Rubin, disputants will more likely litigate when the rule they are concerned with is inefficient, and are less likely to do so when the rule is efficient. For Rubin, this comes from the fact that parties have an incentive to resort to litigation because or when they know that they will have to use the same rule again in the future and anticipate the economic rents that they will gain from using it. According to Priest, this assumption is not necessary: he proposed an extension of Rubin's model in which the incentive for litigation results from the costs that inefficient rules impose on the parties. Then, efficient rules, being less costly, are not litigated while inefficient rules, which are expensive, are litigated and tend to disappear. In both models, a process of natural selection eliminates inefficient rules.

Once again, these models are not without limits. Efficiency depends on the selection of the disputes, or the rules, that will be litigated. This is a problem for two reasons. First, it is far from obvious that parties use courts to settle their disputes when rules are inefficient, which was Rubin's 1977 argument. On the contrary, parties tend to prefer out-of-court settlement even when rules are inefficient (Landes, 1971; Gould, 1973; Tullock, 1971, 1997; Webster, 2004). Second, and a consequence of the preceding remark, individuals may use a strategic criterion to select when to litigate or when to settle (see Priest and Klein, 1984; Bailey and Rubin, 1994). Recently, Fon and Parisi (2003) have extended these models. They take into account the ideological preferences of judges, and show that ideology influences the decision making process and creates a bias in the evolution of rules. Their result echoes the ideas which, among others, Ogus (2002) has put forward on the capacity of judges to behave as a pressure group and to influence the evolution of legal rules. The conclusion Cooter and Kornhauser reached in 1980 is apparently still valid: there are no mechanisms that guarantee the evolution of common law towards greater efficiency.

The role of institutions

Demand side models are also inexpert in demonstrating that common law *is* efficient. It may then be the case, as Zywicki (2003) argues, that a more general model has to be built, in which institutions are explicitly taken into account. The claim is that the efficiency of a legal system depends on the institutional mechanisms that exist and that these constrain both the demand and the supply side of the market, leading the parties to litigate inefficient rules and judges to implement efficient ones. From the perspective of an efficient institutional framework, one of the most important features that a legal system must possess is its capacity to move legal decision making downwards, towards the individuals, and to organize competition among local courts. Therefore, an increase in the degree of decentralization, i.e. in the number of local courts, favors efficiency. In other words, the more common law systems look like customary ones, the more efficient they are. Zywicki argues that his condition was met in the past, until the middle of nineteenth century (on this see also Mulligan, 2004, or Rubin, 1982), but that the institutions of the common law evolved. The capacity of the system to produce efficient rules was eroded and the efficiency of the common law decreased over the years.

Macro-efficiency of common law as systems of rules

The efficiency of common law can be discussed at a second, higher level, which is labelled "macro-efficiency" by Rubin to designate the efficiency of the entire legal system rather than that of specific legal rules. Rubin excludes the analyses, in particular those of Posner, of wealth-maximization and Hicks-Kaldor efficiency, though these analyses undoubtedly have a macro dimension. It thus can be said that Rubin excludes the works that focus on maximization and Pareto efficiency.

From this undoubtedly Hayekian perspective, the economic efficiency of a legal system is a consequence of its social or organizational efficiency: a legal system is (macro-)efficient because and when it allows an efficient coordination of the individual plans of action – in other words, it promotes order – and then *as a consequence* generates economic efficiency. Then, why would common law be efficient? Because it consists of a set of rules and of a legal organization which offers a high level of protection to individual property rights (including intellectual property rights) and individual freedom and, as a counterpart, it limits the capacity of governments to coerce.

The above arguments were empirically tested and supported by time-series and cross-section analyses. Among those studies, one must distinguish the set works gathered under the label "Law and Finance" (La Porta, Lopez de Silanes, and Shleifer, 1999, 2006, 2008; La Porta, Lopez de Silanes, Shleifer and Vishny, 1997, 1998). These are recent analyses that are important because of their "policy" or "political" impact; in particular, because they were promoted by the World Bank in the reports *Doing Business: Benchmarking Business Regulations* (see www.doingbusiness.org, where we are told that "The Doing Business project ... provides objective measures of business regulations and their enforcement across 178 economies and selected cities at the subnational and regional level"). The "Law and Finance" studies use an impressive amount of empirical analyses to evidence the impact of legal rules on the financial development and the growth path of different countries, and to show that Common law countries are more efficient than civil law and socialist law countries. Unfortunately, other empirical works have shown that there is no strong correlation between legal origin and financial development, higher income or faster growth, or even efficient governments (see Musacchio, 2007; Voigt, 2005, for recent studies).

This lack of definite evidence with regard to the macro-efficiency of Common law systems may mean that mechanisms – other than the origin of legal rules – exist that affect economic performance. The latter explanation corresponds to what Salmon (2005, 2006) suggests when he analyses the role yardstick competition plays in the economic results of various legal systems. Alternatively, it may be that the definition of legal systems retained in these analyses is not precise enough. In effect, one must not forget that "law and finance" analyses rest on a crucial assumption: there exist legal traditions, or legal origins or legal families, that are stable over time and that therefore can be used as important categories to explain economic development. However, as stressed earlier, the boundaries between legal traditions are less clear than they were years ago and if a distinction between common law and civil or statute law countries may be maintained for explanatory purposes, it should not be overemphasized. To put it differently, a rigid classification of countries in families may be inaccurate in helping us understand the determinants of economic growth. Other, more precise, criteria are needed that would help to characterize the genuine differences that exist between legal systems and that could then be tested with regard to growth and efficiency (see Acemoglu and Johnson, 2005; Siems, 2007; Voigt, 2005). In particular, judicial independence may be a particularly important factor in explaining variations of income and economic growth. In this respect, Lars Feld and Stefan Voigt (2003, 2004) have shown that countries belonging to the family of socialist systems of law have a significant (negative) impact on growth rates.

References

Summary

The idea that common law legal systems are efficient is as old as law and economics – that is, even older that Director or Coase and the other founders of this tradition. The issue received revived attention in the 70s and the debate about the efficiency of the common law began to take shape. This was initially structured around Posner's positive and normative claims – that the common law *is* and *should be* efficient – and also around the evolutionary arguments used to explain the efficiency of the common law. In effect, in the mid-1970s, many economists interested in law and economics were attracted by neo-Darwinian theories, using the concept of natural selection to explain the evolution of legal rules towards more efficiency: efficient rules survive; they eliminate other, inefficient rules (Rubin, 1977; Priest, 1977; Goodman, 1978; Landes and Posner, 1979; or Hirshleifer, 1982). The models were largely discussed and criticized (see for instance, Cooter and Kornhauser, 1980, and Rizzo, 1980) but a stream of literature nonetheless developed to prove or to qualify the "efficiency of the common law" thesis. From this perspective, Rubin's 2005 article is illuminating for two reasons: first, it surveys the different types of models that have been provided to explain the efficiency of the Common Law; second, he concludes that the Common Law *was* efficient (see also Rubin, 1982); a conclusion that was also reached by Zywicki (2003) and Webster (2004). The first provides a highly original demonstration of its main arguments, taking institutions into account. The second shows that, in contrast to received wisdom, parties tend to choose out-of-court settlements independently of the efficiency of rules.

Further reading

Acemoglu, Daron and Simon Johnson. 2005. "Unbundling Institutions", *Journal of Political Economy,* 113 (5), pp. 949–995.

Aranson, Petere H. 1992. "The Common Law as Central Economic Planning", *Constitutional Political Economy,* 3 (3), pp. 289–319.

Bailey, Martin J. and Paul H. Rubin, "A Positive Theory of Legal Change", *International Review of Law and Economics,* 14, pp. 467–477.

Boettke, Peter J. and Robert Subrick. 2002. "Rule Of Law, Development, And Human Capabilities", in "The Rule of Law, Freedom, and Prosperity", *Supreme Court Economic Review,* edited by Todd J. Zywicki, Vol. 10.

Cooter, Robert and Lewis Kornhauser. 1980. "Can Litigation Improve the Law without the Help of Judges?", *Journal of Legal Studies,* 9, pp. 139–163.

Feld, Lars and Stefan Voigt. 2003. "Economic Growth and Judicial Independence: Cross Country Evidence Using a New Set of Indicators", *European Journal of Political Economy,* 19 (3), pp. 497–527.

Feld, Lars and Stefan Voigt. 2004. "Making Judges Independent – Some Proposals Regarding the Judiciary", CESifo Working Paper Series No. 1260, available at: http://ssrn.com/abstract=597721.

Fon, Vincy and Francesco Parisi. 2003. "Litigation and the Evolution of Legal Remedies: A Dynamic Model", *Public Choice,* 116 (3–4), pp. 419–433.

Goodman, John C. 1978. "An Economic Theory of the Evolution of Common Law", *Journal of Legal Studies,* 7 (2), pp. 393–406.

Gould, John P. 1973. "The Economics of Legal Conflicts", *Journal of Legal Studies*, 2 (2), pp. 279–300.

Harnay, Sophie and Alain Marciano. 2004. "Judicial conformity versus dissidence: an economic analysis of judicial precedent", *International Review of Law and Economics*, 23, pp. 405–420.

Hirshleifer, Jack. 1982. "Evolutionary models in economics and law", *Research in Law and Economics*, 4, pp. 1–60.

Klerman, Daniel. 2004. "Jurisdictional Competition and the Evolution of the Common Hypothesis", *Australian Journal of Legal History*, 8 (1), available at: www.austlii.edu.au/au/journals/AJLH/2004/1.html.

La Porta, Rafael, Florencio Lopez-de-Silanes, and Andrei Shleifer. 1999. "Corporate Ownership around the World", *Journal of Finance*, 54 (2), pp. 471–517.

La Porta, Rafael, Florencio Lopez-de-Silanes, and Andrei Shleifer. 2006. "What Works in Securities Laws?", *Journal of Finance*, 61 (1), pp. 1–32.

La Porta, Rafael, Florencio Lopez-de-Silanes, and Andrei Shleifer. 2008. "The Economic Consequences of Legal Origins", *Journal of Economic Literature*, 46 (2), pp. 285–332.

La Porta, Rafael, Florencio Lopez-de-Silanes, Andrei Shleifer, and Robert Vishny. 1997. "Legal Determinants of External Finance", *Journal of Finance*, 52 (3), pp. 1131–1150.

La Porta, Rafael, Florencio Lopez-de-Silanes, Andrei Shleifer, and Robert Vishny. 1998. "Law and Finance", *Journal of Political Economy*, 106 (6), pp. 1113–1155.

La Porta, Rafael, Florencio Lopez-de-Silanes, Andrei Shleifer, and Robert Vishny. 2000. "Investor Protection and Corporate Governance", *Journal of Financial Economics*, 58 (1), pp. 1–25.

Landes, William M. 1971. "An Economic Analysis of the Courts", *Journal of Law and Economics*, 14 (1), pp. 61–107.

Landes, William M. and Richard A. Posner. 1979. "Adjudication as a Private Good", *Journal of Legal Studies*, 8 (2), pp. 235–284.

Mahoney, P. 2001. "The Common Law and Economic Growth: Hayek Might be Right", *Journal of Legal Studies,* 30 (2), pp. 503–525.

Mulligan, Robert. 2004. "Spontaneously Evolved Social Order versus Positive Legislation in English Constitutional History", *Review of Austrian Economics*, 17 (1), pp. 41–65.

Musacchio, Aldo. 2007. "Do Legal Origins Have Persistent Effects Over Time? A Look at Law and Finance around the World c. 1900", mimeo, Harvard Business School.

Ogus, A. (2002). "The economic basis of legal culture: Network and monopolisation", *Oxford Journal of Legal Studies,* 22(3), pp. 419–434.

Priest, George L. 1977. "The Common Law Process and the Selection of Efficient Rules", *Journal of Legal Studies,* 6 (1), pp. 65–82.

Priest, George L. and Benjamin Klein. 1984. "The Selection of Disputes for Litigation", *Journal of Legal Studies*, XIII (1), pp. 1–55.

Rizzo, Mario. 1980. "The mirage of efficiency", *Hofstra Law Review,* 8, pp. 641–658.

Rowley, Charles K. 1989. "The Common Law in Public Choice Perspective: A Theoretical and Institutional Critique", *Hamline Law Review,* 12 (2), pp. 355–383.

Rubin, Paul H. 1977. "Why is the Common Law Efficient?", *Journal of Legal Studies,* 6 (1), pp. 51–63.

Rubin, Paul H. 1982. "Common Law and Statute Law", *Journal of Legal Studies,* 11 (2), pp. 205–223.

Rubin, Paul H. 2005. "Micro and Macro Legal Efficiency: Supply and Demand", *Supreme Court Economic Review*, 13, pp. 19–34, reprinted in this volume.

Salmon, Pierre. 2005. "L'apport informatifs des rapports Doing Business est précieux mais attention aux effets pervers", in *Mesurer l'efficacité économique du Droit,* edited by Guy Canivet, Marie-Anne Frison-Roche and Michael Klein. Paris: L.G.D.J., pp. 109–122.

Salmon, Pierre 2006. "Political Yardstick Competition and Corporate Governance in the European Union", in *Investor Protection in Europe: Corporate Law Making, The MiFID and Beyond*, edited by Guido Ferrarini and Eddy Wymeersch. Oxford: Oxford University Press, pp. 31–58.

Siems, Mathias M. 2007. "Legal Origins: Reconciling Law and Finance and Comparative Law", *McGill Law Review*, 52, pp. 55–81.

Tullock, Gordon. 1971. *The Logic of Law*, New York and London: Basic Books.

Tullock, Gordon. 1988. "Defending the Napoleonic Code over the Common Law", in Stuart S. Nagel (ed.), *Research in Law and Policy Studies,* 2, pp. 2–27.

Tullock, Gordon. 1997. *The Case Against the Common Law, The Blackstone Commentaries,* Fairfax: Locke Institute.

Voigt, Stefan. 2005. "Are International Merchants Stupid? A Natural Experiment Refutes the Legal Origin Theory", ICER Working paper.

Webster, Thomas J. 2004. "Economic Efficiency and the Common Law", *Atlantic Economic Journal*, 32 (1), pp. 39–48, reprinted in this volume.

Zywicki, Todd. 2003. "The Rise and Fall of Efficiency in the Common Law: A Supply-Side Analysis", *Northwestern University Law Review*, 97 (4), pp. 1551–1634, reprinted in this volume.

Chapter 16

Todd J. Zywicki

THE RISE AND FALL OF EFFICIENCY IN THE COMMON LAW

A supply-side analysis

I. Introduction

FROM ITS INCEPTION, an animating insight of the economic analysis of law has been the observation that the common law process appears to have a strong tendency to produce efficiency-enhancing legal rules.[1] But many recent commentators have also concluded that recent decades have seen an evolution away from this traditional principle, as the common law appears to increasingly reflect interest-group pressures that have attenuated this traditional evolutionary tendency toward efficiency.[2] This duality has deepened the dilemma confronting scholars, requiring an explanation of not only the factors that traditionally drove the common law toward the production of efficient rules but also requiring an explanation of why the evolution in recent years has differed so dramatically from prior eras.[3] It was traditionally thought that the common law process had built into its structure a self-correcting evolution mechanism that led Lord Mansfield to conclude that over time the common law "works itself pure."[4] Some leading scholars continue to adhere to Mansfield's optimism about the self-correcting nature of the common law.[5] In recent years, however, this process of self-correction seems to have gone awry, leading to increased concerns about inefficiency in many areas of the common law and heightened calls for legislative tort reform and restoration of freedom of contract.[6]

Traditional models of the rise and fall of efficiency in the common law, such as those proposed by Paul Rubin and George Priest, have stressed the "demand" side of the production of common law legal rules.[7] They have argued that the driving force in the evolution of the common law is the actions of private litigants that generate a "demand" for the production of legal rules. Rubin and Priest have argued that these litigation efforts by private parties can explain both the common law's historic tendency to produce efficient rules as well as its more recent evolution away from efficiency in favor of wealth redistribution.

This Article revisits the debate over the rise and fall of efficiency in the common law by examining the supply-side conditions of the production of common law legal rules. This Article does not directly challenge the traditional "demand-side" model, but it proposes to supplement the model with a "supply-side" model of the evolution of the common law that examines the institutional incentives and constraints of common law judges over time. It argues that the traditional efficiency of the common law arose in the context of a particular historical institutional setting and that changes in that institutional framework have made the common law more susceptible to rent-seeking pressures, which have undermined the common law's proefficiency orientation. Moreover, it is argued that understanding the supply side constraints and incentives confronting judges is a *necessary condition* for understanding litigant-driven demand-side models. Whether one seeks to understand efficiency or inefficiency in the common law, it is essential to understand the institutional structure confronting judges and the incentives they are provided to produce efficient law. The market for law, like other markets, requires an understanding of both supply and demand conditions in order to identify the resulting equilibrium.

This Article also demonstrates a more general point. In discussing the tendency of institutions to produce efficiency-enhancing rules, it is necessary to consider two factors. The first factor has been well-recognized by previous scholars, namely the features of the institution that are relevant to the production of efficient rules, such as the ability to make use of decentralized information and provide useful feedback to decision-makers. But a second, equally important feature has been largely ignored by previous scholars: the degree to which the institution is resistant to rent-seeking pressures by private parties seeking to manipulate it so as to redistribute wealth to themselves at the expense of overall efficiency. As this Article will demonstrate, it is necessary to consider *both* of these factors to understand the tendencies of an institution. Even if an institution is designed to maximize efficiency in theory, its attempt to do so will be thwarted if the institution is susceptible to rent-seeking pressures by private litigants. Efficiency-enhancing institutions, therefore, must be incentive-compatible to those using the institution and those affected by its outputs. In other words, the institution must not only be capable of collecting and using all of the information necessary to render a sound decision, but the individual actors within the institution must have the correct individual incentives to use this information to produce efficient rules, rather than to reward rent-seeking pressures.

This Article does not seek to reopen the debate over the empirical validity of whether the common law has traditionally tended toward efficiency or whether modern developments have tended away from efficiency. For the sake of argument, this Article will simply take as a given the assumption that although the traditional common law tended toward efficiency, this tendency has been attenuated and even reversed in some areas in recent decades leading to growing inefficiency in the common law.[8]

The Article first describes the traditional demand-side explanation for the rise and fall of efficiency in the common law. It then describes and distinguishes a supply-side model of efficiency in the common law, examining the historical institutional framework that generated the common law. Prior explanations have generally ignored the supply side of the model, in large part because most scholars have made the anachronistic assumption that the institutional structure of the modern common law is fundamentally identical to that of the traditional common law. This Article will show that this assumption is incorrect, and that the modern institutional framework of the common law differs in several important ways from the institutional framework that characterized the common law throughout its early evolution. Certain historical institutional developments, such as a weak doctrine of precedent and a competitive legal order, provided a framework for the common law to evolve largely insulated from rent-seeking pressures and in favor of efficiency-enhancing rules. These institutional features were coupled with doctrinal tendencies in the law, namely freedom of contract and reliance on custom, both of which further tended to improve efficiency and to prevent rent-seeking pressures. The Article then explains how changes in this institutional framework have generated a decline in the efficiency of the common law and a rise in rent-seeking pressures.

II. Demand-side models of legal evolution

A general model of legal evolution

The process of legal evolution can be usefully envisioned as a "market for law." For instance, it has been argued that the outcome of the legislative process results from competing efforts by various interest groups who "bid" for favorable pieces of legislation and those who bid to prevent legislation harmful to their interests.[9] In this interest-group model, favorable legislation is given to the party that "bids" the most for the legislation.[10] This bidding takes many forms but can generally be understood as making financial and in-kind investments designed to help a politician be re-elected or to directly enrich the politician. Those interest groups that can contribute the greatest resources to a candidate are likely to secure favorable legislation; those that are unable or unwilling to contribute resources are likely to be disfavored in the process. Politicians traditionally have been modeled as largely passive "brokers" of these wealth transfers, simply responding to the demands of special interests.[11] This process of special interests trying to influence the law to transfer wealth from the public to themselves and to thereby increase their wealth above what they would receive in a competitive market (i.e., to earn "economic rents") is referred to as "rent-seeking."[12]

In general, parties will be willing to invest resources up to the amount to be transferred in seeking favorable legislation. Consider, for instance, an import quota that, if enacted, would enrich the American steel industry by a total present value of $100 million over the expected life of the legislation (say 10 years), as compared with expected profits without the quota. In such an example, the steel industry would be willing to invest up to $100 million in the form of campaign contributions, media advertising, in-kind campaign help, and the like to pass the quota.[13] Of course, some of the benefit—and thus some of the cost—will also flow to the employees of firms in the steel industry.[14] So the "industry" that benefits includes all relevant actors, such as shareholders, employees, management, etc. In contrast, the costs of the quota will be diffuse and borne by the many consumers of steel and steel products, who will now be forced to pay slightly higher prices for raw steel and goods manufactured with steel. The exact division of the $100 million surplus among these groups is unimportant for current purposes; what matters is the recognition that legal changes can enrich some groups at the expense of others and that rational parties will invest resources so as to bring about legal changes in order to capture these gains, if the benefited parties are sufficiently able to organize to mount an effective lobbying effort.

The demand curve for legal change, therefore, is a function of two variables: (1) the expected total amount of wealth to be transferred by the law in question (V), and (2) the durability of the favorable piece of legislation, defined as the length of time the law will effectively generate wealth (L).[15]

$D = (VL)$

Where

D = demand for a particular legal rule,

V = the annual value of the amounts to be transferred, and

L = the expected longevity of the law and the number of periods over which wealth will be transferred.

The demand, D, for a particular legal rule will be a function of the present value of the expected stream of economic rents that will be generated by a particular legal rule. Parties will be willing to invest greater amounts to secure legal rules that generate greater benefits to them. Thus, the steel industry would be willing to make much larger investments to secure a very strict import quota rather than a mild import quota, because a strict quota will increase industry wealth much more than a mild quota. So as the expected value of V increases for a particular law, parties will be willing to invest greater sums to secure that law's passage. The converse is also true: as parties invest greater sums, then, at the margin, it is more likely that they will secure favorable legislation, so a greater investment of resources will generally increase the value of any legislation obtained.

The value, V, of a favorable legal rule will also be a function of the ability of detrimentally affected parties to avoid paying the costs of a law. Consider, for example, a minimum wage law. An essential element of a minimum wage law is that parties cannot contract around the law by agreeing to pay less than the statutory minimum. For example, imposing a minimum wage on labor increases wages for those who are employed, but it also causes unemployment for other workers and effects a wealth transfer from shareholders to those laborers benefited by the law. If those injured by the law could escape its reach, such as by contracting for other terms, then no one would provide a wealth transfer to the beneficiaries. Making a law such as the minimum wage policy a default rule that the parties could freely alter, therefore, would frustrate the entire purpose of having such a law. Thus, if detrimentally affected parties cannot escape the reach of a law, then wealth can be transferred from them to the benefited groups under that law. By contrast, if escape from the reach of a law by detrimentally affected parties is easy, then the amount of wealth that can be transferred from those groups to beneficiaries is limited.

Parties will also be willing to invest greater amounts to secure laws that generate longer-lasting benefits. Most favorable legislation does not generate benefits in the short-term. Rather, most legislation generates modest benefits over a long period of time. For instance, occupational licensing of attorneys has the effect of increasing the earnings of lawyers over the span of a 40-year career, rather than generating a one-time lump-sum benefit upon graduation.[16] Thus, as longevity, L, increases, meaning that the expected longevity is likely to go up, parties will be willing to invest more in order to secure favorable legislation. For instance, a law that will generate benefits of $1 million per year for 20 years if enacted will be much more valuable to the interest group it favors than will a law that will generate $1 million, but only for one year. Parties will be willing to invest more to secure the enactment of a law of longer duration because this increases the present value of the benefits to be generated over the life of the wealth-transferring law.

Application of the model to common law evolution

Although originally designed to explain the production of legislation, Paul Rubin has argued that change in the common law can be analyzed by applying this general model.[17] We can think of the demand side of the market as private litigants, bringing actions before courts and requesting that the courts produce legal rulings and legal opinions designed to resolve the dispute. Judges can be thought of as providing the supply side of the market, because they produce the service of dispute resolution and because the reasoned legal opinions and precedents they provide are often designed to offer guidance to future litigants.

Rubin's model rests on the relative stakes between the two parties to a given dispute, arguing that as the amount of money at stake in a particular case increases, the willingness of parties to invest resources in order to effectuate legal change increases as well. The stakes in a given dispute will be a function not only of the amount at stake in that particular case, but also of the potential long term value of the precedent generated by that case, which will affect the results of *future* cases. In many situations, this latter variable will be much larger than the former. For instance, if a party—say steel manufacturers—can obtain a legal precedent that makes it difficult for consumers or employees to sue or one that limits the damages that party can recover, then such a precedent is an extremely valuable economic asset. Although avoiding liability in a particular case saves the steel manufacturer damages in that case, a legal rule that makes it more difficult for plaintiffs to recover in future cases promises an ongoing *stream* of future benefits. If a party has the ability and opportunity to influence the evolution of the law in a manner favorable to it, then it will be willing to invest resources in order to garner legal change. Common law rules, therefore, can be thought of as generated by a process similar to legislative statutes, where interest groups "bid" on particular rules and where the legal rules that are passed are those preferred by the highest bidder. In turn, the highest bidder will be the one who has the largest stakes in the case, either the most to win or lose, from proposed legal change.

Rubin's model, therefore, turns on the same two factors as the model of legislative change: the amount of money at issue in the particular case (V) and the period of time over which parties can capture the benefits of a change in the law (L).[18] But there is a fundamental difference between legislative change and common law change. For legislative change, one legislature has no ability to bind the hands of a subsequent legislature. Thus, in theory at least, all legislative bargains can be undone as governing coalitions in the legislature change.[19] For the common law, however, the modern doctrine of *stare decisis* means that, in theory at least, all court decisions will be binding on all subsequent courts. Thus, there is an inherent stability in the common law process that the legislative process lacks. As a result, even if the value of a favorable legal rule is relatively small in any given case, that benefit may be multiplied over many cases over many years and may give rise to a relatively large bounty in present value terms for any group that can capture it. For similar reasons, a constitutional rule protected by supermajoritarian amendment procedures will be more durable than a mere legislative rule, because the constitutional rule will be more difficult to reverse at a later date.[20] In theory, at least, the doctrine of *stare decisis* suggests that common law rules might be more durable than legislative rules. As will be discussed below, however, this does not necessarily mean that common law rules will be able to redistribute greater amounts of wealth than legislative rules, because other factors may also reduce the amount of wealth that can be transferred.

Because of the long-term nature of the economic rents generated by certain economic rules, Rubin observes that repeat players in litigation will be the parties with the greatest incentives to bring litigation designed to generate new precedents. Groups that are better able to organize will also be able to invest greater resources in legal change. Of course, if the stakes in a given case are sufficiently high that parties will be willing to invest large amounts solely on the outcome of the case without concern for the future value of the precedent generated by the case, then there is no reason to engage in collective action to change the law. If both parties to a dispute have equal and sufficiently high stakes, then their investments will tend to cancel out and the law will tend toward efficiency. If both parties have equal but low stakes, such as in small-claims court, then one would expect largely random drift in the doctrinal evolution of the law. If one party has a greater stake in the dispute and is able to solve any relevant collective action problems, however, then Rubin predicts that the law will evolve in a direction favorable to that party.[21]

Rubin argues that this model generally describes the evolution of the common law as a historical matter, both in its early tendency to promote efficiency as well as more recent developments that depart from efficiency. Rubin postulates that, in the nineteenth century (and presumably before), rule making (both common law and statutory) was dominated by individual actors acting independently, rather than by organized special interests acting collectively.[22] This was the case for several reasons. First, most disputes that arose were between two individuals or between an individual and a very small business. Thus, there was little benefit to be captured by a party from strategic litigation because neither party was a frequent litigant. Moreover, each individual usually stood in a reciprocal relationship with all other individuals; thus an individual or small business who is a plaintiff today was equally likely to be a defendant tomorrow, reducing the incentive to litigate for one-sided rules and favoring advocacy in favor of stable and efficient rules. Finally, Rubin argues, the structure of litigation and high costs of communication made it very difficult for groups to solve collective action problems in order to aggregate their interests into a coherent and effective litigation strategy. Thus, for much of the common law's evolution, most litigation was between two individual parties, both with substantially equal stakes in the outcome. The result was that the common law tended toward efficiency.[23]

Subsequent innovations changed this dynamic in some particulars. The "equal stakes" model still describes many areas governed by the common law, which explains the persistent efficiency in many of these areas. Nonetheless, Rubin argues that his model can explain some episodes of dramatic legal change over very short time periods.

He provides two examples to illustrate his point: the adoption of liability-restricting rules for manufacturing firms in nineteenth century England and the adoption of liability-expanding rules in twentieth century America.

First, the industrial revolution brought about the innovation of large-scale manufacturing enterprises. Unlike private parties, these new firms had a strong interest in the path of legal change—especially in areas such as nuisance law and tort law. Rubin argues that this gave them unequal stakes and may have been sufficient to cause them to invest in legal changes to narrow the scope of liability for pollution and workplace accidents.[24]

In recent decades, a more modern and more potent form of strategic legal change has been occasioned by the Association of Trial Lawyers of America (ATLA), the leading trade group of America's tort plaintiff's lawyers. Among its activities, ATLA organizes plaintiff's lawyers into a coherent interest group that effectively lobbies on issues of legal change, and Rubin and Bailey argue that, through these interest group activities, ATLA has created a class of residual claimants for legal change in the tort law. Thus, even though individual tort plaintiffs are not repeat players, tort *lawyers* as a group are. Moreover, tort lawyers benefit from changing the law so as to increase liability, increase litigation, and increase the damages available from tort lawsuits. Thus, they have high stakes in the generation of legal precedents. This combination of high stakes and strong organization has made ATLA an effective litigant for liability-expanding tort law rules.

Rubin suggests that it is unnecessary to consider the supply side of the market for legal change in order for his model to accurately describe reality.[25] Nonetheless, he leaves open the possibility that changes in the supply side of the market, such as changes in the proclivity or ability of judges to supply certain types of legal rules, can supplement his model of legal change.[26] Thus, in understanding the evolution of the common law, it is not necessary to force an either-or choice between demand-side and supply-side theories. In fact, most markets are best understood by examining both sides.[27] The point of this Article is not to offer a supply-side theory as an alternative to demand-side models. Rather, it is to offer a supply-side story as a *supplement* to demand-side stories. As the subsequent discussion will show, there were crucial historical changes in the supply side of the common law "market" that were necessary for Rubin's model of rent-seeking litigation to be feasible. The argument thus builds upon Rubin's demand-side model, especially as it relates to the stake of litigation and the ability to manipulate the path of legal precedent. As this Article will show, Rubin's argument rests on important assumptions about the nature of legal precedent, the ability of parties to manipulate the path of legal evolution, and the ability of successful litigants to involuntarily bind parties to inefficient legal rules by making exit costly. There are, thus, certain institutional arrangements that are necessary for a rent-seeking model of the common law to be feasible and there are certain institutional arrangements that are more resistant to rent-seeking pressures than other institutional frameworks.

George Priest has offered a similar model of the evolution of the common law.[28] Like Rubin, Priest emphasizes the demand-side of the market for common law evolution, grounding his models in the actions of private litigants. Priest argues that inefficient rules will tend to lead to more societal conflict and will thereby be the subject of more litigation over time. Assuming judges randomly reverse a certain percentage of precedents each time the precedents are tested in litigation, Priest argues that the tendency for inefficient precedents to be litigated more often will also cause them to be reversed more often then efficient rules. Over time this will cause a pronounced tendency in the law toward the production and maintenance of efficient legal rules. As with Rubin, Priest's model can be understood as a demand-side model, wherein judges passively respond to the actions of private litigants.

Scholars have offered a variety of criticisms of Priest's model.[29] For current purposes, however, the crucial point to recognize is that, although Priest may be able to provide an explanation for why the common law might evolve toward efficiency, his model provides no explanation of why the common law might evolve *away* from efficiency.[30] This omission is telling in that it is evident that Priest believes that the common law has departed from the efficiency norm in recent years.[31] In explaining these recent trends, Priest has abandoned his demand-side model of common law evolution, instead turning to a supply-side model grounded in an intellectual and ideological revolution among common law judges. This ideological revolution has caused judges to deviate from sound economics in favor of using tort law as an instrument of social justice and insurance. Priest also implicitly concludes that existing institutional constraints are inadequate to constrain judges from reading their personal ideological preferences into the law.[32] As this Article will show, the ability of judges to indulge their ideological preferences is dependent on certain institutional arrangements that make it possible for judges to bind private-decisionmakers and to thereby impose their ideological preferences.

III. A supply-side model of common law efficiency

Supply-side models of common law efficiency have been rare, as demand-side explanations have dominated scholarship. The only prior supply-side model of efficiency was offered by Judge Richard Posner, who argued that common law judges will have a preference or "taste" for efficiency.[33] According to Posner, judges have a "taste" or "preference" for efficient rules that guide their decision-making. Because of limited external constraints on judges, they can indulge their preferences, whatever those preferences may be. According to Posner, the common law system—at least at the appellate level, where most legal rules are formulated—is highly impersonal, meaning that the judge has little ability or inclination to try to decide the case on the basis of which litigant is a "better" or more morally worthy person. Unlike trial judges, appellate judges generally are not intimately acquainted with the particular circumstances and characteristics of litigants and therefore lack the information and inclination to decide cases on subjective assessments of moral worthiness. Moreover, ethical rules usually require judges to recuse themselves from cases in which they have financial interests, rendering the outcome independent from the resulting financial consequences to the parties. As a result, judges will usually have an incentive to treat lawsuits as interactions between two competing economic activities, leading them "almost by default" to weigh the economic value of the two competing activities.[34] Moreover, judges have limited ability to redistribute wealth through common law rules, and Posner believes that judges recognize these limits. Thus, even if judges have preferences that they weigh more highly than efficiency, their institutional constraints will lead them to recognize that these other goals are unobtainable. Furthermore, even if judges have only a weak preference for efficiency, they will pursue this end by default because of their inability to accomplish other competing ends. Given this, Posner argues that judges will act as if they have a "taste" for efficiency that will lead them to seek efficiency in their decisions. But this preference is weak because it is merely by default, given that judges are constrained from pursuing other goals.

There are several problems with this argument. First, it is difficult to verify because we cannot read judges' minds to determine their preferences or the extent to which their preferences explain case outcomes. Second, Posner's assumption seems inconsistent with the observation that many judges are at least as concerned with redistributive goals as efficiency goals.[35] In fact, common experience indicates that many judges have strong tastes for distributional goals, and that they pursue these goals in their judicial role. Third, it fails to explain why the common law might evolve in an efficient manner at some times during history, but inefficiently at other times. Posner also has argued that nineteenth century judges were moral utilitarians, which led them to embrace the primacy of efficiency as a goal. But, of course, this merely restates the "preferences" theory without any further support, albeit with somewhat greater explanation. Fourth, it is questionable whether even the most well-intentioned judge possesses the expertise and knowledge to devise efficient legal rules where he or she desires to do so.[36]

Thus, no prevailing positive theory of the supply-side incentives of judges to produce efficient rules exists.[37] Posner's argument turns on a postulated personal taste of judges for efficiency, institutional constraints that prevent them from pursuing other preferences, and on recognition by judges that it is in fact futile for them to try to accomplish other goals. Rather than postulating an assumption of judicial preferences for efficiency, this Article argues that the driving force in legal evolution on the supply side of the equation is not unprovable assumptions about judicial tastes but rather the incentives and constraints that judges face in carrying out their tasks. Moreover, this Article will offer a supply-side model that dovetails with the demand-side models of common law evolution previously described. In turn, this will force us to focus on the structure of incentives and constraints confronted by judges that encourage or discourage them from pursuing their personal preferences at the expense of litigants and society in general. This Article is an effort to fill this gap by postulating a supply-side model of efficiency in the common law that focuses on the incentives of judges to produce efficient common law rules.

This Part of the Article will show that there were particular institutional arrangements that characterized the common law in its formative period. These institutions made the common law resistant to rent-seeking litigation pressures and help to explain the common law's historic tendency toward the production of efficient rules. This Part also will argue that each of these factors has changed over time, thereby rendering the common law process more susceptible to problems of rent-seeking through litigation. Thus, the focus here is on the constraints that led common law judges to produce efficient rules even where their personal preferences did not incline them to do so. This Article will thus argue that Rubin and Priest's models rest on a previously unacknowledged change in the institutional constraints on judges. The effect of this change in institutional constraints was to increase the possibilities for litigants to transfer wealth through strategic litigation, both through an increasing incentive and opportunity to engage in rent-seeking litigation in terms of the Rubin model, as well as by creating greater agency costs for judges to indulge their ideological preferences in terms of the Priest model.

This Article will highlight several institutional features. First, it will show that Rubin's model rests on a particular understanding of the role of legal precedent and *stare decisis* in the common law. Although it is reasonable to assume the presence of *stare decisis* as a permanent element of the common law system, in reality the doctrine of *stare decisis* was a fairly recent innovation in the common law, replacing a system of much weaker judicial precedent. A system of strong precedent or *stare decisis*, this Article will show, is an essential element for rent-seeking through the common law.

Second, this Article will describe the historic competitive legal order of the traditional common law. During the era in which the common law evolved, litigants had the ability to choose among many different courts and bodies of law to hear their disputes. Judges were paid by fees paid by the parties, providing judges with an incentive to compete for business and to respond to the needs of litigants through the production of efficient legal rules. Moreover, it provided an ease of exit that reduced the ability of parties to involuntarily redistribute wealth away from parties disfavored by doctrinal developments. Parties could opt out of such a legal system and opt in to a concurrent court. This ease of exit limited their rent-seeking opportunities through litigation.

Third, certain legal doctrines limited the ability to use the court system as a mechanism for rent-seeking activity. In particular, the tendency of traditional common law to produce default rules rather than mandatory rules allowed parties to contract around onerous and inefficient legal rules, thereby preserving efficiency through private ordering. The common law's traditionally strong reliance upon custom also created a tendency toward efficiency and insulated the common law from rent-seeking pressures. As this Article will discuss, because custom evolved from decentralized and consensual processes over long periods of time, it tends to be highly resistant to rent-seeking pressures.

Weak precedent versus stare decisis

As discussed above, Paul Rubin has noted that a necessary condition for efficient legal rules to develop is that both parties to a dispute place relatively equal importance on the precedent developed in the case.[38] Where one party has dramatically more to win from a favorable precedent (or more to lose from an unfavorable precedent), that party will be willing to invest greater resources to secure the desired precedent, leading to a tendency for the law to evolve in a direction favorable to that party, even if the new rule is less efficient than the old rule. Rubin argues that in the early era of the common law, most disputes were between two individuals who were not likely to be repeat players, thus neither side had a relatively stronger incentive than the other to fight for precedents uniquely favorable to his cause.[39] Rubin focuses on the demand side of the fight for legal precedent, noting that parties with a greater stake in the outcome of the case will "bid" higher amounts for a favorable precedent. Thus, there would be no systematic pressures to drive the evolution of the common law away from efficiency. This story seems to be both historically and conceptually correct.

History adds an additional element that renders Rubin's story about the evolution of the common law even more powerful. Looking at the "market" for legal precedent we *see* that the demand for a legal precedent will be affected not only by the value of a precedent but also by the durability of the precedent and its ability to transmit rents through time. Thus, if a precedent is less durable, the present value of the precedent will decrease because a favorable precedent will transfer less wealth over time. As a result, litigants will be less willing to invest resources *ex ante* to secure a favorable precedent.[40] Thus, where precedent is not durable, neither side to a dispute has a relatively greater interest in the precedent, thereby producing conditions favorable to the production of efficient rules.

The traditional common law provided these conditions. Although most modern lawyers and scholars conceive of the doctrine of *stare decisis* as a formative element of the common law, this is an ahistorical understanding of the development of the common law.[41] The doctrine of *stare decisis*, the idea that the holding of a particular case is treated as binding upon courts deciding later similar cases, is a late nineteenth-century development and represents a clear doctrinal and conceptual break with the prior history of the common law.[42] The widespread adoption of the principle of *stare decisis* was a pivotal turn in the common law, which provided a necessary condition for later efforts to turn the development of the common law toward special-interest purposes. This is not to say that the adoption of a principle of strict *stare decisis* was undesirable from the perspective of economic efficiency or coordination. But it is important to recognize that the adoption of a system of strict *stare decisis* is a *necessary* condition for the common law to become a vehicle for rent-seeking.[43] Absent *stare decisis* it is impossible to produce long-term stable precedents that generate returns over time. Thus, there are costs to *stare decisis* as well as benefits, with a major cost stemming from the fact that it makes the law more susceptible to use as a vehicle for rent-seeking and the manipulation of judicial precedent. Indeed, discussions of the benefits of *stare decisis* have often ignored these costs. But it is clear that any discussion of the benefits of *stare decisis* must also consider the inherent costs associated with strict *stare decisis* as well. A brief history of the doctrine of precedent under English common law will help to illustrate the difference and will illuminate why the adoption of *stare decisis* enabled the use of the common law for rent-seeking purposes.

Precedent in English legal history

Modern commentators rarely look beyond the eighteenth and nineteenth centuries in seeking the history of the English common law. The formative period of the common law, however, was from the twelfth to the seventeenth centuries, and this is where the investigation must begin.[44] During this period there was no well-developed concept of precedent at all. Writing in the thirteenth century, for instance, Bracton refers to more than 500 cases in his treatise but does not treat them as authoritative statements of the content of the law.[45] In fact, Bracton did not espouse a doctrine of precedent, nor did he even ever use the word "precedent."[46] Bracton was aberrant in even citing cases, as most early learned treatises cited no cases at all.[47] "The author of *Fleta*, writing about forty years after Bracton, refers to one case; Britton, who wrote an epitome of Bracton soon after 1290, refers to none; Littleton in his authoritative work on *Tenures* (ca. 1481?) refers to eleven cases."[48] Bracton himself had to exert great influence to obtain the loan of plea rolls and was one of the few judges of the era willing to wade through the weighty and unorganized rolls.[49] Few other treatise writers, and certainly no lawyers, would have been willing to exert the energy required to obtain possession of the rolls or to engage in the painstaking trouble of reading through the unorganized masses of parchment.[50] As Plucknett bluntly states, "[a]ny use of cases on Bracton's lines by the profession at large, or even by the bench alone, would have been manifestly impossible."[51]

For early common law judges (including even Bracton), cases were merely illustrations as to how respected individuals had decided cases that came before them.[52] "Cases, that is, judicial decisions, could be used to illustrate legal principles, but were not themselves an authoritative source of law."[53] Prior cases served only as persuasive, not binding, authority and were studied for the soundness of their reasoning, not the authority of their holdings. A series of similar decisions might be considered as evidence of the existence of judicial custom, but those customs were also regarded as only persuasive rather than binding. "If a judge did not approve of a previous decision, or even of a previous custom of the court, he might say that it was wrong and disregard it."[54] In fact, the first known use of the term "precedent" was not until 1557, and in that case the court observed that it was ruling *despite* two "presidents" to the contrary.[55] Indeed, Bracton relied on cases primarily to illustrate the ways in which recently decided cases (in his era) had departed from the sounder judicial rulings of earlier eras and to argue that the newer decisions should be ignored.[56] "Bracton first states his principles and then adduces his cases as historical evidence of the accuracy of his statements. This is a vastly different method from" that of precedent—namely, "taking the cases first and deducing rules of law from them."[57] During the formative centuries of the common law, therefore, there was no system of precedent that resembled the current doctrine of *stare decisis*.

In the sixteenth and seventeenth centuries, cases started to become more important as common law courts developed a practice of adhering more strictly in matters of pleading and procedure to their customs and thereby their precedents. But "[t]his principle was not ironclad."[58] Moreover, the principle was adhered to primarily only in procedural matters, not issues of substantive law.[59] Lord Holt observed, for instance, "[t]he law consists not in particular instances and precedents, but in the reason of the law, and *ubi eadem ratio, idem ius*."[60] Even this adherence in procedural matters was not wholly internally adopted by the judges but was produced primarily by the demands of maintaining the externally-imposed jurisdictional lines between the common law and other types of court.[61] Coke relied on the concept of precedent in his battles against the King, arguing for the historical continuity of the common law tradition. Even Coke's reliance on the concept of precedent in the battles against the King cited precedents only as "examples" of the "true rule" and not "in and of themselves authoritative sources of those rules."[62] The decisions of particular cases, or even a group of cases, were still not treated as authoritatively binding on lower courts.

Useful recitations of precedents would not even be technologically feasible until the invention of movable type printing in the fifteenth century and not until the sixteenth century could lawyers easily acquire printed reports of cases.[63] Prior to then, the only authoritative recitation of outcomes (albeit in a highly summary form) were the "plea rolls," which recorded case outcomes and little else. These were quite literally rolls of dusty parchment sewn together, weighing hundreds of pounds and inscribed with handwritten case outcomes.[64] As one scholar has observed, "Plea Rolls were obviously not things which could be produced easily in Court; it was no light matter to search them or have them searched; and there is ample evidence that they were very difficult of access even to prominent counsel."[65] The purpose of the Rolls was to record the results of cases, and in particular, debts owed to the King, not to aid lawyers. The reasoning of the court in reaching a decision was not of import and few lawyers even had access to the rolls.[66] Because the absence of printing made reproduction of the rolls impossible, a lawyer could authoritatively cite a case only if he could in fact access the rolls and identify the case. "When there were no printed records or reports," Hogue asks, "who could verify citations to previous decisions without first obtaining permission to consult the royal plea rolls?"[67]

The inaccessibility and impracticability of the plea rolls led to the development of privately published Year Books that sought to provide some of the information regarding decided cases. But these differed dramatically in form and substance from modern case reporters. The Year Books were intended as teaching tools, not official case reports, and therefore focused on issues of pleading, procedure, and case strategy, rather than case outcomes.[68] In addition to the rulings in the cases, the Year Books attempted to provide a rudimentary recitation of the relevant facts and arguments in the case. But the Year Books were haphazard, fragmentary, and frequently contradictory.[69] Not only did they often contradict each other in describing the reasoning of cases, they often even disagreed on the case names.[70] Their chronology is often questionable, and judges are often found speaking well after they were dead and long periods of time had transpired with little or no reporting of cases.[71] There were often long time lags between the time a case was decided and the publication of its corresponding opinion.[72] Their origins are sometimes questionable, as several manuscripts were purloined from the lawyers who owned them and then were published without their permission, often with various additions from unknown sources.[73] Moreover, they plainly did not serve the same function as the modern law report, as they were reported and used much more casually.[74] Not only did they report less than current case reporters and in a less rigorous style, but they also often reported *more*—such as private comments by judges and even what was said at mock trials in the Inns of Court.[75] The editorial comments of the reporters were interspersed with the rulings of judges; the statements of well-known counsel were cited as authority.[76] Reporters freely elaborated on the arguments actually advanced by counsel and the judges in individual cases.[77] Not only would the reporters criticize judicial rulings, they would criticize the character and wisdom of the judges themselves; one irreverent reporter attached the nickname "Hervey le Hasty" to judge Hervey le Stanton in recognition of his impetuous style.[78]

Judges and lawyers distinguished among the quality of different Year Books depending on the identity of the authors, with more reliable authors holding greater weight than their competitors. Some reporters were of such poor quality that lawyers were forbidden from citing them in certain courts.[79] Often the assessment of a reporter's supposed quality was determined on whether the reporter agreed with the decision the judge sought to render.[80] Moreover, many Year Books contained cases that were translated into English from the archaic French and Latin that had been used for centuries in the common law courts, raising questions about the accuracy of the translations.[81] To the extent that they were invoked as authority, like the use of precedent generally, the reports in the Year Books focused primarily on issues of procedure rather than substance.[82] Although the Year Books were perhaps better than nothing, they certainly did not provide a sound technological basis for a system that relied on the full and accurate presentation of case results and judicial reasoning, such as a system based on strict *stare decisis*[83]

The first credible set of reports was provided by Plowden in the mid-sixteenth century, but it was not until the publication of Coke's Reports that a comprehensive collection of case reports that could be cited as precedent first appeared.[84] Even then, it was clear that Coke used the term "precedent" loosely rather than as binding authority, as evidenced by his willingness to freely distort the opinions in earlier cases through selective quotations and omissions.[85] Plucknett observes of Coke, "[a] case in Coke's *Reports*, therefore, is an uncertain mingling of genuine report, commentary, criticism, elementary instruction, and recondite legal history. The whole is dominated by Coke's personality, and derives its authority from him."[86] Despite Coke's limitations, his *Reports* were substantially better than those that followed in subsequent centuries.[87]

It was not until 1673 that English courts first distinguished between precedent and dictum, a necessary predicate for treating cases as authoritative statements of the law.[88] Prior to that time, judges rarely compared in detail the facts of the cases that came before them with the facts of earlier analogous cases. The distinction between holdings and dictum could not be established until the development of fuller and more accurate case reports that accurately related the facts of the case and the holdings therein. The development of greater reliance on cases as sources of law arose from a combination of three elements.[89] First, the invention of the printing press enabled the reproduction and distribution of uniform copies of cases; in fact, sets of yearbooks were among the first printing projects in England.[90] Second, this enabled a contemporaneous jurisprudential development that allowed cases to be used as authority for a judicial decision rather than for educational purposes.[91] Finally, this led to an attempt to construct a body of substantive law out of these cases, rather than merely a body of pleadings.[92] Despite earlier efforts, however, not until the publication of Burrow's Report in the mid-eighteenth century was there anything approaching an official set of regular reports of judicial decisions of particular courts.[93]

It was thus not until the seventeenth and eighteenth centuries that the "doctrine" of precedent even began to take on some coherence, although this respect for precedent fell far short of *stare decisis*. During this period, Matthew Hale observed that the decisions of courts "do not make a Law properly so-called," meaning that the decision of a court does not bind subsequent parties or judges.[94] Hale observes, however, that these decisions:

> Have a great Weight and Authority in Expounding, Declaring, and Publishing what the Law of the Kingdom is, especially when such Decisions hold a Consonancy and Congruity with Resolutions and Decisions of former times, and though such Decisions are less than a Law, yet they are a greater evidence thereof than the Opinion of any private Persons, as such, whatsoever.[95]

Cases themselves did not make law but illustrated the principles of the law.[96] But Hale emphasized the existence of a series of consistent decisions in analogous cases over time as providing strong evidence of the existence and validity of a rule. Even a settled pattern of cases was still thought susceptible to reconsideration in the light of reason. Hale still stopped well short of the belief that a mere single case could serve as binding precedent on all later cases, as *stare decisis* requires.

It was only in the nineteenth century, therefore, that precedent began to harden into the concept of *stare decisis*, in which the decision of merely one court is interpreted as binding authority on later courts.[97] Blackstone, for instance, contended that it was the obligation of judges to abide by prior precedents.[98] Despite this admonition, common law judges throughout the eighteenth century frequently second-guessed earlier cases and often refused to follow precedents that they thought unsound.[99] As Allen observes, "To sum up the position at the end of the eighteenth century: the application of precedent was powerful and constant, but no Judge would have been found to admit that he was 'absolutely bound' by any decision of any tribunal."[100] It is thus not until the nineteenth century that the modern version of *stare decisis*—the notion that judges are absolutely bound by prior decisions—took hold.'[101]

For the first several centuries of the common law, therefore, single cases standing alone did not make law. Judges generally adhered to the "declaratory theory" of law: that law was "discovered" by judges, rather than "made."[102] *A pattern* of several cases decided in agreement with one another, by contrast, gave rise to a powerful presumption of the correctness of the legal principle. The agreement of several judges in several cases constituted a judicial custom that attested to the wisdom of the rule and its utility in vindicating parties' expectations. As Plucknett stresses, "An important point to remember is that one case constitutes a precedent; several cases serve as evidence of a custom. . . . It is the custom which governs the decision, not the case or cases cited as proof of the custom."[103] He adds, "A single case was not a binding authority, but a well-established custom (proved by a more or less casual citing of cases) was undoubtedly regarded as strongly persuasive."[104] As a result, courts felt free to reject precedents where they believed the case to be wrongly decided.[105] Today, by contrast, a judge is generally believed to be bound by prior cases even when convinced that the prior case was wrongly decided or would work injustice.

Precedent in the American common law

A similar view of precedent prevailed in the United States in the eighteenth and nineteenth centuries.[106] As Professor Caleb Nelson has observed, American lawyers rejected the notion that individual cases themselves constituted the law. They, like English lawyers, believed that the substantive common law rested on principles outside of the regime of *stare decisis*.[107] Given this, it was thought to be illogical to rely on a system of strict *stare decisis* to settle the substantive rules of law. Like the English system, substantive rules were distinguished from procedural practice. Procedural rules rested purely on the need for consistent and predictable practices, rather than on the notion that one procedural rule might be thought "better" than another. Substantive rules, however, required greater reflection and study, rather than slavish adherence to prior decisions. This distinction was reflected in the ready adoption of strict *stare decisis* for procedural rules and a much later acceptance of the doctrine for substantive rules—an evolution that mirrored those in the English common law.[108] Indeed, as Nelson observes, one dictionary definition of the term "precedent" in the eighteenth century was "a form of pleading that courts had found acceptable in the past."[109]

Eighteenth century Americans rejected the idea that particular cases were themselves the law. Rather, like their English contemporaries, Americans saw particular cases as merely evidence of—or reflections of— underlying legal principles.[110] This may be best illustrated in the terms of so-called "reception" laws enacted by the states shortly after independence. Through these state constitutional and legislative rules, the states provided that rules of the English common law remained in place in the new states.[111] Commentators of the time announced, however, that the acceptance of the English common law did not necessarily require acceptance of the entire body of English *cases*. Thus, the states could feel free to reconsider English judicial decisions to the extent that they were thought inappropriate for the American situation.[112] Virginia Chancellor Creed Taylor observed in this vein, "It was the common law we adopted, and not English decisions."[113] Moreover, the need for a critical review of prior cases was not limited to English decisions but applied with equal force to cases decided after Independence by American courts.[114]

Moreover, the case reports in early America were at least as imprecise as in England, if not worse. Although England could at least reasonably rely on the reports of Coke, Plowden, and Burrow during the seventeenth and eighteenth centuries, Americans had few reliable reports until the nineteenth century.[115] Although some colonial lawyers published private notes on cases in their jurisdictions, these volumes focused on the arguments of counsel rather than the court's ruling.[116] Judges often paid little heed to the cases found in private case collections.[117] Like the Year Books, therefore, these reports could not provide a basis for a system of *stare decisis* that relied upon coherent and accurate case reports. Officially published reporters that focused on judicial opinions began to appear in the early nineteenth century but did not become almost universal until the end of the nineteenth century.[118]

As in England, prior cases were all treated as persuasive authority rather than binding authority. It was the sound reasoning of the prior case that demanded respect, not the mere existence of the case. Thus, even in the United States, the decision of a great English common law judge such as Lord Mansfield commanded greater respect than that of a mediocre American judge.[119] But judges showed special deference to a long line of decisions that had all independently reached the same conclusion.[120] The concurrence of many judges through time attested to the wisdom and consensus of a rule, much as social traditions generated through decentralized processes over long periods of time testify to the wisdom and consensus of those practices.[121] Later judges might be reluctant to question this consensus, not because they were compelled to follow the earlier judgments, but because this contrary consensus carried within it great persuasive force. As Professor Nelson observes, however:

> [T]his phenomenon is not quite the same thing as a presumption against
> overruling erroneous precedents. The influence of a series of decisions did
> not rest on the notion that judges should presumptively adhere to past

decisions even when convinced of their error, but rather on the notion that judges should be exceedingly hesitant to find error where a series of their predecessors had all agreed.[122]

But note that it was only because judges could in fact challenge earlier decisions that they thought incorrect that later judges could draw the inference that consensus agreement among prior judges testified to the soundness of the rule.[123] If the rule was unsound, prior judges could have overruled it. By contrast, in a regime of strict *stare decisis*, it is far more difficult to draw strong inferences about the quality of legal rules solely from the agreement of a series of judges in the rule. After all, latter cases in the series may merely be the path-dependent result of earlier erroneous decisions, rather than quality decisions in and of themselves.

Implications of weak precedent for common law efficiency.

Through most of the history of Anglo-American common law, therefore, precedent was flexible and based on the congruence of legal decisions with expectations, reason, and judgment. The convergence of several independently acting judges on similar conclusions attested to the wisdom and consensus support for the rule, rather than the authority of the rule.[124] Precedent was thus more a tradition composed of the decisions of many independent judges acting over time, rather than the sovereign statement of a "law-making" judge.[125] The notion *of stare decisis* as binding precedent was an outgrowth of Benthamite and Hobbesian legal positivism and the belief that law must issue as a sovereign command from the pen of known judicial authors, rather than from the result of a process of spontaneous order.[126] By contrast, the traditional common law judge was not "bound to any past articulation of that law, never absolutely bound to follow a previous decision, and always free to test it against his tradition-shaped judgment of its reasonableness."[127] It was not until the late-eighteenth century, under the influence of Benthamite positivism and technological innovations that made printing and distribution of case reports feasible, that strict *stare decisis* came to supplant weaker forms of judicial precedent.[128]

This historical background is essential to understand the traditional immunity of the common law to efficiency-distorting, rent-seeking influences. Prior to the acceptance of the hard doctrine of *stare decisis*, obtaining a favorable judgment by a party in a given case was of minimal value to that party. Because the decision in that case did not authoritatively bind subsequent courts, each precedent provided minimal long-term value to the parties in the case. This was true even with respect to repeat players and institutional parties who *would* indeed have had such an interest if a doctrine of *stare decisis*, in fact, existed. Moreover, the flexibility of reliance on precedent opened the system to self-correction, so that wrongheaded or inefficient decisions could be reversed at low cost by subsequent courts.

Where there is no *stare decisis*, there is no incentive to engage in rent-seeking litigation because there is no single authority empowered to "make" law.[129] Any rent-seeking legal doctrine can be upset by a subsequent judge who recognizes that the rent-seeking doctrine is inconsistent with reason and community consensus and expectations. Capturing a favorable precedent in a *stare decisis* system increases the value of the flow of wealth generated by that precedent. In fact, the presence of *stare decisis* provides incentives to interest groups to try to manipulate the path of cases that come before courts so as to try to influence which cases are heard first and which ones will, thereby, create *stare decisis*-setting precedents.[130] The absence of binding precedent in the form of *stare decisis* reduces the flow of wealth that can be generated from any given case, thereby eliminating the unequal incentives that often exist for one party or the other to invest heavily in altering the evolution of the law. The incentive to invest resources in rent-seeking is a function of the rules of precedent. As precedent becomes more binding through greater deference by later courts to the decisions of earlier courts, this will increase the incentives to invest resources in order to secure a favorable precedent.

Moreover, the absence of binding *stare decisis* limits agency costs by judges. Because subsequent judges retain the power to reconsider earlier decisions, outlier judges have a limited ability to refashion the law according to their policy preferences. Instead, the law will come to reflect the considered and independent judgment of *many* judges rather than one or a small group of judges seeking to change the direction of the law.

This is not to say that, in the end, a legal regime with weak precedent is more efficient than one with strict *stare decisis*.[131] Although strict adherence to *stare decisis* increases the incentives and opportunities for rent-seeking, there may be countervailing benefits that outweigh these costs. It has been argued that *stare decisis* will tend to increase economic efficiency by increasing the predictability of legal rules.[132] *Stare decisis* also eliminates the need to relitigate issues repeatedly, which conserves time and judicial resources by narrowing the issues in litigation and relieving judges of the need to repeatedly decide settled legal issues. If subsequent judges feel bound by precedent, the *stare decisis* can potentially reduce agency costs. The decision between a regime of *stare decisis* and a weaker adherence to precedent, therefore, is a comparative one. Previous scholars have ignored the rent-seeking incentives created by strict adherence to precedent. Alternatively, this analysis may require revisiting the purpose of *stare decisis*, and, in particular, reexamining the distinction between vertical *stare decisis* in a hierarchical court system and horizontal *stare decisis* in equal courts through time or with coequal jurisdictions. For instance, it may be that vertical *stare decisis* is necessary to create predictability; nonetheless, one might still argue for attenuated use of *stare decisis* through time or for decisions made by coequal courts.[133]

Once the full costs of *stare decisis* (including rent-seeking costs) are recognized, it may be that a different conception of precedent provides a better balance of these offsetting costs and benefits than does *stare decisis*. F.A. Hayek, for instance, argues that precedent should adhere to the more abstract *concepts and principles* that emerge from the accumulation of cases under the common law, rather than by adhering mechanically to the narrow *holdings* in particular cases as binding precedent.[134]

In addition, it may be that different contexts call for different rules of precedent, depending on how these offsetting factors balance out. For instance, where there appears to be unusually high incentives to engage in strategic litigation, the costs of strict *stare decisis* are higher, and thus a less rigid rule of precedent may be appropriate. This may explain, for instance, why the Supreme Court applies a more flexible rule of precedent to prior decisions on constitutional issues than on other issues.[135] Because of the heightened durability and incentives for special-interest litigation regarding constitutional issues, there is a particular concern about parties investing resources to secure favorable precedents in this context, and thus it may be appropriate to apply a less rigid rule of precedent in this setting. A less-rigid adherence to precedent may also be appropriate in situations where the predictability per se of particular rules is not as important; thus the benefits of *stare decisis* may be smaller relative to the costs in terms of incentives to expend resources on strategic litigation.

In weighing the costs and benefits of *stare decisis*, therefore, it is essential to remember that increased rent-seeking will be an inherent part of *every* system that includes *stare decisis*. Because *stare decisis* allows one holding to control the outcome of cases in the future, it will have a capital value to repeat players who will be encouraged to invest resources to alter the future development of the law. Thus, one benefit of *stare decisis* is that it conserves time and judicial resources in subsequent cases because, once decided, an issue does not have to be relitigated repeatedly. But this benefit comes at a cost. The more durable the precedent, the more parties will invest in the *original* case to try to win a favorable precedent. The greater, therefore, will be the incentive to try to manipulate the path of precedent. Thus, the subsequent costs saved by not having to relitigate the issue will be at least partially, and perhaps fully, offset by the higher stakes in the precedent-creating case and the larger investments that parties will be willing to make to secure a favorable precedent. These costs are inherent and cannot be eliminated because so long as there are benefits to be gained by strategic litigation, private parties will be willing to invest resources to try to capture those gains. The proper comparison for purposes of determining whether *stare decisis* is still, in the end, an efficient doctrine must include these inherent rent-seeking costs in the equation.[136]

A competitive legal order

A second important institutional feature that historically influenced the common law's evolution was the competitive, or "polycentric," legal order in which the common law developed. During the era that the common law developed, there were multiple English courts with overlapping jurisdictions over most of the issues that comprise common law.[137] As a result, parties potentially could bring a particular lawsuit in a variety of different courts. In turn, this created competition among these various courts for business. Moreover, there was no clear hierarchy of appellate courts. It further appears that, in general, this competition was conducted on the basis of which court provided the speediest and highest quality judicial system. Some have argued that this should have spawned pro-plaintiff, rather than efficiency-enhancing, legal rules; but, as will be discussed below, this inter-jurisdictional competition was constrained by certain forces that limited the ability of courts to compete for business by providing pro-plaintiff rules.[138] At the same time, this competitive process limited the ability of courts and special interest litigants to use the courts as a mechanism for wealth transfers. America benefited from a similar institutional regime under the doctrine of *Swift* v. *Tyson*,[139] which established jurisdictional competition in America during the nineteenth century, thereby limiting rent-seeking litigation and encouraging the development of efficient law.

Competition among courts in England.

Multiple overlapping jurisdictions.—The common law is generally thought of as purely the law that was created by the King's Bench, primarily in nineteenth-century England. But the King's Bench was just one of several legal systems that existed and thrived through the formative period of the common law's evolution. The common law that emerged in the nineteenth century resulted not just from the decisionmaking of wise judges of the King's Bench, but was rather the result of a long period of competition and collaboration between that court and numerous other courts with jurisdiction to resolve disputes.[140] Legal historian Arthur Hogue cautions, "We should remember that the law enforced in royal courts, and common to all the realm of England, was in competition with concurrent rules enforced in other courts."[141] As the common law courts eventually absorbed these rival courts, "the common law . . . absorbed much, if not all, of the judicial business of its competitors and may have borrowed heavily from them in the process of aggrandizement."[142]

As an initial matter, ecclesiastical courts declared themselves independent from secular authorities with respect to all issues under their scope, claiming exclusive jurisdiction over issues of family law and inheritance and concurrent jurisdiction over many other issues, including contract law.[143] In turn, "[s]ecular law itself was divided into various competing types, including royal law, feudal law, manorial law, urban law, and mercantile law."[144] Within the royal court system alone there were seven types of courts: (1) General Eyres, (2) Common Please, (3) King's Bench, (4) Exchequer, (5) Commissions of Assize, (6) *Oyer* and *Terminer*, and (7) Gaol Delivery.[145] There were many courts, national and local, royal and ecclesiastical, public and private. Although each was formally defined by a particular jurisdiction, their jurisdictional reach often overlapped and even where they did not, the limits were often evaded through the use of fictions designed to circumvent these formal limits.[146]

During the crucial centuries of the evolution of English law, judicial salaries in all courts were paid in large part from the fees paid by litigants, which provided judges with incentives to maximize the number of cases heard and to expand the jurisdictional reach of their court. Holdsworth observes that even though common law judges began earning state-sponsored salaries as early as 1268, these "were by no means regularly paid."[147] The salaries were often years in arrears and remained irregular until the mid-seventeenth century.[148] Through the Middle Ages, therefore, the right to earn income from fees was "the most valuable" and constituted "a considerable sum."[149] In fact, in 1826, when common law judges were denied the right to earn income from fees, their salaries were more than doubled, apparently to compensate for the loss.[150] Many of the chief rivals of the common law courts, such as the law merchant courts, were wholly private institutions that received no government subsidy and thus were even more reliant on litigant fees than were the common law courts. As a result, judges had an incentive to compete for business and to draw cases to their courts.[151]

Many courts had overlapping jurisdictions with one another. In some instances this concurrent jurisdiction was express. But more commonly, this shared jurisdiction arose in defiance of official jurisdictional limits. Courts ferociously sought to expand their own jurisdictions while protecting themselves from the encroachments of others. The King's Bench, the Exchequer, and the Court of Common Pleas heard many of the same cases and were consistently locked in heated conflicts over allegations that one of these courts was exceeding its jurisdictional limits and invading on the proper jurisdiction of a rival.[152] Although they supposedly had independent jurisdictions, through the use of legal fictions and other mechanisms, by 1700, the three could be said to have acquired comparable jurisdictions over most legal claims.[153] Technically, each of the courts was limited in its jurisdictional reach. But these limitations were difficult to define and easily evaded, such as by the use of procedural fictions designed to camouflage actions in order to shoehorn them into particular courts.[154] For instance, church courts held exclusive jurisdiction over matters of testamentary succession and marriages, but it could often be difficult to determine whether particular situations fell under the church's jurisdiction or that of some other court.[155] The use of fictions allowed courts to reclassify the form of pleading in a case, thereby claiming jurisdiction over cases that the court would otherwise lack authority to hear. For instance, the Court of Exchequer had jurisdiction over debts owed to the King, but not debts between two private parties. Nonetheless, it was said that if a creditor owed the King (such as for taxes), then the failure of a debtor to repay a debt imperiled the ability of the creditor to pay the King. As a result, it was said that the Exchequer could hear the dispute between the debtor and creditor.[156] This was a relatively simple fiction, however; the number and complexity of fictions multiplied so as to evade formal jurisdictional limitations.[157] Even the Magna Carta itself arose in large part as a protest by the lords against the King's efforts to infringe upon the jurisdiction of the lords' courts in order to capture those cases for political and financial reasons.[158] In fact, the phrase *"lex terrae"* in Magna Carta arguably referred not only to the common law, but to all of the other jurisdictions in the kingdom, "including ecclesiastical law, admiralty law, martial law, the law of nations, the law merchant, natural law, and . . . 'the law of the state.'"[159]

This created a system of competition among the courts for filings, leading courts to compete to provide the most unbiased, accurate, reasonable, and prompt resolution of disputes.[160] Litigants could "vote with their feet," patronizing those courts that provided the most effective justice. This meant that judges had to respond to their customers, the individuals who actually used the courts, rather than powerful special interests trying to impose rent-seeking rules involuntarily on passive citizens. This competitive process also led courts to recognize the legal innovations of their rivals, generating flexibility and high-quality justice. As Plucknett observes, even though the various courts were rivals, they "were, in fact, on intimate terms. It did not matter so much that they were usually terms of rivalry," he continues, "for even then they kept close watch upon developments in other institutions, and competed in providing the best remedy."[161]

In addition, this competitive process also contributed to the intellectual development of the law. Because of the slipperiness of jurisdictional labels, judges and litigants were required to look beyond mechanical jurisdictional labels to understand the substance of the underlying claims in order to determine whether jurisdiction was appropriate. Because these jurisdictional assaults and defenses took the form of fictions, this required additional skill and understanding to pierce the superficial categorization of a claim to understand the conceptual structure of the underlying action. This need to look beyond form to the underlying substance of the action made the law more coherent and intellectually sound. Moreover, because court systems were constantly borrowing ideas from one another, the development of the law was encouraged. Because the category labels differed from one court to another, in order to adopt a rival's innovation it was necessary to dig below the form to the underlying substance of the claim. To transfer concepts from one court to another thus required courts to abstract away from the forms of pleadings that were unique to each court to coherent conceptual categories that could be transferred from one court to another. Thus, inter-jurisdictional competition forced courts to abstract away from particular cases to higher conceptual categories and provided a powerful impetus for the improvement and rationalization of the law.[162]

As a result of this proliferation of courts with overlapping jurisdictions, Harold Berman observes, "The same person might be subject to the ecclesiastical courts in one type of case, the king's courts in another, his lord's courts in a third, the manorial court in a fourth, a town court in a fifth, [and] a merchants' court in a sixth."[163] Hogue similarly observes:

> Save when a matter of freehold was at issue, Englishmen were not compelled to present their causes before the king's courts. Men were free to take their cases into the local courts of the counties, which administered local, customary law; men might seek justice from the church courts administering rules of canon law, which touched many matters, especially those related to wills and testaments, marriage and divorce, and contracts involving a pledge of faith; feudal barons might accept jurisdiction of a baronial overlord whose court applied rules of feudal custom; townsmen might bring their causes before the court of a borough, which would judge them by rules of the law merchant.[164]

Because of the competitive interaction of these different systems of law, Hogue adds, "All these courts and systems of law deserve mention in an account of the growth of the common law."[165]

Even if the common law is defined as the law of the royal courts, this law was shaped both by the internal dynamics of the various royal courts as well as their interaction with other courts outside the framework of the royal courts.[166] "This arrangement, seemingly impracticable to modern eyes, was a feature of English public life for five centuries."[167] In fact, as late as 1765, Blackstone observed in his *Commentaries* that multiple types of law still prevailed in England, including natural law, divine law, the law of nations, the English common law, local customary law, Roman law (governing Oxford and Cambridge Universities), ecclesiastical law, statutory law, and the law merchant.[168]

In short, a market for law prevailed, with numerous court systems competing for market share in order to increase their fees.[169] This competitive process generated rules that satisfied the demand of consumers (here, litigants) for fairness, consistency, and reasonableness. Although law and economics scholars generally recognize the advantages of markets in ordering individual and social affairs, recent scholars have curiously overlooked this important historical element of the development of the common law's efficiency.[170] But the point was actually recognized by Adam Smith. Smith observed in the *Wealth of Nations*, "The fees of court seem originally to have been the principal support of the different courts of justice in England. Each court endeavoured to draw to itself as much business as it could, and was, upon that account, willing to take cognizance of many suits which were not originally intended to fall under its jurisdiction."[171] Through the use of legal fictions, Smith noted, the courts could evade *de jure* limitations on their respective jurisdictions and thereby compete for the business of litigants. "In consequence of such fictions," Smith observed, "It came in many cases, to depend altogether upon the parties before what court they would chuse to have their cause tried; and each court endeavoured, by superior dispatch and impartiality, to draw to itself as many causes as it could."[172] Smith ascribed the positive evolution of English law to the competition between the various courts:

> The present admirable constitution of the courts of justice in England was, perhaps, originally in a great measure, formed by this emulation, which anciently took place between their respective judges; each judge endeavouring to give, in his own court, the speediest and most effectual remedy, which the law would admit, for every sort of injustice.[173]

In his *Lectures on Jurisprudence*, Smith observed, "Another thing which tended to support the liberty of the people and render the proceedings in the courts very exact, was the rivalship which arose betwixt them."[174] Smith also noted that requiring judges to compete for fees would cause them to work harder and more efficiently, thereby removing incentives for judges to shirk or to indulge their personal preferences.[175]

The presence of a market for law with several competing suppliers provides an important part of the explanation as to why the common law system tended to generate efficient rules. The King's Bench must be understood as just one actor within a system of several competing producers of law. The "common law," therefore, is the law that evolved from this competitive process, and the borrowing, winnowing, and evolutionary process that it generated. As with any market process, therefore, the end result of this process can be understood as a spontaneous order, created by the interactions of the many individuals who comprise the process rather than by a particular identifiable author.[176] Where there are numerous suppliers of a service and individuals can freely choose among them, this competition will limit the ability to use the court system as a mechanism for redistributing wealth. Where authorities lack the power to coerce parties into their jurisdiction and impose their will, it is difficult to enact inefficient rules because parties can exit the disfavored jurisdiction. Merchants, for instance, have long used the law merchant courts (today international commercial arbitration) to escape unwise and overreaching legal rules. The lesson of the historical record is that, under such conditions, the court system responded by providing decisions that reflected widespread consensus and efficiency, rather than the interests of a few well-organized special interests.

Effects of competition on legal development. Moreover, many of the concepts and doctrines later associated with the common law had their genesis in other courts, such as the law merchant, chancery, or ecclesiastical courts. The development of contract law provides a case study of how competition among courts led to the development of efficiency enhancing legal rules. For much of the history of the common law, Berman observes, contract law in the common law courts remained poorly developed and the system of pleading and proof remained highly formal. The common law courts were thus a stagnant, intellectual backwater for dealing with legal issues involving persons rather than land. Land law dominated English law, especially in the common law courts. "Compared with relationships concerning land," Milsom observes, "Other kinds of legal relationship, and in particular those which we talk about under the headings of contract and tort, were of little consequence."[177] Therefore, "If . . . we allow the age to speak for itself, it will not have so much to say about them. And if we mainly allow the records of the king's courts to speak for the age, we shall hear relatively even less."[178]

This "arrested development" of the common law of contract, Fifoot adds, "was due not so much to the paucity of litigation as to the lack of any comprehensive principle under which isolated decisions could be adjusted."[179] This lack of coherent contract doctrine caused litigants to eschew the common law courts as for resolving difficult questions of contract law.[180] The common law courts thus handled routine matters such as "recognizances," which were essentially penal bonds on which creditors could levy upon the failure of the debtor to perform on a contract. They were thus probably not properly characterized as independent contractual obligations at all but rather glorified debt-collection devices.[181] Parties would often use the common law courts in a collusive or even fictitious manner to create a judgment on a debt of record that the creditor could later use to collect upon default.[182] To the extent that this constituted the bulk of the actions in the royal courts, it is easier to understand why the royal courts failed to develop a more robust body of contract defenses and the like. Simpson, for instance, estimates that in the sample year of 1572, 503 actions were brought on bonds in contrast to only three actions brought in assumpsit.[183]

Although legal developments in the common law courts may have ceased during this time, they continued apace in rival jurisdictions. Contract law was highly developed in several of the other courts, leading parties to ignore the royal courts and resolve their disputes elsewhere. These rival courts included local courts, ecclesiastical courts, law merchant courts, and Chancery. Although they will be discussed distinctly here for purposes of exposition, in practice, the boundaries among these systems were highly fluid as there was a great deal of cross-fertilization between them.

(1)   *Local courts.* Local courts resolved many issues of contract law and other forms of personal legal relations for centuries. These courts included both town and feudal courts.[184] Independent local courts in towns and manors gave remedies in cases where the King's courts would not; Plucknett observes that these country courts "developed a reasonable mass of settled practice" for dealing with contract disputes even though they did not have well theorized concept of contract law.[185] These local courts provided a place of first resort for the bulk of Englanders pursuing claims in contract or tort.[186]

(2)   *Ecclesiastical courts.* Ecclesiastical courts were also a major rival. The ecclesiastical courts offered a similarly highly developed body of contract law and other law, leading many laymen to bring their cases in the ecclesiastical courts.[187] William Stubbs notes that the canon law courts "claimed jurisdiction over everything that had to do with the souls of men," a claim that potentially included almost any "region of social obligation."[188] The assertion of authority over all "spiritual matters" meant in practice that the church was able to create a sort of "shadow claim" for almost every claim recognized in other legal jurisdictions, from contract, to debt, to criminal law, to testamentary succession.[189] In addition to this subject matter jurisdiction, "any person could bring suit in an ecclesiastical court, or could remove a case from a secular court

to an ecclesiastical court, even against the will of the other party, on the ground of 'default of secular justice.'"[190] Even though ordinary contracts fell under the jurisdiction of lay courts, breaking a promise, especially one made under oath, was also a sin.[191] As a result, ecclesiastical courts could assert jurisdiction over many contract cases.[192] Whereas the common law required all contracts to be in writing and made under seal, ecclesiastical courts were more flexible.[193] Other areas of the law affecting laymen, such as family law and intestate succession, were almost completely under the jurisdiction of the ecclesiastical courts.[194] Common law innovations in procedural areas also owe a large debt to canon law influence.[195] Even the mundane issues of contract and property law could be characterized as raising spiritual issues that could trigger the church's jurisdiction.[196] The availability of rival courts under independent powers— Pope and King—provided a powerful mechanism for legal development.[197] This was both direct, by the innovations of the ecclesiastical courts, as well as indirect by pressuring other courts to innovate,[198] Also, many of the Chancellors of the Chancery Court were clerics who were trained in the canon law tradition and brought principles of the canon law with them to the Chancery bench.[199] Canon law, as incorporated into the Chancery Courts, was the root of such fundamental equitable principles as the requirements of good faith and fair dealing in transactions, as well as the remedy of specific performance.[200] Canon law also enabled the systematization of the otherwise ad hoc exercise of the Chancellor's discretion.[201] This fierce rivalry between the ecclesiastical courts and other courts persisted for hundreds of years and was ended only when the Reformation brought the church, and hence its courts, under the King's power.[202]

(3)   Law merchant courts. Most important in the realm of commercial law and contracts was the law merchant, or *lex mercatoria*.[203] The law merchant was born in the commercial city-states of Italy in the early medieval period.[204] The birth of the law merchant in Italy was fortuitous, as this also encouraged cross-fertilization between the law merchant and canon law. The universal reach of the church crossing national boundaries also had the effect of universalizing law, creating a type of "law of nations" that could be applied nearly uniformly throughout Europe.[205] As a result, the ecclesiastical law provided a powerful complement to the universalizing nature of the law merchant, which found its expression through the customs of merchants, which were largely universal as well.[206] The canon law offered a long and intellectually robust legal tradition that could be grafted onto the law merchant. Whereas the law merchant was a collection of informal procedures and customary law, the canon law provided an intellectual framework that could be used to organize the law merchant into a coherent legal system. But equally important, the canon law offered an intellectual framework to synthesize the law merchant without creating an oppressive set of procedural and substantive rules that would have the effect of strangling it. For instance, canon law provided a moral grounding for enforcement of practices of good faith and fair dealing, which still serve as the foundation of commercial law and practice today.[207] "[R]unning through all the mass of particular rules" of the canon law system were "two guiding principles that the procedure must be simple and speedy, and the law must be equitable,"[208] These principles provided a powerful organizing standard for the emergence of the law merchant. As Holdsworth observes, these principles justified the "purging of the law of barren technicalities which enabled the merchants" to devise their own procedures and substantive law free from the heavy-hand of

legal formalities.[209] "That the usages and practice of the merchants themselves were the main source of the law is clear from the literature on the subject."[210] In addition, the *lex mercatoria* also reflected influences of Roman law,[211] the *Lex Rhodia* customary commercial law of the Mediterranean identified in the third century,[212] and the influences of the Middle East, where long-distance trade and complex commerce emerged earlier than in Europe.[213]

In fact, much of the fabric of sophisticated contract law was rooted in the law merchant, not the common law courts. Thus, the law merchant offered a range of innovative equitable defenses, such as defenses of fraud, duress, and mistake.[214] The law merchant also developed rules protecting bona-fide purchasers for value well before the common law did.[215] The common law did not adopt these defenses until the incorporation of the law merchant into the common law many years later. Thus, the law merchant modernized contract law well before the common law courts did.[216] Indeed, the law merchant courts themselves faced competition from other courts— the common law courts, ecclesiastical courts, etc.[217] As a result, the law merchant confronted the same competitive pressures to innovate and modernize that the other jurisdictions also confronted.

Founded in the Mediterranean, the law merchant eventually migrated to England through the pressures of international trade as England joined the family of commercial nations.[218] England, in turn, followed the world trend of creating a set of unique courts and a body of procedural and substantive rules that drew merchants into its courts.[219] Disputes between merchants over contracts, notes, or other commercial affairs were tried in these specialized tribunals.[220] As Thomas Scrutton observed, "If you read the [common] law reports of the seventeenth century you will be struck with one very remarkable fact; either Englishmen of that day did not engage in commerce, or they appear not to have been litigious people in commercial matters, each of which alternatives appears improbable."[221] He then provides the answer to his puzzle: "The reason why there were hardly any cases dealing with commercial matters in the Reports of the Common Law Courts is that such cases were dealt with by special Courts and under a special law. That law was an old-established law and largely based on mercantile customs."[222] In fact, the common law courts were jurisdictionally prohibited from hearing cases involving contracts that were made and to be performed outside England because of the inability to collect the relevant facts through the process of a jury trial.[223] The common law also lacked jurisdiction over torts committed abroad.[224] Given the relatively undeveloped nature of the English economy relative to the rest of Europe during the Middle Ages, most large commercial activity was performed by foreign merchants; thus, this jurisdictional limitation barred the common law courts from hearing almost all important commercial litigation.[225] In addition, because many commercial transactions were, by definition, transnational, it was desirable to have a uniform transnational body of law that did not vary according to the nationalities of the contracting parties.[226] The law merchant courts applied to both international and domestic transactions between merchants.[227] Indeed, over time the law merchant rules became available for *all* commercial transactions in which either of the parties was a merchant, including domestic trades,[228] so that during the Stuart era, "the bulk of mercantile litigation was . . . committed to private arbitration."[229] Thus, there was no demand by merchants for the common law to innovate because merchants were satisfied with the rules produced by the *lex mercatoria*.

On the other side, there was little opportunity or social need for the common law to innovate because contract and other disputes were being adequately resolved in the law merchant courts and elsewhere.[230]

Law merchant courts prospered in towns, fairs, and various markets.[231] Medieval trading fairs and major commercial towns provided courts for merchants to resolve disputes over contracts and torts.[232] These were referred to as the courts of "piepowder," so named because the courts heard and ruled on cases before the dust could fall from the feet of the merchants at the fairs.[233] The right to hold a trading fair included within it a right to offer a piepowder court to resolve disputes arising during the fair.[234] These courts offered swift resolution of disputes with a minimum of procedural formalities.[235] Rather than the archaic substantive rules of the common law, the law merchant courts offered law grounded in commercial custom consistent with the merchants' expectations.[236] Juries were composed of merchants themselves, often drawn from multiple nationalities.[237] The *Carta Mercatoria* of 1303 promised protection for foreign merchants, including access to speedy justice in the event of a dispute as well as the promise that any jury would be half composed of foreign merchants.[238] Lawyers were generally barred from the proceedings as disruptive of the speedy and informal resolutions of disputes.[239] The courts of various fairs maintained information networks that made possible the transnational enforcement of judgments. As a result, an unpaid judgment from a fair held in England, for instance, could be enforced against a merchant in a piepowder court in Italy. The failure to perform the judgment resulted not only in punishment to the merchant, but the exclusion of the merchant's fellow countrymen from the fair.[240]

The courts of the Staple also provided their own sets of arbitral merchant courts to resolve disputes arising in the markets of the most important articles of commerce in England, such as wool, woolfells, leather, lead, and tin.[241] Under the "Statute of the Staple," enacted in 1353, common law courts were specifically prohibited from hearing disputes arising from contracts made on the staple markets and the staple courts were expressly instructed to apply the law merchant and commercial custom and not the common law.[242] The jurisdiction of the staple courts was both broad and exclusive, including claims of debt, covenant, and trespass, and excluding the King's courts in all cases but freehold or felony.[243] Under the *Carta Mercatoria*, Edward I expressly granted merchants the right to enter into contracts consistent with commercial custom, rather than forcing them to fit their transactions into the form favored by the common law.[244] As Holdsworth summed up the situation in the era of the flourishing law merchant, "With the merchant, his courts and his law the common law had little concern."[245] In part, this was because of the incompetence of the common law courts to deal credibly with commercial disputes.[246] To understand the common law of England, especially prior to the eighteenth century, therefore, it is crucial to understand the history of the law merchant as a rival jurisdiction to the common law.[247]

Through the leadership of Coke and Mansfield, the law merchant was eventually incorporated into the common law.[248] Under Coke's lead, the common law began to chip away at the jurisdiction of the law merchant courts over commercial disputes beginning in the seventeenth century by increasingly looking to merchant custom as a source of legal understanding.[249] Mansfield completed the revolution in the commercial jurisprudence of the common law courts by incorporating the law merchant into the common law.[250] In so doing, Mansfield overthrew the common law's encrusted and dysfunctional precedent regarding economic relations among merchants to try to increase control of the common law courts over commercial law matters.[251] The law merchant had proven itself responsive to the innovations and needs of commercial practice, whereas the common law remained loyal to archaic doctrines from an earlier age of commerce and earlier technologies. Mansfield largely adopted the law merchant's rules on everything from rules of evidence to the substantive rules of negotiable instruments in response to competitive pressures from the law merchant court system.[252] Modern conceptions of partnership and other business forms originated in the law merchant,[253] as did warranties of quality and the fellow-servant doctrine.[254] In addition, Mansfield made substantial use of special merchant juries as a mechanism for bringing merchant custom into the common law and making it a basis for an integration of merchant practice into the common law.[255] Still other law merchant concepts found their way into the common law through the initial mediation of the Chancery Court, as the Chancery sought to draw business to itself in the great competition with the common law courts.[256]

The stricter form of the incorporation thesis has been questioned in recent years.[257] For current purposes, however, quibbles over the direct historical lineage of the law merchant into the common law are largely beside the point. There is little question that, at the very least, the law merchant courts innovated in the realm of commercial law well before the common law recognized many of these concepts and that the competition among these courts drove the common law under Coke to innovate to preserve its market share.[258] Moreover, it is evident from the historical record that Lord Mansfield was clearly aware of the law merchant and many of its principles. In responding to this interjurisdictional competition, therefore, the rivalry had the effect of driving the common law toward efficiency.

(4)   Chancery court. Finally, standing behind the common law was the Court of Chancery. It was well understood that, in part, the inflexibility and lack of creativity of the common law was justified by the recognition that any undue hardship caused by the common law's rigor could be ameliorated by the equitable remedies available in Chancery. In the name of predictability and consistency, common law therefore adopted bright-line rules that occasionally worked hardship in particular cases.[259] Nonetheless, this hardship was not the end of the story, as it was well recognized that individuals could resort to equity to prevent the injustice.[260] Baker writes, "if the common law remained inflexible, the Chancery was an obvious source of relief. It could give better remedies than the common law courts, and could give remedies where the regular courts gave none."[261] Equity provided a defense where, for instance, a bond was wholly or partially satisfied but not recovered by the debtor.[262] Equity also provided relief in situations of contractual mistake and created the equity of redemption primarily for situations of mistake or bad faith.[263] Chancery could also enforce promises not made through a written sealed document, which the common law required.[264] Among other inconveniences of this common law doctrine was that it made executory promises unenforceable.[265] Given the widespread recognition of the interaction between common law and equity at the time, it would be inaccurate to end one's analysis by merely pointing out the absurdity of some of the common law's rules. Exceptions from the common law's harsh rules were to be sought in Chancery, and Chancery aggressively competed to win business away from the common law.[266]

In principle, the Chancery court could act whenever the operation of the common law would work an injustice, as for a "breach of conscience"[267] or where common law provided no adequate remedy.[268] This mandate was often construed broadly.[269] For example, Chancery relief was available in cases of fraud, forgery, and duress, for which no relief was available at common law.[270] Chancery was also invoked to enforce contracts made abroad, which, as noted, were unenforceable at common law.[271] Chancery could also be invoked to enforce performance where the plaintiff was too poor to afford expensive common law writs or where a rich and powerful defendant was able to exercise undue influence over local judges and jurors.[272]

Chancery could intervene on the basis of the inadequacy of the common law remedy available to a party for a breach of contract, not just because of the inadequacy of the common law conception of contract. This allowed the Chancery court to act to award specific performance of a contract, a remedy unavailable at common law.[273] For a time in the fifteenth and sixteenth centuries, the common law courts feared that Chancery's flexibility and procedural advantages would allow the Chancery courts to displace the common law courts as the dominant legal institutions of England. In fact, the common law courts did lose a substantial number of cases to Chancery.[274] Especially in the latter period of the era of competing courts, the Chancery court provided an ever-present threat and rival to the common law.[275] Merchants and commoners were especially disfavored by the common law's adherence to arcane and expensive legal formalities and, therefore, found recourse in Chancery to enforce their contracts.[276] Spurred by this competition, the common law courts responded by designing procedural and substantive innovations "which would win back the patronage of the litigants and the lawyers who advised them."[277] For instance, Coke's impetus for introducing the law merchant into the common law was in large part a response to the Chancery's earlier successes in doing the same.[278]

Although the competition from other courts to the common law was in the realm of personal law, such as contracts and torts, students of the law will recognize that the Chancery courts played a powerful role in generating improvements to the law of real property as well. In particular, the development of such vehicles as equitable trusts provided individuals with dramatic legal innovations that made it easier for them to execute their legal affairs. It should not be surprising that the great innovation in property forms thus arose during an era of robust inter-jurisdictional competition between the common law and chancery.[279] Absent competition from Chancery, there was no dynamic at work to drive the common law toward innovation in property forms. This led the common law to stagnate. This likely explains the otherwise puzzling *numerus clausus* doctrine of the common law, which limits the forms of property rights that can be designed in real property.[280] Cases involving the ownership and transfer of real property were the sole jurisdiction of the common law courts.[281]

Monopolies generally exercise their monopoly power by restricting supply. In the context of real property law, the common law's monopoly on real property matters may explain the supply restriction on real property forms. Competition, by contrast, should have the effect of increasing supply over the monopoly rate of provision. This seems to be what occurred during the era of flourishing competition between common law and Chancery law, when Chancery developed a number of fictions to evade the common law's monopoly.[282] Through the Statute of Uses the common law was able to "capture . . . the more important of those uses, which had become a new species of property under the fostering hand of the Chancellor."[283] Thus, by imitating the Chancery innovations—and by increasing the forms of property available under the common law—the common law was able to maintain its market share. By contrast, the reinstatement of a monopoly court system brought with it a traditional restriction of supply—in this context, the restrictions of the *numerous clausus* doctrine.[284]

(5)   The common law response. In turn, the common law courts were actively competing with these courts; for example, it appears that the eventual demise of the vibrancy of the local courts was a result of being outbid by the competing common law.[285] In response to the vibrancy of the merchant law courts, common law judges developed the notion of *assumpsit* as a mechanism for adjudicating contract claims that fell outside the traditional "procedural shackles" of debt and covenant that had stymied the development of the common law.[286] Assumpsit allowed the common law for the first time to develop a coherent mechanism for developing a true contract doctrine.[287] In fact, the undeveloped state of traditional contract law may be best evidenced by the fact that assumpsit developed from tort concepts, not from debt actions or any other form of action, because common law simply lacked the intellectual structure to deal with promissory obligations.[288]

At other times, however, this competition was not so benign.[289] For instance, the King's establishment of Admiralty courts in the fourteenth century to compete against local mercantile courts was driven not by the desire to improve the law but to force all foreign trade to pass through these monopolistic organizations, primarily to simplify customs control.[290] Nevertheless, the Admiralty courts expressly rejected the strict pleading requirements of the common law courts, following procedures much more similar to those of the law merchant courts.[291] Similarly, the Reformation predictably narrowed the independent jurisdiction of the ecclesiastical courts on issues of contract law.[292] As for the law merchant, Baker observes that the reasons for its decline are not wholly clear. In large part, it appears to have been a victim of the creeping power of the common law courts, which imposed its own bureaucratic practices and asserted the right to hear appeals from the law merchant courts. Eventually, this creeping legalization of the law merchant courts undermined the flexibility and speed that had attracted merchants to the law merchant courts in the first place.[293]

Regardless of the reason, over time, and especially under Coke's influential leadership, the common law eventually came to displace these competing jurisdictions and to assert control over the commercial law of England. Although this increased the power of the King and the common law judges, Holdsworth observes:

> To the litigant [it] meant much inconvenience. To the commercial law of this country it meant a slower development. But to the common law it meant a capacity for expansion, and a continued supremacy over the law of the future, which consolidated the victories won in the political contests of the 17th century. If Lord Mansfield is to be credited with the honourable title of the founder of the commercial law of this country, it must be allowed that Coke gave to the founder of that law his opportunity.[294]

Similarly, Plucknett observes, "It is therefore not unfair to say that Coke's influence made for the establishment of a supreme common law, and for the abolition or severe restriction of all other forms of law in the country. His triumph therefore introduced a certain narrowness and conservatism which stood in the way of reform."[295]

Thus, even though contract law in the common law courts remained relatively undeveloped during this period, it appears that this gap was filled by local courts, law merchant courts (the *lex mercatoria*), and ecclesiastical courts. Plucknett speculates that the strength of these competing legal systems may explain why the common law remained so undeveloped. He writes:

> It may be said with some fairness that the existence on the one hand of mercantile jurisdictions, and on the other of the spiritual courts which could bring moral pressure to bear, together with the remedies available locally, afford some explanation for the common law courts declining to expend their law of contract . . . . [T]he common law apparently felt that it could abstain with a clear conscience, knowing that the matter was already in the expert hands of the Church and the merchants . . . .[296]

In contrast to the ecclesiastical and law merchant courts, the common law itself developed a relatively inflexible, formalistic, and cumbersome regime.[297] The rigors of the forms of action undermined the coherent evolution of the common law system of contract, causing the common law to lag well behind these other legal regimes that provided the engine for reform of contract law. Church courts were also well ahead of lay courts in the evolution of modern rules of proof and procedure in contract disputes.[298] On the other hand, the absorption of these principles into the common law enabled improvement of the law by extending their reach to all transactions, rather than limiting their application to just the individuals subject to the various specialized jurisdictions, such as merchants or shippers.[299]

Constrained competition and the production of efficient rules. A better understanding of the history of the common law system also provides the answer to Landes and Posner's puzzle as to why competition among courts did not generate pro-plaintiff doctrine in the several courts of the land.[300] In fact, Landes and Posner acknowledge that the historical record appears to be inconsistent with the prediction of their model that courts would compete by generating pro-plaintiff rules.[301] "Why it did not emerge . . . presents an interesting question for further research."[302] Indeed, in the *common law* courts, there was in fact much pro-plaintiff doctrine, such as a notable absence of defenses to contract and the like.[303] These courts were little more than debt collection courts that required little in the way of developed contract jurisprudence and responded in kind.

In the *other* courts, however, such as the *lex mercatoria*, ecclesiastical, and Chancery courts, a different dynamic was at work. In law merchant courts, for instance, legal disputes were characterized by a high degree of reciprocity. Because merchant law was rooted in the customs of traders, this reflected the reciprocal nature of inclusive customs.[304] Merchants could never predict which side of a dispute they would be on. As a result, they did not favor either pro-plaintiff or pro-defendant rules.

Instead, they favored efficient rules that minimized the transaction costs of conducting transactions. In the Staple Courts, the rules of the exchange were established by its members who would be governed by those rules. Because they would be ongoing members of the exchange engaging in repeat, reciprocal transactions, there was a built-in incentive to adopt efficiency-enhancing rules to govern the exchange.

In the trading fairs of the middle ages, a different dynamic was at work. The right to hold a fair was the prerogative of the King, but the King could grant franchises to local lords to hold fairs. With this grant came the power to establish a special law of the fair and a court system to administer it. As with the Staple Courts, this special law of the fair was independent of the royal law. Holdsworth observes, "[T]he administration of the law has always been a profitable thing; and therefore, the grantee of the franchise naturally kept it in his own hands."[305] Because the fair owner was thus the residual claimant of both the proceeds of the fair as well as the ancillary legal system, he had an incentive to maximize the popularity of the fair and the commerce conducted there. With respect to the legal system provided, therefore, the fair owner had a natural incentive to provide timely justice and efficiency-enhancing rules, rather than favoring one party or the other.

Nor would the ecclesiastical courts have been expected to provide pro-plaintiff rules. Rather, the rules provided in these courts reflected the influence of Canon and Roman law. Canon law doctrines reflected the influence of equitable considerations rooted in church teachings, thus the law was required to be fair, equitable, and reasonable, thereby limiting the ability of Canon law courts to compete on a purely pro-plaintiff doctrine. Roman law reflected a heritage similar to that of the law merchant, a body of law that evolved through reciprocity-based interactions that tended to promote individual liberty and private ordering.[306] The Chancery courts reflected many of these same influences of Canon law and Roman law.

In addition, in many of these interactions the parties had a preexisting relationship amenable to private contractual ordering, such as for products liability, medical malpractice, or some other relationship. Traditionally, these were understood as relations of a contractual nature and would thus be driven by the logic of the evolution of contract law, not tort law.[307] Only in recent decades has tort law expanded to fill the areas traditionally governed by contract law. Moreover, as noted, most of the disputes in question arose from conflicts between two individuals, not between institutional repeat players. Under these conditions, reciprocity norms would tend to govern the evolution of legal doctrine, rather than rent-seeking norms. Moreover, conflicts between pure strangers unrelated by contractual or customary relationships were likely very rare during the era in which the common law evolved. Thus, the relevant margin on which courts would have been competing by producing legal doctrine would have been in the far more common situation in which a preexisting relationship between parties existed.

Perhaps most crucial was the fact that, even though parties faced few formal constraints on where to bring their suits, this choice of jurisdiction was actually made *ex ante* rather than *ex post* most of the time. When the parties chose their jurisdiction, therefore, they did not know whether they would be more likely to be the plaintiff or the defendant in any subsequent litigation and so would be unlikely to prefer a biased court over an unbiased one. To be sure, there is no evidence of widespread use of choice of law or choice of forum clauses within contracts. But there were clearly-established norms and expectations as to which court would hear a lawsuit arising under a given contract. Thus, there were a set of default expectations as to which court would hear a given case. These were default expectations to which parties tacitly adhered. For merchants, for instance, it was expected that the law merchant would hear disputes that arose unless some other court (such as common law) was expressly specified.[308] Similarly, Chancery could act only if it could be shown that an inadequate remedy was available at common law or application of common law would work an injustice, thereby further limiting its ability to compete for business through the provision of pro-plaintiff rules.[309] This set of assumptions about the default courts that would hear a given case meant that forum choice was, in fact, *ex ante* and made when the parties were uncertain as to which would be the possible plaintiff or defendant under a subsequent suit. Once a given forum was implicitly chosen *ex ante*, breach of the agreement was enforced by the threat of ostracism against merchants who refused to allow the case to be heard in the agreed-upon forum or failed to abide by the judgment of the court.[310] Ostracism from the merchant community effectively ended the offending merchant's career.[311] Making the choice of forum *ex ante* thus promoted beneficial forum-shopping for efficient law and discouraged forum-shopping for law that systematically favored one party over another.[312]

This also explains why court precedent tended toward efficiency, rather than acting as a random drift between efficiency and inefficiency, as previous models predicted it would.[313] Earlier law and economics scholars focused on the incentives of litigants to push the law toward efficiency or inefficiency. And it is true that where there is weak precedent, litigants do in fact lack such an incentive and random drift may result. But in a competitive legal order, *judges*, rather than litigants, were the residual claimants for the results of legal doctrine. Because judges were paid from legal fees, they would maximize their fees when business increased. And, as the foregoing analysis has demonstrated, a particular court maximized its business through the provision of efficient legal rules, giving judges an incentive to push for efficient rules. As a result, random drift would not result; instead, there would be an incentive for judges to favor efficient rules because they could capture the benefits that accrued from such rules.

When the common law courts swallowed up these other courts, the preexisting body of law flowed directly into the common law. Rather than a piecemeal acceptance of these doctrines, the common law adopted entire bodies of law that had grown up in an environment of reciprocal interactions. This direct incorporation of these entire bodies of law accounts for the sudden appearance of systematic and coherent bodies of law in the common law during a concentrated period in the eighteenth and nineteenth centuries. It also accounts for why the competition among courts generated efficient law, rather than pro-plaintiff law. As the jurisdiction of the royal courts expanded over time, eventually many of the doctrines first developed in these rival courts were absorbed into the common law courts.[314] It was during this period that the common law first adopted the distinction between contract and tort, a distinction that had long prevailed in the law applied in Chancery, Admiralty, Star Chamber, and other royal courts.[315] Notions of unjust enrichment and quasi-contract prevailed in numerous other courts well before being received into the common law, albeit it an altered form.[316] The fundamental concept of negotiability in bills of exchange emerged among merchants as early as the thirteenth century; the common law did not recognize the doctrine until 1603.[317] The concept of respondeat superior, the idea that employers are vicariously liable for the harm caused by the negligence of their employees, was incorporated into the common law from the maritime law of the Admiralty courts and the law merchant.[318] Berman and Reid note that other developments in the common law in the early eighteenth century reflect the powerful influence of courts such as the law merchant and maritime courts.[319]

The discussion here should be qualified in one respect, however, in that it may overstate the differences between the royal courts on one hand and other competing courts on the other. Through the use of legal fictions, it appears that there may have been some changes going on in the current law that were not fully recognized until later dates. As previously noted, legal fictions had long been used by courts seeking to expand their jurisdiction.[320] Beginning in the seventeenth century, however, the courts started using fictions to change the *substantive* laws as well.[321] Through the use of fictions, such as the action of "special assumpsit," the common law courts expanded their jurisdiction to take account of a wide variety of contracts that previously had been subject to the jurisdiction of the Chancery, Admiralty, High Commission, and Star Chamber. Baker argues, for instance, that the recognition of a claim in *assumpsit* merely gave the common law courts an express mechanism for hearing cases that they were deciding already, merely under different procedural headings.[322] Similarly, the common law courts lacked the power to hear cases entered into with traders from other countries; nonetheless, by engaging in jurisdictional fictions the common law was able to assert jurisdiction over the growing commercial practice.[323] Although this served to "unify[ ] the English law of contract," it also hardened contract law doctrines, depriving its contract law of the flexibility that characterized the contract law of the other courts.[324]

Subject to this slight qualification, the history of the English common law suggests that those who examine only the body of law developed in the royal courts prior to the nineteenth century in order to understand the actual "law of England" may be looking in the wrong place. Much legal modernization was actually being carried out in courts other than the common law courts, and those were the courts where parties were litigating their claims. Except for control over land, multiple courts maintained competing jurisdictions with the common law on almost all other matters that touched the personal legal affairs of Englanders. Many of the eventual innovations of the common law courts in later times were merely the absorption of these well-developed bodies of law from other courts into the common law, rather than a fundamental redirection of the common law itself. Moreover, through the use of legal fictions many of these changes, such as the adoption of negligence principles, may have been implicitly operating prior to the nineteenth century although they were not formally announced until then.

Thus, the market for law created by the competitive nature of the historic common law gave rise to a pro-efficiency dynamic of market competition. As Rowley concludes

> The competitive nature of early common law evolution inevitably provided a powerful impulse for the law to reflect the interests of the litigants and, in this sense, to be efficient. For exit, and to a lesser extent

voice, were available weapons to those who became disenchanted with the writs and their court interpretations.[325]

At the same time, this nonhierarchical and decentralized institutional structure insulated the common law from rent-seeking pressures and constrained judges. Judicial agency costs only became a real problem after the centralization of the legal system and the demise of competing legal jurisdictions. Prior to that time, the ability of parties to "vote with their feet" constrained judicial power to pursue personal preferences. Thus, it may be that this need to constrain judicial discretion through stricter *stare decisis* was a response to the breakdown of the traditional mechanism for constraining judges. Given this interdependent relationship between rules of precedent on one hand and the structure of the court system on the other, Judge Kozinski may not be correct in his intuition: "It is entirely possible that lawyers of the eighteenth century, had they been confronted with the regime of rigid precedent that is in common use today, would have reacted with alarm."[326] To be sure, the nature of precedent has changed since the nineteenth century, but this is because the nature of the court system has changed, as well. The demise of a competitive legal order in fact suggests a need for a doctrine of *stare decisis* as a mechanism to control judicial discretion in the absence of the opportunity of parties to choose their court. The common law emerged from this dynamic process of competition, as entrepreneurial competitors created new legal doctrines and copied successful innovations from one another. This helped to create efficiency in the common law and insulate it from public choice influences.

The American experience

Swift *and* Erie.—Through the nineteenth century, the United States had a legal regime similar to the competitive legal order in England. Under the doctrine of *Swift v. Tyson,*[327] which prevailed until *Erie Railroad v. Tompkins,*[328] the United States had a similar system of competing courts with overlapping jurisdictions. Although similar, the systems were not identical, leading to different evolutionary paths. Under *Swift*, common law cases in diversity actions could be brought either under the common law of a particular state or under general federal common law, thereby generating overlapping common law jurisdictions for the same act. Traditional mythology has held that this created an incentive for forum-shopping by plaintiffs seeking pro-plaintiff legal rules, and that as a result, Justice Brandeis rejected the *Swift* doctrine in *Erie*, ruling that there can be no general federal common law.[329] The conclusion that *Swift* should have been abandoned because of rampant negative forum-shopping is questionable.[330] On the other hand, there were some important differences between the English competitive system and the American system under *Swift v. Tyson* that eventually created several problems with the American system. Nonetheless, there is ample evidence that availability of competing courts under *Swift* explains much of the evolution toward efficient legal doctrines in the United States in the nineteenth century. Moreover, *Erie's* abandonment of *Swift* and its replacement with a less competitive regime has reduced a power constraint on rent-seeking in the state courts that has led to many of the problems in common law doctrine in recent years.

The diversity jurisdiction of the federal courts empowers those courts to hear disputes that arise between residents of two different states. Under *Swift v. Tyson*, however, the federal courts provided more than just a forum to diversity disputes. The federal courts also had the power to develop their own common law to apply to those disputes. This effectively gave litigants not only a choice of *forum*, but also a choice of *law*. Moreover, the federal courts and state courts shared jurisdiction within the same geographic area, subject only to the limitation that the disputants could establish diversity.

Recent scholarship has suggested that *Erie* was not animated by excessive forum shopping, but was intended to prevent individuals from escaping inefficient and burdensome state regulation that was generally animated by the influence of special interests.[331] Judges on the lower federal courts, the product of three successive Republican administrations (Harding, Coolidge, and Hoover), were hostile to progressive state laws that interfered with common law principles of freedom of contract.[332] Following *Lochner v. New York*[333] and its progeny, the federal courts relied on time-honored common law principles to strike down those regulations. In response, Roosevelt Supreme Court appointees sought to preclude these diversity cases from reaching the federal courts; *Erie* eliminated much of the incentive to sue in federal court.[334] Brandeis, a progressive, was particularly disturbed by the aggressive approach of the federal courts and sought to deprive the federal courts of this power.[335] Brandeis observed in 1905 that the leading lawyers in the United States were "engaged mainly in supporting the claims of corporations; often in endeavoring to evade or nullify the . . . crude laws by which legislators sought to regulate the power or curb the excesses of corporations."[336] This is ironic, for, as previously noted, the presence of overlapping legal jurisdictions was a source of freedom that allowed individuals to escape the clutches of special interest-oriented legal rules.

Justice Story implicitly recognized the importance of this issue in *Swift*, as his opinion in *Swift* was animated by the desire to allow the federal courts to develop the commercially sophisticated and modern practices of the law merchant.[337] And, in fact, history clearly indicates that the body of commercial law developed in the federal courts during the *Swift* era was substantially more efficient than the law in the state courts.[338] Because federal law was grounded in commercial custom it tended to produce predictable and efficiency enhancing law.[339] By contrast, state law was provincial, ignorant, and dominated by the rent-seeking influences of local special interests.[340] By prohibiting competition between the state and federal legal systems within the same jurisdictions for the same acts, this competition was ended, leaving individuals subject to the regulation of the states. True, competition among different states continued, but this competition is limited and subject to the risks of judicial enforcement (or non-enforcement) of choice-of-law clauses in contracts. The elimination of the ability to forum-shop into federal court, therefore, did not merely eliminate access to one court at the margin; instead, it eliminated access to the many skilled federal judges and the efficiency-enhancing law that they had created over many decades of decision-making.

It was traditionally understood that the diversity jurisdiction of the federal courts was intended not only to serve as an alternative forum to protect out-of-state interests, but also to provide an alternative body of law to protect out-of-state interests, especially creditors.[341] In fact, it was generally understood that it would be largely pointless to provide an alternative forum to litigate cases if the court would still apply parochial state laws that could discriminate against out-of-state interests under the guise of facial neutrality.[342] As Justice Story observed in a different case:

> [I]n controversies affecting citizens of other states, and in no degree aris-
> ing from local regulations, as for instance, foreign contracts of a commer-
> cial nature, I think that it can hardly be maintained, that the laws of a state,
> to which they have no reference however, narrow, injudicious and incon-
> venient they may be, are to be the exclusive guides for judicial decision.
> Such a construction would defeat nearly all of the objects for which the
> constitution has provided a national court.[343]

Tony Freyer echoes Story's analysis, noting that the "national courts were established in order to protect the rights of citizens of different states and nations from
unfavorable local *law*."[344]

Swift created the opportunity for forum-shopping by giving plaintiffs and defendants the choice of whether to sue in state court or in federal court in diversity cases.
As Bridwell and Whitten observe, "This kind of 'forum shopping' was exactly what
the diversity jurisdiction was designed to accomplish."[345] At the time, this choice
actually tended to vindicate the parties' legitimate expectations by establishing a
background of rules to govern the dispute. Like the *ex ante* expectation of forum
choice under the English system, it was generally understood by the parties when
they entered into a contract under the *Swift* system just which court system would
govern a subsequent dispute.[346] Where the exchange took place between individuals
of different states, it was generally supposed that the general customary rules of merchants would apply. By contrast, where the exchange took place between individuals
of the same state, it was generally understood that local law and custom would control, which might differ from general customary law. Indeed, *Swift* v. *Tyson* turned on
the question of the negotiability of a bill drawn in Maine and accepted in New York,
giving it an interstate character from the outset. As a result, Swift was entitled to
rely on the fact that the general principles of the commercial world (*i.e.*, the law
merchant) would apply to govern disputes over the negotiability of the note, rather
than the parochial rules of New York. Popularly elected state judges consistently acted
to deny the rights of out-of-state creditors; federal judges applying law merchant
principles, by contrast, were able to enforce these contracts reliably.

In addition, Justice Story's opinion in *Swift* rests in part on the common
law's distinction between the flexible concept of "precedent" that still prevailed in the
nineteenth century on one hand and the more rigid concept of *stare decisis* that emerged
in the common law in the twentieth century on the other. "It will hardly be contended," Story argues, "that the decisions of courts constitute laws." Echoing English
commentators, Story concludes that judicial decisions "are, at most only evidence of
what the laws are, and are not, of themselves, laws. They are often re-examined,
reversed and qualified by the courts themselves, whenever they are found to be either
defective, or ill-founded, or otherwise incorrect."[347] Under the *Swift* view, judicial
precedent does not become fixed as "law" unless it was enacted by the state legislature
or has become so well-established through time and widespread acceptance of
its reasonableness and usefulness that it is not likely to be overruled.[348] It follows,

therefore, that, just as a subsequent state judge could reconsider the decision of his predecessor, so, too, could a federal judge reconsider the decision of a prior state judge. It was the reason of the rule, rather than its authority, that bound subsequent judges.[349]

Thus, *Swift* did not rest in the belief that the federal courts are animated by some "brooding omnipresence in the sky," as famously caricatured by Oliver Wendell Holmes in his critique of federal common law.[350] Rather, Story's opinion rests on the traditional common law distinction that isolated judicial decisions do not become binding principles of law until they have been tested repeatedly by courts and individual actors. The best law is that which is tested and sifted through time by many judges. Moreover, merchant custom was seen as a surer source of principles than common law precedent.[351] The failure to grasp the essence of the opinion in *Swift* is thus more a reflection of the postivist prejudices of twentieth century scholars than of the naiveté of Justice Story.[352]

To the extent that there is any validity to the traditional criticism of *Swift* that it permitted inefficient forum shopping, these criticisms are clearly overstated. *Erie* itself was a case involving strangers. Even if such stranger cases may give rise to pro-plaintiff legal doctrines, this says nothing at all about whether interjurisdictional competition should be prohibited for situations where the parties have a preexisting relationship.[353] Even in modern society, many so-called "stranger" cases really are not. Most products liability cases, after all, arise from consensual transactions. Moreover, there are likely to be preexisting relationships through insurance companies and other institutions that turn seemingly stranger-based conflicts into semi-contractual cases.[354] Thus, even if it were thought necessary to limit jurisdictional competition where there is no preexisting relationship between the parties, this does not mean that such limits should be imposed where the parties can explicitly or implicitly consent *ex ante* to particular jurisdictions. Indeed, as noted, *Swift* was developed in exactly this sort of case and was only later extended to govern cases with facts such as *Erie*'s.[355] One could easily distinguish cases like *Swift* from cases like *Erie* if one were so inclined.[356]

Erie effectively created a series of territorial monopolies for the production of common law. In fact, unlike the competitive nature of the traditional common law that constrained the ability to use legal doctrine to transfer wealth, *Erie* creates the conditions for effective forum shopping and for the production of pro-plaintiff rules. Thus, jurisdictions such as Alabama have established themselves as providing pro-plaintiff legal regimes within their geographical monopolies.[357] Moreover, there are political dynamics at work in such states that create incentives for lawyers to demand pro-plaintiff rules and for judges to supply those rules.[358] By contrast, defendants have little ability to counteract these tendencies. Contractual choice of law provides parties with the ability to contract *ex ante* for the rules of a particular state, which will tend to promote efficient forum-shopping with respect to contracts that contain those terms.[359] An *ex ante* commitment to arbitration will also place some limits on negative forum-shopping. But these are imperfect responses to the problem of negative forum-shopping. Enforcement of choice-of-law and mandatory arbitration clauses is imperfect,[360] and the growth of tort law into the traditional contract domain over the past several decades[361] makes these remedies an imperfect substitute for full competition by courts with overlapping jurisdiction. Given the permissive jurisdictional rules today, it will be difficult for defendants to force cases to be filed in a less pro-plaintiff state. And as a result of *Erie*, there is no other forum to provide a different substantive law. Thus, whereas states have clear incentives to provide pro-plaintiff rules, there are few countervailing incentives to provide pro-defendant legal doctrines. It is the current regime of geographical monopolies and unlimited choice of forum by plaintiffs that present the real conditions for the development of pro-plaintiff legal rules. Absent competition among court systems, there is little reason to believe that the common law will evolve toward efficiency.

Nonetheless, a closer examination of the *Swift* regime suggests that the American regime was not quite as robust as the English regime. Most crucially, it appears that the federal courts in America did not act under quite as strong incentives to favor efficiency. First, American judges were not paid on the cases that they heard. As a result, they possessed a much greater incentive to shirk on their workload, which was eventually reflected in the massive backlogs of cases that eventually piled up in the federal courts in the waning years of the *Swift* regime.[362] Second, they faced no external constraints that forced them to adhere to norms of reciprocity in adjudication. The law merchant judge, for instance, drew his authority from the commitment to implement merchant custom. Ecclesiastical judges drew their authority from the commitment to act in compliance with equity and church teaching. Federal judges under *Swift* faced no such constraints. Thus, they had limited constraints and limited feedback on their decision-making. Third, the courts erroneously expanded the logic of the case beyond its proper boundaries, thereby allowing pernicious forum shopping that tended to defeat legitimate expectations, rather than the beneficial forum shopping contemplated by Story and which prevailed for most of the nineteenth century.

Summary of the importance of competitive legal order

The competitive legal order of the common law's institutional framework has been crucially important in understanding the rise and fall of efficiency in the common law. As Charles Rowley posits the dilemma, "Neither Hayek nor Posner has presented a convincing explanation as to why, or through what mechanism, the judiciary should be supportive of the law of liberty or the law of efficiency in a largely monopolistic court bureaucracy such as that which characterizes twentieth century Britain and the U.S."[363] During the formative era of the common law, the common law courts were just one of many courts in which litigants could have their claims heard. Each of these courts competed with the others for business, seeking to provide speedy, fair, and effective justice. This competition among courts led to innovation and incentives to provide efficient legal rules. Courts that attempted to turn the law into a mechanism of wealth redistribution were confronted by the inability to coerce unwilling parties to provide those wealth transfers. By contrast, the demise of competitive law in England and the United States has increased the incentives and opportunities for rent-seeking. Litigants have limited ability to exit jurisdictions with inefficient legal regimes.

This historical inquiry also raises questions about *Erie*'s analysis of *Swift*. *Erie* itself and scholars who have studied *Erie* focused only on the evils of forum shopping; few have focused on the possible *benefits* of forum shopping. Positive forum shopping generates experimentation and produces laws conducive to economic efficiency and coordination. By allowing exit from inefficient state regulation, *Swift* also created pressure for the production of efficient law and thereby enabled the production of efficient law. To be sure, some of this competition persists today as a result of the ability to use choice-of-law clauses to exit a particular state's inefficient legal regime.[364] But this ability to exit through choice-of-law is limited, most notably by the requirement of some sort of geographic contacts. By contrast, under the *Swift* regime, federal law and state law were operative within the *same* jurisdiction, greatly heightening the ability of parties to exit and the competition to produce efficient law. Moreover, contacts under current law may often be tenous at best, causing parties to later be surprised by the choice-of-law clause. Under *Swift*, however, parties could always be aware that federal law could apply to the transaction. To be sure, there were forum shopping evils, especially as *Swift* was expanded beyond its original scope. Nonetheless, by eliminating *all* forum shopping between state and federal court, *Erie* effectively threw out the proverbial baby with the bath water, eliminating efficient as well as inefficient forum shopping.

Doctrinal tendencies of the common law

A final factor that tended to promote the efficiency of the common law was that it was traditionally understood primarily as a mechanism for private ordering, rather than for collective goals. This bias was evidenced in at least two important ways that improved the efficiency of the law and reduced its vulnerability to rent-seeking. First, the common law was primarily comprised of a system of default rules, rather than mandatory rules. This allowed individuals the freedom to contract around inefficient common law rules and thereby to create their own wealth enhancing rules. Second, the common law provided great respect for custom that arose through voluntary individual interaction. By enforcing contracts and customs, the common law reinforced the view that the purpose of the law was to enable private ordering by essentially allowing the parties free reign to devise the rules that would govern their transactions.

In many ways the arguments for the efficiency of custom and contract flow from a common source, namely individuals designing their own rules to govern their affairs. Contractual bargains represent express individual choice to arrange affairs in a given way. Custom represents implicit design and acquiescence of individuals in a pattern of affairs that emerges spontaneously, but otherwise is similar to contract. Moreover, this analysis intertwines with the previous arguments about weak precedent and competitive law. As this Article will show, the presence of competition among legal systems forced courts to provide laws conducive to private ordering and therefore, provided laws rooted in custom. The freedom of the parties to choose their law meant that law had to conform to their preferences and expectations. Private parties were not forced, therefore, to fit their behavior into judicially constructed categories. In turn, a legal system based on custom requires a legal system grounded on weak precedent rather than *stare decisis*, so as to preserve the flexibility of customary law.

Default rules and contract. Common law rules historically tended to be default rules, rather than mandatory rules. This meant that the parties could contract around an inefficient common law rule, thereby designing a more efficient rule to govern

378 TODO J. ZYWICKI

the transaction.[365] So long as the benefit from contracting for a tailor-made legal rule exceeded the transaction costs of express contracting, then parties will do so. Voluntary agreements by parties to alter majoritarian default rules by voluntary contract are generally Pareto efficient. Those with subjective or idiosyncratic preferences could thus draft their own tailor-made rules for their particular situations. Thus, even if the efficient rule is the rule that is preferred by most parties, there are other parties who would prefer some alternative arrangement. These parties have a "subjective" valuation that is distinct from the majority preferences.[366] Freedom of contract allows these parties to design contractual arrangements that suit their purposes, while majoritarian default rules are suitable for most contracting parties.[367] Lord Mansfield's views are illustrative: "If the parties do not choose to contract according to the established rule, they are at liberty, as between themselves, to vary it."[368] Allowing these parties to tailor their own rules further enhances economic efficiency.

Moreover, the ability of parties to contract around contract default rules also makes the legal system more resistant to rent-seeking pressures by reducing the incentive for parties to use the court system to try to obtain rules that redistribute wealth rather than promote efficiency.[369] Although the winner in a given case may gain a windfall from the promulgation of an inefficient rule, this windfall will likely be a one-time-only boon. Parties can "exit" the inefficient legal rule by contracting around it, reallocating the risk to the party who is in the best position to bear the risk.[370] Where the parties can contract around an inefficient rule there will be little incentive to seek inefficient rules or for judges to create such rules. Forcing the parties to contract around the inefficient rule, however, requires the use of real economic resources that could otherwise be deployed to a higher social use. The inefficient rule creates deadweight social loss that could be avoided by the promulgation of a more efficient legal rule. At the same time, the ability to contract around the inefficient rule reduces its usefulness as a mechanism for redistributing social wealth on an ongoing basis. Thus, even if judges or interest groups seek to use the common law process to redistribute wealth, the ability to contract around inefficient rules generally makes the common law a very cumbersome and inefficient mechanism for accomplishing the desired end.

Modern law has substantially reduced the ability of parties to contract around inefficient rules, particularly as legislative and mandatory common law rules have increasingly come to squeeze out contract default rules in many areas of society and the economy. Traditionally, the common law was conceived as a set of off-the-rack default rules that could be freely modified by the mutual consent of contracting parties. The whole point of strict products liability, by contrast, was to supplant this regime of default rules with a network of immutable rules that parties were specifically forbidden to contract around. In particular, courts reconceived contractual warranty cases as strict products liability cases. Thus, in *Henningsen v. Bloomfield Motors, Inc.*,[371] the New Jersey Supreme Court ruled that cases involving personal injury from product use would no longer be governed by warranty law, even though warranty law had controlled such actions for 100 years. The New Jersey Supreme Court believed product warranties were tools for exploiting consumers and denied such warranties any future effect.[372]

The replacement of default warranty rules with immutable tort rules was advanced with *Greenman v. Yuba Power Products, Inc.*[373] In *Greenman*, Chief Justice Roger Traynor articulated the standard of strict tort liability for personal injuries caused by products. Traynor concluded that consumers possessed neither the sophistication nor power to freely bargain about warranty terms for mass-produced consumer goods.[374] Moreover, strict liability for manufacturers would provide insurance to injured victims who might not otherwise be covered by insurance. By contrast, Traynor argued, manufacturers were uniformly in a better position to control the risk of product defects and could obtain insurance, the cost of which could be spread among numerous other consumers. Finally, the revolution was complete in 1964 when the American Law Institute adopted the strict liability standard in the Restatement (Second) of Torts, § 402A.[375]

This inability to contract around rules has also imposed a forced uniformity on implied contractual terms, making it virtually impossible for idiosyncratic bargainers to contract around the rule. For instance, parties who place a high subjective value on a particular term or activity may simply be unable to acquire that product at any price because of the inability to make a binding contractual waiver of liability. This is the case even if the individual is knowingly assuming the risk of some particular activity. Thus, there is additional social loss in the form of the opportunity cost of foregone value-creating transfers that would otherwise be executed in the presence of greater contractual freedom.[376] At the very least, the difficulty of drafting a contractual waiver of liability will substantially increase the cost of entering into a contract to partake of the activity. Not only will it be expensive to draft an adequate contractual waiver of liability, but the difficulty in doing so will tend to reduce the number of suppliers of the product, thus raising the costs of finding a trading partner.

By making it impossible to contract out of this regime of mandatory rules, one-size-fits-all legal rules have weakened the dynamic evolution of the common law that allowed for change in response to the needs of those governed by it. This dynamic regime was changed to a regime where all further changes would be required to go through judicial gate-keepers, thereby defeating the private ordering purpose of contract law. As Richard Epstein observed, through this process of legally-imposed uniformity, "The system of product liability was stripped of its powers of self-correction. In essence, *Henningsen, Greenman*, and the Restatement (Second) of Torts reserved to the courts a legal monopoly to fashion the relevant terms and conditions on which all products should be sold in all relevant markets."[377] Epstein concluded that the once-flowing river of the common law that "works itself pure" has arguably been replaced by a "Procrustean bed" of judicially imposed uniformity.[378]

The increased use of mandatory rules has also made the common law more susceptible to rent-seeking pressures. Through mandatory rules, private parties have the ability to impose rules that serve their private ends, rather than general efficiency. Because unwilling parties cannot escape the reach of these rules, they are compelled to provide wealth transfers to rent-seeking interests. In turn, the increased ability to provide such wealth transfers increases the incentives to private parties to invest in lobbying and litigation to secure wealth transferring rules.

Custom. Traditionally the common law tended to enhance efficiency through its heavy reliance on custom and traditions, sifted by judicial reason, as sources of legal principles.[379] Customs that evolve over long periods of time through decentralized, voluntary, and inclusive institutional processes will usually be the source of sound legal principles.[380] Customs that arise spontaneously through the voluntary interactions of many individuals over long periods of time will be subject to testing, feedback, and voluntary acceptance. Such customs have survived testing across the generations as well as by many people within a given community. People in a given community have incorporated those customs into their expectations and behaviors. Thus, there is reason to believe that customs that have survived this process of selection have embedded within them a certain tacit and unarticulated wisdom.[381] As the Ninth Circuit observed in *Hart*, "The common law, at its core, was a reflection of custom, and custom had a built-in flexibility that allowed it to change with circumstance."[382]

Customary law is likely to be most reliable in situations where parties interact in a series of multiple, reciprocal arrangements and disputes.[383] In this evolutionary setting, the efficiency effects of custom are comparable to free contract. As with explicit contractual bargaining, where all parties are aware of a custom and participate in its development, there is reason to believe that the custom reflects consent, consensus, and the basis of individual expectations. Reciprocity makes it likely that any particular party will not always be on the same side in any given dispute, making that party more likely to favor a rule that favors efficiency overall rather than systematically favoring either plaintiffs or defendants. Repeat interactions make it likely that over time the party will, in fact, be on both sides of the transaction over time; it also reduces the likelihood that any particular interaction will be the final one. This symmetry of interaction and repeated dealing creates conditions favorable to the evolution of efficient customs. Thus, the history of the law merchant is accurately identified as a particularly fortuitous institutional arrangement for the generation of efficient legal rules.[384] Chancery also looked to merchant custom for guidance.[385] Blackstone singled out the customs of merchants as an especially important area of customary law.[386] But relations of reciprocity characterize many social and economic interactions, not just those among merchants.[387]

Customs and traditions that arise spontaneously from decentralized and repeated voluntary interactions will also tend to be relatively well protected from public choice pressures and from well organized special interests. For special interests to succeed in the task of using law to redistribute wealth to themselves, they require some point of pressure or leverage by which they can compel other individuals to surrender wealth to them. Customs, however, arise spontaneously from the decentralized and voluntary interactions of many anonymous individuals. Unlike the positivist model that requires a sovereign issuing "top-down" commands, customary law offers a "bottom-up" process as legal rules emerge from the expectations and agreements generated by voluntary agreement and interaction.[388] Thus, there is no point of leverage on which a special interest can press to change the custom in the preferred manner. Moreover, because custom is fluid, attempts to change one element of a customary relationship will tend to be counteracted by other changes. By its very nature, therefore, custom will tend to be highly resilient and highly protected from public choice pressures. Because the common law traditionally was rooted in custom, the common law was similarly resistant to interest group pressures.[389]

Again, the reliance on custom went hand-in-hand with the competitive legal order and weak precedent that characterized the common law. The flexibility and ability of custom to change and adapt over time made it unwise to try to hem in legal change through strict rules of precedent. Moreover, given the choice, parties would have been expected to favor the application of well established and widely shared customary practices to resolve their disputes, rather than the formal and alien concept of the common law. Thus, the heavy reliance on custom in judicial decision-making was in large part a reflection of the fact that this preference was shared by the litigants themselves.

Traditional common law theorists recognized that custom and contract are both rooted in the wellspring of individual consent. This reliance on individual consent reinforced both that the common law was a spontaneous order as well as the notion that the common law was a mechanism for private ordering. Thus, John Selden, one of the most influential common law theorists, placed heavy reliance on the importance of consensual obligations as the foundation for the moral authority of the law.[390] Selden believed that the most important rule of natural law was the absolute obligation of complying with one's contracts, both divine and with humans.[391] He also saw the obligations of customary law as having binding force because he viewed customary law as essentially consensual in nature.[392] Mansfield also stressed the customary basis of commercial transactions.[393]

The American experience, again, was similar. As Bridwell and Whitten observed, the defining characteristic of the federal court's commercial law jurisprudence under *Swift* v. *Tyson* was its willingness to rely on commercial custom to decide cases. State regulation often sought to further some defined public goal, whether for the public good or to benefit discrete special interests. By contrast, the federal courts deferred to the expectations of the parties under the contract, seeking to "discover" their intent and expectations. "[C]ommercial law was . . . customary law."[394] Indeed, the customary basis of law reinforced the federal court's authority over commercial law:

> Under this view of the commercial law as custom, the function of diversity jurisdiction in commercial cases should be apparent. In a customary law system in which the purpose of a grant of subject matter jurisdiction is to protect nonresidents from local bias, the intentions and expectations of the parties to every dispute had to be determined by a tribunal independent of the apprehended local prejudice.[395]

Commercial custom was universal and consistent; thus the federal courts were the appropriate place to implement this uniformity. The role of custom in the modern law has been greatly reduced. Traditionally, courts were highly deferential toward custom. Custom, embedded in a network of private contract and a market, was seen as a powerful institution for transmitting information and for ratifying consent. Custom was seen as an offshoot of contract, a collection of tacit understandings and agreements that implicitly allocated the parties' respective rights and obligations. But, during the liability revolution of recent decades, custom has come to be viewed with the same jaundiced eye as freedom of contract; as freedom of contract came under increasing attack, so did custom.[396] Rather than being viewed as a source of consent and tacit wisdom, custom increasingly was seen as exclusive rather than inclusive, a mechanism for powerful interests to escape liability for the harms they caused. Custom, it was suggested, did not arise spontaneously through voluntary interaction. Rather it was "created" by manufacturers and medical professionals and then "imposed" upon powerless and uninformed buyers. Thus, consumers were not really involved in the evolution of the custom and, to the extent they

appeared to be, their involvement was poorly informed. As with contractual limitations on liability, therefore, it was essential for judges to intervene to second guess the
results of custom. Thus, custom has gradually moved away from being a per se defense
regarding the reasonableness of precautions and instead become mere evidence
of reasonableness.[397] Some form of cost-benefit analysis is the prevailing standard,
"leaving custom with a subordinate role in the overall analysis."[398] Although the roots
of this transition lay in several cases in the early twentieth century, compliance with
custom remained a per se defense against liability in most jurisdictions during most
of the twentieth century. In part, the durability of the defense may have resulted from
the fact that "courts saw it as providing a salutary 'policy' check on potentially vast
liability."[399] During the 1960s and 1970s, however, the evidentiary rule governing
custom gradually came to supplant the rule of treating compliance custom as a per se
defense. Thus, the role of custom in tort law was diminished during the era of the
liability revolution.

More fundamentally, modern lawyers and judges reject the notion that legal rules
should be driven by custom and the spontaneously generated practices of merchants,
consumers, and private actors. Instead, the purpose of law is believed to be to satisfy
articulated social goals, whether economic, social, or moral. Whereas the law was
previously understood as purpose-independent inputs into individual action and the
coordination of individual plans, today it is more accurate to see individual action and
behavior as a means to the accomplishment of prescribed social goals that the law
is designed to accomplish. With this has come the belief that custom is valuable only
if it serves some larger social goal beyond the coordination of the affairs of private
individuals. As a result, law results from political struggle rather than the customs that
emerge from private action.[400]

Summary of contract and custom. The discussion in this subpart has been somewhat
abbreviated, as the underlying concepts are quite well established. For current purposes, however, it is most important to recognize the crucial role of contract
and custom in the rise and fall of the efficiency of the common law. Both tended to
promote efficient rules while also being resistant to rent-seeking pressures.

The adherence to freedom of contract permitted parties to contract around inefficient rules which placed pressure on courts to innovate. If those parties who are
supposed to provide wealth transfers under an inefficient rule are able to escape that
rule through freedom of contract, this will reduce the incentive of litigants to demand
and judges to provide inefficient rules.

The common law's heavy reliance on custom also promoted the efficiency of the
common law. Custom is largely immune to rent-seeking pressures. Custom is diffuse,
decentralized, and consensual; thus there is no point of "leverage" that can be used to
try to manipulate the path of custom's evolution. Thus, judicial reliance on custom
also attenuated rent-seeking pressures as it is difficult to direct the path of customary
evolution.

It may be fairly argued that these doctrinal tendencies—reliance on contract and
custom—are themselves produced by the institutional factors discussed earlier. In
part, this is true. Because courts competed for business, they had to provide rules
favored by the parties and responsive to their needs. These rules were found in the
rules and expectations created by the parties themselves through custom rather than
in judicial precedent. Moreover the inability of courts to bind unwilling parties led to

a reliance on default rules and freedom of contract, rather than to mandatory rules. But these doctrinal tendencies also retain independent significance in that it appears that these factors retained vitality for some time even after the decline of the institutional factors that generated them. Thus, these doctrinal tendencies had a residual effect of perpetuating these legal rules for some time afterward. Moreover, these factors have independent significance in that they were part of the judicial mindset of the traditional common law. Thus, they are independently relevant in explaining the rise and fall of efficiency in the common law. Judges traditionally believed in the propriety of reliance on custom and contract, which had efficiency-enhancing consequences. To the extent that this jurisprudential mindset has changed, this change has been reflected in the rules produced by the common law process.

Summary

For purposes of exposition, the foregoing discussion has distinguished among various different elements of the historical institutional structure of the common law that contributed to its propensity to generate efficient rules. But it should be stressed that each of these elements was closely intertwined with one another and that they all contributed to the formation of a legal system that was quite distinct from the modern common law system. As noted, the practice of weak precedent prevailed during an era of jurisdictional competition and a vision of the law rooted in private ordering. Reflection demonstrates the interconnections between these elements.[401] A fully mature doctrine of *stare decisis* requires a formalized and hierarchical legal system to enforce vertical *stare decisis* through the enforcement by higher courts against lower courts in the hierarchy. Enforcement of horizontal *stare decisis* also requires a formalized legal process for promoting uniformity of the law through time. Both forms of *stare decisis*, therefore, cannot exist without a formal and hierarchical court structure.[402] For instance, assume that the Exchequer Court laid down a ruling. This case would not be binding on any other court in the system, such as ecclesiastical courts, law merchant, or the like. In short, *stare decisis* of the modern type cannot exist in a competitive legal order. Absent a developed concept of *stare decisis*, judges naturally gravitated toward a spontaneous order notion of law, looking for the concepts and logic in the law, rather than the authority of a previously decided case.

Moreover, it is almost certainly no coincidence that the hardened notion of *stare decisis* emerged contemporaneously with the enactment of the Judicature Act of 1873 and the Appellate Jurisdiction Act of 1876.[403] These laws ended the competitive legal order that had prevailed in England for some 600 years, uniting the common law courts and Chancery courts under one hierarchical umbrella. The creation of a hierarchical legal system also made possible for the first time a coherent application of the strict doctrine of *stare decisis*.[404] In turn, this necessitated the creation of a formalized system of case reporting that accurately reported case holdings, rather than the heterogeneous reporting practices of the Year Books. In turn, this motivated the intellectual revolution that shunned the spontaneous order or "declaratory" theory of law in favor of a more positivist conception of the law. This also generated, for the first time, the contention that *stare decisis* was needed to constrain judges from overstepping their proper bounds. Absent *stare decisis*, it was feared, judges would use their power to impose their personal preferences on society. As noted, this concern was traditionally ameliorated by the fact that judges only had persuasive law-making authority because parties could choose to have their case heard in rival jurisdictions. The creation of a hierarchical legal system, however, enabled judges to issue rulings and then compel their enforcement on both current and future parties. This new and vast grant of power to judges raised concerns of judicial lawlessness, thereby putting greater weight on the importance of *stare decisis* in constraining judges.

In the United States, a similar force was at work. *Swift v. Tyson* rested on the institutional freedom that parties had to seek relief in either state or federal courts, each of which developed its own legal system. The intellectual foundation for this system was the notion that the law was a spontaneous order, not a set of isolated cases. Thus, *Swift v. Tyson* also adopted the traditional weaker view of the weight of precedent of the earlier English era. By contrast, the overruling of *Swift* by *Erie* caused both an institutional and intellectual revolution. *Erie* not only required the abandonment of competing legal systems, but also carried with it the positivist notion that legal cases are themselves the law in the same way that discrete statutory enactments of state legislatures are the law. Thus, the declaratory theory of law became untenable as well.

IV. Conclusion

Until the mid-nineteenth century, the institutional and intellectual structure of the common law was very different from its modern form. This is not merely historical pedantry, because it was during this period that the essence of the common law was formed. In particular, the doctrines of the common law that were later recognized as the pro-efficiency doctrines were laid down during this period. But they were laid down in a variety of different courts and only later absorbed into the common law. Subsequent changes undermined the institutional framework that had supported the development of efficiency-enhancing common law rules. These institutional changes provided a necessary condition for the later deviation of the common law process away from efficiency and toward rent-seeking rules.

Paul Rubin's model of efficiency and inefficiency relies on the assumption of the presence of strong precedent *(stare decisis)* that binds later courts through time, on strong court hierarchies that allow superior courts to bind inferior courts (thereby preventing litigant exit), on restrictions to contracting around inefficient rules, and finally, on judicial decisionmaking as the primary source of law rather than custom. Without the presence of these factors, litigants will find it futile to manipulate the evolutionary path of the law because of the inability to maintain the wealth enhancing rule through time or because of the inability to coerce unwilling parties to subject themselves to the rule. During the formative period of the common law, each of these four factors tended toward the production of economic efficiency. By contrast, in the past century, each of these factors has changed, increasing the incentives for rent-seeking litigation and limiting the ability of other parties to escape the reach of these rules through exit or choice. Thus, these supply-side changes were a necessary condition before Rubin's demand-side model could adequately describe reality.

George Priest's model of legal evolution also rests on changes in the supply side of the equation. Priest attributes the rising inefficiency of the common law in recent decades to the pursuit by judges of ideological and redistributive policy preferences. As this Article has demonstrated, for this to occur it first is necessary to have an institutional framework that permits high agency costs for judges such that they can pursue their personal preferences to the exclusion of serving the needs of the parties. The historic system of weak precedent, a competitive legal order, freedom of contract, and customary law insured that judges would be unable to pursue their personal preferences at the expense of the public. As these factors changed over time, however, the legal system became more vulnerable to influence by judges' ideological preferences, thereby creating opportunities for greater judicial control over the path of the law.

Understanding the efficiency and inefficiency of the common law, therefore, requires an understanding of the supply side of common law rule-making. Examining the demand side alone will be insufficient to fully understand the evolutionary process. This Article has provided a model to explain both why the early common law tended toward the production of efficient rules, as well as why the modern common law has increasingly tended toward the production of inefficient rules.

Notes

1   *See* Richard A. Posner, Economic Analysis of Law § 2.2, at 25–27 (5th ed. 1998).

2   The literature on the economic inefficiency of modem American tort law, for instance, is now quite extensive. *See, e.g.*, Peter W. Huber, Liability: The Legal Revolution and its Consequences (1988);The Liability Maze:The Impact of Liability Law on Safety and Innovation (Peter W. Huber & Robert E. Litan eds., 1991); David E. Bernstein, *The Breast Implant Fiasco,* 87 Cal. L. Rev. 457 (1999); George L. Priest, *The Modern Expansion of Tort Liability: Its Sources, Its Effects, and Its Reform,* 5(3) J. Econ. Perspectives 31 (1991). Other scholars have challenged these conclusions. *See* James A. Henderson & Theodore Eisenberg, *The Quiet Revolution in Products Liability: An Empirical Study of Legal Change,* 37 UCLA l. Rev. 479 (1990). *But see* Arthur Havenner, Not Quite a Revolution in Products Liability (Manhattan Institute Judicial Studies Program White Paper, 1991) (challenging Henderson and Eisenberg's conclusions). There have been similar criticisms of tendencies in contract law to principles such as unconscionability to restrict freedom of contract and the enforceability of contracts. *See* Richard A. Epstein, *Unconscionability: A Critical Reappraisal,* 18 J.L. & Econ. 293 (1975); Richard A. Epstein, *The Static Conception of the Common Law,* 9 J. Leg. Stud. 253 (1980); Paul H. Rubin, *The Theory of the Firm and the Structure of the Franchise Contract,* 21 J.L. & Econ. 223 (1978).

3   Indeed, several of those who have criticized the recent developments in common law doctrine are the same scholars who developed the earlier models explaining the tendency of the common law toward efficiency. *See infra* notes 24–27, 30–32 and accompanying text.

4   Omichund v. Barker, 1 Atk. 21, 33 (K.B. 1744).

5   *See* Mark F. Grady, *Legal Evolution* and Precedent, 3 Ann. Rev. L. & Ethics 147 (1995).

6   *See* Todd J. Zywickj, Public Choice and Tort Reform (George Mason University School of Law, Working Paper No. 00–36, 2000), *available at* http://www.law. gmu.edu/faculty/papers/authors.html#z.

7   The discussion here will focus on Priest and Rubin's models as representative of the
     class of models. Numerous related and refined models also exist. A full discussion
     of this body of literature is outside of the scope of this Article. An excellent sum-
     mary of the various models that have been offered, as well as a general survey of
     early developments in the efficiency thesis of law and economics, is presented in
     Peter H. Aranson, *Economic Efficiency and the Common Law: A Critical Survey,* in Law
     and Economics and the Economics of Legal Regulation 51 (J.-Matthias Graf von
     der Schulenburg & Goran Skogh eds., 1986).

8   Making this threshold assumption should not be interpreted as denying the impor-
     tance of those questions or to ignore the fact that a lively debate on those questions
     continues to rage. Reasonable arguments could be made, and in fact have been
     made, on both sides of the question. This Article, however, is concerned with a
     somewhat different inquiry of exploring the evolutionary and institutional mecha-
     nisms at work that might explain these tendencies, assuming that they in fact exist.
     As a result, this paper simply assumes for the sake of argument that such trends do
     in fact exist, and seeks to explain them.

9   For a summary of these models, see Todd J. Zywicki, *Environmental Externalities and
     Political Externalities: The Political Economy of Environmental Regulation and Reform,* 73
     Tul. L. Rev. 845 (1999) [hereinafter Zywicki, *Environmental Externalities*]. *See also*
     William M. Landes & Richard A. Posner, *The Independent Judiciary in an Interest-
     Group Perspective,* 18 J.L. & Econ 875 (1975). The constitutional amendment process
     may similarly be conceived of as a market, as parties bid for desired constitutional
     amendments. *See* Todd J. Zywicki, *Senators and Special Interests: A Public Choice Analysis
     of the Seventeenth Amendment,* 73 Or. L. Rev. 1007 (1994) [hereinafter Zywicki,
     Senators and Special Interests]; Donald J. Boudreaux & A.C. Pritchard, *Rewriting the
     Constitution: An Economic Analysis of the Constitutional Amendment Process,* 62 Fordham
     L. Rev. 111 (1993).

10   This is oversimplified. Often it will be the case that the legislative bargain that is
     struck is the result of a multi-lateral bargain between several interest groups rather
     than a bilateral bargain where one group wins and another loses. *See* Zywicki,
     Environmental Externalities, supra note 9, at 848–56. Rather, it will generally be the
     case that *relatively* well-organized groups will generally be able to take advantage of
     relatively unorganized groups to transfer wealth to themselves. The question of
     how the wins and losses are to be allocated as a distributional matter is a second-
     order question.

11   This is particularly the case with respect to the Chicago School of political econ-
     omy. *See* Chicago Studies in Political Economy (George Stigler ed., 1988). Politicians
     do play an active role in some models. *See* Fred S. McChesney, Money for Nothing:
     Politicians, Rent Extraction, and Political Extortion 7–13 (1997). The Virginia
     School of political economy also has paid greater attention to the role of politicians
     and political entrepreneurship in the special-interest theory of government. For a
     useful overview and comparison of these various intellectual schools (including the
     Rochester School as well), *see* Maxwell L. Stearns, Public Choice and Public Law:
     Readings and Commentary xvii-xxvi (1997).

12   *See* Jonathan R. Macey, *Cynicism and Trust in Politics and Constitutional Theory,* 87
     Cornell L. Rev. 280, 294 n.50 (2002) ("Rent-seeking refers to the lobbying process
     by which special interest groups attempt to procure legislation that transfers wealth
     (economic 'rents') in excess of what the members of such groups could earn in the

competitive marketplace to themselves from the public at large."); *see also* McChesney, *supra* note 11, at 7–13 (describing rent-seeking).

13 *See* Gordon Tullock, *The Welfare Costs of Tariffs, Monopolies, and Theft*, 5 W. Econ. J. 224,228 (1967).

14 *See* Zywicki, *Environmental Externalities, supra* note 9, at 866–68.

15 Stating the point in the form of an equation is not intended to present a formal model of legal change but is intended only to serve an expository purpose in identifying the relevant considerations.

16 Of course, these economic rents are to some extent dissipated by investments to join the profession. Thus, for instance, law schools can charge higher tuition to students and students will be willing to pay higher tuition, because a law degree is required to practice law. Thus, law schools are part of the "industry" that benefits from restrictive licensing of lawyers.

17 *See* Paul H. Rubin, *Why Is the Common Law Efficient?*, 6 J. Leg. Stud. 51 (1977) [hereinafter Rubin, *Why is the Common Law Efficient?*]; *see also* Paul H. Rubin et al., *Litigation Yersus Legislation: Forum Shopping by Rent Seekers*, 107 Pub. Choice 295 (2001); Martin J. Bailey & Paul H. Rubin, *A Positive Theory of Legal Change*, 14 Int'l Rev. L. & Econ. 467, 476 (1994) [hereinafter Bailey & Rubin, Positive Theory]; Paul H. Rubin & Martin J. Bailey, *The Role of Lawyers in Changing the Law*, 23 J. Leg. Stud. 807 (1994); Paul H. Rubin, *Common Law and Statute Law*, 11 J. Leg. Stud. 205 (1982) [hereinafter Rubin, *Common Law and Statute Law*]. Gordon Tullock described a similar model, but less concretely than Rubin. *See* Gordon Tullock, Trials on Trial: A Pure Theory of Legal Procedure 197–206 (1980); *see also* George L. Priest, Selective Characteristics of Litigation, 9 J. Legal Stud. 399 (1980) (suggesting a similar model).

18 *See* Rubin, *Common Law and Statute Law, supra* note 17, at 207.

19 *See* Zywicki, *Senators and Special Interests, supra* note 9, at 1028–29. In practice, of course, there are a large number of constitutional and other internal procedural rules that limit the ability of one legislature to overturn the work of prior legislatures. *See id.*; *see also* Landes & Posner, *supra* note 9, at 878.

20 *See* W. Mark Crain & Robert D. Tollison, *Constitutional Change in an Interest-Group Perspective*, 8 J. Legal Stud. 165, 168–69 (1979); Landes & Posner, *supra* note 9, at 892.

21 *See* Rubin, *Common Law and Statute Law, supra* note 17, at 206 ("[F]or efficiency to result from these models parties to particular disputes must represent symmetrically all future interests in such disputes. If this condition is not satisfied, the models indicate that the law will not be driven toward efficiency. Rather, the law will come to favor those parties which do have future interests in cases of the sort under consideration, whether or not it is efficient for such parties to be victorious."); *see also* Marc Galanter, *Why the "Haves" Come Out Ahead: Speculation on the Limits of Legal Change*, 9 Law & Soc. Rev. 95 (1974).

22 Rubin, *Common Law and Statute Law, supra* note 17, at 211–14.

23 As Rubin notes, this same dynamic meant that statute law also tended toward efficiency during this era. *Id.*

24 He leaves open the question of whether this change was efficiency-enhancing or not. *See id.* at 216–17.

25 Rubin and Bailey stress the point that a strength of their model is that it can explain the evolution of the common law without accounting for changes in judicial preferences. *See* Bailey & Rubin, *Positive Theory, supra* note 17, at 476. This does not rule out the

possibility that legal change may occur as a result of a change in the incentives and constraints facing judges, however, which is the argument advanced in this paper. For an argument of legal evolution rooted in changes in judges' ideological preferences, see Alfred L. Brophy, *Reason & Sentiment: The Moral Worlds and Modes of Reasoning of Antebellum Jurists*, 79 B.U. L. Rev. 1161 (1999) (book review).

26   *See* Bailey & Rubin, *Positive Theory, supra* note 17, at 475–76.

27   *See* Robert Cooter & Lewis Kornhauser, *Can Litigation Improve the Law Without the Help of Judges?'*, 9 J. Legal Stud. 139 (1980).

28   *See* George L. Priest, *The Common Law Process and the Selection of Efficient Rules*, 6 J. Leg. Stud. 65 (1977).

29   For a summary of several of those criticisms, *see* Posner, Economic Analysis of Law, *supra* note 1, § 21.5, at 614.

30   For the common law evolutionary process to trend away from efficiency in Priest's model, it would be necessary for efficient rules to cause more social conflict and therefore to be litigated more often than inefficient rules, which is expressly denied by the assumptions of the model. Thus, Priest's model is a one-way model that can explain the evolution toward efficient rules but not an evolution *away* from efficiency.

31   *See* Priest, *supra* note 2; *see also* George L. Priest, *Products Liability, Law and the Accident Rale, in* Liability: Perspectives and Policies 184 (Robert E. Litan & Clifford Winston eds., 1988).

32   *See* George L. Priest, *The Current Insurance Crisis and Modern Tort Law,* 96 Yale L.J. 1521 (1987) (arguing that modern tort law is the result of judges reading their philosophical ideas into the law); George L. Priest, *Puzzles of the Tort Crisis,* 48 Ohio St. L.J, 497 (1987) (same); George L. Priest, *The Invention of Enterprise Liability: A Critical History of the Intellectual Foundations of Modern Tort Law,* 14 J. Legal Stud. 461 (1985).

33   *See* Posner, *supra* note 1, § 19.2, at 569.

34   *Id.*

35   *See* Zywicki, *supra* note 6; *see also* James E. Krier, Book Review, 122 U. Pa. L. Rev. 1664 (1974) (reviewing Posner, *supra* note 1). Judges may also be concerned with "justice," broadly defined. *See* Gerald P. O'Driscoll, Jr., *Justice, Efficiency, and the Economic Analysis of Law: A Comment on Fried,* 9 J. Leg. Stud. 355 (1980).

36   *See* O'Driscoll, *supra* note 35; Mario J. Rizzo, *The Mirage of Efficiency*, 8 Hofstra L. Rev. 641 (1980); *see also* Edward Stringham, *Kaldor-Hicks Efficiency and the Problem of Central Planning*, 4 Q.J. Austrian Econ. 41 (2001); Gillian K. Hadfield, *Bias in the Evolution of Legal Rules*, 80 Geo. L.J. 583 (1992).

37   There have been several efforts to model and test the prediction that an independent judiciary will be willing to enforce interest-group legislative bargains. *See* Gary M. Anderson et al., *On the Incentives of Judges to Enforce Legislative Wealth Transfers*, 32 J.L. & Econ. 215 (1989); Landes & Posner, *supra* note 9. Others have investigated other aspects of the judicial production of precedents and judicial decisionmaking from an institutional perspective. *See* Stephen M. Bainbridge & G. Mitu Gulati, *How Do Judges Maximize? (The Same Way Everybody Else Does—Boundedly): Rules of Thumb in Securities Fraud Opinions*, 51 Emory L.J. 83 (2002).

38   *See supra* notes 22–23 and accompanying text.

39   *See supra* notes 24–27 and accompanying text.

40   *See* Todd J. Zywicki, *Beyond the Shell and Husk of History: The History of the Seventeenth Amendment and Its Implications for Current Reform Proposals*, 45 Clev. St. L. Rev. 165,

229–30 (1997) (noting that parties will spend less money lobbying for legislation if the expected duration of the legislation is small); Landes & Posner, *supra* note 9.

41   A useful summary of the arguments in favor of stare decisis is provided in Oona A. Hathaway, *Path Dependence in the Law: The Course and Pattern of Legal Change in a Common Law System*, 86 Iowa L. Rev. 601, 650–55 (2001). Precedent as discussed here is horizontal (binding through time) rather than vertical (superior courts binding inferior courts in a hierarchical system). In the time since an initial draft of the current article was authored, debate on this particular issue has become quite spirited. *See* Hart v. Massanari, 266 F.3d 1155 (9th Cir. 2001); Anastasoff v. United States, 223 F.3d 898 (8th Cir. 2000), *vacated as moot en banc*, 235 F.3d 1054 (8th Cir. 2000).

42   Harold J. Berman & Charles J. Reid, Jr., *The Transformation of English Legal Science: From Hale to Blackstone*, 45 Emory L.J. 437, 449 (1996).

43   In fact, it has been argued that where both parties lack a continuing interest in the production of precedent, the result will not be the production of efficient rules but rather "random drift" with no tendency toward the production of efficient or inefficient rules. *See* Rubin, *Why is the Common Law Efficient?, supra* note 17, at 56–57; John C. Goodman, *An Economic Theory of the Evolution of Common Law,* 7 J. Leg. Stud. 393 (1978). As will be shown below, however, this was not the case historically. Even though the parties to the litigation lacked a continuing interest in the production of precedents, the existence of competition between multiple courts and legal systems meant that judges and courts had a continuing interest in the production of precedents. Judges were paid from filing fees; therefore even though private parties were not residual claimants of the long-term value of precedents, judges were. As a result, random drift did not result. *See infra* notes 146–151.

44   The basic structure of the common law and many of its substantive rules, such as many landholding rules, were already established as early as 1135. *See* John Hudson, The Formation of the English Common Law: Law and Society in England from the Norman Conquest to Magna Carta 20–21 (1996); R.C. Van Caenegem, the Birth of the English Common Law 33 (2d ed.1988). Pollock traces the origins of the English common law to the Norman conquest, but allows that "the earliest things which modern lawyers are strictly bound to know" date only to the latter thirteenth century. Sir Frederick Pollock, *English Law Before the Norman Conquest,* 14 L.Q. Rev. 291 (1898), *reprinted in* 1 Select Essays in Anglo-American Legal History 88 (Association of American Law Schools ed., 1968) [hereinafter Select Essays]. Regardless of the exact date, it is evident that the roots of the common law reach well back into the Middle Ages.

45   *See* Berman & Reid, *supra* note 42, at 445; Arthur R. Hogue, Origins of The Common Law 175, 188-91 (1966).

46   *See* Berman & Reid, *supra* note 42, at 445.

47   *See* Hogue, *supra* note 45, at 189; Theodore F.T. Plucknett, a Concise History of The Common Law 343 (5th ed. 1956) ("But it must be observed that whatever use [Bracton] made of cases was necessarily peculiar to himself."). Even as late as the 1760s, Adam Smith cited only a handful of cases in his Lectures on Jurisprudence. *See* Adam Smith, Lectures on Jurisprudence (R.L. Meek et al. eds., 1982).

48   Hogue, *supra* note 45, at 189.

49   *See infra* notes 64-67 and accompanying text (discussing plea rolls).

50   Plucknett, *supra* note 47, at 343. Plucknett observes that the plea rolls are "immense in number and there was and still is no guide to their contents; they have to be read

straight through from beginning to end without any assistance from indexes or head-notes." *Id.*

51   *Id. See also* 1 Sir Frederick. Pollock & Frederic William Maitland, The History of English Law: Before the Time of Edward 1183 (1968) ("By some piece of good fortune Bracton, a royal justice, obtained possession of a large number of rolls. But the ordinary litigant or his advocate would have had no opportunity of searching the rolls, and those who know what these records are like will feel safe in saying that even the king's justices can not have made a habit of searching them for principles of law.").

52   *See* Hogue, *supra* note 45, at 189 ("Bracton's use of cases differs from the modem reference to cases. In the twentieth century the authority of the case decided in a higher court has a binding authority on a lower court. But Bracton and other medieval justices cite cases merely to illustrate or to explain the law."); Berman & Reid, *supra* note 42, at 445; *see also* Plucknett, *supra* note 47, at 260 ("[Bracton] never gives us any discussion of the authority of cases and clearly would not understand the modern implications of stare decisis. Indeed, his cases are carefully selected because they illustrate what he believes the law ought to be, and not because they have any binding authority; he freely admits that at the present moment decisions are apt to be on different lines. Bracton's use of cases, therefore, is not based upon their authority as sources of law, but upon his personal respect for the judges who decided them, and his belief that they raise and discuss questions upon lines which he considers sound.").

53   Berman & Reid, *supra* note 42, at 445; *see also* Hogue, *supra* note 45, at 175–76 ("[Bracton's] use of the judicial decisions of his predecessors was not the same as the sophisticated twentieth-century doctrine of *stare decisis*, requiring a hierarchy of courts, certain conventions in the reporting of cases, and the printed publication of reports."); Plucknett, *supra* note 47, at 344 ("In Bracton's hands a case may illustrate a legal principle, and the enrolment may be historical proof that the principle was once applied, but the case is not in itself a source of law.").

54   Berman & Reid, *supra* note 42, at 445.

55   Harold J. Berman, The *Origins of Historical Jurisprudence: Coke, Selden, Hale*, 103 Yale L.J. 1651,1732(1994).

56   Plucknett, *supra* note 47, at 343–44. Plucknett observes, "Bracton has no hesitation in using cases which we should call out of date or overruled, in order to maintain that the law ought to be something different from what it is. From this it is clear that the whole of Bracton's position would fall if decisions, as such, were in any modern sense a source of law." *Id.* at 344.

57   Plucknett, *supra* note 47, at 344.

58   Berman & Reid, *supra* note 42, at 446.

59   *See* Berman, *supra* note 55, at 1732 ("Prior to Coke, these 'presidents' were largely concerned with procedural matters, and only rarely did judges compare in detail the facts of the cases that came before them with the facts of earlier analogous cases."); Carleton Kemp Allen, Law in The Making 143(2d ed. 1930).

60   C.H.S. Fifoot, Lord Mansfield 16 (1936) (quoting Holt).

61   *Id.* More precisely, rival courts cited precedent in order to expand their jurisdiction at the expense of the King's Bench. A primary purpose of legal fictions was to evade jurisdictional limits so that parties could bring actions in the court of their choice, rather than the *dejure* court that they were entitled to use. *See* J.H. Baker, An Introduction to English Legal History 33 (1971); Hogue, *supra* note 45, at 11

(describing the ability to manipulate pleading forms in order to get access to the court preferred by litigants, notwithstanding formal jurisdictional limits).

62   Berman & Reid, *supra* note 42, at 447.

63   Hogue, *supra* note 45, at 181, 190. The first printed law book, Littleton's *Tenures,* appeared in 1481. *See* Baker, *supra* note 61, at 116.

64   *See* 2 William Holdsworth, A History of English Law 185 (4th ed. 1936). Holdsworth states that the plea rolls were a number of membranes "filed" together at the top, distinguishing them from the Chancery Rolls, which consist of a "continuous strip of parchment made by sewing the membranes together at the top." *Id.* at 185 n. 1.

65   Allen, *supra* note 59, at 139.

66   In fact, one reason Bracton cites a substantially larger number of cases than his peers is that as a judge he had access to the case rolls, whereas most lawyers did not. *See* Hogue, *supra* note 45, at 189. Dan Coquilette observes that the rolls did not record the reasons for the decisions, just the judgment. Moreover, the rolls were closely guarded and available only to a few judges and privileged lawyers. Daniel R. Coquillette, The Anglo-American Legal Heritage: Introductory Materials 147 (1999).

67   Hogue, *supra* note 45, at 171.

68   Often the case outcome will not even be reported, either because the reporter thought it unimportant or simply because he was absent from court the day the ruling was issued. Instead, the reporters focus on the jousting between the judges and the counsel. The case outcome was often thought unimportant because of the absence of the doctrine of stare decisis. It is not until the doctrine of stare decisis emerges that case reports are thought to be valuable for their recitation of the holding and reasoning of the case. For an excellent summary of the uses and content of the Year Books, *see* 2 Holdsworth, *supra* note 64, at 551–56.

69   *See* Hogue, *supra* note 45, at 189-90; Berman & Reid, *supra* note 42, at 446 (noting that "as historical records" private case reports "were often quite unreliable"). Hogue quotes Justice Fitzherbert's observation to one lawyer, "As against your book 1 can produce four books where the contrary has been decided." Hogue, *supra* note 45, at 190 (citing T. Ellis Lewis, *The History of Judicial Precedent*, 47 L.Q. Rev. 411). Fifoot, referring to the "poverty of the Reports," derides them as "uninspiring compilations." *See* Fifoot, *supra* note 60, at 14. In addition, only the decisions of the common law courts were consistently reported. There were numerous other competing court systems in England at the time that decided cases as well but which failed to produce written precedents at all. *See* William S. Holdsworth, *Case Law,* in Essays In Law & History 147, 156 (A.L. Goodhart & H.G. Hanbury eds., 1946); *see also infra* Part III.B.

70   Robert C. Berring, *Legal Research and Legal Concepts: Where Form Molds Substance,* 75 Cal. L. Rev. 15, 18-19 (1987). As one commentator observes, "*Clerk v. Day* was reported in four different books, and in not one of them correctly—not even as to name . . . . Arbitrary spelling of the names of cases is a bibliographical irritation, and sometimes a difficulty. *Fetter v. Beal* . . . is a pretty good disguise for *Fitter v. Veal* . . ." Percy H. Winfield, The Chief Sources of English Legal History 185 n.3 (1925).

71   *See* Baker, *supra* note 61, at 105–07.

72   *See* Hart v. Massanari, 266 F.3d 1155, 1166 (9th Cir. 2001) (noting that Heydon's case was decided in 1584 but Coke's account was not published until 1602); *see also*

Allen Dillard Boyer, *"Understanding, Authority, and Will": Sir Edward Coke and the Elizabethan Origins of Judicial Review*, 39 B.C. L. Rev. 43, 79 (1997).

73   *See* Van Vechten Veeder, *The English Reports, 1537–1865*, *in* 2 Select Essays, *supra* note 44, at 127.

74   *See* Plucknett, *supra* note 47, at 344–45.

75   *Id.* at 348. Plucknett's colorful description captures the essential flavor of these reports:

> A large amount of the material which [the Year Books] contain is hardly strictly necessary for professional purposes. Long and rambling conversations are reported at great length. A large amount of irrelevant material is carefully recorded. There seems to be a definite interest in the personalities of judges and serjeants . . . . One cannot avoid the feeling that the anonymous authors of these Year Books took a great delight in the work of compiling them, whatever the technical object was which they had in view.

Id. at 269.

76   *See* John Maxcy Zane, *The Five Ages of the Bench and Bar of England, in* 1 Select Essays, *supra* note 44, at 625, 650. Reporters were especially attracted to witty put-downs, bungled pleas, and other entertaining items. *See* 2 Holdsworth, *supra* note 64, at 551.

77   5 Holdsworth, *supra* note 64, at 370.

78   Zane, *supra* note 76, at 650; 2 Holdsworth, *supra* note 64, at 551.

79   *See* Frederick G. Kempin, Jr., *Precedent and Stare Decisis: The Critical Years, 1800 to 1850*, 3 Am. J. Leg. Hist. 28, 32 (1959).

80   *See* Holdsworth, *supra* note 69, at 155. Indeed, there is an entire secondary literature concerned solely with identifying the quality and traditional reputations of various reporters. *See, e.g.*, John W. Wallace, The Reporters (4th ed. 1882); Veeder, *supra* note 73, at 123.

81   *See* 5 Holdsworth, *supra* note 64, at 368. French and Latin were the traditional language of the English courts. During the Commonwealth period, however, English was made the official language of the court. Thus, editors were required to translate all of the older reports into English, a task completed with irregular success. *See* Veeder, *supra* note 73, at 127.

82   *See* Plucknett, *supra* note 47, at 268–70.

83   *See* Potter's Historical Introduction to English Law and Its Institutions 277 (A.K.R. Kiralfy ed., 4th ed. 1962) [hereinafter Potter's] ("The form of the manuscript Year Book and the lack of uniformity due to the absence of printed books prevented the citation of cases in the modern way.").

84   Berman, *supra* note 55, at 1733; Veeder, *supra* note 73, at 128.

85   Berman & Reid, *supra* note 42, at 447 ("Coke often distorted the older cases, culling from them the language that supported his own views; he would reach out for anything said by a judge in an earlier case if it seemed to him to reflect a true legal principle."); Veeder, *supra* note 73, at 132 ("In connection with his habit of editing the conclusions of the court in accordance with his own views of the law, it may be added that Coke is not always accurate.").

86   *See* Plucknett, *supra* note 47, at 281. Plucknett further observes of Coke, "In his hands a law report takes the form of a somewhat rambling disquisition upon the case in question. He frequently gives the pleadings, but less often does he tell us the arguments. As for the decision, it is often impossible to distinguish the remarks of

the judge (where it was not Coke himself) from the comments of the reporter. There was no clear boundary in his mind between what a case said and what he thought it ought to say, between the reasons which actually prompted the decision, and the elaborate commentary which he could easily weave around any question." *Id.* Coke provided his own subjective account of the cases and sometimes was the judge or lawyer in the cases he reported. *See* Coquilette, *supra* note 66, at 314.

87   *See* Plucknett, *supra* note 47, at 281 ("The reporters who succeeded Coke are much lesser men . . . . Their reports are frequently short and inaccurate, and sometimes unintelligible. Matters arenot helped by the fact that one case is commonly reported by three or four reporters, for they are often equally bad.").

88   Berman, *supra* note 55, at 1732.

89   *See* Coquilette, *supra* note 66, at 273–74.

90   *Id.* at 273.

91   *Id.* at 274.

92   *Id.*

93   5 Holdsworth, *supra* note 64, at 373 (Burrow's reports); Plucknett, *supra* note 47, at 281.

94   Berman & Reid, *supra* note 42, at 448 (quoting Matthew Hale, The History of the Common Law of England 68 (1713)).

95   *Id.*

96   *See* Holdsworth, *supra* note 69, at 158; *see also id.* at 158 n.4 ("The law does not consist of particular cases, but of general principles, which are illustrated and explained by those cases." (quoting *R. v. Bembridge* (1783))).

97   *See* Bruno Leoni, Freedom and the Law 180 (3d ed. 1991) (distinguishing the concept of "precedent" serving as the generally accepted principle of community from "*binding* precedent in the common-law systems of the Anglo-Saxon countries at the present time").

98   Allen, *supra* note 59, at 147.

99   *Id.*

100   *Id.* at 150.

101   *Id; see also* Potter's, *supra* note 83, at 277.

102   *See* Hart v. Massanari, 266 F.3d 1155, 1165 (9th Cir. 2001); 1 F.A. Hayek, Law, Legislation, And Liberty: Rules And Order (1973); Leoni, *supra* note 97, at 80–85.

103   Plucknett, *supra* note 47, at 347.

104   *Id.; see also* Potter's, *supra* note 83, at 275 ("A bad case could be dismissed as misconceived, but a series of cases in the same sense in all courts would be difficult not to follow.").

105   Plucknett, *supra* note 47, at 347.

106   *See* Caleb Nelson, *Stare Decisis and Demonstrably Erroneous Precedents,* 87 Va. L. Rev. 1, 21–46 (2001); Thomas R. Lee, *Stare Decisis In Historical Perspective: From the Founding Era to the Rehnquist Court,* 52 Vand. L. Rev. 647 (1999). Stare decisis may have taken hold in England later than in America. *See* Kempin, *supra* note 79, at 51.

107   Nelson, *supra* note 106, at 23–24. Nelson describes these as the "external" sources of the law, contrasting them with the "internal" source of precedent. *Id.*

108   *See supra* notes 58–62 and accompanying text.

109   Nelson, *supra* note 106, at 32; *see also id.* at 32 n.115.

110   *See* Nelson, *supra* note 106, at 25–27; Lee, *supra* note 106, at 660.

111   See A.C. Pritchard & Todd J. Zywicki, *Finding the Constitution: An Economic Analysis of Tradition's Role in Constitutional Interpretation*, 77 N.C. L. Rev. 409, 469 n.249 (1999) (describing reception laws).

112   See Nelson, *supra* note 106, at 28; Kempin, *supra* note 79, at 38–42.

113   Quoted in Nelson, *supra* note 106, at 27.

114   See *id*. at 29.

115   See Kempin, *supra* note 79, at 34. There were exceptions for some periods and places, such as Dallas's reports of the Pennsylvania courts and U.S. Supreme Court, but high-quality reporters were rare. I would like to thank Caleb Nelson for pointing out these exceptions.

116   See *id*. at 34–35.

117   See *id*. at 38.

118   See *id*. at 35–36; *see also* Hart v. Massanari, 266 F.3d 1155, 1169 (9th Cir. 2001) (noting rise of official reporters in America).

119   Nelson, *supra* note 106, at 34; Kempin, *supra* note 79, at 38.

120   Nelson, *supra* note 106, at 34.

121   See Pritchard & Zywicki, *supra* note 111, at 489–93.

122   Nelson, *supra* note 106, at 35.

123   See Pritchard & Zywicki, *supra* note 111, at 490–93; *see also* Nelson, *supra* note 106, at 36.

124   See Pritchard & Zywicki, *supra* note 111, at 491; *see also* Donald Lutz, *Political Participation in Eighteenth Century America, in* Toward a Usable Past: Liberty Under State Constitutions 19, 34 (Paul Finkelmaen & Stephen E. Gottlieb eds., 1991); J.G.A. Pocock, *Burke and the Ancient Constitution: A Problem in the History of Ideas, in* J.G.A. Pocock, Politics, Language and Time: Essay on Political Thought and History 202, 213 (1971).

125   See Pritchard & Zywicki, *supra* note 111, at 491; Berman & Reid, *supra* note 42, at 449 (referring to "the traditionary concept of precedent" and distinguishing it from "the strict doctrine of stare decisis that first emerged in the latter nineteenth century").

126   See Gerald J. Postema, Bentham and the Common Law Tradition 213 (1986); *see also* Berman & Reid, *supra* note 42, at 514 (characterizing the strict doctrine of precedent as "essentially a positivist theory, more congenial to the codification movement but grafted onto the doctrine of precedent"). Writing in 1930 Carlton Kemp Allen expressed dismay that his contemporary judges had become to regard "mere decisions *in themselves* as settling disputed point, and of forgetting the fundamental principle which governs the whole employment of precedent." Allen, *supra* note 59, at 157. *See also* Nelson, *supra* note 106, at 38 (noting influence of Bentham on American move toward stricter stare decisis).

127   Allen, *supra* note 59, at 194–95.

128   In fact, stricter *stare decisis* was adopted in the late-Nineteenth Century in part as a mechanism to constrain judicial discretion and judicial law-making. *See* Nelson, *supra* note 106, at 48.

129   See Leoni, *supra* note 97, at 83 ("[Law is] something to be described or to be discovered, not something to be enacted—a world of things that were there, forming part of the common heritage of all . . . citizens. Nobody enacted that law; nobody could change it by any exercise of his personal will.").

130   See Maxwell L. Stearns, Constitutional Process: A Social Choice Analysis of Supreme Court Decision-Making (2000); Maxwell L. Stearns, *Standing Back from the Forest:*

Justiciability and Social Choice, 83 Cal. L. Rev. 1309, 1329–50 (1995); Frank H. Easterbrook, *Ways of Criticizing the Court*, 95 Harv. L. Rev. 802, 817–21 (1982).

131 An excellent discussion of the costs and benefits of a regime of weak precedent rather than strict precedent is presented in Nelson, *supra* note 106, at 54–73.

132 *See* Ronald A. Heiner, *Imperfect Decisions and the Law: On the Evolution of Legal Precedent and Rules*, 15 J. Legal Stud. 227 (1986).

133 For instance, as will be discussed below, the shared jurisdictions of state and federal courts to make common law under the *Swift* v. *Tyson* regime might suggest that neither court be formally bound by the decisions of the other. By contrast, under *Erie R.R. v. Tompkins*, federal courts are bound by the decisions of state courts. *See infra* notes 327–362.

134 *See* 1 Hayek, *supra* note 102. Allen similarly appeals to the principles and concepts of the common law as being of preeminence, not individual case holdings. Allen, *supra* note 59, at 175. This appears to have been the traditional belief of the common law as well. *See* Kempin, *supra* note 79, at 39. Kempin quotes from *Hammond v. Ridgely's Lessee:*

> I cannot perceive why on any principle either of law or policy, an opinion of any court should be deemed of binding authority when the foundation of that opinion is taken away. It is the principle that should govern, the substance and not the shadow. Sound policy does indeed require, that principles laid down, and acted upon by courts of last resort, should not be lightly shaken, as it is to established principles, and not to isolated opinions, that parties look in making their contracts.

> *Id.*

135 *See* William S. Consovoy, *The Rehnquist Court and the End of Constitutional Stare Decisis*: Casey, Dickerson *and the Consequences of Pragmatic Adjudication*, 2002 Utah L. Rev. 53.

136 Many notable scholars have offered economic analyses of stare decisis, but none have previously considered these rent-seeking aspects of stare decisis as a cost of the doctrine. *See, e.g.,* Erin O'Hara, *Social Constraint or Implicit Collusion? Toward a Game Theoretic Analysis of Stare Decisis*, 24 Seton Hall L. Rev. 736 (1993); Lewis Kornhauser, *An Economic Perspective on Stare Decisis*, 65 Chi.-Kent L. Rev. 63 (1989); Jonathan R. Macey, *The Internal and External Costs and Benefits of Stare Decisis*, 65 Chi.-Kent L. Rev. 93 (1989).

137 It should be stressed that even though the analysis here will focus on the English experience, especially with respect to the common law, competitive legal order was not unique to England. Indeed, a competitive legal system was even more developed in continental Europe and persisted longer than in England. See Harold J. Berman, Law and Revolution: The Formation of the Western Legal Tradition (1983); *see also* Tom Bell, *Polycentric Law,* 7 Humane Stud. Rev. 1 (1991), *available at* http://www.theihs.org/libertyguide/hsr/hsr.php/12.html. The focus on England in the current analysis is simply because of the Article's focus on the efficiency of the common law in England and America, but a similar dynamic applied in continental Europe as well.

138 *See* discussion *infra* at notes 300–313 and accompanying text.

139 41 U.S. I (1842).

140 Much of the common law was already developed by the thirteenth century. *See* Charles Rowley, *The Common Law in Public Choice Perspective: A Theoretical and*

Institutional Critique, 12 Hamline L. Rev. 355, 371 (1989); Baker, *supra* note 61, at 9. Baker writes:

> The common law was not all invented in a day, or a year, but arose out a long process of jurisdictional transfer in which many old customs were abandoned but many more were preserved. To appreciate how the ancient customs of England were accommodated to the unifying innovations of the Normans and Angevines, regard must be had not merely to the views of the great men in the king's court at Westminster, but also to what was happening from day to day in the shires, hundreds and boroughs throughout the land.

> *Id.*

141 Hogue, *supra* note 45, at 5.

142 *Id.*

143 Berman, *supra* note 137, at 10; *see also* Coquilette, *supra* note 66, at 183 (noting that Church courts were the most important alternative to royal common law courts).

144 Berman, *supra* note 137, at 10.

145 Hogue, *supra* note 45, at 189.

146 *See infra* notes 154–157 (discussing use of fictions to evade jurisdictional limits).

147 1 Holdsworth, *supra* note 64, at 252.

148 *Id.* at 252.

149 *Id.* at 254.

150 *Id.* at 255.

151 Hudson observes that despite the large number of courts with overlapping jurisdictions "[t]here is little sign of a confusion of courts in Anglo-Norman England" and that "[t]he lack of rigid jurisdictional rules need not have been a disadvantage for disputants." *See* Hudson, *supra* note 44, at 51. "At the same time," he adds, "court-holders may have competed to settle disputes, since doing so could increase their authority and bring profit." *Id.* at 26. *See also* Bruce Lyon, A Constitutional and Legal History of Medieval England 443 (2d ed. 1980); Baker, *supra* note 61, at 31; William M. Landes and Richard A. Posner, *Adjudication as a Private Good*, 8 J. Legal Stud. 235, 235 (1979).

152 *See* Plucknett, *supra* note 47, at 210 (observing that the "competition between the King's Bench, Common Pleas and Exchequer . . . resulted in these three courts having coordinate jurisdiction in many common classes of cases"); Baker, *supra* note 61, at 36 ("[B]efore 1700 the three major courts had acquired comparable jurisdiction over common pleas."); *id.* (noting that although each court had some limited exclusive jurisdiction, "the bulk of ordinary business was shared between the three courts"). Indeed, as noted above, these conflicts over jurisdiction were the primary issues recorded in early published opinions, rather than the substantive results generated in those cases. Only cases involving freehold of land were required to come before the King's courts in the twelfth and thirteenth centuries. *See* Rowley, *supra* note 140, at 371.

153 *See* Baker, *supra* note 61, at 46.

154 *See* Hudson, *supra* note 44, at 26 ("There were not strict rules of jurisdiction determining the court to which every dispute must come."). As noted above, a stricter doctrine of precedent emerged first in this area to police jurisdictional lines among these rival courts. *See* discussion *supra* notes 59–61 and accompanying text.

As Professor Hirsch has observed, the use of fictions to provide legal flexibility is also important with respect to *vertical* stare decisis. Fictions, or "contraptions," provide lower courts with wiggle room to escape the reach of troublesome precedents imposed by superior courts. *See* Adam J. Hirsch, *Inheritance Law, Legal Contraptions, and the Problem of Doctrinal Change*, 79 Or. L. Rev. 527 (2000).

155   *See* S.F.C. Milsom, Historical Foundations of the Common Law 23–24 (2d ed. 1981). Milsom writes:

> [M]any difficulties arose. Testamentary jurisdiction was clearly for the church; but was the church's nominee or some other to represent the dead man in the law courts if he died owing or being owed an enforceable debt? Questions about the fact and validity of marriage were clearly for the church, and therefore questions of legitimacy; but were its determinations to bind the lay courts in deciding upon inheritance? . . . How could the frontier be defined?

> *Id.*

156   For instance, *Hadley* v. *Baxendale*, a chestnut of first-year Contracts courses dealing with the re-coverability of consequential damages for breach of contract, was decided by the Exchequer Court. 9 Ex. 341, 156 Eng. Rep. 145 (1845).

157   *See* Nathan Levy, Jr., *Mesne Process in Personal Actions at Common Law and the Power Doctrine*, 78 Yale L.J. 52 (1968) (describing many of the fictions used by courts to assert jurisdiction over disputes); *see also* Milsom, *supra* note 155, at 61–63 (describing some of the fictions used to allow courts to assert jurisdiction over disputes); Plucknett, *supra* note 47, at 644 (describing development of doctrine of *indebitatus assumpsit* as attempt by King's Bench to infringe on the exclusive jurisdiction of Common Pleas over actions in Debt).

158   *See* Hudson, *supra* note 44, at 225.

159   Mary Elizabeth Basile et al., *Lex Mercatoria* and Legal Pluralism: A Late Thirteenth-Century Treatise and its Afterlife 139 (1998) (quoting Sir Francis Ashley).

160   Some have argued that this competition should have produced a tendency toward pro-plaintiff legal rules in order to induce plaintiffs to choose one court over another. Why this did not occur is discussed *infra* at notes 300–326 and accompanying text.

161   Plucknett, *supra* note 47, at 650.

162   *See id.* ("[S]ince development took the form of modifying the different forms of action, it was inevitable that there should be a good deal of overlapping, and consequently the boundaries between forms of action became obscure. Hence it was all the more easy to emphasize substance above form.").

163   Berman, *supra* note 137, at 10. *See also* Rowley, *supra* note 140, at 371. Rowley notes that other than freehold cases, Englishmen:

> could take their cases to the county courts, which administered local, customary law, or into the church courts, which administered canon law; or into the borough courts which administered the law merchant; or, in the case of feudal barons, into the courts of a baronial overlord which would apply the rules of feudal custom.

> *Id.*

164   Hogue, *supra* note 45, at 5.

165   *Id.*

166   *See* Baker, *supra* note 61, at 9. Baker notes:

> [I]n seeking the origins of the common law it is misleading to study solely the work of the royal judges. Sometimes the reason why a royal court would not allow an action or grant a remedy in a particular case was not that the matter was unknown to 'English law', but that the action pertained to some other jurisdiction or that the remedy was available elsewhere . . . . It is even more essential to understand the balance of jurisdictions when considering the evolution of the common law itself.

> *Id.*

167   *Id.* at 29. Along these lines, Harold Berman writes:

> For some four hundred years these secular legal systems co-existed alongside the canon law, and alongside each other, within every territory of Europe. With the national Protestant Revolutions of the sixteenth and seventeenth centuries, the various co-existing jurisdictions were, in effect, nationalized; nevertheless, the existence of plural jurisdictions and plural bodies of law within each country has remained a significant characteristic of the Western legal tradition at least until the latter part of the twentieth century.

> Harold J. Berman, *The Western Legal Tradition in a Millenial Perspective: Past and Future*, 60 La. L. Rev. 739, 740 (2000).

168   1 William Blackstone, Commentaries on the Law of England 3–27 (1765) (reprinted 1966).

169   *See* Berman, *supra* note 137, at 10 ("Perhaps the most distinctive characteristic of the Western legal tradition is the coexistence and competition within the same community of diverse jurisdictions and diverse legal systems."); *see also* Lon L. Fuller, Anatomy of The Law 123 (1968) ("A possible . . . objection to the view [of law] taken here is that it permits the existence of more than one legal system governing the same population. The answer is, of course, that such multiple systems do exist and have in history been more common than unitary systems."); S.F.C. Milsom, *Introduction, in* Pollock & Maitland, *supra* note 51, at xcv. Milson writes:

> Different and more or less conflicting systems of law, different and more or less competing systems of jurisdiction, in one and the same region, are compatible with a high state of civilization, with a strong government, and with an administration of justice well enough liked and sufficiently understood by those who are concerned.

> *Id.*

170   Exceptions are R. Peter Terrebonne, *A Strictly Evolutionary Model of Common Law*, 10 J. Legal Studies 397, 406–07 (1981); Goodman, *supra* note 43; and Rowley, *supra* note 140. The point is also noted in passing in Tom W. Bell, *The Common Law in Cyberspace*, 97 Mich. L. Rev. 1746, 1768 (1999) and Randy E. Barnett, *The Sound of Silence: Default Rules and Contractual Consent*, 78 Va. L. Rev. 821, 910–11 (1992).

171   Adam Smith, An Inquiry into the Nature and Causes of The Wealth of Nations bk. V, ch. 1, pt. 22, at 241 (Edward Cannan ed., 1976).

172   *Id.* at 241.

173   *Id.* at 241–42.

174   Adam Smith, *Report of 1762–63, in* Lectures on Jurisprudence, *supra* note 47, at 280; *see also* Adam Smith, *Report dated 1766, in* Lectures on Jurisprudence, *supra*

note 47, at 423 ("During the improvement of the law of England there arose rival-
ships among the several courts.").

175   Adam Smith, *Report of 1762–63, in* Lectures on Jurisprudence, *supra* note 47, at 241
("Public services are never better performed than when their reward comes only in
consequence of their being performed, and is proportioned to the diligence
employed in performing them."). Posner has postulated that because judges are
insulated from market pressures they will tend to consume leisure and shirk on
their obligations. *See* Richard A. Posner, *What Do Judges and Justices Maximize?
(The Same Thing Everyone Else Does),* 3 Sup. Ct. Econ. Rev. 1, 13–15, 31 (1994). This
concern about excess judicial consumption of leisure was not merely hypothetical.
Apparently common law judges were notorious for shirking on their duties
when they could get away with it, Burdick quotes the great English legal
historian Sir John Fortescue's comments on the work habits of the common law
judiciary:

> You are to know further, that the judges of England do not sit in the King's
> courts above three hours in the day, that is from eight in the morning till
> eleven. The courts are not open in the afternoon. The suitors of the court
> betake themselves to the *pervise*, and other places, to advise with the Sergeants
> at Law, and other their counsel, about their affairs. The judges when they have
> taken their refreshments spend the rest of the day in the study of the laws,
> reading the Holy Scriptures, and other innocent amusements at their pleasure.
> It seems rather a life of contemplation than of action.

Francis Marion Burdick, *Contributions of the Law Merchant to the Common Law, in* 3
Select Essays, *supra* note 44, at 36. Sir Henry Spellman, by contrast, believed
that the unwillingness of the common law judges to work in the afternoon was
caused by less "innocent amusements":

> It is now to be considered why high courts of justice sit not in the afternoon
> . . . Our ancestors and other northern nations being more prone to distem-
> per and excess of diet used the forenoon only, lest repletion should bring
> upon them drowsiness and oppression of spirits. To confess the truth our
> Saxons were immeasureably given to drunkenness.

Id. at 36 n. 3. Spellman argued that this tendency toward drunkenness also explained
the common law prohibition on providing jurors with meat, drink, fire, or candle
light until they agreed upon their verdict. *Id. See also* Ahmed E. Taha, *Publish or Paris?
Evidence of How Judges Allocate Their Time,* 5 Am. L. & Econ. Rev. (forthcoming 2003)
(providing empirical test of judicial utility functions).

176   *See* 1 Hayek, *supra* note 102, at 94–123 (describing common law as "spontaneous
order").

177   Milsom, *supra* note 169, at xlix.

178   *Id.; see also id.* at lii ("[A]t no time was the action of covenant common in the king's
courts, except as a basis for levying fines . . . ."); Baker, *supra* note 61, at 271
("Compared with the local and ecclesiastical courts, the medieval royal courts
played a limited part in the field of contract.").

179   Fifoot, *supra* note 60, at 14.

180   Thomas Edward Scrutton, *Roman Law Influence in Chancery, Church Courts, Admiralty,
and Law Merchant, in* 1 Select Essays, *supra* note 44, at 208, 238 (quoting J. Davies);
id. at 239 (quoting Blackstone).

181   W.T. Barbour, *The History of Contract in Early English Equity, in* 4 Oxford Studies in Social and Legal History 54 (Paul Vinogradoff ed., 1974) (reprint of 1914 edition).

182   *See* Plucknett, *supra* note 47, at 631.

183   *See* A.W.B. Simpson, A History of The Common Law of Contract: The Rise of The Action of Assumpsit 125 (1987).

184   *See* Baker, *supra* note 61, at 25.

185   Plucknett, *supra* note 47, at 635; Milsom, *supra* note 169, at *l* ("Nobody has ever doubted that most litigation in what we should call contract and tort took place in lesser courts than the king's . . . .").

186   *See* Pollock & Maitland, *supra* note 51, at 109.

187   *See* Berman, *supra* note 167, at 743; Milsom, *supra* note 169, at lii. The strong intellectual framework of the canon law, especially when compared to the English common law, owed much to the incorporation of Roman law into the canon law, which provided a systematic framework of legal principles. *See* Berman, *supra* note 137, at 245.

188   William Stubbs, *The History of the Canon Law in England, in* 1 Select Essays, *supra* note 44, at 248, 270.

189   *See* Stubbs, *supra* note 188, at 270–71. Baker notes that the Church had "pervasive jurisdiction over the lives of most ordinary people." Baker, *supra* note 61, at 112. Stubbs describes the irritation of Henry III and Edward II regarding the extravagant jurisdictional claims of the ecclesiastical courts. *See* Stubbs, *supra* note 188, at 272.

190   Berman, *supra* note 137, at 223.

191   *See* Milsom, *supra* note 155, at 23.

192   Pollock and Maitland observe that as a result of the potentially vast reach of the church's jurisdiction over the pledge of faith, only "[w]ith great difficulty were the Courts Christian prevented from appropriating a vast region in the province of contract." Pollock & Maitland, *supra* note 51, at 128. *See also id.* at 131 ("Large then is the province of ecclesiastical law; but it might have been much larger.").

193   *See* Coquilette, *supra* note 66, at 184–85.

194   *See* Milsom, *supra* note 155, at 23; Scrutton, *supra* note 180, at 226; Berman, *supra* note 137, at 223. The independence and strength of the ecclesiastical courts in England through the end of the Eighteenth-Century at least is suggested by Alexander Hamilton's comparison in the *Federalist Papers* of the Probate Courts in early America "to the spiritual courts in England." The Federalist No. 83 at 502 (Alexander Hamilton) (Clinton Rossiter ed., 1961). The church's jurisdiction to deal with intestate succession arose from its power to decide issues of legitimacy and paternity. Of course, in each of these areas the ecclesiastical courts faced rivals from other jurisdictions seeking to infringe on the Church's jurisdiction.

195   *See* Pollock & Maitland, *supra* note 51, at 134.

196   Stubbs notes that the Bishop of London, for instance, entertained suits alleging that a guild member had breached his oath by improperly revealing "the art and mysteries" of his guild to non-members. *See* Stubbs, *supra* note 188, at 271.

197   *See* Berman, *supra* note 137, at 225 ("Every person in Western Christendom lived under both canon law and one or more secular legal systems.").

198   *See* Milsom, *supra* note 169, at xcviii ("the wide and flexible jurisdiction of the spiritual power was of great service in the middle ages, both in supplementing the justice of secular courts, and in stimulating them by its formidable competition to improve their doctrine and practice").

199   *See* 1 William S. Holdsworth, A History of English Law 241–42 (1903).

200   *Id.* at 241–42 (noting that "the ecclesiastical bias of the chancellors" led them to interpose "good faith and honest dealing" into the Chancery's contract doctrine); *see also* Barbour, *supra* note 181, at 163.

201   Barbour, *supra* note 181, at 158 (noting indirect reception of canon law into Chancery).

202   *See* Stubbs, *supra* note 188, at 270 (noting that "for four hundred years, from the Conquest to the Reformation," the canon law and common law courts "stood side by side, with rival bodies of administrators and rival or conflicting processes"). As Stubbs observes, the ecclesiastical courts had their own bar and educational system as well. *Id.* at 266. Stubbs also observes that many clerics were quite ambivalent about the great activity of the ecclesiastical courts, arguing that it distracted the church from spiritual matters in its focus on secular matters of contract enforcement and the like. *See id.* at 269. Moreover, although the punishment for many wrongs was penance, in practice liable parties would provide civil compensation to commute the term of penance. *See* J. H. Baker, An Introduction to English Legal History 112 (2d ed., 1979).

203   For general overviews of the history and characteristics of the law merchant, see Berman, *supra* note 137, at 333–56 (stressing legal rules) and Bruce L. Benson, The Spontaneous Evolution of Commercial Law, 55 S. Econ. J. 644 (1989) (providing economic analysis of law merchant).

204   *See* 5 Holdsworth, *supra* note 64, at 65–102 (reviewing history of Italian law merchant).

205   Berman observes:

> The mercantile community had its own law, the lex mercatoria, just as the church had its own law, the jus canonicum. The merchants were, of course, members of the church and hence subject to the canon law, but they were also members of the mercantile community and hence subject to the law merchant. When the two bodies of law conflicted, it might not be clear which of the two should prevail.

Berman, *supra* note 137, at 346.

206   *See* 5 Holdsworth, *supra* note 64, at 79–80 (noting overlap between ecclesiastical law and law merchant).

207   *See id.* at 81.

208   *See id.* at 83.

209   *See id.*

210   *See id.* at 130. The first great treatise on the law merchant, Gerard Malynes's *Lex Mercatoria* (published in 1622) was authored by a merchant, not a lawyer. *Id.* at 131–32. Malynes's most prominent successor, Marius (1670), was also a merchant. *See* A.T. Carter, A History of English Legal Institutions 265 (1902).

211   Berman, *supra* note 137, at 339.

212   Leon E. Trakman, The Law Merchant: The Evolution of Commercial Law 8 (1983).

213   Wyndham A. Bewes, The Romance of the Law Merchant; Being an Introduction to the Study of International and Commercial Law with Some Account of the Commerce and Fairs of The Middle Ages 11 (1923). In elevating the purported influence of Middle Eastern legal sources, Bewes also questions the influence of Roman law.

214   *See* Bruce L. Benson, *Law Merchant, in* 2 The New Palgrave Dictionary of Economics and the Law 500, 503 (Peter Newman ed., 1998); Berman, *supra* note 137, at 343; Trakman, *supra* note 212, at 12; *see also* Krell v. Henry, 2 K.B. 740, 748 (1903) (noting Roman Law origins of excuse doctrines such as impossibility and frustration).

215   DouglassC. North, Institutions, Institutional Change and Economic Performance 129 (1990).

216   Basile et al., *supra* note 159, at 136. The authors note:

> At the common law a person's writings could only be pleaded against him if they were sealed and delivered, whereas in a suit between merchants, bills of Lading, Bills of Exchange, being but tickets without Seals, Letters of advice and credences, Policies of assurance, Assignations of Debts, all of which are of no force at the Common Law, are of good credit and force by the Law Merchant.

> *Id. See also* Bewes, *supra* note 213, at 19. Bewes notes:

> Now, it is above all things necessary to bear in mind that the [law merchant] courts enforced the custom of merchants and the customers made the law: and we may as well remember that the two great distinctive elements in the merchants' law, as enforced in their own courts, were good faith and dispatch, for speed and honesty must be obtained, though by means not sanctioned by the common law, which was and ever has been a laggard, and by its halting procedure hinders the rapid course of commercial justice.

> *Id.*

217   *See* Benson, *supra* note 214, at 504 (noting that merchants took disputes to ecclesiastical courts); Basile et al., *supra* note 159, at 126 (noting competition with common law, admiralty courts, conciliar courts, and the Chancery).

218   Although the discussion here focuses primarily on the law merchant as it evolved in fairs, towns, and markets, it should be noted that the term itself also conventionally includes the law developed to govern international trade on the seas, and thus was equally important to the development of mercantile and admiralty law. These two branches of the law merchant were substantially identical; therefore, I discuss only the "commercial" branch here. *See* 1 Holdsworth, *supra* note 199, at 303. Holdsworth states:

> It is clear that both the maritime and commercial law of the Middle Ages grew up amid similar surroundings, governed the relations of persons engaged in similar pursuits, was enforced in similar tribunals. It is not therefore surprising that, from that time to this, the relations between them have always been of the closest.

> *Id.*

219   Holdsworth notes that the law merchant in England evolved in a way different from the rest of Europe, as the law merchant was melded with unique English historical conditions. *See* 5 Holdsworth, *supra* note 64, at 67.

220   Holdsworth distinguishes three distinct periods in the history of the law merchant. In the first, the law merchant was applied provincially in local town courts. In the second, the law merchant emerged as in independent court system, applying a set of unique procedures and applying a universal *lex mercatoria*, rooted in merchant practice rather

than in local law-making. Third, the law merchant was incorporated by Lord Mansfield into the common law as a form of merchant custom, melding the substantive rules of the merchant law with the procedures of the common law. *See* William Searle Holdsworth, *The Development of the Law Merchant and Its Courts, in* 1 Select Essays, *supra* note 44, at 289, 293, *excerpted from* 1 Holdsworth, *supra* note 199, at 300–37. I will focus here on the second period and its incorporation by Lord Mansfield.

221   *See* Thomas Edward Scrutton, *General Survey of the History of the Law Merchant*, 3 Select Essays, *supra* note 44, at 1, 7; *see also* Basile et al., *supra* note 159, at 137.

222   Scrutton, *supra* note 221, at 2; *see also* Burdick, *supra* note 175, at 43. Burdick notes:

> It is apparent . . . that for several centuries there was a true body of law in England which was known as the law merchant. It was as distinct from the law administered by the common law courts, as was the civil or the canon law. It was a part of the unwritten law of the realm, although its existence and its enforcement had been recognized and provided for by statutes. Until the Seventeenth Century, it was rarely referred to in common law tribunals.

> *Id.*

223   *See* 5 Holdsworth, *supra* note 64, at 119, 140; William F. Walsh, A History of Anglo-American Law 367 (2d ed. 1932). Eventually the common law courts were able to use fictions to evade this jurisdictional limitation. *See* 5 Holdsworth, *supra* note 64, at 40 and *infra* notes 320–323 and accompanying text. This jurisdictional barrier was eventually overcome by a fiction in the sixteenth century, but commercial litigation did not become a significant part of the common law until the seventeenth century. *See* Barbour, *supra* note 181, at 76–77; H. W. Arthurs, "Without The Law": Administrative Justice and Legal Pluralism in Nineteenth-Century England 54 (1985).

224   *See* 1 Holdsworth, *supra* note 199, at 307 n.2.

225   *See* 5 Holdsworth, *supra* note 64, at 115.

226   *See* Arthurs, *supra* note 223, at 53.

227   *See* Holdsworth, *supra* note 220, at 298.

228   *See id.* at 292–93, 298; Basile et al., *supra* note 159, at 2 (showing a reproduction of *Lex Mercatoria* and arguing that law merchant applies to transaction involving a merchant's "merchandise"); *id.* at 96 (noting that "merchant" was defined "broadly" to include "all those enfeoffed and resident in the 'five places' [in which merchant courts existed] and by suggesting that 'markets' include the entire geographical area of the same places").

229   Fifoot, *supra* note 60, at 8; *see also* William Mitchell, an Essay on The Early History of The Law Merchant 21 (photo, reprint 1969) (1904) (concluding that the Law Merchant existed and that it was "the private international law of the Middle Ages"); Alexander N. Sack, *Conflicts of Laws in the History of the English Law, in* 3 Law: A Century of Progress 342, 375 (1937) ("For centuries commercial causes were determined by a law of their own, the law merchant.").

230   *See* Walsh, *supra* note 223, at 362. The author states:

> One reason why the law of contract lagged so far behind in its development was that merchants, shippers, and traders had a special law of their own administered in special courts for them alone. . . . This law took care of the controversies arising in connection with business, so that very few questions of this nature arose in the regular courts prior to the seventeenth century.

Id.

231 Holdsworth, *supra* note 220, at 298. The law merchant prevailed in five places: cities, fairs, seaports, market-towns, and boroughs. Basile et al., *supra* note 159, at 23.

232 On the fair courts, *see* Scrutton, *supra* note 221, at 9–11.

233 *Id.* at 9 (referring to court as the Court *Pepoudrous*).

234 *See* Holdsworth, *Development, supra* note 220, at 298.

235 *See* Benson, *supra* note 203, at 650. In fact, one significant advantage of the law merchant courts was that they generally were open for business. The common law courts, by contrast, sat only in the mornings and often disposed of cases at a leisurely pace. *See supra* note 175 and accompanying text (describing practice of common law courts not to meet in the afternoon). By contrast, law merchant court was held twice per day, before and after dinner. Basile et al., *supra* note 159, at 60.

236 Burdick, *supra* note 175, at 40. Often the customs reflected the nature of the merchants themselves. Rather than a "pledge of faith" as under the ecclesiastical law, for example, the merchants instead pointed to the "wetting of a bargain," *i.e.*, buying a drink to memorialize a deal, as an important evidentiary act. *See* Scrutton, *supra* note 180, at 10. The reliance on commercial custom in the *lex mercatoria* would later provide the impetus for Karl Llewellyn's advocacy of the incorporation of commercial custom into Article 2 of the Ucc.

237 *See* Carter, *supra* note 210, at 254–55.

238 *See* 1 Holdsworth, *supra* note 199, at 311.

239 *See* 5 Holdsworth, *supra* note 64, at 96.

240 *See id.* at 98,107.

241 Holdsworth, *supra* note 220, at 302. The staple courts eventually died out with the decline of trade through the staple markets in the sixteenth century. *See* Walsh, *supra* note 223, at 367. These "staple courts" bear a strong resemblance to the private systems of adjudication that currently prevail in various commodities markets. Compare the rules governing the Staple Court provided by *The Little Red Book of Bristol, reprinted in Carter, supra* note 210, at app. III, with Lisa Bernstein's description of the rules governing the National Grain and Feed Association in Lisa Bernstein, *Merchant Law in Merchant Court: Rethinking the Code's Search for Immanent Business Norms*, 144 U. Pa. L. Rev. 1765 (1996).

242 *See* Carter, *supra* note 210, at 261; *see also* Holdsworth, *supra* note 220, at 302. For a general overview of the Courts of Staple, *see* Bernard Edward Spencer Brodhurst, *The Merchants of the Staple, in* 3 Select Essays, *supra* note 44, at 16. The Statute of the Staple provided, in relevant part, "all merchants coming to the staple, their servants and household, shall be ruled by mercantile law *(la lei* marchant) concerning all things touching the staple, and not by the common law of the land, nor by the usage of cities, boroughs, or other towns." Basile et al., *supra* note 159, at 129 (quoting The Statute of the Staple, 1353, 27 Edw. 3, c. 8 (Eng.)). Some recent commentators have argued that, notwithstanding its language, the Statute of the Staple did not actually deprive the common law courts of jurisdiction over these disputes, but that the Statute simply empowered the staple markets to establish additional locations for adjudicating disputes. *See* Charles J. Reid, Jr., *The Early History of the Law of Bills and Notes: A Study of the Origins of Anglo-American Commercial Law*, 53 Bus. Law 835, 837 n.2 (1998) (book review).

243 Holdsworth, *supra* note 220, at 302.

244 Plucknett, *supra* note 47, at 636.

245 Holdsworth, *supra* note 220, at 303.

246 *Id.* at 316 (detailing cases that illustrated "the incompetence of the Common Law Courts to deal with the [commercial] jurisdiction which they claimed").

247 *See* Milsom, *supra* note 169, at xxvii.

248 Some doctrines were incorporated directly into the common law; others were incorporated indirectly, passing first through other courts such as Star Chamber, Admiralty, or Equity, before finally passing into the common law. *See* 5 Holdsworth, *supra* note 64, at 135.

249 *See* Scrutton, *supra* note 221, at 12–13.

250 *Id.* at 13; *see also* Coquillette, *supra* note 66, at 449–53 (discussing Mansfield's commercial law jurisprudence); Daniel R. Coquillette, *Legal Ideology and Incorporation IV: The Nature of Civilian Influence on Modern Anglo-American Commercial Law*, 67 B.U. L. Rev. 877, 948–62 (1987).

251 *See* Fifoot, *supra* note 60, at 93-117 (describing Mansfield's commercial law jurisprudence); Plucknett, *supra* note 47, at 657–70 (describing absorption of merchant law rules into the common law); Bruce L. Benson, *To Arbitrate or To Litigate: That Is the Question*, 8 Eur. J.L. & Econ. 91, 125 (1999); Hogue, *supra* note 45, at 234 ("It was the achievement of Mansfield to incorporate the law merchant into the common law and to fashion what had been a body of special customary law into general rules within a larger system."). Mansfield is often called "the founder of the commercial law" of England. Holdsworth, *supra* note 220, at 331; *see also* Carter, *supra* note 210, at 270.

252 *See* Bruce L. Benson, The Enterprise of Law; Justice Without the State 225–26 (1990). This dynamic continues today, as the inefficiencies and unworkable doctrines of national legal systems have led most cross-border commercial traffic to be governed by systems of commercial arbitration rather than country-specific legal systems. *Id.* at 226–27.

253 *See* Burdick, *supra* note 175, at 48; 5 Holdsworth, *supra* note 64, at 111. An extensive list of the various legal concepts that originated with the law merchant is provided by Berman. *See* Berman, *supra* note 137, at 349–50.

254 5 Holdsworth, *supra* note 64, at 110–11. Walsh observes that a claim for damages for a breach of warranty was recognized under the law merchant some two centuries before the common law. *See* Walsh, *supra* note 223, at 366.

255 *See* Fifoot, *supra* note 60, at 104–05.

256 *See* Burdick, *supra* note 175, at 50. One commentator argues that following the eventual demise of the law merchant as an independent court, but for Mansfield's correction of "the illiberal policy of the common lawyers," merchants would have likely gravitated toward the Chancery to resolve their legal issues. Carter, *supra* note 210, at 250–51.

257 Legal historians dispute whether the law merchant in England offered only expedited procedures, different substantive rules, or both. Recent legal historians have also questioned whether there was in fact an independent set of law merchant courts, or whether this was merely the application of merchant custom in the common law courts. The discussion in the text will follow the traditional view, one which seems to continue to gain the allegiance of the majority of legal historians, from Holdsworth, to Maitland, down to Harold Berman. Revisionists include such notables as Professor James Rogers and J.H. Baker. Rogers, although acknowledging that the "incorporation" thesis remains the dominant belief among legal historians and that law merchant courts developed speedier and streamlined procedures for resolving disputes, argues that the common law's commercial jurisprudence

was "home grown." In this Article, I will adopt the traditional view while rendering no independent assessment of Professor Roger's critique one way or the other. *See* James Steven Rogers, The Early History of the Law of Bills and Notes: A Study of the Origins of Anglo-American Commercial Law 20 (1995). Rogers argues:

> In the standard accounts of the history of commercial law, the law merchant is usually taken to have been a body of substantive law based on mercantile custom, distinct from the common law applied in the central courts. Although this view has won nearly universal acceptance among writers on commercial law, the evidence shows that it is quite inaccurate.

Id. Baker notes that "[i]t might seem absurdly heretical to question the almost universally accepted history" of the incorporation thesis, but nonetheless concludes that Lord Mansfield's eighteenth-century commercial law innovations and the recognition of merchant custom arose internally from the common law, rather than being incorporated from the law merchant courts. *See* J.H. Baker, *The Law Merchant and the Common Law Before 1700, in* The Legal Profession and The Common Law: Historical Essays 341, 343 (J. H. Baker ed. 1986).

258 As Arthur comments, "[i]n a sense, Mansfield's work can be construed as the ultimate triumph of the common law over a rival system. If so, it is a triumph of a peculiar sort: the victorious system in effect adopted as its own the form and substance of the vanquished." Arthurs, *supra* note 223, at 55.

259 Baker details a number of the harsher common law doctrines. *See* Baker, *supra* note 202, at 87. It should be noted, however, that although harsh, some of these rules may not have been as irrational as they appeared at first glance. For instance, the rule that forced debtors to pay twice if they failed to have their bond cancelled upon repayment may not have been a simple-minded rule that sought to avoid "destroying certainty and condoning carelessness." *Id*, at 88. Instead, it was likely an attempt to advance the concept of negotiability in commercial notes. This again points out the mistake of examining the common law in isolation from its larger context of courts. Again, these equitable defenses were later merged into the common law when Chancery was abolished.

260 *See* Coquillette, *supra* note 66, at 186 (noting that "Chancery permitted the common law courts to adhere to strict forms and rules without worrying about the 'hard case' which would make poor precedent if decided compassionately"); *see also* Barbour, *supra* note 181, at 68 ("We do not mean to say that relief [in Chancery] was given in every case in which it was sought, but it is apparent that there was a general belief that in equity wrongs which escaped the common law courts would be remedied."); *id.* at 85 (quoting *Doctor and Student*, "And if such default happen in any person whereby he is without remedy at the common law, yet he may be holden by a subpoena . . . ").

261 *See* Baker, *supra* note 202, at 272; *see also* Margaret E. Avery, *The History of the Equitable Jurisdiction of Chancery Before 1460*, 42 Bull. Inst. Hist. Res. 129, 132 (1969) ("The disadvantages of the common law procedure in the later middle ages are well known: it was rigid, ponderous, expensive and susceptible to many abuses.").

262 *See* Coquillette, *supra* note 66, at 186.

263 *See* 1 Holdsworth, *supra* note 199, at 244; *see also* Avery, *supra* note 261, at 134–35.

264 *See* Avery, *supra* note 261, at 134-35. Perversely, this rule ran both ways in that failure to seal the document made the contract unenforceable, whereas sealing the document made the contract enforceable even if the affixing of the seal was

inadvertent or even if an individual's seal was lost or stolen and improperly affixed. *See* Barbour, *supra* note 181, at 22. Similarly, if the written deed evidencing a debt was destroyed or lost, then the debt itself was destroyed. *Id.* at 100-01. Interestingly, however, seals were not generally required in London or Bristol, leading commercial centers where merchants found the formalities of the common law to be unwieldy and therefore merchant custom eschewed them. *See id.* at 19.

265 *See* Barbour, *supra* note 181, at 19.

266 Avery, *supra* note 261, at 132. Avery states:

> Deficiencies in the substance and execution of the common law were the main reason for the chancellor's intervention, and a study of the Proceedings reveals some of the most serious of these weaknesses, and shows the ways in which the chancellor was able to offer superior remedies, thus attracting suitors to his court.

> *Id.*

267 Barbour, *supra* note 181, at 153.

268 *See id.* at 54–58.

269 *See id.* at 68. Barbour notes:

> Theoretically, appeal is to be made to the chancellor only where there is no remedy at law, but this allowed a very wide latitude to the chancellor's discretion, and in fact, if he chose to assume jurisdiction in a particular case, there was no means of preventing the use of the subpoena. Equity might enjoin a plaintiff from prosecuting an action at law, but the King's Bench or Common Pleas had no process to restrain a petitioner from bringing suit in chancery.

> *Id.* The author also comments:

> The primary limitation imposed on the use of the subpoena lay in the fact that it could be brought only in case the petitioner could show an absence of remedy at law. . . . Such, at all events, was the theory. However, the chancellor did not interpret this limitation strictly; he recognized a variety of circumstances which might produce a failure of legal remedy, and if the constant complaint of serjeants and judges is any criterion, we may assume that in spite of this limitation he found means of invading what was regarded as the peculiar domain of the common law.

> *Id.* at 151. *See also id.* at 75 (noting that inability of itinerant merchants or soldiers to secure a speedy remedy from cumbersome common law process was sufficient grounds for invoking Chancery's jurisdiction). Indeed, some petitioners would plead that the defendant's behavior was animated by witchcraft, invoking equitable jurisdiction on the ground that this constituted a violation of conscience. *See id.* at 68–69.

270 *See* 1 Holdsworth, *supra* note 64, at 243–44,

271 *See* Barbour, *supra* note 181, at 76–77.

272 *Id.* at 78–79.

273 *See* 1 Holdsworth, *supra* note 199, at 243; Barbour, *supra* note 181, at 84.

274 *See* Baker, *supra* note 202, at 36. A dramatic recitation of the struggle between common law and equity is provided by Holdsworth. *See* 1 Holdsworth, *supra* note 199, at 247–51.

275   Farnsworth notes that the impetus for the common law to develop *assumpsit* into a legitimate body of contract law was "encouraged by the fear that the Chancellor would" and that the common law courts were "conscious of the expanding jurisdiction of Chancery and anxious to preserve their own powers." E. Allan Farnsworth, *The Past of Promise: An Historical Introduction to Contract*, 69 Colum. L. Rev. 576, 595 (1969).

276   *See* Barbour, *supra* note 181, at 153 ("The deficiencies of the common law became the more apparent as trade increased; merchants were not prepared to embody their contracts in a highly technical form. The very essence of business development lies in the possibility of fluid and formless agreements which may be easily made and easily changed."); *id.* ("Nor was it only the commercial class which felt the restraint of a rigid and unyielding system of law. There were hosts of 'accords' and 'bargains' among people of humble life, who from ignorance or lack of means did not observe the technicalities of legal forms.").

277   *See* Baker, *supra* note 202, at 37; Barbour, *supra* note 181, at 66 ("In fact, there can be little doubt that the eagerness displayed by certain judges to extend Assumpsit from misfeasance to nonfeasance was prompted by the strong desire to retain jurisdiction that was fast slipping away."). Those courts most threatened by the competition from Chancery, such as the King's Bench, also responded the most dramatically with procedural and substantive improvements. Baker, *supra* note 61, at 37; 2 Holdsworth, *supra* note 64, at 456 (noting that the "competition of chancellor" awakened "even the most conservative common lawyer to the necessity of endeavouring to meet [the] demands" of an economically dynamic society).

278   *See* Burdick, *supra* note 175, at 50; Basile et al., *supra* note 159, at 146–47 (describing growth of commercial cases in Chancery and competition with Admiralty courts for business). Because Chancery and the law merchant were both grounded in concepts of justice and equity, rather than law, it proved much easier for Chancery to digest the law merchant into its processes than it later did for the common law. *See* Carter, *supra* note 210, at 263.

279   *See* 1 Holdsworth, *supra* note 199, at 239; Avery, *supra* note 261, at 138–39 (noting that the increase in Chancery business in the Fifteenth Century came "not from businessmen, but from landowners and that . . . it was a reflection of their desire for greater freedom to dispose of their land as they wished").

280   *See* Thomas W. Merrill & Henry E. Smith, *Optimal Standardization in the Law of Property: The Numerus Clausus Principle*, 110 Yale L.J. 1 (2000).

281   Avery argues that this was primarily to ensure tax collection on land transfers at sale and death. *See* Avery, *supra* note 261, at 143. Barbour notes that notwithstanding this jurisdictional limit, contracts to convey land (e.g., a promissory contract where the deed had not yet been executed) could be enforced in Chancery by specific performance. Barbour, *supra* note 181, at 117.

282   *See* Avery, *supra* note 261, at 141; *id.* at 143 ("Chancery in this period was not a court for the poor and needy . . . it was a tribunal for landowners who wished to escape the restrictions imposed by common law upon their freedom to deal with their lands as they wished.")-

283   *See* 1 Holdsworth, *supra* note 199, at 241.

284   The administration of property in America today largely remains under provision by geographic monopolies at state and local levels. By contrast, contract law is subject to greater choice of law opportunities, creating a degree of competition in the provision of contract terms, enforcement, and remedies. Consistent with the

hypothesis in the text, a diversity of contract terms has proliferated, whereas property law retains the restrictive set of property forms identified by the *numerous clauses* doctrine.

285 *See* Van Caenegem, *supra* note 44, at 33. The greatest competitive advantage of the common law courts was its adoption and regular use of juries. *See id.* at 62–84; *see also* 1 Pollock & Maitland, *supra* note 51, at 203 (describing demise of local courts as result of free choice of litigants).

286 Baker, *supra* note 257, at 354; *see also* Farnsworth, *supra* note 275, at 593–94 (discussing the limits on using existing forms of "covenant" and "debt" from developing into a sophisticated body of contract law).

287 *See* 5 Holdsworth, *supra* note 64, at 117.

288 Barbour, *supra* note 181, at 40; *id.* at 117 ("Assumpsit did not originally lie upon a promise or bargain as such."); *see also* Farnsworth, *supra* note 275, at 594–95.

289 *See* Basile et al., *supra* note 159, at 161; Farnsworth, *supra* note 275, at 592 (noting that the common law "achieved its success [in contract law] less on its intrinsic merits than as a by-product of the victories of the common law courts in their jurisdictional struggles with their competitors").

290 *See* Plucknett, *supra* note 47, at 660 n.2.

291 *See id.* at 661; Holdsworth, *supra* note 220, at 316.

292 *See* Farnsworth, *supra* note 275, at 592.

293 Baker, *supra* note 257, at 352; *accord* 1 Holdsworth, *supra* note 199, at 335. Baker surmises that the judges of the common law may have increased their power because of a perception that the procedural informality and substantive flexibility of the law merchant system was inconsistent with the strictures of due process. *See* Baker, *supra* note 257, at 352–53. Burdick contends without elaborating that the common law judges made a practice out of "enticing or coercing their suitors into the courts of common law." Burdick, *supra* note 175, at 44. On the other hand, many scholars question the purported demise of the law merchant, noting the continued importance of the law merchant in modern times, especially in international arbitration and the rise of arbitration and alternative dispute resolution. *See* Oliver Volckart & Antje Mangels, *Are the Roots of the Modern Lex Mercatoria Really Medieval?*, 65 S. Econ. J. 427, 432 (1999) (noting that almost 90% of all border-crossing commercial transactions contain an arbitration clause). For a general discussion of the importance of the modern law merchant, *see* Bruce L. Benson, *Arbitration in the Shadow of the Law*, *in* 1 The New Palgrave Dictionary of Economics and the Law 93 (1998); Benson, *supra* note 203, at 654–60; Trakman, *supra* note 212.

294 Holdsworth, *supra* note 220, at 319.

295 Plucknett, *supra* note 47, at 284.

296 *Id.* at 636; *see also* Baker, *supra* note 202, at 272; Farnsworth, *supra* note 275, at 592 (noting that there was "no great pressure for enforceability as contracts were not a significant part of the business of the common law courts").

297 Plucknett, *supra* note 47, at 636.

298 *See* Milsom, *supra* note 155, at 25.

299 *See* Holdsworth, *supra* note 220, at 330 (describing law merchant foundation of negotiability principle for bills of exchange and later extension through the common law to all persons); William Cranch, *Promissory Notes Before and After Lord Holt*, *in* 3 Select Essays, *supra* note 44, at 74 (same).

300 William M. Landes and Richard A. Posner, *Adjudication as a Private Good*, 8 J. Legal Stud. 235, 253–54 (1979). It is also interesting to note that, in researching this

article, I did not locate any contemporary evidence that lawyers or litigants thought that courts of the early common law system improperly favored plaintiffs. By contrast, as noted above, the historical record is replete with references to the beneficial effects of competition. The silence in the historical record presents a striking difference from the sustained criticism of America's analogous regime under *Swift v. Tyson*, discussed below.

301   *Id.* at 255. Landes and Posner argue:

> Left unexplained by this analysis is the actual pattern of competition in the English courts during the centuries when the judges were paid out of litigant fees and plaintiffs frequently had a choice among competing courts. There is evidence of competition among the courts for plaintiffs through substantive and procedural innovation, but none (of which we are aware) of the kind of blatant plaintiff favoritism that our economic analysis predicts would emerge in such a competitive setting.

Id. Daniel Klerman has recently challenged this conclusion, arguing that history suggests that competing jurisdictions did, in fact, lead the common law to develop pro-plaintiff rules, and that this tendency was not eliminated until the Crown asserted a monopoly over the English legal system. *See* Daniel Klerman, Jurisdictional Competition and the Evolution of the Common Law (unpublished work presented at George Mason University School of Law, March 19, 2001).

302   Landes & Posner, *supra* note 300, at 255.

303   *See* Klerman, *supra* note 301.

304   *See* Francesco Parisi, *Toward a Theory of Spontaneous Law*, 6 Const. Pol. Econ. 211 (1995); *see also* Vincy Fon & Francesco Parisi, Customary Law and Articulation Theories: An Economic Analysis (George Mason University School of Law, Working Paper No. 02–24, 2002).

305   5 Holdsworth, *supra* note 64, at 94.

306   Leoni, *supra* note 97, at 22. Leoni notes that Roman law was grounded in custom and operated on a system of weak precedent rather than strict stare decisis.

307   Landes and Posner recognize that if this condition is met, then competition among courts may work fine. *See* Landes & Posner, *Adjudication, supra* note 300, at 258 ("The general conclusion is that we can expect more efficient rules of contract and commercial law (including corporation law, which is also based on consensual arrangements) than of tort or criminal law, because parties to contracts face a competitive supply of court systems.").

308   *See* Basile et al., *supra* note 159, at 24 (noting that within the five sites where the law merchant functioned, "mercantile law is always to be upheld unless both parties openly and expressly agree on the common law"); *id.* at 27 (where plaintiff and defendant disagree about which law should prevail, "he who demands mercantile law should always be heard, whether he is the plaintiff or defendant. And the plea should be brought to conclusion according to mercantile law . . . ."). Farnsworth, *supra* note 275, at 592.

310   *See* Benson, *supra* note 203, at 649–50.

311   *Id.*

312   For a similar argument in a modern context, *see* Kimberly A. Moore and Francesco Parisi, *Rethinking Forum Shopping in Cyberspace,* 77 Chi.-Kent L. Rev. 1325, 1339 (2002).

313   *See* discussion *supra* note 43.

314 Holdsworth, *supra* note 220, at 319 n. 1 (enumerating various modern legal doctrines that were developed in rival courts well before their adoption by the common
law courts).

315 Berman & Reid, *supra* note 42, at 462.

316 *Id*. at 467; *see also* Fifoot, *supra* note 60, at 131–32 (describing merchant basis of
quasi-contract as exception to consideration doctrine).

317 Holdsworth, *supra* note 220, at 304. Rogers forcefully argues that the importance
of negotiability, and therefore the role of the law merchant in spurring legal innovation, has been traditionally overemphasized by Holdsworth and others. *See* Rogers,
supra note 257, at 5. Holdsworth, however, identifies several other key common
law concepts that can be traced to law merchant origins. *See* Holdsworth, *supra* note
220, at 327.

318 Berman & Reid, *supra* note 42, at 461–463.

319 *Id*.

320 *See supra* notes 154–157 and accompanying text; *see* also Berman & Reid, *supra* note
42, at 459.

321 *See* Berman & Reid, *supra* note 42, at 459. For more on the use of fictions in the
common law, *see* Henry Sumner Maine, Ancient Law: its Connection with the Early
History of Society and Its Relation to Modern Ideas 16 (1st ed. 1917).

322 Baker, *supra* note 257, at 366–67.

323 *See* Holdsworth, *supra* note 220, at 315.
The common law had not in the past claimed jurisdiction over contracts made or
offences committed abroad, and probably not over contracts made and offences
committed in ports intra fluxum et refluxum maris. Such jurisdiction was coveted.
By supposing these contracts or offences to have been made or committed
in England the Common Law Courts assumed jurisdiction; and thus by a 'new
strange poetical fiction,' and by the help of 'imaginary sign-posts in Cheapside' they
endeavored to capture jurisdiction over the growing commercial business of the
country.
Id. (citations omitted).

324 Berman & Reid, *supra* note 42, at 461.

325 Rowley, *supra* note 140, at 371.

326 Hart v. Massanari, 266 F.3d 1155, 1167 (9th Cir. 2001).

327 41 U.S. 1 (1842).

328 304 U.S. 64(1938).

329 *Id*. at 78. This historical argument obviously mirrors the more theoretical
argument of Landes and Posner. *See* discussion *supra* notes 300-303 and accompanying
text.

330 Clearly I will not attempt a comprehensive analysis of the *Erie* debate in this paper.
As Judge Henry Friendly observed almost 40 years ago, "If a considerable pond of
ink about *Erie* had already accumulated in 1945, this has now become a rather large
lake." *See* Henry J. Friendly, *In Praise of* Erie— *and of the New Federal Common Law*, 39
N.Y.U. L. Rev. 383, 383 (1964). Since then, the lake has expanded into a sea, if not
an ocean. I will seek to add but a few drops to this watershed, as it relates to the
themes of this Article.

331 The historical record is ambiguous on the degree of nonuniformity between private law applied in state and federal court, nor is it clear whether nonuniformity
was more pronounced in some areas of law rather than others. *Compare* Hessel E.
Yntema & George H. Jaffin, *Preliminary Analysis of Concurrent Jurisdiction*, 79 U. Pa.

L. Rev. 869, 881–86 & n.23 (1931) (concluding that there was no substantial problem of nonuniformity) *with* Felix Frankfurter, *Distribution of Judicial Power Between
United States and State Courts*, 13 Cornell L.Q. 499, 524–30 (1928).

332   *See* Maxwell Stearns, *Standing and Social Choice: Historical Evidence*, 144 U. Pa. L.
Rev. 309, 375 (1995).

333   198 U.S. 45 (1905).

334   *See* William A, Braverman, Note, *Janus Was Not a God of Justice: Realignment of Parties
in Diversity Jurisdiction*, 68 N.Y.U. L. Rev. 1072, 1096(1993).

335   Brandeis cursed "bigness and centralization" generally and thus sought to decentral-
ize law-making authority to the states. Tony Freyer, Harmony & Dissonance: *The
Swift and Erie* Cases in American Federalism 150(1981).

336   Freyer, *supra* note 335, at 151.

337   Swift v. Tyson, 41 U.S. 1 (1842). There is substantial commentary on the law
merchant foundations of Swift. *See* Curtis A. Bradley, *The Status of Customary
International Law in U.S. Courts—Before and After Erie*, 26 Denv. J. Int'l L. &
Pol'y 807, 813 (1998); Lawrence Lessig, *Erie-Effects of Volume 110: An Essay on
Context in Interpretive Theory*, 110 Harv. L. Rev. 1785, 1791 (1997); Bradford R.
Clark, *Federal Common Law: A Structural Reinterpretation*, 144 U. Pa. L. Rev. 1245,
1283–85 (1996); William A. Fletcher, *The General Common Law and Section 34 of
the Judiciary Act of 1789: The Example of Marine Insurance*, Harv. L. Rev. 1513,
1517–20 (1984).

338   *See* Randall Bridwell and Ralph U. Whitten, The Constitution and the Common Law:
The Decline of the Doctrines of Separation of Powers and Federalism 5 (1977).

339   *See id.* at 92.

340   *See* Zywicki, *Senators and Special Interests, supra* note 9, at 1019–21 (discussing the
special interest roots of much progressive legislation).

341   *See* Freyer, *supra* note 335, at 20 (noting that prior to Swift, "outright local prejudice against out-of-state creditors" created uncertainty in commercial relations).

342   *Id.* 83.

343   Van Reimsdyk v. Kane, 28 F. Cas. 1062 (C.C.D. R.I. 1812) (No. 16,871) (emphasis
omitted), *rev'd on other grounds sub nom.* Clark v. Van Reimsdyk, 13 U.S. 153 (1815),
quoted in Bridwell & Whitten, *supra* note 338, at 81.

344   Freyer, *supra* note 335, at 32 (emphasis added).

345   Bridwell & Whitten, *supra* note 338, at 91; *see also* Freyer, *supra* note 335, at 26.

346   *See* Bridwell & Whitten, *supra* note 338, at 5 (arguing that federal common law
protected parties' expectations better than did state laws).

347   *Swift*, 41 U.S. at 18; *see also* Freyer, *supra* note 335, at 26.

348   *See* Clark, *Federal Common Law, supra* note 337, at 1291.

349   *See* Bridwell & Whitten, *supra* note 338, at 13 ("If the federal courts had been bound
to follow all state judicial precedents under such a common law process, the non-
resident in a diversity action would thus have been deprived of the independent
forum the Constitution envisioned Congress might provide.").

350   S. Pac. Co. v. Jensen, 244 U.S. 205, 222 (1917) (Holmes, J., dissenting) ("The
common law is not a brooding omnipresence in the sky but the articulate voice of
some sovereign or quasi-sovereign that can be identified . . . ."). Jensen was an admiralty case, but Holmes's critique there was similar to his criticisms of federal common
law under *Swift*. *See also* Kuhn v. Fairmont Coal Co., 215 U.S. 349, 370–72 (1910)
(Holmes, J., dissenting). Freyer observes that notwithstanding Holmes's criticism of
expansions of *Swift*, early in his legal career Holmes helped to edit the Twelfth

Edition of Kent's *Commentaries on American Law*. Drafts of Holmes's work indicate that he seemed to agree with *Swift*, at least as it related to commercial law, but disagreed with its extensions in subsequent cases. Freyer, *supra* note 335, at 86–87.

351 Freyer, *supra* note 335, at 43.

352 In *Kuhn v. Fairmont Coal*, decided in 1910, the Supreme Court adhered to this distinction between settled principles of common law and judicial decisions that had stood the test of time and those judicial decisions that were still subject to reconsideration and analysis. Thus, Justice Harlan wrote there, "Where such local law or custom has been established by repeated decisions of the highest courts of a state, it becomes also the law governing the courts of the United States sitting in that state." *Kuhn*, 215 U.S. at 359. "But where the law has not been thus settled," Harlan added, "it is the right and duty of the Federal courts to exercise their own judgment; as they always do in reference to the doctrines of commercial law and general jurisprudence." *Id.* at n.l (quoting *Bucher v. Cheshire R. Co.*, 125 U.S. 555). In fact, in his dissenting opinion in *Erie*, Justice Butler continued to emphasize that the final authority of the validity of a common law rule was its compliance with tests of reason or long-standing utility. He wrote, "Whenever possible, *consistent with standards sustained by reason and authority constituting the genera! law*, this Court has followed applicable decisions of the state courts." *Erie*, 304 U.S. at 85 (Butler, J., dissenting) (emphasis added).

353 *Swift* was conceived in a case of negotiable instruments, an area of law that is essentially contractual in nature and which is governed today by the Uniform Commercial Code. By the time *of Erie, Swift* had expanded dramatically to govern numerous areas of private law. *See* Jack Goldsmith and Steven Walt, Erie *and the irrelevance of Legal Positivism*, 84 Va. L. Rev. 673, 687 (1998); *see also* Lessig, *supra* note 337, at 1792 (distinguishing contractual relations in Swift from tort law); Bradford R. Clark, *Ascertaining the Laws of the Several States: Positivism and Judicial Federalism After* Erie, 145 U. Pa. L. Rev. 1459, 1475–76 (noting expansion of *Swift* beyond law merchant context); Freyer, *supra* note 335, at 69–72 (noting expansion of *Swift* doctrine beyond original contractual and law merchant roots); Bridwell & Whitten, *supra* note 339, at 96–97 (discussing expansion of *Swift*).

354 *See* Randy E. Barnett, The Structure of Liberty: Justice and the Rule of Law 284–97 (1998); Stephen J. Ware, *Default Rules from Mandatory Rules: Privatizing Law Through Arbitration*, 83 Minn. L. Rev. 703, 751–53 (1999); Stephen J. Ware, *Arbitration & Assimilation*, 77 Wash. U. L.Q. 1053, 1053(1999).

355 *See* Bridwell & Whitten, *supra* note 338, at 97 (criticizing later cases for extending principle of *Swift* beyond its proper bounds).

356 *Id.* at 121 ("It seems absolutely clear that tort law was vastly different in kind from the general customs of the commercial world, and that it should have been treated as a local mater to be controlled by state law as defined in state decisions."). Many of the criticisms of the expansion of *Swift* also are critical of the "public" law extensions of *Swift* rather than private law. For a discussion of those issues, *see* generally Michael G. Collins, *Before* Lochner—*Diversity Jurisdiction and the Development of General Constitutional Law*, 74 Tul. L. Rev. 1263 (2000).

357 *See* Zywicki, *supra* note 6. Indeed, the fact that Erie only prohibited forum-shopping between state and federal court (primarily by defendants under the removal power), and did not prohibit forum-shopping among other state courts, adds further credence to the thesis that Brandeis was more concerned about preserving state regulatory power rather than a principled concern about forum shopping.

358 Often the motivation is for judges to build political support in states with elected judiciaries by redistributing wealth from out-of-state defendants to in-state plaintiffs. *See generally* Alexander Tabarrok & Eric Helland, *Court Politics: The Political Economy of Tort Awards*, 42 J.L. & Econ. 157 (1999). But in some of the most notable plaintiff's "heavens" in Alabama and Mississippi, there is some evidence that the volume of litigation itself provides a substantial economic benefit to the local economy.

359 *See* Erin A. O'Hara & Larry E. Ribstein, *From Politics to Efficiency in Choice of Law*, 67 U. Chi. L. Rev. 1151, 1154 (2000).

360 *See* Stephen J. Ware, Alternative Dispute Resolution §§ 2.25, 2.28 (2001); Stephen J. Ware, *Paying the Price of Process: Judicial Regulation of Consumer Arbitration Agreements*, 2001 J. Dispute Resolution 89, 89 (2001); Stephen J. Ware, *Money, Politics and Judicial Decisions: A Case Study of Arbitration in Alabama*, 15 J.L. & Politics 645, 661–62 (1999).

361 *See generally* P.S. Atiyah, The Rise and Fall of Freedom of Contract (1979); Grant Gilmore, The Death of Contract (1974).

362 Freyer, *supra* note 335, at 76.

363 Rowley, *supra* note 140, at 372.

364 *See* O'Hara & Ribstein, *supra* note 359, at 1154–55.

365 Todd J. Zywicki, *A Unanimity-Reinforcing Model of Efficiency in the Common Law: An Institutional Comparison of Common Law and Legislative Solutions to Large-Number Externality Problems*, 46 Case W. Res. L. Rev. 961, 1002 (1996); Louis De Alessi & Robert J. Staaf, *The Common Law Process: Efficiency or Order?*, 2 Const. Pol. Econ. 107, 116 (1991).

366 James M. Buchanan, *Introduction: L.S.E. Cost Theory in Retrospect, in* L.S.E. Essays on Cost 1 (James M Buchanan & G.F. Thirlby eds., 1981); James M. Buchanan, Cost and Choice: An Inquiry in Economic Theory (1969); Ludwig von Mises, Human Action: A Treatise on Economics (1963); Donald J. Boudreaux et al., *Talk is Cheap: The Existence Value Fallacy*, 29 Envtl. L. 765 (1999); Zywicki, *supra* note 365, at 966-80; Timothy J. Muris, *Cost of Completion or Diminution in Market Value: The Relevance of Subjective Value*, 12 J. Legal Stud. 379 (1983).

367 *See* Luis De Alessi & Robert J. Staaf, *Subjective Value in Contract Law*, 145 J. Institutional & Theoretical Econ. 561 (1989); *see also* Charles J. Goetz & Robert E. Scott, *Enforcing Promises: An Examination of the Basis of Contract*, 89 Yale L.J. 1261 (1980).

368 Quoted in Fifoot, *supra* note 60, at 99.

369 Of course, when combined with a competitive court system, these two features gave parties a great ability to escape inefficient legal rules in favor of preferred rules.

370 *See* generally Ronald Coase, *The Problem of Social Cost*, 3 J.L. & Econ. 1 (1960).

371 161 A.2d 69 (N.J. 1960).

372 As such, their logic followed the intellectual framework pioneered by Friedrich Kessler, that such warranty contracts constituted "contracts of adhesion" and were the result of coercion by corporations rather than bargained-for consent. Friedrich Kessler, *Contracts of Adhesion—Some Thoughts about Freedom of Contract*, 43 Colum. L. Rev. 629, 631–32 (1943).

373 377 P.2d 897 (Cal. 1962).

374 *Id.* at 900–01.

375 Restatement (Second) of Torts § 402A (1965).

376 Robert J. Staaf & Bruce Yandle, *Collective and Private Choice, Constitution, Statutes and the Common Law, in* Economic Analysis of Law—A Collection of Applications 254, 260 (Wolfgang Weigel ed., 1991).

377   Richard A. Epstein, *The Unintended Revolution in Product Liability Law*, 10 Cardozo L. Rev. 2193,2202(1989).

378   Id.

379   *See* Pritchard & Zywicki, *supra* note 111, at 460–68; *see also* Allen, *supra* note 59; Pocock, *supra* note 124, at 202; Robert D. Cooter, *Decentralized Law for a Complex Economy: The Structural Approach to Adjudicating the New Law Merchant*, 144 U. Pa. L. Rev. 1643, 1694 (1996).

380   It is important to note that this observation applies only to "inclusive" customs, such as commercial custom, but not to "exclusive" customs such as a custom race or sex discrimination. The difference is that in the former all affected parties participate in the formation and maintenance of the custom, whereas in the latter one group maintains a custom of receiving benefits while imposing costs on another group, thus the custom is not likely to be efficient with respect to the party bearing the costs.

381   Pritchard & Zywicki, *supra* note 111, at 451–57; Edmund Burke, Reflections on The Revolution in France 34–35 (L. G. Mitchell ed., 1993); F.A. Hayek, The Constitution of Liberty (1960); Michael Oakeshott, *On Being Conservative*, in Rationalism in Politics and Other Essays 407 (1991); Pocock, *supra* note 124, at 379; Michael W. McConnell, *The Role of Democratic Politics in Transforming Moral Convictions into Law*, 98 Yale L.J. 1501, 1504 (1989).

382   Hart v. Massanari, 266 F.3d 1155, 1167 (9th Cir. 2001).

383   "The key conditions are reciprocity and high frequency." Richard A. Epstein, *The Path to the TJ. Hooper: The Theory and History of Custom in the Law of Tort,* 21 J. Legal Stud. 1,11 (1992). *See* also Todd J. Zywicki, The Reciprocity Instinct (George Mason University School of Law, Working Paper October 1, 2001) (on file with author) (specifying conditions for "reciprocal altruism" to survive in nature).

384   Berman, *supra* note 137, at 333–56; Benson, *supra* note 203, at 649–50; Trakman, *supra* note 212, at 8.

385   Barbour, *supra* note 181, at 154.

386   *See* 1 Blackstone, *supra* note 168, at 75.

387   Berman, *supra* note 167, at 757.

388   *See id.* ("[I]n the Western legal tradition, especially in its earlier phases, it has been taken for granted that law comes not only, and not primarily, from the lawmaking power of the state but also, and primarily, from relationships created on the ground by individuals and groups in their interactions with each other. Not the state, not the governmental authorities, but people, the community, has been understood to be a primary source of law . . . . In the past it has been understood that customary law, unofficial law, is a primary source of state law, official law, and that one of the principal functions of state law is to enforce the rights and obligations that arise from customary law.").

389   Pritchard & Zywicki, *supra* note 111, at 460–68; Parisi, *Toward a Theory of Spontaneous Law, supra* note 304, at 212.

390   Berman, *supra* note 55, at 1699.

391   *Id.* Selden derived the sanctity of contractual relations between people from the covenant between God and Noah. Just as Noah's obligations arose from this contractual covenant, Selden believed that covenants between people were imbued with a comparable religious component. *Id.* Berman argues that the obligation of keeping one's contracts was for Selden the "most important rule of natural law." *Id.* (citing Richard Tuck, Natural Rights Theories (1984)).

392   Berman, *supra* note 55, at 1699.

393   Fifoot, *supra* note 60, at 99.

394   Bridwell & Whitten, *supra* note 338, at 66; *see also id.* at 15.

395   *Id.* at 67.

396   *Discussion of Paper by Richard Epstein*, 10 Cardozo L. Rev. 2223, 2238 (1989).

397   Steven Hetcher, *Creating Safe Social Norms in a Dangerous World*, 73 S. Cal. L. Rev. 1, 4–7 (1999).

398   Epstein, *supra* note 383, at 2.

399   Hetcher, *supra* note 397, at 17.

400   *See* Todd J. Zywicki, *Hayek versus Posner on the Economic Analysis of Law*, Rev. Austrian Econ. (forthcoming 2003); *see also* Hayek, *supra* note 102, at 85 ("The law will consist of purpose-independent rules which govern the conduct of individuals towards each other, are intended to apply to an unknown number of further instances, and by defining a protected domain of each, enable an order of actions to form itself wherein the individuals can make feasible plans."); James M. Buchanan, *Good Economics—Bad Law*, 60 Va. L. Rev. 483, 489 (1974) ("The working of 'law,' as an activity, is not guided by nor should it be guided by explicit criteria for 'social improvement.' Law, in this vision, is a stabilizing institution providing the necessary framework within which individuals can plan their own affairs predictably and with minimal external interferences.").

401   *See* Kempin, *supra* note 79, at 32–33.

402   *See* Hart v. Massanari, 266 F.3d 1155, 1175 (9th Cir. 2001).

> The concept of binding precedent could only develop once two conditions were met: The development of a hierarchical system of appellate courts with clear lines of authority, and a case reporting system that enabled later courts to know precisely what was said in earlier opinions. As we have seen, these developments did not come about—either here or in England—until the nineteenth century, long after Article III of the Constitution was written.

> *Id.*

403   *See* 1 Holdsworth, *supra* note 199, at 408.

404   To be sure, there were earlier courts and commentators who advocated a stricter adherence to *stare decisis* in both England and America. But absent a clearly-organized hierarchical legal system, it would not have been possible to effectuate a stricter adherence to precedent in practice.

Chapter 17

Thomas J. Webster

ECONOMIC EFFICIENCY AND THE COMMON LAW

Introduction

D O LEGAL RULES based on the common law in the U.S. result in economically efficient outcomes? The evidence or what there is of it, seems to suggest otherwise. Tullock [1997] noted that while the precise social cost of legal disputes is unknown, it must be substantial and certainly much higher compared to developed economies. Tullock noted that in 1983, the U.S. federal, state, and local spending on civil and criminal justice amounted to almost $40 billion or about $170 per capita. This accounted for about 3 percent of total the U.S. government expenditures. Of this amount, $37 per capita was expended on judicial services [Cooter and Ulen, 1988, p. 478], which "amounts to only a small fraction of the social cost of resolving disputes though the courts, since most of these costs are borne by private parties" [Tullock 1997, p. 45]. Cooter and Ulen [1988] estimated that the labor cost of a full trial was about $400 per hour, not including the cost of court facilities. According to Tullock [1997, p. 52]:

> "Since the early 1960's . . . the U.S. courts have systematically assaulted the classical law of tort dismantling its twin historic pillars—deterrence and compensation—in favor of notions of societal insurance and risk-spreading and undermining the concept of fault as a doctrinal mechanism for limiting tort liability to substantive tortfeasors. [Huber, 1988; Rowley, 1989]. The abandonment of proximate cause in favor of joint and several liability has fired the engines of the rent-seekers who now specifically target deep pockets. The shift from negligence with contributory negligence to comparative negligence or strict liability has induced a sharp increase in moral hazard as plaintiffs lower their own standards of care and has stimulated a sharp increase in tertiary legal costs as the volume of law suits has exploded. The widening of damages to encompass pain and

suffering and loss of companionship damages as well as to anticipate harms
that have not even occurred has made a mockery of the law and has eliminated a wide range of other viable goods and services from the American
market place [Barnes and Stout, 1992, ch. 3]."

Do higher legal costs and resulting economic inefficiencies imply a higher degree
of accuracy in the U.S. court rulings? Is the truth better served in the U.S. courts than
elsewhere? According to Tullock [1980], the available evidence appears to suggest
otherwise. Tullock measured the error rate of the courts by comparing the decisions
of two independent decision-making bodies about a given case. According to Tullock
[1980, p. 32], if the litigants disagree, then one must be wrong. If both agree, then
it is possible that both are wrong. Disagreements between litigants constitute a measure of the courts' minimum error rate. Kalven and Zeisel [1966] found that while
it is not possible to ascertain whether the judges or juries were in error, disagreements occurred in one-fourth of the cases examined. By contrast, Baldwin and
McConnville [1979] found that the error rate in England was only about one in eight,
suggesting that the common law in the U.S. results in economically less efficient
outcomes.

Contrary to this admittedly porous evidence, Posner [1979, 1992] argued that
there is a systemic tendency for common law rules to evolve toward economically
efficient outcomes. According to Posner, litigants will resort to court rulings more
frequently when the existing rules are inefficient and less frequently when the rules
are efficient. Once efficient rules have evolved, the incentive for further litigation is
reduced.

Posner's process-oriented justification for common law efficiency is related
to the utility-maximizing behavior of rational judges who pursue the same instrumental and consumption objectives as private individuals [Posner, 1993]. Because
the judiciary operates on a not-for-profit basis, the salaries of federal judges of
the same rank are not functionally related to professional stature or productivity.
Instead, judges are motivated by prestige and professional recognition within the
legal community [Tullock, 1997, p. 22]. As a result, Posner argued that judges tend
to adhere to the principle of *stare decisis*, in which precedent is binding upon subsequent cases. *Stare decisis* requires that courts behave impartially and universally
when applying the law, and discourages courts "from deciding cases on the basis of
propositions that it would be unwilling to apply to all similarly situated disputants"
[Tullock, 1997, p. 4].

Rubin [1977] argued that when disputants have an ongoing interest in cases as
precedent, then the decision to use the courts to settle disputes and the efficiency of
the common law are intimately related. According to Rubin, disputants are likely to
resort to litigation whenever the relevant legal rules are inefficient. However, they are
less likely to do so when the rules are inefficient. Resulting court rulings reduce the
likelihood of future litigation and increase the probability that efficient rules will persist.
Although Rubin's analysis supports Posner's contention of economic efficiency, this
evolution proceeds from the utility-maximizing decisions of the disputants rather
than from the wisdom of judges.

However, Rubin's results are not general. If only one of the disputants has an
ongoing interest in cases as precedent, as in the case of insurance companies, then

precedent will tend to evolve in favor of that disputant. If neither disputant has an ongoing interest, then the *status quo* is likely to prevail despite the fact that significant inefficiencies may be absorbed by both parties. This is particularly true whenever high court costs may inhibit litigation.

In contrast to Posner and Rubin, Landes [1971], Gould [1973], and Tullock [1971, 1997] determined that the convergence of the common law to economically efficient outcomes is unlikely because it is generally in the litigants' best interest to settle out of court. In particular, Tullock [1997, pp. 22–3] has argued that there ". . . is no obvious reason why judges should be enamored of economic efficiency for its own sake." According to Tullock, scholars of law and economics ". . . have been forced to fall back on dubious arguments concerning the nature of the litigation process . . . to justify their assertion that the common law is economically efficient." Cooter and Kornhauser [1980] modeled legal evolution as a Markov process and found that there is no automatic mechanism to guarantee that the common law converges to economic equilibrium, even when economically inefficient rules are litigated or when judges replace inefficient rules with efficient rules.

The argument presented in this paper supports the latter view that there is no such automatic convergence mechanism because generally it will be in the litigants' best interest to seek an out-of-court settlement. As a result, economically inefficient common law rules will tend to endure to the benefit of the rent seeking activities of many legal professionals. The next two sections will review Rubin's argument that the common law will evolve to yield socially efficient outcomes when both litigants have an ongoing interest in legal cases as precedents. Then, Rubin's model will be reformulated as a two-part, two-person game. In the first part of the game, the decision to litigate is modeled as a two-person, non-cooperative, simultaneous-move game in which the disputants determine whether it is in their best interest to litigate or to pursue an out-of-court settlement. If an out-of-court settlement is a dominant strategy for either player, then the second part of the game will entail bargaining between the disputants until a final settlement is reached. This paper argues that it is generally in the best interest of the disputants to pursue an out-of-court settlement regardless of accident and prevention costs, court costs, and legal precedent, and these factors are important only insofar as they affect the distribution of the gains from an out-of-court settlement. The next section will briefly review the implications of bargaining without impatience and with symmetric and asymmetric impatience. The final section will summarize the main conclusions of this paper.

Is the common law efficient?

Professor Paul Rubin [1977] has argued that the court system is an efficient mechanism for resolving disputes and there is a natural tendency for the common law to evolve over time so as to yield economically efficient court rulings. According to Rubin, this evolutionary tendency toward economic efficiency proceeds from the utility-maximizing decisions of the disputants. At the heart of his argument is the observation that disputants tend to resort to court rulings more often when existing common law rules are inefficient. Once efficient rules have evolved, further litigation is no longer necessary. To demonstrate this, Rubin used the example of an accident involving two disputants, A and B, which costs X. According to Rubin, it will be economically efficient to assign liability for the accident to B if:

$$T_B = S_B + N_B X < S_A + N_A X = T_A, \qquad (17.1)$$

where T_A and T_B represent the present value of accident costs and prevention costs for disputants A and B, respectively. S_A and S_B represent payments for accident avoidance. Condition (1) asserts that economic efficiency requires that disputant B is made liable when $T_B < T_A$. Thus, the most efficient solution is for disputant B to purchase insurance S_B and for there to be N_B accidents. From A's perspective, the legal rule is efficient when there is no incentive to seek an out-of-court settlement. According to Rubin, whether disputant B spends S_B or A spends S_A depends on how the litigants expect the courts to rule. Court rulings are assumed to be based somewhat on precedent.

Let p be the probability that B will win the suit if the case is litigated and that both parties agree on its value. It is further assumed that the value of p is based on legal precedent. If $p > 0.5$, then legal precedent favors B, otherwise A is likely to win the suit if the case is litigated. Given condition (1), economic efficiency requires that liability be assigned to B if $p < 0.5$. If this is the case, then it will pay for B to litigate only if the possibility exists to overturn legal precedent, resulting in an economically efficient court ruling. According to Coase [1960], if condition (1) is satisfied, then it will pay for A to bribe B to avoid accidents. However, Rubin points out that transaction costs may be greater than $(T_A - T_B)$, in which case A will accept the liability. Although Rubin examined the no-bribery and bribery scenarios, the present discussion will focus on the no-bribery scenario.

The issue is whether there is a tendency for the common law to evolve toward economic efficiency. According to Rubin, the critical element is whether the disputants have an ongoing interest in legal cases as precedents. Rubin examined three situations: first, both parties have an ongoing interest; second, only one party has an ongoing interest; and third, neither party has an ongoing interest in the case as precedent. Rubin argued that the common law will evolve toward economic efficiency only when both parties have an ongoing interest in legal cases as precedent. When only one party has an ongoing interest, then legal precedent will tend to evolve in favor of the party that has a stake in future cases but that the outcome may not be efficient. Finally, when neither party has an interest in the outcome, then the common law will remain in stasis, regardless of whether or not the legal rules are efficient. This paper will focus only on the first situation, where both parties have an ongoing interest in legal cases as precedent. In the next section, Rubin's efficiency argument will be reviewed.

The case for efficiency when both parties are interested in precedent

According to Rubin, a litigant has a substantial interest in legal cases as precedent if that party is likely to be involved in similar cases in the future. Rubin defined the criterion whereby a case may or may not be settled out of court. If the rules are inefficient, then there will be an incentive for one of the disputants to litigate until the rule is overturned. If the rules are efficient, then no such incentive exists, in which case the rules will be affirmed. For example, suppose that a case is litigated and the plaintiff B wins. In this case, B is awarded X and saves T_B, which is the present value of accident and prevention costs. On the other hand, if A wins, then A is not liable to pay X and saves T_A in the future, although B will begin to pay T_B. Court costs, which are denoted as C, are assumed to be the same for each litigant, although this assumption is not required. Symbolically, the value to A of an in-court judgment that favors B is given as:

$$V_{A'} = p\,(-\,X) + (1-p)T_A - C. \tag{17.2}$$

The value to B of a favorable in-court judgment is:

$$V_{B'} = p(X) + (1-p)(-T_B) - C. \tag{17.3}$$

According to Rubin, the parties to the suit will settle out of court only if:

$$-V_A > V_B. \tag{17.4}$$

Condition (17.4) asserts that an out-of-court settlement is likely if the expected loss to A from going to court is greater than the expected gain to B from an in-court judgment. If this is the case, then there is room for the disputants to negotiate an out-of-court settlement. If condition (17.4) is not satisfied, then the parties will litigate. If conditions (17.2) and (17.3) are substituted into condition (17.5), then:

$$(1-p)(T_A - T_B) < 2C. \tag{17.5}$$

Condition (17.5) says that if the expected net present value of accident and prevention costs is negative or if the positive value of $(1-p)(T_A - T_B)$ is less than the sum of the litigant's court costs $(2C)$, then it will pay for A to negotiate a settlement. Rubin called the term $(T_A - T_B)$ the cost of the inefficient legal rule. As this term becomes larger or as the probability that A will win increases, the more likely that litigation will occur. Condition (17.5) also implies that a settlement is positively related to court costs. Finally, if the legal rule is efficient $(T_B > T_A)$, then litigation will not occur and economically efficient rules will be affirmed. A will choose to litigate only when the expected net present value of accident and prevention costs are greater than court costs.

A game theoretic approach to economic efficiency

In this section, Rubin's model will be reformulated as a two-part, two-person game. The first part is a two-person, non-cooperative, simultaneous-move game in which the disputants determine whether it is in their best interest to litigate or to seek an out-of-court settlement. If an out-of-court settlement is a strictly-dominant or a weakly-dominant strategy for either disputant, then the disputant will initiate negotiations over the size of a possible settlement.

In the discussion that follows, the author will continue to assume that B is the plaintiff, A is the defendant, p is the probability, B will win the suit, and both parties agree on the value of p, which is based on precedent. Thus, if the disputants litigate, conditions (17.2) and (17.3) define the expected value of an in-court judgment.

Suppose that instead of litigating, the disputants agree to an out-of-court settlement X'. In this case, B will begin to pay T_B while A saves T_A in the future. Symbolically, the value to A of an out-of-court settlement is:

$$V_{A'} = -X' + T_A. \tag{17.6}$$

Similarly, the value to B of an out-of-court settlement is:

$$V_{B'} = X' - T_B. \tag{17.7}$$

The decision to litigate or settle may be modeled as a two-person, non-cooperative, simultaneous move game. The decision to litigate or settle may be illustrated as the payoff matrix of Table 17.1.

The entries in the cells of the payoff matrix do not represent the value of a final settlement from each combination of strategies but rather the initial bargaining position of each litigant. According to Rubin, condition (17.4) asserts that the disputants should seek an out-of-court settlement if $-V_A > V_B$. It is clear from the payoffs in Table 17.1 that it will be in A's best interest to settle whenever $-V_A > -V_{A'}$, or:

$$pX - (1-p)T_A + C > X' - T_A. \tag{17.8}$$

Similarly, it will be in B's best interest to settle whenever $V_B' > V_B$, or:

$$X' - T_A > pX - (1-p)T_B - C. \tag{17.9}$$

What role will the size of the out-of-court proposal have on the disputants' decision to litigate? From conditions (17.8) and (17.9), an increase in the size of a proposed settlement makes it more likely that A will attempt to litigate and B will accept an out-of-court settlement. To see this, re-consider condition (17.8), which may be rewritten as:

$$p(X + T_A) + C > X'. \tag{17.10}$$

Table 17.1

		Disputant B	
		Litigate	Settle
Disputant A	Litigate	(V_A, V_B)	$(V_A, V_{B'})$
	Settle	$(V_{A'}, V_B)$	$(V_{A'}, V_{B'})$

Note: Payoffs (Disputant A, Disputant B)

Condition (17.10) asserts that it will pay for A to settle if the size of the settlement is less than the expected value of the difference between the accident costs and the present value of accident and prevention costs, plus court costs. Condition (17.9) may be rewritten as:

$$X' > p(X + T_B) - C. \tag{17.11}$$

Condition (17.11) asserts that for B to settle, the settlement must be greater than the expected present value of accident and prevention costs, less court costs. Thus, for both parties to agree to an out-of-court settlement it must be the case that:

$$p(X + T_A) + C > X' > p(X + T_B) - C. \tag{17.12}$$

Rearranging condition (17.12), then:

$$T_A + 2C > [(X' + C - pX)/p] - X > T_B. \tag{17.13}$$

Note from condition (17.13) that since T_A, $2C$, and T_B are all positive, then $[(X' + C - pX)/p] - X > 0$, which implies that $X' > pX - C$. This implies that for the disputants to reach an out-of-court agreement, A's proposed settlement must be greater than the expected in-court ruling, less B's court costs. Condition (17.13) also implies that for the litigants to settle:

$$-p(T_A - T_B) < 2C. \tag{17.14}$$

Condition (17.14) asserts that for the disputants to settle, the negative expected value of accident and prevention costs must be less than the sum of the litigants' total court costs. According to Rosen, the legal rule is efficient when $T_B > T_A$. Thus, even when the legal rule is efficient, the disputants may still negotiate an out-of-court settlement provided that the expected net present value of accident and prevention costs are less than the sum of the litigants' court costs. When the expected net present value of accident and prevention costs is greater than the sum of the litigants' court costs, then litigation will take place, even when the legal rules are efficient. What if the legal rules are inefficient ($T_A > T_B$)? In this case, the left side of the inequality in condition (17.14) is unambiguously negative, which guarantees that the disputants will seek an out-of-court settlement whenever court costs are nonnegative. In other words, when the legal rules are inefficient, the strictly-dominant strategy of both disputants is to settle. This result contrasts sharply with Rubin's argument that an out-of-court settlement is only likely whenever the legal rules are inefficient. Thus, by respecifying the Rubin model as a two-person, non-cooperative, simultaneous-move game, the analysis presented here supports the arguments put forth by Landes, Gould, Tullock, and others that it is generally in the disputants' best interest to pursue an out-of-court settlement regardless of whether the common law is efficient. In fact, this paper argues that it will generally be in the disputant's best interest to settle whenever there is any uncertainty regarding the outcome of an in-court judgement precisely because court costs are not trivial.

Condition (17.14) also asserts that disputants tend to resort to the courts when legal rules are efficient and court costs are less than the expected net present value of accident and prevention costs ($T_A - T_B$). However, as noted earlier, U.S. court costs are significant. Thus, even in the presence of efficient legal rules there is a propensity for disputants to settle out of court. The empirical evidence appears to support this conclusion. For example, according to Cooter and Ulen [1988, p. 478], about 95 percent of all civil disputes are settled without recourse to a trial.

The foregoing analysis suggests that regardless of whether legal rules are efficient or inefficient, it is generally the dominant strategy of disputants to settle. Contrary to Rosen's conclusions, there is no automatic tendency for the common law to converge toward efficient outcomes *via* the courts. Thus, an entrenched and inefficient common law will tend to be perpetuated for the benefit of rent-seeking court officers. As Tullock [1997, p. 26] has pointed out:

> "There is a significant element of rent-seeking in the adversarial legal system. Trial lawyers can be viewed from the same perspective as special interest lobbyists. In both cases, government is involved as a vehicle of wealth distribution. The basic difference between the two is that legal proceedings are subject to more stringent procedural rules. Such rules may serve to increase rather than to ameliorate the social waste from rent-seeking and rent-protection. As with much lobbying of Congress, litigation offers some prospect of genuine social product. However, the social product itself tends to be lost in a sea of social waste [Tullock 1995, p. 17]."

Tullock [1997, p. 35] continues:

> ". . . the benign nineteenth century influence of utilitarian philosophy has been swept away dramatically during the twentieth century under the influence of socialist ideology combined with pervasive legal rent-seeking [Tullock, 1996]. . . . Judges, indeed, have found it possible to change legal rules so as to benefit favored special interest groups, most notably the Association of Trial Lawyers of America. . . . Where the judges have not moved, federal and state legislators, dominated by lawyers, have enacted statutes to ensure that legal rent-seeking is profitable for an ever-growing cohort of American attorneys."

The only question left to answer is how much must either disputant receive in order to conclude an out-of-court settlement? The answer depends upon the bargaining patience of the disputants. To simplify the analysis, bargaining between the disputants without impatience is assumed. This is equivalent to assuming that the discounted present value of an out-of-court settlement is zero for both disputants. From condition (17.10) it is known that A will settle for an amount less than $p(X + T_A) + C$ (A's reservation price) and that B will accept any offer that is greater than $p(X + T_B) - C$ (B's reservation price). If A and B come to an agreement, then the gain to both disputants will add up to the difference between A's reservation price and B's reservation price, which in this case is equal to the amount $[p(X + T_A) + C] - [p(X + T_B) - C] = p(T_A - T_B) + 2C$.

How will this gain be distributed between A and B? The answer depends upon who makes the first offer. Suppose that A's dominant strategy is to settle and B's dominant strategy is to litigate. In this case, A will make the first offer. Since A knows that B will reject any offer less than $p(X + T_B) - C$, then that is precisely the amount that A will offer and that B will accept, in which case the entire gain will go to A. For example, suppose A's initial offer to B is $X_1 < p(X + T_B) - C$. Clearly, B will reject this offer and make a counteroffer of $X_2 > p(X + T_B) - C$. If it is assumed that there is no limit to the number of counteroffers and there are no bargaining (transaction) costs, then A's counteroffer will be $X_1 < X_3 < X_2$. As long as A is in a position to make a counteroffer, then A will never accept B's offer as the final one. Since A has the last-mover's advantage, then it will be in B's best interest to accept A's initial offer of:

$$X' = p(X + T_B) - C. \tag{17.15}$$

Suppose, on the other hand, both parties negotiate with symmetric impatience. In this case, the present value of a future out-of-court settlement is positive and the same for both disputants. If it is assumed that both disputants are aware of the costs imposed on the other by failing to come to an agreement, then the final settlement will depend upon who makes the first offer and the number of negotiating rounds. In general, when the discount rate for both disputants is the same, then negotiations will continue until the disputants are indifferent between the expected value of an in-court judgement and the present value of an out-of-court settlement. If there are a large number of negotiating rounds, then the gain to both disputants will be evenly divided. Although, the disputant who makes the final counteroffer will enjoy a slight advantage.

Finally, suppose that both parties negotiate with asymmetric impatience. In this case, the final outcome will depend on the different opportunity costs to both disputants. The greater the disputant's impatience, such as the greater the discount rate, the smaller the gains will be from bargaining. If there are a large number of negotiating rounds, then the gains to the disputants will be inversely proportional to the relative size of the discount rates [Rubenstein, 1982]. Thus, if the discount rate for B is twice as large as the discount rate for A, then A's share of the gain will be approximately twice as large as the share going to B.

What effect will a change in the probability p that B will win the case if litigated, accident costs, court costs, and the present value of accident and prevention costs have on the size of an out-of-court settlement? Recall that B will accept any out-of-court settlement $X' \geq p(X + T_B) - C$ and that A will accept any out of court settlement where $X' < p(X + T_A) + C$. As noted above, the actual out-of-court settlement will depend on which disputant makes the first offer. It is easily seen from these relationships that an increase in legal and court costs C will lower B's reservation bid and raise A's reservation offer. In other words, an increase in legal and court costs C will lower the amount of an out-of-court settlement that B would be willing to accept, and raise the amount of the out-of-court settlement that would make it likely that A will litigate. Conversely, increases in the probability p that B will win the case if litigated, accident costs, or the present value of accident and prevention costs will raise both the reservation bid and offer, for example, increase the amount of the minimum out-of-court settlement.

Summary and conclusions

This paper has examined the argument put forward by Posner [1979, 1992], Rubin [1977], and others that there is a natural tendency for the common law to converge toward economic efficiency. In particular, this paper analyzed Rubin's argument that the decision to use the courts to settle disputes and the efficiency of the common law are related. To demonstrate this, Rubin used the example of an accident involving two disputants, A and B. According to Rubin, if the present value of accident and prevention costs for A is greater than that for B ($T_A > T_B$), then the legal rules are efficient. Rubin's analysis implies that even if the legal rules are inefficient, it may still pay for A to seek an out-of-court settlement, provided that the expected net present value of accident and avoidance costs is less than the sum of the litigants' court costs, otherwise A will litigate. In general, Rubin argues that there is a general tendency for A to litigate until inefficient legal rules are overturned.

By respecifying the Rubin model as a two-person, non-cooperative, simultaneous-move game, the analysis presented in this paper supports the arguments put forth by Landes, Gould, Tullock, and others that it is generally in the litigants' best interest to pursue an out-of-court settlement. Even when the legal rules are inefficient, A's strictly-dominant strategy will be to settle. The analysis also suggests that it may also be in A's best interest to negotiate an out-of-court settlement when the legal rules are efficient if the expected net present value of accident and avoidance costs is less than the litigants' court costs. Finally, it may pay for A to litigate even when the legal rules are efficient if the expected net present value of accident and avoidance costs are greater than the sum of the litigants' court costs.

Rubin's model suggests that if in-court judgments are not socially optimal, then litigants with an ongoing interest in cases as precedents will continue to litigate. In this way, the common law will eventually lead to socially efficient outcomes. By contrast, the analysis presented in this paper seems to suggests that there is a general tendency for the disputants to pursue an out-of-court settlement, regardless of whether the legal rules are efficient or inefficient. The decision to go to court appears not to be based on the efficiency of the legal system but rather on whether the expected costs of not going to court exceed the cost of litigation. This conclusion supports Tullock's [1997, p. 59] contention that the desire of the legal profession to maintain the *status quo* and preserve profit opportunities arising from legal rent-seeking behavior rules out a systemic convergence of the common law toward economic efficiency is unlikely:

> "Essentially, the United States clings to an inefficient legal system which developed in the Middle Ages without much thought and which has evolved across the centuries without serious examination into whether or not its basic premises are sound. Its survival is due in part to tradition and in part because it guarantees large incomes to many of those connected with it. . . . Evidence in support . . . is available from recent experience in the United States where parties increasingly contract out of the American court system committing themselves instead to arbitration. . . . Arbitration appears to be well-liked by those with the foresight to avoid the U.S. court system. In areas where it is applicable, it is set fair to supersede the common law system, introducing a private code system by default."

References

Baldwin, J., McConnville, M. *Jury Trials*, Oxford: The Clarendon Press, 1979.

Barnes, D. W., Stout, L. A. *Cases and Materials on Law and Economics*, St. Paul: West Publishing Co., 1992.

Coase, R. H. "The Problem of Social Costs," *Journal of Law and Economics*, 3, October, 1960, pp. 1–44.

Cooter, R., Kornhauser, L. "Can Litigation Improve the Law Without the Help of Judges?" *Journal of Legal Studies*, 9, 1, 1980, pp. 139–63.

Cooter, R., Ulen, T. *Law and Economics*, Glenview: Scott, Foresman & Co., 1988.

Gould, J. P. "The Economics of Legal Conflicts," *Journal of Legal Studies*, 2, 2, 1973, pp. 279–300.

Huber, P. W. *Liability: The Legal Revolution and its Consequences*, New York: Basic Books, 1988.

Kalven, H., Zeisel, H. *The American Jury*, Boston: Little, Brown & Co., 1966.

Landes, W. M. "An Economic Analysis of the Courts," *Journal of Law and Economics*, 61, 14, 1971, pp. 61–108.

Posner, R. "Utilitarianism, Economics, and Legal Theory," *Journal of Legal Studies*, 8, 1, 1979, pp. 103–40.

—. *Economic Analysis of Law*, Fourth Edition, Boston: Little Brown, 1992.

—. "What Do Judges Maximize?" *Supreme Court Economic Review*, 23, 1993, pp. 1–41.

Rowley, C. W. "The Common Law in Public Choice Perspective," *Hamline Law Review*, 12, 2, 1989, pp. 355–83.

Rubenstein, A. "Perfect Equilibrium in a Bargaining Model," *Econometrica*, 61, 1, 1982, pp. 99–109.

Rubin, P. "Why is the Common Law Efficient?" *Journal of Legal Studies*, 6, 1, January, 1977, pp. 51–61.

Tullock, G. *The Logic of the Law*, New York: Basic Books, 1971.

—. *Trials on Trial: The Pure Theory of Legal Procedure*, New York: Columbia University Press, 1980.

—. "Rent-Seeking and the Law" in Casas-Pardo and F. Schneider (Eds.) *Current Issues in Public Choice*, Aldershot: Edward Elgar Publishing, 1995.

—. "Legal Heresy," *Economic Inquiry*, 24, 1, 1996, pp. 1–19.

—. "The Case Against the Common Law," *The Blackstone Commentaries, No. 1*, Durham, North Carolina: The Locke Institute, 1997.

Chapter 18

Paul H. Rubin

MICRO AND MACRO LEGAL EFFICIENCY

Supply and demand

I. Introduction

A **BASIC QUESTION** for law and economics is the efficiency of law. Hayek, although writing before the law and economics movement and writing from another perspective, had argued that common or judge made law was better than statute law; I return to Hayek's arguments below.[1] Posner has of course argued often and forcefully that the common law is efficient.[2] His arguments are based on examination of particular legal doctrines. I call this the "micro" argument for legal efficiency. The evolutionary models were aimed at explaining this micro efficiency. There is another more recent literature that uses empirical methods to compare various legal systems. This literature generally finds that common law is more efficient than other forms of law. I call this the "macro" argument for efficiency. It is ultimately a Hayekian argument, based on the idea that in common law systems governments have less power than in other systems. I first discuss micro efficiency, and then macro.

II. "Micro" efficiency

Micro efficiency is based on an examination of particular legal doctrines and attempts to determine if they are efficient. This was the method used by Posner.[3] The difficulty with this method of analysis is that often the conclusion regarding the efficiency of a particular rule depends on unmeasured transactions costs of various sorts; if the analysts' intuition about relative magnitudes of costs is incorrect, then doctrines claimed to be efficient may not be so. Nonetheless, Posner's analysis has been the intellectual spark behind the growth of law and economics, and questions of efficiency of the sort he was the first to raise have dominated the literature. Much of this literature may be considered as detailed attempts to answer the positive efficiency question first posed by Posner, and much of the rest aims at deriving normative conclusions as to what is efficient.

This method of analysis is fundamentally different from efficiency analysis in other branches of economics. There, a process (market competition) is postulated and it is shown that the process leads to efficient outcomes. Economists do not generally examine consumers to see if they are equating ratios of marginal utilities to prices, or firms to see if they are charging marginal cost. Rather, the process by which outcomes are generated is shown to lead to efficiency. It is for this reason that many economists are uncomfortable with the efficiency arguments of law and economics. Nonetheless, because this is the standard method in law and economics, any analysis of the efficiency of any particular body of law can be considered as evidence for or against Posner's hypothesis. If some law is found efficient, then this is evidence for the hypothesis. If some law is found inefficient, or if there are proposals for reform, then this is evidence against the hypothesis. In this sense, much of law and economics is aimed at testing this fundamental hypothesis.

A. Evolutionary models

Scholars are of course aware of these difficulties and have sought to identify a process that would lead to efficiency. I first proposed the evolutionary model of legal efficiency in an attempt to solve this problem.[4] The evolutionary models are attempts to explain judicial behavior without resort to preferences or utility functions. Initially, these models aimed at explaining Posner's putative observation that the common law was efficient. It is fair to say that the models failed in this endeavor, perhaps because the law is not so efficient as Posner argued. Nonetheless, these models have had an important impact on the literature because they have called attention to forces other than judicial preferences in explaining the law. The evolutionary models are ultimately based on the model of the litigation process first set forth by Landes.[5]

In the first paper applying an evolutionary model to the common law, I argued that most cases are settled, rather than litigated, and that it is only litigated cases that can lead to legal change. Cases are settled when the expected value to the plaintiff of a case is less than the expected cost to the defendant. This will not occur if stakes are symmetric. However, inefficient laws can sometimes create asymmetric stakes because the inefficiency means that there are deadweight losses than cannot be bargained away in the settlement process. That is, an inefficient rule creates a loss to one party that is greater than the gain to the other because of future stakes in similar type cases. Thus, litigation becomes more likely when rules are inefficient, and so inefficient rules are subject to greater selection pressure, and more likely to be overturned. (Note that this model, like many of its successors, depends on parties having ongoing interests in disputes of a certain sort, rather than merely in the matter at hand.)

Following this initial contribution were several extensions and modifications. Priest argued that inefficient rules generated larger stakes and so were more likely to be litigated, again subjecting them to increased selection pressure.[6] Goodman argued that efficient precedents were worth more to parties who would benefit than inefficient precedents were worth to their beneficiaries, and that parties to whom a decision was worth more would spend more litigating and so would be more likely to win.[7] In other words, efficient precedents were more likely to win in litigation and survive than were inefficient precedents. Katz expanded on this notion in the context of presenting a model of litigation expenditures.[8] Terreborne also presented a model of efficient legal evolution.[9] Stake argued that there were evolutionary forces likely to make property law more efficient than tort law.[10]

Other scholars began critically examining these models, and the general notion of legal efficiency. Tullock has long argued that the English common law process is less efficient than Continental processes.[11] Rizzo argues from an Austrian perspective that the amount of information needed for judges to achieve efficiency is excessive,[12] although Rubin in a critique argues that Rizzo's criticism might apply to efficiency in all of economics, not merely in law and economics.[13] Aranson argues that it is impossible for judges to seek efficiency because the calculations required are equivalent to those required to make central planning work.[14] Hadfield has argued that because judges see only a biased sample of potential cases, depending on the rules in existence, it is impossible for judges to move towards efficiency, even if they desire to do so.[15] Landes and Posner, in a symposium paper published in the *Journal of Legal Studies*, argued that the earlier models had erred by modeling precedent as an all or nothing issue, when the proper question was whether a precedent was stronger or weaker.[16] That is, litigation might strengthen or weaken a precedent without overturning it completely. Thus a party with an interest in overturning an inefficient precedent would also have to consider the possibility that litigation could strengthen as well as weaken the precedent. This consideration greatly weakens the evolutionary pressures for efficiency. Parsons combined Priest's point (that inefficient precedents would lead to increasing litigation) with the Landes and Posner point (that precedents that were litigated might become entrenched) to argue that there is a tendency for the common law to become "reckless" – to favor rules that inefficiently lead to increased accidents.[17] Cooter and Kornhauser present a complex evolutionary model in which there are some tendencies towards efficiency, but in which both efficient and inefficient rules will be observed at any time.[18] This model, and alternative definitions and implications of efficiency, are discussed in Kornhauser.[19] Von Wagenheim presents a model with similar results.[20]

Hirshleifer, building on my discussion of inefficiency when stakes in precedent are asymmetric, provided what may be one of the most useful and influential criticisms of the evolutionary models.[21] Recall that in my original model and in some others, including Goodman[22] and Landes and Posner,[23] evolutionary forces moved the law towards efficiency only if the party with an interest in efficiency had an ongoing interest in the form of the law. Hirshleifer generalized this point to show that the law could come to favor whichever party could most easily organize and mobilize resources for litigation of unfavorable precedents. This movement would be independent of efficiency. I used this point to argue that common law was more like statute law than many want to admit: interest groups could use either common or statute law to achieve their goals.[24] I argued that the apparent efficiency of the common law was because most common law was developed at a time when organization of interest groups was expensive, and that more recently both common and statute law have been subject to interest group pressures. Crew and Twight expanded on this point and found common law less subject to rent seeking than statute law.[25] Rowley and Brough[26] and Barzel[27] find that contract and property might be expected to be efficient, but not tort.

Martin Bailey and I extended this theme in a formal model of the influence of interest groups on the law and we have shown that plaintiffs' attorneys have been responsible for the shape of modern tort law, using an evolutionary mechanism to shape the law.[28] Christopher and John Curran and I modeled an interest group deciding whether to use litigation or lobbying as a method of rent seeking;[29] Osborne presents a similar model.[30] Fon and Parisi provide an additional mechanism to explain expansion of tort (mainly product liability) law: since plaintiffs chose courts in which to file, judges who are in favor of expansive law will see more cases and have more influence than more conservative judges.[31] (I discuss the issue of plaintiff choice of court below.) Although shaped by evolutionary forces, this law is socially quite inefficient.

An interesting set of hypotheses regarding legal evolution is in Roe.[32] Roe argues that the notion of evolution towards efficiency is an important determinant of legal form, but it is not the only determinant. He incorporates three subsidiary notions into an efficiency framework – the importance of initial conditions (borrowed from chaos theory), path dependence, and evolutionary accidents. The result of these processes would be that laws would be well but not perfectly adapted. However, while these notions are interesting, as Roe himself admits, they do not as of yet provide refutable hypotheses. It would be interesting to see if these propositions can be generalized to provide some implications.

In a recent important paper, Zywicki has added what he calls a "supply side" to the efficiency of law models.[33] He points out that the evolutionary models discussed above are "demand side" models, with litigants demanding efficient rules. Following Berman,[34] Zywicki shows that during the formative period of the common law there was competition between several court systems. There was first competition between civil and ecclesiastical courts. Within the civil system, there were royal law, feudal law, manorial law, urban law and mercantile law courts, all competing for the fees and business of litigants. There were courts of the King's Bench, the Exchequer, and the Court of Common Pleas, and four more obscure royal courts as well. Judges were paid from court fees, and all of these courts competed for business and fees; for example, church courts jurisdiction over testamentary succession and over the "sin" of lying involved in a contract breach could be used to increase the domain of these courts. This created an incentive for each court to provide unbiased, accurate and quick resolution of disputes. This is the supply side: judges and courts competed to supply efficient rules to get the business of disputants. Courts could also borrow remedies and rules from each other, which facilitated the evolution and spread of efficient rules and remedies. In this competition, the Law Merchant *(Lex mercatoria)* played a major role in commercial law, including contract law.[35] Ultimately the common law under Mansfield adopted the law merchant and this is the source of the efficient contract and commercial law rules that many have observed in the common law.

It is sometimes argued that choice of courts will lead pro-plaintiff courts to dominate since plaintiffs chose the court in which to file; Fon and Parisi present a modern variant of this argument.[36] It is important to note that in the era of legal competition discussed above, in most circumstances (and particularly in business or contractual disputes) the parties would pick the forum ex ante, so that both would have an incentive to choose efficient courts.[37] Moreover, many disputes that are now governed by tort, such as malpractice and product liability, were then governed by contract, so that ex ante competition also applied in these cases. Thus, in this large class of disputes, there would be no pro-plaintiff bias as might exist when plaintiffs choose courts after a dispute has arisen.

In this view, an important source of efficiency is the existence of competing courts and bodies of law. Where such competition exists, rules will tend towards efficiency. Where competition is lacking, there will be weak or non-existent tendencies for efficiency. This explains the actual path of the common law. In its formative stages, there was competition, and the law became efficient. More recently, there has been less competition, and the law has moved towards some inefficiencies. For example in the U.S., federal and state common law originally competed. Moreover, federal law was more economically efficient and less subject to state level rent seeking. This competition ended in 1938, as a result of the case *Erie Railroad v. Tompkins*.[38] After that period there was less competition as the federal courts were required to use the relevant state law. Choice of law in contracts is still possible, but state judges must ratify this choice. State "long arm" statutes reduce this competition.[39]

Now, arbitrators compete with the courts for commercial business.

What can we say about the evolutionary models? By focusing on the role of litigants and, with the addition of the important Zywicki analysis on the role of competing courts, the models have a good deal of explanatory power. They do not (as first thought) indicate that the common law will always be efficient. However, they do explain both why common law was efficient in the past and why it is now less efficient. They also provide some guidance for methods of channeling the law towards efficiency.[40] Additionally, by demonstrating the difficulty of achieving the goal of efficiency, they have helped scholars to understand when the law may be efficient and when it is likely not to be. Moreover, an important component of the evolutionary models was their focus on the litigation decision as driving legal evolution. Other models of legal evolution, both economic and non-economic, either leave mechanisms for evolution unspecified or assume that the preferences of judges are the driving forces. The economic models were the first to focus on the motives of litigants, realizing that judges can decide only those cases that come before them. As Elliott, in a study of the history of evolutionary models, indicates, "Moreover, the economic school of evolution has broadened our view of the legal system to include the role of litigants, as well as judges, in making law."[41] The literature associated with Priest and Klein on selectivity bias in case selection is a result of the focus on litigants' decisions, which has come out of the evolutionary models.[42]

III. "Macro" efficiency

In addition to the literature that examines the efficiency of particular rules, there is a newer literature examining the overall efficiency of common law. The theoretical basis for this literature is the work of Hayek. Hayek argued that common law was created from the bottom up, rather than from the top down. The recent literature has elaborated this point to argue that common law does a better job than code law of protecting property rights from predation by the state itself.[43]

The two major legal systems in Europe are the common law and code or civil law. Common law is the British legal system, and is now used in former British colonies, including the U.S. It is sometimes referred to a "judge made law" since the law itself is not written down anywhere, but is the product of judicial decisions, and in particular the decision of appellate courts in resolving actual disputes between individuals, or between individuals and the state. Scully identifies 54 countries as using common law.[44] In contrast, legal codes are passed by legislatures and interpreted by judges. Thus, in code countries judges are said to interpret the law, but not make it. In practice, this distinction between the roles of judges is not the major difference between code and common law systems. Rather, as discussed below, the major difference is in the amount of deference given to the state. Scully identifies 94 countries in his sample as following code law. (The term "civil law" refers to code countries, but also to the non-criminal part of the common law and sometimes to non-ecclesiastical law. To avoid confusion, I refer throughout to "code" law.)

If property rights cannot be effectively protected, then there are several detrimental effects on income and wealth. First, people will invest less in creating wealth because returns are uncertain. Second, some people will spend their time in the fundamentally unproductive activity of trying to predate against others as, for example, by becoming thieves, or by becoming corrupt bureaucrats. The potential productivity of these people in producing goods and services is lost to the economy. Third, productive people will spend part of their time and effort in protecting themselves from predators, as by guarding resources from thieves or hiding resources from corrupt tax collectors. The effort spent in these activities is also lost to the economy. Finally, to the extent that people invest in less productive, but more easily protected resources, then the economy becomes less productive. For example, if people invest in gold because it is portable and easily concealed, then the possible productivity of houses or businesses that could have been built is lost.

The modern conception of the "rule of law" was defined by Dicey, "In England no man can be made to suffer punishment or to pay damages for any conduct not definitely forbidden by law; every man's legal rights or liabilities are almost invariably determined by the ordinary Courts of the realm ... These principles mean that there can be no punishment or taking of property without an explicit law, and all persons (including officers of the government) are subject to the power of the courts."[45] Numerous scholars have documented the importance of a rule of law and protection of property rights for economic growth. This has been done both by examining the historical record (time series analysis) and by comparing countries at a point in time (cross section analysis).

A. Time series analysis

Consider first time series or historical analysis. In modern times, the first example was probably North and Thomas.[46] Rosenberg and Birdzell provided a detailed historical analysis of the economic growth of the West in response to property rights and market facilitating institutions.[47] In a recent paper, Acemoglu, Johnson and Robinson show that the major impetus for European growth beginning in the 16th century was Atlantic trade.[48] This trade strengthened the power of merchants and enabled them to obtain changes in institutions that strengthened the power of markets and the rule of law. An interesting approach is in Jones who argues that it was specifically the increase in protection of intellectual property rights that has led to economic growth.[49] Pipes has also argued for the efficiency of a private property regime from a historical, not economic, perspective.[50] The form of property rights can change over time as costs and benefits change; for example, Smith shows that in England land went from individually owned to commons fields (albeit with strict usage rules) back to individuals' use, as values changed.[51]

B. Cross section analysis

There are also numerous cross section studies that find that the existence of economic freedom and a rule of law are associated with higher levels of economic growth. Barro began this line of research, focusing on rates of growth.[52] Scully was also an early pioneer.[53] Other important recent contributions include Barro[54], Hall and Jones[55], Acemoglu, Johnson and Robinson[56], and Knack and Keefer.[57] Rodrik, Subramanian and Trebbi[58] find that institutions, measured either as a "rule of law" variable or as a measure of low risk of expropriation (following Acemoglu, Johnson and Robinson[59]), are much more important than openness or geography in explaining levels of incomes in a sample of eighty countries for 1995. Acemoglu, Johnson and Robinson also find that institutions are more important than geography in explaining incomes.[60] Carlsson and Lunstrom decompose the effect of indices of economic freedom, and find that, while the overall index is significant in explaining economic growth, some components are not significant.[61] Notably for our purposes, they find that the variable "Legal Structure and Security of Private Ownership" is significant and robust in explaining growth.

Scully finds a significant relationship between protection of individual liberties and the common law, " . . . the probability of having one's civil liberties protected is 2.5 times greater in common law nations than in countries with a codified legal tradition."[62] He also finds that Marxist-Leninist and Muslim countries have significantly less political and civil freedom than non-Marxist and non-Muslim countries.[63] Additionally, politically open societies grew at a compound real per capita annual rate of 2.5 percent per annum, compared to a 1.4 percent growth rate for politically closed societies.[64] Societies that obey the rule of law grew at a 2.8 percent rate, compared to a 1.2 per cent rate in societies where state rights take precedence over individual rights. Societies that subscribe to private property rights and a market allocation of resources grew at a 2.8 percent rate, compared to a 1.1 percent rate in nations where private property rights are circumscribed and the government intervenes in resource allocation. Scully summarizes his results, "Thus, societies where freedom is restricted are less than half as efficient in converting resources into gross domestic product as free societies. Alternatively, more than twice the standard of living could be obtained with these same resource endowments in these societies, if liberty prevailed."[65]

La Porta et al. examine the relationship between legal systems and "good" government, where good government is defined as "good-for-economic-development" and includes measures of government intervention, public sector efficiency, provision of public goods, size of the public sector, and political freedom.[66] They find that countries with socialist legal systems are more interventionist, in that they provide less protection to property rights, more regulation and higher tax rates. Systems with French origin legal systems are also more interventionist than common law systems. Scandinavian countries are more interventionist than common law, but German law countries are about the same. Mahoney, in an explicitly Hayekian analysis, compares incomes and legal systems.[67] He looks at growth rates for a sample of 102 countries from 1960–1992. He finds that common law countries grew 0.71 percent faster than did code countries. These results are approximately robust through many alternative specifications. He concludes that common law origin legal systems lead to significantly increased economic growth because they provide more stable property rights and better contract enforcement. Common law has also been shown to be more efficient in governing finance.[68]

C. Why does law matter?

The argument for the importance of institutions is this: There may be differences in incomes between countries because of different amounts of capital per worker, of education, and of technology. But none of these differences are fundamental. Capital is mobile internationally, and it should be profitable for owners of capital to move it to low capital countries by investing in these countries because capital will have higher returns where it is scarcer. Similarly, education should have a higher return in countries with low levels of human capital, and some individuals should find it worthwhile to undertake the investment. Educated persons can also migrate to places where their education is more valuable. Technology is also mobile across countries, through licensing or direct investment. But if institutions differ across countries, and if property rights are not well protected in some countries, then the above results do not hold. For example, capital will not flow into countries where property rights are not secure, even with very high potential returns. Rather, capital may actually flow out of such countries into countries with lower returns but more security. Thus, most scholars studying differences across countries recently have focused on institutions, and particularly the rule of law and the existence of property rights, to explain income differences.

It might appear that less successful countries could adopt institutions from more successful countries and so copy their success. But there are factors limiting this possibility. Powerful individuals or groups would often lose from the adoption of more efficient institutions and are often in a position to block the adoption of these advances.[69] Moreover, because long-term commitments for compensation from those who would gain from new institutions to those who would lose are unworkable, there is no possibility of paying off these elites to get them to allow more efficient institutions.[70]

There may be a link between the macro and micro views of efficiency. Recall that an important source of micro efficiency is the competition between legal systems. But this competition itself is a function of the reduced power of the state in common law systems. Thus, it is more likely that a common law system will allow competition among legal systems, and this competition itself will generate micro efficiency. This point is clearly worth further research.

IV. Future research

There are additional areas for future research suggested by this analysis. First, it would be useful to examine the general issue of the relation between legal efficiency and competition between laws. Anecdotal evidence is consistent with the hypothesis. For example, it is commonly found that societies relying on Islamic law are less efficient and such societies are notorious for relying on the Koran for both civil and religious law.[71] But systematic attention paid to this issue would be worthwhile.

Second, there is room to examine competition between bodies of law in the US setting. For example, arbitration is a body of private law that competes with public law. Benson has studied arbitration in detail.[72] Bernstein has presented an interesting case study of a private legal system.[73] The issue of the feedback from arbitration to public law has been less examined, however. There is room to examine this feedback. Although public judges are no longer paid by litigants' fees (so incentives for creation of efficient law are reduced) there is still some possibility of feedback. The theory advanced here would suggest that this feedback would lead to more efficient public law. Moreover, there are periodic efforts to reduce the scope of arbitration; the effects of these efforts, if successful, would also be worth examining.

Third, there is some legal competition in the form of choice of law in contracts. Ribstein and others have studied choice of law, but again, viewing this issue through the lens described here would also be useful.[74] In particular, as choice of law becomes less constrained, we would expect the underlying law in jurisdictions allowing increased legal choice to become more efficient. The argument here is that increased legal competition has both static and dynamic efficiency implications. The static implications are that parties would choose more efficient laws to govern their dealings when possible. The dynamic implications are that the law itself would become more efficient if increased competition is allowed.

Finally, the issue of the efficiency of non-contractual law, and particularly tort law (including products liability law) is worth further study. The standard view is that when there is choice of legal forum plaintiffs will choose pro-plaintiff venues; Fon and Parisi indicate that this choice will also affect the law through an evolutionary process.[75] But for many years law, including tort law, seems to have been relatively efficient even though there was much legal choice. Zywicki suggests that many issues that are now governed by tort (medical malpractice, product liability) were previously governed by contract, and so ex ante choice governed.[76] However, plaintiffs would have had an incentive to change this rule, and in modern times have succeeded in doing so. It is not clear how legal competition would have led to efficiency in this branch of law. This issue is clearly worth further research, for both academic and policy reasons.

V. Conclusion

Following Posner, law and economics scholars initially focused on the efficiency of particular legal rules – what I call "micro" efficiency. My evolutionary model and similar models were devised to explain this sort of efficiency. More recently, research has examined the overall efficiency of the legal system—what I call "macro" efficiency.

The basic underlying paradigm is Hayekian; it is argued that common law systems give less power to the state than do civil law systems. There is substantial empirical evidence in favor of the macro efficiency of common law. The link between the two may be the willingness of the common law to allow competition between competing legal systems. Recent work by Zywicki has emphasized the benefits of this competition. There is much work to be done examining the implications of legal competition for the shape of the law.

Notes

1   Friedrich Hayek, *The Constitution of Liberty* (Chicago, 1960); Friedrich Hayek, *Law, Legislation and Liberty* (Chicago, 1973).

2   Richard A. Posner, *Economic Analysis of Law* (Little, Brown 1st ed, 1973); Richard A. Posner, *Economic Analysis of Law* (Aspen 5th ed, 2003).

3   Much of my own work is of this type. See, for example, Paul H. Rubin, *Business Firms and the Common Law: The Evolution of Efficient Rules* (Praeger, 1983).

4   Paul H. Rubin, *Why is the Common Law Efficient?*, 6 *J Legal Stud* 51 (1977).

5   William M. Landes, *An Economic Analysis of the Courts*, 14 *J L & Econ* 61 (1971).

6   George L. Priest, *The Common Law Process and the Selection of Efficient Rules*, 6 *J Legal Stud* 65 (1977).

7   John C. Goodman, *An Economic Theory of the Evolution of the Common Law*, 7 *J Legal Stud* 393 (1979).

8   Avery Katz, *Judicial Decisionmaking and Litigation Expenditure*, 8 *Intl Rev L & Econ* 127 (1988).

9   Peter R. Terrebonne, *A Strictly Evolutionary Model of Common Law*, 10 *J Legal Stud* 397 (1981).

10   Jeffrey Evans Stake, *Status and Incentive Aspects of Judicial Decisions*, 79 *Georgetown L J* 1447 (1991).

11   Gordon Tullock, *The Case Against the Common Law* (Carolina Academic, 1997).

12   Mario J. Rizzo, *The Mirage of Efficiency*, 8 *Hofstra L Rev* 641 (1980); Mario J. Rizzo, *Law Amid Flu: The Economics of Negligence and Strict Liability in Tort*, 9 *J Legal Stud* 291 (1980).

13   Paul H. Rubin, *Decision Making and the Efficiency of Law: A Comment on Rizzo*, 9 *J Legal Stud* 319 (1980).

14   Peter H. Aranson, *The Common Law as Central Economic Planning*, 3 *Const Polit Economy* 28 (1992).

15   Gillian K. Hadfield, *Biases in the Evolution of Legal Rules*, 80 *Georgetown L J* 583 (1992).

16   William M. Landes and Richard A. Posner, *Adjudication as a Private Good*, 8 *J Legal Stud* 235 (1979).

17   Wes Parsons, *The Inefficient Common Law*, 92 *Yale L J* 863 (1983).

18   Robert D. Cooter and Lewis A. Kornhauser, *Can Litigation Improve the Law Without the Help of Judges*, 9 *J Legal Stud* 139 (1980).

19   Lewis A. Kornhauser, *A Guide to the Perplexed Claims of Efficiency in the Law*, 8 *Hofstra L Rev* 591 (1980).

20   Georg Von Wagenheim, *The Evolution of Judge Made Law*, 13 *Intl Rev L & Econ* 381 (1993).

21   Jack Hirshleifer, *Evolutionary Models in Economics and Law,* in Paul H. Rubin and Richard Zerbe, eds, 4 *Research in Law and Economics* 1 *JAI* (1982).

22   Goodman, 7 *J Legal Stud* 393 (cited in note 8).

23   Landes and Posner, 8 *J Legal Stud* 235 (cited in note 16).

24   Paul H. Rubin, *Common Law and Statute Law,* 11 *J Legal Stud* 205 (1982).

25   Michael A. Crew and Charlotte Twight, *On the Efficiency of Law: A Public Choice Perspective* 66 *Public Choice* 15 (1990).

26   Charles K. Rowley and Wayne Brough, *The Efficiency of the Common Law: A New Institutional Economics Perspective,* in Rudiger Pethig and Ulrich Schlieper, eds, *Efficiency, Institutions, and Economic Policy: Proceedings of a Worship Held by the Sonderforschungsbereich 5 at the University of Mannheim* 103 (Springer, 1987).

27   Yoram Barzel, *Dispute and Its Resolution: Delineating the Economic Role of the Common Law,* 2 *Am L & Econ Rev* 238 (2000).

28   Martin J. Bailey and Paul H. Rubin, *A Positive Theory of Legal Change,* 14 *Intl Rev L & Econ* 467 (1994); Paul Rubin and Martin J. Bailey, *The Role of Lawyers in Changing the Law,* 23 *J Legal Studies* 807 (1994).

29   Paul H. Rubin, Christopher Curran, and John Curran, *Litigation versus Lobbying: Forum Shopping by Rent-Seekers,* 107 *Public Choice* 295 (2001).

30   Evan Osborne, *What's Yours is Mine: Rent-Seeking and the Common Law,* 5 *Public Choice* 3 (2002).

31   Vincy Fon and Francesco Parisi, *Litigation and the Evolution of Legal Remedies: A Dynamic Model,* 116 *Public Choice* 419 (2003).

32   Mark J. Roe, *Chaos and Evolution in Law and Economics,* 109 *Harv L Rev* 641 (1996).

33   Todd J. Zywicki, *The Rise and fall of Efficiency in the Common Law,* 97 *NW L Rev* 1551 (2003).

34   Harold J. Berman, *Law and Revolution: The Formation of the Western Legal Tradition* (Harvard, 1983).

35   Bruce L. Benson, *The Spontaneous Evolution of Commercial Law,* 55 *S Econ J* 644 (1989).

36   Fon and Parisi, 116 *Public Choice* 419 (cited in note 31).

37   Zywicki, 97 *NW L Rev* 1551 (cited in note 33).

38   *Erie Railroad v Tompkins,* 304 US 64 (1938).

39   Paul H. Rubin, John Calfee, and Mark Grady, BMW vs Gore: *Mitigating the Punitive Economics of Punitive Damages,* 5 *S Ct Econ Rev* 179 (1997).

40   See for example, Paul H. Rubin, *Growing a Legal System in the Post-Communist Economies,* 27 *Cornell Intl L J* 1 (1994); Paul H. Rubin, *Legal Systems as Frameworks for Market Exchanges* in Claude Menard and Mary Shirley, eds, *Handbook of New Institutional Economics* (Kluwer, in press).

41   E. Donald Elliott, *The Evolutionary Tradition in Jurisprudence* 85 *Colum L Rev* 38, 71 (1985).

42   George L. Priest and Benjamin Klein, *The Selection of Disputes for Litigation,* 13 *J Legal Stud* 1 (1984). For an analysis of theories of legal evolution from 1880–1940 (which thus omits analysis of the economic theories), see Herbert Hovenkamp, *Evolutionary Models in Jurisprudence,* 64 *Tex L Rev* 645 (1985).

43   A more complete discussion of these issues in available in Rubin, *Legal Systems as Frameworks* (cited in note 40).

44   Gerald W. Scully, *Constitutional Environments and Economic Growth* (Princeton, 1992).

45   A.V. Dicey, *Introduction to the Study of the Law of the Constitution* 8th ed, available online at http://www.constitution.org/cmt/avd/law_con.htm (1944).

46   Douglas C. North and Robert P. Thomas, *The Rise of the Western World: A New Economic History* (Cambridge, 1973).

47   Nathan Rosenberg and L.E. Birdzell, *How the West Grew Rich: The Economic Transformation of the Western World* (Basic, 1986).

48   Daron Acemoglu, Simon H. Johnson, and James A. Robinson, *The Rise of Europe: Atlantic Trade, Institutional Change and Economic Growth* (MIT working paper, 2002) available online from SSRN, http://papers.ssrn.com/sol3/papers.cfm?abstract_id=355880 (visited June, 29, 2004).

49   Charles I. Jones, *Was an Industrial Revolution Inevitable? Economic Growth Over the Very Long Run* 1(2)(1) *Advances in Macroeconomics,* http://www.bepress.com.proxy.library.emory.edu/bejm/advances/vol1/iss2/art1 (2001).

50   Richard Pipes, *Property and Freedom* (New York, 1999).

51   Henry E. Smith, *Exclusion versus Governance: Two Strategies for Delineating Property Rights,* 31 *J Legal Stud* S453 (2002).

52   Robert Barro, *Economic Growth in a Cross Section of Countries,* 106 *Q J Econ* 407 (1991).

53   Scully, *Constitutional Environments* (cited in note 44).

54   Robert J. Barro, *Determinants of Economic Growth: A Cross Country Study* (MIT, 1997).

55   Robert E. Hall and Charles I. Jones, *Why Do Some Countries Produce So Much More Output Per Worker Than Others?,* 114 *Q J Econ* 83 (1999).

56   Daron Acemoglu, Simon H. Johnson and James A. Robinson, *The Colonial Origins of Comparative Development: An Empirical Investigation,* 91 *Am Econ Rev* 1369 (2001).

57   Stephen Knack and Philip Keefer, *Does Social Capital Have and Economic Payoff? A Cross-Country Investigation* 112 *Q J Econ* 1251 (1997).

58   Dani Rodrik, Arvind Subramanian, and Francesco Treddi, *Institutions Rule: The Primacy of Institutions over Geography and Integration in Economic Development,* NBER working paper 9305, available from SSRN, http://papers.ssrn.com/sol3/papers.cfm?abstract_id=347077 (2002).

59   Acemoglu, Johnson, and Robinson, *Colonial Origins* (cited in note 56).

60   Daron Acemoglu, Simon H. Johnson, and James A. Robinson, *Reversal of Fortune: Geography and Institutions in the Making of the Modern World Income Distribution* (NBER working paper 8460) available at SSRN, http://papers.ssrn.com/sol3/papers.cfm?abstract_id=281865 (2001).

61   Fredrik Carlsson and Susanna Lunstrom, *Economic Freedom and Growth: Decomposing the Effects,* 112 *Public Choice* 335 (2001).

62   Scully, *Constitutional Environments* at 162 (cited in note 44).

63   Id at 161.

64   Id at 176.

65   Id at 179.

66   Rafael La Porta et al., *The Quality of Government,* 15 *J L. Econ. & Org* 222 (1999).

67   Paul G. Mahoney, *The Common Law and Economic Growth: Hayek Might be Right,* 30 *J Legal Stud* 503 (2001).

68   See, for example, Rafael La Porta et al., *Law and Finance,* 106 *J Polit Economy* 1113 (1998).

69   Daron Acemoglu and James A. Robinson, *Economic Backwardness in Political Perspective,* MIT Department of Economics working paper 02–13, available from SSRN, http://papers.ssrn.com/sol3/papers.cfm?abstract_id-303188 (2002).

70   Daron Acemoglu, *Why Not a Political Coase Theorem? Social Conflict, Commitment, and Politics,* 31 *J Comp Econ* 620 (2003).

71   Scully, *Constitutional Environments* (cited in note 44); La Porta et al., 15 *J Law, Econ, & Org* 222 (cited in note 66).

72   Benson, 55 S Econ J 644 (cited in note 34); Bruce L. Benson, *To Arbitrate or to Litigate: That is the Question,* 8 *Eur J L & Econ* 91 (1999).

73   Lisa Bernstein, *Opting Out of the Legal System: Extra Legal Contractual Relations in the Diamond Industry* 21 *J Legal Stud* 115 (1992).

74   See, for example, Erin A. O'Hara and Larry E. Ribstein, *From Politics to Efficiency in Choice of Law,* 67 *U Chi L Rev* 1151 (2000); Bruce H. Kobayashi and Larry E. Ribstein, *Contract and Jurisdictional Competition* in Frank H. Buckley, ed, *The Fall and Rise of Freedom of Contract* (Duke, 1999).

75   Fon and Parisi, 116 *Public Choice* 419 (cited in note 31).

76   Zywicki, 97 *NW L Rev* 1551 (cited in note 33).

Index

For Product Safety Concerns and Information please contact our EU
representative GPSR@taylorandfrancis.com Taylor & Francis Verlag GmbH,
Kaufingerstraße 24, 80331 München, Germany

Printed and bound by CPI Group (UK) Ltd, Croydon, CR0 4YY
08/05/2025
01864436-0001